TAKING SIDES

Clashing Views in
Race and Ethnicity

NINTH EDITION

Selected, Edited, and with Introductions by

Raymond D'Angelo
St. Joseph's College

Herbert Douglas
Rowan University

McGraw Hill

Connect
Learn
Succeed™

Connect
Learn
Succeed™

TAKING SIDES: CLASHING VIEWS IN RACE AND ETHNICITY, NINTH EDITION

Published by McGraw-Hill, a business unit of The McGraw-Hill Companies, Inc., 1221 Avenue of the Americas, New York, NY 10020. Copyright © 2013 by The McGraw-Hill Companies, Inc. All rights reserved. Printed in the United States of America. Previous edition(s) © 2011, 2009, and 2008. No part of this publication may be reproduced or distributed in any form or by any means, or stored in a database or retrieval system, without the prior written consent of The McGraw-Hill Companies, Inc., including, but not limited to, in any network or other electronic storage or transmission, or broadcast for distance learning.

Some ancillaries, including electronic and print components, may not be available to customers outside the United States.

This book is printed on acid-free paper.

Taking Sides® is a registered trademark of the McGraw-Hill Companies, Inc.
Taking Sides is published by the **Contemporary Learning Series** group within the McGraw-Hill Higher Education division.

1 2 3 4 5 6 7 8 9 0 DOC/DOC 1 0 9 8 7 6 5 4 3 2

MHID: 0-07-8050472
ISBN: 978-0-07-8050473
ISSN: 95-83858 (print)
ISSN: (requested)

Managing Editor: *Larry Loeppke*
Senior Developmental Editor: *Jill Meloy*
Content Licensing Specialist: *DeAnna Dausener*
Marketing Director: *Adam Kloza*
Marketing Manager: *Nathan Edwards*
Project Manager: *Jessica Portz*
Cover Designer: *Studio Montage, St. Louis, MO*
Buyer: *Jennifer Pickel*
Media Project Manager: *Sridevi Palani*

Compositor: MPS Limited
Cover Image: © Getty Images RF

Editors/Academic Advisory Board

Members of the Academic Advisory Board are instrumental in the final selection of articles for each edition of TAKING SIDES. Their review of articles for content, level, and appropriateness provides critical direction to the editors and staff. We think that you will find their careful consideration well reflected in this volume.

TAKING SIDES: Clashing Views in RACE AND ETHNICITY
Ninth Edition

EDITORS

Raymond D'Angelo
St. Joseph's College

Herbert Douglas
Rowan University

ACADEMIC ADVISORY BOARD MEMBERS

Preface

This edition of *Taking Sides: Clashing Views in Race and Ethnicity* offers 20 selected issues and 40 readings dealing directly with race and ethnic relations in America. We have selected from historians, sociologists, political scientists, public intellectuals, and others to reflect a wide range of perspectives. The interdisciplinary nature of the selections provides students with much needed different perspectives on issues. At the same time, the issues will be attractive to the different disciplines in colleges and universities that offer courses in race and ethnic relations. We anticipate that this edition may be used in history, sociology, political science, ethnic studies, and psychology courses. We have followed the standard *Taking Sides* format, which includes an issue introduction and postscript. The introduction to each issue prepares the student with a brief background and questions to be considered when reading the selections. The postscript summarizes the debate, and suggests additional sources for research on the topic.

This reader is intended to supplement other texts or case studies in college courses dealing with race and ethnicity. As such, it is designed to provide a range of readings within a framework.

Students are encouraged to develop and structure their own ideas about race and ethnicity. The introductions and postscripts of each issue intentionally do not contain definitive answers. Students should consider the selections along with our editorial comments, and then formulate responsible thinking and discussion.

Changes to This Edition   New to this edition of *Taking Sides: Clashing Views in Race and Ethnicity* are four issues that deal with Native American mascots as racist symbols, the digital divide and racism, children of undocumented immigrants and the question of U.S. citizenship, and the new Jim Crow, mass incarceration of blacks. Reflecting the changing political culture, we try to include the most central and sociologically relevant questions that reflect race and ethnicity today. Indeed, there are choices to be made given the wide range of topics touched by race and ethnicity. Thus, each new edition presents us with difficult selection decisions. Typically, we review and consider over 30 issues and then select 20 based upon relevancy, faculty surveys, and selection potential. The ninth edition has been updated in an effort to provide political relevancy to go along with organization and structure to this field of study. With a focus on American identity, we aim to present various issues dealing with race, ethnicity and immigration as they contribute to the public discourse on the shifting ideology of what is an American in terms of race and ethnicity. Unit 1 deals with race, ethnicity and American identity in a nation of immigrants. Unit 2, new to this edition, explores both new and classic challenges of race and skin color. Unit 3 profiles controversial topics addressing race. Unit 4 is dedicated to immigration. Unit 5 applies a social geographical examination to race and ethnicity.

Supplements An *Instructor's Resource Guide with Test Questions* is available from the publisher for instructors who have adopted *Taking Sides: Clashing Views in Race and Ethnicity* for their course. Also, a general guidebook offers information on methods and techniques for using the debate format in a class-room setting. Interested instructors should contact the publisher. There is an online version of *Using Taking Sides in the Classroom* along with a correspond-ence service for adopters at www.mhhe.com/cls.

Taking Sides: Clashing Views in Race and Ethnicity is only one title of many in the series. Any reader interested in viewing the table of contents for any other titles in the *Taking Sides* series should visit the website at www.mhhe.com/cls.

Acknowledgments This book would not have been possible without many stimulating discussions about race and ethnicity that we have had with students, colleagues, and family members over the years. We wish to recognize the many students we have taught throughout our academic careers at St. Joseph's College and Rowan University. It is their interest and curiosity that helped stimulate our research in this area.

Raymond D'Angelo recognizes that research and scholarship, whether in monographic form or as constructed in this edition of *Taking Sides: Clashing Views in Race and Ethnicity,* is an endless and collaborative process. Without the interaction and informed dialogue with many friends and colleagues in my day-to-day life, staying current and forging ahead with sociological work would not be possible. Within this context, I want to acknowledge the administration of St. Joseph's College for affording me the time and opportunity to complete this project. I wish to thank and acknowledge the following colleagues for their help with this edition. Stephen Rockwell, political scientist and departmental colleague, offered a critique of this edition along with his ideas on the use of Native American mascots. Julie Walsh, a long-time friend and colleague, now a political scientist at American International College, offered ideas and comments on issues new to this edition. Additionally, Dean Richard Greenwald contributed important questions about color blind and post-racial issues. Charles Gallagher of LaSalle University aided with the "Rethinking the Color Line" unit of the reader and granted permission to use the title of his book on race and ethnicity for it.

My participation in the New York University Faculty Resources Network 2009 summer seminar, "Changing Places, Changing Faces: Recent Immigrant Settlement in the United States and Its Consequences," convened by Katharine Donato, sociologist at Vanderbilt University, contributed to my critical under-standing of current immigration issues. Additional scholars who have contrib-uted, knowingly or unknowingly, to my efforts include former professors Robert Washington, Judith Porter, Eugene Schneider, and Robert Perinbanay-agam, along with departmental colleagues Kenneth Bauzon and Mirella Landriscina.

Special appreciation goes to my wife, Susan, and my children, Adam and Olivia. Directly and indirectly, they offer reactions to contemporary race and ethnic relations. Thanks go to my brother, Kenneth, along with my mother and late father, who, in their own way, have shed light and understanding for me on the many controversies stemming from race and ethnic differences they have observed within the American experience.

Herbert Douglas acknowledges the support and encouragement over the years from his siblings. Dr. Corann Okorodudu and the members of the Steering Committee of Africana Studies of Rowan University are recognized for their part to my development as a contributor to the discourse on race and ethnicity. Dr. Nadim Bitar, professor of sociology, University of Toledo, is recognized for the mentoring, guidance, and support he has provided for many years. Roy Silver, professor of sociology, Southeast Community and Technical College of the University of Kentucky, offered his comments and support. The late Ernest Anderson of the Vineland, New Jersey, NAACP is extended recognition for the significant role he played in the sharpening of my insight into race and ethnicity.

We both appreciate the assistance, diligence, and patience of Jill Meloy, senior developmental editor, and Jane Mohr, lead project manager in the McGraw-Hill Contemporary Learning Series. We extend our thanks to them. Together, Raymond D'Angelo and Herb Douglas wish to acknowledge the contribution our parents have made to any successes we have achieved in our academic lives and careers. Without the values that they instilled in us, including a commitment to lifelong learning, this important project would not have been possible for us to achieve.

Raymond D'Angelo
St. Joseph's College

Herbert Douglas
Rowan University

For Our Parents

Contents in Brief

UNIT 1 Race, Ethnicity, and American Identity in a Nation of Immigrants   1

Issue 1. Do We Need a Common Identity?   2
Issue 2. Is Diversity an Inevitable Part of a New American Identity?   30
Issue 3. Do Recent Immigration Trends Challenge Existing Ideas of America's White Identity?   48
Issue 4. Is the Obama Presidency Moving Toward a Post-Racial Society?   72

UNIT 2 Rethinking the Color Line   85

Issue 5. Is Racism a Permanent Feature of American Society?   86
Issue 6. Is the Emphasis on a Color-Blind Society an Answer to Racism?   103
Issue 7. Do Whites Associate Privilege with Their Skin Color?   122
Issue 8. Are Native American Mascots Racist Symbols?   146

UNIT 3 Race Still Matters   165

Issue 9. Is Race Prejudice a Product of Group Position?   166
Issue 10. Does the Digital Divide Reflect American Racism?   192
Issue 11. Is Racial Profiling Defensible Public Policy?   209
Issue 12. Is Affirmative Action Necessary to Achieve Racial Equality?   228

UNIT 4 Immigration: New Faces, Old Questions   245

Issue 13. Does Immigration Contribute to a Better America?   246
Issue 14. Is Today's Immigration Debate Racist?   261
Issue 15. Is There Room for Bilingual Education in American Schools?   276
Issue 16. Should Children of Undocumented Immigrants Have a Birthright to U.S. Citizenship?   294

UNIT 5 The Geography of Race and Ethnicity   305

Issue 17. Are America's Public Schools Resegregating?   306
Issue 18. Is There a Need for a Permanent Voting Rights Act?   324
Issue 19. Do Minorities and Whites Engage in Self-Segregation?   345
Issue 20. Is the Mass Incarceration of Blacks the New Jim Crow?   372

Contents

Preface   iv

Correlation Guide   xvi

Topic Guide   xviii

Introduction   xxi

UNIT 1   RACE, ETHNICITY, AND AMERICAN IDENTITY IN A NATION OF IMMIGRANTS   1

Issue 1.   Do We Need a Common Identity?   2

YES: **Patrick J. Buchanan**, from "Nation or Notion?" *The American Conservative* (October 4, 2006)   5

NO: **Michael Walzer**, from "What Does It Mean to Be an 'American'?" *Social Research* (Fall 1990)   13

Patrick J. Buchanan, a syndicated conservative columnist and author of *The Death of the West: How Dying Populations and Immigrant Invasions Imperil Our Country and Civilizations* (St. Martin's Griffin, 2002), argues that America needs one common identity. He views attempts to change America's historic identity as fraudulent. Michael Walzer, professor at the Institute for Advanced Study, makes the pluralist argument that America cannot avoid its multicultural identity. He explores the ways in which citizenship and nationality are compatible with the preservation of one's ethnic identity, culture, and community.

Issue 2.   Is Diversity an Inevitable Part of a New American Identity?   30

YES: **Henry A. Giroux**, from "Insurgent Multiculturalism and the Promise of Pedagogy," in David Theo Goldberg, ed., *Multiculturalism: A Critical Reader* (Blackwell, 1994)   33

NO: **Lawrence Auster**, abridged from "How the Multicultural Ideology Captured America," *The Social Contract,* vol. 14, no. 3 (Spring 2004)   41

Henry A. Giroux is a writer on multiculturalism and related topics and current Chair of Communication Studies at McMaster University, Ontario, Canada. He emphasizes the need to focus on the cultural categories (black versus white) that are promoted within multiculturalism and diversity in order to understand power relations and other issues that are reflective of racialized identities in society. For Giroux, one significant way to address the problem of inequality is through identity politics. Lawrence Auster is a conservative writer and blogger. He has written extensively on issues pertaining to national identity and ethnic diversity, including *The Path to National Suicide: An Essay on Immigration and Multiculturalism* (American Immigration Control Foundation, 1990). He sees that multiculturalism and diversity have gained popularity as an ideology based on a set of false propositions. For Auster, diversity and multiculturalism are real attacks on European culture.

Issue 3.   Do Recent Immigration Trends Challenge Existing Ideas of America's White Identity?   48

YES: **Charles A. Gallagher,** from "Racial Redistricting: Expanding the Boundaries of Whiteness," in Heather M. Dalmage, ed., *The Politics of Multiracialism: Challenging Racial Thinking* (State University of New York Press, 2004, pp. 59–76)   *51*

NO: **Ellis Cose,** from "What's White, Anyway?" *Newsweek* (September 18, 2000)   *66*

Charles A. Gallagher, author and sociology professor at Georgia State University, argues that America is currently undergoing a "racial redistricting" in which the boundaries of whiteness are expanding to include lighter-skinned people of color (i.e., Asians and some Latinos). Ellis Cose, an African American journalist, argues that the traditional boundaries that determine race and skin color are not what they once were. Although he does not specifically cite ethnicity, Cose furthers the claim that American identity today is an expanding category. The boundaries of whiteness have expanded and are no longer hard and fast.

Issue 4.   Is the Obama Presidency Moving Toward a Post-Racial Society?   72

YES: **Alvin Poussaint,** from "Obama, Cosby, King and the Mountaintop," CNN.com (November 13, 2008)   *75*

NO: **Melissa V. Harris-Perry,** from "Black by Choice," *The Nation* (May 3, 2010)   *79*

Alvin Poussaint, a professor of psychiatry at the Harvard Medical School, has authored many books on child psychiatry with emphasis on African American children. Poussaint uses the election of Barack Obama as the president of the United States as a historical moment that may be the beginning of a post-racial era. Melissa V. Harris-Lacewell is a professor of politics at Tulane University. She is the author of *Barbershops, Bibles, and BET: Everyday Talk and Black Political Thought* (Princeton University Press, 2004). Harris-Lacewell uses President Barack Obama's selection of black as his race in filling out the census to argue that we are not ready for a post-racial society.

UNIT 2   RETHINKING THE COLOR LINE   85

Issue 5.   Is Racism a Permanent Feature of American Society?   86

YES: **Derrick Bell,** from *Faces at the Bottom of the Well: The Permanence of Racism* (Basic Books, 1992)   *89*

NO: **Russell Niele,** from "'Postracialism': Do We Want It?" *Princeton Alumni Weekly* (vol. 110, no. 7, January 13, 2010)   *97*

Derrick Bell, a prominent African American scholar and authority on civil rights and constitutional law, argues that the prospects for achieving racial equality in the United States are "illusory" for blacks. Russell Niele, a lecturer in politics at Princeton, works for the Executive Precept Program sponsored by Princeton's James Madison Program. He has written on affirmative action and the origins of an urban black underclass. Niele argues that American society is moving toward a meritocracy, which is post-racist (not post-racial). For him, race, ethnicity, and religious identity are less determinant than they were in earlier American history.

Issue 6.   Is the Emphasis on a Color-Blind Society an Answer to Racism?   103

YES: **Ward Connerly**, from "Don't Box Me In," *National Review* (April 16, 2001)   *106*

NO: **Eduardo Bonilla-Silva**, from *Racism without Racists: Color-Blind Racism and the Persistence of Racial Inequality in the United States* (Rowman & Littlefield, 2003)   *109*

Ward Connerly is a strong critic of all attempts at racial classification and believes that in order to achieve a racially egalitarian, unified American society, the government and private citizens must stop assigning people to categories delineated by race. To achieve this goal, Mr. Connerly is supporting the enactment of a "Racial Privacy Initiative." Eduardo Bonilla-Silva argues that "regardless of whites' sincere fictions, racial considerations shade almost everything in America" and, therefore, color-blind ideology is a cover for the racism and inequality that persist within contemporary American society.

Issue 7.   Do Whites Associate Privilege with Their Skin Color?   122

YES: **Paul Kivel**, from *Uprooting Racism: How White People Can Work for Racial Justice* (New Society, 1996)   *126*

NO: **Tim Wise**, from "The Absurdity (and Consistency) of White Denial: What Kind of Card Is Race?" www.counterpunch.org/wise04242006.html (April 24, 2006)   *133*

Paul Kivel, a teacher, writer, and antiviolence/antiracist activist, asserts that many benefits accrue to whites solely on the basis of skin color. These benefits range from economic to political advantages and so often include better residential choice, police protection, and education opportunities. Tim Wise, an author of two books on race, argues that whites do not acknowledge privilege. Instead, whites are often convinced that the race card is "played" by blacks to gain their own privilege, something that whites cannot do. Hence, whites simply do not see discrimination and do not attach privilege to their skin color.

Issue 8.   Are Native American Mascots Racist Symbols?   146

YES: **Sonia K. Katyal**, from "The Fight over the Redskins Trademark and Other Racialized Symbols," http://writ.news.findlaw.com/commentary/20091207_katyal.html (December 7, 2009)   *150*

NO: **Arthur J. Remillard**, from "Holy War on the Football Field: Religion and the Florida State University Indian Mascot Controversy," in James A. Vlasich, ed., *Essays in Sports and American Culture* (McFarland, 2005, pp. 104–118 (Edited), chapter 8)   *155*

Sonia K. Katyal, professor of law and author of *Property Outlaws*, discusses the use of Native American mascots in professional sports, with an emphasis on the Washington Redskins and the negative impact of the use of such symbols on Native American peoples and culture. Arthur Remillard, professor of religious studies, recognizes the concern that the use of Native American mascots within non-Native institutions generates. However, he argues that the use of such symbols can be viewed as contributing to respect for Native American culture and its inherent strengths among the American population.

UNIT 3   RACE STILL MATTERS   165

Issue 9.   Is Race Prejudice a Product of Group Position?   166

YES: **Herbert Blumer,** from "Race Prejudice as a Sense of Group Position," *The Pacific Sociological Review* (Spring 1958)   *169*

NO: **Gordon W. Allport,** from "The Young Child," *The Nature of Prejudice* (Perseus Books, 1979)   *177*

Herbert Blumer, a sociologist, asserts that prejudice exists in a sense of group position rather than as an attitude based on individual feelings. The collective process by which a group comes to define other racial groups is the focus of Blumer's position. Gordon W. Allport, a psychologist, makes the case that prejudice is the result of a three-stage learning process.

Issue 10.   Does the Digital Divide Reflect American Racism?   192

YES: **Susan P. Crawford,** from "The New Digital Divide," *The New York Times* (December 3, 2011)   *196*

NO: **Larry Schweikart,** from "Race, Culture, and the 'Digital Divide,'" *Freeman* (vol. 52, no. 5, pp. 44–47, May 2002)   *200*

Susan P. Crawford, professor of law at the Benjamin N. Cordozo School of Law and former special assistant to President Obama for science, technology, and innovation policy, argues that there is a new digital divide that places African Americans and Latinos at the risk of being left behind the Internet revolution. Larry Schweikart, professor of history at the University of Dayton and conservative writer, asserts that "the racial digital divide is largely a myth." He points out that African Americans, when including the workplace, have as equal access as whites to computers. However, where a divide occurs is in home computer ownership.

Issue 11.   Is Racial Profiling Defensible Public Policy?   209

YES: **Scott Johnson,** from "Better Unsafe than (Occasionally) Sorry?" *The American Enterprise* (January/February 2003)   *212*

NO: **David A. Harris,** from "Profiles in Injustice: American Life under the Regime of Racial Profiling," in *Profiles in Injustice: Why Police Profiling Cannot Work* (The New Press, 2002)   *215*

Scott Johnson, conservative journalist and an attorney and fellow at the Clermont Institute, argues in favor of racial profiling. He claims that racial profiling does not exist "on the nation's highways and streets." Johnson accuses David Harris of distorting the data on crimes committed and victimization according to race. For him, law enforcement needs to engage in profiling under certain circumstances in order to be effective. David A. Harris, law professor and leading authority on racial profiling, argues that racial profiling is ineffective and damaging to America's diverse nation. He believes it hinders effective law enforcement.

Issue 12.   Is Affirmative Action Necessary to Achieve Racial Equality?   228

YES: **Robert Staples**, from "Black Deprivation-White Privilege: The Assault on Affirmative Action," *The Black Scholar* (Summer 1995)   *231*

NO: **Roger Clegg**, from "Faculty Hiring Preferences and the Law," *The Chronicle of Higher Education* (May 19, 2006)   *237*

Robert Staples, an African American sociologist, views affirmative action as a positive policy designed to provide equal economic opportunities for women and other minorities. Roger Clegg, general counsel of the Center for Equal Opportunity in Sterling, Virginia, and contributor to *The Chronicle of Higher Education,* argues against affirmative action, citing *Grutter v. Bollinger.* He makes the case for universities to hire the best qualified faculty.

UNIT 4   IMMIGRATION: NEW FACES, OLD QUESTIONS   245

Issue 13.   Does Immigration Contribute to a Better America?   246

YES: **Philippe Legrain**, from "The Case for Immigration: The Secret to Economic Vibrancy," *The International Economy* (Summer 2007, vol. 21, issue 3)   *249*

NO: **Peter Brimelow**, from "Immigration: Dissolving the People," *Alien Nation: Common Sense About America's Immigration Disaster* (Random House, 1995)   *254*

Philippe Legrain is a journalist, economist, and author of *Immigrants: Your Country Needs Them* and *Open World: The Truth About Globalization.* He makes the case that immigration contributes to a better America as well as a better world. His economic argument primarily emphasizes that the flow of immigrants within the global system brings both talent and labor to areas of need. Peter Brimelow, senior editor of *Forbes* and *National Review* magazines, argues that the United States is being overrun by a growing tide of aliens who are changing the character and composition of the nation in manners that are threatening and destructive to its well-being and prospects for future advancement.

Issue 14.   Is Today's Immigration Debate Racist?   261

YES: **Carlos Fuentes**, from "Huntington and the Mask of Racism," *New Perspectives Quarterly* (Spring 2004), pp. 77–81   *264*

NO: **Samuel P. Huntington**, from *The Clash of Civilizations and the Remaking of World Order* (Simon & Schuster, 1996)   *268*

Carlos Fuentes, prominent Mexican writer and social commentator, argues that much of the current immigration debate is racist. For example, he criticizes Samuel Huntington's assessment that Mexican immigrants exploit the United States and represent an unjust burden to the nation. This "mask" of racism appears under the guise of a concern with American national unity. Samuel Huntington, political scientist and Albert J. Weatherhead III, university professor at Harvard University, expresses the concern that Mexican immigrants and, by implication, other Latinos are creating significant problems for America, specifically with reference to assimilation, as their numbers continue to increase within the population. In general, he believes that Latino immigration is a threat to America's national unity.

Issue 15. Is There Room for Bilingual Education in American Schools? 276

YES: **Kendra Hamilton**, from "Bilingual or Immersion? A New Group of Studies Is Providing Fresh Evidence That It's Not the Language of Instruction That Counts, but the Quality of Education," *Diverse Issues in Higher Education* (April 20, 2006) *279*

NO: **Rosalie Pedalino Porter**, from "The Case Against Bilingual Education," *The Atlantic Monthly* (May 1998) *284*

Kendra Hamilton, editor of *Black Issues in Higher Education*, argues that the studies available for assessing the quality of such programs are inconclusive. She makes the argument that the outcomes of bilingual education programs are often jeopardized by the quality of the instruction provided. Thus, the significant question of the quality of the programs is being ignored. Rosalie Pedalino Porter, author of *Forked Tongue: The Politics of Bilingual Education* and affiliate of The Institute for Research in English Acquisition and Development (READ), makes the case against bilingual education. She presents a negative view of the contributions of such programs to the academic achievement of non–English-speaking students. Also, she is greatly concerned that such programs retard the integration of such students within the larger, English-speaking society.

Issue 16. Should Children of Undocumented Immigrants Have a Birthright to U.S. Citizenship? 294

YES: **Eric Foner**, from "Birthright Citizenship Sets America Apart," http://host.madison.com, August 20, 2010 *297*

NO: **George F. Will**, from "An Argument to be Made about Immigrant Babies and Citizenship," *The Washington Post*, March 28, 2010 *299*

Distinguished professor of history at Columbia University, Eric Foner examines the legal and constitutional basis for granting birthright citizenship and argues that this right illuminates the strength of American society. Conservative newspaper columnist and commentator, George F. Will is troubled by the facile tendency to grant birthright citizenship to the children of undocumented immigrants. He views this practice as reflecting a misinterpretation of the Bill of Rights and the Fourteenth Amendment. He vigorously opposes this policy.

UNIT 5 THE GEOGRAPHY OF RACE AND ETHNICITY 305

Issue 17. Are America's Public Schools Resegregating? 306

YES: **Tim Lockette**, from "Unmaking Brown," *Teaching Tolerance* (Spring 2010) *310*

NO: **Ingrid Gould Ellen**, from "Welcome Neighbors?" *Brookings Review* (Winter 1997) *315*

Tim Lockette, a freelance writer in Montgomery, Alabama, and former editor of *Teaching Tolerance,* demonstrates that through certain Supreme Court decisions, the elimination of bus programs, and flawed school choice programs, America's public schools are resegregating. The desegregation effects of the historic 1954 *Brown* decision have been reversed. Ingrid Gould Ellen, writer for *Brookings Review,* argues that neighborhood racial integration is increasing. She thinks researchers must balance their pessimistic findings of resegregation with increased integration.

Issue 18.   Is There a Need for a Permanent Voting Rights Act?   324

YES: Richard M. Valelly, from "Ballots in the Balance: Does the 1965 Voting Rights Act Still Matter?" *The Two Reconstructions: The Struggle for Black Enfranchisement* (University of Chicago Press, 2004)   *327*

NO: Abigail Thernstrom, from "Redistricting, Race, and the Voting Rights Act," *National Affairs* (Spring 2010)   *330*

Richard M. Valelly, the author of *The Two Reconstructions: The Struggle for Black Enfranchisement* (University of Chicago Press, 2004), is a professor of political science at Swarthmore College. Pointing to U.S. history, he fears that without key sections, especially Section 5, of the Voting Rights Act, the black vote will be suppressed. What happened in the 1890s to black disfranchisement can happen again. Abigail Thernstrom, a political scientist, is a senior fellow at the Manhattan Institute in New York. She has written extensively on race and voting rights. She argues that it is time to end race-driven districting and that certain sections, especially Section 5, of the Voting Rights Act of 1965 are no longer needed.

Issue 19.   Do Minorities and Whites Engage in Self-Segregation?   345

YES: Beverly D. Tatum, from "Identity Development in Adolescence," in *Why Are All the Black Kids Sitting Together in the Cafeteria?* (Basic Books, 1997), pp. 52–74   *349*

NO: Debra Humphreys, from *Campus Diversity and Student Self-Segregation: Separating Myths from Facts* (Diversity Web Association of American Colleges and Universities, 1999)   *364*

Beverly D. Tatum, an African American clinical psychologist and president of Spelman College, examines identity development among adolescents, especially black youths, and the behavioral outcomes of this phenomenon. She argues that black adolescents' tendency to view themselves in racial terms is due to the totality of personal and environmental responses that they receive from the larger society. Debra Humphreys is the director of Programs, Office of Education and Diversity Initiatives, at the Association of American Colleges and Universities in Washington, DC. She notes that today's university students are matriculating on very diverse campuses that are "leading to significant educational and social benefits for all college students. In such an environment, students have many opportunities to interact and associate with students of different backgrounds than themselves." She cites research that tends to show that rather than self-segregating, students are interacting across racial and ethnic lines in significant numbers.

Issue 20.   Is the Mass Incarceration of Blacks the New Jim
        Crow?   372

YES: **Michelle Alexander,** from *The New Jim Crow* (The New Press,
    2011)   *375*

NO: **James Forman, Jr.,** from "Racial Critiques of Mass
    Incarceration: Beyond the New Jim Crow," *Racial Critiques*
    (vol. 87, February 26, 2012)   *387*

Michelle Alexander is an associate professor of law at Ohio State
University with a joint appointment at the Kirwan Institute for the Study of
Race and Ethnicity. She draws attention to the racial imbalance in
America's prison population and presents a compelling analysis of the
wide-ranging social costs and divisive racial impact of mass incarceration.
James Forman, Jr., a clinical professor of law at Yale Law School and a
noted constitutional law scholar, affirms the utility of the new Jim Crow
paradigm but argues that it has significant limitations. It obscures
significant facts regarding the history of mass incarceration as well as
black support for punitive criminal justice policy among other deficiencies.

Contributors   399

Correlation Guide

The *Taking Sides* series presents current issues in a debate-style format designed to stimulate student interest and develop critical thinking skills. Each issue is thoughtfully framed with an issue summary, an issue introduction, and an Exploring the Issue section. The pro and con essays—selected for their liveliness and substance—represent the arguments of leading scholars and commentators in their fields.

Taking Sides: Clashing Views in Race and Ethnicity, 9/e is an easy-to-use reader that presents issues on important topics such as *immigration, the digital divide*, and *symbolism*. For more information on *Taking Sides* and other *McGraw-Hill Contemporary Learning Series* titles, visit www.mhhe.com/cls.

This convenient guide matches the issues in **Taking Sides: Race and Ethnicity, 9/e** with the corresponding chapters in two of our best-selling McGraw-Hill Race and Ethnicity textbooks by Desmond/Emirbayer and Aguirre/Turner.

Taking Sides: Race and Ethnicity, 9/e	Racial Domination, Racial Progress: The Sociology of Race in America 1/e by Desmond/Emirbayer	American Ethnicity: The Dynamics and Consequences of Discrimination, 7/e by Aguirre/Turner
Issue 1: Do We Need a Common Identity?	**Chapter 1:** Race in the Twenty-First Century **Chapter 10:** Intimate Life	**Chapter 10:** The Future of Ethnicity in America
Issue 2: Is Diversity an Inevitable Part of a New American Identity?	**Chapter 1:** Race in the Twenty-First Century	**Chapter 10:** The Future of Ethnicity in America
Issue 3: Do Recent Immigration Trends Challenge Existing Ideas of America's White Identity?	**Chapter 1:** Race in the Twenty-First Century **Chapter 3:** Politics	**Chapter 2:** Explaining Ethnic Relations **Chapter 4:** White Ethnic Americans **Chapter 7:** Latinos **Chapter 10:** The Future of Ethnicity in America
Issue 4: Is the Obama Presidency Moving Toward a Post-Racial Society?	**Chapter 3:** Politics **Chapter 11:** Towards Racial Justice	**Chapter 10:** The Future of Ethnicity in America
Issue 5: Is Racism a Permanent Feature of American Society?	**Chapter 1:** Race in the Twenty-First Century **Chapter 11:** Towards Racial Justice	**Chapter 1:** Ethnicity and Ethnic Relations **Chapter 10:** The Future of Ethnicity in America
Issue 6: Is the Emphasis on a Color-Blind Society an Answer to Racism?	**Chapter 11:** Towards Racial Justice	**Chapter 2:** Explaining Ethnic Relations **Chapter 10:** The Future of Ethnicity in America
Issue 7: Do Whites Associate Privilege with Their Skin Color?	**Chapter 2:** The Invention of Race **Chapter 8:** Aesthetics	**Chapter 4:** White Ethnic Americans

Taking Sides: Race and Ethnicity, 9/e	Racial Domination, Racial Progress: The Sociology of Race in America 1/e by Desmond/Emirbayer	American Ethnicity: The Dynamics and Consequences of Discrimination, 7/e by Aguirre/Turner
Issue 8: Are Native American Mascots Racist Symbols?	**Chapter 3:** Politics **Chapter 8:** Aesthetics	**Chapter 6:** Native Americans
Issue 9: Is Race Prejudice a Product of Group Position?	**Chapter 1:** Race in the Twenty-First Century **Chapter 6:** Crime and Punishment	**Chapter 3:** The Anglo-Saxon Core and Ethnic Antagonism
Issue 10: Does the Digital Divide Reflect American Racism?	**Chapter 1:** Race in the Twenty-First Century **Chapter 7:** Education	**Chapter 2:** Explaining Ethnic Relations **Chapter 10:** The Future of Ethnicity in America
Issue 11: Is Racial Profiling Defensible Public Policy?	**Chapter 3:** Politics **Chapter 6:** Crime and Punishment	**Chapter 10:** The Future of Ethnicity in America
Issue 12: Is Affirmative Action Necessary to Achieve Racial Equality?	**Chapter 3:** Politics **Chapter 4:** Economics **Chapter 11:** Towards Racial Justice	**Chapter 2:** Explaining Ethnic Relations **Chapter 10:** The Future of Ethnicity in America
Issue 13: Does Immigration Contribute to a Better America?	**Chapter 3:** Politics **Chapter 4:** Economics	**Chapter 5:** African Americans **Chapter 7:** Latinos **Chapter 8:** Asian and Pacific Island Americans **Chapter 10:** The Future of Ethnicity in America
Issue 14: Is Today's Immigration Debate Racist?	**Chapter 3:** Politics	**Chapter 7:** Latinos **Chapter 8:** Asian and Pacific Island Americans
Issue 15: Is There Room for Bilingual Education in American Schools?	**Chapter 7:** Education	**Chapter 7:** Latinos **Chapter 10:** The Future of Ethnicity in America
Issue 16: Should Children of Undocumented Immigrants Have a Birthright to U.S. Citizenship?	**Chapter 3:** Politics **Chapter 4:** Economics	**Chapter 7:** Latinos
Issue 17: Are America's Public Schools Resegregating?	**Chapter 7:** Education	**Chapter 5:** African Americans **Chapter 8:** Asian and Pacific Island Americans
Issue 18: Is There a Need for a Permanent Voting Rights Act?	**Chapter 3:** Politics	**Chapter 5:** African Americans
Issue 19: Do Minorities and Whites Engage in Self-Segregation?	**Chapter 10:** Intimate Life	**Chapter 2:** Explaining Ethnic Relations
Issue 20: Is the Mass Incarceration of Blacks the New Jim Crow?	**Chapter 3:** Politics **Chapter 6:** Crime and Punishment **Chapter 11:** Towards Racial Justice	**Chapter 2:** Explaining Ethnic Relations **Chapter 5:** African Americans **Chapter 7:** Latinos **Chapter 10:** The Future of Ethnicity in America

Topic Guide

This topic guide suggests how the selections in this book relate to the subjects covered in your course. You may want to use the topics listed on these pages to search the web more easily. On the following pages a number of websites have been gathered specifically for this book. They are arranged to reflect the units of this *Taking Sides* reader. You can link to these sites by going to www.mhhe.com/cls.

All issues, and their articles that relate to each topic are listed below the bold-faced term.

Affirmative Action

12. Is Affirmative Action Necessary to Achieve Racial Equality?

Assimilation

1. Do We Need a Common Identity?
2. Is Diversity an Inevitable Part of a New American Identity?

Bilingualism

15. Is There Room for Bilingual Education in American Schools?

Citizenship

1. Do We Need a Common Identity?
13. Does Immigration Contribute to a Better America?
16. Should Children of Undocumented Immigrants Have a Birthright to U.S. Citizenship?

Civil Rights Movement

12. Is Affirmative Action Necessary to Achieve Racial Equality?
17. Are America's Public Schools Resegregating?
18. Is There a Need for a Permanent Voting Rights Act?

Color Blind

6. Is the Emphasis on a Color-Blind Society an Answer to Racism?
19. Do Minorities and Whites Engage in Self-Segregation?
20. Is the Mass Incarceration of Blacks the New Jim Crow?

Common Identity

1. Do We Need a Common Identity?

Corrections

20. Is the Mass Incarceration of Blacks the New Jim Crow?

Critical Race Theory

5. Is Racism a Permanent Feature of American Society?

Discrimination

7. Do Whites Associate Privilege with Their Skin Color?
12. Is Affirmative Action Necessary to Achieve Racial Equality?
17. Are America's Public Schools Resegregating?
18. Is There a Need for a Permanent Voting Rights Act?
19. Do Minorities and Whites Engage in Self-Segregation?
20. Is the Mass Incarceration of Blacks the New Jim Crow?

Digital Divide

10. Does the Digital Divide Reflect American Racism?

Diversity

2. Is Diversity an Inevitable Part of a New American Identity?
13. Does Immigration Contribute to a Better America?
15. Is There Room for Bilingual Education in American Schools?

16. Should Children of Undocumented Immigrants Have a Birthright to U.S. Citizenship?

Dominant Group

1. Do We Need a Common Identity?
2. Is Diversity an Inevitable Part of a New American Identity?

Economic Issues

13. Does Immigration Contribute to a Better America?

Ethnicity

1. Do We Need a Common Identity?
2. Is Diversity an Inevitable Part of a New American Identity?
13. Does Immigration Contribute to a Better America?
15. Is There Room for Bilingual Education in American Schools?
16. Should Children of Undocumented Immigrants Have a Birthright to U.S. Citizenship?

Hate Ideology

5. Is Racism a Permanent Feature of American Society?
8. Are Native American Mascots Racist Symbols?

Immigration

3. Do Recent Immigration Trends Challenge Existing Ideas of America's White Identity?
13. Does Immigration Contribute to a Better America?
14. Is Today's Immigration Debate Racist?
15. Is There Room for Bilingual Education in American Schools?
16. Should Children of Undocumented Immigrants Have a Birthright to U.S. Citizenship?

Inequality

10. Does the Digital Divide Reflect American Racism?
12. Is Affirmative Action Necessary to Achieve Racial Equality?
17. Are America's Public Schools Resegregating?
18. Is There a Need for a Permanent Voting Rights Act?
19. Do Minorities and Whites Engage in Self-Segregation?
20. Is the Mass Incarceration of Blacks the New Jim Crow?

Melting Pot

1. Do We Need a Common Identity?
2. Is Diversity an Inevitable Part of a New American Identity?

Minority

1. Do We Need a Common Identity?
2. Is Diversity an Inevitable Part of a New American Identity?

Multiculturalism

2. Is Diversity an Inevitable Part of a New American Identity?
15. Is There Room for Bilingua Education in American Schools?
16. Should Children of Undocumented Immigrants Have a Birthright to U.S. Citizenship?

Nativism

3. Do Recent Immigration Trends Challenge Existing Ideas of America's White Identity?
9. Is Race Prejudice a product of Group Position?
13. Does Immigration Contribute to a Better America?
14. Is Today's Immigration Debate Racist?

Native Americans

8. Are Native American Mascots Racist Symbols?

New Jim Crow

20. Is the Mass Incarceration of Blacks the New Jim Crow?

Pluralism

1. Do We Need a Common Identity?
2. Is Diversity an Inevitable Part of a New American Identity?

Popular Culture

8. Are Native American Mascots Racist Symbols?

Post-Racial

4. Is the Obama Presidency Moving Toward a Post-Racial Society?
6. Is the Emphasis on a Color-Blind Society an Answer to Racism?

Prejudice

9. Is Race Prejudice a product of Group Position?

Racial Profiling

11. Is Racial Profiling Defensible Public Policy?

Racism

4. Is the Obama Presidency Moving Toward a Post-Racial Society?
5. Is Racism a Permanent Feature of American Society?
6. Is the Emphasis on a Color-Blind Society an Answer to Racism?
10. Does the Digital Divide Reflect American Racism?
14. Is Today's Immigration Debate Racist?
20. Is the Mass Incarceration of Blacks the New Jim Crow?

Segregation

17. Are America's Public Schools Resegregating?
19. Do Minorities and Whites Engage in Self-Segregation?

Social Justice

11. Is Racial Profiling Defensible Public Policy?
17. Are America's Public Schools Resegregating?
18. Is There a Need for a Permanent Voting Rights Act?
20. Is the Mass Incarceration of Blacks the New Jim Crow?

Stereotypes

8. Are Native American Mascots Racist Symbols?
9. Is Race Prejudice a Product of Group Position?

Supreme Court

12. Is Affirmative Action Necessary to Achieve Racial Equality?
16. Should Children of Undocumented Immigrants Have a Birthright to U.S. Citizenship?
17. Are America's Public Schools Resegregating?

Technology

10. Does the Digital Divide Reflect American Racism?

Undocumented Immigrants

13. Does Immigration Contribute to a Better America?
16. Should Children of Undocumented Immigrants Have a Birthright to U.S. Citizenship?

White Privilege

3. Do Recent Immigration Trends Challenge Existing Ideas of America's White Identity?
7. Do Whites Associate Privilege with Their Skin Color?

Introduction

America is woven of many strands. Our fate is to become one, and yet many.

Ralph Ellison (1952)

Neither the life of an individual nor the history of a society can be understood without understanding both.

C. Wright Mills

History Immigration

From its inception, America emerged as a multiethnic nation. The Anglo-Saxons and other European ethnic groups who came to America during the colonial era met aboriginal people who had been residing on these lands for thousands of years prior to their arrival. As the colonies developed and their economies began to emerge, African slaves were imported to provide labor for the agrarian economy that would emerge. As the economy of the new nation evolved from agrarian pursuits to industrial capitalism, more and more ethnic groups were attracted to these shores to expand the ranks of labor and to pursue their American dream. Over time, the United States experienced multiple waves of immigration, from the old immigration of pre–Civil War times to the new immigrants of the post–Reconstruction Era, extending to include the most recent immigration of Asians and Hispanics that the nation experienced during the 1990s. So, America has developed as a nation of diverse ethnicities and races derived from virtually every corner of the known world. How does one accommodate the interests and the goals of these diverse ethnic and racial groups while maintaining a unified society?

What is an American? How is one to define American identity? (See Unit 1.) The United States gained its reputation in the world as a land of freedom and justice for all who arrived on its shores. This quality of the nation's experience has made America a magnet for peoples seeking liberty, justice, and opportunity for improving the quality of their lives.

In the shifting sands of vocabulary that describe the race and ethnic components of American culture, one contemplates "diversity" and "multiculturalism." Public discourse on these matters takes us on a conceptual journey to explain who Americans are and who Americans are not. For all who are in America—the most recent arrivals together with descendants of the very first to arrive—the meaning of what is an American requires us to reflect upon and analyze the history of race and ethnicity.

Political authority and control to the means of economic production by a dominant Anglo group presented challenges to new immigrants, and later in the nineteenth century, former slaves along with other people of color, especially Native Americans. The popular notion of the American melting pot was problematic. The dominant group demonstrated a sense of superiority over subordinate groups. Ethnocentrism, xenophobia, and nativism were common in early American culture and soon resulted in policy efforts to restrict opportunities for those who did not look like white, Anglo-Saxon Protestants, or practice their values. What price would a non-Anglo have to pay to "become" an American?

An early twentieth-century effort to control American identity can be seen in the Immigration Act of 1924. The Act created immigration quotas based on the percentage of each ethnic group present in America at that time. This legislation had the effect of restricting the immigration of less-favored European ethnic groups such as the Italians and the Poles and created space for the great migration of African Americans from the South to the urban, industrial centers of the North.

We see the struggle for American identity encompassing European ethnics and American blacks as remarkably similar. Both groups were attracted to the northern industrial centers of the United States, seeking economic opportunity that was shrinking in their rural backgrounds. Both groups were deeply religious and anchored by the church in a new urban environment. At the same time, both were vulnerable to being exploited within the labor markets in which they were competing. The competition among racial and ethnic groups within prevailing labor markets is a significant feature of capitalist economies, and the United States was no exception.

Race Segregation

Segregation emerged as the social and legal framework of race relations at the end of the nineteenth century. In the legal arena, the 1896 *Plessy v. Ferguson* became the law of the land and therefore public policy in race relations. The resulting race segregation that proliferated throughout American cities isolated blacks from European ethnic immigrants. It is in this context that an understanding of early twentieth-century race and ethnic relations should be framed. Hence, the early notion of American identity for the most part excluded blacks. Consequently, the late nineteenth to early twentieth-century debate within the black community emerged between Booker T. Washington and W.E.B. DuBois. These leaders were concerned with issues of racial advancement, and they offered competing philosophies and strategies for African Americans to achieve these goals.

The intensity and divisiveness of the race issue in American life were manifested in thousands of lynchings of blacks, forced labor camps, and an ideology of white supremacy. This ideology extended to other peoples of color as seen when Japanese Americans were isolated in internment camps during World War II. Increasingly, blacks and other people of color resided in segregated barrios and ghettos within the core cities of the country. Douglas Massey and Nancy Denton, in *American Apartheid and the Urban Underclass,* refer to this housing segregation as American apartheid.

The Civil Rights Movement and Desegregation

During the slave era, some questioned whether this peculiar institution was compatible with important American values such as those of the Christian religion and the nation's democratic ethos. The abolitionists were among the first to raise such questions, and their movement was a significant historical precursor to the civil rights movement of the post–World War II period. Indeed, the war itself contributed to changing race relations in the states. It was Executive Order 1199 issued by President Harry S. Truman that integrated the armed forces. This was significant in that it is an early example of the employment of an egalitarian principle to effect the racial reform of an American institution. Black soldiers receiving equal treatment while fighting the war would return home to face segregation.

During the 1940s, the NAACP's legal defense team under the leadership of Charles Hamilton Houston mapped out a strategy to dismantle Jim Crow. Public education became the battleground to overturn the "separate but equal" law of the land. Eventually, in 1954 the Supreme Court overturned *Plessy* in the *Brown v. Board of Education* decision. This decision was a watershed of progress in American race relations. Soon, the civil rights movement would address many issues including public accommodations and perhaps, most importantly, voting rights among others.

Gunnar Myrdal's *An American Dilemma* (1944), a landmark critique of American race relations, contributed significantly to the depth and breadth of knowledge on race in that it argued that America lacked the will to change and enforce its creed of equality and justice within the common life of society. C. Vann Woodward's *The Strange Career of Jim Crow* (1955) became a classic study of segregation.

In the 1960s and beyond, the civil rights movement forced America to recognize and confront the phenomenon of institutional racism. There was more to the problem of racial injustice than just individual attitude and behavior. The Civil Rights Act of 1964, along with the Voting Rights Act of 1965 and the Fair Housing Act of 1968, was a key legislative initiative advanced to address racial inequality.

Multiculturalism

With new immigrants of color arriving in significant numbers in the 1990s—coming together with existing minorities within desegregated America—an emphasis on multiculturalism and diversity emerged. So, for example, the 2010 U.S. Census shows a population breakdown of 13 percent Hispanic, 12 percent African American, 3 percent Asian American, and 70 percent white. This contrasts with the demographic profile of the mid-twentieth century in which the minority population consisted primarily of 12 percent black.

Today, we see a country with an increasing Latino population. In this context, multicultural and diversity concerns are affecting a broad spectrum of American institutions extending from the private corporate sector to public education. Further, this calls into question traditional definitions of race and ethnicity. American demographers predict that increasing diversification of the population of the United States will continue unabated for the foreseeable future. Thus, the challenges to the institutional leaders of America to manage diversity properly will be a major challenge of the twenty-first century. The large numbers of recent Latino immigrants have rekindled the debate over national identity. It has exposed fault lines within the Congress, leading to divisions within each political party; it has forced the corporate elite into a defensive position over hiring practices; it has provoked a mass reaction as reflected in the Minutemen, a volunteer group that has assumed a role of southern border security; and it has become a major arena of media presentation.

Race and Ethnicity in the Age of Obama

The Obama election has generated great interest around the world with regard to its impact on race relations within the United States. Many are posing the question: How will the presidency of a person who rose to power on a mantra of change influence issues of race, ethnicity, and diversity that confront American society? Some observers proclaim that America is now poised to enter an age of a post-racial, color-blind society. Others claim that major challenges persist. In these areas of concern, which range from the traditional racism that has confronted the society to the complexity of issues that immigrants are presenting in their attempts to gain acceptance and inclusion within American life, the next few years will reveal the direction of the society. Many of the more cautious observers of the impact of the Obama presidency, especially civil rights advocates, are concerned that his election and the claim that it has ushered in a new post-racial, color-blind society will make it more difficult to address and resolve issues of racial inequality and related concerns with ethnicity and diversity that confront the nation. They view the emergence of the Tea Party activists, a political grassroots conservative movement with strong anti-Obama leanings, as retrograde influences upon attempts to move the nation forward on issues of race, ethnicity, and diversity.

Indicative of the immigration controversy are two events, one near the U.S.-Mexican border and the other on the east coast, which deserve mention. A recent controversial decision in Arizona to allow local police officers to check the immigration status of suspicious people thought to be in America illegally has uncovered a major schism in that state. Is this an invitation for racial profiling (Issue 11)? Anti-Latino sentiment reached an ugly climax in 2008 in eastern Long Island, New York, when an Ecuadorean immigrant was stabbed to death by a white high school student. How widespread is anti-immigrant sentiment throughout America (Issues 13 and 14)? When and how will Congress generate a new federal immigration policy? Will a new policy end the controversy? In Texas, social conservatives abandoned neutral pedagogy in an attempt to revise the social studies public school curriculum standards by emphasizing ideology over historical accuracy. They were relatively successful but failed to pass a motion to rename the slave trade the "Atlantic triangular trade." The Texas State Board of Education's actions illustrate a reaction to diversity's challenge to American identity. If Texas, one of the largest consumers of standardized textbooks in the country, adopts a book, publishers are much more likely to produce and reproduce the book for national consumption. This is seen as one attempt to neutralize any critical assessment of the American historical experience. Another reaction to the challenge of diversity to American identity occurred just last month when the governor of Arizona signed a bill banning the teaching of ethnic studies in Arizona's public schools. Along similar lines, in Virginia, the governor's declaration of "Confederate History Month" ignored any mention of slavery. What do these three examples suggest about the re-formation of a national identity (Unit 1)?

Despite problems and negative reactions, multiculturalism continues to become an increasing factor in American life. The U.S. military, corporations, governments, colleges, universities, and other mainstream institutions continue to reflect increasing American diversity brought on by the lasting effects of the civil rights movement, current immigration patterns, and demographic changes. Will the Obama effect lead to a broadening of the inclusion of African Americans and immigrants of color? How will Americanization take place in the future among the foreign born? One thing is certain; the Obama era will have an impact on race relations within the United States. The nature and content of this impact remain to be seen. The real sociological drama is that American identity continues to be a work in progress.

Trends in the Study of Race and Ethnicity

Race and ethnicity were not focal concerns of American scholarship prior to the dawn of the twentieth century; thus, there was a dearth of course offerings on this subject matter within American colleges and universities. The Chicago School of Sociology is credited with introducing the formal study of race relations in

American colleges and universities in the 1920s. Beginning with Robert Park, a journalist turned sociologist, along with Ernest Burgess and their colleagues, the study of race and ethnic groups emerged as a primary area in twentieth-century history and sociology due to their introduction of such courses at the University of Chicago. Park's cycle of race relations and the idea of assimilation served the country well in terms of policy, as immigrants believed they, and especially their children, would eventually be accepted in their new culture.

Much later in the twentieth century, a pluralist perspective emerged that offered a challenge to the notion of assimilation. Cultural pluralism, a concept noted by Milton Gordon in 1964, refers to the many different cultural systems within the framework of the larger society. When contrasted to assimilation theory, pluralism offers an explanation for the lack of mixing and merging of cultural groups.

It should be noted that the following works on Reconstruction, Ulrich B. Phillips, *American Negro Slavery,* and William Dunning, *Reconstruction, Political and Economic: 1865–1877,* were the primary influences of research and teaching on race prior to the 1950s. The revisionist/reformist scholars who followed them consider both as apologists for slavery and racism. African American intellectuals whose scholarship challenged the perspectives on race presented by Phillips and Dunning found it very difficult to secure publication of their own works. Despite these challenges, black scholars such as Rayford Logan (*The Betrayal of the Negro: From Rutherford B. Hayes to Woodrow Wilson*) and E. Franklin Frazier (*The Negro Family in the United States*) were able to publish works that challenged the traditional notions of race promoted by white scholars of the earlier period.

Some of the most significant challenges to the scholarship and teaching of race that prevailed during the segregation era came from white scholars of a leftist orientation. Two prime examples of this scholarly tradition are the multiple-volume work, *A Documentary History of the Negro People in the United States,* by the Marxist historian Herbert Aptheker; and Philip Foner's *Mrs. Lincoln and Mrs. Keckly: The Remarkable Story of the Friendship between a First Lady and a Former Slave.* In contrast to traditional history books, Howard Zinn, in *A People's History of the United States: 1492–Present,* highlights the contributions of people of color, women, and immigrants to American culture.

Increasingly, the scholarly literature places immigration in the larger context of globalization. For some, immigration has been promoted directly and indirectly by the idea that global trade is the key to economic prosperity. This is seen as the case for rich as well as poor nations and has stimulated the movement of people from sex slaves to field hands. Thus, there is concern with the economic impact of immigration on the existing workforce (Issues 13, 14, and 16). The impact of a revitalized conservatism in politics, government, and society has been attended by challenges to diversity and multiculturalism and a reemphasis on an "American" identity and its concomitant impact on immigration and immigrants (Issues 1, 2, and 6).

Immigrants who came to the United States often received an "industrial welcome." This positive participation in certain labor markets was facilitated by existing shortages of labor within certain sectors of the economy dominated by menial jobs of low status and offering minimal remuneration. A good example of this orientation toward low-wage workers can be seen in the situation faced by immigrant labor from Latin America in agriculture. Workers from the existing American labor markets tend to find farm labor as undesirable and thus they are quite willing for Mexicans and other Latinos to do this "dirty work" of society. However, when immigrants begin to compete with native workers for higher status jobs in pursuit of upward mobility, the result is social conflict between and among such groups.

Social conflict theories offer us important insights into significant areas of race and ethnic relations. Theories of economic competition and cultural conflict are important theoretical perspectives for examining such intergroup relations. Also, Herbert Blumer's theory of group position became another important analytical construct that can be profitably employed to examine competition and conflict within race and ethnic relations (Issue 9).

The inevitable conflicts between and among immigrant groups and racial minorities living in a new country were examined by the emerging social sciences. Within these disciplines, Theodore Adorno, Gordon Allport, Robert Merton, and others applied social scientific thought to prejudice, discrimination, and racism. Some of these problems and issues are explored in this edition (Issue 9).

In the wake of the landmark decision of the U.S. Supreme Court of 1954 and the civil rights movement, new opportunities for advancing the study of race and ethnicity emerged. In the wake of this opening, other scholars including Eric Foner, John Hope Franklin, Thomas Pettigrew, Thomas F. Gossett, Cornel West, and many others proliferated within the academic community to advance this interdisciplinary area of scholarly concern. Emerging in academia now are new programs and college majors whose primary focus is on the unique history and experiences of racial and ethnic groups.

Renewed interest in immigration has emerged in response to changing American demographics. Consider that recent immigration trends show significant growth of the Asian, and especially the Latino, components of the American population (Unit 4). The increasing racial and ethnic diversity of America today is not without its controversy. What is the role of race in an increasingly multicultural society? How does the shift in dominant–subordinate relations affect members of the dominant group? These questions are reviewed in the book under the following issues: Is Diversity an Inevitable Part of a New American Identity? (Issue 2), Is Today's Immigration Debate Racist? (Issue 14) and Are America's Public Schools Resegregating? (Issue 17).

The developments referred to above have occurred at a time when the impact of recent immigrant groups on American society and culture in the twenty-first century may well be transformational. The reality is quite simple—Asian and Latino populations are increasing due to immigration and natural birth rate factors. As a result, the portion of the U.S. population that is represented by these two groups is increasing. Also, the African American population continues to grow, but not at the rate of Latinos or Asians. In responses to these trends, demographers project that people of color collectively will become the majority of the population of the United States by mid-century. Whites will continue to be the largest cohort within the population of the nation but they will no longer be the majority. As a result of these anticipated developments, American leaders and the social institutions with which they are associated will face major challenges to accommodate this new demographic make-up. As the impact of the growing multiculturalism and diversity that is developing intensifies, the nation will be challenged to be more inclusive regarding the membership of the ranks of elites and the opportunities of the members of this new majority to participate more broadly within social institutions. Failure to meet these challenges effectively will threaten the nation's future.

More recent developments in the study of race and ethnicity include the increasing research and publication on white skin privilege (Issue 7) and racial profiling (Issue 11). The emerging scholarship from underrepresented minority scholars of Asian, Latino, and Native American backgrounds suggests an expanding group of thinkers bringing new perspectives and adding to the scholarship of race and ethnic studies. At the same time, we see the proliferation of influential conservative think tanks and media-based talk shows. Thus, current scholarship reflects some of these divisions regarding immigration, national identity, race, and ethnicity in the popular culture.

To the Student

Emphasis on diversity and multiculturalism may reflect a fundamental shift in American culture in terms of the language and vocabulary of American identity. At the same time, healing racial and ethnic issues takes more than changing labels. It requires attitude changes, which are not easy, and institutional changes, which develop slowly in conjunction with public and private policy change. Clearly, disparities in education and economic opportunity persist. Let us begin a reasonable, respectful discussion about important issues, their causes, and possible ways to move forward.

Does "American" constitute multicultural and multiethnic ancestry? Or does it constitute one dominant racial and ethnic group together with many (growing) subordinate groups? We would like to move beyond the "blame the individual" dichotomy versus the "blame society" dichotomy and engage in a discourse that includes the past along with the present demographic reality.

It is our hope that, in the end, students will gain a greater understanding of the diversity that is the American experience. Further, we hope that students will develop the skills to elevate the discourse of race and ethnic issues through reading, respectful discussion, and critical analysis. These issues need sociological scrutiny because without critical thinking, they are so often determined by popular culture and media-influenced ideas. At the same time the student is assessing American culture, he or she can then grasp the individual issue of identity. Without theory and historical perspective, one essentially has no context for ideas that otherwise may reflect a narrow, incomplete picture of the culture.

Some limitations in this didactic approach of study, which positions one selection against another for the purpose of "debate," must be recognized. At times, one side of the issue is clearly and articulately stated, whereas the opposite position lacks these qualities. We have tried to find scholarly representations of different points of view. In the process, however, we have found this to be easier said than done. So, selections from the popular press, often written by public intellectuals reflecting different points of view, are included. Also, we are aware that the issues may have greater complexity than the two positions offered. Clearly, we run the risk of creating a false dichotomy. It is our expectation that the positions included in the reader will generate interest and insight for the student. The carefully selected additional sources appear in the newly created "Exploring the Issue" sections. They are excellent starting points for further research.

Some of the analytical questions may strike the reader as simplistic or even trivial. For example, how can scholars evaluate the permanence of racism in America? Clearly, a definitive yes or no answer ignores a growing body of scholarship concerning racism and related issues. Thus, we seek additional understanding by locating the issue in a debate-style format that enables the student to organize and express his or her ideas while, at the same time, critically examining the stated points of view. The "Exploring the Issue" section following each debate offers students the opportunity for additional research.

Despite its potential limitations, the *Taking Sides* format serves as an introduction to the student as he or she tries to structure thoughts and ideas in these controversial areas. We consider America as a society whose unifying identity is rooted in ethnic and racial diversity. How the diversity plays out— that is, the structures and the forms it takes—is of sociological interest to us. In sum, we want students to explore critically the historical and contemporary experiences of racial and ethnic groups in America.

Issues in This New Edition

This edition builds on our previous four publications (fifth to eighth editions) in consideration of the most recent American trends in the field of race and ethnicity. Our quest to locate and present two sides of a topic covers a wide variety of sources and, at times, we are limited in the selection process due to considerations of space, permissions, and availability of college-level articles. We seek to elevate the treatment of issues on race and ethnicity to a level of responsible scholarship. From time to time, polar opposite positions on a given issue may lead to a more vituperative debate. At other times, after careful study and discussion, different positions may not be viewed as incompatible, but closer to a common ground. Nevertheless, the different positions reflect the evolving nature of American society and culture and deserve to be understood. The net result, we hope, is a deeper and greater understanding of race and ethnicity and their impact upon American culture.

The student or professor familiar with the previous four editions will note that our focus continues to be on American race and ethnic issues. Clearly, in the larger picture, the study of race and ethnicity benefits from a cross-national approach. Although we do not ignore global trends, especially in consideration of immigration, we can do justice to American race and ethnicity only in one volume. We have recommended to our senior editor that global issues of race and ethnicity be considered for a separate publication.

Our decision to focus on American issues is based on the judgment that race, ethnicity, and immigration are fundamental to understanding the American experience and that unresolved issues on these fronts continue to challenge society in the twenty-first century. We have made a concerted effort to move beyond the black–white dichotomy in clear recognition that issues of race and ethnicity are more complex and extensive.

This edition is organized around five concepts: (1) Race, Ethnicity, and American Identity in a Nation of Immigrants, (2) Rethinking the Color Line, (3) Race Still Matters, (4) Immigration: New Faces, Old Questions, and (5) The Geography of Race and Ethnicity. We urge students to understand the persistent role of race and ethnicity in American society and its likely impact on the larger culture as well as on public policy.

Unit 1, "Race, Ethnicity, and American Identity in a Nation of Immigrants," introduces students to the classic question of American identity. What is an American? Specifically, students will contemplate, in the context of race, ethnicity, and American identity, "Who am I?" and "Who are we?" From the early years of the new nation, immigration and slavery confronted both newcomers and those who preceded them. Thus, how to understand the making of an American identity includes consideration of both. Each of the issues in this unit of the book deals with American identity in the context of prevailing ideologies—commonness, diversity, white identity, and the notion of a post-racial society. Students are encouraged to develop a broad, historical perspective on these issues that are still with us today.

Unit 2, "Rethinking the Color Line," deals with challenges to ideas of a new American identity, which have been brought about by recent immigration trends and changes in race relations. In one sense, this unit reflects the convergence of race and immigration. At the same time, emphasis is on the role of race and skin color as American identity shifts. Why is there a current emphasis on a color-blind society? Is this emphasis a new form of racism? Or, is it an effort to transcend race differences politically as well as sociologically? White privilege in America is explored in Issue 7. Is racism a permanent feature of American society? The question of the permanence of racism may at first seem audacious, but its examination will benefit student understanding of race relations. New to this edition is the issue of the use of Native American mascots by professional, collegiate, and high school sports teams. Is this another indication of embedded racism?

Unit 3, "Race Still Matters," deals with the impact of prejudice, discrimination, and the lingering effect of race on minority groups as well as on the larger society. How extensive is racial profiling? The issue of the digital divide adds a contemporary suggestion that, indeed, race still matters. Is the digital divide a new manifestation of American racism? This unit closes with a study of the continuing debate of affirmative action policy.

Unit 4, "Immigration: New Faces, Old Questions," begins with the classic immigration issue—does it make for a better America? This ageless question is positioned in terms of current immigration patterns and society's reaction. Has race become a hidden part of the immigration debate? What policies should be developed concerning current immigration, competition, and conflict over employment and bilingualism? New to this edition is the question of birthright citizenship. Should children of undocumented immigrants have a birthright to American citizenship?

Unit 5, "The Geography of Race and Ethnicity," presents a spatial assessment of segregation, resegregation, and voter redistricting to examine race and ethnicity further. We think the lens of geography is a useful tool for examining issues of racial discrimination in public schools, voting districts, and America's prisons. Why does resegregation occur? Further, a sense of space reflected in the comfort zone of selecting where one chooses to sit, stand, or congregate is seen as a type of personal geography. Why does self-segregation take place, not only among minorities but also among the white majority? This edition closes with a new issue concerning the mass incarceration of blacks. Is this the new Jim Crow?

Editors' Note

We have been engaged in a fascinating and endless four-decade dialogue about race and ethnicity within American society. Putting together this reader and updating it every two years give us the opportunity to examine and frame some of the critical problems and issues of the field. We encourage feedback from our readers. E-mail responses to rdangelo@sjcny.edu.

Raymond D'Angelo
St. Joseph's College

Herbert Douglas
Rowan University

Internet References . . .

United States Census Bureau

The U.S. Census Bureau website presents useful demographic information on ancestry, citizenship, and foreign-born citizens. The links to Hispanic and Asian minority data are extensive. This site is a very good starting point for the serious student to gain background information on race and ethnicity.

www.uscensus.gov

Guide to Sociological Resources

SocioWeb is an excellent starting place for information and research opportunities in the field of sociology including race relations, demography, and population, all of which relate directly to clashing views on race and ethnicity.

www.socioweb.com

American Ethnic Studies: Yale Library Research Guide

At Yale University, this website provides sources for researching ethnic identity including research guides in African American, Latino, Native American, Asian American, and American studies. It is a valuable site for students to begin research in race and ethnic relations, offering multiple links to college libraries and scholarly journals. Includes links to guides, encyclopedias, and dictionaries, along with connections to museums, centers, institutes, and databases.

www.library.yale.edu/rsc/ethnic/internet.html

American Studies: Georgetown University

This website contains the largest bibliography of web-based resources in the field of American studies. The "Race, Ethnicity and Identity" section offers reference and research opportunity for students.

http://cfdev.georgetown.edu/endls/asw/

Pat Buchanan

This is the official website for conservative columnist Pat Buchanan. It offers daily postings and strong position statements from the conservative viewpoint dealing with topics ranging from immigration to international affairs. There are links to several conservative Internet sources.

http://buchanan.org/blog/

Library of Congress (LOC)

This website offers an extensive online collection including areas of interest to students of race and ethnicity. The section titled "American Memory: U.S. History and Culture" presents a good deal of information to the student including an online exhibit of African American history. The LOC also offers an extensive collection in its Hispanic division.

http://memory.loc.gov/ammem/aaohtml/exhibit/aointro.html

Race, Ethnicity, and American Identity in a Nation of Immigrants

*T*here *are a number of concerns that have challenged America throughout its history. Given the fact that immigration has been a significant factor
in shaping the nation, significant concerns with immigration and immigration policies have confronted the American body politic over time. Immigration has challenged the traditional notion of American identity, which
was based upon white, Anglo-Saxon, and Protestant cultural dominance
with minority racial groups such as Native Americans and blacks confined
geographically to reservations and southern plantations. New immigration
raises serious issues concerning the maintenance of an American* unum
*and the melting pot ideal. Recently, increase in the diversity of the Ameri-
can population, to which immigration has been a major contributor, has
brought substantial issues of race relations to the fore. Most recently, Latino
immigration has emerged as a major domestic issue presenting new challenges to American culture and identity. Racial minorities have challenged
the nation to live up to the true meaning of its creed where issues of equity
and social justice are concerned, and these issues and concerns have been
illuminated within the experiences of African Americans and those peoples
of color who have swelled the ranks of America's immigrant experience.
Recent claims that America is moving toward a postracial society represent
a new stab at redefining American identity. Prejudice and discrimination
still remain as obstacles for new immigrants to overcome in pursuit of the
American dream.*

- Do We Need a Common Identity?
- Is Diversity an Inevitable Part of a New American Identity?
- Do Recent Immigration Trends Challenge Existing Ideas of America's White Identity?
- Is the Obama Presidency Moving Toward a Post-Racial Society?

ISSUE 1

Do We Need a Common Identity?

YES: Patrick J. Buchanan, from "Nation or Notion?" *The American Conservative* (October 4, 2006)

NO: Michael Walzer, from "What Does It Mean to Be an 'American'?" *Social Research* (Fall 1990)

Learning Outcomes

After reading this issue, the student should be able to:

- Come away with an understanding of competing views on sources of national identity.
- Understand the concern with national identity in historical context.
- Identify the meaning of important concepts including cultural pluralism and assimilation.
- Properly conceptualize the important scholars associated with American identity and state the significance of their contribution to this issue.
- Link the issue of national identity to subsequent issues in this reader including diversity, immigration, postracial identity, bilingualism, and colorblindness.

ISSUE SUMMARY

YES: Patrick J. Buchanan, a syndicated conservative columnist and author of *The Death of the West: How Dying Populations and Immigrant Invasions Imperil Our Country and Civilizations* (St. Martin's Griffin, 2002), argues that America needs one common identity. He views attempts to change America's historic identity as fraudulent.

NO: Michael Walzer, professor at the Institute for Advanced Study, makes the pluralist argument that America cannot avoid its multicultural identity. He explores the ways in which citizenship and nationality are compatible with the preservation of one's ethnic identity, culture, and community.

T his edition of *Taking Sides: Race and Ethnicity* begins with the complex issue of American identity. Given the different ethnicities and races and varied background differences of the many groups of people who have become Americans, the question of a common identity is inevitable. What is an American? When does an immigrant become an "American"? Indeed, the parallel issues of race and ethnicity are at the heart of the American experience. Hence, to understand American identity is to consider the uniqueness of American culture along with what holds it together. The American identity that was established during the Colonial Period was primarily rooted in Anglo-Saxon German cultural tradition. European immigrant culture dealt with racial differences through the institution of slavery and the isolation of Native Americans on reserve lands. Throughout American history, the ideal of a common American culture has been consistently challenged. Central to the challenges is the changing racial and ethnic composition of the society and the diverse imagery that these changes are producing. These competing cultural groups within the society all expect to be perceived as Americans and to share in a common American identity. This dilemma is fundamental to examination of the assimilation versus pluralism debate. Today's emphasis on diversity and multiculturalism is the latest manifestation of the issue.

Who is eligible to become an American? Until the Civil War, only European American males who owned property could exercise full citizenship. Africans were isolated as slaves on southern plantations, whereas Native Americans were confined to areas of reserve lands. The abolition of slavery led to an immediate—and temporary—citizenship inclusion for former slaves, but the brief historical period known as the Reconstruction Era soon gave way to a century of Jim Crow culture. As segregation advanced in society, Native Americans continued to be confined to reservations. Clearly, racial minority groups were separated from whites. An honest treatment of African Americans did not emerge until the 1950s. To what extent did a common American identity ever exist? Can one confuse the dominant Anglo-Saxon culture of the past with a common ("the" common) American identity?

Patrick Buchanan claims that for the United States to exist, it must have an "ethno-cultural core" and people who believe that they are bound together "by ancestry, history, and destiny." He is critical of a view held by some liberals and neoconservatives, including former President George W. Bush, that multiethnic nations, nations of diversity, such as the United States, can be unified and sustained by belief in a common creed. He rejects any assertion that a diverse nation in which ethnic pluralism prevails can survive simply based on creed as its unifying principle.

In the YES selection, Patrick J. Buchanan believes that immigrants must embrace the language and customs, and the values of American culture before becoming Americans. Thus, he views American identity as threatened by a shift from an emphasis on blood to an emphasis on creed. Buchanan asserts that what is needed to hold a country together is one common identity based upon ancestry and culture. Due to this belief, he is concerned that continued mass immigration from across the world and our current emphasis on multiculturalism and diversity are bases for national suicide.

In the NO selection, Michael Walzer argues that America has no singular national identity. Further, he writes, that to be an American is "to know that

3

and to be more or less content with it." Using the ideas of Horace Kallen, an American philosopher who coined the term "cultural pluralism," Walzer advances the argument that the United States is less a union of states than a union of ethnic, racial, and religious groups.

Walzer maintains that these "unrelated natives" constitute a permanent "manyness" within American society. A dissimilation or unique cultural consciousness. The collectivity of many different racial and ethnic groups that comprise the society does not threaten American culture or its identity. To the contrary, Walzer claims that this diversity is enriching. So, given the tremendous diversity of American people, he views citizenship as the unifying force of society. Neither religion, ethnicity, race, nor any other creed has the unifying force of citizenship in a diverse nation.

Neither Walzer nor Buchanan addresses the question of a common American identity in terms of race and racism. Walzer refers to the difficulties of racial minorities in becoming part of the American *unum*. In contrast, Buchanan believes that multicultural and diverse societies are doomed to disunity. He has written that, "when it comes to the ability to assimilate into the United States, all nationalities, creeds, and cultures are not equal." The legacy of slavery and the long Jim Crow period of American history that followed it have little or no consideration within either of their arguments. This is an important observation when one considers the complexity of the issue of an American identity.

One interesting aspect of American culture is reflected in the tendency to observe and celebrate ethnic holidays. As distinct ethnic groups arrived in the United States, they added to the panoply of such celebrations. The observance of these ethnic holidays did not generate a significant level of resistance until the period of civil rights advancements for African Americans. African American's and Latino's holiday celebrations have been controversial. These celebrations have reignited a concern with core values and American identity. In that regard, African American and Latino holiday celebrations are viewed by those concerned with American identity as a threat to America's core values. It would appear that the concern with core values and identity emerges substantially in response to African American gains. Do celebrations such as St. Patrick's Day and Columbus Day threaten a common American identity? In the same context, what can we say about the celebration of Martin Luther King Day or Black History Month? How much of this celebration of ethnicity is "symbolic," as the sociologist Herbert Gans writes, or do these ethnic celebrations threaten American identity?

As you read this issue, you are urged to keep in mind that each new wave of immigrants challenges American identity. Again and again, the culture and contributions of new immigrants push Americans to ask, should we insist on a common American identity or celebrate our differences? Consider Buchanan's critique of multiculturalism and contrast it with Walzer's ideas of cultural pluralism. Is Buchanan trying to protect and preserve a dominant group culture, or is he intolerant of cultural differences? Does Walzer truly favor pluralism, or does he think a common American identity is impossible? These questions are critical for one to understand and draw conclusions concerning the quest for identity within a changing, diverse multicultural society.

YES

Patrick J. Buchanan

Nation or Notion?

*A*merica *rose from kin and culture, not an abstract proposition.*

In an address to the Young Men's Lyceum in Springfield, Illinois on Jan. 27, 1838, a 28-year-old lawyer spoke on "the Perpetuation of Our Political Institutions." Abe Lincoln asked and answered a rhetorical question:

At what point then is the approach of danger to be expected? I answer, if it ever reach us, it must spring up among us. It cannot come from abroad. If destruction be our lot, we must ourselves be its author and finisher. As a nation of freemen, we must live through all time, or die by suicide.

Lincoln saw ahead a quarter of a century—to civil war.

The question that must be asked a century and a half after Lincoln's death is the one that troubled his generation. Are we on the path to national suicide?

The America of yesterday has vanished, and the America of tomorrow holds promise of becoming a land our parents would not recognize. Considering the epochal changes that have taken place in our country, the political and economic powers working toward an end to national sovereignty and independence, it is impossible to be sanguine about the permanence of the nation.

In Catholic doctrine, death occurs when the soul departs the body, after which the body begins to decompose. So it is with nations.

Patriotism is the soul of a nation. When it dies, when a nation loses the love and loyalty of its people, the nation dies and begins to decompose.

Patriotism is not nation-worship, such as we saw in Europe in the 1930s. It is not that spirit of nationalism that must denigrate or dominate other nations. It is a passionate attachment to one's own country—its land, its people, its past, its heroes, literature, language, traditions, culture, and customs. "Intellectuals tend to forget," wrote Regis Debray, "that nations hibernate, but empires grow old. The American nation will outlast the Atlantic Empire as the Russian nation will outlast the Soviet Empire."

A century ago, the French historian and philosopher Ernest Renan described a nation:

A nation is a living soul, a spiritual principle. Two things, which in truth are but one, constitute this soul, this spiritual principle. One is in the past, the other in the present. One is the common possession of a rich heritage of memories; the other is the actual consent, the desire to live together, the will to preserve worthily the undivided inheritance which has been handed down . . . The nation, like the individual, is the outcome of a long past of efforts, and sacrifices, and devotions . . . To have common glories in the past, a common will in the present; to have done great things together, to will to do the like again—such are the essential conditions of the making of a people.

This community called a nation is much more than a "division of labor" or a "market." Added Renan:

Community of interests is assuredly a powerful bond between men. But . . . can interests suffice to make a nation? I do not believe it. Community of interests makes commercial treaties. There is a sentimental side to nationality; it is at once body and soul; a Zollverein is not a fatherland.

An economic union like the European Union is not a nation. An economy is not a country. An economic system should strengthen the bonds of national union, but the nation is of a higher order than the construct of any economist. A nation is organic; a nation is alive. A constitution does not create a nation. A nation writes a constitution that is the birth certificate of the nation already born in the hearts of its people.

"'Nation'—as suggested by its Latin root nascere, to be born—intrinsically implies a link by blood," wrote Peter Brimelow in National Review in 1992. "A nation in a real sense is an extended family. The merging process through which all nations pass is not merely cultural, but to a considerable extent biological through intermarriage."

Brimelow describes a nation as an "ethno-cultural community—an interlacing of ethnicity and culture," that "speaks one language." He cites the late senator from New York:

In his recent book Pandaemonium, Senator Daniel Patrick Moynihan even used this rigorous definition, in an effort to capture both culture and ethnicity: a nation is a group of people who believe they are ancestrally related. It is the largest grouping that shares that belief.

To be a nation, a people must believe they are a nation and that they share a common ancestry, history, and destiny. Whatever ethnic group to which we may belong, we Americans must see ourselves as of a unique and common nationality—in order to remain a nation.

There is a rival view, advanced by neoconservatives and liberals, that America is a different kind of nation, not held together by the bonds of history and memory, tradition and custom, language and literature, birth and faith, blood and soil. Rather, America is a creedal nation, united by a common commitment to a set of ideas and ideals.

"Americans of all national origins, classes, religions, creeds and colors, have something in common . . . a political creed," wrote Gunnar Myrdal in 1944.

During the battle over Proposition 187 in 1994, when 59 percent of the California electorate voted to cut off welfare to illegal aliens, Jack Kemp and Bill Bennett accepted Myrdal's idea, declaring, "The American national identity is based on a creed, on a set of principles and ideas."

Irving Kristol embraced the Bennett-Kemp view when he compared the United States to the former USSR: "[L]arge nations, whose identity is ideological, like the Soviet Union of yesterday and the United States of today, have ideological interests in addition to more material concerns."

FDR seemed to agree, asserting, "Americanism is a matter of the mind and heart. Americanism is not, and never was, a matter of race and ancestry. A good American is one who is loyal to this country and to our creed of liberty and democracy." To be one nation, said Bill Clinton, all we need to do is define ourselves by "our primary allegiance to the values America stands for and values we really live by."

In his first inaugural address, George W. Bush endorsed the creedal-nation concept: "America has never been united by blood or birth or soil. We are bound by ideals that move us beyond our backgrounds, lift us above our interests, and teach us what it means to be citizens."

To this idea of America as a creedal nation bound together not "by blood or birth or soil" but by "ideals," there is a corollary that has driven immigration policy for 40 years—that people of any culture or continent can be assimilated with equal ease, depending only upon whether they assent to the tenets of our creed.

Demonstrably, this is false. Human beings are not blank slates. Nor can they be easily separated from the abiding attachments of the tribe, race, nation, culture, community whence they came. Any man or woman, of any color or creed, can be a good American. But when it comes to the ability to assimilate into the United States, all nationalities, creeds, and cultures are not equal.

"During my life, I have seen Frenchmen, Italians, Russians, and so on," wrote Joseph de Maistre, "but I must say, as for man, I have never come across him anywhere; if he exists, he is completely unknown to me." Maistre's point, notes Sam Francis, "was that 'tribal behavior' is what makes human beings human. Take it away from 'man' or 'humankind' and what you get is not 'pure man' or 'liberated man' but dehumanization . . ."

Americans are an identifiable people. When traveling abroad, they are recognizable by their speech and mannerisms, not because they have been interrogated on their beliefs in democracy and free markets.

In the most famous depiction of Americans as a new, unique, and separate people, John Jay wrote in Federalist No. 2:

> Providence has been pleased to give this one connected country to one united people—a people descended from the same ancestors, speaking the same language, professing the same religion, attached to the same principles of government, very similar in their manners and customs, and who, by their joint counsels, arms, and efforts, fighting side by side throughout a long and bloody war, have nobly established their general liberty and independence.

"This country and this people seem to have been made for each other," Jay continues, calling his countrymen "a band of brethren." Thus, before the Constitution was ratified, John Jay considered Americans "one united people," "one connected country," and "brethren," of common blood. What holds this "one united people" together? Says Jay: language, faith, culture, and memory.

Each nation's culture, be it that of France, England, or America, gives the nation its particular character. Tom Fleming, editor of Chronicles, notes:

> Culture . . . means the cultivation of a certain kind of character. Cultural institutions . . . are the agents that make us who and what we are. Like Tennyson's Ulysses, you and I can say, 'I am part of all that I have met': the books we read, the music we listen to, the pictures we look at, the prayers we say. A culture is the sum of all these things and many more, including table manners and styles of dress. As an American poet put it, 'The way you wear your hat, the way you drink your tea . . .'

To traditional conservatives, this "creedal nation" exists in the minds of men of words. It is an intellectual construct, to which men can render neither love nor loyalty. For two centuries, men have died for America. Who would lay down his life for the UN, the EU, or a "North American Union"?

When Japan attacked Pearl Harbor, college students stood beside sharecroppers' sons to enlist. These men were not volunteering to defend abstract ideas. For democracy was not attacked. Equality was not attacked. America was attacked. Many had likely never read Jefferson, Hamilton, or Madison, and some would die never having read them. They were patriots united by nationality. They were Americans, and they fought, bled, and died as Americans, no matter what they believed.

Every true nation is the creation of a unique people. Indeed, if America is an ideological nation grounded no deeper than the sandy soil of abstract ideas, she will not survive the storms of this century any more [than] the Soviet Union survived the last. When the regime, party, army, and police that held that ideological nation together lost the will to keep it together, the USSR broke down along the fault lines of nationality, faith, and culture. True nations, held together not by any political creed but by patriotism, emerged from the rubble.

In the great crisis of his empire, Hitler's invasion, Stalin did not call on his subjects to save communism. He called on Russia's sons to defend Mother Russia against the Germanic hordes. Communist to the core, Stalin yet knew that men do not die for secular creeds like Marxism and Leninism, but for the "ashes of their fathers and the temples of their gods."

France considers herself a creedal nation, whose unifying beliefs date to the Enlightenment and Revolution. But when the Revolution tore France to pieces, what held her together through the Napoleonic wars, Sédan, and loss of Alsace, and Verdun, as she divided over ideology and faith, was nationality and culture. Whether monarchical, republican, imperial, or democratic, the French nation and people endure. And if the French cease to be the dominant tribe, adherence to Enlightenment ideas will not save France.

Should America lose her ethnic-cultural core and become a nation of nations, America will not survive. For nowhere on this earth can one find a multicultural, multiethnic, multilingual nation that is not at risk. Democracy is not enough. Equality is not enough. Free markets are not enough to hold a people together.

"Nationalism remains, after two centuries, the most vital political emotion in the world," concedes Arthur Schlesinger, "far more vital than social ideologies such as communism or fascism or even democracy." And inside the nation, "nationalism takes the form of ethnicity and tribalism."

As Samuel Huntington has written:

> America is a founded society created by seventeenth- and eighteenth-century settlers, almost all of whom came from the British Isles . . . They initially defined America in terms of race, ethnicity, culture, and most importantly religion. Then in the eighteenth century they also had to define America ideologically to justify their independence from their home-countrymen.

The ideology was created by colonial elites to justify the breaking of blood ties with their British brethren. But before the ideology came the country.

George Washington had once sought to become an officer in the British army. But by the end of the French and Indian War, he had begun to see the British not as kinsmen but as overlords. In heart and soul, well before the Second Continental Congress, Washington was an American.

After the Boston Tea Party in 1773, Patrick Henry declared, "The distinctions between Virginians, Pennsylvanians, and New Yorkers and New Englanders are no more. I am not a Virginian, but an American." That was two years before Jefferson wrote the first draft of the Declaration of Independence.

The Declaration stated what was already known: the Americans had become a people. In his first draft, Jefferson had written of "our British brethren," who have failed to honor "the ties of our common kindred" and proven themselves "deaf to the voice of . . . consanguinity." These are matters of blood and kinship. The Native Americans shared our continent but were not our kinsmen. To Jefferson and the signers of '76, they were those "merciless Indian Savages, whose known rule of warfare, is an undistinguished destruction, of all Ages, Sexes & Conditions."

"What then is the American, this new man?" was the famous question of the French émigré Henri St. John de Crèvecoeur. To which he gave his classic answer:

> He is an American, who leaving behind all his ancient prejudices and manners, receives new ones from the new mode of life he has embraced, the new government he obeys, and the new rank he holds. The American is a new man, who acts upon new principles . . . Here individuals of all nations are melted into a new race of men.

To preserve this "new race of men," Washington, in a 1792 letter to John Adams, urged that immigrants be spread out among the people.

[T]he policy . . . of [immigration] taking place in a body (I mean settling them in a body) may be much questioned; for, by so doing, they retain the language, habits and principles (good or bad) which they bring with them. Whereas by an intermixture with our people, they or their descendants get assimilated to our customs and laws: in a word soon become one people.

The Father of our country believed that before they could become Americans, immigrants must embrace our language and customs as well as our principles.

For Hamilton, America's success depended on the "preservation of a national spirit and national character" that immigrants must come to share with our native-born. The safety of the republic rested on "love of country" and the "exemption of citizens from foreign bias and prejudice." Assimilation, he wrote, would enable "aliens to get rid of foreign and acquire American attachment . . ."

John Quincy Adams set down the conditions for newcomers: "They must cast off the European skin, never to resume it. They must look forward to their posterity rather than backward to their ancestors . . ."

Theodore Roosevelt echoed Adams's conviction. He thundered again and again against "hyphenated-Americanism." "Either a man is an American and nothing else, or he is not an American at all," said T.R.

This is the traditionalist view: that Americans are a people apart from all others, with far more in common than political beliefs. It is this America that is imperiled by the mass migration of millions from countires whose peoples have never before been assimilated. And if the organic America of the traditionalists dies, the "creedal nation" of Kemp, Kristol, Bennett, and Bush will not survive.

By Jay's definition, can anyone say today that we are "one united people"? We are no longer descended from the same ancestors. The European core—almost 90 percent of all Americans as late as 1965—has fallen well below 70 percent and will be less than half the nation by 2050.

We no longer speak the same language, nor do we insist that immigrants learn English. Of the 9 million living in Los Angeles County, 5 million do not speak English at home. School children in Chicago are taught in 100 languages. The fastest growing radio and TV stations in America broadcast in Spanish.

Nor do Americans any longer profess the same faith. We are no longer Protestant, Catholic, and Jew, as sociologist Will Herberg described us in 1955. We are Protestant, Catholic, Jew, Orthodox, Mormon, Muslim, Hindu, Buddhist, Taoist, Shintoist, Santeria, New Age, voodoo, agnostic, atheist, humanist, Rastafarian, and Wiccan.

We never fought "side by side throughout a long and bloody war." The Greatest Generation is passing on, and if the rest of us recall "a long and bloody war," it was Korea, Vietnam, or Iraq, and not for long did we remain "side by side." For a time the Cold War united us. But that, too, is over.

We are yet "attached to the same principles of government." But this is not enough to hold a nation together. The South was attached to the same principles of government. But that did not prevent it from fighting four bloody years. If

Robert E. Lee could ride across the Long Bridge to Virginia to take up arms against the United States, is it not naïve to believe that scores of millions of aliens without roots here will put America ahead of the homelands they left behind?

Nor do Americans treasure history or revere heroes as we once did. What many still see as a glorious past, others see as shameful history. To many, the discovery of America by the explorers and the winning of the West are no longer seen as heroic events but as matters of which Western man should be ashamed.

Huntington writes, "To reject the central ideas of that doctrine [our political creed] is to be un-American." Two of the central ideas of Huntington's political creed are democracy and equality. How do the Founding Fathers measure up?

Jefferson was a slaveholder who wrote of an "aristocracy of virtue and talent, which nature has wisely provided for the direction of the interests of society . . ." Madison, the author of the Constitution, headed the American Colonization Society, "in the belief that its plan to return slaves to Africa represented the most sensible way out of that long-festering crisis." After Madison's death, leadership passed to Henry Clay, who was eulogized in 1852 by Lincoln.

The unequal treatment of our fellow Americans of African descent for a century after Appomattox was a grave injustice and historic wrong. Nonetheless, we cannot deny that the greatest of our forefathers approved these things. If a belief in equality is the sine qua non of being an American, then the authors of the Declaration of Independence, the Constitution, and the Gettysburg Address do not qualify.

What of a belief in democracy being an indispensable part of the "American Creed"? "Democracy . . . wastes, exhausts, and murders itself. There is never a democracy that did not commit suicide," wrote Adams. "A democracy [is] the only pure republic, but impracticable beyond the limits of a town," added Jefferson. Madison was more negative. Writing in Federalist No. 10, he declared, "democracies have ever been spectacles of turbulence and contention: have ever been incompatible with personal security or the rights of property; and have in general been as short in their lives as they have been violent in their deaths." Said Hamilton: "The ancient democracies, in which the people themselves deliberated, never possessed one feature of good government. Their very nature was tyranny."

If a commitment to democracy is an indispensable element of the American Creed that unites the nation, the Founding Fathers seem not to qualify as 100 percent American.

Whether America is a nation like all others or a different kind of nation is more than an academic question. For who wins the argument determines America's destiny. As Huntington points out, "National interest derives from national identity. We have to know who we are before we can know what our interests are."

The scheme to redefine America's identity as other than what America has always been is a historic fraud, concocted by ideologues to divert the nation away from a traditional foreign policy into crusades to remake the world in a democratist mould.

Inventing a new past for America as a creedal nation—the kind of nation our forefathers would have rebelled against—neoconservatives hope to control a future they see as fulfilling America's mission: to democratize mankind. Americans are being indoctrinated in a fabricated creed that teaches they are being untrue to themselves and faithless to their fathers unless they go abroad in search of monsters to destroy.

Whether America is a traditional nation or an ideological nation is also critical to the immigration debate. For if America is a "propositional nation," then who comes and whence they come do not matter. Indeed, the more who come and assent to the American "proposition," the stronger and better nation we become. That way lies the remaking of America into the first universal nation of Ben Wattenberg's dream and Teddy Roosevelt's nightmare, when he warned against our becoming a "tangle of squabbling minorities" and no longer a nation at all.

Before Americans ever adopted a creed, Americans were a people and America was a nation. Those who equate the creed with the nation rewrite that history to convert America into something she never was: an imperial democracy imposing her ideology on a resisting world, to the ruin of the Republic she was meant to be. And they will turn America into something she cannot survive becoming: a multicultural, multiethnic, multilingual Tower of Babel.

If we are a creedal nation, united by a commitment to democracy, equality, and liberty, with a mandate and mission to impose those ideas and ideals on mankind, we shall have a foreign policy like that of George W. Bush. But if we are a traditional nation, our national interests will be traditional: the defense of our land and the preservation of the lives and liberty of our people.

Language, faith, culture, and history—and, yes, birth, blood, and soil—produce a people, not an ideology. After the ideologies and creeds that seized Germany, Italy, and Russia by the throat in the 20th century were all expunged, Germans remained German, Italians remained Italian, and Russians remained Russian. After three decades of Maoist madness, the Chinese remain Chinese.

"Historically," Huntington writes, "American identity has had two primary components: culture and creed . . . If multiculturalism prevails and if the consensus on liberal democracy disintegrates, the United States could join the Soviet Union on the ash heap of history."

Democracy is not enough. If the culture dies, the country dies.

Michael Walzer  **NO**

What Does It Mean to Be an "American"?

There is no country called America. We live in the United States *of America,* and we have appropriated the adjective "American" even though we can claim no exclusive title to it. Canadians and Mexicans are also Americans, but they have adjectives more obviously their own, and we have none. Words like "unitarian" and "unionist" won't do; our sense of ourselves is not captured by the mere fact of our union, however important that is. Nor will "statist," even "united statist," serve our purposes; a good many of the citizens of the United States are antistatist. Other countries, wrote the "American" political theorist Horace Kallen, get their names from the people, or from one of the peoples, who inhabit them. "The United States, on the other hand, has a peculiar anonymity."[1] It is a name that doesn't even pretend to tell us who lives here. Anybody can live here, and just about everybody does—men and women from all the world's peoples. (The *Harvard Encyclopedia of American Ethnic Groups* begins with Acadians and Afghans and ends with Zoroastrians.[2]) It is peculiarly easy to become an American. The adjective provides no reliable information about the origins, histories, connections, or cultures of those whom it designates. What does it say, then, about their political allegiance?

Patriotism and Pluralism

American politicians engage periodically in a fierce competition to demonstrate their patriotism. This is an odd competition, surely, for in most countries the patriotism of politicians is not an issue. There are other issues, and this question of political identification and commitment rarely comes up; loyalty to the *patrie,* the fatherland (or motherland), is simply assumed. Perhaps it isn't assumed here because the United States isn't a *patrie.* Americans have never spoken of their country as a fatherland (or a motherland). The kind of natural or organic loyalty that we (rightly or wrongly) recognize in families doesn't seem to be a feature of our politics. When American politicians invoke the metaphor of family they are usually making an argument about our mutual responsibilities and welfarist obligations, and among Americans, that is a controversial argument.[3] One can be an American patriot without believing in the mutual responsibilities of American citizens—indeed, for some Americans disbelief is a measure of one's patriotism.

From *Social Research,* vol. 57, no. 3, Fall 1990, pp. 591–614. Copyright © 1990 by New School for Social Research. Reprinted by permission.

Similarly, the United States isn't a "homeland" (where a national family might dwell), not, at least, as other countries are, in casual conversation and unreflective feeling. It is a country of immigrants who, however grateful they are for this new place, still remember the old places. And their children know, if only intermittently, that they have roots elsewhere. They, no doubt, are native grown, but some awkward sense of newness here, or of distant oldness, keeps the tongue from calling this land "home." The older political uses of the word "home," common in Great Britain, have never taken root here: home counties, home station, Home Office, home rule. To be "at home" in America is a personal matter: Americans have homesteads and homefolks and home-towns, and each of these is an endlessly interesting topic of conversation. But they don't have much to say about a common or communal home.

Nor is there a common *patrie,* but rather many different ones—a multitude of fatherlands (and motherlands). For the children, even the grandchildren, of the immigrant generation, one's *patrie,* the "native land of one's ancestors," is somewhere else. The term "Native Americans" designates the very first immigrants, who got here centuries before any of the others. At what point do the rest of us, native grown, become natives? The question has not been decided; for the moment, however, the language of nativism is mostly missing (it has never been dominant in American public life), even when the political reality is plain to see. Alternatively, nativist language can be used against the politics of nativism, as in these lines of Horace Kallen, the theorist of an anonymous America:

> Behind [the individual] in time and tremendously in him in quality are his ancestors; around him in space are his relatives and kin, carrying in common with him the inherited organic set from a remoter common ancestry. In all these he lives and moves and has his being. They constitute his, literally, *natio,* the inwardness of his nativity.[4]

But since there are so many "organic sets" (language is deceptive here: Kallen's antinativist nativism is cultural, not biological), none of them can rightly be called "American." Americans have no inwardness of their own; they look inward only by looking backward.

According to Kallen, the United States is less importantly a union of states than it is a union of ethnic, racial, and religious groups—a union of otherwise unrelated "natives." What is the nature of this union? The Great Seal of the United States carries the motto *E pluribus unum,* "From many, one," which seems to suggest that manyness must be left behind for the sake of oneness. Once there were many, now the many have merged or, in Israel Zangwell's classic image, been melted down into one. But the Great Seal presents a different image: the "American" eagle holds a sheaf of arrows. Here there is no merger or fusion but only a fastening, a putting together: many-in-one. Perhaps the adjective "American" describes this kind of oneness. We might say, tentatively, that it points to the citizenship, not the nativity or nationality, of the men and women it designates. It is a political adjective, and its politics is liberal in the strict sense: generous, tolerant, ample, accommodating—it allows for the survival, even the enhancement and flourishing, of manyness.

On this view, appropriately called "pluralist," the word "from" on the Great Seal is a false preposition. There is no movement from many to one, but rather a simultaneity, a coexistence—once again, many-in-one. But I don't mean to suggest a mystery here, as in the Christian conception of a God who is three-in-one. The language of pluralism is sometimes a bit mysterious—thus Kallen's description of America as a "nation of nationalities" or John Rawls's account of the liberal state as a "social union of social unions"—but it lends itself to a rational unpacking.[5] A sheaf of arrows is not, after all, a mysterious entity. We can find analogues in the earliest forms of social organization: tribes composed of many clans, clans composed of many families. The conflicts of loyalty and obligation, inevitable products of pluralism, must arise in these cases too. And yet, they are not exact analogues of the American case, for tribes and clans lack Kallen's "anonymity." American pluralism is, as we shall see, a peculiarly modern phenomenon—not mysterious but highly complex.

In fact, the United States is not a "nation of nationalities" or a "social union of social unions." At least, the singular nation or union is not constituted by, it is not a combination or fastening together of, the plural nationalities or unions. In some sense, it includes them; it provides a framework for their coexistence; but they are not its parts. Nor are the individual states, in any significant sense, the parts that make up the United States. The parts are individual men and women. The United States is an association of citizens. Its "anonymity" consists in the fact that these citizens don't transfer their collective name to the association. It never happened that a group of people called Americans came together to form a political society called America. The people are Americans only by virtue of having come together. And whatever identity they had before becoming Americans, they retain (or, better, they are free to retain) afterward. There is, to be sure, another view of Americanization, which holds that the process requires for its success the mental erasure of all previous identities—forgetfulness or even, as one enthusiast wrote in 1918, "absolute forgetfulness."[6] But on the pluralist view, Americans are allowed to remember who they were and to insist, also, on *what else they are*.

They are not, however, bound to the remembrance or to the insistence. Just as their ancestors escaped the old country, so they can if they choose escape their old identities, the "inwardness" of their nativity. Kallen writes of the individual that "whatever else he changes, he cannot change his grandfather."[7] Perhaps not; but he can call his grandfather a "greenhorn," reject his customs and convictions, give up the family name, move to a new neighborhood, adopt a new "life-style."

He doesn't become a better American by doing these things (though that is sometimes his purpose), but he may become an American simply, an American and nothing else, freeing himself from the hyphenation that pluralists regard as universal on this side, though not on the other side, of the Atlantic Ocean. But, free from hyphenation, he seems also free from ethnicity: "American" is not one of the ethnic groups recognized in the United States census. Someone who is only an American is, so far as our bureaucrats are concerned, ethnically anonymous. He has a right, however, to his anonymity; that is part of what it means to be an American.

For a long time, British-Americans thought of themselves as Americans simply—and not anonymously: they constituted, so they would have said, a new ethnicity and a new nationality, into which all later immigrants would slowly assimilate. "Americanization" was a political program designed to make sure that assimilation would not be too slow a process, at a time, indeed, when it seemed not to be a recognizable *process* at all. But though there were individuals who did their best to assimilate, that is, to adopt, at least outwardly, the mores of British-Americans, that soon ceased to be a plausible path to an "American" future. The sheer number of non-British immigrants was too great. If there was to be a new nationality, it would have to come out of the melting pot, where the heat was applied equally to all groups, the earlier immigrants as well as the most recent ones. The anonymous American was, at the turn of the century, say, a place-holder for some unknown future person who would give cultural content to the name. Meanwhile, most Americans were hyphenated Americans, more or less friendly to their grandfathers, more or less committed to their manyness. And pluralism was an alternative political program designed to legitimize this manyness and to make it permanent—which would leave those individuals who were Americans and nothing else permanently anonymous, assimilated to a cultural nonidentity.

Citizens

But though these anonymous Americans were not better Americans for being or for having become anonymous, it is conceivable that they were, and are, better American *citizens*. If the manyness of America is cultural, its oneness is political, and it may be the case that men and women who are free from non-American cultures will commit themselves more fully to the American political system. Maybe cultural anonymity is the best possible grounding for American politics. From the beginning, of course, it has been the standard claim of British-Americans that their own culture is the best grounding. And there is obviously much to be said for that view. Despite the efforts of hyphenated Americans to describe liberal and democratic politics as a kind of United Way to which they have all made contributions, the genealogy of the American political system bears a close resemblance to the genealogy of the Sons and Daughters of the American Revolution—ethnic organizations if there ever were any![8] But this genealogy must also account for the flight across the Atlantic and the Revolutionary War. The parliamentary oligarchy of eighteenth-century Great Britain wasn't, after all, all that useful a model for America. When the ancestors of the Sons and Daughters described their political achievement as a "new order for the ages," they were celebrating a break with their own ethnic past almost as profound as that which later Americans were called upon to make. British-Americans who refused the break called themselves "Loyalists," but they were called disloyal by their opponents and treated even more harshly than hyphenated Americans from Germany, Russia, and Japan in later episodes of war and revolution.

Citizenship in the "new order" was not universally available, since blacks and women and Indians (Native Americans) were excluded, but it was never linked to a single nationality. "To be or to become an American," writes Philip Gleason, "a person did not have to be of any particular national, linguistic, religious, or ethnic background. All he had to do was to commit himself to the political ideology centered on the abstract ideals of liberty, equality, and republicanism."[9] These abstract ideals made for a politics separated not only from religion but from culture itself or, better, from all the particular forms in which religious and national culture was, and is, expressed—hence a politics "anonymous" in Kallen's sense. Anonymity suggests autonomy too, though I don't want to claim that American politics was not qualified in important ways by British Protestantism, later by Irish Catholicism, later still by German, Italian, Polish, Jewish, African, and Hispanic religious commitments and political experience. But these qualifications never took what might be called a strong adjectival form, never became permanent or exclusive qualities of America's abstract politics and citizenship. The adjective "American" named, and still names, a politics that is relatively unqualified by religion or national-ity or, alternatively, that is qualified by so many religions and nationalities as to be free from any one of them.

It is this freedom that makes it possible for America's oneness to encompass and protect its manyness. Nevertheless, the conflict between the one and the many is a pervasive feature of American life. Those Americans who attach great value to the oneness of citizenship and the centrality of polit-ical allegiance must seek to constrain the influence of cultural manyness; those who value the many must disparage the one. The conflict is evident from the earliest days of the republic, but I will begin my own account of it with the campaign to restrict immigration and naturalization in the 1850s. Commonly called "nativist" by historians, the campaign was probably closer in its politics to a Rousseauian republicanism.[10] Anti-Irish and anti-Catholic bigotry played a large part in mobilizing support for the American (or American Republican) party, popularly called the Know-Nothings; and the political style of the party, like that of contemporary abolitionists and free-soilers, displayed many of the characteristics of Protestant moralism. But in its self-presentation, it was above all republican, more concerned about the civic virtue of the new immigrants than about their ethnic lineages, its religious critique focused on the ostensible connection between Catholicism and tyranny. The legislative program of the Know-Nothings had to do largely with questions of citizenship at the national level and of public education at the local level. In Congress, where the party had 75 representatives (and perhaps another 45 sympathizers, out of a total of 234) at the peak of its strength in 1855, it seemed more committed to restrict-ing the suffrage than to cutting off immigration. Some of its members would have barred "paupers" from entering the United States, and others would have required an oath of allegiance from all immigrants immediately upon landing. But their energy was directed mostly toward revising the naturalization laws.[11] It was not the elimination of manyness but its disenfranchisement that the Know-Nothings championed.

Something like this was probably the position of most American "nativists" until the last years of the nineteenth century. In 1845, when immi-gration rates were still fairly low, a group of "native Americans" meeting in

Philadelphia declared that they would "kindly receive [all] persons who came to America, and give them every privilege except office and suffrage."[12] I would guess that the nativist view of American blacks was roughly similar. Most of the northern Know-Nothings (the party's greatest strength was in New England) were strongly opposed to slavery, but it did not follow from that opposition that they were prepared to welcome former slaves as fellow citizens. The logic of events led to citizenship, after a bloody war, and the Know-Nothings, by then loyal Republicans, presumably supported that outcome. But the logic of republican principle, as they understood it, would have suggested some delay. Thus a resolution of the Massachusetts legislature in 1856 argued that "republican institutions were especially adapted to an educated and intelligent people, capable of *and accustomed to* self-government. Free institutions could be confined safely only to free men. . . . "[13] The legislators went on to urge a twenty-one-year residence requirement for naturalization. Since it was intended that disenfranchised residents should nonetheless be full members of civil society, another piece of Know-Nothing legislation would have provided that any alien free white person (this came from a Mississippi senator) should be entitled after twelve months residence "to all the protection of the government, and [should] be allowed to inherit, and hold, and transmit real estate . . . the same manner as though he were a citizen."[14]

Civil society, then, would include a great variety of ethnic and religious and perhaps even racial groups, but the members of these groups would acquire the "inestimable" good of citizenship only after a long period of practical education (but does one learn just by watching?) in democratic virtue. Meanwhile, their children would get a formal education. Despite their name, the Know-Nothings thought that citizenship was a subject about which a great deal had to be known. Some of them wanted to make attendance in public schools compulsory, but, faced with constitutional objections, they insisted only that no public funding should go to the support of parochial schools. It is worth emphasizing that the crucial principle here was not the separation of church and state. The Know-Nothing party did not oppose sabbatarian laws.[15] Its members believed that tax money should not be used to underwrite social manyness—not in the case of religion, obviously, but also not in the case of language and culture. Political identity, singular in form, would be publicly inculcated and defended; the plurality of social identities would have to be sustained in private.

I don't doubt that most nativists hoped that plurality would not, in fact, be sustained. They had ideas, if not sociological theories, about the connection of politics and culture—specifically, as I have said, republican politics and British Protestant culture. I don't mean to underestimate the centrality of these ideas: this was presumably the knowledge that the Know-Nothings were concealing when they claimed to know nothing. Nonetheless, the logic of their position, as of any "American" republican position, pressed toward the creation of a politics independent of all the ethnicities and religions of civil society. Otherwise too many people would be excluded; the political world would look too much like Old England and not at all like the "new order of the ages," not at all like "America." Nor could American nativists challenge ethnic and religious pluralism directly, for both were protected (as the parochial schools were protected) by the constitution to which they claimed a passionate attachment. They could only insist that passionate attachment should be the mark of all citizens—and set forth the usual arguments against the seriousness of love at first sight and in favor of long engagements. They wanted what Rousseau wanted: that citizens should find the greater share of their happiness in public (political) rather than in private (social) activities.[16] And they were prepared to deny citizenship to men and women who seemed to them especially unlikely to do that.

No doubt, again, public happiness came easily to the nativists because they felt so entirely at home in American public life. But we should not be too quick to attribute this feeling to the carryover of ethnic consciousness into the political sphere. For American politics in the 1850s was already so open, egalitarian, and democratic (relative to European politics) that almost anyone could feel at home in it. Precisely because the United States was no one's *national* home, its politics was universally accessible. All that was necessary in principle was ideological commitment, in practice, a good line of talk. The Irish did very well and demonstrated as conclusively as one could wish that "British" and "Protestant" were not necessary adjectives for American politics. They attached to the many, not to the one.

For this reason, the symbols and ceremonies of American citizenship could not be drawn from the political culture or history of British-Americans. Our Congress is not a Commons; Guy Fawkes Day is not an American holiday; the Magna Carta has never been one of our sacred texts. American symbols and ceremonies are culturally anonymous, invented rather than inherited, voluntaristic in style, narrowly political in content: the flag, the Pledge, the Fourth, the Constitution. It is entirely appropriate that the Know-Nothing party had its origin in the Secret Society of the Star-Spangled Banner. And it is entirely understandable that the flag and the Pledge continue, even today, to figure largely in political debate. With what reverence should the flag be treated? On what occasions must it be saluted? Should we require schoolchildren to recite the Pledge, teachers to lead the recitation? Questions like these are the tests of a political commitment that can't be assumed, because it isn't undergirded by the cultural and religious commonalities that make for mutual trust. The flag and the Pledge are, as it were, all we have. One could suggest, of course, alternative and more practical tests of loyalty—responsible participation in political life, for example. But the real historical alternative is the test proposed by the cultural pluralists: one proves one's Americanism, in their view, by living in peace with all the other "Americans," that is, by agreeing to respect social manyness rather than by pledging allegiance to the "one and indivisible" republic. And pluralists are led on by the logic of this argument to suggest that citizenship is something less than an "inestimable" good.

Hyphenated Americans

Good it certainly was to be an American citizen. Horace Kallen was prepared to call citizenship a "great vocation," but he clearly did not believe (in the 1910s and '20s, when he wrote his classic essays on cultural pluralism) that one could make a life there. Politics was a necessary, but not a spiritually sustaining activity. It was best understood in instrumental terms; it had to do with the arrangements that made it possible for groups of citizens to "realize and protect" their diverse cultures and "attain the excellence appropriate to their kind."[17] These arrangements, Kallen thought, had to be democratic, and democracy required citizens of a certain sort—autonomous, self-disciplined, capable of cooperation and compromise. "Americanization" was entirely legitimate insofar as it aimed to develop these qualities; they made up Kallen's version of civic virtue, and he was willing to say that they should be common to all Americans. But, curiously perhaps, they did not touch the deeper self. "The common city-life, which depends upon like-mindedness, is not inward, corporate, and inevitable, but external, inarticulate, and incidental . . . not the expression of a homogeneity of heritage, mentality, and interest."[18]

Hence Kallen's program: assimilation "in matters economic and political," dissimilation "in cultural consciousness."[19] The hyphen joined these two processes in one person, so that a Jewish-American (like Kallen) was similar to other Americans in his economic and political activity, but similar only to other Jews at the deeper level of culture.[20] It is clear that Kallen's "hyphenates," whose spiritual life is located so emphatically to the left of the hyphen, cannot derive the greater part of their happiness from their citizenship. Nor, in a sense, should they, since culture, for the cultural pluralists, is far more important than politics and promises a more complete satisfaction. Pluralists, it seems, do not make good republicans—for the same reason that republicans, Rousseau the classic example, do not make good pluralists. The two attend to different sorts of goods.

Kallen's hyphenated Americans can be attentive and conscientious citizens, but on a liberal, not a republican, model. This means two things. First, the various ethnic and religious groups can intervene in political life only in order to defend themselves and advance their common interests—as in the case of the NAACP or the Anti-Defamation League—but not in order to impose their culture or their values. They have to recognize that the state is anonymous (or, in the language of contemporary political theorists, neutral) at least in this sense: that it can't take on the character or the name of any of the groups that it includes. It isn't a nation-state of a particular kind and it isn't a Christian republic. Second, the primary political commitment of individual citizens is to protect their protection, to uphold the democratic framework within which they pursue their more substantive activities. This commitment is consistent with feelings of gratitude, loyalty, even patriotism of a certain sort, but it doesn't make for fellowship. There is indeed *union* in politics (and economics) but union of a sort that precludes intimacy. "The political and economic life of the commonwealth," writes Kallen, "is a single unit and serves as the foundation and background for the realization of the distinctive individuality of each *natio*."[21] Here pluralism is straightforwardly opposed to republicanism: politics offers neither self-realization nor communion. All intensity lies, or should lie, elsewhere.

Kallen believes, of course, that this "elsewhere" actually exists; his is not a utopian vision; it's not a case of "elsewhere, perhaps." The "organic groups" that make up Kallen's America appear in public life as interest groups only, organized for the pursuit of material and social goods that are universally desired but sometimes in short supply and often unfairly distributed. That is the only appearance countenanced by a liberal and democratic political system. But behind it, concealed from public view, lies the true significance of ethnicity or religion: "It is the center at which [the individual] stands, the point of his most intimate social relations, therefore of his intensest emotional life."[22] I am inclined to say that this is too radical a view of ethnic and religious identification, since it seems to rule out moral conflicts in which the individual's emotions are enlisted, as it were, on both sides. But Kallen's more important point is simply that there is space and opportunity *elsewhere* for the emotional satisfactions that politics can't (or shouldn't) provide. And because individuals really do find this satisfaction, the groups within which it is found are permanently sustainable: they won't melt down, not, at least, in any ordinary (noncoercive) social process. Perhaps they can be repressed, if the repression is sufficiently savage; even then, they will win out in the end.

Kallen wasn't entirely unaware of the powerful forces making for cultural meltdown, even without repression. He has some strong lines on the effectiveness of the mass media—though he knew these only in their infancy and at a time when newspapers were still a highly localized medium and the foreign-language press flourished. In his analysis and critique of the pressure to conform, he anticipated what became by the 1950s a distinctively American genre of social criticism. It isn't always clear whether he sees pluralism as a safeguard against or an antidote for the conformity of ethnic-Americans to that spiritless "Americanism" he so much disliked, a dull protective coloring that destroys all inner brightness. In any case, he is sure that inner brightness will survive, "for Nature is naturally pluralistic; her unities are eventual, not primary. . . . "[23] Eventually, he means, the American union will prove to be a matter of "mutual accommodation," leaving intact the primacy of ethnic and religious identity. In the years since Kallen wrote, this view has gathered a great deal of ideological, but much less of empirical, support. "Pluralist principles . . . have been on the ascendancy," writes a contemporary critic of pluralism, "precisely at a time when ethnic differences have been on the wane."[24] What if the "excellence" appropriate to our "kind" is, simply, an American excellence? Not necessarily civic virtue of the sort favored by nativists, republicans, and contemporary communitarians, but nonetheless some local color, a brightness of our own?

Peripheral Distance

This local color is most visible, I suppose, in popular culture—which is entirely appropriate in the case of the world's first mass democracy. Consider, for example, the movie *American in Paris,* where the hero is an American simply and not at all an Irish- or German- or Jewish-American. Do we drop our hyphens when we travel abroad? But what are we, then, without them? We carry with us cultural artifacts of a quite specific sort: *"une danse americaine,"* Gene Kelly tells the French children as he begins to tap dance. What else could he call it, this melted-down combination of Northern English clog dancing, the Irish jig and reel, and African rhythmic foot stamping, to which had been added, by Kelly's time, the influence of the French and Russian ballet? Creativity of this sort is both explained and celebrated by those writers and thinkers, heroes of the higher culture, that we are likely to recognize as distinctively American: thus Emerson's defense of the experimental life (I am not sure, though, that he would have admired tap dancing), or Whitman's democratic inclusiveness, or the pragmatism of Peirce and James.

"An American nationality," writes Gleason, "does in fact exist."[25] Not just a political status, backed up by a set of political symbols and ceremonies, but a full-blooded nationality, reflecting a history and a culture—exactly like all the other nationalities from which Americans have been, and continue to be, recruited. The ongoing immigration makes it difficult to see the real success of Americanization in creating distinctive types, characters, styles, artifacts of all sorts which, were Gene Kelly to display them to his Parisian neighbors, they would rightly recognize as "American." More important, Americans recognize one another, take pride in the things that fellow Americans have made and done, identify with the national community. So, while there no doubt are people plausibly called Italian-Americans or Swedish-Americans, spiritual (as well as political) life—this is Gleason's view—is lived largely to the right of the hyphen: contrasted with real Italians and real Swedes, these are real Americans.

This view seems to me both right and wrong. It is right in its denial of Kallen's account of America as an anonymous nation of named nationalities. It is wrong in its insistence that America is a nation like all the others. But the truth does not lie, where we might naturally be led to look for it, somewhere between this rightness and this wrongness—as if we could locate America at some precise point along the continuum that stretches from the many to the one. I want to take the advice of that American song, another product of the popular culture, which tells us: "Don't mess with mister in-between."[26] If there are cultural artifacts, songs and dances, styles of life and even philosophies, that are distinctively American, there is also an idea of America that is itself distinct, incorporating oneness and manyness in a "new order" that may or may not be "for the ages" but that is certainly for us, here and now.

The cultural pluralists come closer to getting the new order right than do the nativists and the nationalists and the American communitarians. Nonetheless, there is a nation and a national community and, by now, a very large number of native Americans. Even first- and second-generation Americans, as Gleason points out, have graves to visit and homes and neighborhoods to remember *in this country,* on this side of whatever waters their ancestors crossed to get here.[27] What is distinctive about the nationality of these Americans is not its insubstantial character—substance is quickly acquired—but its nonexclusive character. Remembering the God of the Hebrew Bible, I want to argue that America is not a jealous nation. In this sense, at least, it is different from most of the others.

Consider, for example, a classic moment in the ethnic history of France: the debate over the emancipation of the Jews in 1790 and '91. It is not, by any means, a critical moment; there were fewer than 35,000 Jews in revolutionary France, only 500 in Paris. The Jews were not economically powerful or politically significant or even intellectually engaged in French life (all that could come only after emancipation). But the debate nonetheless was long and serious, for it dealt with the meaning of citizenship and nationality. When the Constituent Assembly voted for full emancipation in September 1791, its position was summed up by Clermont-Tonnerre, a deputy of the Center, in a famous sentence: "One must refuse everything to the Jews as a nation, and give everything to the Jews as individuals. . . . It would be repugnant to have . . . a nation within a nation."[28] The Assembly's vote led to the disestablishment of Jewish corporate existence in France, which had been sanctioned and protected by the monarchy. "Refusing everything to the Jews as a nation" meant withdrawing the sanction, denying the protection. Henceforth Jewish communities would be voluntary associations, and individual Jews would have rights against the community as well as against the state: Clermont-Tonnerre was a good liberal.

But the Assembly debate also suggests that most of the deputies favoring emancipation would not have looked with favor even on the voluntary associations of the Jews, insofar as these reflected national sensibility or cultural difference. The future Girondin leader Brissot, defending emancipation, predicted that Jews who became French citizens would "lose their particular characteristics." I suspect that he could hardly imagine a greater triumph of French *civisme* than this—as if the secular Second Coming, like the religious version, awaited only the conversion of the Jews. Brissot thought the day was near: "Their eligibility [for citizenship] will regenerate them."[29] Jews could be good citizens only insofar as they were regenerated, which meant, in effect, that they could be good citizens only insofar as they became French. (They must, after all, have some "particular characteristics," and if not their own, then whose?) Their emancipators had, no doubt, a generous view of their capacity to do that but would not have been generous in the face of resistance (from the Jews or from any other of the corporate groups of the old regime). The price of emancipation was assimilation.

This has been the French view of citizenship ever since. Though they have often been generous in granting the exalted status of citizen to foreigners, the successive republics have been suspicious of any form of ethnic pluralism. Each republic really has been "one and indivisible," and it has been established, as Rousseau thought it should be, on a strong national oneness. Oneness all the way down is, on this view, the only guarantee that the general will and the common good will triumph in French politics.

America is very different, and not only because of the eclipse of republicanism in the early nineteenth century. Indeed, republicanism has had a kind of afterlife as one of the legitimating ideologies of American politics. The Minute Man is a republican image of embodied citizenship. Reverence for the flag is a form of republican piety. The Pledge of Allegiance is a republican oath. But emphasis on this sort of thing reflects social disunity rather than unity; it is a straining after oneness where oneness doesn't exist. In fact, America has been, with severe but episodic exceptions, remarkably tolerant of ethnic pluralism (far less so of racial pluralism).[30] I don't want to underestimate the human difficulties of adapting even to a hyphenated Americanism, nor to deny the bigotry and discrimination that particular groups have encountered. But tolerance has been the cultural norm.

Perhaps an immigrant society has no choice; tolerance is a way of muddling through when any alternative policy would be violent and dangerous. But I would argue that we have, mostly, made the best of this necessity, so that the virtues of toleration, in principle though by no means always in practice, have supplanted the singlemindedness of republican citizenship. We have made our peace with the "particular characteristics" of all the immigrant groups (though not, again, of all the racial groups) and have come to regard American nationality as an addition to rather than a replacement for ethnic consciousness. The hyphen works, when it is working, more like a plus sign. "American," then, is a name indeed, but unlike "French" or "German" or "Italian" or "Korean" or "Japanese" or "Cambodian," it can serve as a second name. And as in those modern marriages where two patronymics are joined, neither the first nor the second name is dominant: here the hyphen works more like a sign of equality.

We might go farther than this: in the case of hyphenated Americans, it doesn't matter whether the first or the second name is dominant. We insist, most of the time, that the "particular characteristics" associated with the first name be sustained, as the Know-Nothings urged, without state help—and perhaps they will prove unsustainable on those terms. Still, an ethnic-American is someone who can, in principle, live his spiritual life as he chooses, *on either side of the hyphen.* In this sense, American citizenship is indeed anonymous, for it doesn't require a full commitment to American (or to any other) nationality. The distinctive national culture that Americans have created doesn't underpin, it exists alongside of, American politics. It follows, then, that the people I earlier called Americans simply, Americans and nothing else, have in fact a more complicated existence than those terms suggest. They are American-Americans, one more group of hyphenates (not quite the same as all the others), and one can imagine them attending to the cultural aspects of their Americanism and refusing the political commitment that republican ideology demands. They might still be good or bad citizens. And similarly, Orthodox Jews as well as secular (regenerate) Jews, Protestant fundamentalists as well as liberal Protestants, Irish republicans as well as Irish Democrats, black nationalists as well as black integrationists—all these can be good or bad citizens, given the American (liberal rather than republican) understanding of citizenship.

One step more is required before we have fully understood this strange America: it is not the case that Irish-Americans, say, are culturally Irish and politically American, as the pluralists claim (and as I have been assuming thus far for the sake of the argument). Rather, they are culturally Irish-American and politically Irish-American. Their culture has been significantly influenced by American culture; their politics is still, both in style and substance, significantly ethnic. With them, and with every ethnic and religious group except the American-Americans, hyphenation is doubled. It remains true, however, that what all the groups have in common is most importantly their citizenship and what most differentiates them, insofar as they are still differentiated, is their culture. Hence the alternation in American life of patriotic fevers and ethnic revivals, the first expressing a desire to heighten the commonality, the second a desire to reaffirm the difference.

At both ends of this peculiarly American alternation, the good that is defended is also exaggerated and distorted, so that pluralism itself is threatened by the sentiments it generates. The patriotic fevers are the symptoms of a republican pathology. At issue here is the all-important ideological commitment that, as Gleason says, is the sole prerequisite of American citizenship. Since citizenship isn't guaranteed by oneness all the way down, patriots or superpatriots seek to guarantee it by loyalty oaths and campaigns against "un-American" activities. The Know-Nothing party having failed to restrict naturalization, they resort instead to political purges and deportations. Ethnic revivals are less militant and less cruel, though not without their own pathology. What is at issue here is communal pride and power—a demand for political recognition without assimilation, an assertion of interest-group politics against republican ideology, an effort to distinguish this group (one's own) from all the others. American patriotism is always strained and nervous because hyphenation makes indeed for dual loyalty but seems, at the same time, entirely American. Ethnic revivalism is also strained and nervous, because the hyphenates are already Americans, on both sides of the hyphen.

In these circumstances, republicanism is a mirage, and American nationalism or communitarianism is not a plausible option; it doesn't reach to our complexity. A certain sort of communitarianism is available to each of the hyphenate groups—except, it would seem, the American-Americans, whose community, if it existed, would deny the Americanism of all the others. So Horace Kallen is best described as a Jewish (-American) communitarian and a (Jewish-) American liberal, and this kind of coexistence, more widely realized, would constitute the pattern he called cultural pluralism. But the different ethnic and religious communities are all of them far more precarious than he thought, for they have, in a liberal political system, no corporate form or legal structure or coercive power. And, without these supports, the "inherited organic set" seems to dissipate—the population lacks cohesion, cultural life lacks coherence. The resulting "groups" are best conceived, John Higham suggests, as a core of activists and believers and an expanding periphery of passive members or followers, lost, as it were, in a wider America.[31] At the core, the left side of the (double) hyphen is stronger; along the periphery, the right side is stronger, though never fully dominant. Americans choose, as it were, their own location; and it appears that a growing number of them are choosing to fade into the peripheral distances. They become American-Americans, though without much passion invested in the becoming. But if the core doesn't hold, it also doesn't disappear; it is still capable of periodic revival.

At the same time, continued large-scale immigration reproduces a Kallenesque pluralism, creating new groups of hyphenated Americans and encouraging revivalism among activists and believers in the old groups. America is still a radically unfinished society, and for now, at least, it makes sense to say that this unfinishedness is one of its distinctive features. The country has a political center, but it remains in every other sense decentered. More than this, the political center, despite occasional patriotic fevers, doesn't work against decentering elsewhere. It neither requires nor demands the kind of commitment that would put the legitimacy of ethnic or religious identification in doubt. It doesn't aim at a finished or fully coherent Americanism. Indeed, American politics, itself pluralist in character, *needs* a certain sort of incoherence. A radical program of Americanization would *really* be un-American. It isn't inconceivable that America will one day become an American nation-state, the many giving way to the one, but that is not what it is now; nor is that its destiny. America has no singular national destiny—and to be an "American" is, finally, to know that and to be more or less content with it.

Notes

1. Horace M. Kallen, *Culture and Democracy in the United States* (New York: Boni & Liveright, 1924), p. 51.

2. *Harvard Encyclopedia of American Ethnic Groups, ed. Stephan Thernstrom* (Cambridge, Mass.: Harvard University Press, 1980).

3. Mario Cuomo's speech at the 1984 Democratic party convention provides a nice example of this sort of argument.

4. Kallen, *Culture and Democracy,* p. 94.

5. *Ibid.,* p. 122 (cf. 116); John Rawls. *A Theory of Justice* (Cambridge, Mass.: Harvard University Press, 1971), p. 527.

6. Quoted in Kallen, *Culture and Democracy,* p. 138; the writer was superintendent of New York's public schools.

7. Kallen, *Culture and Democracy,* p. 94.

8. See Kallen's account of how British-Americans were forced into ethnicity: *Culture and Democracy,* pp. 99f.

9. Philip Gleason. "American Identity and Americanization," in *Harvard Encyclopedia,* p. 32.

10. On the complexities of "nativism," see John Higham, *Send These to Me: Jews and Other Immigrants in Urban America* (New York: Atheneum, 1975). pp. 102–115. For an account of the Know-Nothings different from mine, to which I am nonetheless indebted, S.M. Lipset and Earl Raab, *The Politics of Unreason: Right-wing Extremism in America, 1790–1970* (New York: Harper & Row, 1970), ch. 2.

11. Frank George Franklin, *The Legislative History of Naturalization in the United States* (New York: Arno Press, 1969), chs. 11–14.

12. *Ibid.,* p. 247.

13. *Ibid.,* p. 293.

14. *Ibid.*

15. Lipset and Raab, *Politics of Unreason,* p. 46.

16. Jean-Jacques Rousseau, *The Social Contract,* trans. G. D. H. Cole (New York: E. P. Dutton, 1950), bk. III, ch. 15, p. 93.

17. Kallen, *Culture and Democracy,* p. 61.

18. *Ibid.,* p. 78.

19. *Ibid.,* pp. 114–115.

20. It is interesting that both nativists and pluralists wanted to keep the market free of ethnic and religious considerations. The Know-Nothings, since they thought that democratic politics was best served by British ethnicity and Protestant religion, set the market firmly within civil society, allowing full market rights even to new and Catholic immigrants. Kallen, by contrast, since he understands civil society as a world of ethnic and religious groups, assimilates the market to the universality of the political sphere, the "common city-life."

21. Kallen, *Culture and Democracy,* p. 124.

22. *Ibid.,* p. 200.

23. *Ibid.,* p. 179.

24. Stephen Steinberg, *The Ethnic Myth: Race, Ethnicity, and Class in America* (Boston: Beacon Press, 1981), p. 254.

25. Gleason, "American Identity," p. 56.

26. The song is "Accentuate the Positive," which is probably what I am doing here.

27. Gleason, "American Identity," p. 56.

28. Quoted in Gary Kates, "Jews into Frenchmen: Nationality and Representation in Revolutionary France," *Social Research* 56 (Spring 1989): 229. See also the discussion in Arthur Hertzberg, *The French Enlightenment and the Jews: The Origins of Modern Anti-Semitism* (New York: Schocken, 1970), pp. 360–362.

29. Kates, "Jews into Frenchmen," p. 229.

30. The current demand of (some) black Americans that they be called African-Americans represents an attempt to adapt themselves to the ethnic paradigm—imitating, perhaps, the relative success of various Asian-American groups in a similar adaptation. But names are no guarantees; nor does antinativist pluralism provide sufficient protection against what is all too often an *ethnic*-American racism. It has been argued that this racism is the necessary precondition of hyphenated ethnicity: the inclusion of successive waves of ethnic immigrants is possible only because of the permanent exclusion of black Americans. But I don't know what evidence would demonstrate *necessity* here. I am inclined to reject the metaphysical belief that all inclusion entails exclusion. A historical and empirical account of the place of blacks in the "system" of American pluralism would require another paper.

31. Higham, *Send These to Me,* p. 242.

EXPLORING THE ISSUE

Do We Need a Common Identity?

Critical Thinking and Reflection

1. What are the competing views of Buchanan and Walzer?
2. What is the history of concern with national identity?
3. Compare and contrast pluralism with assimilation.
4. Who are the significant scholars associated with issues of American identity?
5. How is the issue of national identity related to subsequent issues in this reader, including diversity, immigration, postracial identity, bilingualism, and colorblindness?

Is There Common Ground?

Buchanan and Walzer write about a society in which immigration and the changes in the racial and ethnic composition have resulted in an alteration in the perception of identity over time. They are focused on the impact that the diverse components of society have upon the quest for a common identity. Neither of these authors expects America to become a homogenous nation. Immigration and the impact that it is having on society negate prospects for such a development. Arthur Schlesinger Jr., *The Disuniting of America: Reflections on a Multicultural Society* (W.W. Norton, 1992), in "E Pluribus Unum?" suggests that the concern with racial and ethnic issues is undertaken at the expense of American unity. In contrast, Walzer believes that American oneness is based upon common American citizenship. Here, he offers a different view from Buchanan who strongly believes that America needs one common identity. Despite its delicacy the melting pot as the precursor to a common American identity is worthy of students' critical examination.

Additional Resources

Feldstein, Stanley and Lawrence Costello. 1974. *The Ordeal of Assimilation* (Anchor Books).

Gans, Herbert. 1979. "Symbolic Ethnicity: The Future of Ethnic Groups and Cultures in America." *Ethnic and Racial Studies* (2:1, 1–20).

Glazer, Nathan and Daniel Patrick Moynihan. 1970. *Beyond the Melting Pot* (MIT Press).

Gordon, Milton. 1964. *Assimilation in American Life* (Oxford University Press).

Gordon, Milton. 1978. *Human Nature, Class, and Ethnicity* (Oxford University Press).

Handlin, Oscar. 1951. *The Uprooted* (University of Pennsylvania Press).

Novak, Michael. 1973. *The Rise of the Unmeltable Ethnics: Politics and Culture in the Seventies* (Collier).

Parenti, Michael. 1970. "Assimilation and Counter-Assimilation," in Philip Green and Stanford Levison, eds. *Power and Community: Dissenting Essays in Political Science* (Vintage Books).

Park, Robert. 1950. "On Assimilation," in *Race and Culture: Essays on the Sociology of Contemporary Man* (Free Press).

Schlesinger Jr., Arthur. 1992. *The Disuniting of America: Reflections on a Multi-cultural Society* (W.W. Norton).

Steinberg, Stephen. 2001. *The Ethnic Myth: Race, Ethnicity and Class in America* (Beacon Press).

Waters, Mary. 1990. *Ethnic Options: Choosing Identities in America* (University of California Press).

Weisberger, Bernard. 1971. *The American People* (American Heritage).

This website is dedicated to research and education on "the historic vision" of American democracy. The Future of American Democracy Foundation works in close partnership with Yale University Press and the Yale Center for International and Area Studies as a nonprofit, nonpartisan foundation. The site aims to be centrist in its approach. Of particular note to the reader is "Foundation Project III: The American Identity."

http://thefutureofamericandemocracyfoundation.org/

The Center for American Common Culture (Hudson Institute) offers articles, book reviews, speeches and transcripts, and reports on citizenship, assimilation of immigrants, and American common culture. For example, there is a transcript available on the site, "What Makes An American? Historical Perspectives on Immigration," which will add to students' understanding of an American common identity.

http://acc.hudson.org/

E Pluribus Unum: The Bradley Project on America's identity brings together leading social scientists, historians, and journalists to examine critical aspects of American identity including "American National Identity" and "Assimilation and Immigration." Harris Interactive (www .harrisinteractive.com) conducted an overview survey on American identity concluding that the country is facing an identity crisis.

http://bradleyproject.org/

This is the official website for conservative columnist Pat Buchanan. It offers daily postings and strong position statements from the conservative viewpoint dealing with topics ranging from immigration to international affairs. It offers links to several other conservative Internet sources.

http://buchanan.org/blog/

ISSUE 2

Is Diversity an Inevitable Part of a New American Identity?

YES: **Henry A. Giroux**, from "Insurgent Multiculturalism and the Promise of Pedagogy," in David Theo Goldberg, ed., *Multiculturalism: A Critical Reader* (Blackwell, 1994)

NO: **Lawrence Auster,** abridged from "How the Multicultural Ideology Captured America," *The Social Contract,* vol. 14, no. 3 (Spring 2004)

Learning Outcomes

After reading this issue, the student should be able to:

- Understand new notions of American identity.
- Understand how immigration has influenced notions of American identity.
- Examine how more inclusive racial policies have influenced notions of American identity?
- Identify and apply the concepts of multiculturalism and diversity to an examination of American identity.
- Link the issue of diversity to all the other issues in this reader.

ISSUE SUMMARY

YES: Henry A. Giroux is a writer on multiculturalism and related topics and current Chair of Communication Studies at McMaster University, Ontario, Canada. He emphasizes the need to focus on the cultural categories (black versus white) that are promoted within multiculturalism and diversity in order to understand power relations and other issues that are reflective of racialized identities in society. For Giroux, one significant way to address the problem of inequality is through identity politics.

NO: Lawrence Auster is a conservative writer and blogger. He has written extensively on issues pertaining to national identity and ethnic diversity, including *The Path to National Suicide: An Essay on Immigration and Multiculturalism* (American Immigration Control

Foundation, 1990). He sees that multiculturalism and diversity have gained popularity as an ideology based on a set of false propositions. For Auster, diversity and multiculturalism are real attacks on European culture.

W.E.B. DuBois' classic reference to America's race problem, "The problem of the twentieth century is the problem of the color line," can be seen as a precursor to the issue of diversity. Written in 1899, during the peak years of Jim Crow America, DuBois foresaw the next 100 years in terms of the struggle for equality and how race would limit that struggle. Immigration and the multicultural and diverse society resulting from it have served to intensify the color line issues in America. At the same time, as stated in Issues 1 and 13, immigration and the changes it has produced, especially at the turn of the twentieth century, would challenge the dominant American identity. During the early twentieth century there was no emphasis on diversity as something desirable. Ethnic groups, consisting of immigrants from southern and eastern Europe, would seek to claim a part of the new world culture. Indeed, the United States in the early twentieth century and throughout was becoming more and more multicultural. However, diversity, as we know it today, was not a part of the vocabulary of the time. In contrast, cultural emphasis was on assimilation and Americanization.

The emphasis on a need for diversity within American institutions was a positive response to the challenges presented to society by the civil rights movement. The heightened sensitivity toward diversity and the need to be institutionally inclusive became a significant component of the struggles against racism and the racially exclusionary policies that prevailed at this time. As a result of the racial progress that has been achieved, leaders, and decision makers within institutions, ranging from universities to the military and including much of the corporate sector, have increasingly the goal of race and ethnic diversity. Hiring practices, in both the corporate and public sectors of the economy, as well as the admission policies of some colleges and universities, reflected this embrace of diversity as appropriate institutional goals.

As the nation emerged during the post–civil rights era and conservative ideology has been embraced by a substantial portion of the body politic, there has arisen increasing criticism of diversity. One of the leading contributors to this critical discourse is Arthur Schlesinger, Jr., a liberal historian. Critics associate racial diversity with the promotion of separate identities rather than a unifying theme of an American identity. Such critics raise the question of whether it is good for society to emphasize separate racial identities rather than one unifying common identity. Lastly, some critics argue that the emphasis upon racial diversity has contributed to continued racial and ethnic polarization and social conflict within the nation.

With his attack on diversity and multiculturalism, Lawrence Auster writes of the "fraud of inclusion." He argues that a majority culture should not have to include "alien" traditions in order to strengthen its identity. If that is the case, then the majority culture "has no right to exist." According to Auster, whites, especially white liberals, cannot face the reality that multiculturalism does not work. Thus, for Auster, diversity is not an inevitable part of a new American identity. Diversity is intrinsically related to other issues in this edition of *Taking Sides,* especially bilingualism (Issue 15), self-segregation (Issue 19), immigration (Issue 13), and common identity (Issue 1).

In an ideal universe, would we celebrate diversity? Cultural conservatives want everyone to be assimilated to one American culture (Issues 1 and 3). Liberals, including Giroux, strongly favor multiculturalism. They view multiculturalism as one way to address prevailing social, political, and economic inequality. For Giroux, diversity is an inevitable part of a new American identity. On the other hand, Auster sees multiculturalism and diversity as an attack on the traditional American identity, which is rooted within a European cultural context.

The editors urge students to address the issue of diversity within the context of the contentious history of race and ethnic relations in America. The question can be viewed in terms of identity politics (Issue 1), and it can also be viewed as obscuring a proper concern with class and inequality within society. This issue is important because racial and ethnic identity intersect with class as determinants in one's life chances in American society. As students imagine a society without class differences, how does diversity, as we know it, become more important in contributing to a common identity?

YES

Henry A. Giroux

Insurgent Multiculturalism and the Promise of Pedagogy

Introduction

Multiculturalism has become a central discourse in the struggle over issues regarding national identity, the construction of historical memory, the purpose of schooling, and the meaning of democracy. While most of these battles have been waged in the university around curriculum changes and in polemic exchanges in the public media, today's crucial culture wars increasingly are being fought on two fronts. First, multiculturalism has become a "tug of war over who gets to create public culture."[1] Second, the contested terrain of multiculturalism is heating up between educational institutions that do not meet the needs of a massively shifting student population and students and their families for whom schools increasingly are perceived as merely one more instrument of repression.

In the first instance, the struggle over public culture is deeply tied to a historical legacy that affirms American character and national identity in terms that are deeply exclusionary, nativist, and racist. Echoes of this racism can be heard in the voices of public intellectuals such as George Will, Arthur Schlesinger Jr, and George Gilder. Institutional support for such racism can be found in neoconservative establishments such as the Olin Foundation and the National Association of Scholars.

In the second instance, academic culture has become a contested space primarily because groups that have been traditionally excluded from the public school curriculum, and from the ranks of higher education, are now becoming more politicized and are attending higher education institutions in increasing numbers. One consequence of this developing politics of difference has been a series of struggles by subordinate groups over access to educational resources, gender and racial equity, curriculum content, and the disciplinary-based organization of academic departments.

While it has become commonplace to acknowledge the conflicting meanings of multiculturalism, it is important to acknowledge that in its conservative and liberal forms multiculturalism has placed the related problems of white racism, social justice, and power off limits, especially as these might be addressed as part of a broader set of political and pedagogical concerns. In

From *Multiculturalism: A Critical Reader* by David Theo Goldberg, ed. (Blackwell, 1994), pp. 325–343 (excerpts). Copyright © 1994 by Blackwell Publishing Ltd. Reprinted by permission of Blackwell Publishing Ltd/John Wiley & Sons.

what follows, I want to reassert the importance of making the pedagogical more political. That is, I want to analyze how a broader definition of pedagogy can be used to address how the production of knowledge, social identities, and social relations might challenge the racist assumptions and practices that inform a variety of cultural sites, including, but not limited to, the public and private spheres of schooling. Central to this approach is an attempt to define the pedagogical meaning of what I will call an insurgent multiculturalism. This is not a multiculturalism that is limited to a fascination with the construction of identities, communicative competence, and the celebration of tolerance. Instead, I want to shift the discussion of multiculturalism to a pedagogical terrain in which relations of power and racialized identities become paramount as part of a language of critique and possibility.

In part, this suggests constructing "an educational politics that would reveal the structures of power relations at work in the racialization of our social order" while simultaneously encouraging students to "think about the invention of the category of whiteness as well as that of blackness and, consequently, to make visible what is rendered invisible when viewed as the normative state of existence: the (white) point in space from which we tend to identify difference."[2] As part of a language of critique, a central concern of an insurgent multiculturalism is to strip white supremacy of its legitimacy and authority. As part of a project of possibility, an insurgent multiculturalism is about developing a notion of radical democracy around differences that are not exclusionary and fixed, but that designate sites of struggle that are open, fluid, and that will provide the conditions for expanding the heterogeneity of public spaces and the possibility for "critical dialogues across different political communities and constituencies."[3] . . .

Toward an Insurgent Multiculturalism

To make a claim for multiculturalism is not . . . to suggest a juxtaposition of several cultures whose frontiers remain intact, nor is it to subscribe to a bland "melting-pot" type of attitude that would level all differences. It lies instead, in the intercultural acceptance of risks, unexpected detours, and complexities of relation between break and closure.[4]

Multiculturalism like another broadly signifying term is multiaccentual and must be adamantly challenged when defined as part of the discourse of domination or essentialism. The challenge the term presents is daunting given the way in which it has been appropriated by various mainstream and orthodox positions. For example, when defined in corporate terms it generally is reduced to a message without critical content. Liberals have used multiculturalism to denote a pluralism devoid of historical contextualization and the specificities of relations of power or they have depicted a view of cultural struggle in which the most fundamental contradictions "implicating race, class, and gender can be harmonized within the prevailing structure of power relation."[5] For many conservatives, multiculturalism has come to signify a disruptive, unsettling, and dangerous force in American society. For some critics, it has been taken up as a slogan for promoting an essentializing identity politics and various forms of nationalism. In short, multiculturalism can be defined through a variety of ideological constructs, and signifies a terrain of struggle around the reformation of historical memory, national identity, self- and social representation, and the politics of difference.

Multiculturalism is too important as a political discourse to be exclusively appropriated by liberals and conservatives. This suggests that if the concept of multiculturalism is to become useful as a pedagogical concept, educators need to appropriate it as more than a tool for critical understanding and the pluralizing of differences; it must also be used as an ethical and political referent which allows teachers and students to understand how power works in the interest of dominant social relations, and how such relations can be challenged and transformed. In other words, an insurgent multiculturalism should promote pedagogical practices that offer the possibility for schools to become places where students and teachers can become border crossers engaged in critical ethical reflection about what it means to bring a wider variety of cultures into dialogue with each other, to theorize about cultures in the plural, within rather than outside "antagonistic relations of domination and subordination."[6]

In opposition to the liberal emphasis on individual diversity, an insurgent multiculfuralism also must address issues regarding group differences and how power relations function to structure racial and ethnic identities. Furthermore, cultural differences cannot be merely affirmed to be assimilated into a common culture or policed through economic, political, and social spheres that restrict full citizenship to dominant groups. If multiculturalism is to be linked to renewed interests in expanding the principles of democracy to wider spheres of application, it must be defined in pedagogical and political terms that embrace it as a referent and practice for civic courage, critical citizenship, and democratic struggle. Bhikhu Parekh provides a definition that appears to avoid a superficial pluralism and a notion of multiculturalism that is structured in dominance. He writes:

> Multicultualism doesn't simply mean numerical plurality of different cultures, but rather a community which is creating, guaranteeing, encouraging spaces within which different communities are able to grow at their own pace. At the same time it means creating a public space in which these communities are able to interact, enrich the existing culture and create a new consensual culture in which they recognize reflections of their own identity.[7]

In this view, multiculturalism becomes more than a critical referent for interrogating the racist representations and practices of the dominant culture, it also provides a space in which the criticism of cultural practices is inextricably linked to the production of cultural spaces marked by the formation of new identities and pedagogical practices that offers a powerful challenge to the racist, patriarchal, and sexist principles embedded in American society and schooling. Within this discourse, curriculum is viewed as a hierarchical and representational system that selectively produces knowledge, identities, desires, and values. The notion that curriculum represents knowledge that is objective, value free, and beneficial to all students is challenged forcefully as it becomes clear that those who benefit from public schooling and higher education are generally white, middleclass students whose histories, experiences, language, and knowledge largely conform to dominant cultural codes and practices. Moreover, an insurgent multiculturalism performs a theoretical service by addressing curriculum as a form of cultural politics which demands linking the production and legitimation of classroom knowledge, social identities, and values to the institutional environments in which they are produced.

As part of a project of possibility, I want to suggest some general elements that might inform an insurgent multicultural curriculum. First, a multicultural curriculum must be informed by a new language in which cultural differences are taken up not as something to be tolerated but as essential to expanding the discourse and practice of democratic life. It is important to note that multiculturalism is not merely an ideological construct, it also refers to the fact that by the year 2010, people of color will be the numerical majority in the United States. This suggests that educators need to develop a language, vision, and curriculum in which multiculturalism and democracy become mutually reinforcing categories. At issue here is the task of reworking democracy as a pedagogical and cultural practice that contributes to what John Dewey once called the creation of an articulate public. [Historian and intellectual] Manning Marable defines some of the essential parameters of this task.

> Multicultural political democracy means that this country was not built by and for only one group—Western Europeans; that our country does not have only one language—English; or only one religion-Christianity; or only one economic philosophy—corporate capitalism. Multicultural democracy means that the leadership within our society should reflect the richness, colors and diversity expressed in the lives of all of our people. Multicultural democracy demands new types of power sharing and the reallocation of resources necessary to great economic and social development for those who have been systematically excluded and denied.[8]

Imperative to such a task is a reworking of the relationship between culture and power to avoid what Homi Bhabha has called "the subsumption or sublation of social antagonism . . . the repression of social divisions . . . and a representation of the social that naturalizes cultural difference and turns it into a 'second'-nature argument."[9]

Second, as part of an attempt to develop a multicultural and multiracial society consistent with the principles of a democratic society, educators must account for the fact that men and women of color are disproportionately underrepresented in the cultural and public institutions of this country. Pedagogically this suggests that a multicultural curriculum must provide students with the skills to analyze how various audio, visual, and print texts fashion social identities over time, and how these representations serve to reinforce, challenge, or rewrite dominant moral and political vocabularies that promote stereotypes that degrade people by depriving them of their history, culture, and identity.

This should not suggest that such a pedagogy should solely concentrate on how meanings produce particular stereotypes and the uses to which they are put. Nor should a multicultural politics of representation focus exclusively on producing positive images of subordinated groups by recovering and reconstituting elements of their suppressed histories. While such approaches can be pedagogically useful, it is crucial for critical educators to reject any approach to multiculturalism that affirms cultural differences in the name of an essentialized and separatist identity politics. Rather than recovering differences that sustain their self-representation through exclusions, educators need to demonstrate how differences collide, cross over, mutate, and transgress in their negotiations and struggles. Differences in this sense must be understood not through the fixity of place or the romanticization of an essentialized notion of history and experience but through the tropes of indeterminacy, flows, and translations. In this instance, multiculturalism can begin to formulate a politics of representation in which questions of access and cultural production are linked to what people do with the signifying regimes they use within historically specific public spaces.

While such approaches are essential to giving up the quest for a pure historical tradition, it is imperative that a multicultural curriculum also focus on dominant, white institutions and histories to interrogate them in terms of their injustices and their contributions for "humanity." This means, as [author and Harvard professor] Cornel West points out that

> to engage in a serious discussion of race in America, we must begin not with the problems of black people but with the flaws of American society—flaws rooted in historical inequalities and longstanding cultural stereotypes. . . . How we set up the terms for discussing racial issues shapes our perception and response to these issues. As long as black people are viewed as "them," the burden falls on blacks to do all the "cultural" and "moral" work necessary for healthy race relations. The implication is that only certain Americans can define what it means to be American—and the rest must simply "fit in."[10]

In this sense, multiculturalism is about making whiteness visible as a racial category that is, it points to the necessity of providing white students with the cultural memories that enable them to recognize the historically and socially constructed nature of their own identities. Multiculturalism as a radical, cultural politics should attempt to provide white students (and others) with the self-definitions upon which they can recognize their own complicity with, or resistance to, how power works within and across differences to legitimate some voices and dismantle others. Of course, more is at stake here than having whites reflect critically on the construction of their own racial formation and their complicity in promoting racism. Equally important is the issue of making all students responsible for their practices, particularly as these serve either to undermine or expand the possibility for democratic public life.

Third, a multicultural curriculum must address how to articulate a relationship between unity and difference that moves beyond simplistic binarisms. This is, rather than defining multiculturalism against unity or simply for difference, it is crucial for educators to develop a unity-in-difference position in which new hybrid forms of democratic representation, participation, and citizenship provide a forum for creating unity without denying the particular, multiple, and the specific. In this instance, the interrelationship of different cultures and identities become borderlands, sites of crossing, negotiation, translation, and dialogue. At issue is the production of a border pedagogy in which the intersection of culture and identity produces self-definitions that enable teachers and students to authorize a sense of critical agency. Border pedagogy points to a self/other relationship in which identity is fixed as neither other nor the same; instead, it is both and, hence, defined within multiple literacies that become a referent, critique, and practice of cultural translation, a recognition of no possibility of fixed, final, or monologically authoritative meaning that exists outside of history, power, and ideology.

Within such a pedagogical cartography, teachers must be given the opportunity to cross ideological and political borders as a way of clarifying their own moral vision, as a way of enabling counterdiscourses, and, as Roger Simon points out, as a way of getting students "beyond the world they already know in order to challenge and provoke their inquiry and challenge of their existing views of the way things are and should be."[11]

Underlying this notion of border pedagogy is neither the logic of assimilation (the melting pot) nor the imperative to create cultural hierarchies, but the attempt to expand the possibilities for different groups to enter into dialogue to understand further the richness of their differences and the value of what they share in common.

Fourth, an insurgent multiculturalism must challenge the task of merely representing cultural differences in the curriculum; it must also educate students of the necessity for linking a justice of multiplicity to struggles over real material conditions that structure everyday life. In part, this means understanding how structural imbalances in power produce real limits on the capacity of subordinate groups to exercise a sense of agency and struggle. It also means analyzing specific class, race, gender, and other issues as social problems rooted in real material and institutional factors that produce specific forms of inequality and oppression. This would necessitate a multicultural curriculum that produces a language that deals with social problems in historical and relational terms, and uncovers how the dynamics of power work to promote domination within the school and the wider society. In part, this means multiculturalism as a curricula discourse and pedagogical practice must function in its dual capacity as collective memory and alternative reconstruction. History, in this sense, is not merely resurrected but interrogated and tempered by "a sense of its liability, its contingency, its constructedness."[12] Memory does not become the repository of registering suppressed histories, albeit critically, but of reconstructing the moral frameworks of historical discourse to interrogate the present as living history.

Finally, a multicultural curriculum must develop, in public schools and institutions of higher education, contexts that serve to refigure relations between the school, teachers, students, and the wide community. For instance, public schools must be willing to develop a critical dialogue between the school and those public cultures within the community dedicated to producing students who address the discourse and obligations of power as part of a larger attempt at civic renewal and the reconstruction of democratic life. At best, parents, social activists, and other socially-concerned community members should be allowed to play a formative role in crucial decisions about what is taught, who is hired, and how the school can become a laboratory for learning that nurtures critical citizenship and civic courage. Of course, the relationship between the school and the larger community should be made in the interest of expanding "the social and political task of transformation, resistance, and radical democratization.[13] In both spheres of education, the curriculum needs to be decentralized to allow students to have some input into what is taught and under what conditions. Moreover, teachers need to be educated to be border crossers, to explore zones of cultural difference by moving in and out of the resources, histories, and narratives that provide different students with a sense of identity, place, and possibility. This does not suggest that educators become tourists traveling to exotic lands; on the contrary, it points to the need for them to enter into negotiation and dialogue around issues of nationality, difference, and identity so as to be able to fashion a more ethical and democratic set of pedagogical relations between themselves and their students while simultaneously allowing students to speak, listen and learn differently within pedagogical spaces that are safe, affirming, questioning, and enabling.

In this instance, a curriculum for a multicultural and multiracial society provides the conditions for students to imagine beyond the given and to embrace their identities critically as a source of agency and possibility. In addition, an insurgent multiculturalism should serve to redefine existing debates about national identity while simultaneously expanding its theoretical concerns to more global and international matters. Developing a respect for cultures in the plural demands a reformulation of what it means to be educated in the United States and what such an education implies for the creation of new cultural spaces that deepen and extend the possibility of democratic public life. Multiculturalism insists upon challenging old orthodoxies and reformulating new projects of possibility. It is a challenge that all critical educators need to address.

Notes

1. Alice Kessler-Harris, "Cultural Locations: Positioning American Studies in the Great Debate," *American Quarterly,* 44, 3 (1992), p. 310.

2. Hazel Carby, "The Multicultural Wars," in *Black Popular Culture,* ed. Gina Dent (Seattle: Bay Press, 1992), pp. 193–4.

3. Kobena Mercer, "Back to my Routes: A Postscript on the 80s," *Ten.* 8, 2, 3 (1992), p. 33.

4. Trinh T. Minh-Ha, *Woman, Native, Other: Writing Postcoloniality and Feminism* (Bloomington: Indiana University Press, 1989), p. 232.

5. E. San Juan, Jr, *Racial Formations/Critical Transformations: Articulations of Power in Ethnic and Racial Studies in the United States* (Atlantic Highlands, NJ: Humanities Press, 1992), p. 101.

6. Hazel Carby, "Multi-Culture," *Screen Education,* 34 (Spring 1980), p. 65.

7. Bhabha and Parekh, "Identities on Parade: A Conversation," p. 4.

8. Manning Marable, *Black America: Multicultural Democracy* (Westfield, NJ: Open Media, 1992), p. 13.

9. Homi K. Bhabha, "A Good Judge of Character: Men, Metaphors, and the Common Culture," in *Racing Justice, Engendering Power: Essays on Anita Hill, Clarence Thomas, and the Construction of Social Reality,* ed. Toni Morrison (New York: Pantheon, 1992), p. 242.

10. Cornel West, "Learning to Talk of Race," p. 24.

11. Roger I. Simon, *Teaching Against the Grain* (New York: Bergin and Garvey Press, 1992), p. 17.

12. Henry Louis Gates, Jr, "The Black Man's Burden," *Black Popular Culture* ed. Gina Dent (Seattle: Bay Press, 1992), p. 76.

13. Judith Butler, "Contingent Foundations: Feminism and the Question of 'Post modernism'," in *Feminists Theorize the Political,* eds. Judith Butler and Joan Scott (New York: Routledge, 1991), p. 13.

Lawrence Auster

 **NO**

How the Multicultural Ideology Captured America

Paraphrasing Richard Nixon's famous remark about Keynesianism, the Harvard sociologist Nathan Glazer declared some years ago that "We are all multiculturalists now." One's initial response to such an unwanted announcement is to say "What do you mean, *we*?" Yet, even if "we" do not subscribe to multiculturalism, it cannot be denied that over the last twenty years multiculturalism has become the ruling idea of America, seen in every area of life from educational curricula to racial proportionality in private employment and university admissions (ensconced in the U.S. Constitution in *Grutter v. Bollinger*) to the quasi-official establishment of foreign languages to the constant invocations of "diversity" by our political, business, and intellectual elites. How, so quickly and effortlessly, did this alien belief system take over our country? I have elsewhere explained multiculturalism as an expression of the revolutionary increase of racial diversity that was unleashed by the 1965 Immigration Act. In this article, however, I want to look at multiculturalism, not as the inevitable outcome of ethnic diversification, and not as the result of enforced political correctness, but as an ideology that has advanced itself by means of a set of propositions. My purpose is to examine the false arguments of the multiculturalists themselves, and to see how they have used these arguments to fool an all-too-willing American majority into going along with them.

The Fraud of Inclusion

The first principle of multiculturalism—if something so untrue can be called a principle—is the equality of all cultures. According to the multiculturalists, America is an assemblage of racially or ethnically defined subcultures, all of which have equal value, and none of which can claim a privileged position.

The second principle of multiculturalism is inclusion. It is said that minority and non-Western cultures have been unjustly excluded in the past from full participation in our culture, and that in order to correct this historic wrong we must now include them on an equal basis. Moreover, we are told, such inclusion of different cultures does not threaten our culture, but "enriches" it. By this reasoning, if we became (say) an officially bilingual society, with Spanish appearing alongside English on every cereal box and street sign in the land (as is done with the two languages of Canada), our culture would not be harmed

Substantially abridged from *The Social Contract,* vol. 14, no. 3, Spring 2004. Copyright © 2004 by Lawrence Auster. Reprinted by permission of the author.

in the slightest. We would only be including something we once excluded. We would have become something *more,* not *less.* What could be more positive? How could any decent person object?

To answer that question, let us imagine a scenario in which a Western cultural group—say a large population of Italian Catholics—moved en masse into a non-Western country—say in the Moslem Mideast—and demanded that the host society drop all public observance of its majority religion and redefine itself as a multicultural state. When the Moslems react in fear and outrage, the Catholics answer: "What are you so uptight about, brothers? In challenging Islam's past exclusionary practices, we're not *threatening* your religion and way of life, we're *enriching* them." Of course, as even the multiculturalists would admit in this hypothetical instance (since in this scenario it is a non-Western, rather than a Western, culture that is being threatened), such "enrichment" would change Islam into something totally unacceptable to the Moslem majority. By the same logic, if the U.S. Congress were required to conduct all its proceedings in Chinese or Spanish alongside English, that would obviously not "enrich" America's political tradition, but radically disrupt and change it. To say that a majority culture must "include" alien traditions in order to prove its own moral legitimacy is to say that the majority culture, *as* a majority culture, has no right to exist.

Since multiculturalism claims to stand for the sanctity and worth of each culture, the discovery that its real tendency is to dismantle the existing, European-based culture of the United States should have instantly discredited it. Yet whites in general, and conservatives in particular, have continually failed to notice this obvious contradiction. One reason for this failure is that modern conservatives—being race-blind, democratic universalists—tend to see multiculturalism solely as an attack on the ideology of universalism. They don't see multiculturalism as an attack on *a particular culture and people,* namely their own, because as universalists they have no allegiance to that particular culture and people. Thus the typical white conservative today will say that multiculturalism is bad because "it divides us into different groups"— which is of course true. But he rarely says that multiculturalism is bad because "it is destroying *our* culture"—the majority culture and peoplehood of European Americans—since that would imply that he was defending a particular culture rather than a universalist idea. Since conservatives have been unprepared to defend European America as such, they have been unable to point out the true nature of multiculturalism, which is that it is an attack on white Western civilization, and so they have have been unable to oppose multiculturalism effectively.

The Myths of Mainstream Multiculturalism

If inclusion is as obvious a fraud as I have been suggesting, and so evidently directed at the destruction of America's majority culture, why have mainstream Americans been so blind to it? One reason is the multiculturalists' skillful portrayal of multiculturalism as a benign and harmless movement, based on established principles that everyone, except for bigots, embraces.

The general pattern of the "good" multiculturalism goes something like this:

- The multiculturalists say that "respecting other cultures" poses no threat to American culture. This claim goes unchallenged by the leaders of the majority culture, partly because they believe it, partly because they want to appear inclusive rather than alarmist. According to the liberal critic Paul Berman, most academics who supported multiculturalism had no conscious desire to destroy Western intellectual culture. They only wanted to "expand" the Western tradition by including previously overlooked or excluded voices. Seeing multiculturalism as essentially benign, they dismissed the conservatives' attack on it as overwrought.
- But as soon as multiculturalism is admitted into the mainstream, it suddenly turns out that "respecting minority cultures" means nothing less than granting those cultures a form of sovereignty, which means *delegitimizing* the mainstream culture in which the minority cultures have just been included.
- Even though this turn of events has exposed the "moderate" position as radical, anyone who questions it is now placed on the defensive. Almost overnight, what had once been considered radical, and had to conceal itself, has become the mainstream consensus, while what had once been seen as the mainstream consensus, and excluded radicalism, has been silenced.
- Finally, even after this darker side of multiculturalism has been revealed, there is no end of liberals who cry: "But that's not what *I* mean by multiculturalism! I'm in favor of the *good* multiculturalism." As if to say: "This bad multiculturalism is not *really happening*. Therefore I don't have to do anything to oppose it. I'll just keep calling for the good multiculturalism." Meanwhile, like the pod people in *The Invasion of the Body Snatchers*, the bad multiculturalism continues to take over more and more of America's body without anyone seeing that it is happening, until the moment arrives when we discover, in Nathan Glazer's pathetic phrase, that "we are all multiculturalists now."

In order to break down any resistance to multiculturalism, it wasn't enough to portray it as mainstream; it also had to be seen as *inevitable*. The moderate multiculturalists achieved both these ends by means of an audacious myth. America, they told us, has "always" been multicultural. In fact, all the societies that have ever existed have been multicultural. Multiculturalism is simply the human condition, not to be questioned any more than the air we breathe. Many advocates of this view are not multiculturalists *per se* but old-fashioned progressives (or, to put it less politely, international socialists), who have an ingrained hostility toward nationhood, religion, and all other inherited group distinctions, which they see as obstacles to the political and economic unification of mankind. When these progressives say that "all cultures are multicultural," they are not really seeking to emphasize cultural differences (as the radical multiculturalists do), but rather to underscore a universal *sameness* that would render nations—or at least the American nation—obsolete.

Now we come to what is perhaps the most important multicultural myth of all, the belief that inclusion is simply about equality. Equality—or, to be more precise, antiracism—is the sheep's clothing of multiculturalism. The opinion makers of post World War II America carefully taught us that ethnic and cultural differences are of no intrinsic importance and should *never* be a factor in how we treat people. Once our minds had been molded by this simple but powerful idea, we commenced opening the doors of our nation to formerly excluded groups. But each time the doors have been opened and some new group has been admitted, a very strange thing has happened: The ideal of "equality" has suddenly been replaced by the ideal of "diversity." *Now* the opinion makers tell us that the newcomers' ethnic and cultural differences are of supreme importance and must be "respected." *Now* they tell us that we, the host society, must turn ourselves inside out in order to accommodate these differences, to "sensitize" ourselves to them, to "learn" from them. Before we opened the doors, we had been told that to exclude culturally different people from our society was racist. But now that we've let them in, we're told that to expect them to fit into our society is racist.

This bait-and-switch tactic, which is central to the multicultural enterprise, was also used to create a vast "bilingual" education establishment. The reasonable-sounding idea that non-English speaking children should be given special help learning English in order to have an equal opportunity in this country (as stated by the Supreme Court in *Lau v. Nichols*) was soon transformed into the requirement that such children be taught in their native language—often, it turned out, for their entire public school careers. In fact, for most "bilingual" advocates and not a few Hispanic parents, the transmission and preservation of the Spanish language as a major and official language in this country had been their real motive from the start, and it continues to be their real, openly stated, goal to this day. Yet during these past 30 years of controversy over bilingual education, white liberals have consistently failed to hear what the bilingual advocates were plainly telling them. Whites would point to the many documented failures of bilingual education to make children competent in English, thinking that this was a sufficient argument against bilingualism. But as far as the politically active part of the Hispanic community was concerned, Spanish maintenance, not assimilation, was bilingualism's true purpose. Seeing only the "bait" (equality and assimilation) and blind to the "switch" (diversity and ethnic pride), well-meaning whites would periodically call for more effective methods of English instruction for Hispanic youngsters—and then, to their shock, find themselves attacked as "racists." Unnerved, they would beat a quick retreat from the issue, leaving bilingual education in place.

In much the same way, the bait-and-switch has been used to accommodate whites to the browning of America. The belief that all the peoples in the world are "the same as you and me" is used to get the immigration doors opened; as Bob Dole put it at the 1996 Republican Convention, the latest immigrants from Mexico are "as American as the descendants of the Founding Fathers." But as soon as the strangers are within the gates and it has become evident that they are *not* like you and me, the assurances of sameness are replaced by celebrations of difference.

Immigration advocate Earl Shorris admitted in his book, *Latinos: A Biography of the People,* that Hispanics were not assimilating like previous immigrant groups. Optimistic 1960s liberals, he said, seriously underestimated the tenacity of Hispanics' cultural and ethnic differences from the American mainstream. Shorris nevertheless denied that Hispanics are fragmenting America. They are "seeking *their version* of the American dream.—[T]he victories of Latino culture are victories of pluralism. . . . Nothing is taken in return for this enrichment; it is, by definition, a gift." [italics added].

In a rational world, the announcement by an open-borders advocate that the largest immigrant group is not assimilating would have been seen as at least somewhat damaging to the immigrant cause. But Shorris effortlessly turned this embarrassment into a blessing, telling his white liberal readers that, far from being upset, they should be *grateful* for the existence of a rapidly expanding, non-assimilating group that is intruding its own way of life, language, educational standards, and ethnic allegiances into this country.

Shorris had good reason for confidence that he could get away with this obvious ploy. He knew that white people cannot face the reality of ethnic and cultural difference and what it means for this society, because it would destroy their universalist belief that all people and all cultures can get along on a basis of perfect equality. The bait-and-switch almost always works—because whites *want* it to work.

EXPLORING THE ISSUE

Is Diversity an Inevitable Part of a New American Identity?

Critical Thinking and Reflection

1. What are the new and more recent notions of American identity?
2. How has immigration influenced ideas of American identity?
3. How have more inclusive racial policies influenced thinking regarding American identity?
4. Why are multiculturalism and diversity significant for examining American identity?
5. How do other issues in this reader connect to the larger issue of diversity?

Is There Common Ground?

Diversity has been on the increase in America in recent years, so Giroux and Auster examine the impact of diversity in changing American identity. Both are involved in a critique of the contribution of diversity and its social impact on American society. The concept of diversity became popular in 1978, stemming from the *Bakke v. University of California Board of Regents,* when the Supreme Court ruled "that taking into consideration the race of an applicant to the University was acceptable if it served 'the interest of diversity.'" Although seen as a landmark affirmative action case, the notion of diversity became a useful and commonplace concept to understand American identity. Indeed, more than 30 years after *Bakke,* diversity has become a vital part of a discussion of American identity. The concept has expanded from the initial focus on race to include ethnicity, religion, sexual orientation, and other personal characteristics. Ethnicity, along with immigration, has always been part of the national identity dilemma. In this context, diversity has become intertwined with multiculturalism and immigration. However, complicating the diversity issue is what many view as the dilution of the idea of diversity to the point that it has lost its original focus and application. Thus, the editors encourage students to consider race, ethnicity, multiculturalism, and diversity as essential in the public dialogue concerning American identity.

Additional Resources

Blackwell, Angela Glover, Stewart Kwoh, and Manuel Pastor. 2010. *Uncommon Ground: Race and America's Future* (W. W. Norton & Co.).

Davidson, Martin. 2011. *The End of Diversity As We Know It: Why Diversity Efforts Fail and How Leveraging Difference Can Succeed* (Berrett-Koehler Publishers).

Gerteis, Joseph. 2005. "Dealing with Diversity: Mapping Multiculturalism in Sociological Terms." *Sociological Theory* (23:2).

Gordon, Milton. 1964. *Assimilation in American Life: The Role of Race, Religion, and National Origins* (Oxford University Press).

Hirsch, E.D. 1987. "American Diversity and Public Discourse." in *Cultural Literacy: What Every American Needs to Know* (Houghton Mifflin).

Jost, Kenneth. 2007. "Racial Diversity in Public Schools: Has the Supreme Court Dealt a Blow to Integration?" *CQ Researcher* (17:32).

Michaels, Walter Benn. 2006. *The Trouble with Diversity: How We Learned to Love Identity and Ignore Inequality* (Henry Holt & Co.).

Myers, John. 2005. *Minority Voices: Linking Personal Ethnic History and the Sociological Imagination* (Allyn & Bacon).

Myers, John. 2006. *Dominant-Minority Relations in America: Convergence in the New World* (Allyn & Bacon).

Nathan, Rebekah. 2005. *My Freshman Year: What a Professor Learned by Becoming a Student* (Penguin Books).

Parillo, Vincent. 2008. *Diversity in America* (Sage Publications).

Reed, Susan. 2011. *The Diversity Index: The Alarming Truth About Diversity in Corporate America . . . and What Can be Done About It* (AMACOM).

Schlesinger, Arthur M. 1992. *The Disuniting of America: Reflections on a Multicultural Society* (W.W. Norton).

Schrag, Peter. 1999. "The Diversity Defense." *The American Prospect* (September 1).

Schwartz, Benjamin. 1995. "The Diversity Myth." *The Atlantic Monthly* (May). *The Journal of Higher Education.* 2001. Special Issue: "The Social Role of Higher Education." (72:2, 172–204).

Wood, Peter. 2004. *Diversity: The Invention of a Concept* (Encounter Books).

The U.S. Census Bureau website presents useful demographic information on ancestry, citizenship, and foreign-born citizens. The links to Hispanic and Asian minority data are extensive. This site is a very good starting point for the serious students to gain background information on race, ethnicity, and diversity.

www.census.gov/

The website, which is part of the Pew Research Center, chronicles Latinos' experiences in a changing America. It includes demographic data including country of origin profiles, survey data, and current topics including Arizona's new immigration law. The interactive maps offer students a clear understanding of Latino settlement by geography.

http://pewhispanic.org/

This is the website of the progressive think tank, Political Research Associates. It is devoted to supporting movements for a more inclusive democratic society. The site boasts that it keeps an eye on the Right. It produces reports in *The Public Eye,* a journal that advances progressive thinking. Students will find a multicultural critique of anti-immigrant groups.

www.publiceye.org/

ISSUE 3

Do Recent Immigration Trends Challenge Existing Ideas of America's White Identity?

YES: Charles A. Gallagher, from "Racial Redistricting: Expanding the Boundaries of Whiteness," in Heather M. Dalmage, ed., *The Politics of Multiracialism: Challenging Racial Thinking* (State University of New York Press, 2004, pp. 59–76)

NO: Ellis Cose, from "What's White, Anyway?" *Newsweek* (September 18, 2000)

Learning Outcomes

After reading this issue, the student should be able to:

- Comprehend recent immigration trends.
- Understand the concept of racial redistricting.
- Understand how the boundaries of whiteness have expanded over time.
- Comprehend how concern with skin color affects attitudes toward immigration.
- Apply ideas from this issue to the broader issues of immigration.

ISSUE SUMMARY

YES: Charles A. Gallagher, author and sociology professor at Georgia State University, argues that America is currently undergoing a "racial redistricting" in which the boundaries of whiteness are expanding to include lighter-skinned people of color (i.e., Asians and some Latinos).

NO: Ellis Cose, an African American journalist, argues that the traditional boundaries that determine race and skin color are not what they once were. Although he does not specifically cite ethnicity, Cose furthers the claim that American identity today is an expanding category. The boundaries of whiteness have expanded and are no longer hard and fast.

Currently, a debate is raging in the United States regarding the estimated 12 million alleged illegal immigrants that reside here. A recent issue of the *Population Bulletin* devoted to immigration cites U.S. Census data to show that over 1 million immigrants came to the United States in each of the early years of the twenty-first century. Over half of these immigrants came from Latin America, whereas 30 percent came from Asia. Thus, 81 percent of recent immigrants are classified as nonwhite (Issue 14). What are the implications of this trend? Along with the social and demographic issues is the question of race and American identity. Americans have always been concerned with strangers and new immigrants. In one sense, the current concern about white identity and American culture repeats history.

Clearly, one of the consequences of recent immigration patterns is a renewal of the question of race and American identity. Issue 1 deals with the historic question of the need for a common American identity. This issue involves the contemporary tensions of how to incorporate non-European immigrants within an American identity. How do recent immigration trends challenge existing ideas of white identity? The argument made by Charles Gallagher suggests that dominant whites in America view Asians as "driven to assimilate and move up the socioeconomic ladder." Along with some Latinos, Asians are viewed as having values similar to those of the white majority, including hard work, family values, and willingness to assimilate. Gallagher's interpretation of this leads to his notion of racial redistricting. By this, he means expanding the boundaries of whiteness to include these groups.

The reaction to the preponderance of non-European immigrants within America in the twentieth and early twenty-first centuries has often been negative. These non-European groups are seen as a threat by the white majority. Race, however the concept is defined today, is assumed to be a vital part of an American identity. Specifically, whites tend to take for granted that the majority status of whiteness is synonymous with American identity. Demographically, that has always been easy to ascertain. For example, as recently as the 1950s, blacks were 12 percent of the population, whereas Hispanics were 3 percent, and Asians were less than 1 percent. America was, statistically speaking, nearly 85 percent white. In contrast, today whites constitute approximately 70 percent of the population with blacks and Hispanics both at approximately 13 percent and Asians approaching 5 percent.

Also, Asian and Latin American immigration, especially the latter, raises the question of American identity. With this contemporary immigration pattern, does race emerge as a major factor for determined American identity? Should the paradigm for looking at race relations extend beyond the black–white dichotomy and include ethnicity? With all the issues surrounding nineteenth and early twentieth century immigration and its impact on a common American identity, race had much less significance than it has today. European immigrants and their descendants assimilated to the dominant group, and in the process, distanced themselves from nonwhites, such as Native Americans and African Americans.

Charles Gallagher views the unintended consequence of recent immigration trends as the creation of a new racial landscape that is characterized in a nonblack–black dichotomy in place of the older white–black dichotomy. Racial redistricting means expanding those who are accepted as white. This development will benefit some new immigrants and leave others behind because of skin color.

Beginning with his citation of the McCarran-Walter Act of 1952, Ellis Cose argues that nonwhite immigrants no longer have to "paint themselves white in order to become Americans." His position is that American identity increasingly is no longer defined by whiteness. Rather, American identity is slowly changing as the definition of what is white expands its boundaries. In contrast, Gallagher argues that American identity continues to be defined by whiteness. Despite his agreement with Cose that the boundaries of what is considered white are expanding, Gallagher strongly disagrees with the view that whiteness is increasingly irrelevant.

Does Gallagher further the assimilation argument, or does he challenge it? How accurate is Cose in his position that for recent immigrants, race means less than in the past? Does he make the case for a modern pluralist argument? Is he correct in his assumption that whiteness is fading into irrelevance?

Controversy is not new to immigration history. Nineteenth century reactions to "new" immigrants gave rise to nativism that opposed Roman Catholic and Chinese immigrants. The sentiment eventually produced a social and political reaction that led to the National Origins System, a highly restrictionist immigration policy directed at the growing immigration from southern Europe. The dominance of a white, Anglo-Saxon, Protestant culture asserted itself. Other European groups would be accommodated but in limited numbers so as to protect the majority culture rooted in northern and western European background.

Negative reaction to "new" immigrants in the two centuries past continues today. Within the immigration debate, the nativist bias is clearly evident. Whites were able to assimilate, whereas nonwhites faced the challenge that they were unassimilable. The question of white identity persists as the American society becomes ever increasingly multicultural and diverse. What is determined to be an American identity will be reflected in these changing demographics of America. Once again the phrase, "They are not like us," continues to manifest itself to distinguish resident groups from new immigrants. The dynamic alteration of the racial and ethnic character of the nation represents a continuing significant challenge to traditional ideas of American identity.

YES

Charles A. Gallagher

Racial Redistricting: Expanding the Boundaries of Whiteness

My family would object to a biracial relationship if the person I was see-ing were African American. I'm dating someone from El Salvador now and they are okay with the relationship.

> —nineteen-year-old white female college student

My dad would be more upset if the guy was black than if he was Asian. I think this is because of the slavery situation in America, the hatred towards black and vice versa.

> —eighteen-year-old white female college student

We are most likely to see something more complicated: a white-Asian-Hispanic melting pot—a hard to differentiate group of beige Americans—offset by a minority consisting of blacks who have been left out of the melting pot once again.

> —political analyst Michael Lind on the future of interracial relationships

The multiracial movement has raised public awareness that millions of individuals with mixed-race backgrounds do not fit into the racial categories established by the government. What this movement has ignored however, are the ways in which existing racial categories expand to incorporate groups once considered outside of a particular racial category. The social and physi-cal markers that define whiteness are constantly in a state of flux, shifting in response to sociohistoric conditions. Groups once on the margins of white-ness, such as Italians and the Irish, are now part of the dominant group. National survey data and my interviews with whites suggest a process similar to the incorporation of Southern and Eastern Europeans into the "white" race is taking place among certain parts of the Asian and Latino populations in the United States. I argue that the racial category "white" is expanding to include those ethnic and racial groups who are recognized as being socially, culturally, and physically similar to the dominant group.

How borders of whiteness have evolved over time provides theoretical insight into how racial categories are redefined and how this process affects the relative mobility of racial and ethnic groups.[1] Not long ago Italian and Irish immigrants and their children had a racial status that placed them outside the bounds of whiteness.[2] Both of these groups now fit unambiguously under the umbrella of whiteness. Like the process of racialization[3] that transformed Italians and Irish into whites, some light-skinned, middle-class Latinos and multiracial Asians are being incorporated into the dominant group as they define themselves, their interests, and are viewed by others as being like whites. As white respondents in my study made clear, Asians, and to a lesser extent Latinos, were viewed as having the cultural characteristics (a strong work ethic, commitment to family, focus on schooling) that whites believe (or imagine) themselves as possessing. In what was an extension of the model minority myth, many whites in this study saw Asians as potential partners in the demonization of African Americans, further legitimating the existing racial hierarchy.

I argue that we are currently experiencing a "racial redistricting" where the borders of whiteness are expanding to include those groups who until quite recently would have been outside the boundaries of the dominant group. Within the context of contemporary race relations those groups who do not "conform" to cultural and physical expectations of white middle-class norms, namely blacks and dark-skinned Latinos who are poor, will be stigmatized and cut off from the resources whites have been able to monopolize; good public schools, social networks, safe neighborhoods, and access to primary sector jobs. These expanding borders serve to maintain white or nonblack privilege by casting blacks in negative, stereotypical terms. As whites and other nonblack groups inhabit a common racial ground the stigma once associated with interracial relationships between these groups is diminishing. These trends in racial attitudes and how these perceptions may influence mate selection have important implications for multiracial individuals and how racial categories will be defined in the near future.

The initial focus of the twenty individual interviews and eight focus groups (a total of seventy-five randomly picked white college students at a large northeastern urban university) was to examine the political and cultural meaning they attached to being white. What emerged in the interviews was a narrative about their whiteness that was intricately tied to how similar or dissimilar respondents saw other racial groups, why discussions of race relations tended to focus only on blacks and whites, and why Asians, and not blacks, could be absorbed or folded into the dominant group. These interviews revealed that many whites saw Asians and blacks in starkly different terms. At another large urban university in the southeast I administered an open-ended survey to a large undergraduate sociology class asking white respondents if they or any family members would have any reservations about them dating or marrying across the color line. The questionnaire was designed to examine to what extent, if any, white respondents' views about interracial relationships varied by race of the potential partner. Fifty-nine white students of traditional college age participated in the open-ended survey. The trends in these two samples point to how racial attitudes, social distance, and the perception of assimilation may shape dating preferences and how the cultural and pheno-typical expectations that define racial categories change.

Multi or Mono Racial: National Trends

Over the next twenty years we are likely to witness the children of Asian/white and Latino/white unions identifying themselves as many of their parents have already; as whites with multiple heritages where expressions of ancestry are "options" that do not limit or circumscribe life chances. According to the 1990 census, native-born Asian wives were almost equally likely (45 percent) to have a white *or* Asian husband. Almost one third (31.4 percent) of native-born Latinas had white husbands while 54 percent of married American Indian women had white husbands. Only 2.2 percent of black wives had white husbands. The percentage of husbands who had white wives was also quite high; 36 percent of native born Asian, 32 percent of Latino, and 53 percent of American Indian men married white women. Only 5.6 percent of black husbands, however, had white wives.[4]

Self-identifying as white rather than a combination of races is the choice made by a sizable number of multiracial offspring. In fact, a 2000 study by the National Health Interview Surveys allowed respondents to select more than one race but were then asked in a follow-up interview to choose their "main race." More than 46 percent of those who marked white and Asian as their racial identity chose white as their "main race," 81 percent of those who marked white and American Indian marked white as their "main race," whereas only 25 percent of those who marked black and white marked chose white as their "main race."[5] In the 2000 census almost half (48 percent) of the nation's Latino population defined themselves as white.[6]

What is perhaps more important for understanding how the contours of racial categories expand and contract is an examination of the racial defini-tion parents in interracial marriages give to their children. A significant propor-tion of interracial couples where one partner is white and the other is Asian or Latino choose to define their offspring as white.[7] In families where the father was white and the mother was Asian Indian, 93 percent defined their children as white. Where the father was white, 51 percent of Native American, 67 percent of Japanese and 61 percent of Chinese mixed-race families defined their children as white. Only 22 percent white father and black mother unions defined their chil-dren as white. Among white mothers who married nonwhite husbands Waters found "50 percent of the offspring of white mothers and Native American fathers are reported to be white, 43 percent of Japanese/white children are reported as white, 35 percent of Chinese/white children are reported as white, and 58 percent of Korean/white children are reported *by* their parents to be white" while only 22 percent of black/white children were defined as white.[8] Given these trends, it is possible that the progeny of some of these relationships will have the option to self-identify as white and live their lives in white social networks, occupy white neighborhoods, and marry white partners. It is possible then that the white race can "grow" without an influx of "white" immigrants.

Asian Assimilation Versus Black Separatism

One theme that emerged in my interviews was that whites viewed Asians as model minorities driven to assimilate and move up the socioeconomic ladder while blacks were viewed as refusing to adopt the styles, mannerisms, and habits that would aid in their upward mobility. The sense that Asians were working to be part of the system while blacks were not was evident in the following focus group discussion:

Interviewer: Why is our conversation mostly about blacks.

Theresa: Because [Asians] are so quiet.

Martha: That's exactly what I was going to say. They don't make a big deal like the blacks do. They don't jump up and down and scream and yell. They just do their thing.

Theresa: [Asians] don't want to be bothered. They want to get through so that they can have a chance to get into the system, figure it out, work up to what they want and they don't need anyone to bother them. They'll be fine. They can depend on themselves. They know that. I think they figure that if they try and depend on other people or try to make a voice about it they'll just get pushed down.

Interviewer: So why don't they make demands on the system?

Kathleen: I don't think they particularly lose out like the blacks did. And now the American Indians are starting to get more vocal because they've just been pushed down so much. I don't know that [Asians] ever have. I know that during World War II when they were put in the camps and stuff, whatever, but I don't see discrimination against them.

Theresa's comments point to the stages of assimilation some whites believe groups need or should pass through in order to gain upward mobility. The expectation is that groups will learn to work within the ethnic and racial hierarchy, not challenge it. The reference that blacks "jump up and down and scream and yell" suggests that organized resistance and opposition by African Americans to racial inequality is not a legitimate way to bring about social change or create economic opportunity for blacks. If Asians are no longer discriminated against, as Kathleen argues, the reason must be that they have properly integrated themselves in a dominant group. What was implied in many of these exchanges was that whites perceived blacks as not trying hard enough to mirror the beliefs and behaviors of the dominant group while Asians did. Culturally, then, whites view Asians (and Latinos) as fellow immigrants who also worked their way up the racial and ethnic hierarchy; these groups are, as implied by my respondents, kindred spirits.

In sharp contrast to the idea that Asians have been accepted because of individual self-reliance, blacks' wearing clothing that expressed black unity, black nationalism, or critiques of institutional racism (e.g., wearing

Malcolm X shirts or caps) was perceived as intimidating to whites and the antithesis of the assimilation narrative whites see blacks rejecting. The view that Asians wished to be mainstream culturally where blacks did not was evident in this exchange:

Mitch: They just go about and do what they have to do and blend in with the background. They're not so much asserting themselves. They kind of work around you to get done what they have to get done, more than trying to break through a whole blockade of stuff.

Interviewer [addressing Frances]:   Were you going to say something about intimidation?

Frances: I mean, [Asians] don't intimidate us. They don't walk around with Oriental hats or clothes. They don't make a big issue of it. They keep their culture to themselves. If you want to join their culture they don't have a problem with that. If you want to marry an Oriental, granted, that can be a problem. A lot of times that can really be a problem. But, the only problem we would run into would be the parents of the kids our age, because most of them have come from their country but the second generation, *they're American and they know American ways.* There's no pressure.

Mitch: I think there's a lot in the press about discrimination and its time is coming. I mean it's true, though. But, I mean, it's all over the place, stuff about discrimination. It's just becoming like really, really popular for black students to be black and proud and racist. But with Asians it's not that way. I mean there is a magazine *Ebony* for strictly black people—I've never really read it. I mean there is no magazine for just Asian people. There's nothing saying, like, Asian power. But it's [a black focus] all over the place.

That which makes race a salient form of social identity, such as wearing a Malcolm X cap or "black theme" shirts that call for pan-African unity, was viewed by some whites as a form of racial intimidation. The perception that blacks self-segregate and promote separatism by reading a black magazine such as *Ebony* while Asians do not, reflects the belief that Asians and whites have rejected race politics and share a common vision of what it means to be an American. It is important to note that dozens of magazines exist that are directed primarily at Asian and Asian Americans on a wide range of social, cultural, and business topics.

Having a strong work ethic, taking responsibility for your own mobility and embracing assimilation was a point Sharie made to contrast why she believes Koreans have been more successful than blacks:

Interviewer: Why do you think the Koreans have succeeded where the blacks haven't?

Sharie: Because they don't blame anybody. They try. They work, work, work and they succeed. And if they don't succeed they take it and they accept it and they don't blame anybody for it. They just take it and they don't cause any problems. And we don't blame them for anything. They don't do anything to us wrong. They're nice to us. You know what I mean? There shouldn't be a struggle. The black people have every opportunity. We try to give them every opportunity. Look at the schools—if you are a black person you can practically go to school free here, practically. And, uh, and I'm glad to see that there's so many black people going to college and that they're all trying to succeed but they can't blame us all the time.

Interviewer: Whom do they blame?

Sharie: The white society, that we're not giving them enough opportunity. I don't know. I think that's why the Koreans . . .

Interviewer: What do you think that does, the blaming, in terms of what whites think about blacks?

Sharie: That they're losers. That they're putting the blame on somebody who's not—it's an excuse for them—it's your fault; it's the white society's fault. I think it just makes them think less of them. It makes them think that they don't have a work ethic. I mean when we came to this country no one had anything—I mean, they had less than the blacks when they came over to this country, way less. And look at where this country has come. They can work just as hard and succeed way above their expectations if they just stopped and looked at themselves.

This depiction of Asians collectively starting out with "way less" than African Americans yet achieving the American Dream because they are the model minority serves a number of functions; it minimizes social distance between whites and Asians while crafting a narrative where each group can point to the other's immigration experiences and shared upward mobility. What is also shared however, as evidenced in surveys of perceived social distance racial attitudes, is the tendency for both whites and Asians to stereotype blacks.[9]

Asian Passivity, Black Intimidation: Reflections of Social Distance

The theme of black racial intimidation and Asian passivity emerged in this focus group exchange:

James: It's because—I think they're quiet and they're smaller in stature than black people and they seem less threatening. I mean, that's not all of them. You know, I have a couple Asian friends, and they can be loud sometimes, but, I think, as a group they're all right.

Rita: They don't walk around with Mao Tse-tung hats on or shirts that say Asian Power. They're not being threatening. They're acting, they're making themselves useful, not making themselves useful, that's really awful to say, but they're working within the framework that they're given and they're making the best of their opportunities.

James: Maybe it's because of their culture.

Interviewer: So does that mean that since they're not asking for anything so they're not a threat? Is that what goes on?

Jeff: They're not demanding anything—a lot of the time in dealing with the black cause it won't work—please, "can we have equal rights," demanding . . .

Interviewer: So, why is that so different?

Jeff: Because demanding takes on an aggressive stature whereas asking doesn't.

And if I personally see someone being aggressive to me my first impulse is to be aggressive back and, again, that's another vicious circle.

As Rita sees it, Asians work "within the framework" where blacks presumably do not, and unlike blacks, Asians do not use past racial injustices to explain current racial inequities. Rita's reference that Asians do not use racial identity politics (no Mao Tse-tung hats) to advance group interests taps a strong sentiment among whites that the assertion of group rights (demanding "equal rights") to ameliorate racial inequality is a rejection of the ideals that made America great: rugged individualism, embracing an achievement ideology, and believing the socioeconomic playing field is level for all. In the last exchange Jeff explains that race relations between black and whites are tense because blacks are "aggressive" where Asians are not.

The amount of perceived social distance between whites, blacks, and Asians was evident in this exchange concerning which groups whites view as a threat:

Mike: Asians are different about being Asians and blacks are different about being black.

Joshua: You don't usually see Asian Power T-shirts.

Mike: And they're just not militant—that's not the word I'm looking for but it seems like the Asians are like, scholars.

Christel: They seem more complacent.

Lori: Yeah. They laugh at us. You know, they can say, make fun of me now, but . . .

Mike: They're so academic. I don't really think they're worried about finding a place and getting up in the university.

Lori: They're not as concerned with social issues. It doesn't seem like it, anyway.

Interviewer: Are they less threatening as a group?

Mike: They're not threatening, I don't think, to anybody.

Rejecting identity politics, blending in, not being threatening or militant; all these characteristics serve to make blacks cultural outsiders and by contrast, make Asians insiders. In addition to James's earlier comment about Asians being less threatening because they are smaller in stature, a few other respondents identified appearance as central to race relations.

One of the few nontraditional-aged students in the interviews, Pauline, a thirty-eight-year-old student, links color and culture in her explanation of group dynamics.

Interviewer: And why don't we talk about white and Asian?

Pauline: Like I said, I think it's because they're a little more accepted than the blacks.

Interviewer: Why are they more accepted?

Pauline: I think because their skin color is not as dark.

Interviewer: Do you think it's just that, just the skin color?

Pauline: Uh, maybe their culture is more accepted.

Interviewer: In what way?

Pauline: Well, you hear about how, like the Asians, a lot of them have families that believe in respect, respect for the family, so maybe their ideas in those ways are more accepted than the ways that blacks have lived.

Rob uses what he perceives as the physical similarities between whites and Asians also as the reason there seems to be less hostility between whites and Asians than whites and blacks.

Interviewer: It seems that I don't really hear students, that is, white students talk about Asian students that much. They don't seem to be an issue about anything. What's your take on that? I mean, why do you think that is?

Rob: I don't know. That is an interesting perspective. I don't know. I don't know. Maybe it gets down to something as simple as, you know, the contrast of skin color. Maybe it's just that blunt. I don't know.

Interviewer: What do you mean by that, though?

Rob: I mean that if you had a mass of people, just a crowd of people standing right there you could obviously pick out black Americans much easier than you might an Asian. You know what I mean? Because there is an obvious difference. Maybe it's something like that. I don't know. I really don't know.

These exchanges suggest that whites view Asians as having made every effort to assimilate by embracing a work ethic, striving for the American Dream, and doing so in a color-blind fashion.

Many whites in this study saw Asians as possessing similar attitudes, beliefs, ambitions and even viewed Asians as being physically similar to whites, while blacks were seen as aggressive, threatening, and demanding. Herbert Blumer succinctly described how racial identities are constructed and understood by observing: "To characterize another racial group is, by opposition, to define one's own group."[10] However, groups are not only defined through an oppositional relationship; solidarity between groups can emerge when social distance between two groups is less than the social distance of a different, and often more stigmatized group. My respondents' comments suggest that a racial repositioning is taking place where whites imagine Asians as occupying a place within the existing racial hierarchy that minimizes the social distance between whites and Asians, while blacks are placed farther on the social margins.[11]

Shades of Romance: Color, Preference, and Stigma

The focus group interviews above suggest that many whites view Asians as being culturally more similar to them than blacks, a finding that mirrored my survey on interracial relationships. My open-ended questionnaire asked respondents if any family members would "object to you bringing home a romantic partner that was from a different race." An overwhelming majority (86 percent) of the fifty-nine white respondents in my survey said that at least one family member would object to dating outside the white race but most wrote that being involved with Asians and Latinos would be viewed as less of a problem for family members. This finding is consistent with national survey data on intermarriage rates. A Knight Ridder poll in 1997 found that although whites were generally accepting of interracial marriage, 30 percent of respondents opposed black and white unions but were less critical of interracial marriages involving Latinos and Asians.[12] Mary Waters reports that "one in five whites still believes interracial marriage should be outlawed, and a majority of whites, 66 percent, said they would oppose a close relative marrying a black."[13] In their analysis of 1990 General Social Survey data, Herring and Missah found that whites, Jews, Asians, and Hispanics had the greatest opposition to one of their own marrying someone who was black.[14] While there was variation in the levels of opposition to interracial marriages for all groups, marrying someone who was white generated the least amount of disapproval. Using data from a 1992 study of Los Angeles County, Bobo and Smith found an "unambiguously greater average level of hostility to contact with blacks among nonblacks than occurs in reference to any other group."[15] Their survey found that whites, Asians, and Hispanics were more likely to oppose residential integration and interracial marriage with blacks and viewed blacks as being more dependent on welfare, harder to get along with, and less intelligent than other racial and ethnic groups. These attitudes serve as an important backdrop in understanding which racial groups whites might consider as romantic partners and how the resulting multiracial families would be positioned in the U.S. racial hierarchy.

My Father Would Disown Me, . . .

The responses below typify the anger that crossing the color line was imagined to trigger with family members, especially when it was a white female being involved with a black male:

> If I were to bring home a black man or a man of any other racial group home with me, my father would disown me! My father would kick me out of the house and would financially disown me, and never talk to me again. He was raised in a very old fashioned traditional blacks are slaves, lower on the social scale and not anywhere close to being on the same level as the rest of the world. I have never been involved with a black man, but I did go to my senior prom with a black friend. It started a big fight between everyone in my family. (eighteen-year-old white female)
>
> If I were to bring someone home from a different racial background as my boyfriend, my family would be very confused. The person that would be most upset would be my dad. He would completely object to me having a black male date his daughter. My dad grew up in Atlanta, and now works in Atlanta. He is surrounded by the black race all day. He has set in his mind there are blacks and there are niggers. He says the black men and women that speak where people can understand them, and that have respect for people and their things are respectable black people. He will then explain that the niggers in the world that are lazy, disrespectful, stealing, cheating, Ebonics speaking blacks who will never earn respect by him. Don't get me wrong. My dad has black friends too. (nineteen-year-old white female)
>
> My father would object, my mom and dad will both be upset. They said that it looks bad when a white girl is dating a black guy because it looks like she cannot do any better than a black guy. (eighteen-year-old white female)
>
> We moved, as part of the white flight, to a whiter area. A part of why we moved was so that I would date a white girl, in my opinion. (nineteen-year-old white male)

What stands out in these survey responses was that blacks, but not Asian, American Indian, or Latino were the reference group these white respondents used to explain how family members might react to an interracial relationship. Perhaps that as the quintessential racial "other" in the United States "black" was automatically inserted as what was understood as a worst-case scenario for their families. Only a minority of white respondents (14 percent) wrote that their family would be indifferent or supportive of an interracial relationship, a finding that calls into question recent national surveys that suggest America has come to accept interracial relationships.

Asian or Latino—But No Blacks

A number of respondents made it clear that crossing the color line would *only* be a problem if their partner were black.

My dad and brother. I think men are intimidated by other men that are different from them. I do think that there is a big difference from Asian or Latin to black. My dad would be more upset if the guy was black than if he was Asian. I think this is because of the slavery situation in America, the hatred towards black and vice versa. (eighteen-year-old white female)

My ultra-liberal parents wouldn't care. I assume the only race that would shock them (assuming I was still living in the south) is black. Considering the drastic habitual differences and tastes on a general level they would question our compatibility. As for Asians, Latino, Middle Eastern, etc., I've had a diverse group of friends so neither of us would feel awkward. My family would object to a biracial relationship if the person I was seeing was African American. I'm dating someone from El Salvador now and they are okay with the relationship. (nineteen-year-old white female)

Most of my family is pretty open-minded. To be honest, my stepfather wouldn't care unless my partner were African American (black). (twenty-year-old white male)

My dad would object to the relationship the most. He is very traditional. Especially towards a relationship between myself and a guy of African American descent. I have had a relationship with a Filipino-American and he addressed little objection however it was clear that he wasn't thrilled about it. (nineteen-year-old white female)

These last open-ended survey responses and the responses in the epigraph underscore trends in the national survey data discussed at the beginning of this chapter; whites are more willing to cross the color line when their potential mate is not black.

Growing the White Race: Theoretical Predictions

The Multiracial Movement seeks to highlight how the existing racial categories used by government and state agencies deny multiracial people the right to self-definition. Moreover rejecting the monoracial categories imposed on multiracial people is taken as an act of revolution and ultimately such insurgency can bring about positive social change by acknowledging how the idea of race as a socially constructed category reflects power, politics, and the maintenance of white privilege.[16] In a society fixated on creating an infinite amount of consumer choices and willing to impose free market principles on almost every social interaction, the beliefs that undergird the Multiracial Movement would appear to fit easily into post–civil rights race politics. This however, has not happened as evidenced by the relatively small number of multiracial people who could have defined themselves as multiracial in the 2000 census but did not. What appears to be taking place is a reconfiguring of existing racial categories. Richard Alba advises that "rather than speak of the decreasing White population," our collective notion of majority group might undergo a profound redefinition as "some Asians and Hispanics join what has been viewed as 'White' European population."[17] Herbert Gans makes a similar yet more problematic prediction about the future of racial categories:

> [T]oday's multiracial hierarchy could be replaced by what I think of as a dual or bimodal one consisting of "nonblack" and "black" population categories, with a third "residual," category for the groups that do not, or do not yet, fit into the basic dualism. More important, this hierarchy may be based not just on color or other visible bodily features, but also on the distinction between undeserving and deserving, or stigmatized and respectable, races. The hierarchy is new only insofar as the old white–nonwhite dichotomy may be replaced by a nonblack one, but it is hardly new for blacks, who are likely to remain at the bottom once again.[18]

Gans's collapsing of our current racial hierarchy into a dichotomous one where a sizable part of the population is placed in an intergenerational racial holding pattern is consistent with cultural critic Michael Lind's comment in the epigraph which suggests that racial borders may be fluid but the end result will be a further cementing of blacks to the bottom of the racial and economic hierarchy.

Sociologist Mary Waters writes that "[i]n general in the United States, those who are nonwhite racially have not been granted this opportunity by society but have been identified racially by others even if they wanted to disregard their racial or ethnic identity" (emphasis hers).[19] What is of particular importance in Waters's analysis is that the inability to select from the full range of the racial or ethnic options is imposed by "others," a point that underscores the racism on which the one-drop rule was founded. But just as the dominant group can impose measures that exclude individuals from their ranks so too can it create discourse, privilege traits, and stereotypes that assume group behavior. It is not that nonblacks aspire to be white but "in the racial context of the United States, in which Blacks are the defining other, the space exists for significant segments of groups today defined as nonwhite to become White."[20] What is suggested here is that educated, assimilated Asians and Latinos will be accepted into the dominant group. Those Asians and light-skinned Latinos who are well educated, economically secure, and/or with a white partner, may be able to take advantage of and exploit the perks, privileges, and prerogatives of being a member of the dominant group.

Access to amenities such as suburban housing and good schools are linked to race. Reynolds Farley notes that when Asians and Latinos move to metropolitan areas "they find themselves less residentially segregated than blacks."[21] More than one-half of all Asians (50.6 percent) in 1998 lived in suburban areas. Douglas Massey found that "the largest and most segregated Asian communities in the United States are much less isolated than the most integrated Black communities." In addition, he found that class did not lessen the extent to which black communities were racially segregated. "The most affluent blacks," Massey explains, "appear to be more segregated than the poorest Hispanics and Asians; and in contrast to the case of Blacks, Hispanic and Asian segregation levels fall steadily as income rises, reaching low or moderate levels of $50,000 or more."[22] Adelman and associates found that "even when group differences in socio-demographic are controlled, blacks were located in neighborhoods with higher levels of poverty and female headship and fewer college-educated residents than were their non-Hispanic white counterparts."[23] It is likely Asian/white and Latino/white families are part of these suburbanization trends.

But these assertions concerning residential segregation, social isolation, and which racial minorities are denied access to the resource rich middle-class white suburbs also miss what is slowly taking place: white suburbs are absorbing, even welcoming certain multiracial families because they are viewed as being culturally similar to the dominant group. Sociologist Orlando Patterson chides African Americans for not creating the rich and dense web of social networks that result from interethnic and interracial marriages. He argues that "[a]ll other American ethnic groups, including the more recently arrived Asians are intermarrying at record rates. . . . [W]hen one marries into another ethnic group one greatly expands one's social networks."[24] He advises, "[A]fter four centuries of imposed social—although not sexual reproductive—endogamy, Afro-Americans could do with a good deal of exogamy."[25] But Patterson's inability to understand why interracial marriage rates look as they do is analogous to the Multiracial Movement's blind spot on how a sizable part of the multiracial population define themselves or go on to define their children as white rather than multiracial. Patterson suggests that each racial group has a cultural dowry they bring to their marriages. The problem is that in a society structured around white racial dominance Asians and Latinos are defined as having those traits while blacks do not. We are now (or perhaps again) at a unique juncture in the history of racial and ethnic identity construction where racial categories may be mutating. Expanding the boundaries of whiteness to include those groups who subscribe to the existing racial status quo is one way racial dominance is "reorganized." White privilege is not being challenged by the incorporation of new groups into the category "white." It is revitalized as potential challengers to the existing hierarchy are co-opted and rewarded with the perks of membership in the dominant group. What is typically required, however, is that the racist beliefs and practices of the dominant group are internalized by those who join the ranks of the dominant group. In the end the Multiracial Movement may not be able to count on assimilated, economically successful light-skinned Latinos or Asians or their even lighter-skinned multiracial children, because like the Italians and Irish before them, racial redistricting will have allowed them to glide easily into the category "white."

Notes

Michael Lind, "The Beige and the Black," *The New York Times Magazine*, September 6, 1998, 39.

1. See Roediger and Ignatiev. See also Ruth Frankenberg, *White Women, Race Matters: The Social Construction of Whiteness* (Minneapolis: University of Minnesota Press, 1993); Birgit Brander, ed., *The Making and Unmaking of Whiteness* (Durham: Duke University Press, 2001); Ashley W. Doane Jr., "Dominant Group Identity in the United States: The Role of "Hidden"

Ethnicity in Intergroup Relations," *The Sociological Quarterly,* 38, no. 3; Charles A. Gallagher, "White Reconstruction in the University," *Socialist Review,* 24 (1995); Amanda Lewis, "Whiteness Studies: Past Research and Future," *African American Research Perspectives,* 8, no. 1 (2002).

2. See David Roediger; *Towards an Abolition of Whiteness: Essays on Race, Politics, and the Working Class* (New York: Verso, 1994); David Roediger, *The Wages of Whiteness: Race and the Making of the American Working Class* (New York: Verso, 1991); Noel Ignatiev, *How the Irish Became White* (New York: Routledge, 1995); Karen Brodkin Sacks, "How Did Jews Become White Folks?" in *Race,* ed. Steven Gregory and Roger Sanjek (New Brunswick: Rutgers University Press, 1994); Charles A. Gallagher, "White Racial Formation: Into the Twenty-First Century," in *Critical White Studies: Looking Behind the Mirror,* ed. Richard Delgado and Jean Stefancic (Philadelphia: Temple University Press, 1997).

3. Omi and Winant define this process as a "socio-historical process by which racial categories are created, inhabited, transformed and destroyed." Michael Omi and Howard Winant, *Racial Formation in the United States: From the 1960s to the 1990s* (New York: Routledge, 1994), 55.

4. Reynolds Farley, "Racial Issues: Recent Trends in Residential Patterns and Intermarriage," in *Diversity and Its Discontents: Cultural Conflict and Common Ground in Contemporary American Society,* ed. Neil Smelser and Jeffrey Alexander (Princeton: Princeton University Press, 1999), 114–15.

5. Annie E. Casey Foundation, "Using the New Racial Categories in the 2000 Census." . . .

6. U.S. Census.

7. Mary Waters, "Multiple Ethnic Identity Choices," in *Beyond Pluralism: The Conception of Groups and Group Identities in America,* ed. Wendy F. Katlin, Ned Landsman, and Andrea Tyree (Chicago: University of Chicago Press, 1998).

8. Waters, 41.

9. Cedric Herring and Charles Amissah, "Advance and Retreat: Racially Based Attitudes and Public Policy," in *Racial Attitudes in the 1990s: Continuity and Change,* ed. Steven A. Tuch and Jack Martin (Westport: Praeger, 1997), 139.

10. Herbert Blumer, "Race Prejudice as a Sense of Group Position," in *Rethinking the Color Line: Readings in Race and Ethnicity,* ed. Charles A. Gallagher (Mountain View, CA: Mayfield Press, 1999).

11. Michael Omi argues that we should not think about increased rates of intermarriage between white men and Asian women as an "indicator of assimilation" because such a description negates "differences in group power." It may be, as Omi suggests, that the assimilation framework masks patriarchy, sexist stereotypes of Asian women, and group-based inequalities in the name of minimizing social distance but it does not alter the fact that these marriages and the children of these unions challenge and blur existing racial categories. The ability to have both racial and ethnic options in how these individuals construct their identity suggests that under certain conditions the one-drop rule will cease to accurately describe the experiences of certain mixed race individuals. See Michael Omi, "The Changing Meaning of Race," in *America Becoming: Racial Trends and Their Consequences,* ed. Neil Smelser, William J. Wilson, and Faith Mitchell (Washington, DC: National Academy Press, 2001), 258.

12. Anne-Marie Connor, "Interracial Unions Have a Ripple Effect on Families, Society," *Los Angeles Times*. . . .

13. Waters, 43.

14. Cedric Herring and Charles Amissah, "Advance and Retreat: Racially Based Attitudes and Public Policy," in *Racial Attitudes in the 1990s: Continuity and Change,* ed. Steven A. Tuch and Jack Martin (Westport: Praeger, 1997), 139.

15. Lawrence Bobo and Ryan Smith, "From Jim Crow Racism to Laissez-Faire Racism: The Transformation of Racial Attitudes," in *Beyond Pluralism: The Conception of Groups and Group Identities in America,* ed. Wendy Katlin, Ned Landsman, and Andrea Tyree (Chicago: University of Illinois Press), 202.

16. Root, 7.

17. Omi, 258.

18. Herbert Gans, "The Possibility of a New Racial Hierarchy in the Twenty-First Century United States," in *The Cultural Territories of Race,* ed. Michele Lamont (Chicago: University of Chicago Press, 1999), 371.

19. Waters, 29.

20. Jonathan W. Warren and France Winddance Twine, "White Americans, the New Minority?: Non-Blacks and the Ever-Expanding Boundaries of Whiteness," *Journal of Black Studies,* 28, no. 2 (Nov. 1997).

21. Farley, 102.

22. Douglas Massey, "Residential Segregation and Neighborhood Conditions," in *America Becoming: Racial Trends and Their Consequences,* ed. Neil Smelser, William J. Wilson, and Faith Mitchell (Washington, DC: National Academy Press, 2001), 411.

23. Robert Adelman, Hui-shien Tsao, Stewart Tolnay, and Kyle Crowder, "Neighborhood Disadvantage Among Racial and Ethnic Groups: Residential Location in 1970 and 1980," *The Sociological Quarterly,* 42, no. 4.

24. Orlando Patterson, *The Ordeal of Integration: Progress and Resentments in America's Racial Crisis* (Washington, DC: Civitas, 1997), 195.

25. Patterson, 197.

Ellis Cose  **NO**

What's White, Anyway?

In Argentina, where he was born, my acquaintance had always been on solid taxonomic ground. His race was no more a mystery than the color of the clouds. It was a fact, presumably rooted in biology, that he was as white as a man could be. But his move to the United States had left him confused. So he turned to me and sheepishly asked in Spanish, "Am I white or am I Latino?"

Given his fair complexion and overall appearance, most Americans would deem him white, I replied—that is, until he opened his mouth, at which point his inability to converse in English would become his most salient feature. He would still be considered white, I explained, but his primary identity would be as a Latino. For his U.S.-raised children, the relevant order will likely be reversed: in most circles they will simply be white Americans, albeit of Argentine ancestry, unless they decide to be Latino. At any rate, I pointed out, the categories are not exclusive—although in the United States we often act as if they are.

He said he understood, though something in his manner told me he was more confused than ever. Playing the game of racial classification has a way of doing that to you. For though the question—who is white?—is as old as America itself, the answer has often changed. And it is shifting yet again, even as the advantages of whiteness have become murkier than ever.

In the beginning, the benefits were obvious. American identity itself was inextricably wrapped up in the mythology of race. The nation's first naturalization act (passed during the second session of the first Congress in March 1790) reserved the privilege of naturalization for "aliens being free white persons." Only after the Civil War were blacks allowed to present themselves for citizenship, and even then other suspect racial groups were not so favored. Thus, well into the 20th century persons of various ethnicities and hues sued for the purpose of proving themselves white.

In 1922 the case of a Japanese national who had lived in America for two decades made its way to the Supreme Court. Takao Ozawa argued that the United States, in annexing Hawaii, had embraced people even darker than the Japanese—implicitly recognizing them as white. He also made the rather novel, if bizarre, claim that the dominant strain of Japanese were "white persons" of Caucasian root stock who spoke an "Aryan tongue." The high court disagreed. Nonetheless, the following year a high-caste Hindu, Bhagat Singh Thind, asked the same court to accept him as a white Aryan. In rejecting his claim Justice George Sutherland, writing for the court, declared: "It may be true that the blond Scandinavian and the brown Hindu have a common ancestor in the dim reaches of antiquity, but the average man knows perfectly well that there are unmistakable and profound differences between them today." While the children of Europeans quickly became indistinguishable from other Americans, "it cannot be doubted that the children born in this country of Hindu parents would retain indefinitely the clear evidence of their ancestry," concluded Sutherland.

The McCarran-Walter Act, passed in 1952, finally eliminated racial restrictions on citizenship. No longer were East Indians, Arabs and assorted other non-Europeans forced, in a figurative sense, to paint themselves white in order to become Americans.

Today such an exercise seems weird beyond words. But it's worth recalling that even Europeans were not exempt from establishing their racial bona fides. The great immigration debates of the first part of the 20th century were driven in large measure by panic at the prospect of American's gene pool becoming hopelessly polluted with the blood of inferior European tribes. Many of the leading scientists and politicians of the day worried that immigrants from Eastern and Southern Europe—people considered intellectually, morally, and physically inferior—would debase America's exalted Anglo-Saxon-Germanic stock. Such thinking was influenced, among other things, by the rise of eugenics. "The Races of Europe," a book published in 1899 by sociologist William Z. Ripley, was a typical text. Ripley classified Europeans into three distinct races: blond, blue-eyed Teutonics (who were at the highest stage of development); stocky, chestnut-haired Alpines; and dark, slender Mediterraneans. No less a personage than Stanford University president David Starr Jordan bought into the scheme, along with some of the leading lights of Congress. And though "undesirable" European races were never flatly prohibited from eligibility for citizenship, American immigration laws were crafted to favor those presumed to be of finer racial stock. While all whites might be deemed superior to those who were black, yellow or brown, all white "races" were not considered equal to each other.

Gradually America learned to set aside many of its racial preconceptions. Indeed, much of American history has been a process of embracing previously reviled or excluded groups. At one time or another, various clans of Europeans—Poles, Italians, Jews, Romanians—were deemed genetically suspect; but they were subsequently welcomed. They were all, in essence, made white. The question today is whether that process will extend to those whose ancestors, for the most part, were not European.

To some extent it certainly will. That reality struck me some years ago when, in a moment of unguarded conversation, a radio host observed that "white Asians" were in demand for certain jobs. Initially I had no idea what the man was talking about, but as he rattled on I realized he was saying that he considered some Asian-Americans (those with a lighter complexion) to be, for all intents and purposes, as white as himself. In his mind at least, the definition of whiteness has expanded well beyond its old parameters. And

I suspect he is far from alone. This is not to say that Takao Ozawa would be better able today than in 1922 to convince a court that he is Aryan; but he almost certainly could persuade most Americans to treat him like a white person, which essentially amounts to the same thing. America's cult of whiteness, after all, was never just about skin color, hair texture and other physical traits. It was about where the line was drawn between those who could be admitted into the mainstream and those who could not.

Those boundaries clearly are no longer where they once were. And even as the boundaries of whiteness have expanded, the specialness of whiteness has eroded. Being white, in other words, is no longer quite what it used to be. So if Ozawa and his progeny have not exactly become white, they are no longer mired in America's racial wasteland. Indeed, even many Americans with the option of being white—those with, say, one Mexican parent or a Cherokee grandfather—are more than ever inclined to think of themselves as something else. And those for whom whiteness will likely never be an option (most blacks and many darker Hispanics, for instance) are freer to enjoy being whatever they are.

Society, in short, has progressed much since the days when Eastern Europeans felt it necessary to Anglicize their names, when Arabs and East Indians went to court to declare themselves white and when the leading scientists of the day had nothing better to do than to link morality and intelligence to preconceived notions of race. But having finally thrust aside 19th-century racial pseudo-science, we have not yet fully digested the science of the 21st, which has come to understand what enlightened souls sensed all along: that the differences that divided one race from another add up to a drop in the genetic ocean.

Recognizing the truth of that insight is only part of society's challenge. The largest part is figuring out what to do with it, figuring out how, having so long given racial categories an importance they never merited, we reduce them to the irrelevance they deserve—figuring out how, in short, to make real the abstraction called equality we profess to have believed in all along.

EXPLORING THE ISSUE

Do Recent Immigration Trends Challenge Existing Ideas of America's White Identity?

Critical Thinking and Reflection

1. Explain recent immigration trends in terms of race and country of origin.
2. What does Gallagher mean by "racial redistricting"?
3. According to the authors, how have the boundaries of whiteness expanded over time?
4. How does concern with skin color impact attitudes toward immigration?
5. How does the content of this issue apply to the broader issue of immigration?

Is There Common Ground?

Americans and their leaders have promoted an image of the nation as "the land of opportunity." The statue of liberty is a symbolic representation of this image. Immigrants have vigorously responded to this beacon and have arrived to pursue their American dream. The results of this development are apparent and reflective in the diversity that one confronts daily in the United States. Indeed, the racial and ethnic diversity is obvious to anyone. Students should observe that the most recent wave of Latino, Asian, and East Europeans has added to the multicultural character of American identity. Many of these immigrants now reside in large metropolitan areas such as Los Angeles and New York, along with hundreds of other cities and suburbs, which are becoming increasingly diverse.

How will these new immigrants challenge America's traditional idea of white identity? What has recent immigration added to American culture? How has recent immigration challenged American culture? How will the challenges of living in a multicultural society impact the identity of new immigrants? How will these additions change our notion of minority groups? Both Gallagher and Cose agree that the traditional boundaries of whiteness are expanding. They also understand that immigration and the racial and ethnic diversity that is associated with it are major factors in this expansion. Given the expectation that immigration, Latino and Asian, will continue into the foreseeable future, the challenges to America's white identity will intensify.

Additional Resources

Allen, James Paul and Eugene James Turner. 1988. *We Are the People: An Atlas of America's Ethnic Diversity* (Macmillan).

Brodkin, Karen. 1999. *How Did Jews Become White Folks and What That Says About Race in America* (Rutgers University Press).

Cose, Ellis. 1998. *Color Blind: Seeing Beyond Race in a Race Obsessed World* (Harper Perennial).

Foner, Nancy and George Frederickson, eds. 2005. *Not Just Black and White: Historical and Contemporary Perspectives on Immigration, Race and Ethnicity in the United State* (Russell Sage Foundation Publications).

Guglielmo, Jennifer and Salvatore Salerno. 2003. *Are Italians White?: How Race is Made in America* (Routledge).

Huntington, Samuel. 2004. *Who Are We: The Challenges to America's National Identity* (Simon & Schuster).

Ignatiev, Noel. 2008. *How the Irish Became White* (Routledge).

Jacobson, Matthew Frye. 1998. *Whiteness of a Different Color: European Immigrants and the Alchemy of Race* (Harvard University Press).

Lippard, Cameron D. and Charles A. Gallagher, eds. 2010. *Being Brown in Dixie: Race, Ethnicity, and Latino Immigration in the New South* (Lynne Rienner Publishers).

Lipsitz, George. 2006. *The Possessive Investment in Whiteness: How White People Profit from Identity Politics* (Temple University Press).

McDermott, Monica and Frank Samson. 2005. "White Racial and Ethnic Identity in the United States" *Annual Review of Sociology* (31: August, 245–261).

Olson, James. 2002. *Equality Deferred: Race, Ethnicity, and Immigration in America Since 1945* (Wadsworth Books).

Pinder, Sherrow. 2011. *Whiteness and Racialized Ethnic Groups in the United States: The Politics of Remembering* (Lexington Books).

Roediger, David R. 2006. *Working Toward Whiteness: How America's Immigrants Became White. The Strange Journey From Ellis Island to the Suburbs* (Basic Books).

Rubin, Lillian. 1995. "Is This a White Country, or What?" in *Families on the Fault Line* (Harper Perennial).

Schlesinger, Arthur, Jr. 1992. *The Disuniting of America: Reflections on a Multicultural Society* (W.W. Norton).

Takaki, Ronald. 1993. *A Different Mirror: A History of Multicultural America* (Little, Brown).

Waters, Mary. 1997. in Juan F. Perea, ed. *Immigrants Out! The New Nativism and the Anti-Immigrant Impulse in the United States* (New York Press).

Waters, Mary. 1998. "Multiple Ethnic Identity Choices," in Wendy F. Katlin, Ned Landsman, and Andrea Tyree, eds. *Beyond Pluralism: The Conception of Groups and Group Identities in America* (University of Chicago Press).

Intended for the general public, this daily Internet publication deals with important issues primarily those of national security and the state of American culture. Students will find an interesting archived article, "Sole Loyalty: The Politics of Immigration Reform" (June 9, 2011), which relates to the ideas of Gallagher and Cose.

www.americanthinker.com/

This is the site of a webzine, "The Occidental Observer," which is dedicated to white identity, interests, and culture. It is edited by Kevin MacDonald, a professor of psychology at California State, Long Beach. Its content focuses on "white identity, white interests, and the culture of the west."

www.theoccidentalobserver.net/

ISSUE 4

Is the Obama Presidency Moving Toward a Post-Racial Society?

YES: **Alvin Poussaint**, from "Obama, Cosby, King and the Mountaintop," CNN.com (November 13, 2008)

NO: **Melissa V. Harris-Perry**, from "Black by Choice," *The Nation* (May 3, 2010)

Learning Outcomes

After reading this issue, the student should be able to:

- Explain the meaning of post-racial.
- Distinguish between post-racial and post-racist society.
- Explain black and white differences in perceptions of a post-racial society.
- Examine the evidence employed to support the post-racial thesis.
- Understand President Obama's position on a post-racial society?

ISSUE SUMMARY

YES: Alvin Poussaint, a professor of psychiatry at the Harvard Medical School, has authored many books on child psychiatry with emphasis on African American children. Poussaint uses the election of Barack Obama as the president of the United States as a historical moment that may be the beginning of a post-racial era.

NO: Melissa V. Harris-Lacewell is a professor of politics at Tulane University. She is the author of *Barbershops, Bibles, and BET: Everyday Talk and Black Political Thought* (Princeton University Press, 2004). Harris-Lacewell uses President Barack Obama's selection of black as his race in filling out the census to argue that we are not ready for a post-racial society.

The election of President Obama has caused many Americans, including some prominent African Americans, to conclude that American society has entered a post-racial phase of development. Supporters of the post-racial thesis cite what they claim is an increasing acceptance of interracial couples and marriages as evidence. Others argue that the emergence of the Internet and social networking sites and processes have served to neutralize color line considerations (Issue 10). Based on the available evidence as indicated above, many Americans are convinced that a post-racial era is emerging in society.

Black progress achieved during Reconstruction was followed by the backlash and regression of disfranchisement, the terrorism of the lynch mobs associated with the Ku Klux Klan, and the social construction of segregation. These repressive efforts were designed to subordinate African Americans within American society and keep them "in their place." The progress of the civil rights movement was followed by a backlash against these reforms and is highlighted by the continuing attacks on affirmative action policy. In the politics of today, conservative candidates, such as Ron Paul of Texas, question the legitimacy of the Civil Rights Act of 1964 and other areas of racial progress.

The idea of an American society that moves beyond the issues of race and skin color can be seen as utopian. Does the post-racial concept refer to a society in which acceptance and inclusion across color lines have become normative and race truly no longer matters?

To consider the prefix "post" in any context (e.g., postmodern, postcolonial, postwar, etc.) suggests that a society or an era of history has moved beyond one reality to begin another. However, the argument for a post-racial society does not deny the existence of race issues, nor does it imply that race no longer matters. Those who support the post-racial idea employ the election of an African American to the presidency to signal a dramatic improvement in race relations. Thus, the debate for a post-racial America can be seen as an attempt at a new beginning in race relations.

In his keynote address at "The Race in America" Conference at the University of Pittsburgh, June 3, 2010, Julian Bond, a veteran civil rights leader and former chairman of the National Association for the Advancement of Colored People (NAACP), stated that housing segregation was the vital arena of the fight for equality today. He observed the following concerning the need for progress on this issue, "it's so key to all of the other myriad problems which people of color face if you're segregated to one part of town, you're away from the best jobs, the best schools, the best opportunities." Clearly, Bond and the NAACP do not agree with the post-racial thesis.

The achievement of substantial progress, such as that of the civil rights legislation of the 1960s, is often perceived within substantial elements of the white majority as evidence of the solution to the problems of the color line. Despite such thinking on the part of whites, the data available on the gaps between whites, blacks, and others within society reveal the contrary. These data demonstrate that racial inequality still exists in many vital areas of social concern, including life expectancy, poverty, and incarceration rates, among others.

Conscious of media images, especially those communicated through television, Alvin Poussaint, an African American child psychiatrist, in the YES selection, predicts that Barack Obama's election will shape the (race) perceptions of a generation of children, black and white. Poussaint, a former script consultant to *The Cosby Show,* expresses hope and concern for positive racial images. The effect that *The Cosby Show* had on children of all races was its positive image of blacks. Despite the recognition of racial discrimination in the country, Poussaint sees the Obama family as a great symbol of positive imagery, which leads many Americans to think that we are at the beginning of a post-racial era.

On the contrary, in the NO selection, Melissa V. Harris-Lacewell argues that President Obama's self-identification as black, in the U.S. Census survey, is "recognition that the legal and historical realities of race are definitive." She points out that Obama's candidacy disrupted the very idea of whiteness. By overturning stereotypes of blacks, Obama appeals to Americans seeking to put race behind them and enter a post-racial status that allows America to transcend blackness. However, Harris-Lacewell is troubled by this development—a perceived growing tendency to declare victory over racism and the rush to describe a new post-racial society.

Major segments of the American population including blacks, whites, and other minorities are not prepared to draw the conclusion that America is entering a post-racial era. David Brooks, a prominent conservative news commentator, opined in a challenging op-ed piece in *The New York Times,* "The End of Integration" (July 6, 2007) that whites do not want to live this way. Subsequently, in a television interview, he claimed that Americans did not view integration as positive. One can challenge Brooks' assessment, but given the persistence of segregation and other forms of discrimination (see Units 3 and 5), it is difficult to see how African Americans and others can anticipate the demise of this reality in the short term. How is it possible that a post-racial America can emerge simply based upon one event such as a presidential election within society?

The emergence of a post-racial America would be a profound transformation of this society. Given the salience of race within the American experience, virtually every social institution would be affected in some manner. So, students should not underestimate the magnitude of the challenges that this transformation would require. Therefore, it is critical that students examine all aspects of this issue. Is the goal of a post-racial society for America achievable? If so, how can it be achieved? The challenges are daunting!

YES

Alvin Poussaint

Obama, Cosby, King and the Mountaintop

(**C**NN)—Rev. Martin Luther King Jr. told followers the night before he was killed that he had been "to the mountaintop" and seen the promised land of racial equality. Last week's election of Barack Obama was the equivalent of taking all African-Americans to that peak, says Dr. Alvin Poussaint.

In his view, Obama's victory last week wasn't just a political triumph. It was a seismic event in the history of black America.

Poussaint has made it his life's work to study how African-Americans see themselves and how the larger society sees them.

From the days of the civil rights movement through the 1980s, when he was a script consultant on "The Cosby Show," to today, he has been a leader in assessing how images of black people in the media shape perceptions. Poussaint, who is 74, is professor of psychiatry at Judge Baker Children's Center in Boston and at Harvard Medical School.

At a key point in the civil rights movement, Poussaint moved to Mississippi and worked for the Medical Committee for Human Rights, in Jackson, from 1965 to 1967, helping care for civil rights workers and aiding the desegregation of hospitals and other health care institutions.

Poussaint met Bill Cosby in the 1970s and has worked with him on a variety of books and shows, most recently co-authoring a book with Cosby. He was interviewed by CNN on Wednesday.

CNN: What do you think is the long-term impact of the election of Barack Obama as a symbol and a message to the black community in America?

Dr. Alvin Poussaint: We're going to have a generation of children—if he's in there for eight years—being born in 2009, looking at television and images, hearing before they can talk, absorbing it in their brain and being wired to see the visual images of a black man being president of the United States and understanding very early that that's the highest position in the United States.

So I think that's going to be very powerful in its visual imagery . . . and they're going to see these images constantly on television, probably offsetting a lot of the negative imagery that they may see in shows and videos and sometimes in stereotypic comedy.

These images will also make black parents proud. Although there are many barriers to this, it might put back on the table the importance of the two-parent family. . . . Maybe it will do something for couples and bring black men and black women closer together.

The sense of pride may carry over into family life, the same way it is being carried over now into the life of the church already. At black churches this past Sunday, all of them were talking about Obama and being ambassadors for Obama—in other words, suggesting that now that he's president, that black people should take the high road.

The big problem with all of this is that if there's high expectations that somehow the social ills that the black community faces will suddenly evaporate, they're going to be disappointed—because the economy, the economic crisis is a major issue that's going to affect the black community, making things worse. . . . So there's going to be more unemployment, more poor people, more black homeless and more poverty. . . .

Obama's also going to have a positive effect on the white community. Way back in the 1960s, I used to go to Atlanta when it was segregated and even after it started desegregating. When you went downtown to restaurants, you would walk in as a black person and they would kind of act like, "What are you doing here?" You weren't welcome, you know, you just felt it.

And Maynard Jackson became the first black mayor, and I felt a whole change in the tone of the city. You went places and when you walked in, people had to consider: "Is this someone who knows the mayor, this black person?" And so I think they began to treat all black people better because black people were now in power. . . . This may help to eradicate stereotypes that they hold. . . .

So this may have a spinoff effect . . . maybe more blacks will break through the glass ceiling in corporations, more blacks may, because of their newfound confidence, become more civically engaged, run for office.

CNN: What if he had lost, what would the impact have been then?

Poussaint: A lot of black people would have concluded that he lost because of his race, and the black people who had no faith in the system in the first place would have continued to feel that way, maybe even more strongly, and maybe even have more anger at the institutions that have authority over them and that they see as white-controlled.

CNN: Obama is taking over at a time of tremendous international and national challenges. Every president has setbacks. What would be the impact of setbacks on a political level?

Poussaint: Nearly everybody that you hear talk about it realizes that he's inheriting a horrible situation. In fact one of the black leaders joked about how, as soon as things are falling apart in the country, that they hand it over to a black person—"Here, you take it."

People are saying that he's just been dealt a terrible hand and is going to have to work very hard to be successful and they're rooting for him and hoping. There's a mindset right now of "What can we do to help Obama?"

And I don't think it's just black people saying it, it's all the people who voted for him, young people and women, the workers, the unions—"What can we do to help him be successful, and undo the mess that we're in?"

CNN: What do you make of the idea that "The Cosby Show" made America more ready to vote for a black man to be president?

Poussaint: I don't know, you can't study this stuff scientifically. The intent when the Cosby show came on . . . was to present a black family that was not the old stereotypical family that white people laughed at in a sitcom. And we wanted the show to have a universality, in terms of a mother, a father, wonderful children, a lot of love being shown, an emphasis on education.

Today if you have 12 or 15 million viewers of a show a week, it's number one. Well, Cosby was bringing in about 60 million people a week. So this had a deep effect on white children, Latino children, and even many adults, what their images of black people were.

So that's why Karl Rove reached into the hat the other day and said this was the beginning of the post-racial era, because it made white people embrace this black family like a family of their own and fall in love with it.

It probably played some role at chipping away at those negative images, which made white people . . . more ready to embrace a lot of things, including Tiger Woods and Oprah Winfrey and Denzel Washington and Will Smith. Certainly when Obama gets on the scene, people don't say, "What kind of black family is that? We haven't seen any black family like that."

Because that's what they said about the Cosby show, . . . that this doesn't represent a black family, this is fantasy. And it wasn't fantasy, because there were black families like that in 1984, and there are many more black families like that in the middle class and upper-middle class today.

CNN: You were a consultant on the Cosby show. How did that come about?

Poussaint: I knew him and his wife. When the show was coming on, he called me and said he wanted me to . . . be a production consultant to keep this a positive show without stereotyping: "I want you to read and critique every single script before it goes into production, anything you want to say to make this family psychologically believable, living in reality." He wanted the story lines to have a plot that made sense. . . . He told me to weed out what he called put-down humor, which he felt was too prevalent, particularly on a lot of black shows where you make fun of people.

I was allowed to comment on anything, from the clothes to some of the people they were casting, to making sure there was a wide range of colors on the show in terms of complexion, what's on the reading table, what cultural activities the kids are going to, what colleges they're applying to. . . .

CNN: You co-authored a book with Bill Cosby. What's the message of that book?

Poussaint: It's called, "Come on People: On the Road from Victims to Victors." The message is, don't be helpless and hopeless and see yourself as a victim and wallow in failing and think that's your lot in life. What you have to do is take the high road and you have to work hard to try to achieve against the odds. . . .

Most of the black people are where they are today because we succeeded against the odds, we didn't allow the racism out there to totally squelch us. And we feel that spirit is being lost, particularly in low-income communities and sometimes among middle-income people too. And we felt they had to adopt more of an attitude of being victors.

And victors are active, they try to do their best, they take education very seriously. And Obama's a good example—if he took a victim's attitude and said, "Well, a black man could never get elected president of the United States," which a lot of us felt like, he wouldn't have run for the presidency. So he adopted what we call a victor's attitude—"I'm going to go for it, it may be a longshot, but it's possible."

CNN: What do you compare the Obama victory to in terms of significance?

Poussaint: The civil rights movement's success in getting the civil rights bill of '64 and the Voting Rights Act of '65, that opened things mightily for the black communities all over the country. Obviously getting those bills and those accomplishments—forget about The Cosby Show—the voting rights bill played a significant role in Obama's victory.

CNN: Does Obama's victory as a historical moment equal those?

Poussaint: It equals those but it has a more powerful visual symbolism. It's like people are going from [Martin Luther] King, who was moving us toward the mountaintop . . . to Obama, people saying [we're] getting to the mountaintop and now being able to gaze down. So it's the fruition of a movement beginning in slavery. . . . We were in slavery for 250 years, and then Jim Crow segregation for another 100, and we've been struggling for freedom. Obama represents us winning our freedom—like "free at last, free at last, free at last."

But it's not really true. We still have racial discrimination in the country, we're still going to have racial injustice.

Melissa V. Harris-Lacewell

 **NO**

Black by Choice

President Obama created a bit of a stir in early April when he completed his Census form. In response to the question about racial identity the president indicated he was "Black, African American or Negro." Despite having been born of a white mother and raised in part by white grandparents, Obama chose to identify himself solely as black even though the Census allows people to check multiple answers for racial identity.

This choice disappointed some who have fought to ensure that multiracial people have the right to indicate their complex racial heritage. It confused some who were surprised by his choice not to officially recognize his white heritage. It led to an odd flurry of obvious political stories confirming that Obama was, indeed, the first African-American president.

When Obama marked his Census form, he offered another lesson in what has been an intensive if unintentional seminar on the social construction of race. In just a few years, decades of multiple racial formations have been projected onto him at hyperspeed; it's a bit like watching those nature films that show the growth of an apple tree from a seed in just thirty seconds. When Hillary Clinton held a significant lead among black voters, media outlets regularly questioned if Obama was "black enough" to earn African–American electoral support. When the Rev. Jeremiah Wright dominated the news cycle, the question shifted to whether Obama was "too black" to garner white votes. By the final months of the campaign, Obama's opponents charged that he was a noncitizen, a Muslim and a terrorist. In less than two years a single body had been subjected to definitions ranging from insufficiently black, to far too black, to somehow foreign and frightening.

But Obama did more than disrupt standard definitions of blackness; he created a definitional crisis for whiteness. Imagine for a moment that a young American falls into a Rip Van Winkle sleep in 1960. He awakens suddenly in 2008 and learns that we are in the midst of a historic presidential election between a white and a black candidate. He learns that one candidate is a Democrat, a Harvard Law School graduate, a lecturer at the conservative University of Chicago Law School. He also discovers that this candidate is married to his first wife, and they have two children who attend an exclusive private school. His running mate is an Irish Catholic. The other candidate is a Republican. He was an average student who made his mark in the military. This candidate has been married twice, and his running mate is a woman whose teenage daughter is pregnant out of wedlock.

Now ask our recently awakened American to guess which candidate is white and which is black. Remember, his understanding of race and politics was frozen in 1960, when a significant number of blacks still identified themselves as Republican, an Ivy League education was a marker of whiteness and military service a common career path for young black men. Remember that he would expect marriage stability among whites and sexual immorality to mark black life. It's entirely possible that our Rip would guess that Obama was the white candidate and McCain the black one.

By displaying all these tropes of traditional whiteness, Obama's candidacy disrupted the very idea of whiteness. Suddenly whiteness was no longer about educational achievement, family stability or the command of spoken English. One might argue that the folksy interventions of Sarah Palin were a desperate attempt to reclaim and redefine whiteness as a gun-toting ordinariness that eschews traditional and elite markers of achievement.

Obama's whiteness in this sense is frightening and strange for those invested in believing that racial categories are stable, meaningful and essential. Those who yearn for a postracial America hoped Obama had transcended blackness, but the real threat he poses to the American racial order is that he disrupts whiteness, because whiteness has been the identity that defines citizenship, access to privilege and the power to define national history.

In 1998 Toni Morrison wrote that Bill Clinton was the first "black president" because he "displays almost every trope of blackness: single-parent household, born poor, working-class, saxophone-playing, McDonald's-and-junk-food-loving boy from Arkansas." Ten years later the man who truly became America's first black president displayed few of these tropes. Instead he was a scholarly, worldly, health food–eating man from Hawaii. In this sense, Obama was the white candidate in 2008, and a substantial portion of white voters preferred Obama's version of whiteness to that of McCain and Palin.

Which brings us back to Obama's Census choice. Despite his legitimate claims on whiteness, he chose to call himself black. As historian Nell Painter documents in her new book *The History of White People*, white identity was a heavily policed and protected border for most of American history. A person born to an African parent and a white parent could be legally enslaved in America until 1865. From 1877 until 1965 that person would have been subject to segregation in public accommodations, schools, housing and employment. In 1896 the Supreme Court established the doctrine of separate but equal in the case of Homer Plessy, a New Orleans Creole of color whose ancestry was only a small fraction African. President Obama's Census self-identification was a moment of solidarity with these black people and a recognition that the legal and historical realities of race are definitive, that he would have been subject to all the same legal restrictions had he been born at another time. So in April, Obama did as he has done repeatedly in his adult life: he embraced blackness, with all its disprivilege, tumultuous history and disquieting symbolism. He did not deny his white parentage, but he acknowledged that in America, for those who also have African heritage, having a white parent has never meant becoming white.

EXPLORING THE ISSUE

Is the Obama Presidency Moving Toward a Post-Racial Society?

Critical Thinking and Reflection

1. What is the meaning of a post-racial society?
2. What is the difference between a post-racial and a post-racist society?
3. What are the different perceptions of a post-racial society?
4. What is the basis for the argument for a post-racial society?
5. Does President Obama embrace the post-racial thesis? Explain.

Is There Common Ground?

Poussaint and Harris-Lacewell are concerned with overcoming the legacy of racism and its impact on American society. Both of these African American scholars have lived during the civil rights era and have witnessed the changes in race relations that have occurred in American society. Specifically, they have observed the impact of desegregation upon American society. Interestingly, in an interview in *Rolling Stone* (May 10, 2012), the president himself has commented on this issue, stating, "I never bought into the notion that by electing me, somehow we are entering into a post-racial period. I've seen in my own lifetime how racial attitudes have changed and improved, and anybody who suggests that they haven't isn't paying attention or is trying to make a rhetorical point. . . . Because we all see it every day, and me being in this Oval Office is a testimony to changes that have been taking place." There are many factors that students must consider in exploring this issue, including comparative data on unemployment rates, incarceration (Issue 20), income and wealth inequity, and the persistence of segregated schools (Issue 17). The goal of a post-racial society, that is one which transcends race, is a noble ideal but to many Americans, it is unrealistic.

Additional Resources

Blackwell, Angela Glover, Stewart Kwoh, and Manuel Pastor. 2010. *Uncommon Ground: Race and America's Future* (W. W. Norton & Co.).

Brown, Michael K. 2003. *Whitewashing Race: The Myth of a Color-Blind Society* (University of California Press).

Funderberg. Lisa. 1995. *Black, Whites, Other: Biracial Americans Talk About Race and Identity* (Harper Perennial).

Harris-Perry, Melissa A. 2011. *Sister Citizen: Shame, Stereotypes, and Black Women in America* (Yale University Press).

Kennedy, Randall. 2004. *Interracial Intimacies: Sex, Marriage, Identity, and Adoption* (Vintage).

Kennedy, Randall. 2012. *The Persistence of the Color Line: Racial Politics and the Obama Presidency* (Vintage).

Leonardo, Zeus. 2009. *Race, Whiteness, and Education* (Routledge).

Maillard, Kevin and Rose Villazor, eds. 2012. *Loving v. Virginia in a Post-Racial World: Rethinking Race, Sex and Marriage* (Cambridge University Press).

McWhorter, John. 2009. "Obamakids: And the 10-Year-Olds Shall Lead Us," *New York Magazine* (August 18).

Murray, Charles. 2012. *Coming Apart: The State of White America 1960–2010* (Crown Forum).

O'Hearn, Claudine. 1998. *Half and Half: Writers on Growing Up Biracial and Bicultural* (Pantheon).

Page, Clarence. 2000. "How Race Counts in the 2000 Census." *The Chicago Tribune* (March 15).

Parker, Frank R. 1966. "The Damaging Consequences of the Rehnquist Court'sCommitment to Color-Blindness Versus Racial Justice." *The American University Law Review* (45, February 3).

Spencer, Ranier. 2009. "Mixed-Race Chic." *The Chronicle Review* (55, May 29).

Touré. 2011. *Who's Afraid of Post-Blackness?* (Free Press).

Williams, Patricia J. 2009. "Talking About Not Talking About Race." *New York Magazine* (August 18).

Williams, Patricia J. 2010. "Not-Black by Default." *The Nation* (May 10).

Williams, Thomas Chatterton. 2012. "As Black as We Wish to Be." *The New York Times* (March 18).

Wise, Tim. 2009. *Between Barack and a Hard Place: Racism and White Denial in the Age of Obama* (City Lights Publisher).

Wise, Tim. 2010. *Colorblind: The Rise of Post-Racial Politics and the Retreat from Racial Equity* (City Lights Publisher).

This daily news site is produced by a multiracial team of writers who believe America can become improved and united by racial justice. The information on the site is published by the Applied Research Center, which is a "racial justice think tank." It contains many subject areas ranging from criminal justice to arts and culture. There is a relevant section on how young people think, act, and talk about race.

http://colorlines.com/

This is the website of the Public Broadcasting Station, which contains a wealth of information on race and ethnicity along with current information on many social and cultural topics. It is listed here because the student may find current issues such as a colorblind society, post-racial identity, along with immigration and ethnicity concerns well researched. A thorough explanation of the documentary,

82

"Race: The Power of an Illusion," exposes the student to in-depth personal accounts of people responding to the issue of colorblind identity.

www.pbs.org/

The *Journal of Blacks in Higher Education* website is dedicated to research and sharing of information about African Americans in higher education. Along with daily news articles and research projects, the site offers information about African American accomplishments, college enrollment trends, racial gaps in public as well as higher education and links to related online articles of interest. The student will find a number of articles on post-racial identity on the site.

www.jbhe.com/

Established by Ward Connerly (Issue 6) and Dusty Rhodes, president of *National Review,* in 1996, The American Civil Rights Institute is dedicated to educating the public on the harms of racial and gender preferences in federal, state, and local programs. It hosts a blog to which Roger Clegg (Issue 12) opines about affirmative action and related topics. It offers several links to like-minded sites including those dedicated to answering the critics of Connerly's civil rights initiatives explored in (Issue 6, "Is the Emphasis on a Color-Blind Society an Answer to Racism?"

www.acri.org/

This is the site of the American Civil Rights Coalition. It was founded by Ward Connerly (Issue 6) and Dusty Rhodes, president of *National Review,* and is related to The American Civil Rights Institute. In the "News and Articles" section is a copy of "The Obama Era: Post Racial or Most Racial?" a report of the American Civil Rights Coalition, which argues that with the election of Obama, America is more race conscious than prior to the "post-racial" era.

www.acrc1.org/media/

Internet References . . .

Brookings

America's oldest think tank, the Brookings Institute, sponsors this website. It offers students high-quality research on many relevant topics dealing with race, ethnicity, and immigration. Over the past 90 years, its research has contributed to countless public policy decisions in large part because of its centrist approach.

http://brookings.edu

The Heritage Foundation

This is the website for the well-known conservative think tank, The Heritage Foundation, which states that it is committed to building an America where freedom, opportunity, prosperity, and civil society flourish. The site offers information including research on many issues including race, ethnicity, and immigration.

www.heritage.org

The American Enterprise Institute

The website for the American Enterprise Institute for Public Policy Research (AEI) indicates that it is a conservative think tank, founded in 1943. It is associated with neoconservative thought and policy recommendations. Approximately 35 conservative public intellectuals and activists contribute to the site.

www.aei.org

Latin American Network Information Center: University of Texas

The Latin American Network Information Center sponsors this website. It seeks to facilitate access to Internet-based information to, from, or on Latin America. It provides information about Latin America for students, teachers, and researchers, and potential research to hundreds of sites on Hispanics in the United States. There are excellent academic resources available on the site.

www1.lanic.utexas.edu

Policy and People

This website offers current information on national issues including immigration, education, and other social issues. It aims to take the spotlight off politics and politicians and put it back on policy and the people. The site is nonpartisan and nonprofit, featuring moderates, liberals, and conservatives. It highlights national policy debates.

www.citizenjoe.org

Rethinking the Color Line

*T*he period from World War II to the present has brought renewed challenges to American society where issues of race and identity are concerned. Returning soldiers, including Japanese Americans, African Americans, and Latino Americans among others, were unprepared to accept existing patterns of race relations and the color-based inequities that prevailed within the nation. Many were prepared to struggle for identity and equality opportunities to pursue the American dream. Such sentiments and emergent discontents within minority communities and progressive white communities led to the creation of organizations such as the Japanese American Citizenship League, La Raza, and others that would challenge the notion that America was "a white man's country." Racial and ethnic stereotypes were commonplace during this period. A powerful civil rights movement emerged to challenge the constitutional, legal, and social realities of Jim Crow. Also, black power and red power advocates emerged with identity, culture, and inequality as focal concerns of their demands for change. American elites in the society in which they led were again challenged to confront these issues with meaningful responses to the mounting demand for change. The following four issues are an attempt to examine some of these challenges and the responses that they generated within mainstream American society.

- Is Racism a Permanent Feature of American Society?
- Is the Emphasis on a Color-Blind Society an Answer to Racism?
- Do Whites Associate Privilege with Their Skin Color?
- Are Native American Mascots Racist Symbols?

ISSUE 5

Is Racism a Permanent Feature of American Society?

YES: Derrick Bell, from *Faces at the Bottom of the Well: The Permanence of Racism* (Basic Books, 1992)

NO: Russell Niele, from "'Postracialism': Do We Want It?" *Princeton Alumni Weekly* (vol. 110, no. 7, January 13, 2010)

Learning Outcomes

After reading this issue, the student should be able to:

- Develop a sophisticated understanding of the influence of racism in the development of American society.
- Develop a conceptual distinction between discrimination and racism.
- Comprehend different forms of racism, including individual and institutional racism.
- Understand the reification of racism.
- Explain Niele's idea of a post-racist society.
- Understand why Niele promotes meritocracy as a goal.

ISSUE SUMMARY

YES: Derrick Bell, a prominent African American scholar and authority on civil rights and constitutional law, argues that the prospects for achieving racial equality in the United States are "illusory" for blacks.

NO: Russell Niele, a lecturer in politics at Princeton, works for the Executive Precept Program sponsored by Princeton's James Madison Program. He has written on affirmative action and the origins of an urban black underclass. Niele argues that American society is moving toward a meritocracy, which is post-racist (not post-racial). For him, race, ethnicity, and religious identity are less determinant than they were in earlier American history.

The persistence of ideological and institutional racism within the United States has given rise to a debate over the prospects for ridding American society of this glaring contradiction. On one side of this debate are those who believe that a proper examination of the American experience and the treatment of African Americans and other peoples of color throughout history lead to the conclusion that racism is unlikely to be eroded in this country and will continue to challenge the American creed. The other side comprises those who advance the more optimistic view concerning race relations within the United States. Members of this camp claim that the destructive impact of racism is declining in this country, and that any lagging progress of African Americans is due to factors other than racial discrimination.

Racist ideology has been employed throughout the nation's history in attempts to justify institutional policies and practices such as slavery and segregation. Despite the substantial efforts of supporters of a racially egalitarian society, the reification of racism is a continuing reality of this nation.

Derrick Bell is a proponent of the thesis that racism is a permanent feature of American society. His classic proposition is supported by an analysis of some of the most important aspects of African Americans' historical development. Bell reminds us that despite the fact of significant progress for some blacks of the United States, the legacy of slavery has left a significant portion of the race "with life-long poverty and soul-devastating despair. . . ."

Bell believes that race consciousness is so imbedded in whites that it is virtually impossible to rise above it. He argues that "few whites are able to identify with blacks as a group" and tend to view them through "comforting racial stereotypes." Bell cites a number of examples of the destructive impact of racial bonding among whites upon blacks' efforts to progress within society. He points out that even poor whites have tended to support institutions such as slavery and segregation rather than coalescing with blacks to fight against common class–based social disadvantages such as unemployment and poverty. Given this record of race relations, it is impossible for Bell to accept the claim that racism has been largely overcome in the United States. To the contrary, he feels strongly that a critical and proper examination of the history of black–white relations supports the conclusion that racism is a permanent feature of American society.

In the YES selection, Bell argues that, "Black people will never gain full equality in this country." For him the legacy of institutional discrimination that was reflected in slavery continues through the exclusionary policies of racial segregation that has left blacks "at the bottom of the well." Additionally, Bell views certain roles that blacks play in the society, such as the scapegoat, as contributing to the permanence of racism. Who will play these roles? He also views the color-coded perceptions and behaviors that dominate social interaction between the "races" as so culturally imbedded as to be virtually impossible to overcome.

In the NO selection, Russell Niele does not agree with Bell that racism is a permanent strain of the fabric of American society. Niele believes that America is moving toward a meritocracy based on talent and hard work, which neutralizes racism. Thus, he opposes Bell's position that racism is a permanent feature of American society. Niele views American society as post-racist. Traditional forms of identity, in his view, are less determinant of opportunity for social advancement today than they were in earlier American history. He cites progress within the institutions of society that have been achieved by blacks and other minorities as strong evidence of a post-racist America.

The reader would benefit from expanding his or her perspective for dealing with the issue to include ideas and concepts dealing with social and cultural values. This is a debate in itself. That is, do structural conditions such as racism, discrimination, and lack of opportunity lead to inequality and poverty? Or, is poverty attributed to individual factors including socialization and value formation? Bell makes a structural argument to explain the permanence of racism. Niele cites Harvard sociologist, William Julius Wilson's thesis of the declining significance of race, which is reflected in more opportunities for formal education, including higher education leading to significant social and economic advantages. Nieie places more emphasis on the individual, hence his argument for meritocracy.

Racism has played a major role in the formation and ongoing development of the American society. Given this existential reality, it is not difficult to understand that some observers and analysts of American race relations, when confronted with the inequality that persists between blacks and whites in society, would blame this phenomenon on racial discrimination. Those who support this argument view racism as a continuing and permanent reality of American society.

In developing their views on this issue, students may consider a 2008 racial controversy started by white radio talk show host Don Imus' on-air comments about the predominantly black Rutgers University women's basketball team is instructive. The host referred to the team as "nappy-headed hoes" and "jigaboos." Is this an example of media perpetuated racism? Does it contribute to the continuity and perhaps permanence of racism in American culture? Moreover, increasingly popular talk radio, which at times promotes public hatred of minority groups, is at the center of the controversy. Students may want to use additional talk radio examples in their discussion of the permanence of racism and the persistence of discrimination.

American presidents who have addressed the state of race relations in the United States have tended to state some variant of the following assessment: we have made significant progress but that we have a long way to go. Even President Obama, the nation's first African American president, acknowledges that substantial racial progress has been made in the United States. His election is a testament to this fact. However, he does not embrace the claim that the United States has become a post-racial (Issue 4) society, that is, a society where racial egalitarianism is the organizing principle of race relations. Considering this point, students are reminded that the idea of meritocracy has been more of an ideal than a reality for the African American experience. Prior the civil rights era, the nation was challenged to apply the meritocratic ideal. Americans continue to struggle to achieve the vision of an egalitarian society.

YES

Derrick Bell

Faces at the Bottom of the Well: The Permanence of Racism

Divining Our Racial Themes

In these bloody days and frightful nights when an urban warrior can find no face more despicable than his own, no ammunition more deadly than self-hate and no target more deserving of his true aim than his brother, we must wonder how we came so late and lonely to this place.

—Maya Angelou

When I was growing up in the years before the Second World War, our slave heritage was more a symbol of shame than a source of pride. It burdened black people with an indelible mark of difference as we struggled to be like whites. In those far-off days, survival and progress seemed to require moving beyond, even rejecting slavery. Childhood friends in a West Indian family who lived a few doors away often boasted—erroneously as I later learned—that their people had never been slaves. My own more accurate—but hardly more praiseworthy—response was that my forebears included many free Negroes, some of whom had Choctaw and Blackfoot Indian blood.

In those days, self-delusion was both easy and comforting. Slavery was barely mentioned in the schools and seldom discussed by the descendants of its survivors, particularly those who had somehow moved themselves to the North. Emigration, whether from the Caribbean islands or from the Deep South states, provided a geographical distance that encouraged and enhanced individual denial of our collective, slave past. We sang spirituals but detached the songs from their slave origins. As I look back, I see this reaction as no less sad, for being very understandable. We were a subordinate and mostly shunned portion of a society that managed to lay the onus of slavery neatly on those who were slaves while simultaneously exonerating those who were slaveholders. All things considered, it seemed a history best left alone.

Then, after the Second World War and particularly in the 1960s, slavery became—for a few academics and some militant Negroes—a subject of fascination and a sure means of evoking racial rage as a prelude to righteously repeated demands for "Freedom Now!" In response to a resurrection of interest in our past, new books on slavery were written, long out-of-print volumes republished. The new awareness reached its highest point in 1977 with the television version of Alex Haley's biographical novel, *Roots*. The highly successful miniseries informed millions of Americans—black as well as white—that slavery in fact existed and that it was awful. Not, of course, as awful as it would have been save for the good white folks the television writers had created to ease the slaves' anguish, and the evil ones on whose shoulders they placed all the guilt. Through the magic of literary license, white viewers could feel revulsion for slavery without necessarily recognizing American slavery as a burden on the nation's history, certainly not a burden requiring reparations in the present.

Even so, under pressure of civil rights protests, many white Americans were ready to accede to, if not applaud, Supreme Court rulings that the Constitution should no longer recognize and validate laws that kept in place the odious badges of slavery.

As a result, two centuries after the Constitution's adoption, we did live in a far more enlightened world. Slavery was no more. Judicial precedent and a plethora of civil rights statutes formally prohibited racial discrimination. Compliance was far from perfect, but the slavery provisions in the Constitution[1] did seem lamentable artifacts of a less enlightened era.

But the fact of slavery refuses to fade, along with the deeply embedded personal attitudes and public policy assumptions that supported it for so long. Indeed, the racism that made slavery feasible is far from dead in the last decade of twentieth-century America; and the civil rights gains, so hard won, are being steadily eroded. Despite undeniable progress for many, no African Americans are insulated from incidents of racial discrimination. Our careers, even our lives, are threatened because of our color. Even the most successful of us are haunted by the plight of our less fortunate brethren who struggle for existence in what some social scientists call the "underclass." Burdened with life-long poverty and soul-devastating despair, they live beyond the pale of the American dream. What we designate as "racial progress" is not a solution to that problem. It is a regeneration of the problem in a particularly perverse form.

According to data compiled in 1990 for basic measures of poverty, unemployment, and income, the slow advances African Americans made during the 1960s and 1970s have definitely been reversed. The unemployment rate for blacks is 2.5 times the rate for whites. Black per-capita income is not even two thirds of the income for whites; and blacks, most of whom own little wealth or business property, are three times more likely to have income below the poverty level than whites. If trends of the last two decades are allowed to continue, readers can safely—and sadly—assume that the current figures are worse than those cited here.[2]

Statistics cannot, however, begin to express the havoc caused by joblessness and poverty: broken homes, anarchy in communities, futility in the public schools. All are the bitter harvest of race-determined unemployment in a society where work provides sustenance, status, and the all-important sense of self-worth. What we now call the "inner city" is, in fact, the American equivalent of the South African homelands. Poverty is less the source than the status of men and women who, despised because of their race, seek refuge in self-rejection. Drug-related crime, teenaged parenthood, and disrupted and disrupting family life all are manifestations of a despair that feeds on self. That despair is bred anew each day by the images on ever-playing television sets, images confirming that theirs is the disgraceful form of living, not the only way people live.

Few whites are able to identify with blacks as a group—the essential prerequisite for feeling empathy with, rather than aversion from, blacks' self-inflicted suffering, as expressed by the poet Maya Angelou in this introduction's epigraph. Unable or unwilling to perceive that "there but for the grace of God, go I," few whites are ready to actively promote civil rights for blacks. Because of an irrational but easily roused fear that any social reform will unjustly benefit blacks, whites fail to support the programs this country desperately needs to address the ever-widening gap between the rich and the poor, both black and white.

Lulled by comforting racial stereotypes, fearful that blacks will unfairly get ahead of them, all too many whites respond to even the most dire reports of race-based disadvantage with either a sympathetic headshake or victim-blaming rationalizations. Both responses lead easily to the conclusion that contemporary complaints of racial discrimination are simply excuses put forward by people who are unable or unwilling to compete on an equal basis in a competitive society.

For white people who both deny racism and see a heavy dose of the Horatio Alger myth as the answer to blacks' problems, how sweet it must be when a black person stands in a public place and condemns as slothful and unambitious those blacks who are not making it. Whites eagerly embrace black conservatives' homilies to self-help, however grossly unrealistic such messages are in an economy where millions, white as well as black, are unemployed and, more important, in one where racial discrimination in the workplace is as vicious (if less obvious) than it was when employers posted signs "no negras need apply."

Whatever the relief from responsibility such thinking provides those who embrace it, more than a decade of civil rights setbacks in the White House, in the courts, and in the critical realm of media-nurtured public opinion has forced retrenchment in the tattered civil rights ranks. We must reassess our cause and our approach to it, but repetition of time-worn slogans simply will not do. As a popular colloquialism puts it, it is time to "get real" about race and the persistence of racism in America.

To make such an assessment—to plan for the future by reviewing the experiences of the past—we must ask whether the formidable hurdles we now face in the elusive quest for racial equality are simply a challenge to our commitment, whether they are the latest variation of the old hymn "One More River to Cross." Or, as we once again gear up to meet the challenges posed by these unexpected new setbacks, are we ignoring a current message with implications for the future which history has already taught us about the past?

Such assessment is hard to make. On the one hand, contemporary color barriers are certainly less visible as a result of our successful effort to strip the law's endorsement from the hated Jim Crow signs. Today one can travel for thousands of miles across this country and never see a public facility designated as "Colored" or "White." Indeed, the very absence of visible signs of discrimination creates an atmosphere of racial neutrality and encourages whites to believe that racism is a thing of the past. On the other hand, the general use of so-called neutral standards to continue exclusionary practices reduces the effectiveness of traditional civil rights laws, while rendering discriminatory actions more oppressive than ever. Racial bias in the pre-*Brown* era was stark, open, unalloyed with hypocrisy and blank-faced lies. We blacks, when rejected, knew who our enemies were. They were not us! Today, because bias is masked in unofficial practices and "neutral" standards, we must wrestle with the question whether race or some individual failing has cost us the job, denied us the promotion, or prompted our being rejected as tenants for an apartment. Either conclusion breeds frustration and alienation—and a rage we dare not show to others or admit to ourselves.

Modern discrimination is, moreover, not practiced indiscriminately. Whites, ready and willing to applaud, even idolize black athletes and entertainers, refuse to hire, or balk at, working with blacks. Whites who number individual blacks among their closest friends approve, or do not oppose, practices that bar selling or renting homes or apartments in their neighborhoods to blacks they don't know. Employers, not wanting "too many of them," are willing to hire one or two black people, but will reject those who apply later. Most hotels and restaurants who offer black patrons courteous—even deferential—treatment, uniformly reject black job applicants, except perhaps for the most menial jobs. When did you last see a black waiter in a really good restaurant?

Racial schizophrenia is not limited to hotels and restaurants. As a result, neither professional status nor relatively high income protects even accomplished blacks from capricious acts of discrimination that may reflect either individual "preference" or an institution's bias. The motivations for bias vary; the disadvantage to black victims is the same.

Careful examination reveals a pattern to these seemingly arbitrary racial actions. When whites perceive that it will be profitable or at least cost-free to serve, hire, admit, or otherwise deal with blacks on a nondiscriminatory basis, they do so. When they fear—accurately or not—that there may be a loss, inconvenience, or upset to themselves or other whites, discriminatory conduct usually follows. Selections and rejections reflect preference as much as prejudice. A preference for whites makes it harder to prove the discrimination outlawed by civil rights laws. This difficulty, when combined with lackluster enforcement, explains why discrimination in employment and in the housing market continues to prevail more than two decades after enactment of the Equal Employment Opportunity Act of 1965 and the Fair Housing Act of 1968.

Racial policy is the culmination of thousands of these individual practices. Black people, then, are caught in a double bind. We are, as I have said, disadvantaged unless whites perceive that nondiscriminatory treatment for us will be a benefit for them. In addition, even when nonracist practices might bring a benefit, whites may rely on discrimination against blacks as a unifying factor and a safety valve for frustrations during economic hard times.

Almost always, the injustices that dramatically diminish the rights of blacks are linked to the serious economic disadvantage suffered by many whites who lack money and power. Whites, rather than acknowledge the similarity of their disadvantage, particularly when compared with that of better-off whites, are easily detoured into protecting their sense of entitlement vis-à-vis blacks for all things of value. Evidently, this racial preference expectation is hypnotic. It is this compulsive fascination that seems to prevent most whites from even seeing—much less resenting—the far more sizable gap between their status and those who occupy the lofty levels at the top of our society.

Race consciousness of this character, as Professor Kimberlè Crenshaw suggested in 1988 in a pathbreaking *Harvard Law Review* article, makes it difficult for whites "to imagine the world differently. It also creates the desire for identification with privileged elites. By focusing on a distinct, subordinate 'other,' whites include themselves in the dominant circle—an arena in which most hold no real power, but only their privileged racial identity."

The critically important stabilizing role that blacks play in this society constitutes a major barrier in the way of achieving racial equality. Throughout history, politicians have used blacks as scapegoats for failed economic or political policies. Before the Civil War, rich slave owners persuaded the white working class to stand with them against the danger of slave revolts—even though the existence of slavery condemned white workers to a life of economic privation. After the Civil War, poor whites fought social reforms and settled for segregation rather than see formerly enslaved blacks get ahead. Most labor unions preferred to allow plant owners to break strikes with black scab labor than allow blacks to join their ranks. The "them against us" racial ploy—always a potent force in economic bad times—is working again: today whites, as disadvantaged by high-status entrance requirements as blacks, fight to end affirmative action policies that, by eliminating class-based entrance requirements and requiring widespread advertising of jobs, have likely helped far more whites than blacks. And in the 1990s, as through much of the 1980s, millions of Americans—white as well as black—face steadily worsening conditions: unemployment, inaccessible health care, inadequate housing, mediocre education, and pollution of the environment. The gap in national incomes is approaching a crisis as those in the top fifth now earn more than their counterparts in the bottom four fifths combined. The conservative guru Kevin Phillips used a different but no less disturbing comparison: the top two million income earners in this country earn more than the next one hundred million.

Shocking. And yet conservative white politicians are able to gain and hold even the highest office despite their failure to address seriously any of these issues. They rely instead on the time-tested formula of getting needy whites to identify on the basis of their shared skin color, and suggest with little or no subtlety that white people must stand together against the Willie Hortons, or against racial quotas, or against affirmative action. The code words differ. The message is the same. Whites are rallied on the basis of racial pride and patriotism to accept their often lowly lot in life, and encouraged to vent their frustration by opposing any serious advancement by blacks. Crucial to this situation is the unstated understanding by the mass of whites that they will accept large disparities in economic opportunity in respect to other whites as long as they have a priority over blacks and other people of color for access to the few opportunities available.

This "racial bonding" by whites means that black rights and interests are always vulnerable to diminishment if not to outright destruction. The willingness of whites over time to respond to this racial rallying cry explains—far more than does the failure of liberal democratic practices (re black rights) to coincide with liberal democratic theory—blacks' continuing subordinate status. This is, of course, contrary to the philosophy of Gunnar Myrdal's massive midcentury study *The American Dilemma*. Myrdal and two generations of civil rights advocates accepted the idea of racism as merely an odious holdover from slavery, "a terrible and inexplicable anomaly stuck in the middle of our liberal democratic ethos." No one doubted that the standard American policy making was adequate to the task of abolishing racism. White America, it was assumed, *wanted* to abolish racism.[3]

Forty years later, in *The New American Dilemma*, Professor Jennifer Hochschild examined what she called Myrdal's "anomaly thesis," and concluded that it simply cannot explain the persistence of racial discrimination. Rather, the continued viability of racism demonstrates "that racism is not simply an excrescence on a fundamentally healthy liberal democratic body, but is part of what shapes and energizes the body." Under this view, "liberal democracy and racism in the United States are historically, even inherently, reinforcing; American society as we know it exists only because of its foundation in racially based slavery, and it thrives only because racial discrimination continues. The apparent anomaly is an actual symbiosis."

The permanence of this "symbiosis" ensures that civil rights gains will be temporary and setbacks inevitable. Consider: In this last decade of the twentieth century, color determines the social and economic status of all African Americans, both those who have been highly successful and their poverty-bound brethren whose lives are grounded in misery and despair. We rise and fall less as a result of our efforts than in response to the needs of a white society that condemns all blacks to quasi citizenship as surely as it segregated our parents and enslaved their forebears. The fact is that, despite what we designate as progress wrought through struggle over many generations, we remain what we were in the beginning: a dark and foreign presence, always the designated "other." Tolerated in good times, despised when things go wrong, as a people we are scapegoated and sacrificed as distraction or catalyst for compromise to facilitate resolution of political differences or relieve economic adversity.

We are now, as were our forebears when they were brought to the New World, objects of barter for those who, while profiting from our existence, deny our humanity. It is in the light of this fact that we must consider the haunting questions about slavery and exploitation contained in Professor Linda Myers's *Understanding an Afrocentric World View: Introduction to an Optimal Psychology*, questions that serve as their own answers.

We simply cannot prepare realistically for our future without assessing honestly our past. It seems cold, accusatory, but we must try to fathom with her "the mentality of a people that could continue for over 300 years to kidnap an estimated 50 million youth and young adults from Africa, transport them across the Atlantic with about half dying unable to withstand the inhumanity of the passage, and enslave them as animals."

As Professor Myers reminds us, blacks were not the only, and certainly not America's most, persecuted people. Appropriately, she asks about the mindset of European Americans to native Americans. After all, those in possession of the land were basically friendly to the newcomers. And yet the European Americans proceeded to annihilate almost the entire race, ultimately forcing the survivors onto reservations after stealing their land. Far from acknowledging and atoning for these atrocities, American history portrays whites as the heroes, the Indian victims as savage villains. "What," she wonders, "can be understood about the world view of a people who claim to be building a democracy with freedom and justice for all, and at the same time own slaves and deny others basic human rights?"

Of course, Americans did not invent slavery. The practice has existed throughout recorded history, and Professor Orlando Patterson, a respected scholar, argues impressively that American slavery was no worse than that practiced in other parts of the world.[4] But it is not comparative slavery policies that concern me. Slavery is, as an example of what white America has done, a constant reminder of what white America might do.

We must see this country's history of slavery, not as an insuperable racial barrier to blacks, but as a legacy of enlightenment from our enslaved forebears reminding us that if they survived the ultimate form of racism, we and those whites who stand with us can at least view racial oppression in its many contemporary forms without underestimating its critical importance and likely permanent status in this country.

To initiate the reconsideration, I want to set forth this proposition, which will be easier to reject than refute: *Black people will never gain full equality in this country. Even those herculean efforts we hail as successful will produce no more than temporary "peaks of progress," short-lived victories that slide into irrelevance as racial patterns adapt in ways that maintain white dominance. This is a hard-to-accept fact that all history verifies. We must acknowledge it, not as a sign of submission, but as an act of ultimate defiance.*

We identify with and hail as hero the man or woman willing to face even death without flinching. Why? Because, while no one escapes death, those who conquer their dread of it are freed to live more fully. In similar fashion, African Americans must confront and conquer the otherwise deadening reality of our permanent subordinate status. Only in this way can we prevent ourselves from being dragged down by society's racial hostility. Beyond survival lies the potential to perceive more clearly both a reason and the means for further struggle.

In this book, Geneva Crenshaw, the civil rights lawyer—protagonist of my earlier *And We Are Not Saved: The Elusive Quest for Racial Justice,* returns in a series of stories that offer an allegorical perspective on old dreams, long-held fears, and current conditions. The provocative format of story, a product of experience and imagination, allows me to take a new look at what, for want of a better phrase, I will call "racial themes." Easier to recognize than describe, they are essentials in the baggage of people subordinated by color in a land that boasts of individual freedom and equality. Some of these themes—reliance on law, involvement in protests, belief in freedom symbols—are familiar and generally known. Others—the yearning for a true homeland, the rejection of racial testimony, the temptation to violent retaliation—are real but seldom revealed. Revelation does not much alter the mystique of interracial romance or lessen its feared consequences. Nor does the search ever end for a full understanding of why blacks are and remain this country's designated scapegoats. . . .

The goal of racial equality is, while comforting to many whites, more illusory than real for blacks. For too long, we have worked for substantive reform, then settled for weakly worded and poorly enforced legislation, indeterminate judicial decisions, token government positions, even holidays. I repeat. If we are to seek new goals for our struggles, we must first reassess the worth of the racial assumptions on which, without careful thought, we have presumed too much and relied on too long.

Let's begin.

Notes

1. According to William Wiecek, ten provisions in the Constitution directly or indirectly provided for slavery and protected slave owners.

2. Not all the data are bleak. While the median family income for black families declined in the 1970s and 1980s, the proportion of African American families with incomes of $35,000 to $50,000 increased from 23.3 to 27.5 percent. The proportion with incomes above $50,000 increased by 38 percent, from 10.0 to 13.8 percent. The overall median income for blacks declined though: while the top quarter made progress, the bottom half was sliding backward, and the proportion of blacks receiving very low income (less than $5,000) actually increased.

3. According to Myrdal, the "Negro problem in America represents a moral lag in the development of the nation and a study of it must record nearly everything which is bad and wrong in America. . . . However, . . . not since Reconstruction has there been more reason to anticipate fundamental changes in American race relations, changes which will involve a development toward the American ideals."

4. He suggests: "The dishonor of slavery . . . came in the primal act of submission. It was the most immediate human expression of the inability to defend oneself or to secure one's livelihood. . . . The dishonor the slave was compelled to experience sprang instead from that raw, human sense of debasement inherent in having no being except as an expression of another's being."

'Postracialism': Do We Want It?

I often have asked students in my politics precept classes to perform the following thought experiment. "You're going to die tomorrow and will be reincarnated the next day. God offers you two choices. Either you will be reborn into a white working-class family in a lower-middle-income, white-ethnic community in Brooklyn, or you will be reborn into an upper-middle-class, black professional family, living in an upper-middle-class neighborhood in Forest Hills, Queens. You will not remember your present incarnation and have no reason to maintain any continuity with it. Which rebirth do you choose?"

Some readers may be surprised to learn that 90 to 100 percent of students of all races to whom I have posed this question say they would rather be reborn into the upper-middle-class black professional family living in an affluent neighborhood than into the white working-class family living in more modest circumstances. White skin color may still have its privileges in America, but they seem to these post-civil-rights-era students much less important than class advantages.

The most nuanced and perceptive answer I ever got to the question came from a black female student: "If I knew that I would have the same academic talent that I have now," the student explained, "I would choose the poor white family. Having white skin still has many advantages, and it is easy to get a high-paying job in this country if you are smart in school." But, she continued, if she were an average or below-average student, she'd prefer to be born into the rich black family—because affluence brings many advantages, and it's difficult for mediocre students to find lucrative jobs regardless of their race.

This student didn't know it, but she was reflecting what labor economists and other social scientists have been saying for many years: Since the middle of the last century, America has been experiencing a "declining significance of race"—the title of a book by Harvard sociologist William Julius Wilson—and a corresponding rise in the significance to social and economic advancement of formal education and developed cognitive skills. While these latter factors are related in important ways to family and neighborhood background, they also are tied intimately to individual talent and temperament. America has become a very kind place to the academically talented, hardworking, and ambitious students of all races and ethnicities—that is, the sorts of people who wind up at places like Princeton.

Which brings up the case of Barack Obama. What better example is there of how far talent, ambition, hard work, and a focus on what one wants to

Niele, Russell. From *Princeton Alumni Weekly*, vol. 110, no. 7, January 13, 2010, pp. 49–51.
Copyright © 2010 by Princeton Alumni Weekly. Reprinted by permission.

achieve in life can take you today in America than Barack Obama's meteoric career as Ivy League student, *Harvard Law Review* editor, community organizer, law school professor, local politician, U.S. senator, best-selling author, and ultimately president of the United States? I have serious problems with many of Obama's stated views. But it is clear that Obama is a man of great talent, oratorical and otherwise, and that his success in so many fields of endeavor and his ability to do so well among white voters in the 2008 election are the culmination of a long-term trend in America toward greater appreciation of merit, regardless of one's ethnicity, gender, or race.

When one considers that 63 percent of respondents in a 1958 Gallup poll said that if their political party "nominated a generally well-qualified man for president and he happened to be a Negro" they would not vote for him, one gets a sense of how far America has advanced along the meritocratic path. While many black voters—and some guilt-ridden whites—no doubt voted for Obama because of his race, his impressive showing among white independents and young people clearly was based on the perception that he was a fresh voice and a gifted speaker with many talents of intellect and temperament that would make for an effective national leader.

The Obama success has provoked the claim that we have entered an era of a "postracial America." At first blush the phrase strikes me as Utopian silliness, since it ignores the inevitable intergroup tensions and hostilities that are inextricably a part of any multiracial, multiethnic, multireligious society. Nevertheless, insofar as "postracial" conveys the idea not of utopian transformation but of the more modest claim that the many racial, ethnic, and religious identity groups to which Americans belong are considerably less important than they once were in determining success in America, the phrase conveys an important truth.

Race, ethnicity, and religious identity clearly are less important determinants of who gets ahead in the United States today than was the case in the long period of WASP ascendancy—hence my students' preference for being born into a well-to-do black family over a poor white one. Barack Obama's election is only the latest development in a long evolutionary process that accelerated after the Second World War, by which members of various minority groups have ascended to positions of power and influence. It is an important milestone—like the election of John Kennedy as the first Catholic president—though it is not the Holy Grail.

To use an older phrase of classical liberalism, it is part of an important and much-welcomed trend in which careers are increasingly "open to the talents." The widespread belief in this principle is one reason so many Americans continue to oppose race- and ethnicity-based preferences in employment and other areas of American life, and why a majority of the members of the U.S. Supreme Court have been eager to invalidate most such policies through the vehicle of the 14th Amendment's equal-protection clause.

But for many there is a sinister undertone to the phrase "postracial." Michael Eric Dyson *93, for instance, has said that while it surely is good that America should seek to become "postracist," it is not good to strive to become "post-racial"—at least if that means people must abandon their cherished racial and ethnic identities to become full Americans. Here I find myself in agreement with my fellow Princetonian (though I have disagreed sharply with Dyson on many other issues concerning race). *E pluribus unum* ("out of many, one") is one of America's foundational ideals, affirming two equally important principles: We must show respect for particularized diversities (the *pluribus),* while at the same time affirming the importance of participation in a more encompassing civic and political realm (the *unum*) in which those diversities are transcended, without being destroyed.

This means that it is OK to have what older theorists of assimilation called "layered identities," so that Irish-Americans, Italian-Americans, Chinese-Americans, African-Americans, Mormon Americans, Jewish Americans, and all those who cherish their "hyphenated and hybrid attachments" can be no less Americans than WASP Americans or those who have no group identity other than their American nationality. While all individuals and groups in the United States are called upon to affirm certain basic tasks and ideals—like respecting democracy and the rule of law, seeing to it that their children become educated and learn English, respecting the Constitution—the idea of liberty in America generally has encompassed the notion that outside the limited civic and political realm where we share a national identity, people are free to seek happiness and fulfillment in their particularized communities. A "postracial America" for many would mean the destruction of these communal attachments and hybrid identities, the toleration of which, I believe, has contributed to America's relative success in assimilating the diverse peoples of the globe.

The Harvard philosopher Horace Kallen, who wrote in the period between the two world wars, had many wise things to say on these matters. Resisting the extreme Anglo-Saxon assimilationists of his day who enjoined against "hyphenated Americanism" and who reached menacing proportions in the 3-million-strong Ku Klux Klan of the 1920s, Kallen, a Jew, spoke of America as a "multiplicity within unity" of peoples from many diverse ethnic and religious communities. It was within these "organic" communities, Kallen wrote, that we nurture our "preferences of the herd type in which the individual feels freest and most at ease," and it was important for the well-being of everyone, he believed, that citizens not be required to abandon these communal attachments to become fully American.

Around the same time Kallen was defending hyphenated Americanism, the historian Marcus Hansen was fleshing out his law of immigrant succession: What the second generation often tries to forget about its ancestral roots, subsequent generations desperately try to recover and preserve. Hansen and Kallen understood that we all crave a sense of belonging and place, and that America offers the cherished freedom for people to mold and select their own place-defining narratives.

Today, in a "postracist" (but not "post-racial") America, this freedom has become more appealing than ever. Its presence is one reason America remains a magnet for diverse peoples around the world. Together with "careers open to the talents" and our open-market system, it is a freedom we all must seek to preserve. . . .

EXPLORING THE ISSUE

Is Racism a Permanent Feature of American Society?

Critical Thinking and Reflection

1. What is the historical influence of racism on American society?
2. What is the difference between discrimination and racism?
3. Explain the various forms of racism and employ contemporary examples?
4. What is the reification of racism? Offer some examples.
5. What does Niele mean by a post-racist society?
6. What is a meritocracy? What is Niele's argument in favor of it? Is a true meritocracy possible in the United States?

Is There Common Ground?

The struggle to overcome racism has persisted from the Civil War to the present. Racism has consistently challenged major American values including racial equality and meritocracy. Despite the gains of the civil rights movement and changing attitudes on race, it is clear that racism has not vanished. Will racism ever go away? Both Bell and Niele would agree that there has been significant progress in race relations including a decline in racism. Neither of these authors goes so far as to suggest that we are on the threshold of eliminating racism in America. However, the debate over such a policy goal within society serves to illuminate the salience of "race" and the establishment of distinct color-coded racial categories in influencing the development of social relations within modern societies such as the United States and South Africa. In this regard, students should recognize that racism has developed new and different, more covert forms within society (see unit 5). This is a critical point in one's exploration of the permanence of racism.

Additional Resources

Almaguer, Tomas. 1994. *Racial Fault Lines: The Historical Origins of White Supremacy in California* (University of California Press).

Banfield, Edward. 1970. *The Unheavenly City* (Little, Brown).

Blackmon, Douglas A. 2008. *Slavery by Another Name: The Re-Enslavement of Black Americans from the Civil War to World War II* (Doubleday).

Bonilla-Silva, Eduardo. 2001. *White Supremacy and Racism in the Post Civil Rights Era* (Rienner).

Bonilla-Silva, Eduardo. 2003. *Racism Without Racists: Color-Blind Racism and the Persistence of Racial Inequality in the United States* (Rowman & Littlefield.)

Bulmer, Martin and John Solomos, eds. 1999. *Racism* (Oxford Press).

Cox, Oliver Cromwell. 1848. *Caste, Class and Race: A Study in Social Dynamics* (Modern Reader Paperbacks).

Crouch, Stanley. 1997. *The All-American Skin Game, or, The Decoy of Race* (New York, NY: Vintage Books).

Douglas, Herbert. 2005. "Migration and Adaptations of African American Families Within Urban America," in *Minority Voices: Linking Personal Ethnic History and the Sociological Imagination Relations* by John Myers (Allyn & Bacon).

Frazier, E. Franklin. 1939. *The Negro Family in the United States* (University of Chicago Press).

Harrison, Lawrence E. 1992. *Who Prospers? How Cultural Values Shape Economic and Political Success* (Basic Books).

Jaspin, Elliot. 2007. *Buried in the Bitter Waters: The Hidden History of Racial Cleansing in America* (Basic Books, 2007).

Jordan, Winthrop. 1968. *White Over Black: American Attitudes Toward the Negro, 1550–1812* (The University of North Carolina Press).

Kelley, Robin. 1997. *Yo' Mama's Disfunktional: Fighting the Culture Wars in Urban America* (Beacon).

Lewis, Oscar. 1966. *La Vida: A Puerto Rican Family in the Culture of Poverty, San Juan and New York* (Random House).

Lipsitz, George. 2006. *The Possessive Investment in Whiteness: How White People Profit from Identity Politics* (Temple University Press).

Lipsitz, George. 2011. *How Racism Takes Place* (Temple University Press).

Loewen, James. 2006. W. *Sundown Towns: A Hidden Dimension of American Racism* (Touchstone).

Myrdal, Gunnar. 1944. *An American Dilemma* (Harper).

Pfaelzer, Jean. 2007. *Driven Out: The Forgotten War against Chinese Americans* (Random House).

Rhoden, William. 2006. *Forty Million Dollar Slaves: The Rise, Fall, and Redemption of the Black Athlete* (Crown Publishers).

Royster, Deidre. 2003. *Race and the Invisible Hand: How White Networks Exclude Black Men from Blue-Collar Jobs* (University of California Press).

Sports Illustrated. 1968. "The Black Athlete—A Shameful Story." Documents racism in professional and collegiate sports during the 1950s and 1960s. (29: July, 1–5).

Washington, Harriet, A. 2008a. *Medical Apartheid: The Dark History of Medical Experimentation on Black Americans from Colonial Times to the Present* (Doubleday).

Washington, Harriet, A. 2008b. "Apology Shines Light on Racial Schism in Medicine." *The New York Times* (July).

Wilson, William Julius. 1978. *The Declining Significance of Race: Blacks and Changing American Institutions* (University of Chicago Press).

Wilson, William Julius. 1990. *The Truly Disadvantaged* (University of Chicago Press).

This is the website for the Southern Poverty Law Center (SPLC), which was founded by Morris Dees and Joe Levin. Located in Alabama, the center is internationally known for many tolerance programs including education programs, tracking of hate groups, and its legal victories against white supremacists. It offers educational and community programs for those interested in dismantling bigotry.

www.splcenter.org/

For an international perspective coming out of the United Kingdom, the website Working Against Racism (WAR) is sponsored by trade unions. Among other things, it offers an extensive bibliography of sources on racism in Europe. Further, the student can look into anti-racism research projects in France, Belgium, Italy, Bulgaria, and England.

www.workingagainstracism.org/

The human rights organization, Amnesty International, advocates for human rights in more than 150 countries. Although it is international in scope, the site covers pertinent news from the United States. It offers the student exposure to race conflict beyond America.

www.amnesty.org/

ISSUE 6

Is the Emphasis on a Color-Blind Society an Answer to Racism?

YES: **Ward Connerly**, from "Don't Box Me In," *National Review* (April 16, 2001)

NO: **Eduardo Bonilla-Silva**, from *Racism without Racists: Color-Blind Racism and the Persistence of Racial Inequality in the United States* (Rowman & Littlefield, 2003)

Learning Outcomes

After reading this issue, the student should be able to:

- Develop an accurate conceptualization of what it means to be color-blind.
- Identify and explain the significant components of the color-blind ideology.
- Develop an informed understanding of the goals being pursued by advocates of a color-blind society.
- Comprehend the challenges that must be overcome in order to create a color-blind society.
- Identify and explain the functions of racial classification within American society.
- Identify and explain negative impacts of color-blind ideology when applied to minority communities.
- Apply color-blind ideology to contemporary society.

ISSUE SUMMARY

YES: Ward Connerly is a strong critic of all attempts at racial classification and believes that in order to achieve a racially egalitarian, unified American society, the government and private citizens must stop assigning people to categories delineated by race. To achieve this goal, Mr. Connerly is supporting the enactment of a "Racial Privacy Initiative."

NO: Eduardo Bonilla-Silva argues that "regardless of whites' sincere fictions, racial considerations shade almost everything in America" and, therefore, color-blind ideology is a cover for the racism and inequality that persist within contemporary American society.

Skin color has played a pivotal role in determining the legal and social status of individuals and groups throughout American history. Slavery within the United States developed as a racial institution in which blackness defined one's status as a bonded person and the distinction between black and white facilitated the establishment of the social controls necessary to maintain the effectiveness of this mode of economic production. The miscegenation among blacks and whites during the Slave Era resulted in the production of persons of biracial identities, octoroons and quadroons, and these interracial groups were components of a racial hierarchy based upon skin color. The status of the free African Americans of this period was above that of the slaves but below the biracial groups, thus reflecting the color-based status differentiations that informed the social structure of antebellum American society.

In the wake of the Civil War and Reconstruction, racial segregation emerged as the defining mode of race relations within the United States. The Segregation Era was defined by a color–caste system of race relations that was designed to promote the overt exclusion of blacks from meaningful institutional participation and power within society in order to maintain white dominance within society. Signs that read "whites only" and "colored" were quite common throughout this period and defined employment opportunities available to members of the two races and the access of blacks to housing, schools, and other public accommodations that were available within the society.

The *de jure* segregation of American society persisted until it was overtaken by the civil rights movement of the 1960s, but *de facto* segregation (issue 17) remains a prominent feature of the social order of the United States, despite the reforms of the last half-century. Baby boomers within today's African American and white populations bare memories of being socialized and conditioned by the restraining values of this color–caste system of race relations.

Despite the efforts of Martin Luther King and other supporters of civil rights and social justice for African Americans and others of color, the United States is still a nation within which color-consciousness and color-coded decision making are broadly prevalent. The American language and culture are laden with color-coded references such as whites/people of color, black neighborhood/white neighborhood, chocolate cities/vanilla suburbs, and many others. Even within the growing Latino population the tendency to apply color-coding to identify people is prevalent (Issue 14). Despite this fact, in the media and elsewhere there is a tendency to assign Latinos collectively a "brown" identity.

In June 1994, the publishers of *Time Magazine* were so confident that the American public would respond to color-coded communications, that they darkened the image of OJ Simpson appearing on one of its covers. This dramatized the image of the sinister black male stereotype and crime. This color-coded presentation is a contradiction of the publishers' claim to be race-neutral. Although part of the culture advances the idea of color-blindness, with *Time Magazine* we see a mainstream publication use of color to distinguish and define racial differences. This is an obvious contradiction as relates to the color-blind thesis. This interesting paradox has the guise of appearing to be race-neutral. Some observers like Bonilla-Silva argue that color-blindness is a new form of racism—that is, on the one hand, there is a denial of race differences, but on the other, there is a perpetuation of racial stereotypes.

Ward Connerly strongly argues in favor of the promise of a color-blind society. For him, America is becoming increasingly homogeneous where race is concerned and racial discrimination is seen as irrelevant today. Connerly is representative of African Americans who view color-based policies such as affirmative action as obscuring the fact that their success is based on merit, rather than skin color. He embraces the idea that America is increasingly an equal opportunity society.

In contrast, Eduardo Bonilla-Silva views color-blind ideology as a fiction and a new manifestation of racism. For him, the question remains, how do whites explain the contradiction between the notion of a color-blind society and the color-coded inequality that persists in America? For Bonilla-Silva, it is color-blind racism, the new racial ideology. He asks, if all of the society is color-blind, to whom do African Americans and other racial minorities assert their grievances over disadvantage?

Students should be aware that the promotion of a color-blind ideology as social reform raises significant questions. Given the reality of a color-conscious American culture that has lasted for nearly four centuries, how plausible is the achievement of this goal? Is the color-blind thesis as benign as it appears? What is the potential impact of color-blind ideology on black identity? Red? Yellow? Brown? Does color-blind ideology serve as a mask for white privilege? Does the promotion of color-blind ideology undermine civil rights and social justice organization and advocacy? These are among the salient questions that confront this issue.

Ward Connerly

Don't Box Me In

A few weeks ago, I was having dinner with a group of supporters following a lecture. One of those in attendance was a delightful woman who applauded my efforts to achieve a colorblind government. She strongly urged me to stay the course, promised financial support for my organization—the American Civil Rights Institute—and proclaimed that what we are doing is best for the nation.

Then, an odd moment occurred, when she said, "What you're doing is also best for your people." I flinched, took a couple of bites of my salad, and gathered my thoughts. I thought: *"My people"? Anyone who knows me knows that I abhor this mindset. But this dear lady doesn't know all my views or the nuances of race. She has innocently wandered into a racial thicket and doesn't have a clue that she has just tapped a raw nerve. Do I risk offending her by opening this issue for discussion? Do I risk losing her financial support by evidencing my distaste for what she has said? Perhaps it would be best to ignore the moment and let my staff follow up in pursuit of her support.*

I concluded that the situation demanded more of me than to believe that she was incapable of understanding what troubled me about her comment. So, I did what comes naturally in such situations—I politely confronted her. "What did you mean when you referred to 'my people' a moment ago?" I asked. "The black race," she responded. "What is your 'race'?" I asked. She said, "I'm Irish and German." I plowed ahead. "Would it affect your concept of my 'race' if I told you that one of my grandparents was Irish and American Indian, another French Canadian, another of African descent, and the other Irish? Aren't they all 'my people'? What about my children? They consist of my ingredients as well as those of their mother, who is Irish. What about my grandchildren, two of whom have a mother who is half Vietnamese?" The lady was initially awestruck. But that exchange produced one of the richest conversations about race I have ever had.

This discussion is one that an increasing number of Americans are having across our nation. It is one that many more would *like* to have. Thanks to the race questions placed in the 2000 Census, a great number of people are beginning to wonder about this business of their "race."

From its inception, America has promised equal justice before the law. The Declaration of Independence and the Constitution stand as monuments to the Founders' belief that we can fashion a government of colorblind laws, a unified nation without divisible parts. Unfortunately, they had to compromise on that vision from the beginning. To create a government, they had to protect the international slave trade until 1808. After that time, with the slave trade forever banned, they hoped and believed the slave system would wither away.

In a second concession of their principles to material interests, the Founders also agreed to count slaves as only three-fifths of a person. This compromise stemmed not from a belief that slaves were less than human; rather, slaveowning states wanted to count slaves as whole persons in deciding how large their population was, but not count them at all in deciding how much the states would pay in taxes. The infamous three-fifths compromise was the unfortunate concession.

To distinguish slaves from non-slaves, governments established various race classifications. Unfortunately, these classifications continued long after the Civil War amendments formally repudiated them. After all, once everyone was free to enjoy all the privileges and immunities of American citizenship, there was no longer a need to classify people by race. In hindsight, we recognize that, after nearly a century of race classifications imposed by the state, these classifications had become part of the way average Americans saw themselves, as well as others. Over the next half-century, scientists began to recognize that these race classifications don't exist in nature. We had created them, to justify an inhuman system.

Even as science reached these conclusions, however, these classifications played ever more important roles in American life. Poll taxes and literacy tests; separate bathroom facilities, transportation, water fountains, neighborhoods—the entire Jim Crow system relied on these state-imposed race classifications. And with science unable to distinguish a black person from a non-black person, the government relied on the infamous "one-drop rule": If you have just one drop of "black blood," you're black.

Although the Supreme Court struck down the "separate but equal" legal structure, the Court failed to eliminate the race classifications that sustained all the forms of segregation and discrimination the Court was trying to eliminate. We have seen the actual expansion of the groups being classified. On some level, though, I'm sure we really do want to become "one nation . . . indivisible." Witness the tenfold increase in "multiracial" families since 1967. In its decision that year—aptly named *Loving v. Virginia*—the Supreme Court ruled that anti-miscegenation laws (those forbidding people of different races to marry) were unconstitutional. While it took some time for us to shed the taboos against interracial dating and marriage, today there are more "multiracial" children born in California than there are "black" children. When Benjamin Bratt and Julia Roberts began dating, no one cared that they were an interracial couple. So too with Maury Povich and Connie Chung. Love has become colorblind.

The time has come for America to fulfill the promise of equal justice before the law and for the nation to renounce race classifications. To that end, I am preparing to place the Racial Privacy Initiative (RPI) before California voters on the March 2002 ballot. This initiative would prohibit governments in California from classifying individuals by race, color, ethnicity, or national origin. Much to my surprise, just submitting RPI to the state in preparation for gathering signatures has generated controversy. The American Civil Liberties Union has called it a "racist" initiative, and various proponents of race preferences have said it will "turn back the clock on civil rights."

In drafting RPI, we have exempted medical research and have proposed nothing that would prevent law-enforcement officers from identifying particular individuals, so long as those methods are already lawful. To guarantee that laws against discrimination are enforced, we have exempted the Department of Fair Employment and Housing from the provisions of RPI for ten years.

Getting the government out of the business of classifying its citizens and asking them to check these silly little race boxes represents the next step in our nation's long journey toward becoming one nation. Getting rid of these boxes will strike a blow against the overbearing race industry that has grown like Topsy in America. It will help free us from the costly and poisonous identity politics and the racial spoils system that define our political process. It will clip the wings of a government that has become so intrusive that it classifies its citizens on the basis of race, even when citizens "decline to state." Enacting the Racial Privacy Initiative is the most significant step we can take to bring Americans together.

I ask all Americans who share the goal of a united America to join in this endeavor to fulfill our Founders' promise of colorblind justice before the law. For my part, I just don't want to be boxed in.

Eduardo Bonilla-Silva  **NO**

Racism without Racists: Color-Blind Racism and the Persistence of Racial Inequality in the United States

The Strange Enigma of Race in Contemporary America

> There is a strange kind of enigma associated with the problem of racism. No one, or almost no one, wishes to see themselves as racist; still, racism persists, real and tenacious.

> —Albert Memmi, *Racism*

Racism without "Racists"

Nowadays, except for members of white supremacist organizations, few whites in the United States claim to be "racist." Most whites assert they "don't see any color, just people"; that although the ugly face of discrimination is still with us, it is no longer the central factor determining minorities' life chances; and, finally, that like Dr. Martin Luther King Jr., they aspire to live in a society where "people are judged by the content of their character, not by the color of their skin." More poignantly, most whites insist that minorities (especially blacks) are the ones responsible for whatever "race problem" we have in this country. They publicly denounce blacks for "playing the race card," for demanding the maintenance of unnecessary and divisive race-based programs, such as affirmative action, and for crying "racism" whenever they are criticized by whites. Most whites believe that if blacks and other minorities would just stop thinking about the past, work hard, and complain less (particularly about racial discrimination), then Americans of all hues could "all get along."

But regardless of whites' "sincere fictions," racial considerations shade almost everything in America. Blacks and dark-skinned racial minorities lag well behind whites in virtually every area of social life; they are about three times more likely to be poor than whites, earn about 40 percent less than whites, and have about a tenth of the net worth that whites have. They also receive an inferior education compared to whites, even when they attend integrated institutions. In terms of housing, black-owned units comparable to white-owned ones are valued at 35 percent less. Blacks and Latinos also have less access to the entire housing market because whites, through a variety of exclusionary practices by white realtors and homeowners, have been successful in effectively limiting their entrance into many neighborhoods. Blacks receive impolite treatment in stores, in restaurants, and in a host of other commercial transactions. Researchers have also documented that blacks pay more for goods such as cars and houses than do whites. Finally, blacks and dark-skinned Latinos are the targets of racial profiling by the police that, combined with the highly racialized criminal court system, guarantees their over-representation among those arrested, prosecuted, incarcerated, and if charged for a capital crime, executed. Racial profiling in the highways has become such a prevalent phenomenon that a term has emerged to describe it: driving while black. In short, blacks and most minorities are, "at the bottom of the well."

How is it possible to have this tremendous degree of racial inequality in a country where most whites claim that race is no longer relevant? More important, how do whites explain the apparent contradiction between their professed color blindness and the United States' color-coded inequality? I contend that whites have developed powerful explanations—which have ultimately become justifications—for contemporary racial inequality that exculpate them from any responsibility for the status of people of color. These explanations emanate from a new racial ideology that I label *color-blind racism*. This ideology, which acquired cohesiveness and dominance in the late 1960s, explains contemporary racial inequality as the outcome of nonracial dynamics. Whereas Jim Crow racism explained blacks' social standing as the result of their biological and moral inferiority, color-blind racism avoids such facile arguments. Instead, whites rationalize minorities' contemporary status as the product of market dynamics, naturally occurring phenomena, and blacks' imputed cultural limitations. For instance, whites can attribute Latinos' high poverty rate to a relaxed work ethic ("the Hispanics are mañana, mañana, mañana—tomorrow, tomorrow, tomorrow") or residential segregation as the result of natural tendencies among groups ("Does a cat and a dog mix? I can't see it. You can't drink milk and scotch. Certain mixes don't mix.").

Color-blind racism became the dominant racial ideology as the mechanisms and practices for keeping blacks and other racial minorities "at the bottom of the well" changed. I have argued elsewhere that contemporary racial inequality is reproduced through "new racism" practices that are subtle, institutional, and apparently nonracial. In contrast to the Jim Crow era, where racial inequality was enforced through overt means (e.g., signs saying "No Niggers Welcomed Here" or shotgun diplomacy at the voting booth), today racial practices operate in "now you see it, now you don't" fashion. For example, residential segregation, which is almost as high today as it was in the past, is no longer accomplished through overtly discriminatory practices. Instead, covert behaviors such as not showing all the available units, steering minorities and whites into certain neighborhoods, quoting higher rents or prices to minority applicants, or not advertising units at all are the weapons of choice to maintain separate communities. In the economic field, "smiling face" discrimination ("We don't have jobs now, but please check later"), advertising job openings in mostly white networks and ethnic newspapers, and steering highly educated people of color into poorly remunerated jobs or jobs with limited opportunities for mobility are the new ways of keeping minorities in a secondary position. Politically, although the Civil Rights struggles have helped remove many of the obstacles for the electoral participation of people of color, "racial gerrymandering, multimember legislative districts, election runoffs, annexation of predominantly white areas, at-large district elections, and anti–single-shot devices (disallowing concentrating votes in one or two candidates in cities using at-large elections) have become standard practices to disenfranchise" people of color. Whether in banks, restaurants, school admissions, or housing transactions, the maintenance of white privilege is done in a way that defies facile racial readings. Hence, the contours of color-blind racism fit America's "new racism" quite well.

Compared to Jim Crow racism, the ideology of color blindness seems like "racism lite." Instead of relying on name calling (niggers, Spics, Chinks), color-blind racism otherizes softly ("these people are human, too"); instead of proclaiming God placed minorities in the world in a servile position, it suggests they are behind because they do not work hard enough; instead of viewing interracial marriage as wrong on a straight racial basis, it regards it as "problematic" because of concerns over the children, location, or the extra burden it places on couples. Yet this new ideology has become a formidable political tool for the maintenance of the racial order. Much as Jim Crow racism served as the glue for defending a brutal and overt system of racial oppression in the pre–Civil Rights era, color-blind racism serves today as the ideological armor for a covert and institutionalized system in the post–Civil Rights era. And the beauty of this new ideology is that it aids in the maintenance of white privilege without fanfare, without naming those who it subjects and those who it rewards. It allows a President to state things such as, "I strongly support diversity of all kinds, including racial diversity in higher education," yet, at the same time, to characterize the University of Michigan's affirmation action program as "flawed" and "discriminatory" against whites. Thus whites enunciate positions that safeguard their racial interests without sounding "racist." Shielded by color blindness, whites can express resentment toward minorities; criticize their morality, values, and work ethic; and even claim to be the victims of "reverse racism." This is the thesis I will defend to explain the curious enigma of "racism without racists."

Whites' Racial Attitudes in the Post–Civil Rights Era

Since the late 1950s surveys on racial attitudes have consistently found that fewer whites subscribe to the views associated with Jim Crow. For example, whereas the majority of whites supported segregated neighborhoods, schools, transportation, jobs, and public accommodations in the 1940s, less than a quarter indicated they did in the 1970s. Similarly, fewer whites than ever now seem to subscribe to stereotypical views of blacks. Although the number is still high (ranging from 20 percent to 50 percent, depending on the stereotype), the proportion of whites who state in surveys that blacks are lazy, stupid, irresponsible, and violent has declined since the 1940s.

These changes in whites' racial attitudes have been explained by the survey community and commentators in four ways. First, are the *racial optimists*. This group of analysts agrees with whites' common sense on racial matters and believes the changes symbolize a profound transition in the United States. Early representatives of this view were Herbert Hyman and Paul B. Sheatsley, who wrote widely influential articles on the subject in *Scientific American*. In a reprint of their earlier work in the influential collection edited by Talcott Parsons and Kenneth Clark, *The Negro American,* Sheatsley rated the changes in white attitudes as "revolutionary" and concluded,

> The mass of white Americans have shown in many ways that they will not follow a racist government and that they will not follow racist leaders. Rather, they are engaged in the painful task of adjusting to an integrated society. It will not be easy for most, but one cannot at this late date doubt the basic commitment. In their hearts they know that the American Negro is right.

In recent times, Glenn Firebaugh and Kenneth Davis, Seymour Lipset, and Paul Sniderman and his coauthors, in particular, have carried the torch for racial optimists. Firebaugh and Davis, for example, based on their analysis of survey results from 1972 to 1984, concluded that the trend toward less antiblack prejudice was across the board. Sniderman and his coauthors, as well as Lipset, go a step further than Firebaugh and Davis because they have openly advocated color-blind politics *as the* way to settle the United States' racial dilemmas. For instance, Sniderman and Edward Carmines made this explicit appeal in their recent book, *Reaching Beyond Race,*

> To say that a commitment to a color-blind politics is worth undertaking is to call for a politics centered on the needs of those most in need. It is not to argue for a politics in which race is irrelevant, but in favor of one in which race is relevant so far as it is a gauge of need. Above all, it is a call for a politics which, because it is organized around moral principles that apply regardless of race, can be brought to bear with special force on the issue of race.

The problems with this optimistic interpretation are twofold. First, as I have argued elsewhere, relying on questions that were framed in the Jim Crow era to assess whites' racial views today produces an artificial image of progress. Since the central racial debates and the language used to debate those matters have changed, our analytical focus ought to be dedicated to the analysis of the new racial issues. Insisting on the need to rely on old questions to keep longitudinal (trend) data as the basis for analysis will, by default, produce a rosy picture of race relations that misses what is going on on the ground. Second, and more important, because of the change in the normative climate in the post–Civil Rights era, analysts must exert extreme caution when interpreting attitudinal data, particularly when it comes from single-method research designs. The research strategy that seems more appropriate for our times is mixed research designs (surveys used in combination with interviews, ethno-surveys, etc.), because it allows researchers to cross-examine their results.

A second, more numerous group of analysts exhibit what I have labeled elsewhere as the *racial pesoptimist* position. Racial pesoptimists attempt to strike a "balanced" view and suggest that whites' racial attitudes reflect progress and resistance. The classical example of this stance is Howard Schuman. Schuman has argued for more than thirty years that whites' racial attitudes involve a mixture of tolerance and intolerance, of acceptance of the principles of racial liberalism (equal opportunity for all, end of segregation, etc.) and a rejection of the policies that would make those principles a reality (from affirmative action to busing).

Despite the obvious appeal of this view in the research community (the appearance of neutrality, the pondering of "two sides," and this view's "balanced" component), racial pesoptimists are just closet optimists. Schuman, for example, has pointed out that, although "White responses to questions of principle are . . . more complex than is often portrayed . . . they nevertheless do show in almost every instance a positive movement over time." Furthermore, it is his belief that the normative change in the United States is real and that the issue is that whites are having a hard time translating those norms into personal preferences.

A third group of analysts argues that the changes in whites' attitudes represent the emergence of a *symbolic racism*. This tradition is associated with the work of David Sears and his associate, Donald Kinder. They have defined symbolic racism as "a blend of anti-black affect and the kind of traditional American moral values embodied in the Protestant Ethic." According to these authors, symbolic racism has replaced biological racism as the primary way whites express their racial resentment toward minorities. In Kinder and Sanders's words:

> A new form of prejudice has come to prominence, one that is preoccupied with matters of moral character, informed by the virtues associated with the traditions of individualism. At its center are the contentions that blacks do not try hard enough to overcome the difficulties they face and that they take what they have not earned. Today, we say, prejudice is expressed in the language of American individualism.

Authors in this tradition have been criticized for the slipperiness of the concept "symbolic racism," for claiming that the blend of antiblack affect and individualism is new, and for not explaining why symbolic racism came about. The first critique, developed by Howard Schuman, is that the concept has been "defined and operationalized in complex and varying ways." Despite this conceptual slipperiness, indexes of symbolic racism have been found to be in fact different from those of old-fashioned racism and to be strong predictors of whites' opposition to affirmative action. The two other critiques, made forcefully by Lawrence Bobo, have been partially addressed by Kinder and Sanders in their recent book, *Divided by Color*. First, Kinder and Sanders, as well as Sears, have made clear that their contention is not that this is the first time in history that antiblack affect and elements of the American Creed have combined. Instead, their claim is that this combination has become *central* to the new face of racism. Regarding the third critique, Kinder and Sanders go at length to explain the transition from old-fashioned to symbolic racism. Nevertheless, their explanation hinges on arguing that changes in blacks' tactics (from civil disobedience to urban violence) led to an onslaught of a new form of racial resentment that later found more fuel in controversies over welfare, crime, drugs, family, and affirmative action. What is missing in this explanation is a materially based explanation for why these changes occurred. Instead, their theory of prejudice is rooted in the "process of socialization and the operation of routine cognitive and emotional psychological processes."

Yet, despite its limitations, the symbolic racism tradition has brought attention to key elements of how whites explain racial inequality today. Whether this is "symbolic" of antiblack affect or not is beside the point and hard to assess, since as a former student of mine queried, "How does one test for the unconscious?"

The fourth explanation of whites' contemporary racial attitudes is associated with those who claim that whites' racial views represent a *sense of group position*. This position, forcefully advocated by Lawrence Bobo and James Kluegel, is similar to Jim Sidanius's "social dominance" and Mary Jackman's "group interests" arguments. In essence, the claim of all these authors is that white prejudice is an ideology to defend white privilege. Bobo and his associates have specifically suggested that because of socioeconomic changes that transpired in the 1950s and 1960s, *a laissez-faire racism* emerged that was fitting of the United States' "modern, nationwide, postindustrial free labor economy and polity." Laissez-faire racism "encompasses an ideology that blames blacks themselves for their poorer relative economic standing, seeing it as the function of perceived cultural inferiority."

Some of the basic arguments of authors in the symbolic and modern racism traditions and, particularly, of the laissez-faire racism view are fully compatible with my color-blind racism interpretation. As these authors, I argue that color-blind racism has rearticulated elements of traditional liberalism (work ethic, rewards by merit, equal opportunity, individualism, etc.) for racially illiberal goals. I also argue like them that whites today rely more on cultural rather than biological tropes to explain blacks' position in this country. Finally, I concur with most analysts of post–Civil Rights' matters in arguing that whites do not perceive discrimination to be a central factor shaping blacks' life chances.

Although most of my differences with authors in the symbolic racism and laissez-faire traditions are methodological, I have one central theoretical disagreement with them. Theoretically, most of these authors are still snarled in the prejudice problematic and thus interpret actors' racial views as *individual psychological* dispositions. Although Bobo and his associates have a conceptualization that is closer to mine, they still retain the notion of prejudice and its psychological baggage rooted in interracial hostility. In contrast, my model is not anchored in actors' affective dispositions (although affective dispositions may be manifest or latent in the way many express their racial views). Instead, it is based on a materialist interpretation of racial matters and thus sees the views of actors as corresponding to their systemic location. Those at the bottom of the racial barrel tend to hold oppositional views and those who receive the manifold wages of whiteness tend to hold views in support of the racial status quo. Whether actors express "resentment" or "hostility" toward minorities is largely irrelevant for the maintenance of white privilege. As David Wellman points out in his *Portraits of White Racism,* "[p]rejudiced people are not the only racists in America."

Key Terms: Race, Racial Structure, and Racial Ideology

One reason why, in general terms, whites and people of color cannot agree on racial matters is because they conceive terms such as "racism" very differently. Whereas for most whites racism is prejudice, for most people of color racism is systemic or institutionalized. Although this is not a theory book, my examination of color-blind racism has etched in it the indelible ink of a "regime of truth" about how the world is organized. Thus, rather than hiding my theoretical assumptions, I state them openly for the benefit of readers and potential critics.

The first key term is the notion of *race.* There is very little formal disagreement among social scientists in accepting the idea that race is a socially constructed category. This means that notions of racial difference are human creations rather than eternal, essential categories. As such, racial categories have a history and are subject to change. And here ends the agreement among social scientists on this matter. There are at least three distinct variations on how social scientists approach this constructionist perspective on race. The first approach, which is gaining popularity among white social scientists, is the idea that because race is socially constructed, it is not a fundamental category of analysis and praxis. Some analysts go as far as to suggest that because race is a constructed category, then it is not real and social scientists who use the category are the ones who make it real.

The second approach, typical of most sociological writing on race, gives lip service to the social constructionist view—usually a line in the beginning of the article or book. Writers in this group then proceed to discuss "racial" differences in academic achievement, crime, and SAT scores as if they were truly racial. This is the central way in which contemporary scholars contribute to the propagation of racist interpretations of racial inequality. By failing to highlight the social dynamics that produce these racial differences, these scholars help reinforce the racial order.

The third approach, and the one I use in this book, acknowledges that race, as other social categories such as class and gender, is constructed but insists that it has a *social* reality. This means that after race—or class or gender—is created, it produces real effects on the actors racialized as "black" or "white." Although race, as other social constructions, is unstable, it has a "changing same" quality at its core.

In order to explain how a socially constructed category produces real race effects, I need to introduce a second key term, the notion of *racial structure.*

When race emerged in human history, it formed a social structure (a racialized social system) that awarded systemic privileges to Europeans (the peoples who became "white") over non-Europeans (the peoples who became "nonwhite"). Racialized social systems, or white supremacy for short, became global and affected all societies where Europeans extended their reach. I therefore conceive a society's racial structure as *the totality of the social relations and practices that reinforce white privilege.* Accordingly, the task of analysts interested in studying racial structures is to uncover the particular social, economic, political, social control, and ideological mechanisms responsible for the reproduction of racial privilege in a society.

But why are racial structures reproduced in the first place? Would not humans, after discovering the folly of racial thinking, work to abolish race as a category as well as a practice? Racial structures remain in place for the same reasons that other structures do. Since actors racialized as "white"—or as members of the dominant race—receive material benefits from the racial order, they struggle (or passively receive the manifold wages of whiteness) to maintain their privileges. In contrast, those defined as belonging to the subordinate race or races struggle to change the status quo (or become resigned to their position). Therein lies the secret of racial structures and racial inequality the world over. They exist because they benefit members of the dominant race.

If the ultimate goal of the dominant race is to defend its collective interests (i.e., the perpetuation of systemic white privilege), it should surprise no one that this group develops rationalizations to account for the status of the various races. And here I introduce my third key term, the notion of *racial ideology.* By this I mean *the racially based frameworks used by actors to explain and justify* (dominant race) or *challenge* (subordinate race or races) *the racial status quo.* Although all the races in a racialized social system have the *capacity* of developing these frameworks, the frameworks of the dominant race tend to become the master frameworks upon which *all* racial actors ground (for or against) their ideological positions. Why? Because as Marx pointed out in *The German Ideology,* "the ruling *material* force of society, is at the same time its ruling *intellectual* force." This does not mean that ideology is almighty. In fact, ideological rule is always partial. Even in periods of hegemonic rule, such as the current one, subordinate racial groups develop oppositional views. However, it would be foolish to believe that those who rule a society do not have the power to at least color (pun intended) the views of the ruled.

Racial ideology can be conceived for analytical purposes as comprising the following elements: common frames, style, and racial stories. The frames that bond together a particular racial ideology are rooted in the group-based conditions and experiences of the races and are, at the symbolic level, the representations developed by these groups to explain how the world is or ought to be. And because the group life of the various racially defined groups is based on hierarchy and domination, the ruling ideology expresses as "common sense" the interests of the dominant race, while oppositional ideologies attempt to challenge that common sense by providing alternative frames, ideas, and stories based on the experiences of subordinated races.

Individual actors employ these elements as "building blocks . . . for manu-
facturing versions on actions, self, and social structures" in communicative situations. The looseness of the elements allows users to maneuver within various
contexts (e.g., responding to a race-related survey, discussing racial issues with
family, or arguing about affirmative action in a college classroom) and produce
various accounts and presentations of self (e.g., appearing ambivalent, tolerant, or strong minded). This loose character enhances the legitimating role of
racial ideology because it allows for accommodation of contradictions, exceptions, and new information. As Jackman points out about ideology in general:
"Indeed, the strength of an ideology lies in its loose-jointed, flexible application.
An ideology is a political instrument, not an exercise in personal logic: consistency is
rigidity, the only pragmatic effect of which is to box oneself in."

Before I can proceed, two important caveats should be offered. First,
although whites, because of their privileged position in the racial order, form a
social group (the dominant race), they are fractured along class, gender, sexual
orientation, and other forms of "social cleavage." Hence, they have multiple
and often contradictory interests that are not easy to disentangle and that predict *a priori* their mobilizing capacity (Do white workers have more in common
with white capitalists than with black workers?). However, because all actors
awarded the dominant racial position, regardless of their multiple structural
locations (men or women, gay or straight, working class or bourgeois) benefit
from what Mills calls the "racial contract," *most* have historically endorsed the
ideas that justify the racial status quo.

Second, although not every single member of the dominant race defends
the racial status quo or spouts color-blind racism, *most* do. To explain this point
by analogy, although not every capitalist defends capitalism (e.g., Frederick
Engels, the coauthor of *The Communist Manifesto,* was a capitalist) and not
every man defends patriarchy (e.g., *Achilles Heel* is an English magazine published by feminist men), *most* do in some fashion. In the same vein, although
some whites fight white supremacy and do not endorse white common sense,
most subscribe to substantial portions of it in a casual, uncritical fashion that
helps sustain the prevailing racial order. . . .

If instead one regards racial ideology as in fact changing, the reliance on
questions developed to tackle issues from the Jim Crow era will produce an artificial image of progress and miss most of whites' contemporary racial nightmares.

Despite my conceptual and methodological concerns with survey
research, I believe well-designed surveys are still useful instruments to glance
at America's racial reality. Therefore, I report survey results from my own
research projects as well as from research conducted by other scholars whenever appropriate. My point, then, is not to deny attitudinal change or to condemn to oblivion survey research on racial attitudes, but to understand whites'
new racial beliefs and their implications as well as possible. . . .

One Important Caveat

The purpose of this book is not to demonize whites or label them "racist."
Hunting for "racists" is the sport of choice of those who practice the "clinical

approach" to race relations—the careful separation of good and bad, tolerant and intolerant Americans. Because this book is anchored in a structural
understanding of race relations, my goal is to uncover the collective practices
(in this book, the ideological ones) that help reinforce the contemporary racial
order. Historically, many good people supported slavery and Jim Crow. Similarly, most color-blind whites who oppose (or have serious reservations about)
affirmative action, believe that blacks' problems are mostly their own doing,
and do not see anything wrong with their own white lifestyle are good people,
too. The analytical issue, then, is examining how many whites subscribe to an
ideology that ultimately helps preserve racial inequality rather than assessing
how many hate or love blacks and other minorities.

   . . . Since color-blind racism is the dominant racial ideology, its tenta-
cles have touched us all and thus most readers will subscribe to some—if not
most—of its tenets, use its style, and believe many of its racial stories. Unfortunately, there is little I can do to ease the pain of these readers, since when one
writes and exposes an ideology that is at play, its supporters "get burned," so
to speak. For readers in this situation (good people who may subscribe to many
of the frames of color blindness), I urge a personal and political movement
away from claiming to be "nonracist" to becoming "antiracist." Being an anti-
racist begins with understanding the institutional nature of racial matters and
accepting that all actors in a racialized society are affected *materially* (receive
benefits or disadvantages) and *ideologically* by the racial structure. This stand
implies taking responsibility for your unwilling participation in these practices
and beginning a new life committed to the goal of achieving real racial equality. The ride will be rough, but after your eyes have been opened, there is no
point in standing still.

EXPLORING THE ISSUE

Is the Emphasis on a Color-Blind Society an Answer to Racism?

Critical Thinking and Reflection

1. Define color-blind ideology.
2. What are the significant components of the color-blind ideology?
3. What are the goals of the proponents of America assuming a color-blind identity?
4. What are the challenges of creating a color-blind society? Explain.
5. How does Ward Connerly view racial classification? What are the functions of this classification?
6. What are the limits of color-blind ideology for racial minorities?
7. Locate contemporary examples to apply color-blind ideology.

Is There Common Ground?

The YES and NO selections by Connerly and Bonilla-Silva are reflective of the profound and persistent influence of racism in the historical development of American society. Both of these writers are focused on the question, how do we overcome racism in society? Given its troubled racial history, is a color-blind transformation of American society possible? One of the highlights of the civil rights movement was the speech delivered by Dr. Martin Luther King, Jr., during the March on Washington of August 1963. King notes that since color-conscious practices are the source of black disadvantage, policies that address these problems should be color-conscious. Exhibiting the soaring oratory to which the nation and world had become accustomed, this drum major of civil rights advocacy espoused a profound vision of an American future in which people are not judged by the color of their skins, but, rather, by the content of their character as they seek civil rights, equity, and respect for their humanity and human dignity within society. King's words have been used by both sides of the color-blind issue. Connerly would argue that if King were alive today, he would support the color-blind thesis. Bonilla-Silva, on the other hand, would argue that King would never recognize the current color-blind ideology as a basis for racial progress because of persistent race prejudice and discrimination within society. Does color-blind mean blind to racism? Is a color-blind vision utopian, or is it a pragmatic achievable vision for the American future?

Additional Resources

Bonilla-Silva, Eduardo. 2003. *Racism without Racists: Color-Blind Racism and the Persistence of Racial Inequality in the United States* (Rowman & Littlefield).

Brodkin, Karen. 1999. *How Did Jews Become White Folks and What That Says About Race in America* (Rutgers University Press).

Cose, Ellis. 1998. *Color Blind: Seeing Beyond Race in a Race Obsessed World* (Harper Perennial).

Cuomo, Chris J. and Kim Q. Hall. 1999. *Whiteness: Feminist Philosophical Reflections* on *Who Is White?: Latinos, Asians, and the Black/Nonblack Divide* (Rowman & Littlefield Publishers).

Dobratz, Betty A. and Stephanie Shanks-Meile. 1997. *White Power, White Pride!: The White Separatist Movement in the United States* (Twayne Publishers).

Goldfield, D.R. 1990. *Black, White, and Southern: Race Relations and Southern Culture, 1940 to the Present* (Louisiana State University Press).

Guglielmo, Jennifer and Salvatore Salerno. 2003. *Are Italians White?: How Race is Made in America* (Routledge).

Ignatiev, Noel. 2008. *How the Irish Became White* (Routledge).

King, Martin Luther. 1964. *Why We Can't Wait* (Harper Collins).

King, Martin Luther. 1967. *Where Do We Go from Here: Chaos or Community?* (Harper & Row).

King, Martin Luther. 1987. *Stride Toward Freedom* (Harper Collins).

Leonardo, Zeus. 2009. *Race, Whiteness, and Education* (Routledge).

Lovato, Robert. 2006. "A New Vision of Immigration." *The Nation* (March 6).

Mann, Coramae, Marjorie Zatz, and Nancy Rodriguez. 2006. *Images of Color, Images of Crime: Readings* (Oxford University Press).

Roediger, David. 2002. *Colored White: Transcending the Racial Past* (University of California Press).

Russell-Brown, Katheryn K. 2008. *The Color of Crime: Racial Hoaxes, White Fear, Black Protectionism, Police Harassment, and Other Macroaggressions* (New York University Press).

"The Obama Era: Post Racial or Most Racial?" 2011. The American Civil Rights Coalition (June). www.acrc1.org/media/The_Obama_Era_Post_Racial_or_Most_Racial-5[2].pdf

Walker, Samuel, Cassia Spohn, and Miriam DeLeon. 2011. *The Color of Justice: Race, Ethnicity and Crime In America*, 5th ed. (Wadsworth Publishing).

Williams, Patricia. 1997. *Seeing a Color Blind Future* (Farrar, Straus and Giroux).

Wise, Tim. 2009. *Between Barack and a Hard Place: Racism and White Denial in the Age of Obama* (City Lights Publisher).

Wright, Lawrence. 1999. "One Drop of Blood." *The New Yorker* (July 12).

Yancey, George. 2006. *Beyond Racial Gridlock: Embracing Mutual Responsibility* (IVP Books).

The *Journal of Blacks in Higher Education* website is dedicated to research and sharing of information about African Americans in higher education. Along with daily news articles and research projects, the site offers information about African American accomplishments, college enrollment trends, racial gaps in public as well as higher education and links to related online articles of interest. The student will find archived articles related to racism and color-blindness as a new form of racism on the site.

www.jbhe.com/

Established by Ward Connerly and Dusty Rhodes, president of *National Review*, in 1996, The American Civil Rights Institute is dedicated to educating the public on the harms of racial and gender preferences in federal, state, and local programs. It hosts a blog to which Roger Clegg Issue 12) opines about affirmative action and related topics. It offers several links to like-minded sites including those dedicated to answering the critics of Connerly's civil rights initiatives.

www.acri.org/

This is the site of the American Civil Rights Coalition. It was founded by Ward Connerly and Dusty Rhodes, president of *National Review* and is related to The American Civil Rights Institute. In the "News and Articles" section is a copy of "The Obama Era: Post Racial or Most Racial?" a report of the American Civil Rights Coalition, which argues that with the election of Obama, America is more race-conscious than prior to the "post-racial" era. Thus, Connerly justifies his efforts to remove racial classifications from the U.S. Census.

www.acrc1.org/media/

ISSUE 7

Do Whites Associate Privilege with Their Skin Color?

YES: Paul Kivel, from *Uprooting Racism: How White People Can Work for Racial Justice* (New Society, 1996)

NO: Tim Wise, from "The Absurdity (and Consistency) of White Denial: What Kind of Card Is Race?" www.counterpunch.org/wise04242006.html (April 24, 2006)

Learning Outcomes

After reading this issue, the student should be able to:

- Comprehend how white skin privilege is concretely manifested within society according to Kivel and Wise.
- Critically examine how skin color has been fundamental to the determination of racial identity in American culture.
- Establish the relationship between white skin privilege and racial discrimination.
- Critically examine the evidence that is presented in support of the claim of white skin privilege.
- Examine the contribution of white skin privilege to the existence of disadvantaged minorities in the United States.
- Explain the difficulties many whites face in accepting the contention that white skin privilege is a fact of life in America.
- Explain the meaning and function of the "race card."

ISSUE SUMMARY

YES: Paul Kivel, a teacher, writer, and antiviolence/antiracist activist, asserts that many benefits accrue to whites solely on the basis of skin color. These benefits range from economic to political advantages and so often include better residential choice, police protection, and education opportunities.

NO: Tim Wise, an author of two books on race, argues that whites do not acknowledge privilege. Instead, whites are often convinced that the race card is "played" by blacks to gain their own privilege, something that whites cannot do. Hence, whites simply do not see discrimination and do not attach privilege to their skin color.

W.E.B. DuBois has reminded us of the centrality of skin color when he noted that issues of color would dominate human relations of the twentieth century. In the United States, African American children tend to exhibit a keen understanding of the impact of color in race relations when they repeat the following line from blues singer Big Bill Broonzy's 1951 composition, "Black, Brown and White":

> If you're white, you're alright!
> If you're brown, stick around!
> And, if you're black, get back!

These lines were uttered routinely by black American children during their developmental years during the Jim Crow era. It reminds us of the salience of skin color for racial identity.

There is a consensus view among scholars that racial distinctions were not a primary factor influencing human relations in the premodern world. The more substantial influence of race within society tends to be a more recent phenomenon influencing modern cultures and civilizations, especially institutional arrangements such as slavery and segregation. So, the issue of white skin privilege falls in the larger context of race identity in American history.

The history of race relations within the United States is properly examined by employing a white super-ordination black-subordination paradigm. Many Americans have grown accustomed to blacks occupying the lower strata of American class structure. Some Americans tend to view this pattern of race relations as normal. Whites who are accustomed to the social reality, which has been presented here, are challenged to rationalize their position within society. Denial of the existence of privilege is a significant component of this rationalization.

Clearly, the formation of racial consciousness and its impact upon society are vital areas of scholarly investigation in a world characterized by nations of increasing racial/ethnic diversity. Naomi Zack, in *Thinking about Race*, explains the rise of whiteness studies in perspective. Most recent immigration and demographic trends have led to what has been called "the browning of America." A significant increase in Latino and Asian immigration, along with white–nonwhite intermarriage, symbolizes the decrease in the number of whites as a majority. Many scholars see this browning as having the effect of stimulating an increase of white self-awareness.

Throughout the world, although whites do not constitute a majority, they are a dominant-group (people who have the most wealth, power, and possessions). This is an important sociological consideration. The reality of privilege is so embedded within dominant group status that to recognize and admit its reality is alien to most whites. Whites are often asked to think about race from a minority point of view. Throughout one's years of formal education, there is an emphasis upon tolerance and understanding, which enable dominant-group whites to appreciate minority-group experiences. Despite the built-in limitations of viewing things from the point of view of another race, color shifting can enable one to view one's own race differently.

Paul Kivel sees race privilege as white, middle-class privilege. It is not something to be earned; it is viewed as a birthright. It comes with economic, social, and political benefits. Tim Wise, in contrast, argues that whites are oblivious to the notion of skin privilege. Further, he uses the white allegation of "playing the race card," which is directed at blacks, to demonstrate that whites do not think that skin privilege exists.

Many Americans believe that white skin privilege is a myth. It is common for such persons to assert that if such a privilege existed in the past, it would have been overtaken by the reforms of the civil rights era and the color-blind, race-neutral (deracialized) environment that has resulted from these developments. Such observers of current social trends tend to cite the significant expansion of the African American middle class, the more visible presence of blacks and other people of color within American institutions, most especially within the professions, and the increasing profile of black and minority athletes in support of their claim.

These assertions of racial progress, while valid, do not answer the question of whether or not white skin privilege exists. There is copious empirical evidence that significant inequity in such vital areas as wealth, income, education, employment, etc., exists between whites and people of color, especially blacks and Latinos. Both groups are disproportionately represented within the lower strata of the class structure. How does one explain this persistent advantage of whites over others? Is it due to white intellectual superiority? Can it be explained by the assertion that whites are more industrious and motivated? Or, is white skin privilege part of it?

The emerging body of literature on whiteness studies raises questions of privilege in the context of being white. Wise links this with white denial of racism and a "blaming the victim" attitude of blacks. He writes that blacks use racism as a crutch for their own inadequacies. In contrast, Kivel's straightforward presentation lists how whites benefit directly from color. He does not consider denial of racism and neither does he view playing the race card as a factor in white privilege.

This issue will challenge students in several ways. First, the notion of white privilege should expand the boundaries of the discussion of race relations. Second, unlike most issues in this edition, the positions elicited are not strongly opposite to each other. By using Kivel and Wise's concepts, the student will need to deconstruct the concepts and challenge both pieces. Kivel and Wise both write about white privilege and their ideas overlap. At the same time, Wise interprets the attitude held by whites that there is no such thing as white skin privilege. Historically, since race in the United States has been divided into black or white—one had to be either—a black person was defined as someone having black ancestors. The increasing diversity of the American population has rendered traditional race and ethnic categories, regardless of how familiar they are, inadequate. Expanded populations of Asians, Hispanics, and Middle Easterners, for example, challenge the traditional black–white dichotomy employed in research on race relations. The historical mixing of the races that occurred in the United States resulted in the rule of hypo-descent, or "the one drop rule," and rigidly enforced the black–white dichotomy. Intermarriage across racial lines is undermining the black–white dichotomy in research.

Why, in the American experience, did mixed-race people become categorized as black? How would you define whiteness? Why do blacks and whites have such divergent views on racial matters? Is the emphasis on examining white privilege another way to argue for minorities and against the majority group? Is white skin privilege a functional form of discrimination?

YES

Paul Kivel

Uprooting Racism: How White People Can Work for Racial Justice

White Benefits, Middle-Class Privilege

It is not necessarily a privilege to be white*, but it certainly has its benefits. That's why so many of us gave up our unique histories, primary languages, accents, distinctive dress, family names and cultural expressions. It seemed like a small price to pay for acceptance in the circle of whiteness. Even with these sacrifices it wasn't easy to pass as white if we were Italian, Greek, Irish, Jewish, Spanish, Hungarian, or Polish. Sometimes it took generations before our families were fully accepted, and then usually because white society had an even greater fear of darker skinned people.

Privileges are the economic "extras" that those of us who are middle class and wealthy gain at the expense of poor and working class people of all races. Benefits, on the other hand, are the advantages that all white people gain at the expense of people of color regardless of economic position. Talk about racial benefits can ring false to many of us who don't have the economic privileges that we see many in this society enjoying. But just because we don't have the economic privileges of those with more money doesn't mean we haven't enjoyed some of the benefits of being white.

We can generally count on police protection rather than harassment. Depending on our financial situation, we can choose where we want to live and choose neighborhoods that are safe and have decent schools. We are given more attention, respect and status in conversations than people of color. We see people who look like us in the media, history books, news and music in a positive light. (This is more true for men than for women, more true for the rich than the poor.) We have more recourse to, and credibility within, the legal system (again taking into account class and gender). Nothing that we do is qualified, limited, discredited or acclaimed simply because of our racial background. We don't have to represent our race, and nothing we do is judged

---

*I draw on important work on privilege done by Peggy McIntosh, "White Privilege and Male Privilege: A Personal Account of Coming to See Correspondences through Work in Women's Studies," Center for Research on Women, Wellesley College, MA 02181 (1988), as well as material from *Helping Teens Stop Violence,* Allan Creighton with Paul Kivel, Hunter House, Alameda CA (1992).

as a credit to our race, or as confirmation of its shortcomings or inferiority. There are always mitigating factors, and some of us have these benefits more than others. All else being equal, it pays to be white. We will be accepted, acknowledged and given the benefit of the doubt. Since all else is not equal we each receive different benefits or different levels of the same benefits from being white.

These benefits start early. Most of them apply less to white girls than white boys, but they are still substantial. Others will have higher expectations for us as children, both at home and at school. We will have more money spent on our education, we will be called on more in school, we will be given more opportunity and resources to learn. We will see people like us in the textbooks, and if we get into trouble adults will expect us to be able to change and improve, and therefore will discipline or penalize us less or differently than children of color.

These benefits continue today and work to the direct economic advantage of every white person in the United States. First of all, we will earn more in our lifetime than a person of color of similar qualifications. We will be paid $1.00 for every $.60 that a person of color makes. We will advance faster and more reliably as well.

There are historically derived economic benefits too. All the land in this country was taken from Native Americans. Much of the infrastructure of this country was built by slave labor, incredibly low-paid labor, or by prison labor performed by men and women of color. Much of the housecleaning, childcare, cooking and maintenance of our society has been done by low-wage earning women of color. Further property and material goods were appropriated by whites through the colonization of the West and Southwest throughout the 19th century, through the internment of Japanese Americans during World War II, through racial riots against people of color in the 18th, 19th and 20th centuries, and through an ongoing legacy of legal manipulation and exploitation. Today men and women and children of color still do the hardest, lowest paid, most dangerous work throughout the country. And we white people, again depending on our relative economic circumstances, enjoy plentiful and inexpensive food, clothing and consumer goods because of that exploitation.

We have been taught history through a white-tinted lens which has minimized our exploitation of people of color and extolled the hardworking, courageous qualities of white people. For example, many of our foreparents gained a foothold in this country by finding work in such trades as railroads, streetcars, construction, shipbuilding, wagon and coach driving, house painting, tailoring, longshore work, brick laying, table waiting, working in the mills, furriering or dressmaking. These were all occupations that Blacks, who had begun entering many such skilled and unskilled jobs, were either excluded from or pushed out of in the 19th century. Exclusion and discrimination, coupled with immigrant mob violence against Blacks in many northern cities (such as the anti-black draft riots of 1863), meant that recent immigrants had economic opportunities that Blacks did not. These gains were consolidated by explicitly racist trade union practices and policies which kept Blacks in the most unskilled labor and lowest paid work.

It is not that white Americans have not worked hard and built much. We have. But we did not start out from scratch. We went to segregated schools and universities built with public money. We received school loans, V.A. loans, housing and auto loans when people of color were excluded or heavily discriminated against. We received federal jobs, military jobs and contracts when only whites were allowed. We were accepted into apprenticeships, training programs and unions when access for people of color was restricted or nonexistent.

Much of the rhetoric against more active policies for racial justice stem from the misconception that we are all given equal opportunities and start from a level playing field. We often don't even see the benefits we have received from racism. We claim that they are not there.

Think about your grandparents and parents and where they grew up and lived as adults. What work did they do? What are some of the benefits that have accrued to your family because they were white?

Look at the following benefits checklist. Put a check beside any benefit that you enjoy that a person of color of your age, gender and class probably does not. Think about what effect not having that benefit would have had on your life. (If you don't know the answer to any of these questions, research. Ask family members. Do what you can to discover the answers.)

White Benefits Checklist

- My ancestors were legal immigrants to this country during a period when immigrants from Asia, South and Central America or Africa were restricted.
- My ancestors came to this country of their own free will and have never had to relocate unwillingly once here.
- I live on land that formerly belonged to Native Americans.
- My family received homesteading or landstaking claims from the federal government.
- I or my family or relatives receive or received federal farm subsidies, farm price supports, agricultural extension assistance or other federal benefits.
- I lived or live in a neighborhood that people of color were discriminated from living in.
- I lived or live in a city where red-lining discriminates against people of color getting housing or other loans.
- I or my parents went to racially segregated schools.
- I live in a school district or metropolitan area where more money is spent on the schools that white children go to than on those that children of color attend.
- I live in or went to a school district where children of color are more likely to be disciplined than white children, or more likely to be tracked into nonacademic programs.
- I live in or went to a school district where the textbooks and other classroom materials reflected my race as normal, heroes and builders of the United States, and there was little mention of the contributions of people of color to our society.
- I was encouraged to go on to college by teachers, parents or other advisors.

- I attended a publicly funded university, or a heavily endowed private university or college, and/or received student loans.
- I served in the military when it was still racially segregated, or achieved a rank where there were few people of color, or served in a combat situation where there were large numbers of people of color in dangerous combat positions.
- My ancestors were immigrants who took jobs in railroads, streetcars, construction, shipbuilding, wagon and coach driving, house painting, tailoring, longshore work, brick laying, table waiting, working in the mills, furriering, dressmaking or any other trade or occupation where people of color were driven out or excluded.
- I received job training in a program where there were few or no people of color.
- I have received a job, job interview, job training or internship through personal connections of family or friends.
- I worked or work in a job where people of color made less for doing comparable work or did more menial jobs.
- I have worked in a job where people of color were hired last, or fired first.
- I work in a job, career or profession, or in an agency or organization in which there are few people of color.
- I received small business loans or credits, government contracts or government assistance in my business.
- My parents were able to vote in any election they wanted without worrying about poll taxes, literacy requirements or other forms of discrimination.
- I can always vote for candidates who reflect my race.
- I live in a neighborhood that has better police protection, municipal services and is safer than that where people of color live.
- The hospital and medical services close to me or which I use are better than that of most people of color in the region in which I live.
- I have never had to worry that clearly labeled public facilities, such as swimming pools, restrooms, restaurants and nightspots were in fact not open to me because of my skin color.
- I see white people in a wide variety of roles on television and in movies.
- My race needn't be a factor in where I choose to live.
- My race needn't be a factor in where I send my children to school.
- I don't need to think about race and racism everyday. I can choose when and where I want to respond to racism.

What feelings come up for you when you think about the benefits that white people gain from racism? Do you feel angry or resentful? Guilty or uncomfortable? Do you want to say "Yes, but . . . "?

Again, the purpose of this checklist is not to discount what we, our families and foreparents, have achieved. But we do need to question any assumptions we retain that everyone started out with equal opportunity.

You may be thinking at this point, "If I'm doing so well how come I'm barely making it?" Some of the benefits listed previously are money in the bank for each and every one of us. Some of us have bigger bank accounts—much bigger. According to 1989 figures, 1 percent of the population controls about 40 percent of the wealth of this country (*New York Times,* April 17, 1995 "Gap in Wealth in United States called Widest in West"). In 1992, women generally made about 66 cents for every dollar that men made (Women's Action Coalition p. 59).

Benefits from racism are amplified or diminished by our relative privilege. People with disabilities, people with less formal education, and people who are lesbian, gay or bi-sexual are generally discriminated against in major ways. All of us benefit in some ways from whiteness, but some of us have cornered the market on significant benefits from being white to the exclusion of the rest of us.

The opposite of a benefit is a disadvantage. People of color face distinct disadvantages many of which have to do with discrimination and violence. If we were to talk about running a race for achievement and success in this country, and white people and people of color lined up side by side as a group, then every white benefit would be steps ahead of the starting line and every disadvantage would be steps backwards from the starting line before the race even began.

The disadvantages of being a person of color in the United States today include personal insults, harassment, discrimination, economic and cultural exploitation, stereotypes and invisibility, as well as threats, intimidation and violence. Not every person of color has experienced all the disadvantages described below, but they each have experienced some of them, and they each experience the vulnerability to violence that being a person of color in this country entails.

Institutional racism is discussed in detail in parts five, six, and seven. But the personal acts of harassment and discrimination experienced directly from individual white people can also take a devastating toll. People of color never know when they will be called names, ridiculed or have comments made to them or about them by white people they don't know. They don't know when they might hear that they should leave the country, go home or go back to where they came from. Often these comments are made in situations where it isn't safe to confront the person who made the remark.

People of color also have to be ready to respond to teachers, employers or supervisors who have stereotypes, prejudices or lowered expectations about them. Many have been discouraged or prevented from pursuing academic or work goals or have been placed in lower vocational levels because of their racial identity. They have to be prepared for receiving less respect, attention or response from a doctor, police officer, court official, city official or other professional. They are not unlikely to be mistrusted or accused of stealing, cheating or lying, or to be stopped by the police because of their racial identity. They may also experience employment or housing discrimination or know someone who has.

There are cultural costs as well. People of color see themselves portrayed in degrading, stereotypical and fear-inducing ways on television and in the movies. They may have important religious or cultural holidays which are not recognized where they work or go to school. They have seen their religious practices, music, art, mannerisms, dress and other customs distorted, "borrowed," ridiculed, exploited or otherwise degraded by white people.

If they protest they may be verbally attacked by whites for being too sensitive, too emotional or too angry. Or they may be told they are different from other people of their racial group. Much of what people of color do, or say, or how they act in racially mixed company is judged as representative of their race.

On top of all this they have to live with the threat of physical violence. Some are the survivors of racial violence or have had close friends or family who are. People of color experience the daily toll of having to plan out how they are going to respond to racist comments and racial discrimination whenever it might occur.

In the foot race referred to above for jobs, educational opportunities or housing, each of these disadvantages would represent a step backward from the starting line *before the race even started.*

Although all people of color have experienced some of the disadvantages mentioned above, other factors make a difference in how vulnerable a person of color is to the effects of racism. Economic resources help buffer some of the more egregious effects of racism. Depending upon where one lives, women and men from different racial identities are treated differently. Discrimination varies in form and ranges from mild to severe depending on one's skin color, ethnicity, level of education, location, gender, sexual orientation, physical ability, age and how these are responded to by white people and white-run institutions.

Is it hard for you to accept that this kind of pervasive discrimination still occurs in this country? Which of the above statements is particularly hard to accept?

There is ample documentation for each of the effects of racism on people of color listed above. In many workshops we do a stand-up exercise using a list of disadvantages for people of color to respond to. Those of us who are white are often surprised and disturbed about how many people of color stand when asked if they have experienced these things.

Most of us would like to think that today we have turned the tide and people of color have caught up with white people. We would like to believe (and are often told by other white people) that they enjoy the same opportunities as the rest of us. If we honestly add up the benefits of whiteness and the disadvantages of being a person of color, we can see that existing affirmative action programs don't go very far toward leveling the playing field.

The benefits of being white should be enjoyed by every person in this country. No one should have to endure the disadvantages that people of color experience. In leveling the playing field we don't want to hold anyone back. We want to push everyone forward so that we all share the benefits.

When we talk about the unequal distribution of benefits and disadvantages, we may feel uncomfortable about being white. We did not choose our skin color. Nor are we guilty for the fact that racism exists and that we have benefitted from it. We are responsible for acknowledging the reality of racism and for the daily choices we make about how to live in a racist society. We are only responsible for our own part, and we each have a part.

Sometimes, to avoid accepting our part, we want to shoot the bearer of bad news. Whether the bearer is white or a person of color, we become angry at whoever points out a comment or action that is hurtful, ignorant or abusive. We may accuse the person of being racist. This evasive reaction creates a debate about who is racist, or correct, or good, or well-intentioned, not about what to do about racism. It is probably inevitable that, when faced with the reality of the benefits and the harm of racism, we will feel defensive, guilty, ashamed, angry, powerless, frustrated or sad. These feelings are healthy and need to be acknowledged. Because they are uncomfortable we are liable to become angry at whoever brought up the subject.

Acknowledge your feelings and any resistance you have to the information presented above. . . . Yes, it is hard and sometimes discouraging. For too long we have ignored or denied the realities of racism. In order to make any changes, we have to start by facing where we are and making a commitment to persevere and overcome the injustices we face.

We can support each other through the feelings. We need a safe place to talk about how it feels to be white and know about racism. It is important that we turn to other white people for this support. Who are white people you can talk with about racism?

When people say, "We all have it hard," or "Everyone has an equal opportunity," or "People of color just want special privileges," how can you use the information in this book to respond? What might be difficult about doing so? What additional information or resources will you need to be able to do this with confidence? How might you find those resources?

Tim Wise  **NO**

The Absurdity (and Consistency) of White Denial: What Kind of Card Is Race?

Recently, I was asked by someone in the audience of one of my speeches, whether or not I believed that racism—though certainly a problem—might also be something conjured up by people of color in situations where the charge was inappropriate. In other words, did I believe that occasionally folks play the so-called race card, as a ploy to gain sympathy or detract from their own short-comings? In the process of his query, the questioner made his own opinion all too clear (an unambiguous yes), and in that, he was not alone, as indicated by the reaction of others in the crowd, as well as survey data confirming that the belief in black malingering about racism is nothing if not ubiquitous.

It's a question I'm asked often, especially when there are several high-profile news events transpiring, in which race informs part of the narrative. Now is one of those times, as a few recent incidents demonstrate: Is racism, for exam-ple, implicated in the alleged rape of a young black woman by white members of the Duke University lacrosse team? Was racism implicated in Congresswoman Cynthia McKinney's recent confrontation with a member of the Capitol police? Or is racism involved in the ongoing investigation into whether or not Barry Bonds—as he is poised to eclipse white slugger Babe Ruth on the all-time home run list—might have used steroids to enhance his performance?*

Although the matter is open to debate in any or all of these cases, white folks have been quick to accuse blacks who answer in the affirmative of play-ing the race card, as if their conclusions have been reached not because of careful consideration of the facts as they see them, but rather, because of some irrational (even borderline paranoid) tendency to see racism everywhere. So too, discussions over immigration, "terrorist" profiling, and Katrina and its aftermath often turn on issues of race, and so give rise to the charge that as regards these subjects, people of color are "overreacting" when they allege racism in one or another circumstance.

Asked about the tendency for people of color to play the "race card," I responded as I always do: First, by noting that the regularity with which whites respond to charges of racism by calling said charges a ploy, suggests that the race card is, at best, equivalent to the two of diamonds. In other words, it's not much of a card to play, calling into question why anyone would play it (as if it were really going to get them somewhere). Secondly, I pointed out that white reluctance to acknowledge racism isn't new, and it isn't something that manifests only in situations where the racial aspect of an incident is arguable. Fact is, whites have always doubted claims of racism at the time they were being made, no matter how strong the evidence, as will be seen below. Finally, I concluded by suggesting that whatever "card" claims of racism may prove to be for the black and brown, the denial card is far and away the trump, and whites play it regularly: a subject to which we will return.

Turning Injustice into a Game of Chance: The Origins of Race as "Card"

First, let us consider the history of this notion: namely, that the "race card" is something people of color play so as to distract the rest of us, or to gain sympathy. For most Americans, the phrase "playing the race card" entered the national lexicon during the O.J. Simpson trial. Robert Shapiro, one of Simpson's attorneys famously claimed, in the aftermath of his client's acquittal, that co-counsel Johnnie Cochran had "played the race card, and dealt it from the bottom of the deck." The allegation referred to Cochran's bringing up officer Mark Fuhrman's regular use of the "n-word" as potentially indicative of his propensity to frame Simpson. To Shapiro, whose own views of his client's innocence apparently shifted over time, the issue of race had no place in the trial, and even if Fuhrman was a racist, this fact had no bearing on whether or not O.J. had killed his ex-wife and Ron Goldman. In other words, the idea that O.J. had been framed because of racism made no sense and to bring it up was to interject race into an arena where it was, or should have been, irrelevant.

That a white man like Shapiro could make such an argument, however, speaks to the widely divergent way in which whites and blacks view our respective worlds. For people of color—especially African Americans—the idea that racist cops might frame members of their community is no abstract notion, let alone an exercise in irrational conspiracy theorizing. Rather, it speaks to a social reality about which blacks are acutely aware. Indeed, there has been a history of such misconduct on the part of law enforcement, and for black folks to think those bad old days have ended is, for many, to let down their guard to the possibility of real and persistent injury.[1]

So if a racist cop is the lead detective in a case, and the one who discovers blood evidence implicating a black man accused of killing two white people, there is a logical alarm bell that goes off in the head of most any black person, but which would remain every bit as silent in the mind of someone who was white. And this too is understandable: for most whites, police are the helpful folks who get your cat out of the tree, or take you around in their patrol car for fun. For us, the idea of brutality or misconduct on the part of such persons seems remote, to the point of being fanciful. It seems the stuff of bad TV dramas, or at the very least, the past—that always remote place to which we can consign our national sins and predations, content all the while that whatever demons may have lurked in those earlier times have long since been vanquished.

To whites, blacks who alleged racism in the O.J. case were being absurd, or worse, seeking any excuse to let a black killer off the hook—ignoring that blacks on juries vote to convict black people of crimes every day in this country. And while allegations of black "racial bonding" with the defendant were made regularly after the acquittal in Simpson's criminal trial, no such bonding, this time with the victims, was alleged when a mostly white jury found O.J. civilly liable a few years later. Only blacks can play the race card, apparently; only they think in racial terms, at least to hear white America tell it.

Anything But Racism: White Reluctance to Accept the Evidence

Since the O.J. trial, it seems as though almost any allegation of racism has been met with the same dismissive reply from the bulk of whites in the U.S. According to national surveys, more than three out of four whites refuse to believe that discrimination is any real problem in America.[2] That most whites remain unconvinced of racism's salience—with as few as six percent believing it to be a "very serious problem," according to one poll in the mid 90s[3]— suggests that racism-as-card makes up an awfully weak hand. While folks of color consistently articulate their belief that racism is a real and persistent presence in their own lives, these claims have had very little effect on white attitudes. As such, how could anyone believe that people of color would somehow pull the claim out of their hat, as if it were guaranteed to make white America sit up and take notice? If anything, it is likely to be ignored, or even attacked, and in a particularly vicious manner.

That bringing up racism (even with copious documentation) is far from an effective "card" to play in order to garner sympathy, is evidenced by the way in which few people even become aware of the studies confirming its existence. How many Americans do you figure have even heard, for example, that black youth arrested for drug possession for the first time are incarcerated at a rate that is forty-eight times greater than the rate for white youth, even when all other factors surrounding the crime are identical?[4]

How many have heard that persons with "white sounding names," according to a massive national study, are fifty percent more likely to be called back for a job interview than those with "black sounding" names, even when all other credentials are the same?[5]

How many know that white men with a criminal record are slightly more likely to be called back for a job interview than black men without one, even when the men are equally qualified, and present themselves to potential employers in an identical fashion?[6]

How many have heard that according to the Justice Department, Black and Latino males are three times more likely than white males to have their vehicles stopped and searched by police, even though white males are over four times more likely to have illegal contraband in our cars on the occasions when we are searched?[7]

How many are aware that black and Latino students are about half as likely as whites to be placed in advanced or honors classes in school, and twice as likely to be placed in remedial classes? Or that even when test scores and prior performance would justify higher placement, students of color are far less likely to be placed in honors classes?[8] Or that students of color are 2–3 times more likely than whites to be suspended or expelled from school, even though rates of serious school rule infractions do not differ to any significant degree between racial groups?[9]

Fact is, few folks have heard any of these things before, suggesting how little impact scholarly research on the subject of racism has had on the general public, and how difficult it is to make whites, in particular, give the subject a second thought.

Perhaps this is why, contrary to popular belief, research indicates that people of color are actually reluctant to allege racism, be it on the job, or in schools, or anywhere else. Far from "playing the race card" at the drop of a hat, it is actually the case (again, according to scholarly investigation, as opposed to the conventional wisdom of the white public), that black and brown folks typically "stuff" their experiences with discrimination and racism, only making an allegation of such treatment after many, many incidents have transpired, about which they said nothing for fear of being ignored or attacked.[10] Precisely because white denial has long trumped claims of racism, people of color tend to underreport their experiences with racial bias, rather than exaggerate them. Again, when it comes to playing a race card, it is more accurate to say that whites are the dealers with the loaded decks, shooting down any evidence of racism as little more than the fantasies of unhinged blacks, unwilling to take personal responsibility for their own problems in life.

Blaming the Victims for White Indifference

Occasionally, white denial gets creative, and this it does by pretending to come wrapped in sympathy for those who allege racism in the modern era. In other words, while steadfastly rejecting what people of color say they experience— in effect suggesting that they lack the intelligence and/or sanity to accurately interpret their own lives—such commentators seek to assure others that whites really do care about racism, but simply refuse to pin the label on incidents where it doesn't apply. In fact, they'll argue, one of the reasons that whites have developed compassion fatigue on this issue is precisely because of the overuse of the concept, combined with what we view as unfair reactions to racism (such as affirmative action efforts which have, ostensibly, turned us into the victims of racial bias). If blacks would just stop playing the card where it doesn't belong, and stop pushing for so-called preferential treatment, whites would revert back to our prior commitment to equal opportunity, and our heartfelt concern about the issue of racism.

Don't laugh. This is actually the position put forward recently by James Taranto of the *Wall Street Journal*, who in January suggested that white reluctance to embrace black claims of racism was really the fault of blacks themselves, and the larger civil rights establishment.[11] As Taranto put it: "Why do blacks and whites have such divergent views on racial matters? We would argue that it is because of the course that racial policies have taken over the past forty years."

He then argues that by trying to bring about racial equality—but failing to do so because of "aggregate differences in motivation, inclination and aptitude" between different racial groups—policies like affirmative action have bred "frustration and resentment" among blacks, and "indifference" among whites, who decide not to think about race at all, rather than engage an issue that seems so toxic to them. In other words, whites think blacks use racism as a crutch for their own inadequacies, and then demand programs and policies that fail to make things much better, all the while discriminating against them as whites. In such an atmosphere, is it any wonder that the two groups view the subject matter differently?

But the fundamental flaw in Taranto's argument is its suggestion—implicit though it may be—that prior to the creation of affirmative action, white folks were mostly on board the racial justice and equal opportunity train, and were open to hearing about claims of racism from persons of color. Yet nothing could be further from the truth. White denial is not a form of backlash to the past forty years of civil rights legislation, and white indifference to claims of racism did not only recently emerge, as if from a previous place where whites and blacks had once seen the world similarly. Simply put: whites in every generation have thought there was no real problem with racism, irrespective of the evidence, and in every generation we have been wrong.

Denial as an Intergenerational Phenomenon

So, for example, what does it say about white rationality and white collective sanity, that in 1963—at a time when in retrospect all would agree racism was rampant in the United States, and before the passage of modern civil rights legislation—nearly two-thirds of whites, when polled, said they believed blacks were treated the same as whites in their communities—almost the same number as say this now, some forty-plus years later? What does it suggest about the extent of white folks' disconnection from the real world, that in 1962, eighty-five percent of whites said black children had just as good a chance as white children to get a good education in their communities?[12] Or that in May, 1968, seventy percent of whites said that blacks were treated the same as whites in their communities, while only seventeen percent said blacks were treated "not very well" and only 3.5 percent said blacks were treated badly?[13]

What does it say about white folks' historic commitment to equal opportunity—and which Taranto would have us believe has only been rendered inoperative because of affirmative action—that in 1963, three-fourths of white Americans told *Newsweek*, "The Negro is moving too fast" in his demands for equality?[14] Or that in October 1964, nearly two-thirds of whites said that the Civil Rights Act should be enforced gradually, with an emphasis on persuading employers not to discriminate, as opposed to forcing compliance with equal opportunity requirements?[15]

What does it say about whites' tenuous grip on mental health that in mid-August 1969, forty-four percent of whites told a Newsweek/Gallup National Opinion Survey that blacks had a better chance than they did to get a good paying job—two times as many as said they would have a worse chance? Or that forty-two percent said blacks had a better chance for a good education than whites, while only seventeen percent said they would have a worse opportunity for a good education, and eighty percent saying blacks would have an equal or better chance? In that same survey, seventy percent said blacks could have improved conditions in the "slums" if they had wanted to, and were more than twice as likely to blame blacks themselves, as opposed to discrimination, for high unemployment in the black community.[16]

In other words, even when racism was, by virtually all accounts (looking backward in time), institutionalized, white folks were convinced there was no real problem. Indeed, even forty years ago, whites were more likely to think that blacks had better opportunities, than to believe the opposite (and obviously accurate) thing: namely, that whites were advantaged in every realm of American life.

Truthfully, this tendency for whites to deny the extent of racism and racial injustice likely extends back far before the 1960s. Although public opinion polls in previous decades rarely if ever asked questions about the extent of racial bias or discrimination, anecdotal surveys of white opinion suggest that at no time have whites in the U.S. ever thought blacks or other people of color were getting a bad shake. White Southerners were all but convinced that their black slaves, for example, had it good, and had no reason to complain about their living conditions or lack of freedoms. After emancipation, but during the introduction of Jim Crow laws and strict Black Codes that limited where African Americans could live and work, white newspapers would regularly editorialize about the "warm relations" between whites and blacks, even as thousands of blacks were being lynched by their white compatriots.

From Drapetomania to Victim Syndrome— Viewing Resistance as Mental Illness

Indeed, what better evidence of white denial (even dementia) could one need than that provided by "Doctor" Samuel Cartwright, a well-respected physician of the 19th century, who was so convinced of slavery's benign nature, that he concocted and named a disease to explain the tendency for many slaves to run away from their loving masters. Drapetomania, he called it: a malady that could be cured by keeping the slave in a "child-like state," and taking care not to treat them as equals, while yet striving not to be too cruel. Mild whipping was, to Cartwright, the best cure of all. So there you have it: not only is racial oppression not a problem; even worse, those blacks who resist it, or refuse to bend to it, or complain about it in any fashion, are to be viewed not only as exaggerating their condition, but indeed, as mentally ill.[17]

And lest one believe that the tendency for whites to psychologically pathologize blacks who complain of racism is only a relic of ancient history, consider a much more recent example, which demonstrates the continuity of this tendency among members of the dominant racial group in America.

A few years ago, I served as an expert witness and consultant in a discrimination lawsuit against a school district in Washington State. Therein, numerous examples of individual and institutional racism abounded: from death threats made against black students to which the school district's response was pitifully inadequate, to racially disparate "ability tracking" and disciplinary action. In preparation for trial (which ultimately never took place as the district finally agreed to settle the case for several million dollars and a commitment to policy change), the school system's "psychological experts" evaluated dozens of the plaintiffs (mostly students as well as some of their parents) so as to determine the extent of damage done to them as a result of the racist mistreatment. As one of the plaintiff's experts, I reviewed the reports of said psychologists, and while I was not surprised to see them downplay the damage done to the black folks in this case, I was somewhat startled by how quickly they went beyond the call of duty to actually suggest that several of the plaintiffs exhibited "paranoid" tendencies and symptoms of borderline personality disorder. That having one's life threatened might make one a bit paranoid apparently never entered the minds of the white doctors. That facing racism on a regular basis might lead one to act out, in a way these "experts" would then see as a personality disorder, also seems to have escaped them. In this way, whites have continued to see mental illness behind black claims of victimization, even when that victimization is blatant.

In fact, we've even created a name for it: "victimization syndrome." Although not yet part of the DSM-IV (the diagnostic manual used by the American Psychiatric Association so as to evaluate patients), it is nonetheless a malady from which blacks suffer, to hear a lot of whites tell it. Whenever racism is brought up, such whites insist that blacks are being encouraged (usually by the civil rights establishment) to adopt a victim mentality, and to view themselves as perpetual targets of oppression. By couching their rejection of the claims of racism in these terms, conservatives are able to parade as friends to black folks, only concerned about them and hoping to free them from the debilitating mindset of victimization that liberals wish to see them adopt.

Aside from the inherently paternalistic nature of this position, notice too how concern over adopting a victim mentality is very selectively trotted out by the right. So, for example, when crime victims band together—and even form what they call victim's rights groups—no one on the right tells them to get over it, or suggests that by continuing to incessantly bleat about their kidnapped child or murdered loved one, such folks are falling prey to a victim mentality that should be resisted. No indeed: crime victims are venerated, considered experts on proper crime policy (as evidenced by how often their opinions are sought out on the matter by the national press and politicians), and given nothing but sympathy.

Likewise, when American Jews raise a cry over perceived anti-Jewish bigotry, or merely teach their children (as I was taught) about the European Holocaust, replete with a slogan of "Never again!" none of the folks who lament black "victimology" suggests that we too are wallowing in a victimization mentality, or somehow at risk for a syndrome of the same name.

In other words, it is blacks and blacks alone (with the occasional American Indian or Latino thrown in for good measure when and if they get too uppity) that get branded with the victim mentality label. Not quite drapetomania, but also not far enough from the kind of thinking that gave rise to it: in both cases, rooted in the desire of white America to reject what all logic and evidence suggests is true. Further, the selective branding of blacks as perpetual victims, absent the application of the pejorative to Jews or crime victims (or the families of 9/11 victims or other acts of terrorism), suggests that at some level white folks simply don't believe black suffering matters. We refuse to view blacks as fully human and deserving of compassion as we do these other groups, for whom victimization has been a reality as well. It is not that whites care about blacks and simply wish them not to adopt a self-imposed mental straightjacket; rather, it is that at some level we either don't care, or at least don't equate the pain of racism even with the pain caused by being mugged, or having your art collection confiscated by the Nazis, let alone with the truly extreme versions of crime and anti-Semitic wrongdoing.

See No Evil, Hear No Evil, Wrong as Always

White denial has become such a widespread phenomenon nowadays, that most whites are unwilling to entertain even the mildest of suggestions that racism and racial inequity might still be issues. To wit, a recent survey from the University of Chicago, in which whites and blacks were asked two questions about Hurricane Katrina and the governmental response to the tragedy. First, respondents were asked whether they believed the government response would have been speedier had the victims been white. Not surprisingly, only twenty percent of whites answered in the affirmative. But while that question is at least conceivably arguable, the next question seems so weakly worded that virtually anyone could have answered yes without committing too much in the way of recognition that racism was a problem. Yet the answers given reveal the depths of white intransigence to consider the problem a problem at all.

So when asked if we believed the Katrina tragedy showed that there was a lesson to be learned about racial inequality in America—any lesson at all— while ninety percent of blacks said yes, only thirty-eight percent of whites agreed.[18] To us, Katrina said nothing about race whatsoever, even as blacks were disproportionately affected; even as there was a clear racial difference in terms of who was stuck in New Orleans and who was able to escape; even as the media focused incessantly on reports of black violence in the Superdome and Convention Center that proved later to be false; even as blacks have been having a much harder time moving back to New Orleans, thanks to local and federal foot-dragging and the plans of economic elites in the city to destroy homes in the most damaged (black) neighborhoods and convert them to non-residential (or higher rent) uses.

Nothing, absolutely nothing, has to do with race nowadays, in the eyes of white America writ large. But the obvious question is this: if we have never seen racism as a real problem, contemporary to the time in which the charges are being made, and if in all generations past we were obviously wrong to the point of mass delusion in thinking this way, what should lead us to conclude that now, at long last, we've become any more astute at discerning social reality than we were before? Why should we trust our own perceptions or instincts on the matter, when we have run up such an amazingly bad track record as observers of the world in which we live? In every era, black folks said they were the victims of racism and they were right. In every era, whites have said the problem was exaggerated, and we have been wrong.

Unless we wish to conclude that black insight on the matter—which has never to this point failed them—has suddenly converted to irrationality, and that white irrationality has become insight (and are prepared to prove this transformation by way of some analytical framework to explain the process), then the best advice seems to be that which could have been offered in past decades and centuries: namely, if you want to know about whether or not racism is a problem, it would probably do you best to ask the folks who are its targets. They, after all, are the ones who must, as a matter of survival, learn what it is, and how and when it's operating. We whites on the other hand, are the persons who have never had to know a thing about it, and who—for reasons psychological, philosophical and material—have always had a keen interest in covering it up.

In short, and let us be clear on it: race is not a card. It determines whom the dealer is, and who gets dealt.

Notes

*Personally, I have no idea whether or not Barry Bonds has used anabolic steroids during the course of his career, nor do I think the evidence marshaled thus far on the matter is conclusive, either way. But I do find it interesting that many are calling for the placement of an asterisk next to Bonds' name in the record books, especially should he eclipse Ruth, or later, Hank Aaron, in terms of career home runs. The asterisk, we are told, would differentiate Bonds from other athletes, the latter of which, presumably accomplished their feats without performance enhancers. Yet, while it is certainly true that Aaron's 755 home runs came without any form of performance enhancement (indeed, he, like other black ball-players had to face overt hostility in the early years of their careers, and even as he approached Ruth's record of 714, he was receiving death threats), for Ruth, such a claim would be laughable. Ruth, as with any white baseball player from the early 1890s to 1947, benefited from the "performance enhancement" of not having to compete against black athletes, whose abilities often far surpassed their own. Ruth didn't have to face black pitchers, nor vie for batting titles against black home run sluggers. Until white fans demand an asterisk next to the names of every one of their white baseball heroes—Ruth, Cobb, DiMaggio, and Williams, for starters—who played under apartheid rules, the demand for such a blemish next to the name of Bonds can only be seen as highly selective, hypocritical, and ultimately racist. White privilege and protection from black competition certainly did more for those men's game than creotine or other substances could ever do for the likes of Barry Bonds.

1. There is plenty of information about police racism, misconduct and brutality, both in historical and contemporary terms, available from any number of sources. Among them, see Kristian Williams, *Our Enemies in Blue*. Soft Skull Press, 2004. . . .

2. *Washington Post*. October 9, 1995: A22.

3. Ibid.

4. "Young White Offenders get Lighter Treatment," 2000. *The Tennessean.* April 26: 8A.

5. Bertrand, Marianne and Sendhil Mullainathan, 2004. "Are Emily and Greg More Employable Than Lakisha and Jamal? A Field Experiment in Labor Market Discrimination." June 20.

6. Pager, Devah. 2003. "The Mark of a Criminal Record." *American Journal of Sociology.* Volume 108: 5, March: 937–75.

7. Matthew R. Durose, Erica L. Schmitt and Patrick A. Langan, *Contacts Between Police and the Public: Findings from the 2002 National Survey.* U.S. Department of Justice, (Bureau of Justice Statistics), April 2005.

8. Gordon, Rebecca. 1998. *Education and Race.* Oakland: Applied Research Center: 48–49; Fischer, Claude S. et al., 1996. *Inequality by Design: Cracking the Bell Curve Myth.* Princeton, NJ: Princeton University Press: 163; Steinhorn, Leonard and Barabara Diggs-Brown, 1999. *By the Color of Our Skin: The Illusion of Integration and the Reality of Race.* NY: Dutton: 95–96.

9. Skiba, Russell J. et al., *The Color of Discipline: Sources of Racial and Gender Disproportionality in School Punishment.* Indiana Education Policy Center, Policy Research Report SRS1, June 2000; U.S. Centers for Disease Control and Prevention, *Youth Risk Behavior Surveillance System: Youth 2003*, Online Comprehensive Results, 2004.

10. Terrell, Francis and Sandra L. Terrell, 1999. "Cultural Identification and Cultural Mistrust: Some Findings and Implications," in *Advances in African American Psychology*, Reginald Jones, ed., Hampton VA: Cobb & Henry; Fuegen, Kathleen, 2000. "Defining Discrimination in the Personal/Group Discrimination Discrepancy," *Sex Roles: A Journal of Research.* September; Miller, Carol T. 2001. "A Theoretical Perspective on Coping With Stigma," *Journal of Social Issues.* Spring; Feagin, Joe, Hernan Vera and Nikitah Imani, 1996. *The Agony of Education: Black Students in White Colleges and Universities.* NY: Routledge.

11. Taranto, James. 2006. "The Truth About Race in America—IV," Online Journal (*Wall Street Journal*), January 6.

12. The Gallup Organization, *Gallup Poll Social Audit, 2001. Black-White Relations in the United States, 2001 Update*, July 10: 7–9.

13. The Gallup Organization, *Gallup Poll*, #761, May, 1968.

14. "How Whites Feel About Negroes: A Painful American Dilemma," *Newsweek*, October 21, 1963: 56.

15. The Gallup Organization, *Gallup Poll #699*, October, 1964.

16. Newsweek/Gallup Organization, *National Opinion Survey*, August 19, 1969.

17. Cartwright, Samuel. 1851. "Diseases and Peculiarities of the Negro Race," *DeBow's Review.* (Southern and Western States: New Orleans), Volume XI.

18. Ford, Glen and Peter Campbell, 2006. "Katrina: A Study-Black Consensus, White Dispute," *The Black Commentator*, Issue 165, January 5.

EXPLORING THE ISSUE

Do Whites Associate Privilege with Their Skin Color?

Critical Thinking and Reflection

1. How is white skin privilege manifested within American society?
2. What role does skin color play in the acquisition of one's racial identity?
3. How is white skin privilege related to racial discrimination?
4. What is the evidence of white skin privilege?
5. Has white skin privilege contributed to the existence of disadvantaged minorities? How has this contributed to racial stratification, poverty, and inequality?
6. Why do most whites resist the claim of white skin privilege?
7. What is the "race card"? What is its meaning and function?

Is There Common Ground?

Wise and Kivel recognize that a macro-level analysis of the white skin privilege issue reveals that whites are in an advantageous position over blacks and other racial minorities in society. Their socioeconomic status is higher, and institutional placement, power, and influence tend to be higher for whites. Both Wise and Kivel are also interested in overcoming the impact of white skin privilege in American diverse society. They both recognize differences in real-life experiences of whites and minorities such as racial profiling. Wise cites several surveys to indicate white reluctance to acknowledge racism. Essentially, he argues that blacks and whites see the world differently. The white assertion that blacks play the race card is noted in many examples including the relationship between the police and both the black and white communities. Distrust of the police among blacks (see Issues 11 and 20) is more than conventional wisdom; it is a reflection of real-life experiences. At the same time, whites' view of the police reflects a different real-life experience, which Wise sees as white privilege. However, many do not recognize this as privilege. Thus, the idea of white privilege is difficult, if not impossible, for most whites to recognize because for centuries the culture has associated race with minority blacks in the United States. White privilege is taken for granted by whites, many of whom tend to see their life experiences as universally normal.

Additional Resources

Barnes, Annie S. 2000. *Everyday Racism: A Book for All Americans* (Sourcebooks, Inc.).

Berry, Brewton. 1969. *Almost White* (Collier-Macmillan Books).

Binzen, Peter. 1970. *Whitetown, USA: A Firsthand Study of How the "Silent Majority" Lives, Learns, Works and Thinks* (Vintage).

Bonilla-Silva, Eduardo. 2001. *White Supremacy and Racism in the Post-Civil Rights Era* (Lynn Rienner Publishers).

Brodkin, Karen. 1999. *How Did Jews Become White Folks and What That Says About Race in America* (Rutgers University Press).

Doane, Ashley and Eduardo Bonilla-Silva. 2003. *White Out: The Continuing Significance of Racism* (Routledge).

Fanon, Franz. 1967. *Black Skin, White Masks* (New York: Grove Press).

Fine, Michelle, Lois Weis, Linda Powell Pruitt, and April Burns. 2004. *Off White: Readings on Power, Privilege, and Resistance* (Routledge).

Gallagher, Charles. *Rethinking the Color Line: Readings in Race and Ethnicity*, 5th ed. (McGraw-Hill).

Guglielmo, Jennifer and Salvatore Salerno. 2003. *Are Italians White?: How Race Is Made in America* (Routledge).

Ignatiev, Noel. 2008. *How the Irish Became White* (Routledge).

Jensen, Robert. 2005. *The Heart of Whiteness: Confronting Race, Racism and White Privilege* (City Lights Publishers).

Jordan, Winthrop. 1968. *White over Black: American Attitudes Toward the Negro, 1550–1812* (The University of North Carolina Press).

Lipsitz, George. 2006 *The Possessive Investment in Whiteness: How White People Profit from Identity Politics* (Temple University Press).

Lipsitz, George. 2011. *How Racism Takes Place* (Temple University Press).

Roediger, David R. *Working Toward Whiteness: How America's Immigrants Became White* (Basic Books).

Rosenkranz, Mark. 2009 *White Male Privilege: A Study of Racism in America 50 Years After the Voting Rights Act*, 3rd en. (Law Dog Books).

Rothenberg, Paula. 2011. *White Privilege: Essential Readings on the Other Side of Racism* (Worth Publishers).

Stanley Crouch, Stanley. 2004. *The Artificial White Man: Essays on Authenticity* (Basic Books).

Sullivan, Shannon. 2006. *Revealing Whiteness: The Unconscious Habits of Racial Privilege* (Indiana University Press).

Williams, Lind, Faye. 2003. *The Constraint of Race: Legacies of White Skin Privilege in America* (The Pennsylvania State University Press).

Wise, Tim. 2005. *White Like Me: Reflections on Race from a Privileged Son* (Soft Skull Press).

This daily news site is produced by a multracial team of writers who believe America can become improved and united by racial justice. The information on the site is published by the Applied Research Center, which is a "racial justice think tank." It contains many subject areas ranging from criminal justice to arts and culture. There is a relevant section on how young people think, act, and talk about race.

http://colorlines.com/

This is the website of the Public Broadcasting Station, which contains a wealth of information on race and ethnicity along with current information on many social and cultural topics. It is listed here because the student may find current issues such as a colorblind society, post-racial identity, along with immigration and ethnicity concerns well researched. A thorough explanation of the documentary, "Race: The Power of an Illusion," exposes the student to in-depth personal accounts of people responding to the issue of colorblind identity.

www.pbs.org/

This is the site of a webzine, "The Occidental Observer," which is dedicated to white identity, interests, and culture. It is edited by Kevin MacDonald, a professor of psychology at California State, Long Beach. Its content focuses on "white identity, white interests, and the culture of the west."

www.theoccidentalobserver.net

ISSUE 8

Are Native American Mascots Racist Symbols?

YES: Sonia K. Katyal, from "The Fight over the Redskins Trademark and Other Racialized Symbols," http://writ.news.findlaw.com/commentary/20091207_katyal.html (December 7, 2009)

NO: Arthur J. Remillard, from "Holy War on the Football Field: Religion and the Florida State University Indian Mascot Controversy," in James A. Vlasich, ed., *Essays in Sports and American Culture* (McFarland, 2005, pp. 104–118 (Edited), chapter 8)

Learning Outcomes

After reading this issue, the student should be able to:

- Understand the relationship between stereotyping and the use of Native American mascots.
- Begin to understand the cultural diversity that exists among Native American tribes and nations.
- Understand why most Native American groups do not approve of the use of Indian mascots as symbols of sports teams.
- Understand why some Native American groups, in fact, approve of the use of Indian mascots as symbols for sports teams.
- Understand the commercial reasons why Indian mascots are used by colleges, universities, and professional sports teams.
- Develop a critical understanding of how religion as an organizing theme is employed to develop arguments on both sides of this issue.
- Understand how Native Americans respond to the use of their cultural symbols by outsiders.

ISSUE SUMMARY

YES: Sonia K. Katyal, professor of law and author of *Property Outlaws*, discusses the use of Native American mascots in professional sports, with an emphasis on the Washington Redskins and the negative impact of the use of such symbols on Native American peoples and culture.

NO: Arthur Remillard, professor of religious studies, recognizes the concern that the use of Native American mascots within non-Native institutions generates. However, he argues that the use of such symbols can be viewed as contributing to respect for Native American culture and its inherent strengths among the American population.

The identities and cultures of Native Americans, the American Indian, are little understood by many non-Indian Americans. These aboriginal Americans are properly identified as members of tribes, nations, and/or American citizens. All Native Americans were awarded citizenship as a result of the passage of the Indian Citizenship Act of 1924. The lack of understanding of Native American history and cultures throughout mainstream America has been detrimental to developing positive relations among Native peoples and new Americans. Throughout American history, Native Americans have struggled to maintain the integrity of their cultures. The issue presented here is a current manifestation of these struggles.

America is a diverse society and its people are challenged to learn to respect others and to develop a proper sensitivity toward their differing racial backgrounds and ethnic cultures. One of the challenges of living in a multiethnic and multiracial society is the ability of members to recognize differences without associating "the other" with claims of inferiority. The tendency to view those who are different in culture or other attributes through stereotyping is a common practice. Such stereotypes tend to be negative and hostile to those that they claim to represent. The failure to rise above stereotyping is a source of social conflict, both past and present, and is deleterious to the progress of a society.

Native Americans were influenced positively by the civil rights and Black Power movements of the 1960s. As a result, during this period many Native Americans identified with an emergent Red Power ideology. This political philosophy emphasized the need to strengthen the cultural heritage and historical legacy of Native peoples. They were insistent that the history and culture of aboriginal people be respected. Red Power advocates also promote the right to self-determination for Native Americans. It shall also be noted that during the 1960s and beyond, Native Americans have inserted themselves into the national discourse on problems and policies impacting their lives and the nation in ways unseen earlier in the twentieth century.

There is a tendency in the United States to use mascots allegedly based upon Native American cultures and experiences as symbols for commercial purposes including the promotion of college and professional sports organizations. Thus, when one explores the nation's popular culture, one is confronted with references to the Washington Redskins, Atlanta Braves, Golden

State Warriors, Kansas City Chiefs, and Cleveland Indians among others. At the collegiate level, we find the Florida State Seminoles, the Central Michigan Chippewas, and many others. Observing fan behavior at football and baseball stadiums across the nation often presents one with various versions of the "tomahawk chop" on display. This practice has come under increasing scrutiny and criticism from Native Americans and their supporters and is a source of social discord.

Symbols can provide us with a window through which the nature and content of a culture can be perceived and understood. However, the quality and correctness of such perceptions are important to the maintenance of social cohesion and can be very problematic. Non-Indians need to be more respectful and sensitive when dealing with stereotypical representations of Native Americans.

Sonia K. Katyal points out that the use of Native American mascots in professional sports has a negative impact on Native American peoples and culture. She argues that the use of these mascots as commercial symbols is insensitive, racially hostile, and damaging to the interest and well-being of Native Americans. She views the imagery that is presented within these mascots as offensive since they often reflect caricatures of what Native Americans are perceived to be.

She reminds us that Native Americans are seeking legal redress over issues of misuse of Indian mascots. In their petitions, the Indian plaintiffs argue that "the term 'Redskin' was and is a pejorative, derogatory, denigrating, offensive, scandalous, contemptuous, disreputable, disparaging, and racist denigration for a Native American person." They seek to eliminate such offensive references to their cultural heritage.

On the other hand, Arthur Remillard claims that the use of such mascots indicates respect and appreciation for the strength and value of Native Americans' cultural heritage. He argues that these symbols often are promoting values such as honor, courage, leadership, and perseverance in the face of difficulties. He cites a survey from *Sports Illustrated* (March 4, 2002) and other evidence that seems to indicate support for the use of these mascots from Seminoles and some other Native American groups. Many schools, in agreement with Remillard, continue to use Native American mascots and other imagery and make the claim that such use generates interest in Native American culture and history. Further, they argue that such imagery honors Native American culture.

Remillard's selection presents a contrasting survey in *Indian Country Today* (August 8, 2001) in which 81 percent of the Natives responding "indicated use of American Indian names, symbols, and mascots are predominantly offensive and deeply disparaging to Native Americans." Seventy-five percent of those surveyed believe that this abuse of symbols is a violation of antidiscrimination laws.

Dealing with this issue, one must be reminded that there are more than 500 Native American nations and tribes that are recognized by the Bureau of Indian Affairs of the U.S. government. The Seminoles are simply one group among many and their views do not always conform to those of other groups.

This cultural diversity is reflective of significant distinctions in culture, religion, and world view. So it should not be a surprise to learn that Native Americans differ on issues that they confront within American society.

Increasingly, the United States is a nation of diversity—a multicultural society. This is an immutable fact of life whether some among us like it or not. There is no going back. So, essentially the people of the nation are confronted with two choices, and the latter one is stark. One can embrace the reality of national diversity, identify that which we share in common, seek solutions to issues that divide us and move forward together. We can also choose to emphasize differences, focus on divisive concerns, and mortgage the nation's future. This is the crossroad where we stand today.

YES

Sonia K. Katyal

The Fight over the Redskins Trademark and Other Racialized Symbols

A few weeks ago, the Supreme Court declined to hear a case involving the trademark for the Washington Redskins. That decision left in place a lower court ruling stating that the plaintiffs had waited too long to bring a case for trademark cancelation—thus triggering the doctrine of laches, under which suits brought too late are barred. Around the same time, a federal judge in North Dakota prohibited the State Board of Education from immediately retiring the Fighting Sioux moniker of the University of North Dakota.

But neither controversy is truly over, and the underlying issue of racialized representations is likely to be discussed and litigated for years to come. With respect to the Washington Redskins, a different set of plaintiffs—and an entirely new case, filed in August 2006—is waiting in the wings to challenge the trademark on the grounds of its disparaging content. In the UND case, the judge imposed a temporary restraining order on the ground that the state board could not unilaterally alter the deadline without ensuring the tribes' participation. A new hearing has been set.

The legal cases against racially-hostile mascots can be complicated, raising issues related to both intellectual property rights and the First Amendment. Yet the ethical case against such representations could hardly be clearer.

The Widespread Use of American Indian Mascots, and the Damage It Causes

Both of the cases discussed above are painful legacies of an era in advertising that relied on the use of racial or ethnic minorities as the basis for logos, without much attention to the psychological harms such logos can cause, particularly in an educational context.

Sherman Alexie's partly-autobiographical novel *The Absolutely True Diary of a Part-Time Indian* makes the point well. Its fourteen-year-old Native American protagonist courageously decides to attend—and play basketball—at a prestigious all-white high school. As the only boy from the reservation, he faces a daily tirade of taunts: An illustration shows a series of cloud-like white figures bearing down on a small, skinny, bedraggled boy, calling him "Chief,"

Katyal, Sonia. From *Findlaw.com,* December 7, 2009, pp. Online. Copyright © 2009 by Findlaw. Reprinted by permission.

150

"Sitting Bull," "Tonto," "Squaw Boy," and of course, "Redskin." There is one glaring exception to his solitary confinement as the sole Native American at his school. Every time he plays basketball, he is greeted on the court by the image of the school mascot: a hook-nosed, buck-toothed version of an American Indian, sporting feathers and an angry scowl.

For a moment, put yourself in the shoes of Alexie's protagonist: You are fourteen, and saddled with all the challenges that adolescence brings—from acne, to bad fashion, to painful insecurities—on top of the differences you are trying so desperately to overcome as a Native American growing up in the United States. In this sense, Alexie's character is no different than many other children who are asked to overcome tremendous cultural barriers in search of an education. But there is one thing that makes Alexie's character's experience unique: Every day that he excels in basketball, the one activity that enables him to surpass the racial divide between himself and his classmates, the ubiquitous image of the school mascot reminds him of his limitations.

No other race gets singled out for this sort of caricature, so often and so regularly, in this day and age. The toll such mascots take cannot be justified ethically, no matter how the litigation is resolved.

The Suit to Retire the Washington Redskins Logo

Back in 1972, as Suzan Harjo, one of the plaintiffs in the Redskins case, recounts in the book *Team Spirits* (edited by C. Richard King and Charles Springwood), this kind of harm motivated a Native American coalition to respectfully ask the team's attorney to change the name of the Washington Redskins team. They asked him to imagine an NFL in which "the other teams are known as the New York Kikes, the Chicago Polocks, the San Francisco Dagoes, the Detroit Niggers, the Los Angeles Spics, etc."

Their efforts were largely met with silence until twenty years later, when, in 1992, a group of native leaders from diverse tribes sued to request the trademark's cancellation. That year, thousands of Native Americans protested at the Super Bowl in Minneapolis. Speaking to Congress, Suzan Harjo commented, "We have emotional scarring that is taking place . . . the highest rate of teenage suicide of any population in this country, which comes from low self-esteem, which comes from having those kids' elders . . . mocked, dehumanized, cartooned, stereotyped. That is what is causing the deaths of many of our children. We can't be polite about these problems anymore."

Washington Post columnist Richard Cohen agreed: "It hardly enhances the self-esteem of an Indian youth to always see his people—himself—represented as a cartoon character. And always, the caricature is suggestive of battle, of violence—the Indian warrior, the brave, the chief, the warpath, the beating of tom-toms. . . . Its time the Redskins changed their name. A rose by any other name would smell as sweet, but a team that insists on retaining an offensive name just plain stinks."

In the Washington Redskins case, a U.S. Patent and Trademark Office panel agreed with the plaintiffs that the term "Redskins" was disparaging, and ordered cancellation of the trademark. But U.S. District Judge Colleen

Kollar-Kotelly overturned that ruling, claiming that "[t]here is no evidence in the record that addresses whether the use of the term 'redskin(s)' in the context of a football team and related entertainment services would be viewed by a substantial composite of Native Americans, in the relevant time frame, as disparaging." Yet one plaintiff had observed, for example, that "Redskins" is "the absolute, unquestionably worst term. . . . There is no context in which the term 'Redskins' is not offensive."

Sadly, we seem to have made little progress since that decision.

The Problem of Commercial Insensitivity Against Native Americans

Americans have proved increasingly and rightly sensitive about representations that are racially derogatory. Thirty plus years ago, American advertising was littered with objectionable stereotypes of people of color. Today, many of those brands have since retired. Even Aunt Jemima has been given a "liberation makeover," replacing her kerchief with a short bobbed haircut, crisp white sweater, set of pearls, and shining smile. Miley Cyrus faced sharp criticism when she was photographed pretending to be Asian by "slanting" her eyes. A few years ago, there was a national outcry when Abercrombie & Fitch put out a white T-shirt featuring caricatures of Asians with slanted eyes and rice-paddy hats that said, "Wong Brothers Laundry Service—Two Wongs Can Make It White," along with other, similarly themed shirts. Immediately after a public outcry, the shirts were pulled off of the shelves, and the company issued a public statement: "We are truly and deeply sorry we've offended people."

Yet even as African-American and Asian-American stereotypes are widely decried, stereotypical—and sometimes shocking—caricatures of Native Americans persist largely without complaint: The cigar store Indian; the sports team mascot; and the ubiquitous Halloween costume, complete with feathered headdress, are just the most prominent examples.

Fans who think nothing of doing a "tomahawk chop" or exhorting their team to "scalp the enemy" do not always see or understand how those attitudes feed into the longstanding, pervasive harms that minorities often face when their culture is thoughtlessly mocked. Not only do these stereotypes fail to recognize the living reality of Native Americans, but they also suggest that Native culture, unlike any other, is safe to make fun of.

The Benefits to Fans Are Far Outweighed by the Costs to Native Americans

Some fans of teams with Native American mascots insist that they are trying to honor—or represent—our country's Native history, and point out that in some cases, it was a desire to "honor" Native Americans that led to the mascots being created. But today, virtually every America Indian advocacy group, and a long list of powerful non-native groups, including the NAACP and the National Education Association, have spoken out against such mascots.

The American Psychological Association, along with many other researchers, has documented a link between self-esteem and racially hostile mascots, pointing out that their use has a negative effect on all students (not just Native students). Testament to the harm that is caused can be found in the fact that, in every case where a Native American mascot exists, there is also a group of Native Americans students and their parents, pleading with the school to change the name.

In 2005, the National Collegiate Athletic Association laudably instituted a policy barring schools from hosting NCAA championships if they use Native American nicknames, mascots, or imagery. Yet many of these decisions have raised tremendous controversy—for instance, at UND and the University of Illinois. Even today, we still witness the image of the "Fighting Sioux," at UND; the startling caricature of "Chief Wahoo" of the Cleveland Indians; and the use of Native American references in the names of the Chicago Blackhawks and Atlanta Braves.

Some students might take these symbols lightly, but their Native American classmates do not. Consider the words of Charlene Teters, a University of Illinois graduate: "When I first arrived here 10 years ago, it was with a great deal of excitement. I was honored to be here amongst you, attending the University of Illinois, a Big Ten University. I came full of dreams. But what I found . . . was a community permeated with Indian concoctions, a campus bar with a neon sign, HOME OF THE DRINKING ILLINI, a sorority MISS ILLINI SQUAW contest. Fraternity brothers wearing colored paper headdresses to go to the bar to drink, and act out negative stereotypes of Indians. My dream . . . turned to a nightmare."

With many other Native Americans sharing Teters's view, it is no wonder that a plethora of organizations, including the U.S. Commission on Civil Rights, have urged schools to retire these images on the grounds that they perpetuate racial hostility. Even if some folks enjoy these images, the simple truth is that they cause more harm than good to the very population they most affect.

We need not recite the harsh statistics surrounding Native Americans— vast disparities in health care, public safety and education, not to mention the high suicide and dropout rates among youth—to ask ourselves whether such mascots perpetuate harms that are already faced by a group that, quite simply, deserves better treatment at the hands of mainstream marketing.

The Second Washington Redskins Case Is Now on the Horizon

The first Washington Redskins case was filed by a superstar group of Native American activists and scholars, from different tribes, all of whom also served as plaintiffs. Among them was Vine Deloria, Jr., long considered the father of Native American law.

The members of today's second group of plaintiffs are similarly impressive. They are from a variety of tribes, geographies, and walks of life, and they include

Native American youth leaders such as Amanda Blackhorse, Marcus Briggs, and Courtney Tsotigh. Together, they argue that the term "Redskin" "was and is a pejorative, derogatory, denigrating, offensive, scandalous, contemptuous, disreputable, disparaging, and racist denigration for a Native American person."

They too have filed a petition for the cancellation of the trademark "Washington Redskins." But the difference is that they are all much younger than the earlier generation of plaintiffs, potentially minimizing or obviating the laches defense that ended the first Washington Redskins case.

It seems like poetic justice that the very people now leading the charge in the new filing are a group of Native American youth leaders. After all, they are the ones who perhaps feel the racial effects of stereotyping the most. Recently, I saw a photo taken during the 1992 protests at the World Series, and it gave me pause. It showed a young Native American teenager, hair pulled back, proudly standing before the camera with a handwritten sign that read in large black letters, "I am not a Mascot." Seventeen years later, he is still as right as he was then.

Arthur J. Remillard

 **NO**

Holy War on the Football Field: Religion and the Florida State University Indian Mascot Controversy

America's late 19th century saw entertainment spectacles such as Buffalo Bill's Wild West Show feeding a growing Euro-American fascination with the American Indian. From these circus like events, audiences began constructing a limited image of Indianness. Many performers, such as Sitting Bull, were from Lakota and Sioux reservations, thus leading onlookers to conflate the entirety of Indian culture with these traditions. Buffalo Bill's version of the Indian also became valuable for a generation searching for new models of manliness. Starting in the 1920s, Ralph Hubbard introduced Plains Indian culture to the Boy Scouts of America in his attempt to emphasize a primitive form of manhood that valued strength and durability—gender traits that he feared the youth of modern America desperately lacked. America's post–World War II era galvanized Buffalo Bill's Indian on the silver screen with a plethora of Wild West films. These movies created a radical dialectic where Indians were typically either horse-mounted warriors terrorizing the American West or trustworthy sidekicks like the Lone Ranger's laconic partner, Tonto. These films made Indians into fictionalized typecasts from another time and place who all shared a common culture and identity. For the majority of Americans, Hollywood's Indian was their only encounter with Native culture.

Institutes of higher learning contributed to the cultural trend of adopting reductive versions of Indianness. The University of Wisconsin at Lacrosse first introduced the idea, naming themselves the "Indians" in 1909, and many others followed suit in the 1920s, '30s, and '40s. In contemporary America, however, the use of Indian mascots by professional and university athletic teams has come under heavy criticism from Indian and non–Indian advocates. The opposition has argued that such images unnecessarily demean and stereotype Indian culture in ways that would be unacceptable if applied to any other minority/religious/ethnic group.

Finding merit in such arguments, the United States Commission on Civil Rights released a statement in 2001 calling for "an end to the use of Native American images and team names by non–Native schools." The Commission concluded that public institutions employing Indian mascots both "teach all

Remillard, Arthur. From *Horsehide, Pigskin, Oval Tracks And Apple Pie: Essays on Sport And American Culture*, December 12, 2005, pp. 104–118 (Edited). Copyright © 2005 by McFarland & Co. Reprinted by permission.

students that stereotyping of minority groups is acceptable," and "block genuine understanding of contemporary Native people as fellow Americans." Adding a legislative voice, on March 3, 2003, Congressman Frank Pallone, Jr., a Democrat from New Jersey, introduced a bill entitled "Native Act to Transform Imagery in Various Environments." Pallone labeled Indian mascots "offensive" and counter to the ideals and goals of American education. His bill proposed a solution that would "provide funding for the establishment of an incentive program for schools to eliminate the use of names and symbols that are offensive to Native American people." Professional, civic, and educational groups have also added a voice to the debate. The Modern Language Association, the National Education Association, the NAACP, the Presbyterian Church, U.S.A., and the United Methodist Church all have issued statements decrying the use of Indian mascots.

Responding to the criticisms, a host of colleges and universities, such as Adams State, Eastern Michigan, Dartmouth, Marquette, and Stanford, have retired their respective Indian mascots. The Florida State University "Seminoles" have yet to do the same. . . .

Indian scholars C. Richard King and Charles Fruehling Springwood have argued, however, that FSU's mascot ultimately stereotypes the Seminole culture and thereby promotes racially insensitive images of Indianness. While insisting the practice surrounding the mascot "is much more than kids having fun," the authors do not grant FSU immunity. Instead, King and Springwood attempt to show how the mascot "vividly illustrates popular prejudices about Indians" by keeping alive images from an Indian past wrought with oppression—a history that Hollywood's Indian has only helped enable. For these scholars, the mascot debate is far from being a trifling issue. Instead, it represents a continuation of the lengthy and misguided history of America's unwillingness to take Indian culture seriously. A historical and cultural survey shows that the university's mascot has more in common with Buffalo Bill's Wild West Show than the actual Seminole culture. FSU's Seminole rides a horse and throws a spear, yet the Seminoles of Florida had no horses to ride nor spears to throw. Still, the university maintains its claim that it accurately depicts this Indian culture. . . .

The Popular Religion of Football

Indian monikers were common when Florida State University held a student vote in 1947 to determine their mascot. The students faced six options on the ballot: the Statesmen, Rebels, Tarpons, Fighting Warriors, Crackers, and Seminoles. With 381 votes, the Seminole became the new mascot in "commemoration of the tribe of Indians whose descendants still live in the Florida Everglades." Since its adoption, the former tribal leader Osceola has been a key image in the mix of Seminole mascots. The controversial Osceola show, which includes a flaming spear, galloping horse, and 80,000 screaming football fans, began on September 16,1978, during a home game against Oklahoma State. Florida State won the game, and the show has since become a collegiate legend. Sportswriter Richard Billingsley called the pregame ritual "one of the most recognizable, revered, and respected traditions of all time." Moreover, he credited FSU for "maintain[ing] their mascot with dignity, respect, and the goodwill and wishes of the Seminole Tribe."

Many of FSU's fans who agree with Billingsley often talk about the Seminole using religious language. Systematically explaining the virtues of each symbol, one fan stated, "To us, the 'war path' is our journey to make the best possible life we can for ourselves." "[Osceola's horse "Renegade"] is not simply a horse, but rather the educational system on which we are attempting to ride, so that we can move with greater speed and stability towards our own personal futures." Finally, Osceola "is the courage within each of us. He represents our ability to lead, have confidence, and to not settle, but rather to go for our goals, and with hope, attain what we desire." Such sentiments are common among FSU's legions of followers who have a great sense of pride for their mascot.

Supporters also find virtue in the warring acumen of the Seminoles and regularly draw parallels between the Seminole wars of the mid–19th century and the tenaciousness of their football team. "FSU selected the Seminoles," one fan noted, "because they wanted to reflect in their teams the 'never say die' spirit of the Florida Seminole and the bravery and cohesiveness of that tribe" who faced near-certain death at the hands of Federal troops. The virtues heralded by this fan echo the quest for primitive manhood sought by Hubbard and the Boy Scouts. Osceola is a model of courage, bravery, and determination—all virtues born from warfare. Just as Hubbard wanted to reinforce a model of manhood that derived from a nostalgic image of pre-industrial America, FSU fans look to the warring history of early Florida. Thus, for FSU supporters, critics who claim the mascot is demeaning simply are not aware of its privileged place amid the sacred ground of FSU's athletic legacy.

For Florida State football fans, the Seminole represents all that is true and good about their athletic heritage. In his 1992 book, *Saint Bobby and the Barbarians,* journalist Ben Brown presented an account of FSU's 1991 championship season. It was no mistake that Brown labeled FSU's head coach Bobby Bowden a "Saint." For the fans of the team, Bowden is the transcendent figure who brought a struggling team to national prominence. For supporters, the Seminole mascot is a symbol that combines Bowden, FSU football, and their meteoric rise to success. As such, the Seminole is coveted, cherished, and loved just as much as "Saint Bobby" is. As the Indian opposition began leveling attacks against this symbol, therefore, fans rose quickly to its defense and struggled to retain a profoundly important part of their popular religious faith.

"White Man's Hollywood"

The Indian opposition has a difficult battle. It must convince an unwilling population that FSU's religious devotion to the Seminole mascot does not honor, but instead perpetuates a history of misunderstanding. Humor has helped its cause. At a protest over similar problems in Illinois, poster boards displayed pithy phrases such as, "Imagine the Pope dancing at half-time," and "How would you like Jesus on a butt cushion?" Arguably, one of the most notorious examples of humorous comparison comes from Wade Churchill's article "Crimes against Humanity." Churchill first tentatively accepts that Indian mascots represent "good clean fun," but then imagines what other minority mascots might look like. After proposing team names like the "Galveston 'Greaser'" and "San Diego 'Spics,'" Churchill turns his focus to faith. "Have a religious belief? Let's all go for the gusto and gear up the Milwaukee 'Mackerel Snappers' and Hollywood 'Holy Rollers.' The Fighting Irish of Notre Dame can be rechristened the 'Drunken Irish' or 'Papist Pigs.'" Churchill's point is both sarcastic and clear. Indians are small in number and their religious world has long been the subject of abuse, misunderstanding, and mistreatment. America's mainline religions would not stand for the trivialization of their faith on the football field—especially by people who failed to understand the essence of such a religion. Churchill simply asks that institutions like Florida State respect Indian culture and religion as they would any of America's mainline faiths.

A central concern for the Indian opposition is the viability of their religious heritage. While mascots might not employ obvious religious symbols, it is worth noting that Indian religion often coexists with practically every element of Indian life. "If you pull on the thread of 'Native American religion,'" Joel Martin wrote, "you end up pulling yourself into the study of Native American culture, art, history, economics, music, dance, politics, and almost everything else." For the opposition, schools like FSU that use, misuse, and mock Indian traditions, objects, and people, subsequently extend such insults to Indian religion. As a result, a concern for the vitality of their sacred symbols feeds the opposition's concern. . . .

Indian Approval

. . . FSU's most effective means for deflecting the criticisms of the opposition has been the assent of Seminole officials. The March 4, 2002, issue of *Sports Illustrated* cited a survey conducted by the Peter Harris Research Group that asked a diverse sample of 352 Indians living both on and off reservations whether they disapproved of Indian mascots. The results showed 81 percent of the respondents affirming that colleges and high schools should keep their Indian mascots, and 83 percent saying professional teams should do the same. Most of those surveyed thought that Indian mascots had an endearing quality. Much like Notre Dame's fans for their "Fighting Irish," respondents considered the mascots harmless, spirited, and entertaining, rather than demeaning. Furthermore, a majority were not offended by the Redskins mascot of Washington DC's professional football team—a logo that is arguably the most insulting to those opposing Indian mascots.

In some respects, the Florida Seminoles seem to share this sentiment—a point that FSU supporters are not shy about sharing. In a rebuttal to critics within his own professional organization, FSU dean of Arts and Science Donald Foss quoted James E. Billie, the former chairman of the Florida Seminole tribe, as declaring, "I am proud of all those who are by birth or choosing a Seminole!" Foss also cited Jerry Haney, chairman of the Oklahoma Seminoles, as saying,

"I think that the Seminole/Florida State relationship has been a big shot in the arm for us. I think just about everybody out here is supportive of the Florida State Seminoles." On July 2001, however, Haney signed an official statement from the Council of the Five Civilized Tribes "to eliminate the stereotypical use of American Indian names and images as mascots in sports and other events." Nevertheless, writing a similar response, former FSU president Sandy D'Alemberte referred to Miss Seminole Nation of 1995–96 who thanked the university for "promoting our tribe" as she affirmed Billie's assertion: "We're behind it—we're supporting it." Also coming to the defense of the mascot, Florida State Senator Jim King quoted Jim Shore, the official lawyer for the Florida Seminoles, as saying, "We're not offended, why should they [protesters] be offended?"

Indian assent has been the most difficult hurdle for the opposition to maneuver. Statistics and statements on the issue combine to offer a sense that the opposition is small and misdirected. Indeed, the *Sports Illustrated* poll offered convincing numerical evidence to show that Indians remain generally apathetic toward the mascot issue. The opposition argues that this poll, just like the entire issue of Indian assent, is misleading. C. Richard King and Ellen J. Staurowsky noted the various limitations of the study and went on to cite statistics from an August 8, 2001, poll conducted by *Indian Country Today*. In this study 81 percent of the Indian respondents "indicated use of American Indian names, symbols and mascots are predominantly offensive and deeply disparaging to Native Americans." Furthermore, 75 percent maintained that the use of Indian mascots by non–Indian schools "should be seen as a violation of anti-discrimination laws" and 73 percent believed such situations created hostile learning environments for Indians attending such schools. . . .

In spite of the Oklahoma Seminoles' ambiguity, hazy statistics, and the misleading nature of Indian assent, statements of approval coming from tribal leaders have been invaluable for supporters. In their minds, such statements serve as ultimate rebuttals to any criticism. For the opposition, however, the approvals of Seminole leaders fail to account for the Indians outside of tribal power structures. . . .

Conclusion

The arguments over an Indian mascot at FSU involve a discussion of symbols—their purpose, meaning, and function. Anthropologist Clifford Geertz maintains that through symbols, people contact the religious. Symbols are, in other words, conduits of the divine. Critics of this thesis might accept only half of the argument, questioning the claim that football is religious. Clearly, churches and football stadiums serve entirely different purposes, and Indian symbols, such as feathers and tomahawks, have religious value due to their functions in various ritual practices. But why is this latter point so easy to determine? Is it because Indians say that these symbols are religious? Indeed, someone's word does have value for determining what is and is not religious, but it should not put an end to the discussion. Otherwise, we might construct too narrow a definition of religion, or we might call something religious that is without sacred value.

Religious scholar Joseph Price calls American sports "a form of popular religion." As Price explains, sports are not institutional religious bodies in the traditional sense, but they do offer fans opportunities to reconnect with the transcendent. Many FSU supporters find transcendent value in the embodied virtues of the Seminole mascot. The Seminole mascot is, therefore, a highly cherished part of FSU's popular religious faith. Virtue is the religious center of the Seminole mascot, and the manner by which FSU supporters virulently defend their symbol serves to demonstrate its importance. To them, the Seminole mascot is more than a novelty; it is a way of experiencing the world. . . .

EXPLORING THE ISSUE

Are Native American Mascots Racist Symbols?

Critical Thinking and Reflection

1. How do mores and attitudes change over time?
2. Are Native Americans monolithic, or do they exist as distinct tribes and nations with their own histories and cultures?
3. Explain the negative critique of the use of Native American cultural and religious symbols. How does the longtime use and popular acceptance of Native American mascots contribute to unintended consequences such as perpetuating racism? Examine other areas of popular culture, which may contain controversial symbols and caricatures offensive to racial and ethnic groups.
4. Why do some Native American groups approve of the use of Native American symbols as mascots for sports teams?
5. What are the commercial benefits that accrue from the use of Indian mascots?
6. How is religion employed by both Remillard and Katyal to develop their respective positions on this issue?
7. How do Native Americans respond when others use their cultural symbols?

Is There Common Ground?

The use of Native American cultural symbols by professional and collegiate sports teams has generated significant controversy in recent years. Katyal and Remillard both are aware that social conflict, including the Indian wars, has substantially influenced the relationship between Native Americans and the predominant white society. They agree that the use of Native American symbols as mascots is a source of controversy within the nation. Both of these scholars advance a religious argument to make their case. They recognize that this issue arises from the legacy of conflict that has attended Native American relations with mainstream America throughout history. Recent developments in this relationship influenced by the civil rights movement, the Red Power Movement, and related activist organizations have demanded increased sensitivity in the treatment of Native American history and culture. This is the basis upon which the current debate over the use of Native symbols as mascots has arisen. In response to this controversy the U.S. Commission on Civil Rights has called for an end to the use of Native American images and team names by non-Native schools. Also, many colleges, universities, and high schools have decided to eliminate traditional mascots that utilize Indian cultural and religious symbols. Included among the 2,000 schools that have given up their Indian-based mascots are Stanford University (Indians to Cardinals), St. John's University (Redmen to Red Storm), and Miami of Ohio (Redskins to Redhawks), along with several high schools. However, other schools, such as Florida State University, have defended this practice with the claim that their utilization honors Native American religion and cultural heritage.

Additional Resources

Aleiss, Angela. 2008. *Making the White Man's Indian: Native Americans and Hollywood Movies* (Praeger Press).

Brown, Dee. 1970. *Bury My Heart at Wounded Knee: An Indian History of the American West* (Holt Paperbacks).

Brune, Michelle Lyn. 2011. *A Qualitative Study of a Native American Mascot at "Public University"* (ProQuest, UMI Dissertation Publishing).

Davey, Monica. 2010. "Insult or Honor? More Than 2000 Schools Have Given Up Indian Mascots in Response to Protests from Native Americans," *New York Times Upfront* (Scholastic, Inc., February 8).

Deloria, Vine and Lytle Clifford. 1983. *American Indians, American Justice* (University of Texas Press).

Ehle, John. 1997. *Trail of Tears: The Rise and Fall of the Cherokee Nation* (Anchor Books Doubleday).

King, C. Richard. 2001. "Charles Freuling Springwood and Vine Deloria," in *Team Spirits: The Native American Mascots Controversy* (University of Nebraska Press).

King, C. Richard. 2006. *Native Athletes in Sport and Society* (Bison Books).

King, C. Richard. 2010. *The Native American Mascot Controversy: A Handbook* (Scarecrow Press).

Majerol, Veronica. 2012. "Insult or Honor? Indian Themed Mascots Are Traditions for Thousands of Schools and Pro Sports Teams in the U.S.," *New York Times Upfront* (Scholastic, Inc., March 5).

Nichols, Roger. 2004. *American Indians in U.S. History* (Oxford University Press).

Owens, Louis. 2001. *I Hear the Train: Reflections, Inventions, Refractions* (University of Oklahoma Press).

Price, S. and Andrea Woo. 2002. "The Indian Wars," *Sports Illustrated* (March 4, pp. 66–71).

Rhoden, William. 1992. "Sports of The Times: A New View of History," *The New York Times* (January 25).

Rockwell, Stephen. 2010. *Indian Affairs and the Administrative State in the Nineteenth Century* (Cambridge University Press).

Rumbaut, G., ed., *Origins and Destinies: Immigration, Race, and Ethnicity in America* (Wadsworth Publishers).

Sledge, Rob. 2005. *It's a Jungle Out There: Mascot Tales from Texas High Schools* (Statehouse Press).

Smallwood, James. 2004. *The Indian Texans (Texans All)* (Texas A & M University Press).

Snip, C. Matthew. 1996. "The First Americans: American Indians," in Silvia Pedraza and Rubin Spindel, Carol. 2002. *Dancing at Halftime: Sports and the Controversy over Indian Mascots* (New York University Press).

Springwood, Charles F. and C. Richard King. 2001. "Playing Indian: Why Native American Mascots Must End," *Chronicle of Higher Education* (December 9).

Treuer, Antokn. 2012. *Everything You Wanted to Know About Indians but Were Afraid to Ask* (Borealis Books).

Vlasich, James A. 2005. *Horsehide, Pigskin, Oval Tracks and Apple Pie: Essays on Sport and American Culture* (McFarland & Company).

Zirin, Dave. 2009. *People's History of Sports in the United States: 250 Years of Politics, Protest, and Play* (New York: New Press).

This is the website of the American Indian Sports Teams Mascots, Tokens, Nicknames, Logos and Associated Symbols. It offers a critique of the *Sports Illustrated* (March 4, 2002) article on Indian symbols and mascots used by sports teams. Other offerings include newspaper articles, books, and other materials related to the "American Indian" sports team mascot issue.

http://aistm.org/

The purpose of this site is to provide "a cyber-place for Earth's indigenous peoples." It is a nonprofit site dedicated to foster communications between native and nonnative peoples and to conduct research of indigenous people's use of technology. The site provides coverage of Native American news.

www.nativeweb.org/

This is the website of American Indian resources. It is a library of Native American literature, culture, education, history, issues, and language, which contains several links to related websites dealing with Native American issues. There are also links to articles and journals based at colleges and universities in the United States. Additionally, the student can find information about American Indian schools, colleges, and universities.

www.lang.osaka-u.ac.jp/~krkvls/

The Native American Rights Fund (NARF) is the largest nonprofit law firm dedicated to defending the rights of Indian tribes. Its website focuses on law and contains a National Indian Law Library. Additionally, the site offers current news reports dealing with Indian law from local court to Supreme Court decisions and their impact on Indians.

www.narf.org/

This is the website for the Akwesasne Native American newspaper, *Akwesasne Notes*. It is one of the leading newspapers of American Indians. The site offers links to various reports and publications dealing with Native American issues.

www.ratical.org/AkwesasneNs.html

Internet References . . .

Southern Poverty Law Center

This is the website for the Southern Poverty Law Center (SPLC), which was founded by Morris Dees and Joe Levin. Located in Alabama, the Center is internationally known for many tolerance programs including education programs, tracking of hate groups, and its legal victories against white supremacists. It offers educational and community programs for those interested in dismantling bigotry.

www.splcenter. org

NAACP

This website offers information, news, and trends dealing with African Americans. The 50th year commemoration of the 1954 decision, *Brown v. Board of Education,* is explored in detail on the site. The official NAACP publication, *The Crisis,* is available, as are past issues through the site's archives section. Additional information revolving around race relations is presented daily, including a Congressional Report.

www.naacp.org

Museum of Racist Memorabilia

This is the website for the Jim Crow Museum of Racist Memorabilia located in Michigan. It contains information and illustrations on popular cultural racist memorabilia. The site promotes the scholarly examination of historical and contemporary expressions of racism. The virtual tour reveals several caricatures and an informative essay on racist images.

www.ferris.edu/jimcrow/

Black Agenda Report

The Journal of African American Thought and Action is published every Wednesday on this website. It promotes a critically progressive agenda and offers links to approximately 75 progressive websites. Twenty-first century policy issues including labor, immigration, and reparations for African Americans are discussed. Glen Ford is the executive editor.

www.blackagendareport.com

Civil Rights Movement

This is a website dedicated to the history of the southern civil rights movement, also referred to as the Southern Freedom Movement (1951–1968). It contains a history, timeline, and bibliography along with original documents dealing with the civil rights movement. For students doing research, the site offers links, categorized by specific topics, to both scholarly and popular information on the movement.

www.crmvet.org/

UNIT 3

Race Still Matters

*A*t a time when an African American is president of the United States, one may find it difficult to accept that race still matters in this country. Issues of race have challenged the nation from the Colonial Era to the present. Traditionally, race developed as a biological concept. The criteria that were established to place human beings within distinct racial categories were biological in nature and included such features as skin color, prognathism, and cranial configuration, among others. As a result of research and scientific discovery, including the Human Genome Project that is currently under way, the biological basis of racial categories has been refuted. Yet, the idea of race has been retained as a social construction that provides a basis for distinguishing and treating human groups other than one's own. Clearly, race still matters. How does it matter? Race affects where one lives, goes to school, and worships. Race is a significant factor in the distribution of income and wealth. Race is a factor in terms of crime and punishment. Race influences one's life chances.

- Is Race Prejudice a Product of Group Position?
- Does the Digital Divide Reflect American Racism?
- Is Racial Profiling Defensible Public Policy?
- Is Affirmative Action Necessary to Achieve Racial Equality?

ISSUE 9

Is Race Prejudice a Product of Group Position?

YES: Herbert Blumer, from "Race Prejudice as a Sense of Group Position," *The Pacific Sociological Review* (Spring 1958)

NO: Gordon W. Allport, from "The Young Child," *The Nature of Prejudice* (Perseus Books, 1979)

Learning Outcomes

After reading this issue, you should be able to:

- Gain a proper understanding of the group position thesis.
- Properly understand how the group position thesis is employed to explain race prejudice.
- Identify and explain the central thesis that Allport advances to explain how prejudice is acquired.
- Understand the relationship between the acquisition of a racial identity and race prejudice.
- Explain the distinction between individual prejudice and institutional prejudice.
- Apply the group position thesis to the examination of critical issues of race relations, including racial stratification, racial conflict, and segregation.
- Understand the psychological and sociological approaches to explain prejudice.

ISSUE SUMMARY

YES: Herbert Blumer, a sociologist, asserts that prejudice exists in a sense of group position rather than as an attitude based on individual feelings. The collective process by which a group comes to define other racial groups is the focus of Blumer's position.

NO: Gordon W. Allport, a psychologist, makes the case that prejudice is the result of a three-stage learning process.

The nature of prejudice is a critical focus of research concerning intergroup relations. Where does prejudice come from? How and under what circumstances do we acquire it? What are its characteristics? Is prejudice an individual personality trait or, is it a product of structural factors such as group position or economic factors? Ill feelings and overt hostility can reflect prejudice, but so can quiet benign beliefs. The many theories that explain prejudice can be categorized into those that attribute prejudice to individual personality, and those that see prejudice resulting from larger structural factors.

Herbert Blumer begins his group position argument in the context of dominant-subordinate group analysis. Members of the dominant group will, in addition to feelings of superiority, "feel a proprietary claim to certain areas of privilege and advantage." Suspicions of subordinate group members exist because of a fear that the minority group "harbors design on the prerogatives of the dominant race." Although Blumer uses psychological concepts such as feelings, superiority, and distinctiveness, his focus is not on the individual. Rather it rests on the process of image formation. Image formation takes place in the public domain including newspapers, film, and other media. "Careless ignorance of the facts" is often part of the image formation. Surely Blumer believes that prejudice is learned. Nevertheless, his analysis transcends mere "learning."

The analysis of the collective process through which one group defines another involves a historical analysis. Group position is formed in a process defined by the dominant group and redefines subordinate groups. Hence, attitudes are formed from the dominant group perspective.

When the position of the dominant group is challenged, race prejudice emerges. According to Blumer, this may occur in different ways. For example, it may be an affront to feelings or an attempt to transgress racial boundaries. Reaction to interracial marriage or the racial integration of a neighborhood may provoke a "defensive reaction" on the part of the dominant group. Generalizations of the minority group often lead to fear. Disturbed feelings are marked by hostility. Thus, Blumer suggests that race prejudice becomes a protective device. Prejudice is associated with the belief that gains for other (racial and ethnic) groups will result in losses for one's own—a zero sum game.

Examining how prejudice is learned, Gordon Allport stresses the first six years of a child's life, especially the role of the parents in transferring ideas as creating an atmosphere in which the child "develops prejudice as his style of life." The psychological factors exhibited during childrearing, including how the child is disciplined, loved, and threatened, translate into fear or hatred that may ultimately be directed at minorities. A rigid home environment in which parents exercise strict control is more likely to lead to prejudice among the children than a less rigid upbringing. Tolerance results from a less strict childrearing style.

Allport explains that there are three stages of learning prejudice. In the first stage, the pregeneralized learning period, the child learns linguistic categories before he/she is ready to apply them. For example, ethnic and racial slurs are not yet applied to specific groups. Nevertheless, the categories are learned. The second stage in learning prejudice, the period of total rejection, occurs when children connect the labels of groups to be rejected with the individuals in minority groups. For example, Allport argues, by the fifth grade, children tend to choose their own racial group. However, as children grow older and mature, they lose the tendency to overgeneralize about minorities. The third stage, differentiation, sets in often during the later years of high school. By then, the "escape clauses" or exceptions to stereotypes are incorporated into the individual's attitude. So, the limited early learning experiences are replaced by the wider experiences that come with adolescence.

The NO selection by Allport is part of his more comprehensive social psychological account of how prejudice is learned. The emphasis on personality traits formed during early childhood contrasts with Blumer's group position thesis.

We recommend that the student consider both positions to complete a study of prejudice. In this issue we urge students to search for similarities, along with the differences, between Allport and Blumer. Does Blumer reject the notion that prejudice is learned? Does Allport ignore the collective process? If your answer is "no" to these two questions, then how can you build a theory of prejudice?

Film and other components of popular culture have tended to stereotyped images of African Americans and other minorities throughout much of American history. D.W. Griffith's controversial film, *Birth of a Nation,* illustrates this tendency to stereotype blacks and other minorities. The film, originally *The Clansmen,* presented to the country's dominant white population an image of emancipated blacks with exaggerated physical features and association with negative behavioral patterns. The stereotyped images of black men included an alleged desire for white women, and the threat that they represented in that regard. In the Jim Crow America that evolved after Reconstruction, many whites formed such images of blacks derived from available popular cultural images.

Both Blumer and Allport associate prejudice with attitudes of individuals, whether the cause is psychological or sociological. Beyond individual prejudice is institutional prejudice, which, along with institutional discrimination, cannot be ignored in the study of prejudice. For example, institutional racism was the law of the land before the 1954 *Brown* decision. The "separate but equal" doctrine stemming from the landmark *Plessy* case enabled institutions such as schools to discriminate. Institutional prejudice was a "normal" part of American culture and reflected the negative stereotyping of blacks. One of the consequences of institutional prejudice led to self-segregation. Although the country has moved away from legal segregation, the latent effect of institutional prejudice today leads to self-segregation. Students will find Issue 19 ("Do Minorities and Whites Engage in Self-Segregation?") closely related to this discussion of prejudice.

Given the history of the persistence of prejudice and the discrimination that flows from it, it is difficult to envision a society in which the vestiges of prejudice are eliminated. The persistence of prejudice is a continuing challenge to the diverse American society due to the social conflict that it has been generating. So students are challenged to develop strategies through which prejudice can be confronted. Overcoming prejudice is vital to the achievement of a more cohesive and unified America in the future.

YES

Herbert Blumer

Race Prejudice as a Sense of Group Position

In this paper I am proposing an approach to the study of race prejudice different from that which dominates contemporary scholarly thought on this topic. My thesis is that race prejudice exists basically in a sense of group position rather than in a set of feelings which members of one racial group have toward the members of another racial group. This different way of viewing race prejudice shifts study and analysis from a preoccupation with feelings as lodged in individuals to a concern with the relationship of racial groups. It also shifts scholarly treatment away from individual lines of experience and focuses interest on the collective process by which a racial group comes to define and redefine another racial group. Such shift, I believe, will yield a more realistic and penetrating understanding of race prejudice.

There can be little question that the rather vast literature on race prejudice is dominated by the idea that such prejudice exists fundamentally as a feeling or set of feelings lodged in the individual. It is usually depicted as consisting of feelings such as antipathy, hostility, hatred, intolerance, and aggressiveness. Accordingly, the task of scientific inquiry becomes two-fold. On one hand, there is a need to identify the feelings which makeup race prejudice—to see how they fit together and how they are supported by other psychological elements, such as mythical beliefs. On the other hand, there is need of showing how the feeling complex has come into being. Thus, some scholars trace the complex feelings back chiefly to innate dispositions; some trace it to personality composition, such as authoritarian personality; and others regard the feelings of prejudice as being formed through social experience. However different may be the contentions regarding the makeup of racial prejudice and the way in which it may come into existence, these contentions are alike in locating prejudice in the realm of individual feeling. This is clearly true of the work of psychologists, psychiatrists, and social psychologists, and tends to be predominantly the case in the work of sociologists.

Unfortunately, this customary way of viewing race prejudice overlooks and obscures the fact that race prejudice is fundamentally a matter of relationship between racial groups. A little reflective thought should make this very clear. Race prejudice presupposes, necessarily, that racially prejudiced individuals think of themselves as belonging to a given racial group. It means,

From *Pacific Sociological Review,* Spring 1958. Copyright © 1958 by Pacific Sociological Association. Reprinted by permission.

169

also, that they assign to other racial groups those against whom they are prejudiced. Thus, logically and actually, a scheme of racial identification is necessary as a framework for racial prejudice. Moreover, such identification involves the formation of an image or a conception of one's own racial group and of another racial group, inevitably in terms of the relationship of such groups. To fail to see that racial prejudice is a matter (a) of the racial identification made of oneself and of others, and (b) of the way in which the identified groups are conceived in relation to each other, is to miss what is logically and actually basic. One should keep clearly in mind that people necessarily come to identify themselves as belonging to a racial group; such identification is not spontaneous or inevitable but a result of experience. Further, one must realize that the kind of picture which a racial group forms of itself and the kind of picture which it may form of others are similarly products of experience. Hence, such pictures are variable, just as the lines of experience which produce them are variable.

The body of feelings which scholars, today, are so inclined to regard as constituting the substance of race prejudice is actually a resultant of the way in which given racial groups conceive of themselves and of others. A basic understanding of race prejudice must be sought in the process by which racial groups form images of themselves and of others. This process, as I hope to show, is fundamentally *a collective process*. It operates chiefly through the public media in which individuals who are accepted as the spokesmen of a racial group characterize publicly another racial group. To characterize another racial group is, by opposition, to define one's own group. This is equivalent to placing the two groups in relation to each other, or defining their positions *vis-à-vis* each other. It is the *sense of social position* emerging from this collective process of characterization which provides the basis of race prejudice. The following discussion will consider important facets of this matter.

I would like to begin by discussing several of the important feelings that enter into race prejudice. This discussion will reveal how fundamentally racial feelings point to and depend on a positional arrangement of the racial groups. In this discussion I will confine myself to such feelings in the case of a dominant racial group.

There are four basic types of feelings that seem to be always present in race prejudice in the dominant group. They are (1) a feeling of superiority, (2) a feeling that the subordinate race is intrinsically different and alien, (3) a feeling of proprietary claim to certain areas of privilege and advantage, and (4) a fear and suspicion that the subordinate race harbors designs on the prerogatives of the dominant race. A few words about each of these four feelings will suffice.

In race prejudice there is a self-assured feeling on the part of the dominant racial group of being naturally superior or better. This is commonly shown in a disparagement of the qualities of the subordinate racial group. Condemnatory or debasing traits, such as laziness, dishonesty, greediness, unreliability, stupidity, deceit, and immorality, are usually imputed to it. The second feeling, that the subordinate race is an alien and fundamentally different stock, is likewise always present. "They are not of our kind" is a common way in which this is likely to be expressed. It is this feeling that reflects, justifies, and promotes the social exclusion of the subordinate racial group. The combination of these two feelings of superiority and of distinctiveness can easily give rise to feelings of aversion and even antipathy. But in themselves they do not form prejudice. We have to introduce the third and fourth types of feeling.

The third feeling, the sense of proprietary claim, is of crucial importance. It is the feeling on the part of the dominant group of being entitled to either exclusive or prior rights in many important areas of life. The range of such exclusive or prior claims may be wide, covering the ownership of property such as choice lands and sites; the right to certain jobs, occupations, or professions; the claim to certain kinds of industry or lines of business; the claim to certain positions of control and decision-making as in government and law; the right to exclusive membership in given institutions such as schools, churches, and recreational institutions; the claim to certain positions of social prestige and to the display of the symbols and accoutrements of these positions; and the claim to certain areas of intimacy and privacy. The feeling of such proprietary claims is exceedingly strong in race prejudice. Again, however, this feeling even in combination with the feeling of superiority and the feeling of distinctiveness does not explain race prejudice. These three feelings are present frequently in societies showing no prejudice, as in certain forms of feudalism, in caste relations, in societies of chiefs and commoners, and under many settled relations of conquerors and conquered. Where claims are solidified into a structure which is accepted or respected by all, there seems to be no group prejudice.

The remaining feeling essential to race prejudice is a fear or apprehension that the subordinate racial group is threatening, or will threaten, the position of the dominant group. Thus, acts or suspected acts that are interpreted as an attack on the natural superiority of the dominant group, or an intrusion into their sphere of group exclusiveness, or an encroachment on their area of proprietary claim are crucial in arousing and fashioning race prejudice. These acts mean "getting out of place."

It should be clear that these four basic feelings of race prejudice definitely refer to a positional arrangement of the racial groups. The feeling of superiority places the subordinate people *below;* the feeling of alienation places them *beyond;* the feeling of proprietary claim excludes them from the prerogatives of position; and the fear of encroachment is an emotional recoil from the endangering of group position. As these features suggest, the positional relation of the two racial groups is crucial in race prejudice. The dominant group is not concerned with the subordinate group as such but it is deeply concerned with its position *vis-à-vis* the subordinate group. This is epitomized in the key and universal expression that a given race is all right in "its place." The sense of group position is the very heart of the relation of the dominant to the subordinate group. It supplies the dominant group with its framework of perception, its standard of judgment, its patterns of sensitivity, and its emotional proclivities.

It is important to recognize that this sense of group position transcends the feelings of the individual members of the dominant group, giving such members a common orientation that is not otherwise to be found in separate feelings and views. There is likely to be considerable difference between the ways in which the individual members of the dominant group think and feel about the subordinate group. Some may feel bitter and hostile, with strong antipathies, with an exalted sense of superiority and with a lot of spite; others may have charitable and protective feelings, marked by a sense of piety and tinctured by benevolence; others may be condescending and reflect mild contempt; and others may be disposed to politeness and considerateness with no feelings of truculence. These are only a few of many different patterns of feeling to be found among members of the dominant racial group. What gives a common dimension to them is a sense of the social position of their group. Whether the members be humane or callous, cultured or unlettered, liberal or reactionary, powerful or impotent, arrogant or humble, rich or poor, honorable or dishonorable—all are led, by virtue of sharing the sense of group position, to similar individual positions.

The sense of group position is a general kind of orientation. It is a general feeling without being reducible to specific feelings like hatred, hostility, or antipathy. It is also a general understanding without being composed of any set of specific beliefs. On the social psychological side it cannot be equated to a sense of social status as ordinarily conceived, for it refers not merely to vertical positioning but to many other lines of position independent of the vertical dimension. Sociologically it is not a mere reflection of the objective relations between racial groups. Rather, it stands for "what ought to be" rather than for "what is." It is a sense of where the two racial groups *belong*.

In its own way, the sense of group position is a norm and imperative—indeed a very powerful one. It guides, incites, cows, and coerces. It should be borne in mind that this sense of group position stands for and involves a fundamental kind of group affiliation for the members of the dominant racial group. To the extent they recognize or feel themselves as belonging to that group they will automatically come under the influence of the sense of position held by that group. Thus, even though given individual members may have personal views and feelings different from the sense of group position, they will have to conjure with the sense of group position held by their racial group. If the sense of position is strong, to act contrary to it is to risk a feeling of self-alienation and to face the possibility of ostracism. I am trying to suggest, accordingly, that the locus of race prejudice is not in the area of individual feeling but in the definition of the respective positions of the racial groups.

The source of race prejudice lies in a felt challenge to this sense of group position. The challenge, one must recognize, may come in many different ways. It may be in the form of an affront to feelings of group superiority; it may be in the form of attempts at familiarity or transgressing the boundary line of group exclusiveness; it may be in the form of encroachment at countless points of proprietary claim; it may be a challenge to power and privilege; it may take the form of economic competition. Race prejudice is a defensive reaction to such challenging of the sense of group position. It consists of the disturbed feelings, usually of marked hostility, that are thereby aroused. As such, race prejudice is a protective device. It functions, however shortsightedly, to preserve the integrity and the position of the dominant group.

It is crucially important to recognize that the sense of group position is not a mere summation of the feelings of position such as might be developed independently by separate individuals as they come to compare themselves with given individuals of the subordinate race. The sense of group position refers to the position of group to group, not to that of individual to individual. Thus, *vis-à-vis* the subordinate racial group the unlettered individual with low status in the dominant racial group has a sense of group position common to that of the elite of his group. By virtue of sharing this sense of position such an individual, despite his low status, feels that members of the subordinate group, however distinguished and accomplished, are somehow inferior, alien, and properly restricted in the area of claims. He forms his conception as a representative of the dominant group; he treats individual members of the subordinate group as representative of that group.

An analysis of how the sense of group position is formed should start with a clear recognition that it is an historical product. It is set originally by conditions of initial contact. Prestige, power, possession of skill, numbers, original self-conceptions, aims, designs, and opportunities are a few of the factors that may fashion the original sense of group position. Subsequent experience in the relation of the two racial groups, especially in the area of claims, opportunities, and advantages, may mould the sense of group position in many diverse ways. Further, the sense of group position may be intensified or weakened, brought to sharp focus or dulled. It may be deeply entrenched and tenaciously resist change for long periods of time. Or it may never take root. It may undergo quick growth and vigorous expansion or it may dwindle away through slow-moving erosion. It may be firm or soft, acute or dull, continuous or intermittent. In short, viewed comparatively, the sense of group position is very variable.

However variable its particular career, the sense of group position is clearly formed by a running process in which the dominant racial group is led to define and redefine the subordinate racial group and the relations between them. There are two important aspects of this process of definition that I wish to single out for consideration.

First, the process of definition occurs obviously through complex interaction and communication between the members of the dominant group. Leaders, prestige bearers, official, group agents, dominant individuals, and ordinary laymen present to one another characterizations of the subordinate group and express their feelings and ideas on the relations. Through talk, tales, stories, gossip, anecdotes, messages, pronouncements, news accounts, orations, sermons, preachments and the like definitions are presented and feelings are expressed. In this usually vast and complex interaction separate views run against one another, influence one another, modify each other, incite one another, and fuse together in new forms. Correspondingly, feelings which are expressed meet, stimulate each other, feed on each other, intensify each other, and emerge in new patterns. Currents of view and currents of feeling come into being; sweeping along to positions of dominance and serving as polar points for the organization of thought and sentiment. If the interaction becomes increasingly circular and reinforcing, devoid of serious inner opposition, such currents grow, fuse, and become strengthened. It is through such a process that a collective image of the subordinate group is formed and a sense of group position is set. The evidence of such a process is glaring when one reviews the history of any racial arrangement marked by prejudice.

Such a complex process of mutual interaction with its different lines and degrees of formation gives the lie to the many schemes which would lodge the cause of race prejudice in the makeup of the individual—whether in the form of innate disposition, constitutional makeup, personality structure, or direct personal experience with members of the other race. The collective image and feelings in race prejudice are forged out of a complicated social process in which the individual is himself shaped and organized. The scheme, so popular today, which would trace race prejudice to a so-called authoritarian personality shows a grievous misunderstanding of the simple essentials of the collective process that leads to a sense of group position.

The second important aspect of the process of group definition is that it is necessarily concerned with *an abstract image* of the subordinate racial group. The subordinate racial group is defined as if it were an entity or whole. This entity or whole—like the Negro race, or the Japanese, or the Jews—is necessarily an abstraction, never coming within the perception of any of the senses. While actual encounters are with individuals, the picture formed of the racial group is necessarily of a vast entity which spreads out far beyond such individuals and transcends experience with such individuals. The implications of the fact that the collective image is of an abstract group are of crucial significance. I would like to note four of these implications.

First, the building of the image of the abstract group takes place in the area of the remote and not of the near. It is not the experience with concrete individuals in daily association that gives rise to the definitions of the extended, abstract group. Such immediate experience is usually regulated and orderly. Even where such immediate experience is disrupted the new definitions which are formed are limited to the individuals involved. The collective image of the abstract group grows up not by generalizing from experiences gained in close, first-hand contacts but through the transcending characterizations that are made of the group as an entity. Thus, one must seek the central stream of definition in those areas where the dominant group as such is characterizing the subordinate group as such. This occurs in the "public arena" wherein the spokesmen appear as representatives and agents of the dominant group. The extended public arena is constituted by such things as legislative assemblies, public meetings, conventions, the press, and the printed word. What goes on in this public arena attracts the attention of large numbers of the dominant group and is felt as the voice and action of the group as such.

Second, the definitions that are forged in the public arena center, obviously, about matters that are felt to be of major importance. Thus, we are led to recognize the crucial role of the "big event" in developing a conception of the subordinate racial group. The happening that seems momentous, that touches deep sentiments, that seems to raise fundamental questions about relations, and that awakens strong feelings of identification with one's racial group is the kind of event that is central in the formation of the racial image. Here, again, we note the relative unimportance of the huge bulk of experiences coming from daily contact with individuals of the subordinate group. It is the events seemingly loaded with great collective significance that are the focal points of the public discussion. The definition of these events is chiefly responsible for the development of a racial image and of the sense of group position. When this public discussion takes the form of a denunciation of the subordinate racial group, signifying that it is unfit and a threat, the discussion becomes particularly potent in shaping the sense of social position.

Third, the major influence in public discussion is exercised by individuals and groups who have the public ear and who are felt to have standing, prestige, authority, and power. Intellectual and social elites, public figures of prominence, and leaders of powerful organizations are likely to be the key figures in the formation of the sense of group position and in the characterization of the subordinate group. It is well to note this in view of the not infrequent tendency of students to regard race prejudice as growing out of the multiplicity of experiences and attitudes of the bulk of the people.

Fourth, we also need to perceive the appreciable opportunity that is given to strong interest groups in directing the lines of discussion and setting the interpretations that arise in such discussion. Their self-interests may dictate the kind of position they wish the dominant racial group to enjoy. It may be a position which enables them to retain certain advantages, or even more to gain still greater advantages. Hence, they may be vigorous in seeking to manufacture events to attract public attention and to set lines of issue in such a way as to predetermine interpretations favorable to their interests. The role of strongly organized groups seeking to further special interest is usually central in the formation of collective images of abstract groups. Historical records of major instances of race relations, as in our South, or in South Africa, or in Europe in the case of the Jew, or on the West Coast in the case of the Japanese show the formidable part played by interest groups in defining the subordinate racial group.

I conclude this highly condensed paper with two further observations that may throw additional light on the relation of the sense of group position to race prejudice. Race prejudice becomes entrenched and tenacious to the extent the prevailing social order is rooted in the sense of social position. This has been true of the historic South in our country. In such a social order race prejudice tends to become chronic and impermeable to change. In other places the social order may be affected only to a limited extent by the sense of group position held by the dominant racial group. This I think has been true usually in the case of anti-Semitism in Europe and this country. Under these conditions the sense of group position tends to be weaker and more vulnerable. In turn, race prejudice has a much more variable and intermittent career, usually becoming pronounced only as a consequence of grave disorganizing events that allow for the formation of a scapegoat.

This leads me to my final observation which in a measure is an indirect summary. The sense of group position dissolves and race prejudice declines when the process of running definition does not keep abreast of major shifts in the social order. When events touching on relations are not treated as "big events" and hence do not set crucial issues in the arena of public discussion; or when the elite leaders or spokesmen do not define such big events vehemently or adversely; or where they define them in the direction of racial harmony; or when there is a paucity of strong interest groups seeking to build up a strong adverse image for special advantage—under such conditions the sense of group position recedes and race prejudice declines.

The clear implication of my discussion is that the proper and the fruitful area in which race prejudice should be studied is the collective process through which a sense of group position is formed. To seek, instead, to understand it or to handle it in the arena of individual feeling and of individual experience seems to me to be clearly misdirected.

Gordon W. Allport  **NO**

The Young Child

How is prejudice learned? We have opened our discussion of this pivotal problem by pointing out that the home influence has priority, and that the child has excellent reasons for adopting his ethnic attitudes ready-made from his parents. We likewise called attention to the central role of identification in the course of early learning. In the present chapter we shall consider additional factors operating in preschool years. The first six years of life are important for the development of all social attitudes, though it is a mistake to regard early childhood as alone responsible for them. A bigoted personality may be well under way by the age of six, but by no means fully fashioned.

Our analysis will be clearer if at the outset we make a distinction between *adopting* prejudice and *developing* prejudice. A child who adopts prejudice is taking over attitudes and stereotypes from his family or cultural environment. . . . Parental words and gestures, along with their concomitant beliefs and antagonisms, are transferred to the child. He adopts his parents' views. . . .

But there is also a type of training that does not transfer ideas and attitudes directly to the child, but rather creates an atmosphere in which he *develops* prejudice as his style of life. In this case the parents may or may not express their own prejudices (usually they do). What is crucial, however, is that their mode of handling the child (disciplining, loving, threatening) is such that the child cannot help acquire suspicions, fears, hatreds that sooner or later may fix on minority groups.

In reality, of course, these forms of learning are not distinct. Parents who *teach* the child specific prejudices are also likely to *train* the child to develop a prejudiced nature. Still it is well to keep the distinction in mind, for the psychology of learning is so intricate a subject that it requires analytical aids of this type.

Child Training

We consider now the style of child training that is known to be conducive to the *development* of prejudice. (We shall disregard for the time being the learning of specific attitudes toward specific groups.)

From *The Nature of Prejudice* (Basic Books, 1979), pp. 297–311. Copyright © 1979 by Gordon W. Allport. Reprinted by permission of Basic Books, a member of Perseus Books Group, LLC via Rightslink.

One line of proof that a child's prejudice is related to the manner of his upbringing comes from a study of Harris, Gough, and Martin.[1] These investigators first determined the extent to which 240 fourth-, fifth-, and sixth-grade children expressed prejudiced attitudes toward minority groups. They then sent questionnaires to the mothers of these children, asking their views on certain practices in child training. Most of these were returned with the mothers' replies. The results are highly instructive. Mothers of prejudiced children, *far more often* than the mothers of unprejudiced children, held that

> Obedience is the most important thing a child can learn.
>
> A child should never be permitted to set his will against that of his parents.
>
> A child should never keep a secret from his parents.
>
> "I prefer a quiet child to one who is noisy."
>
> (In the case of temper tantrums) "Teach the child that two can play that game, by getting angry yourself."

In the case of sex-play (masturbation) the mother of the prejudiced child is much more likely to believe she should punish the child; the mother of the unprejudiced child is much more likely to ignore the practice.

All in all, the results indicate that pervasive family atmospheres do definitely slant the child. Specifically, a home that is suppressive, harsh, or critical—where the parents' word is law—is more likely to prepare the groundwork for group prejudice.

It seems a safe assumption that the mothers who expressed their philosophies of child training in this questionnaire actually carried out their ideas in practice. If so, then we have strong evidence that children are more likely to be prejudiced if they have been brought up by mothers who insist on obedience, who are suppressive of the child's impulses, and who are sharp disciplinarians.

What does such a style of child training do to a child? For one thing it puts him on guard. He has to watch his impulses carefully. Not only is he punished for them when they counter the parents' convenience and rules, as they frequently do, but he feels at such times that love is withdrawn from him. When love is withdrawn he is alone, exposed, desolate. Thus he comes to watch alertly for signs of parental approval or disapproval. It is they who have power, and they who give or withhold their conditional love. Their power and their will are the decisive agents in the child's life.

What is the result? First of all, the child learns that power and authority dominate human relationships—not trust and tolerance. The stage is thus set for a hierarchical view of society. Equality does not really prevail. The effect goes even deeper. The child mistrusts his impulses: he must not have temper tantrums, he must not disobey, he must not play with his sex organs. He must fight such evil in himself. Through a simple act of projection . . . the child comes to fear evil impulses in others. They have dark designs; their impulses threaten the child; they are not to be trusted.

If this style of training prepares the ground for prejudice, the opposite style seems to predispose toward tolerance. The child who feels secure and loved whatever he does, and who is treated not with a display of parental power (being punished usually through shaming rather than spanking), develops basic ideas of equality and trust. Not required to repress his own impulses, he is less likely to project them upon others, and less likely to develop suspicion, fear, and a hierarchical view of human relationships.[2]

While no child is always treated according to one and only one pattern of discipline or affection, we might venture to classify prevailing home atmospheres according to the following scheme:

Permissive treatment by parents

Rejective treatment

    suppressive and cruel (harsh, fear-inspiring)

    domineering and critical (overambitious parents nagging and dissatisfied with the child as he is)

Neglectful

Overindulgent

Inconsistent (sometimes permissive, sometimes rejective, sometimes overindulgent)

Although we cannot yet be dogmatic about the matter, it seems very likely that rejective, neglectful, and inconsistent styles of training tend to lead to the development of prejudice.[3] Investigators have reported how impressed they are by the frequency with which quarrelsome or broken homes have occurred in the childhood of prejudiced people.

> Ackerman and Jahoda made a study of anti-Semitic patients who were undergoing psychoanalysis. Most of them had had an unhealthy homelife as children, marked by quarreling, violence, or divorce. There was little or no affection or sympathy between the parents. The rejection of the child by one or both parents was the rule rather than the exception.[4]

These investigators could not find that specific parental indoctrination in anti-Semitic attitudes was a necessary element. It is true that the parents, like the children, were anti-Semitic, but the authors explain the connection as follows:

> In those cases where parents and children are anti-Semitic, it is more reasonable to assume that the emotional predispositions of the parents created a psychological atmosphere conducive to the development of similar emotional dispositions in the child, than to maintain the simple imitation hypothesis.[5]

In other words, prejudice was not *taught* by the parent but was *caught* by the child from an infected atmosphere.

Another investigator became interested in paranoia. Among a group of 125 hospital patients suffering from fixed delusional ideas, he found that the majority had a predominantly suppressive and cruel upbringing. Nearly three-quarters of the patients had parents who were either suppressive and cruel or else domineering and overcritical. Only seven percent came from homes that could be called permissive.[6] Thus many paranoias in adult years can be traceable to a bad start in life. We cannot, of course, equate paranoia and prejudice. Yet the rigid categorizing indulged in by the prejudiced person, his hostility, and his inaccessibility to reason are often much like the disorder of a paranoiac.

Without stretching the evidence too far, we may at least make a guess: children who are too harshly treated, severely punished, or continually crit-icized are more likely to develop personalities wherein group prejudice plays a prominent part. Conversely, children from more relaxed and secure homes, treated permissively and with affection, are more likely to develop tolerance.

Fear of the Strange

Let us return again to the question whether there is an inborn source of preju-dice.... [We] reported that as soon as infants are able (perhaps at six months of age) to distinguish between familiar and unfamiliar persons, they sometimes show anxiety when strangers approach. They do so especially, if the stranger moves abruptly or makes a "grab" for the child. They may show special fear if the stranger wears eyeglasses, or has skin of an unfamiliar color, or even if his expressive movements are different from what the child is accustomed to. This timidity usually continues through the preschool period—often beyond. Every visitor who has entered a home where there is a young child knows that it takes several minutes, perhaps several hours, for the child to "warm up" to him. But usually the initial fear gradually disappears.

We reported also an experiment where infants were placed alone in a strange room with toys. All of the children were at first alarmed and cried in distress. After a few repetitions they became entirely habituated to the room and played as if at home. But the biological utility of the initial fear reaction is obvious. Whatever is strange is a potential danger, and must be guarded against until one's experience assures one that no harm is lurking.

The almost universal anxiety of a child in the presence of strangers is no more striking than his rapid adaptability to their presence.

> In a certain household a Negro maid came to work. The young children in the family, aged three and five, showed fear and for a few days were reluctant to accept her. The maid stayed with the family for five or six years and came to be loved by all. Several years later, when the children were young adults, the family was discussing the happy period of Anna's services in the household. She had not been seen for the past ten years, but her memory was affectionately held. In the course of the conversation it came out that she was colored. The children were utterly astonished. They insisted that they had never known this fact, or had completely forgotten it if they ever knew it.

Situations of this type are not uncommon. Their occurrence makes us doubt that instinctive fear of the strange has any necessary bearing upon the organi-zation of permanent attitudes.

Dawn of Racial Awareness

The theory of "home atmosphere" is certainly more convincing than the theory of "instinctive roots." But neither theory tells us just when and how the child's ethnic ideas begin to crystallize. Granted that the child possesses relevant emotional equipment, and that the family supplies a constant undertone of acceptance or rejection, anxiety or security, we still need studies that will show how the child's earliest sense of group differences develops. An excellent setting for such a study is a biracial nursery school.

In investigations conducted in this setting, it appears that the earliest age at which children take any note of race is two and a half.

> One white child of this age, sitting for the first time beside a Negro child, said, "Dirty face." It was an unemotional remark, prompted only by his observing a wholly dark-skinned visage—for the first time in his life.

The purely sensory observation that some skins are white, some colored, seems in many cases to be the first trace of racial awareness. Unless there is the quiver of fear of the strange along with this observation, we may say that race difference at first arouses a sense of curiosity and interest—nothing more. The child's world is full of fascinating distinctions. Facial color is simply one of them. Yet we note that even this first perception of racial difference may arouse associations with "clean" and "dirty."

The situation is more insistent by the age of three and a half or four. The sense of dirt still haunts the children. They have been thoroughly scrubbed at home to eradicate dirt. Why then does it exist so darkly on other children? One colored boy, confused concerning his membership, said to his mother, "Wash my face clean; some of the children don't wash well, especially colored children."

> A first grade teacher reports that about one white child in ten refuses to hold hands during games with the solitary Negro child in the classroom. The reason apparently is not "prejudice" in any deep-seated sense. The rejective white children merely complain that Tom has dirty hands and face.

Dr. Goodman's nursery school study shows one particularly revealing result. Negro children are, by and large, "racially aware" earlier than are white children.[7] They tend to be confused, disturbed, and sometimes excited by the problem. Few of them seem to know that they are Negroes. (Even at the age of seven one little Negro girl said to a white playmate, "I'd hate to be colored, wouldn't you?")

The interest and disturbance take many forms. Negro children ask more questions about racial differences; they may fondle the blond hair of a white child; they are often rejective toward Negro dolls. When given a white and Negro doll to play with, they almost uniformly prefer the white doll; many slap the Negro doll and call it dirty or ugly. As a rule, they are more rejective of Negro dolls than are white children. They tend to behave self-consciously when tested for racial awareness. One Negro boy, being shown two baby dolls alike save for color, is asked, "Which one is most like you when you were a baby?"

> Bobby's eyes move from brown to white; he hesitates, squirms, glances at us sidewise—and points to the white doll. Bobby's perceptions relevant to race, feeble and sporadic though they are, have some personal meaning—some ego-reference.

Especially interesting is Dr. Goodman's observation that Negro children tend to be fully as active as white children at the nursery school age. They are on the whole more sociable—particularly those who are rated as high on "racial awareness." A larger proportion of the Negro children are rated as "leaders" in the group. Although we cannot be certain of the meaning of this finding, it may well come from the fact that Negro children are more highly stimulated by the dawning awareness of race. They may be excited by a challenge they do not fully understand, and may seek reassurance through activity and social contacts for the vague threat that hangs over them. The threat comes not from nursery school, where they are secure enough, but from their first contacts with the world outside and from discussions at home, where their Negro parents cannot fail to talk about the matter.

What is so interesting about this full-scale activity at the nursery school age is its contrast to the adult demeanor of many Negroes who are noted for their poise, passivity, apathy, laziness—or whatever the withdrawing reaction may be called. . . . [We] noted that the Negro's conflicts sometimes engender a quietism, a passivity. Many people hold that this "laziness" is a biological trait of Negroes—but in the nursery school we find flatly contradictory evidence. Passivity, when it exists as a Negro attribute, is apparently a learned mode of adjustment. The assertive reaching out of the four-year-old for security and acceptance is ordinarily doomed to failure. After a period of struggle and suffering the passive mode of adjustment may set in.

Why is there, even in the dawning race awareness of four-year-olds, a nebulous sense of inferiority associated with dark skin? A significant part of the answer lies in the similarity between dark pigmentation and dirt. A third of Dr. Goodman's children (both Negro and white) spoke of this matter. Many others no doubt had it in their minds, but did not happen to mention it to the investigators. An additional part of the answer may lie in those subtle forms of learning—not yet fully understood—whereby value-judgments are conveyed to the child. Some parents of white children may, by word or act, have conveyed to their children a vague sense of their rejection of Negroes. If so, the rejection is still only nascent in the four-year-old, for in virtually no case could the investigators find anything they were willing to label "prejudice" at this age level. Some of the Negro parents, too, may have conveyed to their children a sense of the handicaps of people with black skin, even before the children themselves knew their own skin was black.

The initial damage of associated ideas seems inescapable in our culture. Dark skin suggests dirt—even to a four-year-old. To some it may suggest feces.

Brown is not the aesthetic norm in our culture (in spite of the popularity of chocolate). But this initial disadvantage is by no means insuperable. Discriminations in the realm of color are not hard to learn: a scarlet rose is not rejected because it is the color of blood, nor a yellow tulip because it is the color of urine.

To sum up: four-year-olds are normally interested, curious, and appreciative of differences in racial groups. A slight sense of white superiority seems to be growing, largely because of the association of white with cleanness—cleanliness being a value learned very early in life. But contrary associations can be, and sometimes are, easily built up.

> One four-year-old boy was taken by train from Boston to San Francisco. He was enchanted by the friendly Negro porter. For fully two years thereafter he fantasied that he was a porter, and complained bitterly that he was not colored so that he could qualify for the position.

Linguistic Tags: Symbols of Power and Rejection

Earlier we discussed the immensely important role of language in building fences for our mental categories and our emotional responses. This factor is so crucial that we return to it again—as it bears on childhood learning.

In Goodman's study it turned out that fully half the nursery school children knew the word "nigger." Few of them understood what the epithet culturally implies. But they knew that the word was potent. It was forbidden, taboo, and always fetched some type of strong response from the teachers. It was therefore a "power word." Not infrequently in a temper tantrum a child would call his teacher (whether white or colored) a "nigger" or a "dirty nigger." The term expressed an emotion—nothing more. Nor did it always express anger—sometimes merely excitement. Children wildly racing around, shrieking at play might, in order to enhance their orgies, yell "nigger, nigger, nigger." As a strong word it seemed fit to vocalize the violent expenditure of energy under way.

One observer gives an interesting example of aggressive verbalization during wartime play:

> Recently, in a waiting room, I watched three youngsters who sat at a table looking at magazines. Suddenly the smaller boy said: "Here's a soldier and an airplane. He's a Jap." The girl said: "No, he's an American." The little fellow said: "Get him, soldier. Get the Jap." The older boy added, "And Hitler too." "And Mussolini," said the girl. "And the Jews," said the big boy. Then the little fellow started a chant, the others joining in: "The Japs, Hitler, Mussolini, and the Jews! The Japs, Hitler, Mussolini, and the Jews!"[8] It is certain that these children had very little understanding of their bellicose chant. The names of their enemies had an expressive but not a denotative significance.

One little boy was agreeing with his mother, who was warning him never to play with niggers. He said, "No, Mother, I never play with niggers. I only play with white and black children." This child was developing aversion to the term "nigger," without having the slightest idea what the term meant. In other words, the aversion is being set up prior to acquiring a referent.

Other examples could be given of instances where words appear strong and emotionally laden to the child (goy, kike, dago). Only later does he attach the word to a group of people upon whom he can visit the emotions suggested by the word.

We call this process "linguistic precedence in learning." The emotional word has an effect prior to the learning of the referent. Later, the emotional effect becomes attached to the referent.

Before a firm sense of the referent is acquired, the child may go through stages of puzzlement and confusion. This is particularly true because emotional epithets are most likely to be learned when some exciting or traumatic experience is under way. Lasker gives the following example:

> Walking across the playground, a settlement worker found a little Italian boy crying bitterly. She asked him what was the matter. "Hit by Polish boy," the little man repeated several times. Inquiry among the bystanders showed that the offender was not Polish at all. Turning again to her little friend, she said, "You mean, hit by a big naughty boy." But he would not have it thus and went on repeating that he had been hit by a Polish boy. This struck the worker as so curious that she made inquiries of the little fellow's family. She learned that he lived in the same house with a Polish family and that the Italian mother, by constantly quarreling with her Polish neighbor, had put into the heads of her children the notion that "Polish" and "bad" were synonymous terms.[9]

When this lad finally learns who Poles are, he already will have a strong prejudice against them. Here is a clear case of linguistic precedence in learning.

Children sometimes confess their perplexity concerning emotional tags. They seem to be groping for proper referents. Trager and Radke, from their work with kindergarten, first- and second-grade children, give several examples:[10]

Anna   When I was coming out of the dressing room, Peter called me a dirty Jew.

Teacher   Why did you say that, Peter?

Peter (earnestly)   I didn't say it for spite. I was only playing.

Johnny (helping Louis pull off his leggings)   A man called my father a goy.

Louis   What's a goy?

Johnny   I think everybody around here is a goy. But not me. I'm Jewish.

> On being called a "white cracker" by a Negro boy in the class, the teacher said to her class, "I am puzzled by the meaning of two words. Do you know what 'white cracker' means?"
> A number of vague answers were received from the children, one being "You're supposed to say it when you're mad."

Even while the child is having difficulty with words, they have a great power over him. To him they are often a type of magic, of verbal realism. . . .

> A little boy in the South was playing with the child of the washer-woman. Everything was going smoothly until a neighbor white child called over the fence, "Look out, you'll catch it."
> "Catch what?" asked the first white child.
> "Catch the black. You'll get colored too."
> Just this assertion (reminding the child, no doubt, of expressions such as "catch the measles") frightened him. He deserted his colored companion then and there, and never played with him again.

Children often cry if they are called names. Their self-esteem is wounded by any epithet: naughty, dirty, harum-scarum, nigger, dago, Jap, or what not. To escape this verbal realism of early childhood, they often reassure themselves, when they are a little older, with the self-restorative jingle: Sticks and stones may break my bones, but names can never hurt me. But it takes a few years for them to learn that a name is not a thing-in-itself. As we saw earlier verbal realism may never be fully shaken off. The rigidity of linguistic categories may continue in adult thinking. To some adults "communist" or "Jew" is a dirty word—and a dirty thing—an indissoluble unity, as it may be to a child.

The First Stage in Learning Prejudice

Janet, six years of age, was trying hard to integrate her obedience to her mother with her daily social contacts. One day she came running home and asked, "Mother, what is the name of the children I am supposed to hate?"

Janet's wistful question leads us into a theoretical summary of the present chapter.

Janet is stumbling at the threshold of some abstraction. She wishes to form the right category. She intends to oblige her mother by hating the right people when she can find out who they are.

In this situation we suspect the preceding stages in Janet's developmental history:

1. She identifies with the mother, or at least she strongly craves the mother's affection and approval. We may imagine that the home is not "permissive" in atmosphere, but somewhat stern and critical. Janet may have found that she must be on her toes to please her parent. Otherwise she will suffer rejection or punishment. In any event, she has developed a habit of obedience.
2. While she has apparently no strong fear of strangers at the present time, she has learned to be circumspect. Experiences of insecurity with people outside the family circle may be a factor in her present effort to define her circle of loyalties.
3. She undoubtedly has gone through the initial period of curiosity and interest in racial and ethnic differences. She knows now that human beings are clustered into groups—that there are important

distinctions if only she can identify them. In the case of Negro and white the visibility factor has helped her. But then she discovered that subtler differences were also important; Jews somehow differed from gentiles; wops from Americans; doctors from salesmen. She is now aware of group differences, though not yet clear concerning all the relevant cues.

4. She has encountered the stage of linguistic precedence in learning. In fact, she is now in this stage. She knows that group X (she knows neither its name nor its identity) is somehow hate-worthy. She already has the emotional meaning but lacks the referential meaning. She seeks now to integrate the proper content with the emotion. She wishes to define her category so as to make her future behavior conform to her mother's desires. As soon as she has the linguistic tag at her command, she will be like the little Italian boy for whom "Polish" and "bad" were synonymous terms.

Up to the present, Janet's development marks what we might call the first stage of ethnocentric learning. Let us christen it the period of *pregeneralized* learning. This label is not altogether satisfactory, but none better describes the potpourri of factors listed above. The term draws attention primarily to the fact that the child has not yet generalized after the fashion of adults. He does not quite understand what a Jew is, what a Negro is, or what his own attitude toward them should be. He does not know even what *he* is—in any consistent sense. He may think he is an American only when he is playing with his toy soldiers (this type of categorizing was not uncommon in wartime). It is not only in ethnic matters that thoughts are prelogical from an adult point of view. A little girl may not think that her mother is her mother when the latter is working at the office; and may not regard her mother as an officeworker when she is at home tending the family.[11]

The child seems to live his mental life in specific contexts. What exists here and now makes up the only reality. The strange-man-who-knocks-at-the-door is something to be feared. It does not matter if he is a delivery man. The Negro boy at school is dirty. He is not a member of a race.

Such independent experiences in concrete procession seem to furnish the child's mind. His pregeneralized thinking (from the adult's point of view) has sometimes been labeled "global," or "syncretistic," or "prelogical."[12]

Now the place of linguistic tags in the course of mental development is crucial. They stand for adult abstractions, for logical generalizations of the sort that mature adults accept. The child learns the tags before he is fully ready to apply them to the adult categories. They prepare him for prejudice. But the process takes time. Only after much fumbling—in the manner of Janet and other children described in this chapter—will the proper categorizing take place.

The Second Stage in Learning Prejudice

As soon as Janet's mother gives a clear answer to Janet, she will in all probability enter a second period of prejudice—one that we may call the period of *total rejection*. Suppose the mother answers, "I told you not to play with

Negro children. They are dirty; they have diseases; and they will hurt you. Now don't let me catch you at it." If Janet by now has learned to distinguish Negroes from other groups, even from the dark-skinned Mexican children, or Italians—in other words, if she now has the adult category in mind—she will undoubtedly reject all Negroes, in all circumstances, and with considerable feeling.

The research of Blake and Dennis well illustrates the point.[13] It will be recalled that these investigators studied Southern white children in the fourth and fifth grades (ten- and eleven-year-olds). They asked such questions as, "Which are more musical—Negroes or white people?" "Which are more clean?"—and many questions of a similar type. These children had, by the age of ten, learned to reject the Negro category *totally*. No favorable quality was ascribed to Negroes more often than to whites. In effect, whites had all the virtues; Negroes, none.

While this totalized rejection certainly starts earlier (in many children it will be found by the age of seven or eight), it seems to reach its ethnocentric peak in early puberty. First- and second-grade children often elect to play with, or sit beside, a child of different race or ethnic membership. This friendliness usually disappears in the fifth grade. At that time children choose their own group almost exclusively. Negroes select Negroes, Italians select Italians, and so on.[14]

As children grow older, they normally lose this tendency to total rejection and overgeneralization. Blake and Dennis found that in the 12th grade the white youth ascribed several favorable stereotypes to Negroes. They considered them more musical, more easygoing, better dancers.

The Third Stage

Thus, after a period of *total rejection,* a stage of *differentiation* sets in. The prejudices grow less totalized. Escape clauses are written into the attitude in order to make it more rational and more acceptable to the individual. One says, "Some of my best friends are Jews." Or, "I am not prejudiced against Negroes—I always loved my black Mammy." The child who is first learning adult categories of rejection is not able to make such gracious exceptions. It takes him the first six to eight years of his life to learn total rejection, and another six years or so to modify it. The actual adult creed in his culture is complex indeed. It allows for (and in many ways encourages) ethnocentrism. At the same time, one must give lip service to democracy and equality, or at least ascribe some good qualities to the minority group and somehow plausibly justify the remaining disapproval that one expresses. It takes the child well into adolescence to learn the peculiar double-talk appropriate to prejudice in a democracy.

Around the age of eight, children often *talk* in a highly prejudiced manner. They have learned their categories and their totalized rejection. But the rejection is chiefly verbal. While they may damn the Jews, the wops, the Catholics, they may still *behave* in a relatively democratic manner. They may play with them even while they talk against them. The "total rejection" is chiefly a verbal matter.

Now when the teaching of the school takes effect, the child learns a new verbal norm: he must talk democratically. He must profess to regard all races and creeds as equal. Hence, by the age of 12, we may find *verbal* acceptance, but *behavioral* rejection. By this age the prejudices have finally affected conduct, even while the verbal, democratic norms are beginning to take effect.

The paradox, then, is that younger children may talk undemocratically, but behave democratically, whereas children in puberty may talk (at least in school) democratically but behave with true prejudice. By the age of 15, considerable skill is shown in imitating the adult pattern. Prejudiced talk and democratic talk are reserved for appropriate occasions, and rationalizations are ready for whatever occasions require them. Even conduct is varied according to circumstances. One may be friendly with a Negro in the kitchen, but hostile to a Negro who comes to the front door. Double-dealing, like double-talk, is hard to learn. It takes the entire period of childhood and much of adolescence to master the art of ethnocentrism.

Notes and References

1. D. B. Harris, H. G. Gough, W. E. Martin. Children's ethnic attitudes: II, Relationship to parental beliefs concerning child training. *Child Development,* 1950, 21, 169–181.

2. These two contrasting styles of child training are described more fully by D. P. Ausubel in *Ego Development and the Personality Disorders.* New York: Grune & Stratton, 1952.

3. The most extensive evidence is contained in researches conducted at the University of California. See: T. W. Adorno, Else Frenkel-Brunswik, D. J. Levinson, R. N. Sanford, *The Authoritarian Personality,* New York: Harper, 1950; also, Else Frenkel-Brunswik, Patterns of social and cognitive outlook in children and parents, *American Journal of Orthopsychiatry,* 1951, 21, 543–558.

4. N. W. Ackerman and Marie Jahoda. *Anti-Semitism and Emotional Disorder.* New York: Harper, 1950, 45.

5. *Ibid.,* 85.

6. H. Bonner. Sociological aspects of paranoia. *American Journal of Sociology,* 1950, 56, 255–262.

7. Mary E. Goodman. *Race Awareness in Young Children.* Cambridge: Addison-Wesley, 1952. Other studies have confirmed the fact that Negro children are race-aware before white children: e.g., Ruth Horowitz, Racial aspects of self-identification in nursery school children, *Journal of Psychology,* 1939, 7, 91–99.

8. Mildred M. Eakin. *Getting Acquainted with Jewish Neighbors.* New York: Macmillan, 1944.

9. B. Lasker. *Race Attitudes in Children.* New York: Henry Holt, 1929, 98.

10. Helen G. Trager and Marian Radke. Early childhood airs its views. *Educational Leadership,* 1947, 5, 16–23.

11. E. L. Hartley, M. Rosenbaum, and S. Schwartz. (Children's perceptions of ethnic group membership. *Journal of Psychology,* 1948, 26, 387–398.

12. *Cf.* H. Werner. *Comparative Psychology of Mental Development.* Chicago: Follett, 1948. J. Piaget. *The Child's Conception of the World.* New York: Harcourt, Brace, 1929, 236. G. Murphy. Personality. New York: Harper, 1947, 336.

13. R. Blake and W. Dennis. The development of stereotypes concerning the Negro. *Journal of Abnormal and Social Psychology,* 1943, 38, 525–531.

14. J. H. Criswell. A sociometric study of race cleavage in the classroom. *Archives of Psychology,* 1939, No. 235.

EXPLORING THE ISSUE

Is Race Prejudice a Product of Group Position?

Critical Thinking and Reflection

1. What is Blumer's group position thesis?
2. Illustrate the relationship between group position and the acquisition of race prejudice with examples.
3. How does Allport explain prejudice?
4. How are racial identity and race prejudice related?
5. What is the distinction between individual prejudice and institutional prejudice?
6. To what issues of race relations can the group position thesis be applied? Explain.
7. Compare and contrast the psychological approach to prejudice with the sociological approach?

Is There Common Ground

Allport and Blumer both are involved in research to determine how prejudice is acquired. Clearly, there is no one theory that offers a complete explanation of prejudice. However, when we consider theories together or debate differing positions advanced in this issue, we gain insight and understanding. The basic dilemma is whether or not prejudice results from personality traits best revealed through psychological theories, or whether prejudice is more social and cultural, reflecting Blumer's idea of group position. Utilizing both approaches will help us see how social learning takes place. At this point, we can ask another question concerning the relationship between attitudes and behavior.

To study race prejudice is to consider the role of attitudes and individual feelings in one's life. Still unclear to us is the relationship of attitudes to behavior. Does race prejudice lead to discriminatory practice? Does the prejudiced person behave differently from the nonprejudiced person? Sociologist Robert Merton suggests that prejudice and discrimination are linked in ways that are determined by different social environments. He developed categories to demonstrate that one can be prejudiced and not discriminate, or one cannot be prejudiced but nevertheless discriminate.

Additional Resources

Adorno, Theodore. 1950. *The Authoritarian Personality* (Harper & Row).

Allport, Gordon. 1979. *The Nature of Prejudice* (Perseus).

Ausdale, Van Debra and Joe Feagin. 2001. *The First R: How Children Learn Race and Racism* (Rowman & Littlefield Publishers).

Clark, Kenneth. 1963. *Prejudice and Your Child* (Beacon Press).

Doob, Christopher Bates. 1996. *Racism: An American Cauldron* (HarperCollins).

Duckett, John. 1992. "Psychology and Prejudice: A Historical Analysis and Integrative Framework," *American Psychologist.*

Jacobs, Bruce A. 1999. *Race Manners: Navigating the Minefield between Black and White Americans* (Arcade).

Pettigrew, Thomas. 1980. "Prejudice," in Stephen Thernstrom, ed., *Harvard Encyclopedia of Ethnic Groups* (Harvard University Press).

Porter, Judith. 1971. *Black Child, White Child: The Development of Racial Attitudes* (Harvard University Press).

Sinkler, George. 1972. *The Racial Attitudes of American Presidents: From Abraham Lincoln to Theodore Roosevelt* (Anchor).

Williams, Patricia. 1995. *The Rooster's Egg: On the Persistence of Prejudice* (Harvard University Press).

Documentary Films

Elliot, Jane. 1995. *Blue-Eyed* (California Newsreel).

Griffith, D.W. 1915. *The Birth of a Nation* (Epoch Producing Co.).

Riggs, Marlon. 1987. *Ethnic Notions* (California Newsreel).

Riggs, Marlon. 1991. *Color Adjustment* (California Newsreel).

Wah, L.M. 1994. *The Color of Fear* (Stir Fry Productions).

This website offers "educational resources and information on prejudice, discrimination, multiculturalism and diversity." Its goal is to promote tolerance and limit bias in society. Basically, the site is organized to supplement *Understanding Prejudice and Discrimination* (McGraw-Hill), however, all pages and features of the site are free and open to anyone.

www.understandingprejudice.org/

The Teaching Tolerance website is a project of the Southern Poverty Law Center. It offers a magazine, *Teaching Tolerance*, along with other publications dealing with tolerance appropriate for children up to high school. It is useful for college students in that they can read firsthand how tolerance is taught in the classroom.

www.tolerance.org/

This website was created by two social psychologists, Steven Stroessner of Barnard College and Catherine Good of Baruch College, CUNY. It is a resource for faculty, students, and the general public interested in learning about stereotype threat. The site contains summaries of research, an extensive bibliography, and information on stereotypes, especially the negative effects of stereotypes.

www.reducingstereotypethreat.org/

ISSUE 10

Does the Digital Divide Reflect American Racism?

YES: **Susan P. Crawford,** from "The New Digital Divide," *The New York Times* (December 3, 2011)

NO: **Larry Schweikart,** from "Race, Culture, and the 'Digital Divide,'" *Freeman* (vol. 52, no. 5, pp. 44–47, May 2002)

Learning Outcomes

After reading this issue, the student should be able to:

- Know what is meant by "the digital divide."
- Explain the important factors that determine changes in the digital divide.
- Explain the historical context of the digital divide.
- Assess the role of government and policy concerning high-speed access to the Internet.
- Understand issues of social inequity in an information-driven world.
- Debate the underlying causes of the digital divide.

ISSUE SUMMARY

YES: Susan P. Crawford, professor of law at the Benjamin N. Cordozo School of Law and former special assistant to President Obama for science, technology, and innovation policy, argues that there is a new digital divide that places African Americans and Latinos at the risk of being left behind the Internet revolution.

NO: Larry Schweikart, professor of history at the University of Dayton and conservative writer, asserts that "the racial digital divide is largely a myth." He points out that African Americans, when including the workplace, have as equal access as whites to computers. However, where a divide occurs is in home computer ownership.

The term "digital divide" first became part of the public discourse in 1996. The term's initial descriptive use was to highlight what was labeled as "new illiteracy," computer illiteracy, reflective of the fact that at that time only 3 percent of the nation's schools were connected to the Internet. In 2000, *CQ Researcher* reported that, ". . . more than 90 percent of K-12 public schools are on the Internet." Finding funds for computers in schools was one part of addressing the problem of the new illiteracy. The other problem was connecting to the Internet. "Net Days" were held in many school districts across the country whereby volunteers turned out to connect schools, libraries, and other government offices to the Internet. Now, 12 years into the twenty-first century, the Internet has become a powerful tool for education and job creation. Clearly, building this new part of the telecommunications infrastructure (similar to the power grid, roads, and rail lines) is an important part of America's competitive future in the global economy. It has led to a debate over the role of government regulations in planning and building telecommunications for the future. Thus, we see the classic liberal versus conservative approaches to problems and issues related to America's digital future. Conservatives, like Larry Schweikart, anticipate that the market will lead to a more widespread delivery of services and, eventually, the digital divide will shrink. Susan Crawford, on the other hand, points to a "new digital divide."

The digital divide, now viewed as the inequity of home Internet access among different groups, persists although some of the early technological gaps have closed. It is not yet clear why those gaps have closed. Some argue that the free-market system will eventually close the divide. Others stress the need for government programs to bridge the digital divide.

As difficult as it may be for college students to believe, 40 percent of Americans still lack high-speed Internet access despite President Obama's announcement in early 2011 that he wanted to usher every American into the "digital age" by increasing broadband access across the nation. Although the divide can apply to any social group including those determined by age, education, region, and income, for the purposes of this issue, the digital divide will apply to racial and ethnic groups. Hence, for us the digital divide describes the racial and ethnic gap in access to technological resources. The importance of the computer, its role in public education or as a necessary home product to connect to the Internet, cannot be overstated.

A report in *The Journal of Blacks in Higher Education* (Winter 2004–2005) points out that despite the relatively equal access of computers in schools, blacks remain far behind whites in computer usage at home (61 percent of white households in contrast to 37 percent of black households). Further, a large gap persists when Internet access is considered with whites having almost twice as much access as blacks.

One of the uses of a computer for young students is working on papers and assignments. However, getting access to the Internet is another. Students who can e-mail (and text and use Twitter) and easily connect to the Internet become much more aware of opportunities ranging from research-topic websites to SAT-prep websites. Now, imagine the disadvantages of students who do not have home computers. Thus, blacks and Latinos communicate with each other at a rapid rate via text messaging and cell phones. However, those same students are much less likely than white students to complete research papers, take a SAT-prep course, or complete a college search online. As President Obama has said, "This [the issue] isn't just about a faster Internet or finding a friend on Facebook, it's about connecting every corner of America to the digital age." Basic computer skills are a requirement for practically every job today.

In 2010, 35 percent of blacks and 33 percent of Latinos did not have a home computer, compared to 20 percent of whites and 14 percent of Asians. Computer usage and broadband adoption are strongly correlated with income and education. A Department of Commerce report, "Exploring the Digital Nation: Computer and Internet Use at Home," points out that lower income families, people with less education, those with disabilities, blacks, Hispanics, and rural residents generally lagged the national average in both broadband adoption and computer use.

Addressing this issue with its rapidly shifting data on Internet use, Larry Schweikart suggests that the digital divide is largely a myth. Historically, he points out, there have always been gaps in technology. There were haves and have-nots in the use of farming technology, television ownership, automobile ownership, and telephone service. However, Schweikart argues that those technological gaps have been relatively transient. Eventually, like telephone use, the have and have-not gap in computer ownership and Internet access will be leveled. Thus, he argues that the attention given to the digital divide is, in large part, the creation of a myth.

Recently, *The Journal for Blacks in Higher Education* reported that, "A new study by the National Urban League Policy Institute has found a narrowing of the digital divide in access to broadband Internet services" (May 17, 2012). The new study reveals that 67 percent of whites have access to broadband Internet service compared to 56 percent of blacks. Compare these numbers with a 2009 study that found 65 percent of whites and only 46 percent of blacks had broadband Internet access. On the surface, there appears to be a narrowing of the digital divide as blacks have increased access and use of the Internet. However, the researchers point out that the narrowing of the gap is due to the fact that African Americans are more likely than whites to use smartphones. For many blacks, smartphones are their only access to the Internet. However, "whites are more likely to have broadband access through computer terminals at home."

Susan Crawford argues that despite inexpensive web access that has "brought millions to the Internet," racial minorities still lag behind whites in wired Internet access at home. Indeed, computer ownership has increased among all race and ethnic groups as has the ownership of technological devices. However, Crawford focuses on a "new digital divide," one in which high-speed access to the Internet has resulted in a racial and ethnic gap. She points out, in agreement with the JBHE report, that looking at ownership of the smartphone distorts the digital divide issue. The smartphone is not a substitute for wired access to the Internet. Her position is illustrated with the examples of online job applications and online education, which are much more difficult, and sometimes impossible, to access "from a remote location using wireless."

According to Crawford, by 2040 African Americans and Latinos will compose more than half of the American labor force. These are the very groups who are at risk in being left behind in the Internet revolution. Why are there such uneven rates of technology use by different racial groups? Can the inequality be attributed to poverty and underfunded schools? How can we explain the new digital divide? The good news is that broadband Internet is spreading rapidly.

The introduction of the digital divide as a key issue in race and ethnicity gives us an opportunity to raise related concerns stemming from the Internet Revolution, especially the use of social media. One of these concerns is the role of race in social media identity management. The early days of the Internet were filled with utopian visions that race could disappear online. A *New Yorker* cartoon from the early 1990s showed a dog sitting at a computer saying to another dog, "On the Internet, nobody knows you're a dog." However, sociologists and communications professors such as Peter Chow-White, co-author of *Race after the Internet*, point out that as long as structural inequities in society exist, they will be reflected on the Internet as they are in other social institutions. Danah Boyd, of the Harvard Berkman Center for Internet and Society, pointed to a form of "white flight" from MySpace to Facebook when the latter went through a period of rapid expansion in 2006–07. It is unclear whether this was due to covert racism or invisible factors contributing to self-segregation. What is clear is that online behavior patterns resembled those of society for all the races. Currently, Facebook data reports that 11 percent of all its U.S. users are black and 9 percent are Latino.

To grasp the implications of this issue, students are encouraged to consider the following questions: Is this underrepresentation of blacks and Latinos due to issues of poverty and income inequality? What role do underfunded schools play in this inequity? Why are blacks and Latinos moving so quickly to mobile web access? Will mobile web access be the great equalizer?

YES

Susan P. Crawford

The New Digital Divide

For the second year in a row, the Monday after Thanksgiving—so-called Cyber Monday, when online retailers offer discounts to lure holiday shoppers—was the biggest sales day of the year, totaling some $1.25 billion and overwhelming the sales figures racked up by brick-and-mortar stores three days before, on Black Friday, the former perennial record-holder.

Such numbers may seem proof that America is, indeed, online. But they mask an emerging division, one that has worrisome implications for our economy and society. Increasingly, we are a country in which only the urban and suburban well-off have truly high-speed Internet access, while the rest—the poor and the working class—either cannot afford access or use restricted wireless access as their only connection to the Internet. As our jobs, entertainment, politics and even health care move online, millions are at risk of being left behind.

Telecommunications, which in theory should bind us together, has often divided us in practice. Until the late 20th century, the divide split those with phone access and those without it. Then it was the Web: in 1995 the Commerce Department published its first look at the "digital divide," finding stark racial, economic and geographic gaps between those who could get online and those who could not.

"While a standard telephone line can be an individual's pathway to the riches of the Information Age," the report said, "a personal computer and modem are rapidly becoming the keys to the vault." If you were white, middle-class and urban, the Internet was opening untold doors of information and opportunity. If you were poor, rural or a member of a minority group, you were fast being left behind.

Over the last decade, cheap Web access over phone lines brought millions to the Internet. But in recent years the emergence of services like video-on-demand, online medicine and Internet classrooms have redefined the state of the art: they require reliable, truly high-speed connections, the kind available almost exclusively from the nation's small number of very powerful cable companies. Such access means expensive contracts, which many Americans simply cannot afford. While we still talk about "the" Internet, we increasingly have two separate access marketplaces: high-speed wired and second-class wireless. High-speed access is a superhighway for those who can afford it, while racial minorities and poorer and rural Americans must make do with a bike path.

Just over 200 million Americans have high-speed, wired Internet access at home, and almost two-thirds of them get it through their local cable company. The connections are truly high-speed: based on a technological standard called Docsis 2.0 or 3.0, they can reach up to 105 megabits per second, fast enough to download a music album in three seconds.

These customers are the targets for the next generation of Internet services, technology that will greatly enhance their careers, education and quality of life. Within a decade, patients at home will be able to speak with their doctors online and thus get access to lower-cost, higher-quality care. High-speed connections will also allow for distance education through real-time video-conferencing; already, thousands of high school students are earning diplomas via virtual classrooms.

Households will soon be able to monitor their energy use via smart-grid technology to keep costs and carbon dioxide emissions down. Even the way that wired America works will change: many job applications are already possible only online; soon, job interviews will be held by way of videoconference, saving cost and time.

But the rest of America will most likely be left out of all this. Millions are still offline completely, while others can afford only connections over their phone lines or via wireless smartphones. They can thus expect even lower-quality health services, career opportunities, education and entertainment options than they already receive. True, Americans of all stripes are adopting smartphones at breakneck speeds; in just over four years the number has jumped from about 10 percent to about 35 percent; among Hispanics and African-Americans, it's roughly 44 percent. Most of the time, smartphone owners also have wired access at home: the Pew Internet and American Life Project recently reported that 59 percent of American adults with incomes above $75,000 had a smartphone, and a 2010 study by the Federal Communications Commission found that more than 90 percent of people at that income level had wired high-speed Internet access at home.

But that is not true for lower-income and minority Americans. According to numbers released last month by the Department of Commerce, a mere 4 out of every 10 households with annual household incomes below $25,000 in 2010 reported having wired Internet access at home, compared with the vast majority—93 percent—of households with incomes exceeding $100,000. Only slightly more than half of all African-American and Hispanic households (55 percent and 57 percent, respectively) have wired Internet access at home, compared with 72 percent of whites.

These numbers are likely to grow even starker as the 30 percent of Americans without any kind of Internet access come online. When they do, particularly if the next several years deliver subpar growth in personal income, they will probably go for the only option that is at all within their reach: wireless smartphones. A wired high-speed Internet plan might cost $100 a month; a smartphone plan might cost half that, often with a free or heavily discounted phone thrown in.

The problem is that smartphone access is not a substitute for wired. The vast majority of jobs require online applications, but it is hard to type up a résumé on a hand-held device; it is hard to get a college degree from a remote location using wireless. Few people would start a business using only a wireless connection.

It is not just inconvenient—many of these activities are physically impossible via a wireless connection. By their nature, the airwaves suffer from severe capacity limitations: the same five gigabytes of data that might take nine minutes to download over a high-speed cable connection would take an hour and 15 minutes to travel over a wireless connection.

Even if a smartphone had the technical potential to compete with wired, users would still be hampered by the monthly data caps put in place by AT&T and Verizon, by far the largest wireless carriers in America. For example, well before finishing the download of a single two-hour, high-definition movie from iTunes over a 4G wireless network, a typical subscriber would hit his or her monthly cap and start incurring $10 per gigabyte in overage charges. If you think this is a frivolous concern, for "movie" insert an equally large data stream, like "business meeting."

Public libraries are taking up the slack and buckling under the strain. Nearly half of librarians say that their connections are insufficient to meet patrons' needs. And it is hard to imagine conducting a job interview in a library.

In the past, the cost of new technologies has dropped over time, and eventually many Americans could afford a computer and a modem to access a standard phone line. Phone service—something 96 percent of Americans have—was sold at regulated rates and the phone companies were forced to allow competing Internet access providers to share their lines.

But there is reason to believe this time is different. Today, the problem is about affording unregulated high-speed Internet service—provided, in the case of cable, by a few for-profit companies with very little local competition and almost no check on their prices. They have to bear all the cost of infra-structure and so have no incentive to expand into rural areas, where potential customers are relatively few and far between. (The Federal Communications Commission recently announced a plan to convert subsidies that once sup-ported basic rural telephone services into subsidies for basic Internet access.)

The bigger problem is the lack of competition in cable markets. Though there are several large cable companies nationwide, each dominates its own fragmented kingdom of local markets: Comcast is the only game in Philadelphia, while Time Warner dominates Cleveland. That is partly because it is so expensive to lay down the physical cables, and companies, having paid for those networks, guard them jealously, clustering their operations and spending tens of millions of dollars to lobby against laws that might oblige them to share their infrastructure.

Cable's only real competition comes from Verizon's FiOS fiber-optic serv-ice, which can provide speeds up to 150 megabits per second. But FiOS is avail-able to only about 10 percent of households. AT&T's U-verse, which has about 4 percent of the market, cannot provide comparable speeds because, while it uses fiber-optic cable to reach neighborhoods, the signal switches to slower copper lines to connect to houses. And don't even think about DSL, which carries just a fraction of the data needed to handle the services that cable users take for granted.

Lacking competition from other cable companies or alternate delivery technologies, each of the country's large cable distributors has the ability to raise prices in its region for high-speed Internet services. Those who can still afford it are paying higher and higher rates for the same quality of service, while those who cannot are turning to wireless.

It doesn't have to be this way, as a growing number of countries demonstrate. The Organization for Economic Cooperation and Development ranks America 12th among developed nations for wired Internet access, and it is safe to assume that high prices have played a role in lowering our standing. So America, the country that invented the Internet and still leads the world in telecommunications innovation, is lagging far behind in actual use of that technology.

The answer to this puzzle is regulatory policy. Over the last 10 years, we have deregulated high-speed Internet access in the hope that competition among providers would protect consumers. The result? We now have neither a functioning competitive market for high-speed wired Internet access nor government oversight.

By contrast, governments that have intervened in high-speed Internet markets have seen higher numbers of people adopting the technology, doing so earlier and at lower subscription charges. Many of these countries have required telecommunications providers to sell access to parts of their networks to competitors at regulated rates, so that competition can lower prices.

Meanwhile, they are working toward, or already have, fiber-optic networks that will be inexpensive, standardized, ubiquitous and equally fast for uploading and downloading. Many of those countries, not only advanced ones like Sweden and Japan but also less-developed ones like Portugal and Russia, are already well on their way to wholly replacing their standard telephone connections with state-of-the-art fiber-optic connections that will even further reduce the cost to users, while significantly improving access speeds.

The only thing close is FiOS. But, according to Diffraction Analysis, a research firm, it costs six times as much as comparable service in Hong Kong, five times as much as in Paris and two and a half times as much as in Amsterdam. When it comes to the retail cost of fiber access in America, we do about as well as Istanbul.

The new digital divide raises important questions about social equity in an information-driven world. But it is also a matter of protecting our economic future. Thirty years from now, African-Americans and Latinos, who are at the greatest risk of being left behind in the Internet revolution, will be more than half of our work force. If we want to be competitive in the global economy, we need to make sure every American has truly high-speed wired access to the Internet for a reasonable cost.

Race, Culture, and the "Digital Divide"

Prior to the September 11 attacks and the stock market slump, one of the hottest policy issues debated by technology scholars was the so-called racial "digital divide," a term concocted to portray "haves and have nots" in the world of the Internet. The paper "Bridging the Digital Divide: The Impact of Race on Computer Access and Internet Use" is typical: "[S]ome social scientists are beginning to examine carefully the policy implications of current demographic patterns of Internet access and usage."[1] Former Vice President Al Gore suggested several policy proposals for closing the "digital divide," and President Bill Clinton's "Call to Action for American Education" proposed universal Internet access for students.

Studying race or group behavior is dubious at best; in today's climate, it's even dangerous, since racial groupings are used by collectivists to serve a political agenda. Nevertheless, it is useful to examine the claims being made. Thomas Sowell has cautioned that culture, for example, is a far more important factor in economic activity than race, and in the case of the digital divide, the "experts" may be examining racial characteristics when they should be considering cultural effects. There is also substantial new data showing that Americans are racially intermarrying more frequently. The Census Bureau threw up its hands in frustration trying to count mixed-race Americans in the last census.

That said, let's examine the new arguments about the digital divide, pretending for a moment that race was a factor in computer access and use.

First, although many readers may have trouble recalling a time without computer technology, it is still relatively new. Nevertheless, the Internet has filtered through the social strata from the top down faster than any other technology in history. According to Joel Kotkin and Ross DeVol's working paper for the Milken Institute, here is how fast selected products spread to 25 percent of the population:

> Internet usage in 2001 reached 176 million Americans, 62 percent of the population, according to one Nielsen survey, up from 57 percent just a year earlier. Still, "digital dividers" sound the alarm. Jesse Jackson claimed that differences in Internet use between whites and blacks are "classic apartheid."[2] Research shows that differences in Internet use

Schweikart, Larry. From *The Freeman: Ideas on Liberty*, Vol. 52, No. 5, May 2002, pp. 44–47. Copyright © 2002 by Foundation for Economic Education. Reprinted by permission.

have little to do with income. Instead, computer access has played the pivotal role, according to Thomas Novak and Donna Hoffman of Vanderbilt University.[3]

To solve the "problem" (with "problem" defined as any differences between groups), obviously all the government needs to do is to make sure that regardless of income, everyone has access to a computer.

Not so fast. Other evidence shows that blacks in high numbers have computer access at work—virtually equal to that of whites—and that if one holds income and education constant, blacks are more likely to have computer access at work than whites.[4] This statistic makes sense considering that blacks, in far higher proportions than whites, work for state, local, or the federal government, where computers are provided.

Does education explain the "divide"? There appears to be a link between education and computer access, but a tenuous one. Both British and American studies have shown that more highly educated people tend to use the Internet more, although the notion that pinheaded "friendless nerds" comprise the majority of "surfers" is baseless: one U.K. study found that "internet users lead more sociable lives than non-surfers."[5] However, before researchers jump the gun to claim a link between education levels and Net use, existing studies would have to go much further to hold constant the quality of education in racial comparisons, something that is seldom done.

Divide Myth

When the rhetoric is stripped away, it appears that the racial "digital divide" is largely a myth, and to the extent it does exist, it is somewhat correlated to education and somewhat correlated to access to computers. Aha, say the "digital dividers," maybe racial groups don't have equal access to computers.

Computer access can mean having a computer at work or at home, but researchers have tried to argue that having access only at work won't cut it. Where a sharper divide occurs is in home computer ownership; 44 percent of whites have access to home computers compared to 29 percent of blacks. For this reason, at least one study claims, whites are more likely to use the Internet for information on a regular basis.[6] Net-use rates correlate to having a home computer and a computer at work. The Vanderbilt study found that this was just about the only instance in which "race matters"—when students lacked a computer at home. "White, but not African American students," wrote the researchers, "are able to take advantage of non-traditional access locations including homes of friends and relatives with home computers, and libraries and community centers with Internet access."[7] Even so, the study admitted more blacks were on line than is popularly thought and that the number was growing. As blacks became more familiar with the Internet, the authors concluded (apparently somewhat glumly), they would "catch up" to whites.

These findings pull the rug out from under the advocates of government provision of computer "access" through schools and public facilities. The key is not "access," but attitude. Clearly, having access to public education did not close the "education gap." Access to income-maintenance and welfare programs did not close the "income gap." And now, with large numbers of computers at schools and public facilities, the researchers claim (surprise!) that free computers in public settings have not significantly closed the "digital gap." Of course, to some extent, big-government types will use these studies for the perverse claim that we need to provide computers to low-income people in their homes. Indeed, in supporting tax-funded computer access for the homeless, the Digital Divide Network claimed that "Americans have long agreed that certain communications tools are so fundamental that their provision should not be left to the vagaries of the marketplace alone."[8]

Cultural Differences

The "digital divide" involves cultural differences and experience levels that no government policies can address. For instance, another Vanderbilt study "found interesting differences in media use between whites and African Americans that also deserve further probing. For example, although the rate of home PC ownership among African Americans is flat or even decreasing, their rates of cable and satellite dish penetration are increasing dramatically. At a minimum, our results suggest that African Americans may make better immediate prospects than whites for Internet access through cable modems and satellite technology."[9]

A British researcher found that there is a "huge divide" between those who surf the Net and those who do not. They differ in many respects, including income and education. Moreover, surfers "simply watch less television."[10] Once again, the "experts" are in a quandary, because as far as I know, races don't demonstrate broadly different patterns of television viewing—some, to be sure, but even then, further analysis of the data points back to cultural, not racial, differences.

Are there differences in how races use the Internet? A broad study done in August 2000 by the Pew Internet & American Life Project, found significant differences in Net usage between blacks and whites. For example, blacks were 69 percent more likely than whites to have listened to music online, 45 percent more likely than online whites to play a game, and 12 percent more likely to "browse just for fun." They were also nearly 40 percent more likely to have looked for information about jobs online and 65 percent more likely to seek religious information. But whites were slightly more likely to obtain financial information, and they purchased more products over the Internet.[11] However, the races were approximately equal in their use of the Net to get political news or information.

Contrast white and black use of the Web with Asians, who obtain news from it at an even higher rate than whites, download music more often than blacks, and get political information more often than either blacks or whites. Asians are also more likely than blacks to search for jobs and conduct work-related research on the Net, or to buy or sell stocks online than whites. They are, however, less likely than blacks to search for health information or listen to music online.[12]

The implications of these findings suggest trouble for those who think they can eliminate whatever "digital divide" that may exist through government programs. Buried in these studies is evidence that the members of racial or ethnic groups use the Internet differently—whites more for business and product purchases, blacks more for entertainment and spiritual growth, Asians for work research and political news.

That the patterns of technology use across racial and ethnic groups are not uniform should come as no surprise. Sowell has pointed out that ethnic groups have had different paths to economic success. He has documented the propensity of the Irish, for example, to dominate police and fire departments in eastern urban areas, seeing those jobs as a path to social acceptance and stability. On the other hand, Lebanese, coming from a commercial background, disproportionately go into grocery businesses, and blacks have disproportionately entered government employment and opened auto dealerships. Asians have focused on mathematics and engineering more heavily than other groups.[13]

One use of the Internet is not necessarily better than another—but there are clear differences that would manifest themselves in income, much the way a person who used his car to haul goods would have a different return on his vehicle from someone who polished it up for car shows on the weekend.

Market Bridges Divide

The fact is that the free market has moved rapidly to span the "digital divide" by making technology more accessible.[14] Computers have become so inexpensive that almost anyone can own one, and Internet access is also cheap. What critics of the "digital divide" do not grasp is that people make choices about their resources. Of course, people will accept a free computer . . . or a free television, or a free Thanksgiving turkey. But when pressed to spend their own money on goods or services, it becomes clearer what aspects of their lives people value most. Unless the big-government advocates are ready to start regulating the number of hours that people watch television, the state can hand out computers like free movie passes without any impact on incomes.

All that minority groups need to finish bridging the "digital divide" is to gain further hands-on experience, which will come as younger generations learn the tools of the computer age. There are also work habits that must be adopted if the Internet is to assist in wealth creation. But acquiring them in cyberspace is no different from learning them at McDonald's. Once these habits are established, the benefits of Internet access can become fully realized.

One cannot, however, ignore the implications of using the Net more for entertainment than for work. It is almost a given that the next generation of computer-related products will be in the realm of the "telecosm," George Gilder's name for the ethereal world of data in the telecommunications networks.[15] Gilder has argued that computers themselves will become less important and valuable as more information, and even operating systems, are stored on the Net and downloaded as needed. If that is true, what counts are skills, not hardware. And if Gilder is right, there will be more distractions than ever on the Net, requiring more discipline to block out entertainment and to bore in on wealth creation.

In short, racial aggregates may indeed have different use patterns when it comes to the Internet, but these are largely attributable to different cultural emphases. If this constitutes a "digital divide," so be it. But do we really want government to dictate our Internet habits? Different people have different views on how best to use the Internet. When the call for "equal access" to the Net proves insufficient to change people's perceptions about how they value their online time, will we next hear calls to "train" people to use the Internet in "preferred" ways? Let us hope that the freedom enabled by the telecosm prophesied by Gilder does not become another tool to divide the races. That would truly be a disastrous "digital divide."

Notes

1. Thomas P. Novak and Donna L. Hoffman, "Bridging the Digital Divide: The Impact of Race on Computer Access and Internet Use," February 2, 1998, working paper available at wwww2000.ogsm.vanderbilt.edu/papers/race/science.html, and published as "Bridging the Racial Divide on the Internet," Science, April 17, 1998, pp. 390–91. References here are to the Internet version.

2. Quoted in Adam D. Thierer, "How Free Computers Are Filling the Digital Divide," Heritage Foundation Backgrounder, No. 1361, April 20, 2000, p. 2.

3. Novak and Hoffman.

4. Ibid.

5. Duncan Graham-Row and Will Knight, "Internet Users More Chic Than Geek," New Scientist, November 26, 2001, at www.newscientist.com/news/news.jsp?id=ns99991606.

6. Novak and Hoffman.

7. Ibid.

8. Kevin Taglang, "A Low-Tech, Low-Cost Tool for the Homeless," www.digitaldividenetwork.org/content/stories/index.cfm?key=204.

9. Donna L. Hoffman, Thomas P. Novak, and Ann E. Schlosser, "The Evolution of the Digital Divide: How Gaps in Internet Access May Impact Electronic Commerce," available online at www.ascusc.org/jcmc/vol5/issue3/hoffman.html.

10. Graham-Row and Knight.

11. Tom Spooner and Lee Rainie, "African-Americans and the Internet," Pew Online Life Report, October 22, 2000, available at www.pewinternet.org/reports/toc.asp?Report=25.

12. Tom Spooner, Lee Rainie, and Peter Meredith, "Asian Americans and the Internet: The Young and the Connected," Pew Online Life Report, December 12, 2001, available at www.pewinternet.org/reports/toc.asp?Report=52.

13. Thomas Sowell, The Economics and Politics of Race (New York: William Morrow, 1983).

14. Donald L. Alexander, "Internet Access: Government Intervention or Private Innovation?" Working Paper, Mackinac Center for Public Policy, December 1999.

15. George Gilder, *Telecosm: How Infinite Bandwidth Will Revolutionize Our World* (New York: Free Press, 2000).

EXPLORING THE ISSUE

Does the Digital Divide Reflect American Racism?

Critical Thinking and Reflection

1. What is the current digital divide?
2. What are the factors that determine increases as well as decreases in the digital divide?
3. How has technological inequity responded to the spread of technology?
4. What is the role of government in high-speed access to the Internet? What role does the marketplace play?
5. What is the risk of leaving some minority groups behind in the Internet revolution?
6. Discuss the causes of the digital divide.

Is There Common Ground?

Throughout the introduction to this issue we have emphasized the significant role and impacts that high technology is having upon virtually every aspect of contemporary life. Both Crawford and Schweikart recognize the important role that technology plays today. The post–World War II scientific revolution and the technological advances that were generated by it continue to have a transforming effect upon the economy and new social reality of American culture. The pace and scope of these changes have been dramatic, especially from the perspective of those who are a product of industrial society. The impact of high technology has been vast and includes mass communications, mass travel, mass transportation, and economic production, along with social media. The examination of this issue occurs at a time when high-tech devices are being utilized to rally people to organize social protests and revolutions that have resulted in the overthrow of presidents. At the same time, there is a concern that the ownership, distribution, and use of new technology are inequitable. So, one of the concerns that challenges policymakers and the American public is the preparation of workers to function in a twenty-first century, high-technology economy. Why are African Americans lagging in access and usage of the new high technology? The digital divide tends to be treated as a black–white divide, with the locus of the divide being the home. Since the individual spends a significant amount of time at work, extending the research on this issue to include the workplace will be useful in developing a more comprehensive examination of this issue.

Additional Resources

Banks, Adam. 2006. *Race, Rhetoric and Technology: Searching for Higher Ground* (Mahwah, NJ: Lawrence Earlham Associates and the National Council of Teachers of English).

Bonk, Curtis. 2011. *The World Is Open: How Web Technology Is Revolutionizing Education* (Jossey-Bass).

Collins, Allan and Richard Halverson. 2009. *Rethinking Education in the Age of Technology: The Digital Revolution and Schooling in America* (New York: Teachers College Press).

Compaine, Benjamin M. 2001. *Digital Divide: Facing a Crisis or Creating a Myth?* (Cambridge, MA: MIT Press).

Crawford, Susan. 2011. "The New Digital Divide," *The New York Times* (December 4).

Cuban, Larry. 2003. *Oversold and Underused: Computers in the Classroom* (Harvard University Press).

Gilder, George. 2000. *Telecosm: How Infinite Bandwidth Will Revolutionize Our World* (New York: Free Press).

Kirkpatrick, David. 2010. *The Facebook Effect: The Inside Story of the Company that Is Connecting the World* (New York: Simon & Schuster).

Mack, Reneta Lawson. 2001. *The Digital Divide: Standing at the Intersection of Race & Technology* (Durham, NC: Carolina Academic Press).

Marriott, Michel. 2006. "Blacks Turn to Internet Highway and Digital Divide Starts to Close." *The New York Times* (March 31).

Monrow, Barbara. 2004. *Crossing the Digital Divide: Race, Writing and Technology in the Classroom* (New York: Teachers College Press).

Mossberger, Karen, Caroline Tolbert, and Mary Stansbury. 2003. *Virtual Inequality: Beyond the Digital Divide* (Washington, DC: Georgetown University Press).

Nakamura, Lisa. 2002. *Cybertypes: Race, Ethnicity and Identity on the Internet* (Routledge).

Nakamura, Lisa. 2007. *Digitizing Race: Visual Cultures of the Internet* (University of Minnesota Press).

Nakamura, Lisa and Peter Chow-White, eds. 2011. *Race After the Internet* (Routledge).

Norris, Peppa. 2001. *Digital Divide: Civic Engagement, Information Poverty, and the Internet Worldwide* (Cambridge).

Papacharissi, Zizi. 2010. *A Networked Self: Identity, Community and Culture on Social Network Sites* (Routledge).

Selfe, Cynthia, L. 1999. "Teaching English across the Technological/Wealth Gap," *English Journal* (July, pp. 48–54).

Thierer, Adam D. 2000. "How Free Computers Are Filling the Digital Divide," *Heritage Foundation Backgrounder* (April (no. 1361)).

U.S. Department of Commerce. 2011. "Exploring the Digital Nation: Computer and Internet Use at Home." Available online at www.esa.doc.gov/

The Pew Internet and American Life Project website is one of seven projects that make up the Pew Research Center. It is a nonpartisan, nonprofit "fact tank" that provides information on American participation in technology including social networking, Internet usage, and mobile devices. This site is highly recommended to the student because it offers current data and dozens of related articles on the divide.

www.pewinternet.org

This website primarily deals with teaching and learning in grades K-12. The site, operated by the George Lucas Education Foundation, hopes to use social media to "inspire, inform, and accelerate positive change in schools" to improve learning for students. It offers a status report on the digital divide from 2002 with links to research projects.

www.edutopia.org/digital

The Center for Media Justice seeks to create media and cultural conditions to strengthen social movements for social justice, economic equality, and human rights. It shares an agenda for media justice and activism including commentary on technology and an equitable digital future.

http://centerformediajustice.org

The National Urban league is a civil rights organization dedicated to economic empowerment. The National Urban League Policy Institute website "advances the National Urban League's mission of economic empowerment and civil rights through advocacy, research, policy analysis, and publications." If offers major publications and reports including, "The State of Black America 2010 Jobs: Responding to the Crisis."

www.nul.org/content/national-urban-league-policy-institute

This is the website for the Economics and Statistics Administration of the Department of Commerce. It offers economic analysis and oversees the U.S. Census Bureau and the Bureau of Economic Analysis (BEA). Essential for the digital divide issue is its report, "Exploring the Digital Nation: Computer and Internet Use at Home." The entire report is available through a link.

www.esa.doc.gov/

The Berkman Center for Internet and Society at Harvard University states that its mission is to explore and understand cyberspace through study and assessment. It looks at the impact of the Internet on society. This website offers current news articles along with research project reports.

http://cyber.law.harvard.edu/

ISSUE 11

Is Racial Profiling Defensible Public Policy?

YES: Scott Johnson, from "Better Unsafe than (Occasionally) Sorry?" *The American Enterprise* (January/February 2003)

NO: David A. Harris, from "Profiles in Injustice: American Life under the Regime of Racial Profiling," in *Profiles in Injustice: Why Police Profiling Cannot Work* (The New Press, 2002)

Learning Outcomes

After reading this issue, the student should be able to:

- Understand racial profiling as a police procedure.
- Develop an informed comprehension of the goals of racial profiling.
- Discern the significant racial assumptions that underlie this policy.
- Critically examine the impacts of racial profiling on police–community relations.
- Critically examine the impact of profiling on targeted groups.
- Understand and explain the relationship between racial stereotyping and racial profiling.
- Understand the impact of racial profiling upon the rights of American citizens.
- Analyze the available criminal justice data for determining the effectiveness of racial profiling.

ISSUE SUMMARY

YES: Scott Johnson, conservative journalist and an attorney and fellow at the Clermont Institute, argues in favor of racial profiling. He claims that racial profiling does not exist "on the nation's highways and streets." Johnson accuses David Harris of distorting the data on crimes committed and victimization according to race. For him, law enforcement needs to engage in profiling under certain circumstances in order to be effective.

NO: David A. Harris, law professor and leading authority on racial profiling, argues that racial profiling is ineffective and damaging to America's diverse nation. He believes it hinders effective law enforcement.

The issue of racial profiling has raised many questions concerning society's commitment to the rule of law and the protection of individual rights as provided within the Constitution of the United States. The current controversy over racial profiling entered the public consciousness when the issue emerged in New Jersey and other states that were forced to respond to mounting criticisms of law enforcement practices and policies. Due to the vigorous campaign that was launched against this policy by the Black Ministerial Conference of New Jersey, the ACLU, and other black and Latino leaders and organizations, racial profiling appeared to lose some support.

However, due to the events of September 11, 2001, and the ensuing declaration of a war on terrorism, public attitudes on this issue seem to have shifted, and many Americans now view it as necessary to secure the nation against a growing threat to national security. It is important to examine this issue within the context of the tragic events of September 11.

In response to the September 11 terrorist attacks, there has been a perceptible shift in the focus of racial profiling from the war on drugs to a war on terrorism that tends to target Arabs and Muslims, both citizens and immigrants, as suspects. The treatment that members of these groups have received from the police, the U.S. Immigration and Customs Enforcement (ICE), and other national security agencies has caused many of their members to reconsider their status and identity within the American society. So, racial profiling is having disconcerting effects on Arabs and Muslims of the United States and is producing negative perceptions of this country within their extended communities throughout the world.

Consider the following example. During a congressional primary race in Georgia (August 2006), a challenger to Representative Cynthia McKinney said, "an abundant number of contributors to Mrs. McKinney's campaign have Palestinian and Arab surnames. Now I could accuse her of being under the control of terrorists." Is this an ethnic slur that is the product of stereotyping and profiling? Does the use of Arab-baiting score political points? If so, why? Significant evidence is available to demonstrate the ineffectiveness of racial profiling. Yet, people are standing in the netting of racial profiling based on suspicions derived from racial stereotyping, thus exposing the contradictory nature of this practice.

It is important to note that there was a significant increase in the Latino and Asian populations of the United States during the 1990s. As a result of this increase in immigration, the minority population of the nation has continued to grow and now approaches 100 million. These demographic changes in the United States' population make it clear that managing diversity is one of the most significant challenges facing the current and future leadership of the nation. Hence, the issue of racial profiling will become more relevant in the future.

Scott Johnson suggests that racial profiling is a reasonable and appropriate response to the challenges that confront the nation in its attempts to prevent crime and to maintain social order effectively. In developing his argument in favor of profiling, Scott Johnson contends that the data available on crime rates and arrests by race do not support the claim of racially biased policing as claimed by David Harris and others. Johnson views the opponents of racial profiling as undermining the effectiveness of law enforcement by denying them such a tool. He claims that the restrictions upon profiling will impact disproportionately upon the security of minority victims of crime. Thus, Johnson believes that the profiling of members of certain groups as potential perpetrators of crime is reasonable and effective. From his perspective, "better safe than sorry."

In addition to viewing racial profiling as morally wrong, David Harris argues that there are other salient reasons for opposing this practice. Thus, he is concerned that the police are targeting persons with dark skins without proper reference to probable cause, an important principle of American law.

To Harris, treating an entire group as potential criminals based on the wrongdoing of a small cohort of its members violates the equal protection principle of the Fourteenth Amendment of the Constitution of the United States, a significant value of the nation's political culture.

Harris is also convinced that racial profiling is an ineffective practice of law enforcement, and he presents an empirical argument to support his claim. Additionally, David Harris is concerned that racial profiling is having a corrosive impact on the relationship between the police and the African American, Latino, and other minority communities they are responsible to protect and to serve. He believes that such treatment of minority groups can only result in a diminution of respect for law enforcement and a polarization between the police and members of these communities, thus making effective law enforcement more difficult to achieve.

The actions of the Oklahoma City bomber, Timothy McVeigh, a white American active in an antigovernment militia, did not result in racial profiling. What does that suggest about racial profiling? Are members of antigovernment militias who congregate in remote areas and sharpen their military skills with illegal guns and ammunition being targeted in accordance with a "white" terrorist profile? How can America balance its egalitarian commitment with the profiling of Arabs/Muslims?

To place the issue of racial profiling in perspective, readers must confront the topics of race, crime, national security, and criminal justice. How does our concern with effective law enforcement contribute to racial profiling? Does the culture of the police contribute to racial profiling? Is racial profiling unequal treatment of citizens under the Constitution and the law? Are minority police officers a response to this problem? Is there a basis for an antipolice culture within the African American community?

YES

Scott Johnson

Better Unsafe than (Occasionally) Sorry?

David Harris is the University of Toledo law professor who provided much of the intellectual heft behind the war on racial profiling. His 1999 report for the American Civil Liberties Union, which has filed most of the anti-profiling law suits, was entitled "Driving While Black: Racial Profiling on the Nation's Highways." In 2002 he expanded his argument into a book.

The national ruckus Harris helped stir up has, among other results, made it hard for security personnel to use intelligent profiles to uncover potential terrorists in airports, at our national borders, and at visa offices abroad. That is a mistake that has already come to haunt the U.S. horribly. . . . And so long as anti-profiling crusaders prevent law enforcement officials from carefully applying profiling tools, Americans will continue to be needlessly exposed to potential re-runs of September 11.

Harris and his compatriots are clever enough to present themselves as friends of law enforcement, who are just trying to help the police do a better job. Harris himself purports to object to racial profiling mostly because it's "ineffective." But the reality is that he has launched a broad and misguided attack on America's law enforcement and criminal justice systems. Like most of the activists who have turned the campaign against racial profiling into a crusade, Harris practices a shoddy form of racial politics with which we have become all too familiar.

The thesis at the heart of the anti-profiling complaint—that racial disparities in crime rates and arrests reflect racially biased policing—is torn to shreds by basic criminological data. David Harris argues that crime rates are equal among racial groups, and arrests, convictions, and incarcerations are unequal simply because police, prosecutors, and courts systematically pick on minorities because of the color of their skin. The logic of his argument ends in a demand for justice by racial quota.

The contention that crime is committed at equal rates by members of various ethnic groups is the central premise of the ACLU's anti-profiling argument. If that premise is false, their argument fails. And the stakes are high. The issue of alleged ethnic discrimination by police has taken on a heightened importance amidst the war on terrorism. Many of the profiling issues that began as farce over traffic enforcement stops are now replaying themselves in the war on terror as potential tragedies.

From *The American Enterprise*, vol. 14, no. 1, January/February 2003, pp. 28–30. Copyright © 2003 by American Enterprise Institute. Reprinted by permission.

Contrary to the view of the world propounded by David Harris and the ACLU, racial disparities in law enforcement generally reflect racial disparities in crime rates. It is true that racial disparities exist at many stages of our criminal justice system. Blacks have been arrested, convicted, and incarcerated at rates far exceeding those of whites for as long as official data on the subject have been compiled. Middle Eastern Arabs have been disproportionately associated with air terrorism for more than a generation.

These disparities have been studied for evidence of systematic discrimination, and it is now widely accepted among serious scholars, such as Professor Michael Tonry of the University of Minnesota Law School, that higher levels of arrests and incarceration in the U.S. by ethnicity result substantially from higher levels of crime, not racial bias. Sometimes the magnitude of the racial disparities in crime rates is huge. The black murder rate is seven to ten times the white murder rate.

Harris claims that disparities in arrest and incarceration rates are a function of systemic law enforcement bias. Finding that the best national data do not agree, he arbitrarily declares the data wrong: Citing statistics from the National Crime Victimization Survey, he correctly states that more than 50 percent of violent crimes are unreported. Harris then absurdly implies that it is among these unreported crimes that the otherwise undetected white criminals are hiding.

Harris's argument on this basic point does not reflect well on his methods. He makes such claims not only against cops, but against all parts of our justice system. According to him, "Just as with arrest statistics, incarceration rates measure not crime but the activity of people and institutions responsible for determining criminal sentences." In other words: Judges are racists too, just trust me.

Harris implies that if law enforcers just weren't so darn fixated on Arabs, blacks, and other minority groups, officials would discover that comparable levels of crime and terrorism are committed by whites, and just left unpunished. But we have statistics on the race of perpetrators as identified by the victims of unreported crimes. And guess what? They closely track the racial identity of perpetrators in reported crimes. Harris omits this inconvenient fact brought to light by the National Crime Victimization Survey, even though he relies on that same survey to build other parts of his argument.

The anti-profilers' campaign against law enforcement is particularly bizarre and perverse given that minorities are vastly more likely to be victims of crimes. What kind of "civil rights campaign" prevents the police from incapacitating criminals who prey on minority groups? If police flinch from law enforcement for fear of generating bad arrest data that will label them racist, the great harm that follows will fall disproportionately on law-abiding residents of lower-income neighborhoods.

The controversy over "racial profiling" originated in data regarding traffic stops and airport searches that disproportionately affect blacks and ethnic minorities. In his book, Harris traces profiling back to Operation Pipeline, the 1986 Drug Enforcement Administration effort to enlist highway police in interdicting illegal drugs as they are transported by distributors on the nation's highways. Harris's argument that Operation Pipeline resulted in unfair racial profiling by highway patrollers in New Jersey, Maryland, and elsewhere is predicated on studies that falsely assume there are no ethnic differences in driving behavior, and that all ethnicities violate traffic laws at the same high rate. It is also based on the assertion that drug violations are roughly equal across groups.

But a definitive study commissioned by the New Jersey attorney general and designed by the Public Service Research Institute of Maryland found that on the New Jersey Turnpike blacks speed twice as much as white drivers—and are actually stopped less than their speeding behavior would predict. (The study was released after Harris's book had been published.) Elsewhere, Harris conflates statistics on drug use among racial groups (roughly equal) with statistics on drug distribution (as far as we can tell, not close to equal). It is drug distributors that highway patrol officers are seeking out, not drug users.

Several of the studies used by profiling opponents to indict police show nearly equal "hit" rates between whites and blacks despite the fact that blacks were searched at higher rates. (Hit rates are the rates at which searches result in the discovery of contraband.) In Maryland, "73 percent of those stopped and searched on a section of Interstate 95 were black, yet state police reported that equal percentages of the whites and blacks who were searched had drugs or other contraband," groused the *New York Times*. "Studies have shown that being black substantially raises the odds of a person being stopped and searched by the police—even though blacks who are stopped are no more likely than whites to be carrying drugs," complained the *New Republic* last year. What these statistically misleading statements overlook is that if the hit rates are about equal, there is no discrimination. It appears the police are focusing on legitimately suspicious behavior, and not simply picking on people by ethnicity.

The war on racial profiling has obscured two important facts: Racial profiling does not exist where the ACLU has persuaded everyone it does, such as on the nation's highways and streets. And it does not exist where it should, in the nation's airports and airlines.

Unfortunately, the facts have yet to catch up with the myths promoted by opponents of criminal profiling. Many Americans—including many of our leaders in politics and law enforcement—continue to treat profiling as illegitimate, as if it were disproved and discredited. That is the product of a political campaign, not of scholarly research. And it is a policy which leaves innocent Americans far more exposed to danger than they ought to be.

 **NO**

Profiles in Injustice: American Life under the Regime of Racial Profiling

Sergeant Rossano Gerald

Sergeant First Class Rossano Gerald, a black man, had made the United States Army his life. He served in Operation Desert Storm in Iraq, winning the Bronze Star, and in Operation United Shield in Somalia. His nineteen-year military career has included postings both in the United States and overseas. Military service runs deep in Sergeant Gerald's family; he describes himself as an "army brat" who grew up on military bases.

One blazing hot August day in 1998, Sergeant Gerald and his twelve-year-old son, Gregory, were on their way to a big family reunion in Oklahoma. Almost as soon as they crossed into Oklahoma from Arkansas, an Oklahoma Highway Patrol officer stopped their car. He questioned them, warning Sergeant Gerald not to follow cars in front of him too closely, then allowed him to leave. (Gerald denies following any other cars too closely; because he had noticed several highway patrol cars as he entered the state, he had been driving with extra caution.) But less than half an hour farther into Oklahoma, another highway patrol officer stopped Sergeant Gerald again, this time accusing him of changing lanes without signaling. Sergeant Gerald denied this, and he told the officer that another officer had just stopped him.

Despite Sergeant Gerald's having produced a valid driver's license, proof of insurance, and army identification, the troopers—several squad cars had arrived by now—asked to search his car. Sergeant Gerald politely refused; after answering numerous questions, Sergeant Gerald asked many times that the officer in charge call his commanding officer at his base. The highway patrol officers refused each request. Instead, the police put Sergeant Gerald and Gregory into a squad car, turned off the air conditioning, and turned on the car's fan, which blew suffocatingly hot air into the vehicle; they warned Sergeant Gerald and Gregory that the police dogs present would attack them if they tried to escape.

When Sergeant Gerald still refused to allow them to search his car, the troopers told him that Oklahoma statutes allowed them to search (a blatant

From *Profiles in Injustice: Why Police Profiling Cannot Work* (The New Press, 2002), pp. 1–15. Copyright © 2002 by David A. Harris. Reprinted by permission of The New Press. www .thenewpress.com misstatement of the law), and they had a drug-sniffing dog search the vehicle. Sergeant Gerald knew something about these animals; as part of his army duties, he'd worked with military police officers using drug-detection dogs. The dog never gave any signal that it smelled drugs, but the troopers told Sergeant Gerald that the dog had "alerted" them to the presence of narcotics and that they were going to search his car.

For what seemed like hours in the oppressive heat, Sergeant Gerald—now in handcuffs in the backseat of a patrol car—watched as officers used a variety of tools to take apart door panels, consoles, even the inside of the car's roof; at one point they announced that they had found a "secret compartment" in the car's floor. (It was actually a factory-installed footrest.) The troopers attempted to block his view of the search by raising the hoods on their vehicles, and one of them deactivated a patrol car video-evidence camera. They went through every item in the luggage, questioning Sergeant Gerald about Gregory's plane tickets home, which they found in one of the suitcases. (Gregory lived with his mother in northern Indiana, and Sergeant Gerald planned to put him on a plane home after the reunion.) Meanwhile, Gregory was moved to another police car against his father's express wishes; he was made to sit in the front while a dog barked and growled at him from the backseat and a police officer asked him about his father's "involvement" in drug trafficking.

After two and a half hours—and no recovery of any drugs—the police released Sergeant Gerald with a warning ticket. When he asked them what they planned to do about the mess they had made of his car and his personal belongings, they gave him a screwdriver. Their parting words to him: "We ain't good at repacking." Damage to the car amounted to more than a thousand dollars.

Sergeant Gerald filed a lawsuit to contest his mistreatment. Although he has little taste or desire for litigation, he felt he owed it to his son, Gregory, to show that people who have power cannot abuse others with impunity. "I'm an authority figure myself," Sergeant Gerald says. "I don't want my son thinking for one minute that this kind of behavior by anyone in uniform is acceptable." The lawsuit ended with a settlement of seventy-five thousand dollars paid to Sergeant Gerald and Gregory, even as state officials still denied any wrongdoing. "I think I serve my country well," Sergeant Gerald said. "I never want my son to see racism like this happen." Gregory, he said, remains "scarred" by the experience.

Judge Filemon Vela

In 1980, President Carter appointed Filemon Vela United States District Judge for the Southern District of Texas. Vela had been an elected state judge for six years before that, following a career in private practice. Judge Vela's chambers are in Brownsville, Texas, just across the Rio Grande from Matamoros, Mexico. Brownsville has a long history of connection with Mexico; many of its 130,000 citizens are of Mexican descent. Judge Vela's own great-grandfather came to Texas from Mexico in the 1860s. People know Judge Vela not only for what he does in his courtroom, but also for his activities in the community. His bedrock beliefs in education and straight talk led him to help organize and direct a program in which young male and female convicts serving drug sentences come to local high schools to tell the students how involvement with drugs and violence stole their futures. Judge Vela plays the Ted Koppel role in these sessions, asking the inmates about everything from their fear of prison rape to their shame at having embarrassed their families. Judge Vela's wife, Blanca Vela, is the mayor of Brownsville; between their friends, families, and their many personal and professional acquaintances, they know almost everyone in the city who is involved in politics and civic life.

In 1997, the area around Brownsville became the focus of intense immigration enforcement. "Operation Rio Grande" increased the number of agents in the area from seven hundred to twelve hundred by the end of 1999 and poured sophisticated equipment and resources into the effort. The stepped-up activity paralleled similar operations in California, West Texas, and other illegal immigration hot spots. The result was a strong, proactive Border Patrol presence, enough to affect almost everyone of Mexican descent.

During the summer of 1999, Judge Vela and three members of his staff drove to Laredo, one of the cities in south Texas where Judge Vela holds court on a regular basis. The four rode in a Ford Explorer. A Border Patrol agent, who'd been sitting in a vehicle parked next to the side of the road, pulled them over. The agent asked Judge Vela and the others in the car about their citizenship. After they had answered, Judge Vela asked the agent why he had stopped the car. "He said he stopped us because there were too many people in the vehicle," Vela says, though the Explorer could certainly have held more passengers. Only then did Judge Vela tell the agent who he was; he also said that he felt that the agent did not have legal grounds to stop them. Though the agent quickly ended the encounter, telling Judge Vela and his staff they could go, Vela made a complaint to the officer's superiors—not so much about the conduct of the particular officer involved but rather about the practices and policies that led him to make an unjustified stop. As a judge, he was keenly aware that for any search that uncovers contraband to "stand up in court," the stop of the car that led to the search had to be legal. If the stop was illegal, a judge would have to throw out the evidence—and a criminal would go free. It's not at all surprising that Judge Vela's complaint was taken seriously by the Border Patrol; he received assurances that Border Patrol agents would get more training and education to teach them to stop motorists only with a legal basis.

Almost exactly a year after his first encounter with the Border Patrol, Judge Vela was again on his way to Laredo to preside in court, driving on the same road, this time as the passenger of an assistant U.S. attorney. His staff was riding in another vehicle, traveling along with them. Again, a Border Patrol agent pulled the car over; again, Judge Vela—an American citizen, an attorney, and a federal judge—had to answer questions about his citizenship. Once again, Judge Vela asked why the agent stopped them. The answer this time: the car had tinted windows. Judge Vela filed another complaint, but he was not surprised that a second incident had occurred.

Judge Vela talks about these experiences with candor and a touch of humor. He feels that although it is important to speak out, he cannot allow himself to be defined or embittered by what has happened. "If I ever catch myself being affected by these kinds of things, I should not allow myself to sit [as a judge]," he says. Yet it is clear that these experiences have confirmed for him that everyone in the Hispanic community is a target of immigration enforcement, regardless of whether they are citizens, or of their status or station in life. "If they stop us . . . we who are attorneys, we who study law . . . then my goodness, what will they do to persons who do not have our place?" he wonders. "If they can do it to you and me," he says, referring to himself, his staff, and the assistant U.S. attorney who were with him, "who won't they do it to?" Vela has taught American law and constitutionalism on behalf of the Unites States government to attorneys, judges, and other officials all over the world, particularly in Latin America, and he believes with all his heart that the United States and its Constitution are something special, something unique—something worth preserving. "But if you let these things happen, it will deteriorate." He worries that something is badly out of balance. Another Hispanic judge in Brownsville, who has also experienced the Border Patrol's tactics firsthand, puts it this way: "It feels like occupied territory. It does not feel like we're in the United States of America."

Minhtran Tran and Quyen Pham

With school out for the year, Minhtran Tran and Quyen Pham went shopping one morning at a strip of stores in Garden Grove, a city of approximately 150,000 in Orange County, California. Neither girl, both fifteen-year-old honor students, had a police record or had had any contact at all with law enforcement. When they decided to leave and went to a pay phone outside the stores, police from Garden Grove's gang suppression unit drove up, got out of their cars, and confronted them and a third young Asian girl. The police accused them of making trouble and asked them whether they belonged to a gang, allegedly because they were wearing gang clothing. Officers then put the three girls up against a wall and took photographs of them with a Polaroid camera. None of the girls consented; in fact, the police never asked for their permission, let alone the permission of their parents. The "gang attire" they were alleged to have been wearing could have described the clothing of a million other teenagers that day: form-fitting shirts and oversized baggy pants. The police also took down information from the girls, including height, weight, age, hair and eye color, their home addresses, and the names of the schools they attended.

Minhtran Tran and Quyen Pham may have felt disturbed by their treatment that day, but they received a worse shock later. Other kids they knew who went to the Garden Grove Police Station later that day told the girls that they saw the Polaroid pictures the police had taken of them pinned up on a prominent bulletin board. The girls found this hard to understand; police had not charged or cited them, and they hadn't done anything. They felt that the police had labeled them criminals and treated them as gang members because they were Asians dressed in a certain way. Eventually, along with other young Asian Americans, the two girls became the plaintiffs in a lawsuit against the Garden Grove Police Department.

The photographing of the high school honor students by police did not happen by accident. Rather, it came about as part of a set of practices put in place as a deliberate effort to fight gangs in California. With an influx of Asian immigrants to the West Coast over the last twenty-five years, including refugees from Southeast Asia, the region's Asian population has surged. The growth of any immigrant population typically contributes to the problems one customarily finds in any city or suburban area, including crime and gangs. The Asian population is no different, despite the model minority stereotype, and in the early 1990s southern California communities began to make a concerted effort to combat what they saw as a rising menace.

One of the first examples of the effort came in a thirty-page report, entitled "Asian Gangs in Little Saigon: Identification and Methods of Operation." The document, written by Detective Mark Nye of the Westminster Police Department, explored many aspects of Orange County's Asian youth gangs, from what they did to how they dressed to which cars they drove. The report discussed many different demographic groups, including female gang members. Nye warned that "female gang members in some cases dress very similar to male gang members. They will wear baggy, loose fitting clothing, baggy pants, oversized shirts, usually untucked, and in some cases baseball caps." (Parents will recognize this description of clothing as the nearly ubiquitous uniform of the American teenager—Asian, African American, Hispanic, or white.) Female members of Asian gangs, Nye said, looked enough like their male counterparts that they "can be mistakenly identified as males." And in a catch-22 that makes it difficult to see how any young Asian woman could avoid being labeled as a gang member, Nye said that Asian girls who did not dress in typical gang attire were really just in "disguise."

Robert Wilkins

In the early morning hours of a Monday in May 1992, Robert Wilkins and three members of his extended family were driving to Washington, D.C. from Chicago. The four, all African Americans, had traveled together to Chicago a few days before for the funeral of Wilkins's grandfather, the family patriarch. As they drove along an interstate highway outside of Cumberland, Maryland, a Maryland State Police car pulled them over. Wilkins's cousin had been at the wheel when Wilkins noticed that the stop had lasted some time and that the trooper had brought his cousin to the rear of their rental car, where he could not be seen. Wilkins and his uncle got out to see what was happening.

Wilkins's decision to get out of the car and investigate made perfect sense. He had exactly the right training to deal with a situation like this. A graduate of Harvard Law School, Wilkins was himself a criminal defense lawyer. He practiced with Washington, D.C.'s Public Defender Service, one of the most highly regarded public defender offices in the nation. Wilkins had considerable seasoning not only in the ins and outs of criminal and constitutional law, but also in the nuances of police tactics and street stops. He was a skilled trial lawyer, accustomed to speaking his mind in court crisply, authoritatively, and carefully, even though he was a soft-spoken person. He also had considerable experience dealing with police officers.

Wilkins's cousin, who had been driving, told him that the trooper wanted consent to search the car. It was true; the trooper showed Wilkins a consent-to-search form—a piece of paper that, if signed, would indicate that the trooper had obtained voluntary consent to a search of the car. "I explained to him who I was and that I was a public defender in Washington, D.C.," Wilkins said, "and I understood clearly what our rights were and what his rights were, and that we didn't want to have the car searched." The trooper's reply, though perhaps showing a lack of understanding of the law, was just as clear as Wilkins's statement had been. "He looked at me," Wilkins said, "and he said, 'Well, if you don't have anything to hide, then what's the problem?'"

Undoubtedly, most ordinary people would have given in to the officer's demand at this point, but Wilkins was not so easily intimidated. "I thought to myself that this is the exact, most inappropriate response that the law enforcement officer can give," he said. Just asserting your rights "shouldn't make you suspicious." Wilkins held firm; he told the officer that he and his family wanted to be left alone.

The trooper seemed genuinely puzzled and surprised. Giving the trooper credit for frankness, Wilkins remembers his explanation. "He said, 'Well, this is routine, no one ever objects.' I said I don't know what other people do and that may be the case that nobody else does, but we object." The trooper, perhaps sensing that he was not going to get to search the car the easy way, began to play hardball. He told Wilkins that he and his family would have to wait for a drug-sniffing dog. Wilkins continued to stand his ground, calmly but firmly. He told the trooper that *United States v. Sharpe,* a U.S. Supreme Court decision, said that he could not detain Wilkins and his family without some fact-based suspicion, and he asserted that there was nothing even remotely suspicious about the family. Though Wilkins clearly had the law on his side, the trooper didn't care to debate the issue. He told Wilkins that these searches were "just routine procedure" because the police had been having "problems with rental cars and drugs." (Wilkins and his family were driving a Virginia-registered rental car; the license plate, with its first letter *R,* showed this.) "He wasn't rude, he was firm," Wilkins recalls. "He just made clear, 'Look, you know, this is procedure. . . . You're gonna have to wait here for this dog.'" Even offering to show the trooper the program from his grandfather's funeral did not change anything. By this time, other troopers had arrived. Though they saw Wilkins begin to write down names and badge numbers on a pad, the troopers were undeterred; in fact, Wilkins remembers that at least one seemed quite amused by his insistence on his rights.

And the way the trooper wanted it was, in the end, the way it went. The family was held until the dog arrived. Despite their strenuous objections, all of them were forced to get out of the car and stand in the dark and the rain by the side of the road as the dog—so reminiscent to Wilkins and his family of the dogs turned loose on blacks in the South by police in civil rights confrontations—sniffed every inch of the exterior of the car. And only after this careful search turned up nothing were they allowed to leave—with a $105 ticket, though the trooper had originally told them they would receive only a warning. It was only later that Wilkins learned he'd been stopped because of a written profile (prepared by the Maryland State Police) that described him perfectly—a black male in a rental car.

❧

All four of these stories may sound like egregious examples of police run amok, the work of rogue officers. But the truth is that these situations were the result of a well-known, well-used law enforcement technique that has spread all over the country. It has become known as "racial profiling"—and it describes life for millions of Americans who happen to be black, brown, or Asian. What happened to Sergeant Gerald, Judge Vela, Minhtran Tran and Quyen Pham, and Robert Wilkins is not uncommon at all among people like them. They have lived with these practices for many years—even if the rest of the nation has become aware of racial profiling only recently.

Racial profiling grew out of a law enforcement tactic called *criminal* profiling. *Criminal* profiling has come into increasing use over the last twenty years, not just as a way to solve particular crimes police know about but also as a way to predict who may be involved in as-yet-undiscovered crimes, especially drug offenses. *Criminal* profiling is designed to help police spot criminals by developing sets of personal and behavioral characteristics associated with particular offenses. By comparing individuals they observe with profiles, officers should have a better basis for deciding which people to treat as suspects. Officers may see no direct evidence of crime, but they can rely on noncriminal but observable characteristics associated with crime to decide whether someone seems suspicious and therefore deserving of greater police scrutiny.

When these characteristics include race or ethnicity as a factor in predicting crimes, *criminal* profiling can become *racial* profiling. Racial profiling is a crime-fighting strategy—a government policy that treats African Americans, Latinos, and members of other minority groups as criminal suspects on the assumption that doing so will increase the odds of catching criminals. Many in law enforcement argue that it makes sense to use race or ethnicity in criminal profiles because there is a strong statistical association between membership in minority groups and involvement in crime. Having black or brown skin elevates the chances that any given person may be engaged in crime, especially drug crime, the thinking of police and many members of the public goes. The disproportionately large number of minorities reflected in arrest and incarceration statistics is further proof, the argument continues, that skin color is a valid indicator of a greater propensity to commit crime. Supporters of racial profiling arrive, therefore, at the conclusion that focusing police suspicion on blacks, Latinos, Asians, and other minorities makes perfect sense. Racial profiling is nothing more than rational law enforcement.

If racial profiling is what directs police suspicion at minorities, it is high-discretion police tactics that put these suspicions into action, turning profiles into police investigations. These high-discretion methods allow police to detain, question, and search people who have exhibited no concrete evidence of wrongdoing—something the law would almost never otherwise allow. But thanks to the U.S. Supreme Court, which has widened the permissible scope of police discretion and vastly increased law enforcement power at the same time that profiling has come into wide use, these tactics are all perfectly legal. For example, police officers can use traffic enforcement as a legal excuse to "fish" for evidence, even though officers have observed no criminal conduct. Officers can also ask for "voluntary" consent to search, without even a whisper of a reason to think the citizen asked has done anything wrong. And officers can also "stop and frisk" pedestrians without the probable cause they need in other circumstances.

Taken at face value, we could say that racial profiling is morally and ethically wrong. It is clearly unconscionable to treat an individual as a criminal suspect simply because a small number of individuals from the same racial or ethnic group are criminals. But in a society dedicated to equal justice under law, such a practice also undermines our commitment to individual civil rights. Enforcing the law on the basis of racial and ethnic calculations therefore also offends the Constitution. All Americans are guaranteed "the equal protection of the law"; there are few values closer to the core of our political culture. Enforcing the law in a racially or ethnically biased way violates this central principle.

Racial profiling also damages the relationship between police departments and the communities they serve. Almost all police departments today describe themselves as service oriented; community policing, a philosophy of law enforcement that features partnerships between police and the citizens they serve, has become the accepted and applauded orthodoxy everywhere. Yet profiling, which treats all citizens of particular racial and ethnic groups as potential criminals, can do nothing but alienate these same citizens from their police. It breaks down the trust that must be at the heart of any true partnership, and it threatens to defeat community policing's best efforts to fight crime and disorder. Racial profiling reinforces the preexisting fissures of race in our society. By putting citizens in categories by race and ethnicity to determine which ones should be regarded as suspicious and therefore worthy of greater police scrutiny, we divide ourselves into "the good" and "the bad," the citizen and the criminal.

. . . Apart from the moral, ethical, and constitutional arguments against racial profiling, which have increasingly been embraced by Americans of all colors in recent years, new data now offer an irrefutable statistical argument against the practice. Despite the widespread belief that racial profiling, reprehensible though it may be, is an effective and efficient way of catching criminals—a "rational" approach to law enforcement—newly collected information about "hit rates" gives the lie to this assumption: the numbers just don't add up. Data emerging from studies done over the last few years demonstrate conclusively that hit rates—the rates at which police actually find contraband on people they stop—run contrary to long-held "commonsense" beliefs about the effectiveness of racial profiling. The rate at which officers uncover contraband in stops and searches is *not* higher for blacks than for whites, as

most people believe. Contrary to what the "rational" law enforcement justification for racial profiling would predict, *the hit rate for drugs and weapons in
police searches of African Americans is the same as or lower than the rate for whites.*
Comparing Latinos and whites yields even more surprising results. Police catch
criminals among Latinos at *far lower rates* than among whites. These results
hold true in studies done in New York, Maryland, New Jersey, and other places.
We see the same results in data collected by the U.S. Customs Service, concerning the searches it does of people entering the country at airports: the hit rate
is lower for blacks than it is for whites, and the hit rate for Latinos is lower still.

Other data also yield startling surprises. For example, while it is true that
automobile stops sometimes result in large seizures of drugs, this rarely happens.
In fact, police usually find nothing at all; when they do find drugs, it is almost
always very small amounts. The quantities discovered seldom exceed enough
for personal use and often amount to even less—so-called trace amounts that
can be detected but not used. Of course, what we see on the evening news
are the big seizures; we seldom hear about the small ones and never about
the far more numerous times that officers come up empty-handed. We come
away with the mistaken impression that these tactics are not only rational and
fair but successful—when nothing could be further from the truth. All of this
exposes the rational law enforcement argument as, at best, the product of a
set of mistaken assumptions. If blacks and Latinos who are stopped as a result
of racial profiling are no more likely or are even less likely to be in possession
of drugs or other contraband than whites, it simply doesn't make sense to
enforce the law in this way. And if the net results are not a constant parade
of big-time seizures of contraband but mostly "dry holes" and tiny amounts,
there's no real payoff. If "rational" law enforcement seems to make sense, that
is only because we are selective in our interpretations of facts and limited in
our vision of what police do and in the effects these actions have.

Even if we were to overlook racial profiling's moral, legal, and social flaws,
it simply does not work as a law enforcement tactic. And it is a way of enforcing the law that we almost surely would not accept in other circumstances.
Suppose, for example, that profiles focused not on race and ethnicity but on
poverty. We can imagine appearance characteristics for poverty that would
prove almost as easy to observe as skin color: clothing and personal appearance, the physical condition and age of vehicles, and the neighborhood in
which a person lives. Yet we would almost certainly object if police consistently stopped, questioned, and searched almost everyone who looked poor.
The assumption that police should treat *all* poor people as criminal suspects
because *some* poor people commit crimes would—and should—outrage us. Yet
this is precisely what is happening when we police with racial profiles—except,
of course, that the burden is likely to be distributed not by poverty, but by race
and ethnicity.

It would be easy to assume that racial profiling has its roots only in the
racism of individual racist police officers—that the officers who engage in this
practice are bigots whom we should simply root out of the police force. Surely
there are bigots among police officers, but there are also bigots in every other
profession. The great majority of police officers are good people who make

use of racial profiling unintentionally. They do so not because they are big-oted or bad, but because they think it is the right way to catch criminals. Racial profiling is an institutional practice—a tactic accepted and encouraged by police agencies as a legitimate, effective crime-fighting tool. It is a method full of assumptions that have, for too long, gone untested, unexamined, and unchallenged. And when we do challenge it—push hard on its underlying premises and look at real data—policing with racial profiles cannot be said to be a rational response to crime. It is instead a misdirected attack on a difficult set of problems that causes its own damage to innocent individuals, to policing, to society, and to the law itself. Racial profiling is based not on real evidence but on distorted ideas about crime and an overly narrow view of how to attack it. We can do better; in fact, we must do better. The task of this book is to get us beyond the inaccurate, incorrect, and misleading ways in which we think about crime and how to fight it.

EXPLORING THE ISSUE

Is Racial Profiling Defensible Public Policy?

Critical Thinking and Reflection

1. How does racial profiling work as a police procedure?
2. What are the goals of those in favor of racial profiling?
3. What assumptions about race underlie racial profiling policy?
4. How has racial profiling affected police–community relations?
5. What is the impact of racial profiling on minorities in America?
6. What is the relationship between racial stereotyping and racial profiling? Provide examples.
7. What constitutional issues are at stake with racial profiling?
8. What trends of racial profiling are supported by the data?

Is There Common Ground?

The social awareness of and the concern with racial profiling are associated with the larger issues of crime control and homeland security. Neither Johnson nor Harris denies that racial profiling is one stratagem of law enforcement in the United States. Both of these scholars are quite aware of the social controversy and legal and constitutional concerns that arise from the practice of racial profiling. Against this background a number of questions arise. What is the validity of such a practice in a nation committed to the role of law? Further, the debate over racial profiling serves to illuminate a major division in American politics between the advocates of human rights and individual liberties and others who are willing to relinquish the protection of certain rights in the interests of law and order and national security. Racial minorities tend to view such policies as unwarranted assaults on their human dignity, and counterproductive to achieving the goals of the wars on drugs, crime, and terrorism. Others are concerned that instead of promoting national security, this policy has alienated minorities and immigrant groups and has raised serious concerns around the world. There is a growing perception within the international community that racial profiling is compromising the U.S. government's commitments to the rule of law and to equal rights and social justice. What needs to be done to insure public safety without predetermining suspects based on their skin color or ethnicity?

Additional Resources

Cole, David. 2000. *No Equal Justice: Race and Class in the American Criminal Justice System* (New Press).

Collum, Joseph. 2010. *The Black Dragon: Racial Profiling Exposed* (Jigsaw Press).

"Critical Racial and Ethnic Studies: Profiling and Reparations." 2004. *American Behavorial Scientist* (March). Six articles deal with examples of racial profiling.

Del Carmen, Alejandro. 2007. *Racial Profiling in America* (Prentice-Hall).

Glover, Karen. 2009. *Racial profiling: Research, Racism, and Resistance* (Roman & Littlefield Publishers).

Harris, David. 2002. *Profiles in Injustice: Why Racial Profiling Cannot Work* (The New Press).

Herman, Susan. 2012. "Who's Watching the Watchers?" *Civil Liberties: The American Civil Liberties Union National Newsletter* (Winter, pp. 4–5).

Holbert, Steve and Lisa Rose. 2004. *The Color of Guilt & Innocence: Racial Profiling and Police Practices in America* (Page Marque Press).

Kennedy, Randall. 1998. *Race, Crime and the Law* (Vintage).

MacDonald, Heather. 2003. *Are Cops Racist?* (Ivan R. Dee).

Mamr, Coramae Richey and Marjorie Sue Zatz, eds., 2002. *Race, Crime and Criminal Justice* (Roxbury Publishing).

McCarthy, Andrew. 2005. "Unreasonable Searches." *National Review* (August 29).

Meeks, Kenneth. 2002. *Driving While Black: What to Do if You Are a Victim of Racial Profiling* (Broadway Books).

Peek, Lori. 2010. *Behind the Backlash: Muslim Americans after 9/11* (Temple University Press).

Rusell, Katheryn K. 1999. *The Color of Crime: Racial Hoaxes, White Fear, Black Protectionism, Police Harassment, and Other Macroaggressions—Critical America Series* (New York University Press).

Walker, Samuel, Cassia Spohn, and Meriam Delone. 1999. *The Color of Justice: Race, Ethnicity, and Crime in America* (Wadsworth).

Withrow, Brian L. 2006. *Racial Profiling: From Rhetoric to Reason* (Pearson Education).

Withrow, Brian L. 2010. *The Racial Profiling Controversy* (Looseleaf Law Publications Inc.).

The website of the American Civil Liberties Union offers well-researched information on many different social and political issues including immigrant rights, racial justice including racial profiling, technology and liberty, and voting rights. The racial profiling page references the current Arizona state profiling controversy, Department of Justice data, as well as a link to the entire Racial and Ethnic Profiling Report of the U.N. Committee on the Elimination of Racial Discrimination.

www.aclu.org/

The United States Department of Justice website contains information about the agency and its mission to enforce law and defend the interests of the United States. The mission extends to crime control and fair administration of justice. It contains a copy of the department's "Fact Sheet: Racial Profiling." The student will find access to data on research along with news releases on relevant topics.

www.justice.gov/

ISSUE 12

Is Affirmative Action Necessary to Achieve Racial Equality?

YES: Robert Staples, from "Black Deprivation-White Privilege: The Assault on Affirmative Action," *The Black Scholar* (Summer 1995)

NO: Roger Clegg, from "Faculty Hiring Preferences and the Law," *The Chronicle of Higher Education* (May 19, 2006)

Learning Outcomes

After reading this issue, the student should be able to:

- Develop an informed understanding of racial discrimination and employment.
- Comprehend the meaning of affirmative action as a social policy.
- Develop a proper understanding of the function/application of affirmative action within the hiring process.
- Identify the "protected classes" that are the focus of affirmative action policy.
- Develop an understanding of the constitutional and legal foundations upon which affirmative action policy is based.
- Critically examine the claim that groups who are not associated with affirmative action have received preferential treatment and institutional favoritism throughout much of the nation's history.
- Critically examine the social impact of affirmative action policy.

ISSUE SUMMARY

YES: Robert Staples, an African American sociologist, views affirmative action as a positive policy designed to provide equal economic opportunities for women and other minorities.

NO: Roger Clegg, general counsel of the Center for Equal Opportunity in Sterling, Virginia, and contributor to *The Chronicle of Higher Education*, argues against affirmative action, citing

Grutter v. Bollinger. He makes the case for universities to hire the best qualified faculty.

Affirmative action emerged as a primary policy of government to remedy prevailing racial discrimination and to promote equal opportunity consistent with the requirements of the Civil Rights Act of 1964. Yet, despite its noble intentions, the application of this policy that attempts to end bias and promote racial diversity has provoked much controversy. Those who favor affirmative action programs such as Professor Robert Staples reject the premise that the United States has achieved the status of a color-blind society, thus obviating the need for the preferences that they provide for members of the "protected classes." Rather, he views American society as one afflicted with an embedded racism that persists today. So, Staples is concerned that the attack on affirmative action is part of a plan designed to maintain white privilege at the expense of the continued suffering and subordination of African Americans and other minorities including women within society.

Staples points out that affirmative action is not a "black" program. Rather, he concludes that affirmative action programs were initiated to provide equal economic opportunities for minorities and women. Thus, Staples is very critical of politicians and others who play the "race card" by promoting the myth that most of the benefits of affirmative action programs accrue to blacks, when in fact the primary beneficiaries are white females. To Staples, the targeting of blacks in such a fashion reflects a historical tradition of scapegoating blacks within a strategy of "divide and conquer" politics.

Racial politics are a significant aspect of American political life. Staples locates the attack on affirmative action policies as a significant manifestation of the white backlash against civil rights advancements since the 1960s. He decries the tendency of the opponents of these policies to use them to target African Americans, a group that represents a relatively small minority (12.5%) among the potential beneficiaries of affirmative action, while ignoring the fact that white women are the majority of those targeted for the assistance, which they provide. So, Staples has concluded that the opponents of affirmative action will have accomplished the elimination of an "innocuous" remedial program that has achieved some progress in the pursuit of society's diversity goals if their efforts to abolish such programs are successful.

Opponents of affirmative action view such reforms as bad public policy. As one who tends to view the policy negatively, Roger Clegg believes that affirmative action programs violate the principle of equal opportunity and promote the untenable notion that a group is entitled to a guarantee of success. He believes that this evolutionary orientation of affirmative action is divisive and contributes significantly to the perpetuation of racial intolerance within the nation.

Roger Clegg and other opponents of affirmative action think that such programs are no longer necessary because African Americans and other members of the "protected classes" have made sufficient progress. He and others raise questions about merit in employment and education. Further, Clegg expresses concern that the recognition of black achievement will be undermined by such policies. Legitimate concerns about divisiveness and a backlash against such policies are also raised.

Another concern expressed by opponents of this issue is the claim that affirmative action reinforces feelings of self-doubt and stifles individual initiatives among blacks and other minorities, thus causing them to miss opportunities for advancement that are available to them. They also deny blacks and others the full opportunity to promote the perception within the dominant culture that their hiring was based on merit rather than quotas or preferential hiring.

Robert Staples and proponents of affirmative action policies must confront the fact that these programs are not applied properly in certain situations. In its 1978 ruling in the *Bakke* case and the recent *Bollinger* case, the court found that racial or gender-based quotas are impermissible applications of affirmative action policies. So, gender or racial preferences that are based on some numerical scheme that utilizes a point system to give protected class members an advantage are unconstitutional and must be changed. Quotas, therefore, are unacceptable in affirmative action policy.

Supporters of affirmative action programs embrace the proposition that the goal of achieving racial diversity within the institutions of society is a compelling national interest. They believe that social institutions should reflect the diverse composition of America's population within the profile of their employees. Those who affirm support for such programs are concerned that they will not be able to meet their diversity goals if affirmative action is curtailed or abolished. It is not just the traditional members of the civil rights community who express such concerns.

Leaders of the military establishment and the private corporate world have expressed such concerns, and they were the basis for the *amicus curae* briefs that were filed in support of the University of Michigan's affirmative action policies before the U.S. Supreme Court. Their concern is based on a clear understanding that education and life experiences garnered within diverse environments are vital preparation for one to meet the challenges and function effectively in an increasingly global and multicultural social reality. The achievement of racial and class diversity within educational settings, from preschool to graduate school, is a critical component of any meaningful response to these concerns.

YES

Robert Staples

Black Deprivation-White Privilege: The Assault on Affirmative Action

The current furor over affirmative action has many of us perplexed. Some-how, black Americans have shifted, in image, from being violent criminals, drug dealers, wife beaters, sexual harassers, welfare cheaters and underclass members to privileged members of the middle-class, who acquired their jobs through some racial quota system at the expense of white males who had superior qualifications for those same jobs. It is a testament to the ingenuity of white male politicians, using the race card, that they can exploit the histori-cally ingrained prejudice against black Americans in the direction of the small black middle-class. For the last twenty-five years, the use of racial code issues, such as law and order, revising the welfare system and the tax revolt has served to transform the southern states from a Democratic stronghold to a Republi-can majority among its white population.

However, Republicans are increasingly becoming victims of their own success. White Democratic candidates have become as vigilantly anti-crime and welfare as their Republican opponents. In the Louisiana gubernatorial race of 1995, even the black candidates reached out to those whites seeking harsher sentences for criminals, the overwhelming majority of offenders being black in that particular state. While this situation illustrates that there is no honor among thieves, i.e. politicians, it also demonstrates that the diminish-ing returns of the racial code issues have created a dilemma among the Repub-lican right. Into this void steps the issue of affirmative action, an innocuous program devised more than thirty years ago by President John F. Kennedy to increase the employment of blacks in the public sector. It was expanded by President Richard M. Nixon, who personally believed blacks were intellectu-ally inferior, to include other people of color and white women.

All this occurred at a time when white males held an almost total monop-oly of all top and mid-level professional and managerial jobs in the US. Blacks and women who were qualified could not penetrate the barriers to white col-lar employment except in very special niches for white women (e.g. nursing, home economics or teaching) and a small number of professional blacks who serviced the black community. Subsequently, there was some reduction in the exclusive white male monopoly in the white collar occupations and affirma-tive action was only one of the reasons for the change. The shift from a manu-facturing to a service-based economy was a big factor in increasing female

From *The Black Scholar*, vol. 25, no. 3, Summer 1995, pp. 2–6. Copyright © 1995 by The Black Scholar. Reprinted by permission.

employment. And the racial violence of the late 1960s convinced the ruling elites that some blacks had to be brought into white dominated institutions to bring about racial tranquility.

As for affirmative action, there is no consensus on what it is, who are its beneficiaries or what it has achieved. I will not try to define it, since the practice runs the gamut from including people of color and women in the pool of applicants for vacant positions to establishing explicit racial and gender quotas in some institutional spheres. The beneficiaries are generally blacks, Latinos, American Indians, sometimes Asians and women, the disabled, and military veterans. It is estimated that as many as five million people of color have gotten their jobs directly through affirmative action. However, such figures cannot be validated because affirmative action operates in such a complex and convoluted way.

What we do know is that there has been a small shift in the number of blacks who can be regarded as middle-class. Most estimates are generally in the range of one-third of the Afro-American population. The progress for black women has been greater, as recent census figures show that among young black college graduates, women earn more than men. The progress for white women is more complicated to measure, because the majority of them are married to white men and share the same standard of living. Nonetheless, there has been some economic and educational progress for all affected groups and affirmative action is, at least, partly responsible for this progress because it requires employers to be racial and gender inclusive. What has been overshadowed in this debate is that these groups make up about 70 percent of the American population. White males, the alleged victims of affirmative action compose about 30 percent of the population and still hold about 75 percent of the highest earning occupations in this country, and 95 percent at the very top.

Somehow, some way, this whole issue has been distorted into a prevailing belief that white men are the victims of affirmative action and that their rights have been trampled on. Underlying this belief is the assumption that white males are entitled to 100 percent of the high paying occupations, as they had prior to 1965, because they are intellectually superior to people of color and women. That such a notion could have any credence should be absurd on the face of it. Still, it will be upheld in an initiative on the California ballot in 1996, as it was in July of 1995, when the University of California Regents abolished affirmative action in admissions and employment. And this occurred in a state where half the population are people of color and white, non-Hispanic, males compose twenty percent of the state's population.

I will now address the issue of affirmative action in the state of California and at the University of California, where I have lived and taught for the last three decades. About the state: it is a mosaic of geographic, cultural, social and political elements. Its borders house both the radicals of Berkeley and the John Birch Society of Orange County. Not only is California the most populous of the 50 states, it is one of the most racially diverse. Latinos, Asians, blacks and American Indians make up one half of the state's population. Politically it can be a progressive state, since blacks and women have held a higher number of elective offices there than in any other state. Yet, in the last thirty years the state has experienced (1) the passage of a state proposition to legalize racial discrimination in housing, which was declared unconstitutional by the courts, (2) the uprooting of every black person, by white groups, from their homes in the town of Taft, (3) the election of a member of the Ku Klux Klan as the Democratic candidate for a US Congressional seat and (4) the passage of proposition 187, which denies medical treatment and education to undocumented aliens and their children, most of whom are considered people of color.

With this historical backdrop, the Board of Regents of the University of California met in San Francisco on July 20, 1995 to vote on the issue of abolishing affirmative action in admissions and employment. Until this date, there had been no ground swell of public desire to end a program that had existed for 25 years, in a state where blacks and Latinos compose 40 percent of the pool of potential students. But, the Governor, Pete Wilson, who is running for the Republican nomination for president, was way behind in the polls and needed to show he could actually do something about this "wedge issue" that the Republican party discovered in 1995. Typical of 1990s politics, Wilson has a black man, Ward Connerly, himself a beneficiary of affirmative action, to lead the fight to abolish affirmative action. All those involved in the university—the faculty, administration, student groups and alumni were opposed to its abolishment. The vote was a mere formality, as almost all the white male regents were Republican appointees, and by a vote of 15–10, became the first public university to abolish affirmative action.

One would think it a risky political move in a state where people of color make up 50 percent of the population. However, because many Latinos and Asians are recent immigrants, some undocumented, the voting population is 80 percent white. As Mark Di Camillo, of the California Poll commented, "when you do public opinion polling, you see that whites are much more sensitive to issues that relate to the future of California and the position of whites. They probably have greater concern about their own self-interest." Of course, a substantial number of Asians and some Latinos were also opposed to affirmative action at the University of California. The issue is often framed as a black/white one, though blacks make up only 8 percent of the state's population, less than 6 percent of the UC student body and 2 percent of the faculty. By far, the greatest beneficiaries of affirmative action, due to their larger numbers, are white women. Yet they are hardly mentioned in this debate, partly because they are also 52 percent of white voters and their husbands depend on them for their standard of living. The polls show that about two-thirds of white women would vote to abolish affirmative action.

It is not clear what effect the UC Regents' votes will have on the racial and gender balance of the UC campuses. The president of the University of California, Jack Petalson, issued a statement saying, "Few significant changes are likely because UC's employment and contracting programs are governed by state and federal laws, regulations, executive orders and the US Constitution." Because affirmative action is such an innocuous program, it has created strange political bedfellows. Richard Butler, a leading white supremacist and head of the Church of Jesus Christ Christian Aryan Nation hailed Governor Wilson for his support of the UC Regents' decision. He said that "Wilson is beginning to wake up to Aryan views." At the same time, arch conservatives such as Jack Kemp and William Bennett, who are not running for public office, have reaffirmed their support for affirmative action.

This whole debate tends to obscure some of the real issues for the black community. As Jesse Jackson has noted, "There is substantial evidence that affirmative action is inadequately enforced and too narrowly applied." Blacks hold only 4 percent of professional and managerial positions in the US and are a fraction of 1 percent of senior managers in America's major corporations. At the same time, almost a majority of black males are not in the civilian labor force. About 25 percent of young black males are in prison, on probation or parole. Even if white males can reclaim that 4 percent of the executive positions, it will do little to restore them to the 100 percent monopoly they once held.

An essential piece of the attack on affirmative action is that it unfairly discriminates against white males. To accept this premise is to assume that every white male is superior to every woman and person of color. Why else should they control 100 percent of the top positions in the society: for example, in the government contract set asides about 25 percent of the work is often delegated to people of color and women. Presumably, the other 75 percent is held by "deserving" white males. If that aspect of affirmative action is eliminated, white males will get all the hundreds of billions of dollars in taxpayer funds that go to private companies. As for how white males have achieved such an advantage in this one sphere, far in excess of their percentage of the population, it may have more to do with the fact that other white males are making the decisions on whom to award those contracts—not on the merits of a true competition for them.

The center of the white male argument is that they possess skills other groups do not have, particularly as measured by their performance on standardized tests. Thus, they pretend that those tests are valid measures of merit and use them to exclude all but white males from the top paying occupations. It is, indeed, true that they are better test takers than women and people of color—in part because they created and administer the tests. Other research, also by white males, suggests that many of those exams have no relevance to job performance, contain a cultural bias that favors middle-class Anglo males and are not required for most jobs in the US. In many cases, affirmative action was a tool to consider other—often more relevant—measures to evaluate job applicants. And the opponents of affirmative action are hard pressed to name many cases where individuals, hired under affirmative action, lack the necessary skills to do a job for which they are hired.

In reality, most people in this country are capable of performing well at a variety of occupations, because most of what they learn, in performing occupational tasks, is on the job itself. Since there are not enough desirable and high paying jobs for all the qualified applicants, the system devises arbitrary screening devices such as educational requirements and standardized tests to weed out people. Because white males in the US are socialized into a sense of entitlement to the most prestigious and highest paying positions, they are generally better positioned to take advantage of the arbitrary screening devices. Moreover, studies over the years have found that between 35–65 percent Americans find their jobs through contacts made via the friends and kinship network, a practice that partly accounts for the white male dominance of senior positions in both the private and public sector.

Affirmative action has experienced some abuses. Why people of color and women are held responsible for the abuses is a mystery, since white males are chiefly responsible for administering affirmative action programs. The greatest abuses seem to occur in the contract set asides, where a few blacks and Latinos have served as fronts to get government contracts that actually go to Anglo contractors. Another problem has been the classification of racial minorities. Because people with a small percentage of Indian ancestry can live as white Americans, they face no disadvantage different from other whites in this society. Yet, they have often qualified for affirmative action treatment. The problem of white usurpation of Indian identity was so prevalent that American Indians wanted to retain their original name, albeit a misnomer, because so many whites were claiming the title of Native Americans and receiving benefits designed for oppressed American Indians.

Some opponents of affirmative action have suggested replacing its racial/gender components with that of socioeconomic status, which would also include poor whites. Of course poor whites are already included in university recruitment and admission of students, as well as being part of the disabled and military veteran category. However it is unfair to equate a low socioeconomic status with the disadvantages of race and gender. A poor white male who gets a college education and a middle-class job simply increases the number of white males in the ruling elite. His problems are over, while women and people of color will continue to encounter glass ceilings in education and employment. And blacks who are middle-class do not escape anything but the economic problems associated with being black. Because the oppression is aimed at the entire group, the political remedies should go to all visible members of the black population.

Finally, this attack on affirmative action is nothing more than a replay of history for Afro-Americans. Slavery was defended with a variety of rationalizations, including the inferiority of blacks, the need to make blacks Christians and the slaveowners' property rights. Racial segregation in schools was defended by the separate but equal doctrine. Southern apartheid was maintained politically under the states' rights defense. Now, we have the anomaly of having white males, a third of the population who make up 95 percent of those who run America, control and distribute 90 percent of the nation's wealth, trying to portray themselves as victims because women and people of color finally broke their grip on all the society's resources. Their attack on affirmative action can only be characterized as political and economic overkill.

However, despite its absurdity, the assault has the potential to succeed. Politicians have had the wisdom to target blacks as the main recipients of affirmative action, while ignoring the fact that white women make up as much as 80 percent of the beneficiaries. This allows them to get the votes of white women, who may act on their interests as whites and ignore their interests as women. To the degree that they empathize and share households with white males, they have less to lose. Single white women, female heads-of-households and lesbians, will be sacrificed on the altar of larger white interests. Blacks, historically, make a convenient scapegoat for the decline of capitalism and the whites who are casualties of that decline. While they comprise a small percentage of those subject to affirmative action, they remain a national target of prejudice and stereotyping in every corner of the nation.

The notion of a color blind society, with no need for affirmative action, is a fantasy at this point. Race is the most divisive variable extant in the US. Whites commonly betray their class interests on its behalf and individual life chances for both blacks and whites are a direct function of it. Affirmative action is but one tool—not a very effective one—to mitigate its effect. The attack on it is part of a white plan to make people of color their servants again, while they continue to obligate them to pay taxes to subsidize white privilege. What whites may find is they may not want to live in the world they are creating.

Roger Clegg  **NO**

Faculty Hiring Preferences and the Law

Since the U.S. Supreme Court's rulings on affirmative action in 2003, colleges have begun to reconsider how they give preference to students according to race, ethnicity, and sex—not only in admissions, but in financial aid, internships, and various other programs. They need to do the same thing now for employment preferences. It is an open and ugly secret that many colleges still weigh such factors in faculty hiring decisions. That practice is flatly at odds with, among other laws, Title VII of the 1964 Civil Rights Act, which bans employers from such discrimination. In fact, legal challenges concerning faculty hiring are mounting, and it is emerging as the next big front in the battle against racial preferences.

Consider the collision between law and common practice in higher education at every stage of the employment process:

Posting job notices. Advertisements for job applicants commonly single out minority and female candidates as especially welcome. But Title VII specifically makes it generally illegal "to print or publish or cause to be printed or published any notice or advertisement relating to employment . . . indicating any preference . . . based on race, color, religion, sex, or national origin." My organization, the Center for Equal Opportunity, has recently suggested that the U.S. Equal Employment Opportunity Commission spell out what that means for academic institutions, whose refusal to follow the law makes them virtually unique among employers. We are also challenging ads that seem to suggest not just preference but racial exclusivity.

Offering graduate fellowships. Another track to a faculty position is through a graduate fellowship. In early February, the U.S. Department of Justice forced the Southern Illinois University system to end its policy of giving preferential treatment to minority groups and women in its awarding of such fellowships. The department had argued that, because such positions are typically paid, discrimination in selection for them would violate Title VII. The university denied that it had done anything illegal, but said it would open its paid fellowships to all applicants.

My organization had brought that matter to the Justice Department's attention after students and faculty members unhappy with the university's

From *The Chronicle of Higher Education,* May 19, 2006, pp. B13. Copyright © 2006 by Roger Clegg. Reprinted by permission of the author.

approach contacted us. That illuminates an important point: Surveys, like a 1996 study by the Roper Center for Public Opinion Research and a 2000 study in Connecticut by the Center for Survey Research and Analysis, show that most professors are opposed to preferences. Many are happy to bring such discrimination to the attention of federal agencies or private antidiscrimination organizations.

Defining the applicant pool.   Once applications have been received, some colleges deliberately halt the process if they don't think the pool is "diverse" enough. They will then insist on adding candidates—so long, of course, as those candidates are members of a minority group or female.

But a panel for the U.S. Court of Appeals for the Seventh Circuit ruled last August in *Rudin v. Lincoln Land Community College* that such a practice constitutes evidence of illegal discrimination. And rightly so. It is fair to assume that the practice is going to result in some instances where a non-"diversity" candidate, who would have been hired absent the practice, won't get hired. Further, there will be situations in which the pool does not contain a diversity candidate, and so the college will add such a candidate, but in doing so will not add a nondiversity candidate with the same or better qualifications. In those instances, too, a nondiversity candidate is denied an employment opportunity.

Setting aside special funds for "targets of opportunity."   Colleges sometimes establish special pools of money from which a department can draw to hire underrepresented minority scholars whenever there is an opportunity to do so; those minority scholars are called "targets of opportunity." But such pools are indistinguishable from the racially exclusive scholarships for students that colleges have, quite rightly, been abandoning—and that the federal government has, quite rightly, been successfully challenging. Indeed, the Justice Department challenged an "opportunity hire" program as illegally discriminatory against white males in a June 17, 2005, letter to a university.

Jonathan Bean, a professor of history at Southern Illinois University at Carbondale, and an expert on and critic of racial preferences, has observed that those pools of money have been "like the weather—many people complained about them, but nobody did anything about them." "But," he predicts, "that is about to change, as more professors and universities conclude that the racially exclusive approach is legally untenable."

Making hiring decisions.   Colleges, when they hire, often grant preferences to women or "underrepresented minorities" ("underrepresented" being a clever way to avoid having to give a preference to some minority groups, like Asians or Arab Americans). The bias is supposedly justified by one of three rationales, but none has any legal merit.

The first and oldest justification is that discrimination in favor of a minority person is somehow fair because members of that racial group have historically been discriminated against. That is illogical, inasmuch as the individual beneficiary is not claimed to have been an actual victim. The courts have in all events rejected that "societal discrimination" rationale—for instance,

Justice Sandra Day O'Connor's 1989 opinion in *City of Richmond v. J.A. Croson Company,* citing Justice Lewis F. Powell Jr.'s opinions in *Wygant v. Jackson Board of Education* and *Regents of the University of California v. Bakke.* Hiring preferences, then, can be justified only when evidence exists that the particular employer was at some point discriminating.

The Supreme Court's Title VII decisions—like *Steelworkers v. Weber* and *Johnson v. Transportation Agency*—likewise require showing a "manifest imbalance" in a "traditionally segregated" position. In 2006 it seems unlikely that many faculties will be able to point to any recent discrimination against "underrepresented minorities," when colleges have been cheerfully discriminating in their favor for years, if not decades.

The second excuse is a desire for greater faculty diversity. But that justification has fared no better in the courts. While discrimination in the name of student-body diversity has been narrowly upheld in the Supreme Court's latest decisions on affirmative action, Title VII—the law that applies specifically to hiring—explicitly declines to carve out a "bona fide occupational qualification" for race. So it is unlikely that a court, particularly the current Supreme Court, would make one up.

Nor has any federal court. In the leading case on the matter, *Taxman v. Board of Education of the Township of Piscataway* (1996), the U.S. Court of Appeals for the Third Circuit refused to carve out a diversity exception for faculty-employment discrimination under Title VII. The Fifth Circuit has ruled the same way, and there is no federal decision to the contrary.

In addition, it is important to note that the Justice Department rejected the "diversity" rationale when it moved against Southern Illinois University a few months ago. The rationale proves too much: It could be used to discriminate against women and members of minority groups if they become "overrepresented."

The third excuse is a desire to provide more "role models" for underrepresented minority students. But the Supreme Court rejected the role-model justification for employment discrimination with respect to teachers 20 years ago in *Wygant v. Jackson Board of Education.* Justice Powell wrote, "Carried to its logical extreme, the idea that black students are better off with black teachers could lead to the very system the Court rejected in *Brown v. Board of Education.*" Besides, are we to believe that white students cannot be inspired by black teachers, or black students by white teachers, or either by Asian or Latino teachers?

Setting pay differences. Colleges sometimes offer pay bonuses to faculty hires of the right color. That is flatly prohibited by Title VII for all colleges, and by the Constitution for all state colleges (and by the Equal Pay Act with respect to sex discrimination). Here again, the Justice Department has recently fired a warning shot, successfully confronting Langston University this year on behalf of a white female professor who was paid less than her African and African-American counterparts.

Retaliating against complainants. Title VII is explicit that colleges may not retaliate against faculty members or applicants who challenge illegal discrimination. The EEOC recently brought a successful lawsuit—which was settled this year for $125,000—against Macalester College for retaliating against a white male professor who complained to the provost that he had been discriminated against.

Sometimes the pressure to engage in hiring discrimination is brought to bear on colleges from the outside—specifically, from accreditation authorities. The Center for Equal Opportunity, the Center for Individual Rights, the National Association of Scholars, and five of the seven members of the U.S. Commission on Civil Rights have asked that the Education Department not renew the accreditation authority of the American Bar Association's Council of the Section of Legal Education and Admissions to the Bar because the ABA is attempting to use that authority to coerce law schools into using illegal preferences in student admissions and faculty hiring. My organization has also asked the Education Department and Justice Department to jointly investigate past abuses of this sort by the ABA.

Colleges that refuse to conform their hiring practices to the law risk hefty legal judgments—and they will have to pay not only their own lawyers but also the opposing side's. Unlike most cases, in which you pay only your own lawyers, win or lose, the civil-rights laws provide for such lawyer "fee shifting." Bean points out that his (state) university ultimately concluded that it should not "spend taxpayer dollars defending the indefensible"; presumably, private colleges would be even more reluctant to waste their own money. Bean also notes that, "after years of brazen racial discrimination on all fronts, colleges have left a trail of evidence that could be used against them in court." He's right.

The law aside, neither the interests of students nor the research mission of a college are furthered by hiring less than the best-qualified faculty members. Nor does a double standard in hiring and promotion encourage faculty collegiality.

Universities are free—indeed, they are obliged—to make sure that women and minority groups—underrepresented and otherwise—are not discriminated against. They are free to make sure that their hiring committees "cast a wide net," not relying on old-boy networks but instead trying to ensure the best possible applicant pool from which to draw. That sort of affirmative action is fine. Affirmative discrimination is not.

EXPLORING THE ISSUE

Is Affirmative Action Necessary to Achieve Racial Equality?

Critical Thinking

1. What is the relationship between racial discrimination and employment?
2. Define affirmative action.
3. How is affirmative action applied in the hiring process?
4. What groups are protected under affirmative action policies?
5. How have the courts applied the Constitution and the law in determining affirmation cases?
6. Outside the "protected classes," what groups have received preferential treatment in hiring, college admissions, housing, and other areas of society?
7. What is the impact of affirmative action in the workplace and the society at-large?

Is There Common Ground?

Clegg and Staples agree that there is a legacy of racial discrimination in employment throughout the United States. It is the failure of the nation to provide equal opportunities for all that is the genesis of affirmative action policy. Students should be aware of the tendency to focus the discussion of this issue on African Americans, a tendency that obscures the fact that women, Latinos, and other minorities are all members of the protected class. Sociologist Orlando Patterson argues "no issue better reveals the American tension between principle and pragmatism than the debate over affirmative action." The principles of fairness, equality, and meritocracy all inform this debate. The discourse on affirmative action policies contains significant misconceptions. It is difficult to comprehend or accept a claim that a limited policy of affirmative action is an adequate response to the legacy of slavery and racial segregation that continues to challenge the nation. On the other hand, any racial preferences call into question the prevailing commitment to equal opportunity. The U.S. Supreme Court 2003 decision rendered its highly anticipated ruling on *Grutter v. Bollinger* concerning the University of Michigan Law School's affirmative action policy. The justices ruled that race may be employed as one factor among others in the decision-making processes of college admissions. Thus, the Court upheld the "Bakke standard" that was enunciated by Justice Powell within the ruling on that case in 1978. Since that earlier decision, a standard that permits the use of race as one factor among others has prevailed within the admission policies of the nation's colleges and universities.

Additional Resources

Carter, Stephen. 1991. *Reflections of an Affirmative Action Baby* (HarperCollins).

Cohen, Carl. 2001. "Race Preference and the Universities–A Final Reckoning." *Commentary* (September).

Curry, George E. and Cornel West, eds., 1996. *The Affirmative Action Debate* (Perseus Books).

Dworkin, Ronald. 1998. "Is Affirmative Action Doomed?" *The New York Review of Books* (November 5).

Mills, Nicholaus, ed., 1994. *Debating Affirmative Action: Race, Gender, Ethnicity, and the Politics of Inclusion* (Delta).

Murray, Charles. 1984. "Affirmative Racism," *The New Republic* (December 31).

Patterson, Orlando. 2003. "Affirmative Action: The Sequel," *The New York Times* (June 6).

Steele, Shelby. 1990. *The Content of Our Character* (St. Martin's Press).

The Black Scholar. 2003. The entire issue is devoted to an analysis of the rulings on admissions policy at the University of Michigan (Fall/Winter).

Thernstrom, Stephan and Abgail Thernstrom. 1999. "Racial Preferences: What We Now Know," *Commentary* (February).

Thomas, Clarence. 1987. "Affirmative Action Goals and Timetables: Too Tough? Not Tough Enough!" *Yale Law and Policy Review* (Summer).

West, Cornel. 1992. "Equality and Identity," *The American Prospect* (Spring).

Wilkins, Roger. 1995. "Racism Has Its Privileges," *The Nation* (March 22).

The NAACP website offers information, news, and trends dealing with African Americans. The official NAACP publication, *The Crisis,* is available as are past issues through the site's archives section. Information on affirmative action along with other relevant topics is contained on the site.

www.naacp.org/

This is the website for the American Association for Affirmative Action, which is a non profit organization dedicated to the promotion of affirmative action to achieve equal opportunity. It is an association of professionals who manage "affirmative action, equal opportunity, diversity and other human resource programs." The site book store sells hard to find books on affirmative action and related topics.

www.affirmativeaction.org/

Internet References . . .

Pew Hispanic Center

The website, which is part of the Pew Research Center, chronicles Latinos' experiences in a changing America. It includes demographic data including country of origin profiles, survey data, and current topics including Arizona's new immigration law. The interactive maps offer students a clear understanding of Latino settlement by geography.

http://pewhispanic.org/

Immigration Policy Center

This is the website of the Immigration Policy Center, a Division of the American Immigration Law Foundation. It offers data and research on several aspects of immigration including asylum, refugees, undocumented immigrants, the labor market, and enforcement of immigrant policy.

www.immigrationpolicy.org

Immigration History Research Center: University of Minnesota

The University of Minnesota Immigration Research Center, with a focus on research sources for European immigrants, seeks to promote the history of the American immigrant experience. It offers an extensive bibliography of manuscripts and monographs on European immigrant groups.

www.ihrc.umn.edu/

United States Citizenship and Immigration Services

This is the home page of the United States Citizenship and Immigration Services (USCIS). It offers up-to-date information on U.S. immigration law and policy.

http://uscis.gov/graphics/index.htm

Ellis Island Foundation

The website of the Ellis Island Foundation enables almost everyone a chance to research his or her family history. It contains an American family immigration history center.

www.ellisisland.org/

American Civil Liberties Union

This website covers current information on immigrants' rights and issues of civil rights, including voting rights. It reviews Supreme Court decisions and other legislative action. The archives section offers a wealth of information on race and ethnic legal cases throughout American history. There is an interesting section on racial profiling.

www.aclu.org

Immigration: New Faces, Old Questions

*T*he struggles for civil rights and social justice and the increasing immigration of Asians and Latinos have led to an increased emphasis on diversity and multiculturalism within American society. Recent census data have confirmed that significant immigration of Asians and Latinos is altering the demographic composition of the American population. How are these various peoples of color to be included within the prevailing institutions of the society? What are the appropriate strategies for achieving policies of institutional inclusion? Are multiculturalism and increasing racial diversity contributing to the strength of American institutions and social life, or are these phenomena contributing to racial polarization and disunity within the nation? Persistent challenges in a constantly changing America include the resegregation of America's public schools, bilingualism, racial and ethnic diversity, and the model minority status of Asian Americans.

- Does Immigration Contribute to a Better America?
- Is Today's Immigration Debate Racist?
- Is There Room for Bilingual Education in American Schools?
- Should Children of Undocumented Immigrants Have a Birthright to U.S. Citizenship?

ISSUE 13

Does Immigration Contribute to a Better America?

YES: Philippe Legrain, from "The Case for Immigration: The Secret to Economic Vibrancy," *The International Economy* (Summer 2007, vol. 21, issue 3)

NO: Peter Brimelow, from "Immigration: Dissolving the People," *Alien Nation: Common Sense About America's Immigration Disaster* (Random House, 1995)

Learning Outcomes

After reading this issue, the student should be able to:

- Explain how the global labor market functions and impacts immigration.
- Understand the role of immigrant diversity within the U.S. labor market.
- Assess the role of foreign labor on the United States.
- Evaluate the significance of remittances on world poverty.
- Understand the use of the Fourteenth Amendment of the constitution, specifically, the birthright citizenship clause.
- Explain why some Americans favor and others oppose current American immigration policy.

ISSUE SUMMARY

YES: Philippe Legrain is a journalist, economist, and author of *Immigrants: Your Country Needs Them* and *Open World: The Truth About Globalization*. He makes the case that immigration contributes to a better America as well as a better world. His economic argument primarily emphasizes that the flow of immigrants within the global system brings both talent and labor to areas of need.

NO: Peter Brimelow, senior editor of *Forbes* and *National Review* magazines, argues that the United States is being overrun by a growing tide of aliens who are changing the character and composition of the nation in manners that are threatening and destructive to its well-being and prospects for future advancement.

It is common within America to refer to the country as a nation of immigrants. Virtually all of the people of the United States are either immigrants or their descendants. So, as stressed in other parts of this book, immigration is a significant theme of the American experience. Newcomers have made innumerable contributions to the creation and development of the American nation. The earliest European immigrant populations converted the lands that they colonized into viable western-style political and economic entities, which were transformed by the American Revolution into an independent republic, the United States of America. Foreign-born peoples explored the West, broke the sod of the prairie lands by the sweat of their brows, and contributed to those developments that resulted in the establishment of agriculture as a vital component of economic progress while expanding the frontiers/boundaries of this emergent and dynamic nation.

Despite the fact that virtually all members of the current population of the United States are either immigrants or their descendants, concerns with immigrants and immigration policies have confronted the nation throughout history. One reason for this reality is the fact that historically, the United States has promoted the imagery within the world that the nation is a welcoming bastion of *freedom* and *democracy* and a land of virtually unlimited economic opportunities. Not surprisingly, this nation has served as a magnet for peoples seeking freedom from tyranny and oppression and opportunities to improve the material circumstances of their lives. Thus, the United States has experienced continuing waves of immigration throughout its history, and these influxes of new peoples have raised concerns within segments of the public and political leadership over the potential for deleterious impacts of these foreigners upon American culture and society.

The current immigration debate has revealed a broad spectrum of opinions regarding this issue. Immigration hawks—people hostile to the new immigrants—pressure-elected officials to tighten restrictions, making illegal immigration a felony offense, and to protect the border with fencing. Some hawks would like to see illegal immigrants returned to their country of origin. Interestingly, former President Bush, a conservative, took a middle-ground position on the issue. He proposed a guest worker program and opportunities for resident illegal immigrants to gain citizenship.

On the other side, "immigration doves" are favorable to new immigrants. These doves oppose "criminalizing" illegal immigrants and propose an amnesty program for undocumented aliens. The supporters of new immigrants oppose the tendency to blame some of America's economic problems on the new arrivals. Immigrant supporters claim that immigrants make America a better place through cultural enrichment, economic advancement through both labor and entrepreneurial initiatives, and enhancement of the political culture.

Philippe Legrain argues that immigrant labor is essential to the maintenance of economic vitality and the continuing prosperity of societies. He claims that nations gain economically from accepting both low- and high-skilled immigrant labor. To support his argument, Legrain cites evidence that immigrants do not harm American workers. He views immigrant labor as beneficial to both rich and poor countries. The rich nations acquire needed labor and an enriched talent pool. The poor nations receive remittances that lift some of their people from abject poverty and provide a boost for the local economy.

In contrast, Peter Brimelow is disturbed by the current immigration policies of the U.S. government and, according to his view, the self-inflicted problems they present to the nation. Among his concerns are the increasing numbers of Hispanics and Asians, who are exerting a negative impact upon the demographic composition and character of the American society and its culture. Brimelow also expresses more traditional concerns that tend to link immigrant populations to crime and expanding prison populations, and to the rising costs of health care, education, and other human services.

Peter Brimelow views the nation's current immigration policies as out of control and permitting millions of foreign-born persons, both legal and illegal, to arrive on America's shores. He views immigrants as persons who are distorting the demographic composition of society and requiring increasing levels of financial expenditures to support human services and other social support systems. Brimelow asserts that they contribute little or nothing economically beneficial or required to the nation. Thus, he advocates substantial reform of current immigration policy with an emphasis on restricting newcomers from the global South.

In evaluating this issue, readers are urged to balance the country's historical immigrant past with contemporary patterns of immigration. At the same time, readers should note that there has always been a hostile reaction to immigration, whether it was nineteenth-century nativism or twenty-first century new nativism.

As capitalist industrial and commercial developments emerged to dominate the U.S. economy, immigrants and their children provided the requisite labor to extract the resources necessary to operate the factories producing the goods and services of this emergent economy. Ultimately, "Americanized" children of immigrants made significant contributions to the building of modern American institutions while exerting leadership to move this nation forward to achieve a preeminent position in the world.

Brimelow is concerned that America is becoming an "alien nation." He believes that mass immigration is out of control and inflicting harm on the nation. In this context, Brimelow raises concern for American social problems that are heavily affected by immigrants, such as crime, health care, and education. For him, the benefits of immigration do not outweigh the social costs. Legrain, in contrast to Brimelow, places great emphasis upon the economic contributions of new immigrants to American life. His argument directly challenges Brimelow's in that the benefits of immigration clearly outweigh the social costs.

Descendants of immigrants sometimes disagree regarding immigration policy. At what point does an immigrant, or his descendants, identify more with the dominant culture than with his immigrant culture? Perhaps an answer to this question will aid in understanding the immigration issue. Immigrants are often taking jobs that otherwise would go to American citizens. Are those who are already here fearful of losing jobs? Do those who are opposed to immigration perceive a cultural threat in terms of the language, customs, and values of Latinos and other immigrants? One needs to address these questions in order to understand the controversy that immigration generates within American society.

YES

Philippe Legrain

The Case for Immigration: The Secret to Economic Vibrancy

There is a contradiction at the heart of our globalizing world: while goods, services, and capital move across borders ever more freely, most people cannot. No government except perhaps North Korea's would dream of banning crossborder trade in goods and services, yet it is seen as perfectly normal and reasonable for governments to outlaw the movement across borders of most people who produce goods and services. No wonder illegal immigration is on the rise: most would-be migrants have no other option.

This is perverse. Immigrants are not an invading army; they are mostly people seeking a better life. Many are drawn to rich countries such as the United States by the huge demand for workers to fill the low-end jobs that their increasingly well-educated and comfortable citizens do not want. And just as it is beneficial for people to move from Alabama to California in response to market signals, so too from Mexico to the United States.

Where governments permit it, a global labor market is emerging: international financiers cluster in New York and London, information technology specialists in Silicon Valley, and actors in Hollywood, while multinational companies scatter skilled professionals around the world. Yet rich-country governments endeavor to keep out Mexican construction workers, Filipino care workers, and Congolese cooks, even though they are simply service providers who ply their trade abroad, just as American investment bankers do. And just as it is often cheaper and mutually beneficial to import information technology services from Asia and insurance from Europeans, it often makes sense to import menial services that have to be delivered on the spot, such as cleaning. Policymakers who want products and providers of high-skilled services to move freely but people who provide less-skilled services to stay put are not just hypocrites, they are economically illiterate.

From a global perspective, the potential gains from freer migration are huge. When workers from poor countries move to rich ones, they too can make use of advanced economies' superior capital and technologies, making them much more productive. This makes them—and the world—much better off. Starting from that simple insight, economists calculate that removing immigration controls could more than double the size of the world economy. Even a small relaxation of immigration controls would yield disproportionately big gains.

Yet many people believe that while the world would gain, workers in rich countries would lose out. They fear that foreigners harm the job prospects of local workers, taking their jobs or depressing their wages. Others fret that immigrants will be a burden on the welfare state. Some seem to believe that immigrants somehow simultaneously "steal" jobs and live off welfare.

Governments increasingly accept the case for allowing in highly skilled immigrants. The immigration bill before the Senate would tilt U.S. policy in that direction, establishing a points system that gives preference to university graduates. Such skills-focused points systems are in vogue: Canada and Australia employ one; Britain is introducing one; and other European countries are considering them.

For sure, as the number of university graduates in China, India, and other emerging markets soars in coming decades, it will be increasingly important for the United States to be able to draw on the widest possible pool of talent—not just for foreigners' individual skills and drive, but for their collective diversity.

It is astonishing how often the exceptional individuals who come up with brilliant new ideas happen to be immigrants. Twenty-one of Britain's Nobel Prize winners arrived in the country as refugees. Perhaps this is because immigrants tend to see things differently rather than following the conventional wisdom, perhaps because as outsiders they are more determined to succeed.

Yet most innovation nowadays comes not from individuals, but from groups of talented people sparking off each other—and foreigners with different ideas, perspectives, and experiences add something extra to the mix. If there are ten people sitting around a table trying to come up with a solution to a problem and they all think alike, then they are no better than one. But if they all think differently, then by bouncing ideas off each other they can solve problems better and faster. Research shows that a diverse group of talented individuals can perform better than a likeminded group of geniuses.

Just look at Silicon Valley: Intel, Yahoo!, Google, and eBay were all co-founded by immigrants, many of whom arrived as children. In fact, nearly half of America's venture capital-backed start-ups have immigrant founders. An ever-increasing share of our prosperity comes from companies that solve problems, be they developing new drugs, video games, or pollution-reducing technologies, or providing management advice. That's why, as China catches up, America and Europe need to open up further to foreigners in order to stay ahead.

Diversity also acts as a magnet for talent. Look at London: it is now a global city, with three in ten Londoners born abroad, from all over the world. People are drawn there because it is an exciting, cosmopolitan place. It's not just the huge range of ethnic restaurants and cultural experiences on offer, it's the opportunity to lead a richer life by meeting people from different backgrounds: friends, colleagues, and even a life partner.

Yet it is incorrect to believe that rich countries only need highly skilled immigrants, still less that bureaucrats can second-guess through a points system precisely which people the vast number of businesses in the economy need. America and Europe may increasingly be knowledge-based economies, but they still rely on low-skilled workers too. Every hotel requires not just managers and marketing people, but also receptionists, chambermaids, and waiters. Every hospital requires not just doctors and nurses, but also many more cleaners, cooks, laundry workers, and security staff. Everyone relies on road-sweepers, cabdrivers, and sewage workers.

Many low-skilled jobs cannot readily be mechanized or imported: old people cannot be cared for by a robot or from abroad. And as people get richer, they increasingly pay others to do arduous tasks, such as home improvements, that they once did themselves, freeing up time for more productive work or more enjoyable leisure. As advanced economies create high-skilled jobs, they inevitably create low-skilled ones too.

Critics argue that low-skilled immigration is harmful because the new-comers are poorer and less-educated than Americans. But that is precisely why they are willing to do low-paid, low-skilled jobs that Americans shun. In 1960, over half of American workers older than 25 were high school dropouts; now, only one in ten are. Understandably, high-school graduates aspire to better things, while even those with no qualifications don't want to do certain dirty, difficult, and dangerous jobs. The only way to reconcile aspirations to opportunity for all with the reality of drudgery for some is through immigration.

Fears that immigrants threaten American workers are based on two fallacies: that there is a fixed number of jobs to go around, and that foreign workers are direct substitutes for American ones. Just as women did not deprive men of jobs when they entered the labor force too, foreigners don't cost Americans their jobs—they don't just take jobs; they create them too. When they spend their wages, they boost demand for people who produce the goods and services that they consume; and as they work, they stimulate demand for Americans in complementary lines of work. An influx of Mexican construction workers, for instance, creates new jobs for people selling building materials, as well as for interior designers. Thus, while the number of immigrants has risen sharply over the past twenty years, America's unemployment rate has fallen.

But do some American workers lose out? Hardly any; most actually gain. Why? Because, as critics of immigration are the first to admit, immigrants are different to Americans, so that they rarely compete directly with them in the labor market; often, they complement their efforts—a foreign child-minder may enable an American nurse to go back to work, where her productivity may be enhanced by hard-working foreign doctors and cleaners—while also stimulating extra capital investment.

Study after study fails to find evidence that immigrants harm American workers. Harvard's George Borjas claims otherwise, but his partial approach is flawed because it neglects the broader complementarities between immigrant labor, native labor, and capital. A recent National Bureau of Economic Research study by Gianmarco Ottaviano and Giovanni Peri finds that the influx of foreign workers between 1990 and 2004 raised the average wage of U.S.-born workers by 2 percent. Nine in ten American workers gained; only one in ten, high school dropouts, lost slightly, by 1 percent.

Part of the opposition to immigration stems from the belief that it is an inexorable, once-and-for-all movement of permanent settlement. But now that travel is ever cheaper and economic opportunities do not stop at national borders, migration is increasingly temporary when people are allowed to move freely. That is true for globe-trotting businessmen and it is increasingly so for poorer migrants too: Filipino nurses as well as Polish plumbers.

Britain's experience since it opened its borders to the eight much poorer central and eastern European countries which joined the European Union in 2004 is instructive. All 75 million people there could conceivably have moved, but in fact only a small fraction have, and most of those have already left again. Many are, in effect, international commuters, splitting their time between Britain and Poland. Of course, some will end up settling, but most won't. Most migrants do not want to leave home forever: they want to go work abroad for a while to earn enough to buy a house or set up a business back home.

Studies show that most Mexican migrants have similar aspirations. If they could come and go freely, most would move only temporarily. But perversely, U.S. border controls end up making many stay for good, because crossing the border is so risky and costly that once you have got across you tend to stay.

Governments ought to be encouraging such international mobility. It would benefit poor countries as well as rich ones. Already, migrants from poor countries working in rich ones send home much more—$200 billion a year officially, perhaps twice that informally (according to the Global Commission on International Migration)—than the miserly $100 billion that Western governments give in aid. These remittances are not wasted on weapons or siphoned off into Swiss bank accounts; they go straight into the pockets of local people. They pay for food, clean water, and medicines. They enable children to stay in school, fund small businesses, and benefit the local economy more broadly. What's more, when migrants return home, they bring new skills, new ideas, and capital to start new businesses. Africa's first internet cafes were started by migrants returning from Europe.

The World Bank calculates that in countries where remittances account for a large share of the economy (11 percent of GDP on average), they slash the poverty rate by a third. Even in countries which receive relatively little (2.2 percent of GDP on average), remittances can cut the poverty rate by nearly a fifth. Since the true level of remittances is much higher than official figures, their impact on poverty is likely to be even greater.

Remittances can also bring broader economic benefits. When countries are hit by a hurricane or earthquake, remittances tend to soar. During the Asian financial crisis a decade ago, Filipino migrants cushioned the blow on the Philippines' economy by sending home extra cash—and their dollar remittances were worth more in devalued Filipino pesos. Developing country governments can even borrow using their country's expected future remittances as collateral. Even the poorest countries, which receive $45 billion in remittances a year, could eventually tap this relatively cheap form of finance, giving them the opportunity of faster growth.

By keeping kids in school, paying for them to see a doctor, and funding new businesses, remittances can boost growth. A study by Paola Guiliano of Harvard and Marta Ruiz-Arranz of the International Monetary Fund finds that in countries with rudimentary financial systems, remittances allow people to invest more and better, and thus raise growth. When remittances increase by one percentage point of GDP, growth rises by 0.2 percentage points.

John Kenneth Galbraith said, "Migration is the oldest action against poverty. It selects those who most want help. It is good for the country to which they go; it helps break the equilibrium of poverty in the country from which they come. What is the perversity in the human soul that causes people to resist so obvious a good?"

Part of the answer is that people tend to focus their fears about economic change on foreigners. Other fears are cultural; more recently, these have got mixed up with worries about terrorism. Mostly, this is illogical: Christian Latinos are scarcely likely to be a fifth column of al Qaeda operatives, as Pat Buchanan has suggested. But logic scarcely comes into it. Psychological studies confirm that opposition to immigration tends to stem from an emotional dislike of foreigners. Intelligent critics then construct an elaborate set of seemingly rational arguments to justify their prejudice.

In *Who Are We: The Challenges to America's National Identity,* Harvard academic Samuel Huntington warns that Latino immigrants are generally poor and therefore a drain on American society, except in Miami, where they are rich and successful, at Americans' expense. Ironically, when he shot to fame by warning about a global "clash of civilizations," he lumped Mexicans and Americans together in a single civilization; now he claims that Latinos in the United States threaten a domestic clash of civilizations. He frets that Latinos have until recently clustered in certain cities and states, and then that they are starting to spread out. Immigrants can't win: they're damned if they do and damned if they don't.

Rich-country governments should not let such nonsense define their policies. Opening up our borders would spread freedom, widen opportunity, and enrich the economy, society, and culture. That may seem unrealistic, but so too, once, did abolishing slavery or giving women the right to vote.

Peter Brimelow

 **NO**

Immigration:
Dissolving the People

There is a sense in which current immigration policy is Adolf Hitler's post-humous revenge on America. The U.S. political elite emerged from the war passionately concerned to cleanse itself from all taints of racism or xenophobia. Eventually, it enacted the epochal Immigration Act (technically, the Immigration and Nationality Act Amendments) of 1965.

And this, quite accidentally, triggered a renewed mass immigration, so huge and so systematically different from anything that had gone before as to transform—and ultimately, perhaps, even to destroy—the one unquestioned victor of World War II: the American nation, as it had evolved by the middle of the 20th century.

Today, U.S. government policy is literally dissolving the people and electing a new one. You can be for this or you can be against it. But the fact is undeniable.

"Still," *Time* magazine wrote in its fall 1993 "Special Issue on Multiculturalism," "for the first time in its history, the U.S. has an immigration policy that, for better or worse, is truly democratic."

As an immigrant, albeit one who came here rather earlier than yesterday and is now an American citizen, I find myself asking with fascination: What can this possibly mean? American immigration policy has always been democratic, of course, in the sense that it has been made through democratic procedures. Right now, as a matter of fact, it's unusually undemocratic, in the sense that Americans have told pollsters long and loudly that they don't want any more immigration; but the politicians ignore them.

The mass immigration so thoughtlessly triggered in 1965 risks making America an alien nation—not merely in the sense that the numbers of aliens in the nation are rising to levels last seen in the 19th century; not merely in the sense that America will become a freak among the world's nations because of the unprecedented demographic mutation it is inflicting on itself; not merely in the sense that Americans themselves will become alien to each other, requiring an increasingly strained government to arbitrate between them; but, ultimately, in the sense that Americans will no longer share in common what Abraham Lincoln called in his first inaugural address "the mystic chords of memory, stretching from every battlefield and patriotic grave, to every living heart and hearth stone, all over this broad land."

From *Alien Nation: Common Sense About America's Immigration Disaster* by Peter Brimelow (Random House, 1995). Copyright © 1995 by Peter Brimelow. Reprinted by permission of the author. www.vdare.com

Alexander James Frank Brimelow is an American, although I was still a British subject and his mother a Canadian when he shot into the New York delivery room, yelling indignantly, one summer dawn in 1991. This is because of the 14th Amendment to the U.S. Constitution. It states in part:

"All persons born or naturalized in the United States, and subject to the jurisdiction thereof, are citizens of the United States and of the State wherein they reside."

The 14th Amendment was passed after the Civil War in an attempt to stop Southern states denying their newly freed slaves the full rights of citizens. But the wording is general. So it has been interpreted to mean that any child born in the United States is automatically a citizen. Even if its mother is a foreigner. Even if she's just passing through.

I am delighted that Alexander is an American. However, I do feel slightly, well, guilty that his fellow Americans had so little choice in the matter.

But at least Maggy and I had applied for and been granted legal permission to live in the United States. There are currently an estimated 3.5 million to 4 million foreigners who have just arrived and settled here in defiance of American law. When these illegal immigrants have children in the United States, why those children are automatically American citizens too.

And right now, two-thirds of births in Los Angeles County hospitals are to illegal-immigrant mothers.

All of which is just another example of one of my central themes:

The United States has lost control of its borders—in every sense. A series of institutional accidents, of which birthright citizenship is just one, has essentially robbed Americans of the power to determine who, and how many, can enter their national family, make claims on it—and exert power over it.

In 1991, the year of Alexander's birth, the Immigration and Naturalization Service reported a total of over 1.8 million legal immigrants. That was easily a record. It exceeded by almost a third the previous peak of almost 1.3 million, reached 84 years earlier at the height of the first great wave of immigration, which peaked just after the turn of the century.

The United States has been engulfed by what seems likely to be the greatest wave of immigration it has ever faced. The INS [Immigration and Naturalization Service] estimates that 12 million to 13 million legal and illegal immigrants will enter the United States during the 1990s. The Washington, D.C.-based Federation for American Immigration Reform (FAIR), among the most prominent of the groups critical of immigration policy, thinks the total will range between 10 million and 15 million.

It's not just illegal immigration that is out of control. So is legal immigration. U.S. law in effect treats immigration as a sort of imitation civil right, extended to an indefinite group of foreigners who have been selected arbitrarily and with no regard to American interests.

The American immigration debate has been a one-way street. Criticism of immigration, and news that might support it, just tends not to get through.

For example, the United States is in the midst of a serious crime epidemic. Yet almost no Americans are aware that aliens make up one-quarter of the prisoners in federal penitentiaries—almost three times their proportion in the population at large.

Indeed, many problems that currently preoccupy Americans have an unspoken immigration dimension.

Two further instances:

- The health care crisis. Americans have been told repeatedly that some 30 million to 40 million people in the country have no health insurance at any one point in time. Typically, nobody seems to know how many are immigrants. But immigrants certainly make up a disproportionate share—particularly of the real problem: the much smaller hard core, perhaps 6 million, that remains uninsured after two years.
- The education crisis. Americans are used to hearing that their schools don't seem to be providing the quality of education that foreigners get. Fewer of them know that the U.S. education system is also very expensive by international standards. Virtually none of them know anything about the impact of immigration on that education system.

Yet the impact of immigration is clearly serious. For example, in 1990 almost one child in every 20 enrolled in American public schools either could not speak English or spoke it so poorly as to need language-assistance programs. This number is increasing with striking speed: Only six years earlier, it had been one child in 31.

Current law is generally interpreted as requiring schools to educate such children in their native language. To do so, according to one California estimate, requires spending some 65 percent more per child than on an English-speaking child. And not merely money but, more importantly, teacher time and energy are inevitably being diverted from America's children.

My thesis is that the immigration resulting from current public policy:

- Is dramatically larger, less skilled and more divergent from the American majority than anything that was anticipated or desired.
- Is probably not beneficial economically—and is certainly not necessary.
- Is attended by a wide and increasing range of negative consequences, from the physical environment to the political.
- Is bringing about an ethnic and racial transformation in America without precedent in the history of the world—an astonishing social experiment launched with no particular reason to expect success.

Some of my American readers will be stirring uneasily at this point. They have been trained to recoil from any explicit discussion of race.

Because the term "racist" is now so debased, I usually shrug off such smears by pointing to its new definition: anyone who is winning an argument with a liberal. Or, too often, a libertarian. And, on the immigration issue, even some confused conservatives.

This may sound facetious. But the double standards are irritating. Anyone who has got into an immigration debate with, for example, Hispanic activists must be instantly aware that some of them really are consumed by the most intense racial animosity—directed against whites. How come what's sauce for the goose is not sauce for the gander?

I have indeed duly examined my own motives. And I am happy to report that they are pure. I sincerely believe I am not prejudiced—in the sense of committing and stubbornly persisting in error about people, regardless of evidence—which appears to be the only rational definition of "racism." I am also, however, not blind.

Race and ethnicity are destiny in American politics. And, because of the rise of affirmative action quotas, for American individuals too.

My son, Alexander, is a white male with blue eyes and blond hair. He has never discriminated against anyone in his little life (except possibly young women visitors whom he suspects of being baby-sitters). The sheer size of the so-called "protected classes" that are now politically favored, such as Hispanics, will be a matter of vital importance as long as he lives. And their size is basically determined by immigration.

For Americans even to think about their immigration policy, given the political climate that has prevailed since the 1960s, involves a sort of psychological liberation movement. In Eugene McCarthy's terms, America would have to stop being a colony of the world. The implications are shocking, even frightening: that Americans, without feeling guilty, can and should seize control of their country's destiny.

If they did, what would a decolonized American immigration policy look like? The first step is absolutely clear:

The 1965 Immigration Act, and its amplifications in 1986 and 1990, have been a disaster and must be repealed.

It may be time for the United States to consider moving to a conception of itself more like that of Switzerland: tolerating a fairly large foreign presence that comes and goes, but rarely, if ever, naturalizes. It may be time to consider reviving a version of the bracero program, the agricultural guest-worker program that operated from the 1940s to the 1960s, allowing foreign workers to move in and out of the country in a controlled way, without permanently altering its demography and politics.

This new conception may be a shock to American sensibilities. Many Americans, like my students at the University of Cincinnati Law School, are under the charming impression that foreigners don't really exist. But they also tend to think that, if foreigners really do exist, they ought to become Americans as quickly as possible.

However, the fact is that we—foreigners—are, in some sense, all Americans now, just as Jefferson said everyone had two countries, his own and France, in the 18th century. That is why we are here, just as the entire world flocked to Imperial Rome. The trick the Americans face now is to be an empire in fact, while remaining a democratic republic in spirit. Avoiding the Romans' mistake of diluting their citizenship into insignificance may be the key.

EXPLORING THE ISSUE

Does Immigration Contribute to a Better America?

Critical Thinking and Reflection

1. How does the global labor market function and impact immigration?
2. How does increasing diversity affect immigration and the U.S. labor market?
3. How does the demand for labor abroad impact the United States?
4. What are remittances? How do they contribute to fighting world poverty?
5. What is controversial about the birthright citizenship clause of the Fourteenth Amendment to the Constitution? Why do some want to eliminate it?
6. Why do some Americans think immigration is good, whereas others think it is not good for America?

Is There Common Ground?

Both Brimelow and Legrain recognize that immigration is having a dynamic impact upon the American society and its culture. The multiethnic and multiracial character of the United States continues to change. It was recently reported that the number of births for minorities collectively has exceeded that of whites for the first time in American history. This development clearly indicates that the American future will be one in which whites are no longer the majority of the nation's population. Such a development represents a profound change and subsequent challenge to a society, which was historically perceived as "a white man's country." Both sides of this issue must face these indisputable facts as they confront the challenges of immigration. What is it that really makes for a better America? Now that immigration has reemerged as a major policy concern of American government, the need for a comprehensive reform of policy is necessary. The public debate has entertained topics such as border patrol, quotas, English-only demands, labor competition, amnesty, national security, and cost–benefit analysis. These immigration-related issues have been the source of controversy throughout history and are likely to continue.

Additional Resources

Allen, James Paul and Eugene James Turner. 1988. *We Are the People: An Atlas of America's Ethnic Diversity* (Macmillan).

Chomsky, Aviva. 2007. *They Take Our Jobs!: And 20 Other Myths About Immigration* (Beacon Press).

Custard, Glynn. 2005. "Where Are My Juice and Crackers," *The American Spectator* (July/August).

Daniels, Roger. 1990. *A History of Immigration and Ethnicity in American Life* (Harper Perrennial).

Gonzalez, Juan. 2011. *Harvest of Empire: A History of Latinos in America* (Penguin Books).

Handlin, Oscar. 1951. *The Uprooted: The Epic Story of the Great Migrations That Made the American People* (Grossett and Dunlap).

"Immigration: Should African American Workers Be Worried?" 2006. *The Crisis* (July/August).

Judis, John. 2006. "Border War," *The New Republic* (January 16).

Jacoby, Tamar. 2000. "In Asian America," *Commentary* (July/August).

Krikorian, Mark. 2005. "Re: Immigration," *National Review* (May 23).

Legrain, Philippe. 2007. *Immigrants: Your Country Needs Them* (Princeton University Press).

Maldonado-Denis, Manuel. 1980. *The Emigration Dialectic: Puerto Rico and the USA* (International Publishers).

Martin, Philip and Gottfried Zurcher, 2008. "Managing Migration: The Global Challenge," *Population Bulletin* (March).

O'Sullivan, John. 2004. "Amnesty Again," *National Review* (January 26).

O'Sullivan, Joh. 2005. "The GOP's Immigration Problem," *National Review* (September 12).

Rodriguez, Clara. 2000. *Changing Race: Latinos, the Census, and the History of Ethnicity in the United States* (New York University Press).

Shenton, James P. and Kevin Kenny. 1997. *Ethnicity and Immigration* (American Historical Association).

Thernstrom, Stephan. 1980. *Harvard Encyclopedia of American Ethnic Groups* (Harvard University Press).

This is the website of the progressive think tank, Political Research Associates. It is devoted to supporting movements for a more inclusive democratic society. The site boasts that it keeps an eye on the Right. It produces reports and a journal, *The Public Eye,"* that advances progressive thinking. Students will find a multicultural critique of anti-immigrant groups.

www.publiceye.org/

The latest data on immigration trends in the United States and worldwide are available on the website of the Migration Policy Institute. The MPI Data Hub provides migration facts, statistics, and maps. Available on the site is the 2010 American Community Survey and census data on the foreign born by state. Also, the National Center on Immigrant

Integration Policy is an important part of the site, and it presents a wealth of information on immigration.

www.migrationinformation.org/

The heading of this website reads, Center of Immigration Studies: Low-immigration, Pro-immigrant. It offers information about legal and illegal immigration in the United States. Although the organization is nonpartisan, its position on immigration is that the current high levels of immigration make it hard to achieve national objectives including homeland security, public education, and a living wage. Thus, it is seen as anti-immigration but pro-immigrant.

www.cis.org/

The National Immigration Forum website advocates "for the value of immigrants and immigration to our nation." Primarily, it is concerned with immigration reform, citizenship, border and interior enforcement, and state and local immigration developments. It provides daily press clippings on immigration. The site is sensitive to the role of racism in today's immigration issue.

www.immigrationforum.org/

ISSUE 14

Is Today's Immigration Debate Racist?

YES: **Carlos Fuentes**, from "Huntington and the Mask of Racism," *New Perspectives Quarterly* (Spring 2004), pp. 77–81

NO: **Samuel P. Huntington**, from *The Clash of Civilizations and the Remaking of World Order* (Simon & Schuster, 1996)

Learning Outcomes

After reading this issue, the student should be able to:

- Explain the global migration crisis.
- Understand the history of population movements.
- Explain why some scholars view Mexican immigration as a threat to American civilization.
- Explain why some scholars argue that racism drives an American anti-Mexican sentiment.
- Understand the laws of the labor market.
- Connect attitudes of race to attitudes on immigration.
- Comprehend and explain how cultural conflict is a significant focus of the treatment of this issue.
- Answer according to Carlos Fuentes, how have Mexicans contributed to the growth of the American economy?
- Explain how the "brown menace" and "the mask of racism" are employed to highlight this issue.

ISSUE SUMMARY

YES: Carlos Fuentes, prominent Mexican writer and social commentator, argues that much of the current immigration debate is racist. For example, he criticizes Samuel Huntington's assessment that Mexican immigrants exploit the United States and represent an unjust burden to the nation. This "mask" of racism appears under the guise of a concern with American national unity.

NO: Samuel Huntington, political scientist and Albert J. Weatherhead III, university professor at Harvard University, expresses the concern that Mexican immigrants and, by implication, other Latinos are creating significant problems for America, specifically with reference to assimilation, as their numbers continue to increase within the population. In general, he believes that Latino immigration is a threat to America's national unity.

Immigration is one of the most significant themes of the American experience. The dynamism reflected in the development of the culture and economy, along with the increasing diversity within the nation's population, has been influenced primarily by waves of immigrants arriving on these shores. The ebb and flow of migration has been influenced by factors such as wars, economic downturns, and nativist policies such as anti-immigration laws. Immigration is a fact of life in America. It has never been completely terminated and given the history, prospects for such cessation are bleak at best.

It is an undeniable historical fact that the vast majority of more than 300 million people comprising the population of the United States migrated to this country or are descendants of migrants from a foreign land. Most came voluntarily, impelled by the promise of a better life, whereas others arrived in the chains of bondage of American slavery. However, despite the fact that the United States is a nation whose people are mostly descendants of migrants and immigrants, the policies that define and regulate their status within society are a continuing source of controversy.

Those who favor immigration offer many arguments in support of the thesis that these newcomers are good for the nation. Immigrants are viewed by supporters as sources of cultural enrichment and renewal. Immigrants are also viewed as cheap labor that can contribute to continuing economic vitality, especially within societies with aging populations. In today's urban America, immigrants are given credit for the revitalization of neglected and deteriorating neighborhoods. Opponents of immigration base their negative assessments on claims of alleged contribution to crime, welfare dependency, and taking jobs from America's poor and minorities, among other concerns.

The often-unstated claim is that Mexican immigrants threaten Anglo-Saxon heritage. For example, a reaction to Mexican and other Latino immigrants has resulted in the creation of an English-only movement. There is considerable criticism of and reaction to bilingualism today (Issue 15). In many states, local initiatives aim to reduce or eliminate signs and forms in Spanish. Samuel Huntington notes that immigrants arriving in the United States are increasingly from non-western societies with cultures that are distant from America's dominant culture. This cultural distance that he observes is viewed as a major barrier to assimilation and the unity of the nation.

The current controversy over immigration is intertwined with issues of homeland security, especially border security. Despite the fact that the northern border—Canada—is much longer, the focus on the United States' southern border—Mexico—has become the major domestic political issue regarding immigration policy. Would Swedes concentrated on our borders constitute the same reactions as Latinos? Why is there less concern with security on the Canadian border?

Swirling about this issue are concerns with low wages, crime, a permanent underclass, linguistic ethnocentrism, and the issue of race. Hence, one can see that the current controversy is a continuation of restrictive immigration policy aimed primarily at people of color. In this regard, one should note the passage of the Chinese Exclusion Act of 1882 and the anti-Japanese Gentleman's Agreement of 1907. Both were directed at potential immigrants of color.

Carlos Fuentes defends current immigration trends and attacks Huntington for developing a "mask of racism." He accuses Huntington of promoting an image of Mexican immigrants as "the brown menace"—a major threat to American society. In contrast to Huntington and other critics of Latino immigrants including Mexicans, Fuentes stresses the economic and cultural benefits that Mexican and other Latino immigrants bring to America.

In April 2006, there were major demonstrations throughout the country in support of immigrants' rights. Since Latinos tend to be concentrated within the southwestern states of Texas, New Mexico, Arizona, and California, along with Florida, these states are the major focus for this issue. At the same time the Latino population is spreading throughout the country. With the increasing numbers and growing regional political influence of Latinos, a nativist reaction has gained momentum. How much of this reaction and resistance to Latino immigration is racist?

In confronting this issue students need to be aware of significant facts regarding the evolution of U.S.–Mexican relations. This is necessary because Mexicans within the American population tend to be viewed as aliens. An important fact to observe is that states including Texas, New Mexico, Arizona, and California were once Mexican territory. Mexico lost these territories as a result of its conflicts with the United States. Place names throughout the southwest such as San Francisco, San Diego, Los Angeles, and San Antonio are reflective of the Mexican presence and influence in that area of the country.

The editors recommend that this issue be studied in both a social context and an economic context. For example, contemporary political solutions dealing with the current illegal immigration debate includes additional issues such as amnesty for illegal immigrants, guest worker programs, border security, and concern with the extensive use of the Spanish language in the United States. In exploring this issue, students should be clear about the manner in which populations increase within a society. There are two ways by which population growth occurs, immigration and natural increase. Even if America wers able to seal its borders effectively, the Latino and other immigrant populations would continue to expand due to the excess of births over deaths. The impact of these groups upon American culture and identity will persist into the future. Students should consider Issues 1 and 2 as background to a fuller comprehension of this issue. Additionally, students should consider the following questions that arise from this issue: Do immigrants take jobs? Do immigrants contribute to economic expansion? Do immigrants serve as a reserve "army" of the unemployed and thus drag down wages? Do immigrants create opportunity? How much of a factor do you think race contributes to the current public reaction to immigration—both legal and illegal?

YES

Carlos Fuentes

Huntington and the Mask of Racism

"**T**he best Indian is a dead Indian." "The best nigger is a nigger slave." "The yellow threat." "The red threat." The Puritanism one finds at the base of WASP culture (White, Anglo Saxon, and Protestant) in the United States of America expresses itself, from time to time, with shocking color. Now, another of these forceful and freely expressed simplistic ideas can be added to the colorful expressions already mentioned: "The Brown Menace."

The proponent of this idea is Professor Samuel P. Huntington, the tireless voice of alarm with respect to the menace that the idea of the "other" represents for the foundational soul of white, protestant, Anglo-Saxon United States of America. That there existed (and, still, exists) an indigenous-"America" (Huntington uses the United States as a name for the entire continent) prior to the European colonization is of no concern to him. That besides Anglo-America, there existed a prior French-"America" (Louisiana) and, even, a Russian-America (Alaska) is of no interest to Huntington. What worries him is Hispanic-America, the America of Ruben Dario, the America that speaks Spanish and believes in God. For Huntington, this brown danger is an indispensable danger for a nation that requires, in order to exist, an identifiable external menace. Moby Dick, the white whale, is a symbol of this attitude which, fortunately, not all North Americans share, including John Quincy Adams, the sixth president of the North American nation, who warned his countrymen: "Let us not go out into the world in search of monsters to destroy."

Huntington, in his *Clash of Civilizations,* discovers his necessary external monster (once the USSR and "the red danger" disappeared) in an Islam poised to assault the borders of Western Civilization, in an attempt to outdo the feats of Saladino, the Sultan, who captured Jerusalem in 1187. As a result, Huntington outdoes the Christian Crusade of Richard the Lion Hearted in the Holy Land. Huntington the Lion Hearted's anti-Islamic Crusade expresses the profound racism in his heart and, in similar manner, his profound ignorance of the true *kulturkampf* evident in the Islamic world. Islam is not poised to invade the West. Islam is living, from Algeria to Iran, its own cultural and political battle between conservatives and Islamic liberals. It is a vertical battle, deep within, not a horizontal one of expansion.

From *New Perspectives Quarterly,* Spring 2004, pp. 77–81. Copyright © 2004 by Center for the Study of Democratic Institutions (CSDI) CSDI. Reprinted by permission of NPQ.

The Mexican as Exploiter

Huntington's new crusade is directed against Mexico and the Mexicans that live, work, and enrich life in the northern nation. As far as Huntington is concerned, Mexicans do not live—they invade; they do not work—they exploit; and, they do not enrich—they impoverish, since poverty is part [of] a Mexican's natural condition. All of this, when taking into account the number of Mexicans and Latin Americans in the United States, constitutes a cultural threat for that which Huntington dares to mention: the Anglo-American, Protestant, and Anglo speaking white race.

Are Mexicans invading the US? No, they are simply obeying the laws of the job market. There are job offers for Mexicans because there is a North American labor need. If some day, there were to exist full employment in Mexico, the US would have to find cheap labor from another country for the jobs whites, Saxons, and Protestants—naming them as does Huntington—do not want to fill, since they have either surpassed these levels of employment, or because they have grown old, due to the fact that the economy of the US has passed from the industrial period, to the post-industrial, technological, information age.

Do Mexicans exploit the US? According to Huntington, Mexicans constitute an unjust burden for the US economy: they receive more than they give back.

All of this is false. California earmarks a billion dollars a year to educate the children of immigrants. But if it were to do otherwise—listen up, Schwarzenegger—the state would lose $16 billion a year in federal aid to education. Similarly, Mexican migrant workers pay $29 billion a year more in taxes than the services they receive.

The Mexican immigrant, far from being an impoverishing burden, as assumed by Huntington, creates wealth for all economic levels. At the most humble worker level, the expulsion of Mexican immigrants would be ruinous for the US. John Kenneth Galbraith (the kind of North American that Huntington cannot be) writes the following: "If all the undocumented people in the US were to be expelled, the effect on the North American economy . . . would be nothing less than disastrous. . . . Fruit and vegetables in Florida, Texas and California would not be harvested. The price of food products would rise to incredible levels. The Mexican people that want to come to the US are necessary, and clearly add to everyone's well-being." (The Nature of Mass Poverty)

On another level, the Hispanic migrant, as Gregory Rodriguez from Pepperdine University tells us, has the highest number of salaried individuals per family than any other ethnic group. So, too, is his level of family cohesiveness. The result is that, while the father of the family may have arrived barefoot and soaking wet, the descendents of migrants have attained income levels comparable to those of Asian and Caucasian laborers. By the second and third generation, 55 percent of Hispanic households are owners of their own homes, compared to 71 percent of white households and 44 percent of black households.

I would like to add to the figures given by Professor Rodriguez the fact that in Los Angeles County alone, the number of businesses created by Hispanic migrants rose from 57,000 in 1987 to 210,000 last year. Since 1990, the purchasing power of Hispanics has risen 65 percent. Furthermore, the Hispanic American economy in the US generates almost $400 billion a year—more than the Gross National Product of Mexico.

Do we Hispanics exploit or contribute, Mr. Huntington?

Mexican Balkanization

According to Huntington, the sheer numbers and customs of Mexican migrants will end up Balkanizing the US. North American unity has absorbed the European immigrant (including Jews and Arabs, who are not specifically mentioned by Huntington) because the immigrant of old, such as Chaplin in the movie of the same name, came from Europe, crossed the ocean and being white and Christian assimilated quickly into Anglo-Saxon culture and forgot his language and native customs, something which might surprise the Italians in *The Godfather* and the Central Europeans in *The Deer Hunter*.

No. Only the Mexicans and the Hispanics, in general, are separatists. These people have conspired to create a separate Hispanic American nation, the soldiers of a re-conquest of the territories lost in the Mexican-American War of 1848.

If we were to turn the page over, we would find English to be the most spoken Western language. Does Huntington ever think that this fact reveals to all a silent North American invasion of the entire world? Would we Mexicans, Chileans, French, Egyptians, Japanese and Hindi be justified in prohibiting English to be spoken in our respective countries? To stigmatize the Spanish language as a divisive, practically subversive, factor demonstrates the racist, divisive and provocative spirit of Professor Huntington.

To speak a second (or a third or fourth language) is a sign of culture throughout the world excepting, it would seem, in the Monolingual Eden invented by Huntington. To establish the requirement of a second language in the US (as occurs in Mexico and in France) would eliminate the Satanic effects that Huntington attributes to the language of Cervantes. Hispanic speakers in the US do not form impenetrable nor aggressive groups. They adapt themselves rapidly to English and, at times, conserve the use of Spanish, thus, enriching the accepted multiethnic and multicultural character of the US.

All in all, mono-lingualism is a curable disease. Many of us Latin Americans speak English without fear of being contaminated. Huntington presents us with an image of the US as a fearful trembling giant attacked by Spanish speakers. His tactic is fear of the "other," so favored by fascist mentalities.

No. The Mexican and the Hispanic, in general, contribute to the wealth of the US. They give more than they receive. They wish to integrate themselves in the North American nation. They attenuate the cultural isolationism that has led the governments in Washington to so many disastrous international situations. They advocate a political diversification that has been brought about by Afro-Americans, Native Americans, the Irish, Poles, Russians and Italians, Swedes and Germans, Arabs and Jews.

The Mexican Menace

Huntington brings to the fore a musty anti-Mexican racism that I knew, all to well, as a child studying in the North American capital. *The Volume Library*, a one volume encyclopedia published in 1928 in New York, said the following: "One reason for Mexican poverty is the predominance of its racial inferiority." "No dogs nor Mexicans allowed," read the signs written on numerous restaurant facades in Texas during the Thirties. Today, the Latino electorate is seduced with mixed phrases in Spanish by many candidates, among them Gore and Bush during the last electoral process. It is an electoral campaign tactic (similar to Bush's recent migration proposal).

But for us, Mexicans, Spaniards and Hispanic Americans, what is certain is that language is a factor of pride and unity. Five hundred million men and women speak Spanish around the world. But, it is not a fear factor, nor a menace. If Huntington fears the Hispanic Balkanization of the US and wishes to blame Latin America for its incapacity to establish democratic governments and economic development, we, at least, have lived without nationalistic separatisms since the dawn of Independence.

Perhaps what unites us is what Huntington believes disunites: the multicultural nature of the Spanish language. As Hispanic Americans and Spanish speakers, we are, also, Indo-European and Afro-American. We are the descendants of one nation, Spain, which cannot be understood without its racial multiplicity and Celt-Iberian, Greek, Phoenician, Roman, Arabic, Judaic, Gothic linguistic system. We speak a language with Celt-Iberian followed by Latin roots, enriched by a good portion of Arabic words and set in place by the Jews of the 13th century in the court of Alphonse the Wise.

With all we have mentioned, we are winners, not losers. The loser is Huntington, isolated in his imaginary land of Anglo speaking, white and Protestant racial purity. Even, if, in a curiously benevolent way, he offers his space to "Christianism." Most assuredly, Israel and Islam are menaces to be equally condemned as are Mexico and Hispanic America, and, by extension today's Spain, for their undesirable incursions into the old territories of Huntington's Kingdom.

An idle question: Who will become the next Moby Dick of Captain Ahab Huntington?

Samuel P. Huntington

 **NO**

The Clash of Civilizations and the Remaking of World Order

Immigration

If demography is destiny, population movements are the motor of history. In centuries past, differential growth rates, economic conditions, and governmental policies have produced massive migrations by Greeks, Jews, Germanic tribes, Norse, Turks, Russians, Chinese, and others. In some instances these movements were relatively peaceful, in others quite violent. Nineteenth-century Europeans were, however, the master race at demographic invasion. Between 1821 and 1924, approximately 55 million Europeans migrated overseas, 34 million of them to the United States. Westerners conquered and at times obliterated other peoples, explored and settled less densely populated lands. The export of people was perhaps the single most important dimension of the rise of the West between the sixteenth and twentieth centuries.

The late twentieth century has seen a different and even larger surge in migration. In 1990, legal international migrants numbered about 100 million, refugees about 19 million, and illegal migrants probably at least 10 million more. This new wave of migration was in part the product of decolonization, the establishment of new states, and state policies that encouraged or forced people to move. It was also, however, the result of modernization and technological development. Transportation improvements made migration easier, quicker, and cheaper; communications improvements enhanced the incentives to pursue economic opportunities and promoted relations between migrants and their home country families. In addition, as the economic growth of the West stimulated emigration in the nineteenth century, economic development by non-Western societies has stimulated emigration in the twentieth century. Migration becomes a self-reinforcing process. "If there is a single 'law' in migration," Myron Weiner argues, "it is that a migration flow, once begun, induces its own flow. Migrants enable their friends and relatives back home to migrate by providing them with information about how to migrate, resources to facilitate movement, and assistance in finding jobs and housing." The result is, in his phrase, a "global migration crisis." . . .

In the United States immigrants constituted 8.7 percent of the population in 1994, twice that of 1970, and made up 25 percent of the people in

From *The Clash of Civilizations and the Remaking of World Order* by Samuel P. Huntington (Simon & Schuster, 1996), pp. 198–204, 206. Copyright © 1996 by Samuel P. Huntington. Reprinted by permission of Simon & Schuster Adult Publishing Group and Georges Borchardt, Inc., for the estate of Samuel P. Huntington.

California and 16 percent of those in New York. About 8.3 million people entered the United States in the 1980s and 4.5 million in the first four years of the 1990s. . . .

Public opposition to immigration and hostility toward immigrants manifested itself at the extreme in acts of violence against immigrant communities and individuals, which particularly became an issue in Germany in the early 1990s. More significant were increases in the votes for right-wing, nationalist, anti-immigration parties. . . .

The immigration issue came to the fore somewhat later in the United States than it did in Europe and did not generate quite the same emotional intensity. The United States has always been a country of immigrants, has so conceived itself, and historically has developed highly successful processes for assimilating newcomers. In addition, in the 1980s and 1990s unemployment was considerably lower in the United States than in Europe, and fear of losing jobs was not a decisive factor shaping attitudes toward immigration. The sources of American immigration were also more varied than in Europe, and thus the fear of being swamped by a single foreign group was less nationally, although real in particular localities. The cultural distance of the two largest migrant groups from the host culture was also less than in Europe: Mexicans are Catholic and Spanish-speaking; Filipinos, Catholic and English-speaking.

Despite these factors, in the quarter century after passage of the 1965 act that permitted greatly increased Asian and Latin American immigration, American public opinion shifted decisively. In 1965 only 33 percent of the public wanted less immigration. In 1977, 42 percent did; in 1986, 49 percent did; and in 1990 and 1993, 61 percent did. Polls in the 1990s consistently show 60 percent or more of the public favoring reduced immigration. While economic concerns and economic conditions affect attitudes toward immigration, the steadily rising opposition in good times and bad suggests that culture, crime, and way of life were more important in this change of opinion. "Many, perhaps most, Americans," one observer commented in 1994, "still see their nation as a European settled country, whose laws are an inheritance from England, whose language is (and should remain) English, whose institutions and public buildings find inspiration in Western classical norms, whose religion has Judeo-Christian roots, and whose greatness initially arose from the Protestant work ethic." Reflecting these concerns, 55 percent of a sample of the public said they thought immigration was a threat to American culture. While Europeans see the immigration threat as Muslim or Arab, Americans see it as both Latin American and Asian but primarily as Mexican. When asked in 1990 from which countries the United States was admitting too many immigrants, a sample of Americans identified Mexico twice as often as any other, followed in order by Cuba, the Orient (nonspecific), South America and Latin America (nonspecific), Japan, Vietnam, China, and Korea.

Growing public opposition to immigration in the early 1990s prompted a political reaction comparable to that which occurred in Europe. Given the nature of the American political system, rightist and anti-immigration parties did not gain votes, but anti-immigration publicists and interest groups became more numerous, more active, and more vocal. Much of the resentment focused on the 3.5 million to 4 million illegal immigrants, and politicians responded. As in Europe, the strongest reaction was at the state and local levels, which bear most of the costs of the immigrants. As a result in 1994, Florida, subsequently joined by six other states, sued the federal government for $884 million a year to cover the education, welfare, law enforcement, and other costs produced by illegal immigrants. In California, the state with the largest number of immigrants absolutely and proportionately, Governor Pete Wilson won public support by urging the denial of public education to children of illegal immigrants, refusing citizenship to U.S.-born children of illegal immigrants, and ending state payments for emergency medical care for illegal immigrants. In November 1994 Californians overwhelmingly approved Proposition 187, denying health, education, and welfare benefits to illegal aliens and their children.

Also in 1994 the Clinton administration, reversing its earlier stance, moved to toughen immigration controls, tighten rules governing political asylum, expand the Immigration and Naturalization Service, strengthen the Border Patrol, and construct physical barriers along the Mexican boundary. In 1995 the Commission on Immigration Reform, authorized by Congress in 1990, recommended reducing yearly legal immigration from over 800,000 to 550,000, giving preference to young children and spouses but not other relatives of current citizens and residents, a provision that "inflamed Asian-American and Hispanic families." Legislation embodying many of the commission's recommendations and other measures restricting immigration was on its way through Congress in 1995–96. By the mid-1990s immigration had thus become a major political issue in the United States, and in 1996 Patrick Buchanan made opposition to immigration a central plank in his presidential campaign. The United States is following Europe in moving to cut back substantially the entry of non-Westerners into its society. . . .

Can either Europe or the United States stem the migrant tide? France has experienced a significant strand of demographic pessimism, stretching from the searing novel of Jean Raspail in the 1970s to the scholarly analysis of Jean-Claude Chesnais in the 1990s and summed up in the 1991 comments of Pierre Lellouche: "History, proximity and poverty insure that France and Europe are destined to be overwhelmed by people from the failed societies of the south. Europe's past was white and Judeo-Christian. The future is not."[1] The future, however, is not irrevocably determined; nor is any one future permanent. The issue is not whether Europe will be Islamicized or the United States Hispanicized. It is whether Europe and America will become cleft societies encompassing two distinct and largely separate communities from two different civilizations, which in turn depends on the numbers of immigrants and the extent to which they are assimilated into the Western cultures prevailing in Europe and America.

While Muslims pose the immediate problem to Europe, Mexicans pose the problem for the United States. Assuming continuation of current trends and policies, the American population will, as the figures in Table 1 show, change dramatically in the first half of the twenty-first century, becoming almost 50 percent white and 25 percent Hispanic. As in Europe, changes in immigration policy and effective enforcement of anti-immigration measures could

Table 1

U.S. Population by Race and Ethnicity (in percentages)

	1995	2020 Est.	2050 Est.
Non-Hispanic white	74%	64%	53%
Hispanic	10	16	25
Black	12	13	14
Asian & Pacific Islander	3	6	8
American Indian & Alaskan Native	<1	<1	1
Total (Millions)	263	323	394

Source: U.S. Bureau of the Census. *Population Projections of the United States by Age, Sex, Race, and Hispanic Origin: 1995 to 2050* (Washington: U.S. Government Printing Office, 1996), pp. 12–13.

change these projections. Even so, the central issue will remain the degree to which Hispanics are assimilated into American society as previous immigrant groups have been. Second and third generation Hispanics face a wide array of incentives and pressures to do so. Mexican immigration, on the other hand, differs in potentially important ways from other immigrations. First, immigrants from Europe or Asia cross oceans; Mexicans walk across a border or wade across a river. This plus the increasing ease of transportation and communication enable them to maintain close contact and identity with their home communities. Second, Mexican immigrants are concentrated in the southwestern United States and form part of a continuous Mexican society stretching from Yucatan to Colorado. Third, some evidence suggests that resistance to assimilation is stronger among Mexican migrants than it was with other immigrant groups and that Mexicans tend to retain their Mexican identity, as was evident in the struggle over Proposition 187 in California in 1994. Fourth, the area settled by Mexican migrants was annexed by the United States after it defeated Mexico in the mid-nineteenth century. Mexican economic development will almost certainly generate Mexican revanchist sentiments. In due course, the results of American military expansion in the nineteenth century could be threatened and possibly reversed by Mexican demographic expansion in the twenty-first century.

The changing balance of power among civilizations makes it more and more difficult for the West to achieve its goals with respect to weapons proliferation, human rights, immigration, and other issues. To minimize its losses in this situation requires the West to wield skillfully its economic resources as carrots and sticks in dealing with other societies, to bolster its unity and coordinate its policies so as to make it more difficult for other societies to play one Western country off against another, and to promote and exploit differences among non-Western nations. The West's ability to pursue these strategies will be shaped by the the nature and intensity of its conflicts with the challenger civilizations, on the one hand, and the extent to which it can identify and develop common interests with the swing civilizations, on the other.

Note

1. Raspail's *Le Camp des Saints* was first published in 1973 (Paris. Editions Robert Laffront) and was issued in a new edition in 1985 as concern over immigration intensified in France. The novel was dramatically called to the attention of Americans as concern intensified in the United States in 1994 by Matthew Connelly and Paul Kennedy, "Must It Be the Rest Against the West?" *Atlantic Monthty*, v. 274 (Dec. 1994). pp. 61ff., and Raspail's preface to the 1985 French edition was published in English in *The Social Contract*, v. 4 (Winter 1993–94), pp. 115–117.

EXPLORING THE ISSUE

Is Today's Immigration Debate Racist?

Critical Thinking and Reflection

1. What is the global migration crisis?
2. How do population movements reflect social and economic world conditions?
3. What is Huntington's perceived threat of Mexican immigration to the United States?
4. What is Fuentes' critique of Huntington?
5. What are the laws of the job market? How do they influence global migration?
6. What is the relationship between one's racial attitudes and one's immigration attitude?
7. How is a reference to cultural conflict employed in the debate?
8. How does Fuentes explain the contribution of Mexicans to the growth of the U.S. economy?
9. What does Huntington mean by the "brown menace"? What does Fuentes mean by the "mask of racism"?

Is There Common Ground?

While growing up in America, one was most often exposed to a perspective on the Mexican, and by extension the Latino, which tended to devalue the people and their culture. They were stereotyped as slothful, less intelligent, and best suited for menial labor, and predisposed toward violence, among other characteristics assigned to them. Mexican immigrants tended to be referred to as "wetbacks," that is, people who swam across the Rio Grande River and arrived in America illegally. They were subjected to a significant application of the nativist bias especially during the 1930s when anti-immigration sentiment was high. The current immigration debate is focused on the approximately 12 million illegal immigrants living in the United States. Despite the fact that the discussion of this issue so often occurs within the juxtaposition of legal immigration versus illegal immigration, the social concerns generated by these new immigrants are not limited to the dichotomy indicated. Students should note that the 12 million illegal immigrants are disproportionately Latinos as distinct from the European immigrants who preceded them. Clearly, these newcomers are changing the demographic character; that is, the color composition of American society, and their impact upon social structure, culture, economy, and politics are transparent and can only increase in the future. Some American citizens view these newcomers and the impact they are having upon society as uplifting. Others view the new immigrants as potential threats to order and progress. They are also viewed as a threat to American identity and culture (Issue 1). One should ask, as the Latino population expands in the United States, how will that impact the immigration debate?

Additional Resources

Chavez, Leo R. 2008. *The Latino Threat: Constructing Immigrants, Citizens, and the Nation* (Stanford University Press).

Foner, Nancy and George Frederickson, eds., 2005. *Not Just Black and White: Historical and Contemporary Perspectives on Immigration, Race and Ethnicity in the United States* (Russell Sage Foundation Publications).

Gonzalez, Juan. 2011. *Harvest of Empire: A History of Latinos in America* (Penguin Books).

Handlin, Oscar. 1951. *The Uprooted: The Epic Story of the Great Migrations that Made the American People* (Grosset & Dunlap).

Handlin, Oscar. 1959. *The Newcomers: Negroes and Puerto Ricans in a Changing Metropolis* (Harvard University Press).

Huntington, Samuel. 2004. *Who Are We: The Challenges to America's National Identity* (Simon & Schuster).

Johnson, Kevin. 2009. *Opening the Flood Gates: Why America Needs to Rethink Its Borders and Immigration Laws* (New York University Press).

Judis, John B. 2006. "Border War," *The New Republic* (January 16).

Kretsedemas, Philip. 2012. *The Immigration Crucible: Transforming Race, Nation and the Limits of the Law* (Columbia University Press).

Lippard, Cameron D. and Charles A. Gallagher, eds., 2010. *Being Brown in Dixie: Race, Ethnicity, and Latino Immigration in the New South* (Lynne Rienner Publishers).

Lowenstein, Roger. 2006. "The Immigration Equation," *The New York Times Magazine* (July 9).

Lukens, Patrick A. 2012. *A Quiet Victory for Latino Rights: FDR and the Controversy Over Whiteness* (Arizona State University Press).

Marrow, Helen. 2011. *New Destination Dreaming: Immigration, Race, and Legal Status in the Rural American South* (Stanford University Press).

Mazon, Mauyricio. 1988. *The Zoot-Suit Riots: The Psychology of Symbolic Annihilation* (University of Texas Press).

Odem, Mary E. 2009. *Latino Immigrants and the Transformation of the U. S. South* (University of Georgia Press).

Olson, James. 2002. *Equality Deferred: Race, Ethnicity, and Immigration in America Since 1945* (Wadsworth Books).

Pegan, Eduard, Obregon. 2006. *Murder at the Sleepy Lagoon: Zoot Suits, Race, and Riot in Wartime L. A.* (University of North Carolina Press).

Robinson, Lori, Paul Cuadros, and Alysia Tate. 2004. "Strength in Numbers," *The Crisis* (January/February).

Rodriguez, Gregory. 2008. *Mongrels, Bastards, Orphans and Vagabonds: Mexican Immigration and the Future of Race in America* (Vintage).

Roediger, David R. 2006. *Working toward Whiteness: How America's Immigrants Became White: The Strange Journey From Ellis Island to the Suburbs* (Basic Books).

This is the website for the Southern Poverty Law Center (SPLC), which was founded by Morris Dees and Joe Levin. Located in Alabama, the center is internationally known for many tolerance programs including education programs, tracking of hate groups, and its legal victories against white supremacists. The Center recently listed 1,018 hate groups in the United States for 2011, many of them anti-immigrant and racist. The site also offers educational and community programs for those interested in dismantling bigotry.

www.splcenter.org/

The Federation for American Immigration Reform (FAIR) website advocates for immigration policies that "will best serve American environmental, societal, and economic interests today and into the future." It offers data, maps, legislative news coverage, and statements on immigration issues. FAIR has been cited as an anti-immigrant hate group by the Southern Poverty Law Center.

www.fairus.org/

The heading of this website reads, Center of Immigration Studies: Low-immigration, Pro-immigrant. It offers information about legal and illegal immigration in the United States. Although the organization is nonpartisan, its position on immigration is that the current high levels of immigration make it hard to achieve national objectives including homeland security, public education, and a living wage. Thus, it is seen as anti-immigration but pro-immigrant.

www.cis.org/

The National Immigration Forum website advocates "for the value of immigrants and immigration to our nation." Primarily, it is concerned with immigration reform, citizenship, border and interior enforcement, and state and local immigration developments. It provides daily press clippings on immigration. The site is sensitive to the role of racism in today's immigration issue.

www.immigrationforum.org/

275

ISSUE 15

Is There Room for Bilingual Education in American Schools?

YES: Kendra Hamilton, from "Bilingual or Immersion? A New Group of Studies Is Providing Fresh Evidence That It's Not the Language of Instruction That Counts, but the Quality of Education," *Diverse Issues in Higher Education* (April 20, 2006)

NO: Rosalie Pedalino Porter, from "The Case Against Bilingual Education," *The Atlantic Monthly* (May 1998)

Learning Outcomes

After reading this issue, the student should be able to:

- Develop a meaningful understanding of a bilingual approach to education.
- Comprehend and critically examine the assumptions on which bilingual education programs are based.
- Exhibit an informed understanding of the goals of bilingual education as articulated by advocates.
- Understand how the current concern with immigration influences the debate on this issue.
- Understand how race influences the debate on this issue.
- Identify and explain the negative impacts of this policy according to its critics.
- Identify the challenges facing the continuation of bilingual educational programs in America today.

ISSUE SUMMARY

YES: Kendra Hamilton, editor of *Black Issues in Higher Education*, argues that the studies available for assessing the quality of such programs are inconclusive. She makes the argument that the outcomes of bilingual education programs are often jeopardized by the quality of the instruction provided. Thus, the significant question of the quality of the programs is being ignored.

NO: Rosalie Pedalino Porter, author of *Forked Tongue: The Politics of Bilingual Education* and affiliate of The Institute for Research in English Acquisition and Development (READ), makes the case against bilingual education. She presents a negative view of the contributions of such programs to the academic achievement of non–English-speaking students. Also, she is greatly concerned that such programs retard the integration of such students within the larger, English-speaking society.

The changing demographics of the American population and, most especially, the rapid increase in the Latino population have brought new challenges to the nation. It is important to note that in the last decade Latinos have become the largest minority group in America. One area of concern that has emerged in association with increasing immigration to the United States is reflective of the society's efforts to provide equal educational opportunities for all. So, the question of how best to educate non–English-speaking students, especially Latinos, has arisen. Public schools across the nation have responded to this challenge by developing and implementing comprehensive bilingual language programs that feature English as a second language. The U.S. federal government had passed legislation that facilitated this development, including The Bilingual Education Act (1968), also known as Title VII. However, it was eliminated as part of a larger "school reform" measure known as No Child Left Behind in 2002.

Bilingual education is not new to America. Such programs were introduced from the eighteenth through the twentieth centuries to facilitate the academic progress of European immigrants. Despite this historical experience, bilingual educational programs have come under increasing scrutiny in recent years, and opposition to such initiatives has grown. The value of such programs as reflected in the academic outcomes and progress, which they generate among non–English-speaking students, is increasingly questioned.

Rosalie Pedalino Porter is a strong opponent of bilingual education programs. In support of her position, she states that accumulated research does not support any claim of educational efficacy for such programs. Additionally, she argues that such programs tend to reinforce the separate cultural identity of non–English-speaking students and the speaking of the native language rather than a proper adaptation to the English-speaking society.

Kendra Hamilton offers a different analysis and argues that there is no conclusive evidence that bilingual education is superior to English immersion classes. However, Hamilton makes the case for bilingualism. In fact, she references a study by Dr. Tim Shanahan that is a synthesis of all the available research on second-language literacy. He concludes, "in fact, kids did somewhat better if they received some amount of instruction in their home language." Further, Hamilton is concerned that a significant question regarding this issue is being ignored. She argues that a consideration of the quality of instruction in bilingual education is critical to any assessment of the outcomes it produces.

The editors want to remind students that bilingual education is one component of the concern with immigrants and immigration policy. It is also reflective of the concern that many Americans and their leaders are expressing on issues of identity and assimilation within American culture. The English-only movement is a manifestation of these concerns.

Further questions for students to consider are as follows: How are issues on immigration and identity (Issues 1, 2, and 3) related to one's position on bilingualism? Does a bilingual education complicate the increasing demands on educational resources? In your educational experience, how has exposure to languages other than English enhanced or diminished your appreciation of American culture? How can educators best assess bilingual education programs? Does bilingualism threaten assimilation into American culture?

In developing a stance on this issue, we encourage students to place significant emphasis on two developments. First, the increasing Latino population and second, the nation's growing dependence on Latino and other minority labor within the economy. It is important that these workers acquire the education and skills to meet the challenge of the twenty-first century. Failure to do so will place the nation in jeopardy in maintaining its position in the world economy. Wherever one stands on this issue, it is more important that Latinos acquire the best education that society can provide. Should it be through bilingual programs or via English immersion?

YES

Kendra Hamilton

Bilingual or Immersion? A New Group of Studies Is Providing Fresh Evidence That It's Not the Language of Instruction That Counts, but the Quality of Education

Eight years ago, Proposition 227 virtually eliminated bilingual education in California's K-12 schools. Since then, the English-only approach has made inroads in states like Arizona and Massachusetts, where ballot initiatives have created even more restrictive "English immersion" programs than California's. In Colorado, backers of a failed ballot initiative are trying again, this time with a campaign for a constitutional amendment.

But a group of new studies is providing fresh evidence of what many researchers have been saying all along: English immersion has more political appeal than educational merit.

"We're saying it's not possible given the data available to definitively answer the question 'which is better—bilingual or immersion?'" says Dr. Amy Merickel, co-author of "Effects of the Implementation of Proposition 227 on the Education of English Learners K-12." The five-year, $2.5 million study was conducted for the state of California by the American Institutes for Research and WestEd.

"We don't see conclusive evidence that bilingual education is superior to English immersion, and we don't see conclusive evidence for the reverse," Merickel says. "We think it's the wrong question. It's not the model of instruction that matters—it's the quality."

Dr. Tim Shanahan, professor of curriculum and instruction at the University of Illinois-Chicago and director of its Center for Literacy, agrees.

Shanahan and a team of more than a dozen researchers from institutions across the nation recently completed a synthesis of all the available research on literacy, including second language literacy for the U.S. Department of Education.

"When we looked at all the past attempts to get at this issue and analyzed their data, essentially what we concluded was that, in fact, kids did somewhat better if they received some amount of instruction in their home language," Shanahan says. "How much? It was not clear from the available data. What should it look like? That wasn't entirely clear either. But across the board, the impact of some instruction in home language seemed to be beneficial.

"But one of the things that surprised me and that stood out for me was the sheer volume of the research that was not devoted to these issues," he adds. "If you look at the data, most of the research is on [which] language of instruction [is better]. That issue has so sucked up all the oxygen that all those other issues of quality clearly are being neglected."

Such conclusions run sharply counter to the assertions of many defenders of English immersion. In 1997, millionaire Ron Unz began a campaign against bilingual education, forming an advocacy organization with a simple name and message—English for the Children. That organization helped push Proposition 227 to a landslide victory in California, claiming 61 percent of the vote. Two years later, citing dramatic gains on test scores for immigrant children, the English for the Children movement moved to Arizona, where Proposition 203 notched 63 percent of the vote. In 2002, Massachusetts followed suit with Question 2, which was passed with 70 percent support. But in Colorado, voters rejected the English-immersion philosophy, turning it down 55 percent to 44 percent at the polls.

But the movement began to fizzle after 2002. The offices of English for the Children have closed, and studies have consistently been punching holes in core tenets of the English-only argument.

First to fall were the "dramatic gains" in test scores. Proponents of English-immersion stated emphatically that test scores for immigrant students had shot up 40 percent between 1998 and 2000. But research teams from Stanford University, Arizona State University and others pointed out that scores had risen for all students during that period. They also noted that the rising test scores were due to the fact that California had introduced a new achievement test and not to the effects of Prop 227.

More damning was the failure of Prop 227 to hold up its central promise. English for the Children had repeatedly claimed that results could be achieved with only a one-year transition period for English learners.

"The one-year limit is a fantasy," says Dr. Stephen Krashen, professor emeritus at the University of Southern California's Rossier School of Education. "In California and Arizona, English learners are currently gaining less than one level per year out of five, where level five means 'ready for the mainstream.'"

"That means that a child starting with no English will take at least five years before 'transitioning.' In Massachusetts, after three years of study, only half of the English learners are eligible to be considered for regular instruction," he says.

Merickel's AIR/WestEd research team noted several exemplary programs during the course of their study. Some of the programs were bilingual, others were English immersion and some were "dual immersion"—providing instruction in both Spanish and English.

Prop 227 has actually been a useful tool, she says, for forcing the state to focus much-needed attention on the non-English speaking population. Some former foes of the proposition, she says, "have come to see it as a positive thing."

But Shelly Spiegel-Coleman, president of Californians Together, an advocacy coalition formed in 1998, isn't willing to go so far.

"The truth is Prop 227 was a horrible blow for us, but if that was all that happened to us since 1998, we could have galvanized attention, made our points" and worked to ease the law's most restrictive elements, she says.

But Prop 227 was the first of a wave of reform movements, each more restrictive than its predecessor. First came a flurry of one-size-fits-all, skill-based reading programs, crafted to meet the curricular needs specified in Prop 227.

"They allow no accommodation for non-native speakers, and they're sweeping the country," Spiegel-Coleman says.

And then there are the harsh accountability systems mandated by No Child Left Behind.

"There are these people who have so much invested in these English-only reading programs and accountability systems who do not want to admit that what they're doing is wrong for kids," Spiegel-Coleman says.

Indeed, the stakes in these political battles over education could not be higher. According to U.S. Census figures, the number of children living in homes where English is not the primary language more than doubled from 1979 to 1999, from 6 million to 14 million. California was home to more than 1.4 million English learners—or nearly 40 percent of all such public school students in the nation (excluding Puerto Rico).

These "language minority" students face formidable obstacles in school, according to the National Center for Education Statistics. The dropout rate is 31 percent for language minority children who speak English, compared with 51 percent for language minority kids who do not and only 10 percent for the general population.

"At some point," says Shanahan, "we better get serious about immigration, about integrating immigrants as productive, tax-paying and social security-supporting parts of our work force. To do these things, they have to be able to do the work that we do in the United States—that means we have to be making quality choices to provide them with a quality education."

But the discussion about quality has only begun, says Shanahan, noting that his review found only 17 studies concerned with educational quality, compared with more than 450 studies examining types of reading programs.

Meanwhile the discussion about the language of instruction—a discussion Shanahan says is deeply political—seems never-ending.

RELATED ARTICLE: Six myths about bilingual education.

Myth 1: Bilingual programs are mostly concerned with maintaining the ethnic culture of the family.

Response: While some bilingual programs encourage development of a student's native language after English has been mastered, the major goal of bilingual education is the rapid acquisition of English and mastery of academic subjects.

Myth 2: Bilingual education doesn't work; it prevents children from acquiring English.

Response: Scientific studies consistently show that children in bilingual programs typically score higher on tests of English than do children in all-English immersion programs. In fact, three major reviews coming to this conclusion were published last year in professional, scientific journals.

Myth 3: Children languish in bilingual programs for many years, never learning enough English to study in mainstream classes.

Response: According to a recent report from New York City for children entering school at kindergarten and grade 1, only 14 percent were still in bilingual education after six years. From data provided by the state of Texas, I have estimated that for those who started at kindergarten, only 7 percent were still in bilingual education after grade 5.

Most students in bilingual programs in upper grades are those who came to the United States at an older age. These late-comers face a daunting task: Many come with inadequate preparation in their country of origin, and need to acquire English as well as assimilate years of subject matter knowledge.

Myth 4: Bilingual programs teach only in the native language.

Response: Some critics have claimed that bilingual education requires that children spend five to seven years mastering their native language before they can learn English. This is not correct. In properly organized bilingual programs, English is introduced immediately. ESL [English as a Second Language instruction] begins from the first day, and subjects are taught in English as soon as they can be made comprehensible. Research confirms that English is not delayed by bilingual education. According to one study of bilingual programs, by the time children are in third grade, 75 percent of their subject matter is in English, and it is 90 percent by grade 5.

Myth 5: Immigrants, especially Spanish-speakers, are refusing to learn English.

Response: They aren't refusing to learn English. According to the most recent census, only 7 percent of those who said another language was spoken at home cannot speak English. These figures include newcomers. Census data also tells us that Spanish speakers are acquiring English at the same rate as other groups.

Spanish speakers born in the United States report that they speak, read and write English better than they do Spanish by the time they finish high school. One does, of course, occasionally run into immigrants who don't speak English. These are usually new arrivals, or those who have not been able to find the time or opportunity to acquire English.

Myth 6: Bilingual education is not done in other countries, only in the United States.

Response: Bilingual education is not the most widely used approach for children acquiring a second language, but it is widespread. Most European countries provide bilingual education for immigrant children, and studies done by European scholars show that children in these programs acquire the second language of the country as well as and usually better than those in "immersion" programs. There are also numerous programs for the languages spoken by indigenous minority communities. No member of the European Economic Community has passed the equivalent of California's Proposition 227.

Rosalie Pedalino Porter  **NO**

The Case Against
Bilingual Education

Bilingual education is a classic example of an experiment that was begun with the best of humanitarian intentions but has turned out to be terribly wrongheaded. To understand this experiment, we need to look back to the mid-1960s, when the civil-rights movement for African-Americans was at its height and Latino activists began to protest the damaging circumstances that led to unacceptably high proportions of school dropouts among Spanish-speaking children—more than 50 percent nationwide. Latino leaders borrowed the strategies of the civil-rights movement, calling for legislation to address the needs of Spanish-speaking children—Cubans in Florida, Mexicans along the southern border, Puerto Ricans in the Northeast. In 1968 Congress approved a bill filed by Senator Ralph Yarborough, of Texas, aimed at removing the language barrier to an equal education. The Bilingual Education Act was a modestly funded ($7.5 million for the first year) amendment to the Elementary and Secondary Education Act of 1965, intended to help poor Mexican-American children learn English. At the time, the goal was "not to keep any specific language alive," Yarborough said. "It is not the purpose of the bill to create pockets of different languages through the country . . . but just to try to make those (children) fully literate in English."

English was not always the language of instruction in American schools. During the eighteenth century classes were conducted in German, Dutch, French, and Swedish in some schools in Pennsylvania, Maryland, and Virginia. From the mid nineteenth to the early twentieth century, classes were taught in German in several cities across the Midwest. For many years French was taught and spoken in Louisiana schools, Greek in Pittsburgh. Only after the First World War, when German was proscribed, did public sentiment swing against teaching in any language but English.

These earlier decisions on education policy were made in school, church, city, or state. Local conditions determined local school policy. But in 1968, for the first time, the federal government essentially dictated how non-English-speaking children should be educated. That action spawned state laws and legal decisions in venues all the way up to the Supreme Court. No end of money and effort was poured into a program that has since become the most controversial arena in public education.

~❦~

In simplest terms, bilingual education is a special effort to help immigrant children learn English so that they can do regular schoolwork with their English-speaking classmates and receive an equal educational opportunity. But what it is in the letter and the spirit of the law is not what it has become in practice. Some experts decided early on that children should be taught for a time in their native languages, so that they would continue to learn other subjects while learning English. It was expected that the transition would take a child three years.

From this untried experimental idea grew an education industry that expanded far beyond its original mission to teach English and resulted in the extended segregation of non-English-speaking students. In practice, many bilingual programs became more concerned with teaching in the native language and maintaining the ethnic culture of the family than with teaching children English in three years.

Beginning in the 1970s several notions were put forward to provide a rationale, after the fact, for the bilingual-teaching experiment. José Cárdenas, the director emeritus of the Intercultural Development Research Association in San Antonio, and Blandina Cárdenas (no relation), an associate professor of educational administration at the University of Texas at San Antonio, published their "theory of incompatibilities." According to this theory, Mexican-American children in the United States are so different from "majority" children that they must be given bilingual and bicultural instruction in order to achieve academic success. Educators were convinced of the soundness of the idea—an urgent need for special teaching for non-English-speaking children—and judges handed down court decisions on the basis of it.

Jim Cummins, a bilingual-education theorist and a professor of education at the University of Toronto, contributed two hypotheses. His "developmental interdependence" hypothesis suggests that learning to read in one's native language facilitates reading in a second language. His "threshold" hypothesis suggests that children's achievement in the second language depends on the level of their mastery of their native language and that the most-positive cognitive effects occur when both languages are highly developed. Cummins's hypotheses were interpreted to mean that a solid foundation in native-language literacy and subject-matter learning would best prepare students for learning in English. In practice these notions work against the goals of bilingual education—English-language mastery and academic achievement in English in mainstream classrooms.

Bilingual education has heightened awareness of the needs of immigrant, migrant, and refugee children. The public accepts that these children are entitled to special help; we know that the economic well-being of our society depends on maintaining a literate population with the academic competence for higher education and skilled jobs. The typical complaint heard years ago, "My grandfather came from Greece [or Sicily or Poland] and they didn't do anything special for him, and he did okay," no longer figures in the public discussion.

Bilingual education has brought in extra funding to hire and train paraprofessionals, often the parents of bilingual children, as classroom aides. Career programs in several school districts, among them an excellent one in Seattle that was in operation through early 1996, pay college tuition for paraprofessionals so that they may qualify as teachers, thus attracting more teachers from immigrant communities to the schools. Large school districts such as those in New York and Los Angeles have long had bilingual professionals on their staffs of psychologists, speech therapists, social workers, and other specialists.

Promoting parental understanding of American schools and encouraging parental involvement in school activities are also by-products of bilingual education. Workshops and training sessions for all educators on the historical and cultural backgrounds of the rapidly growing and varied ethnic communities in their districts result in greater understanding of and respect for non-English-speaking children and their families. These days teachers and school administrators make an effort to communicate with parents who have a limited command of English, by sending letters and school information to them at home in their native languages and by employing interpreters when necessary for parent-teacher conferences. In all these ways bilingual education has done some good.

·◦◎◦·

But has it produced the desired results in the classroom? The accumulated research of the past thirty years reveals almost no justification for teaching children in their native languages to help them learn either English or other subjects—and these are the chief objectives of all legislation and judicial decisions in this field. Self-esteem is not higher among limited-English students who are taught in their native languages, and stress is not higher among children who are introduced to English from the first day of school—though self-esteem and stress are the factors most often cited by advocates of bilingual teaching.

The final report of the *Hispanic Dropout Project* (issued in February) states,

> While the dropout rate for other school-aged populations has declined, more or less steadily, over the last 25 years, the overall Hispanic dropout rate started higher and has remained between 30 and 35 percent during that same time period . . . 2.5 times the rate for blacks and 3.5 times the rate for white non-Hispanics.

About one out of every five Latino children never enters a U.S. school, which inflates the Latino dropout rate. According to a 1995 report on the dropout situation from the National Center on Education Statistics, speaking Spanish at home does not correlate strongly with dropping out of high school; what does correlate is having failed to acquire English-language ability. The NCES report states,

For those youths that spoke Spanish at home, English speaking ability was related to their success in school. . . . The status dropout rate
for young Hispanics reported to speak English 'well' or 'very well'
was . . . 19.2 percent, a rate similar to the 17.5 percent status dropout
rate observed for enrolled Hispanic youths that spoke only English at
home.

In the past ten years several national surveys of the parents of limited-
English schoolchildren have shown that a large majority consider learning
English and having other subjects taught in English to be of much greater
importance than receiving instruction in the native language or about the
native culture. In 1988 the Educational Testing Service conducted a national
Parent Preference Study among 2,900 Cuban, Mexican, Puerto Rican, and
Asian parents with children in U.S. public schools. Although most of the parents said they wanted special help for their children in learning English and
other subjects, they differed on whether their children should be taught in
their native languages. Asian parents were the most heavily opposed to the
use of native languages in the schools. Among Latino groups, the Puerto Rican
parents were most in favor, the Mexicans somewhat less, and the Cubans least
of all. A large majority of the parents felt that it is the family's duty, not the
school's, to teach children about the history and traditions of their ancestors.
When Mexican parents were asked if they wanted the school to teach reading
and writing in Spanish and English, 70 percent answered yes. But when they
were asked if they wanted Spanish taught in school if it meant less time for
teaching English, only 12 percent were in favor.

In the most recent national survey of Latino parents, published by
the Center for Equal Opportunity, in Washington, D.C., 600 Latino parents
of school-age children were interviewed (in Spanish or English) in five U.S.
cities—Houston, Los Angeles, Miami, New York, and San Antonio. A strong
majority favored learning English as the first order of business for their children, considering it more important than learning other subjects, and much
more important than reading and writing in Spanish.

Having begun quietly in the 1980s and gained momentum in the 1990s,
Latino opposition to native-language teaching programs is now publicly
apparent. Two actions by communities of Latino parents demonstrate this
turn of events.

A hundred and fifty parents with children in Brooklyn public schools
filed a lawsuit in September of 1995, charging that because their children routinely remained segregated in bilingual programs in excess of three years, and
in some cases in excess of six years, contrary to section 3204 (2) of the State
Education Law, these children were not receiving adequate instruction in English, "the crucial skill that leads to equal opportunity in schooling, jobs, and
public life in the United States."

New York State law limits participation in a bilingual program to three years, but an extension can be granted for up to three years more if an individual review of the student's progress seems to warrant it. And here is the nub of the lawsuit: thousands of students are routinely kept in native-language classrooms for six years or longer without even the pretense of individual progress reviews.

Unfortunately, even with the help of a strong champion of their cause, Sister Kathy Maire, and the pro bono services of a prestigious New York law firm, Paul, Weiss, Rifkind, Wharton & Garrison, the parents lost their case. Under New York law these parents in fact have the right not to enroll their children in bilingual classes, or to remove them from bilingual classes, but in practice pressure from school personnel is almost impossible to overcome. Teachers and principals tell parents that their children will fail in English-language classrooms. They play on ethnic pride, asserting that children of a Latino background need to be taught in Spanish to improve their self-esteem.

In May of last year the Court of Appeals of the State of New York ruled that there could be no further appeals. But the publicity attracted by the case may encourage other Latino parents to take action on behalf of their children. And one concrete improvement has already occurred: the New York City Board of Education announced an end in 1996 to the automatic testing for English-language skills that children with Spanish surnames had undergone when they started school.

On the other coast an equally irate group of Latino parents moved against the Ninth Street School in Los Angeles. Seventy families of mostly Mexican garment workers planned the protest through Las Familias del Pueblo, a community organization that provides after-school child care. Typical of the protesters are Selena and Carlos (I have changed their names because they are undocumented immigrants), who left the poverty of a rural Mexican village in 1985 to come to work in Los Angeles. Their children were born in Los Angeles, but the school insisted that they not be taught in English until they had learned to read and write in Spanish, by the fourth or fifth grade. The parents complained to the school for years that children who lived in Spanish-speaking homes and neighborhoods needed to study in English in the primary grades, when children find it easier to learn a language than they will later on.

Persistent stonewalling by administrators finally moved the parents to keep their children out of school for nearly two weeks in February of 1996, a boycott that made national news. The parents demanded that their children be placed in English-language classes, a demand that has since been met. The school administrators waited too long to make this change: the previous spring only six students (about one percent of enrollment) had been deemed sufficiently fluent in English to "graduate" to regular classrooms in the next school year.

In the early 1970s almost all the students in bilingual classes spoke Spanish. Today, of the three million limited-English students in U.S. public schools, more than 70 percent speak Spanish at home; the rest speak any of 327 other languages. California alone enrolls 1.4 million limited-English children in its schools—one of every four students in the state. According to the

1990 U.S. census, 70 percent of limited-English students are concentrated in California, Florida, Illinois, New Jersey, New York, and Texas.

❧

Controversy over native-language education is at the boil in California. In our most multicultural state, where minorities now constitute 46 percent of the population, a revolution is brewing. In 1987 the California legislature failed to reauthorize the Bilingual-Bicultural Education Act, allowing it to expire. However, the California Department of Education immediately notified all school districts that even without the state law the same requirements would be enforced and bilingual programs continued. In July of 1995 the State Board of Education announced two major policy changes: the "preference" for native-language programs would henceforth be revoked and school districts would be given as much flexibility as possible in choosing their own programs; and school districts were ordered to be more diligent in recording evidence of student achievement than in describing the teaching methods used.

Yet in two years only four school districts have succeeded in obtaining waivers from the department, permitting them to initiate English-language programs for limited-English students. Why should schools have to seek waivers when no state or federal law, no court decision, no state policy bars them from teaching in English? The most important case to date is that of the Orange Unified School District, with 7,000 limited-English students.

Orange Unified applied in early May of . . . [1997] for permission to focus on English-language teaching in kindergarten through sixth grade while using a small amount of Spanish. The Department of Education strongly opposed the district, as did the California Association for Bilingual Education, California Rural Legal Assistance, and the organization Multicultural Education, Training, and Advocacy (META). Local Latino activists publicly criticized the district's change of plan, and some bilingual teachers resigned.

Nevertheless, the Board of Education . . . [in] July [of 1997] granted Orange permission to try an English-language program for one year. A lawsuit was filed, and a temporary restraining order granted. But . . . [in] September [1997], U.S. District Court Judge William B. Shubb lifted the restraining order. In his seventeen-page decision the judge wrote, "The court will not second-guess the educational policy choices made by educational authorities." And he added a ruling with much broader application:

> It is clear that "appropriate action" does not require "bilingual education." . . . The alleged difference between two sound LEP [Limited-English Proficient] educational theories—ESL [English as a Second Language] and bilingual instruction—is inadequate to demonstrate irreparable harm.

The federal court ruling allowed Orange to proceed with its English-language program. But the case was returned to Sacramento County Superior Court, where Judge Ronald B. Robie ruled that nothing in California state law requires primary-language instruction, and therefore no waiver is needed for a district to provide an English-language program; and that federal law permits educational programs not to include native-language instruction. Soon after Robie's ruling the Board of Education rescinded the policy that schools must obtain waivers in order to eliminate bilingual programs. Although the court decision may be appealed, these two actions signal a victory for Orange Unified and have implications for other California districts as well. The legal battle has already cost the Orange district $300,000, which no doubt would have been better spent on students. It is estimated that the new program will cost an additional $60,000 the first year, but the superintendent of Orange Unified schools, Robert French, says, "We're not doing this to save money. We're doing this to save kids."

Ron Unz, a Silicon Valley entrepreneur, has long been concerned about the California education system's failures, especially as they affect its 1.4 million limited-English students. He has decided to put his time, energy, and money into an initiative—"English for the Children"—meant to give all California voters a say on the language of public education. If the initiative passes, in elections to be held on June 2 [1998], it will give "preference" to English-language programs for immigrant children, reduce the length of time children may remain in special programs, and make the state spend $50 million a year to teach English to adults. Bilingual programs will be allowed only in localities where parents actually request native-language teaching for their children.[1]

. . . [In] November [1997], Unz and the co-chairman of the drive, Gloria Matta Tuchman, submitted more than 700,000 signatures to put the petition on the California ballot. The drive has the support of several Latino leaders in California, most notably Jaime Escalante, who is its honorary chairman. Escalante is the Los Angeles high school teacher whose success in teaching his Latino students advanced calculus gained him national fame in the film *Stand and Deliver*.

Though some opponents characterize the petition as "anti-immigrant," Unz and Matta Tuchman have strong pro-immigrant credentials. In 1994 Unz ran against the incumbent Pete Wilson in the Republican primary for governor and forcefully opposed the referendum to deny schooling and health benefits to illegal immigrants—a referendum that passed with Wilson's support. Matta Tuchman is a recognized Latina advocate for improved schooling for all immigrant children, but especially Spanish-speakers. The measure is likely to pass, some believe with strong ethnic support. A *Los Angeles Times* poll . . . [in] October [1997] found Latino voters backing the initiative by 84 percent, and Anglos by 80 percent. A more recent survey showed a reduced amount of support—66 percent of respondents, and 46 percent of Latinos, in favor. But whether or not the initiative passes, bilingual education has had a sufficient trial period to be pronounced a failure. It is time finally to welcome immigrant children into our society by adding to the language they already know a full degree of competency in the common language of their new country—give these children the very best educational opportunity for *inclusion*.

Note

1. It did pass.—Eds.

EXPLORING THE ISSUE

Is There Room for Bilingual Education in American Schools?

Critical Thinking and Reflection

1. What are the working components of a bilingual education program? What distinguishes bilingual education programs from traditional education programs?
2. What are the assumptions about teaching and learning on which bilingual education programs are based?
3. What are the goals of bilingual education?
4. How does the current controversy concerning Latino immigration influence this issue?
5. How do lingering racial concerns influence the discussion of bilingualism?
6. What are the negative impacts as identified by critics of bilingualism? Explain their significance.
7. Why is bilingual education under attack today?

Is There Common Ground?

In considering this issue, it is noteworthy to remind readers that bilingual education programs involve the teaching of English along with a secondary language. Some classes are taught in a native language and some are taught in English. As noted above, bilingual education is not new to American public education. Prior to the reform era of the 1960s, American educators tended to accept that the best method for educating immigrants and incorporating them within the wider American society was through "Americanization." Today, this is called the English immersion approach. Some of this history is detailed in Porter's "The Case Against Bilingual Education." The rise of bilingualism can be dated to the late 1960s when American educators became increasingly concerned with the challenge of providing equal opportunities for quality education to all students. Not without controversy early on, bilingualism spread rapidly within America's public schools. At the same time, a backlash developed that culminated in a California initiative to end bilingual education in public schools, Proposition 227. In 1998, the measure passed by a wide margin among voters. The quality of such programs and the outcomes that they produced in student learning and advancement came under serious questioning. Criticisms ranged from the claim that they perpetuated separate identities to the notion that they retarded assimilation.

Additional Resources

Carger, Chris Liska. 1996. *Of Borders and Dreams: A Mexican-American Experience of Urban Education* (New York: Teachers College Press).

Chavez, Leo R. 2008. *The Latino Threat: Constructing Immigrants, Citizens, and the Nation* (Stanford University Press).

Crawford, James, ed., 1992. *Language Loyalties: A Source Book on the Official English Controversy* (University of Chicago Press).

Donegan, Craig. 1996. "Debate Over Bilingualism: Should English Be the Nation's Official Language," *CQ Researcher* (January 19).

Forrest, S.N. 2004. "Implications of No Child Left Behind on Family Literacy in a Multicultural Community," *The Clearing House* (September/October, pp. 41–45).

Gonzalez, Juan. 2011. *Harvest of Empire: A History of Latinos in America* (Penguin Books).

Hakuta, Kenji. 1987. *The Mirror of Language: The Debate On Bilingualism* (Basic Books).

Hart, P.K. 2006. "Why Juan Can't Read," *Texas Monthly* (October).

Krashen, Stephen. 1999. *Condemned Without a Trial: Bogus Arguments Against Bilingual Education* (Heinemann).

May, Stephen. 2011. *Language and Minority Rights: Ethnicity, Nationalism and the Politics of Language* (Routledge).

Montano, Theresa et al. 2005. "The DEbilingualization of California's Prospective Bilingual Teachers." *Social Justice* (32:3).

Olivos, Edward M. and Lilia Sarmiento. 2006. "Is There Room for Biliteracy? Credentialing California's Future Bilingual Teachers," *Issues in Teacher Education* (15:Spring(l)).

Porter, Rosalie Pedalino. 1996. *Forked Tongue: The Politics of Bilingual Education* (Transaction Publishers).

Porter, Rosalie Pedalino. 2011. *American Immigrant: My Life in Three Languages* (Transaction Publishers).

Potowski, Kim. 2010. *Language Diversity in the USA* (Cambridge University Press).

Robinson, Lori, Paul Cuadros and Alysia Tate. 2004. "Strength in Numbers," *The Crisis* (January/February).

Soto, Lourdes Diaz and Christine Sleeter. 1996. *Language, Culture, and Power: Bilingualism Families and the Struggle for Quality Education* (State University of New York Press).

Suarez-Orozco, Marcelo and Mariela Paez, eds., 2002. *Latinos: Remaking America* (University of California Press).

Zamudio, Margaret, Christopher Russell, Francisco Rios, and Jacquelyn Bridgeman. 2010. *Critical Race Theory Matters: Education and Ideology* (Routledge).

This Hoover Institution of Stanford University collects and distributes knowledge and ideas about "peace, personal freedom and to the safeguards of the American system." It seeks to "limit government intrusion into the lives of individuals." With a broad range of topics including international affairs, the site is the source of obtaining several books and academic journals. It contains a critique of bilingual education.

www.hoover.org/

The website of the National Association for Bilingual Education is "devoted to representing Bilingual Learners and Bilingual Education professionals." Its mission is to advocate for bilingualism in a variety of ways including research, education, and professional development. It contains current news stories dealing with bilingualism and related topics.

www.nabe.org/

The mission of the ProEnglish website is to work to adopt laws and support individual state efforts to declare English the official language of the United States. It claims to be the nation's leading English language advocacy group. Rosalie Porter is the chair of the board of the site.

www.proenglish.org/

ISSUE 16

Should Children of Undocumented Immigrants Have a Birthright to U.S. Citizenship?

YES: Eric Foner, from "Birthright Citizenship Sets America Apart," http://host.madison.com, August 20, 2010

NO: George F. Will, from "An Argument to be Made about Immigrant Babies and Citizenship," *The Washington Post*, March 28, 2010

Learning Outcomes

After reading this issue, the student should be able to:

- Understand the criteria established for the granting of citizenship to children of undocumented immigrants.
- Identify and explain significant American values that are supportive of granting birthright citizenship.
- Comprehend and explain why a critical examination of the Fourteenth Amendment is crucial to the discussion of this issue.
- Understand how both Foner and Will employ the U.S. Constitution and the law to support their ideas.
- Understand birthright citizenship within the context of the larger current immigration issue.

ISSUE SUMMARY

YES: Distinguished professor of history at Columbia University, Eric Foner examines the legal and constitutional basis for granting birthright citizenship and argues that this right illuminates the strength of American society.

NO: Conservative newspaper columnist and commentator, George F. Will is troubled by the facile tendency to grant birthright citizenship to the children of undocumented immigrants. He views this practice as reflecting a misinterpretation of the Bill of Rights and the Fourteenth Amendment. He vigorously opposes this policy.

As the 2012 presidential election campaign intensifies, immigration policy looms large as an issue that might decide the outcome in key states. This development reflects the growing strength of Latinos within the electorate, especially in states such as Texas, Colorado, New Mexico, Arizona, and California, among others. Several states, including Arizona, Alabama, and Georgia, have passed laws that supporters of immigration view as draconian and anti-Hispanic. The failure to pass the Dream Act (development, relief, and education, for alien minors), a measure that would provide a pathway to citizenship for those who complete a college degree or serve in the military, has added to the controversy.

The legislative initiatives that have been passed in states mentioned above have generated significant social protest and a test of the constitutionality of such laws that is pending within the U.S. Supreme Court. This issue and related concerns have tended to resurface at various times throughout American history. For example, it was a major issue during the early 1920s and in response the nation passed several anti-immigration statues such as the Immigration Act of 1921. America's engagement of these issues often occurs during periods of national distress. The current economic crisis and the fears engendered by the challenges to homeland security, be they real or imagined, inform the current debate. Unfortunately, the discussion of such issues is often attended by references that reflect racism and nativist bias.

Eric Foner, a historian and civil rights expert, is a strong proponent of birthright citizenship. He believes that all children born in the United States, regardless of the status of their parents, should be granted this constitutional right. Foner reviews relevant constitutional and legal support for birthright citizenship and finds that this policy is firmly grounded in the law. To Foner, birthright citizenship is supported by the Equal Protection clause of the Fourteenth Amendment of the U.S. Constitution. Further, he states that "the Supreme Court has consistently ruled that birthright citizenship applies to every American-born child and equal protection of the laws to citizens and noncitizens alike."

Professor Foner believes that the willingness of America to accept and assimilate immigrants is a positive testament regarding the nation's culture and values. He also embraces the notion that favorable policies toward immigrants, including birthright citizenship, have contributed much to overcoming the troubled legacy of slavery and related toxic dimensions of the American experience.

George F. Will, a popular conservative commentator and newspaper columnist, presents an argument in opposition to granting birthright citizenship to the children of illegal immigrant parents. He is concerned that this policy offers positive incentives to illegal immigration. Denying birthright citizenship to such children would make a contribution to the lessening of illegal immigration to the United States in the minds of thinkers such as George F. Will. He argues that there is no legal or constitutional impediment to the passage of legislation by the Congress of the Unites States that would put an end to this practice.

Will bases the substance of his argument primarily on the writing of Professor Lino Graglia of the University of Texas Law School. Thus, he has concluded that the granting of birthright citizenship to children of undocumented immigrants based on the first clause of the Fourteenth Amendment is flawed policy. He states that to employ this clause in such a manner reflects a misinterpretation of this language. He notes, "If those who wrote and ratified the 14th Amendment *had* imagined laws restricting immigration—and had anticipated waves of illegal immigration—is it reasonable to presume they would have wanted to provide the reward of citizenship to the children of the violators of those laws? Surely not."

As is the case with most conservatives, George F. Will believes that immigrants are a burden to the nation (see Issues 13 and 14). In the NO selection, he articulates a specific concern with immigrants taking advantage of our social welfare system. He is likely to agree with those who view immigrants as a source of cultural degradation, crime, drug abuse, and other social problems.

The United States continues to be challenged by issues of multiculturalism and diversity, including immigration and birthright citizenship. These challenges and the ensuing conflicts that they generate continue to exist despite the fact that the United States is increasingly a multiethnic, multiracial nation. Demographers anticipate that by 2042 people of color collectively will comprise a majority of the population of the United States. Los Angeles has already crossed this threshold. These changing demographics within the American population pose serious challenges for the nation's future.

The issue of birthright citizenship has arisen at time when immigration has emerged as one of the primary social and political issues confronting the nation. It is a major focus of the debates within the current (2012) presidential campaign. Restrictive immigration laws have been passed by state legislators and local governments across the nation, and more states are considering such initiatives. It is one of the most divisive issues that confrons the nation today. In light of its political implications, students should locate their treatment of this issue within the larger issues of immigration reform. Further, students should consider the impact the denial of citizenship to children of undocumented immigrants poses for American family values.

YES

Eric Foner

Birthright Citizenship Sets America Apart

New York—For almost 150 years Americans have believed that anyone born here, whatever his or her origins, can be a good citizen. There is no reason to believe the children of illegal immigrants are any different.

Congress should think long and hard before tampering with this essential American principle embodied in the 14th Amendment. Approved by Congress in 1866 at the outset of Reconstruction and ratified two years later, the amendment establishes the principle of birthright citizenship. With minor exceptions, all persons born in this country are American citizens, whatever the status of their parents.

Several senators and conservative political commentators are now demanding that the amendment be reinterpreted or rewritten so as to exclude the children of illegal immigrants.

Bitter conflicts about who should be an American citizen are hardly new, nor are efforts to exclude those deemed for one reason or another undesirable. The very first naturalization law, enacted in 1790, barred nonwhite immigrants from ever becoming citizens. This prohibition was lifted for Africans in 1870 but lasted into the mid-20th century for Asians.

The Civil War transformed the debate over citizenship. In a sense, the 14th Amendment wrote into the Constitution the results of the Union's triumph and the destruction of slavery. It begins by defining . . . citizens [as] all persons born or naturalized in the U.S. "and subject to the jurisdiction thereof"—language meant to exclude Indians, deemed to be citizens of their respective tribes, and American-born children of foreign diplomats. It goes on to bar states from depriving these citizens of life, liberty or property or denying them the "equal protection of the laws."

The most important change in the Constitution since the Bill of Rights, the 14th Amendment was intended, first, to establish beyond doubt the citizenship of the 4 million emancipated slaves.

But the Republicans who controlled Congress also had a larger purpose. "It is a singular fact," the abolitionist Wendell Phillips wrote in 1866, "that, unlike all other nations, this nation has yet a question as to what makes or constitutes a citizen." The 14th Amendment established the first national definition of citizenship.

Did Congress intend birthright citizenship to apply to the children of illegal residents? No such group existed in 1866; at the time, just about anyone who wished to enter the country was free to do so. Only later were certain groups singled out for exclusion—prostitutes, polygamists, lunatics, anarchists, and, starting in 1882, the entire population of China.

Not until 1924 was the Border Patrol established, in connection with the law setting nationality quotas for immigration. Initially, its purpose was to keep "undesirable" Europeans—Italians, Greeks, and other southern Europeans—from sneaking across the Mexican border.

Until 1965, there were no numerical limits on immigration from countries in the Western Hemisphere, so the issue of illegal Mexican immigrants, which so alarms today's critics of the 14th Amendment, didn't arise.

The closest analogy in 1866 to today's illegal aliens were immigrants from Asia. The Chinese aroused considerable hostility among white Americans, especially on the West Coast, and with an eye on congressional elections, the amendment's opponents charged that it would make citizens of Chinese children born in this country. The amendment's authors didn't retreat in the face of blatant racism. They chose their words carefully; when they wrote "all persons," they meant it.

The Supreme Court has consistently ruled that birthright citizenship applies to every american-born child and equal protection of the laws to citizens and noncitizens alike.

The juxtaposition of the 14th Amendment with the bar on the naturalization of Asian immigrants long affected Asian-American life. In the early 20th century, California barred aliens ineligible for citizenship from owning land, so Asian parents transferred title to their homes and farms to their citizen children. Not until World War II was China given a quota (all of 105 persons per year) of immigrants eligible for naturalization. Only with the immigration reform of 1965 did Asians achieve the same status as other immigrants.

The 14th Amendment made the Constitution what it is today: a document that guarantees the equal rights of all Americans and to which individuals and groups who feel they are being denied equality can appeal. As the 19th century Republican editor George William Curtis wrote, it was part of a process that changed the government from one "for white men" to one "for mankind."

Adopted as part of the effort to purge the nation of the legacy of slavery, birthright citizenship remains an eloquent statement about the nature of our society and a powerful force for immigrant assimilation. In a world where most countries limit access to citizenship via ethnicity, culture or religion, it sets our nation apart.

George F. Will  **NO**

An Argument to Be Made about Immigrant Babies and Citizenship

A simple reform would drain some scalding steam from immigration arguments that may soon again be at a roiling boil. It would bring *the interpretation of the 14th Amendment* into conformity with what the authors of its text intended, and with common sense, thereby removing an incentive for illegal immigration.

To end the practice of "birthright citizenship," all that is required is to correct the misinterpretation of that amendment's first sentence: "All persons born or naturalized in the United States, and subject to the jurisdiction thereof, are citizens of the United States and of the state wherein they reside." From these words has flowed the practice of conferring citizenship on children born here to illegal immigrants.

A parent from a poor country, writes professor Lino Graglia of the University of Texas law school, "can hardly do more for a child than make him or her an American citizen, entitled to all the advantages of the American welfare state." Therefore, "It is difficult to imagine a more irrational and self-defeating legal system than one which makes unauthorized entry into this country a criminal offense and simultaneously provides perhaps the greatest possible inducement to illegal entry."

Writing in the Texas Review of Law and Politics, Graglia says this irrationality is rooted in a misunderstanding of the phrase "subject to the jurisdiction thereof." What was this intended or understood to mean by those who wrote it in 1866 and ratified it in 1868? The authors and ratifiers could not have intended birthright citizenship for illegal immigrants because in 1868 *there were and never had been any illegal immigrants because no law ever had restricted immigration.*

If those who wrote and ratified the 14th Amendment *had* imagined laws restricting immigration—and had anticipated huge waves of illegal immigration—is it reasonable to presume they would have wanted to provide the reward of citizenship to the children of the violators of those laws? Surely not.

The *Civil Rights Act of 1866* begins with language from which the 14th Amendment's citizenship clause is derived: "All persons born in the United States, *and not subject to any foreign power,* excluding Indians not taxed, are hereby declared to be citizens of the United States." (Emphasis added.) The explicit exclusion of Indians from birthright citizenship was not repeated in the 14th Amendment because it was considered unnecessary. Although Indians were at least partially subject to U.S. jurisdiction, they owed allegiance to their tribes, not the United States. This reasoning—divided allegiance—applies equally to exclude the children of resident aliens, legal as well as illegal, from birthright citizenship. Indeed, today's regulations issued by the departments of Homeland Security and Justice stipulate:

> "A person born in the United States to a foreign diplomatic officer accredited to the United States, as a matter of international law, is not subject to the jurisdiction of the United States. That person is not a United States citizen under the 14th Amendment."

Sen. Lyman Trumbull of Illinois was, Graglia writes, one of two "principal authors of the citizenship clauses in 1866 act and the 14th Amendment." He said that "subject to the jurisdiction of the United States" meant subject to its "complete" jurisdiction, meaning "not owing allegiance to anybody else." Hence children whose Indian parents had tribal allegiances were excluded from birthright citizenship.

Appropriately, in 1884 the Supreme Court held that children born to Indian parents were not born "subject to" U.S. jurisdiction because, among other reasons, the person so born could not change his status by his "own will without the action or assent of the United States." And "no one can become a citizen of a nation without its consent." Graglia says this decision "seemed to establish" that U.S. citizenship is "a consensual relation, requiring the consent of the United States." So: "This would clearly settle the question of birthright citizenship for children of illegal aliens. There cannot be a more total or forceful denial of consent to a person's citizenship than to make the source of that person's presence in the nation illegal."

Congress has heard testimony estimating that more than two-thirds of all births in Los Angeles public hospitals, and more than half of all births in that city, and nearly 10 percent of all births in the nation in recent years, have been to mothers who are here illegally. Graglia seems to establish that there is no constitutional impediment to Congress ending the granting of birthright citizenship to those whose presence here is "not only without the government's consent but in violation of its law."

EXPLORING THE ISSUE

Should Children of Undocumented Immigrants Have a Birthright to U.S. Citizenship?

Critical Thinking and Reflection

1. What are the criteria for establishing citizenship in the United States? How do these criteria apply to the children of undocumented immigrants?
2. What important American values does Foner identify in support of birthright citizenship?
3. What protections provided by the Fourteenth Amendment apply to birthright citizenship?
4. How does Eric Foner use the Fourteenth Amendment to support his position? How does George F. Will use the Fourteenth Amendment to develop his position?
5. Why has this become such a controversial issue today?
6. How has recent public policy such as Obama's proposed Dream Act sought to resolve the issue of birthright citizenship?

Is There Common Ground?

Immigrants continue to view America as a land of opportunity, and so they continue to take great risks to come here. Immigrants are and, for the foreseeable future, will be a significant component of the American population. So the question arises, what is an appropriate immigration policy for the United States? Within the immigration debates, the issue of birthright citizenship for children of undocumented immigrants has arisen. Both George F. Will and Eric Foner have joined this debate offering distinct, conflicting views on the matter. Angela Glover Blackwell, founder and CEO of PolicyLink, a website to advance economic and social equity, suggests that the fate of America hinges on how Americans react to changing demographics. Her concern is that, given the increasing number and percentage of people of color in the United States and their low socioeconomic status, it is in everyone's interest to ensure that America invests in their future. Minorities will be the majority and failure to invest in them will place the nation's future in jeopardy. Blackwell is concerned that there is a major challenge in the country reflective of a prevailing mindset that tends to view this emerging majority as "an unsolvable problem rather than targeting them for investments to secure the nation's future." Blackwell's idea transcends the debate. Whether children become American citizens through their birthright or other means, the fact is that they are going to live in the United States. We must prepare them for the future by investing in education, training, and necessary skills including new technology because it is in the best interests of the nation.

Additional Resources

Blackwell, Angela Glover, Stewart Kwoh, and Manuel Pastor. 2010. *Uncommon Ground: Race and America's Future* (W.W. Norton & Co.).

Chavez, Leo. 2008. *The Latino Threat: Constructing Immigrants, Citizens, and the Nation* (Stanford University Press).

De Genova, Nicholas and Ana Yolanda Ramos-Zayas. 2003. *Latino Crossings: Mexicans, Puerto Ricans, and the Politics of Race and Citizenship* (Routledge).

Gonzalez, Juan. 2011. *Harvest of Empire: A History of Latinos in America* (Penguin Books).

Meyer, Howard. 2000. *The Amendment that Refused to Die: A History of the Fourteenth Amendment* (Toronto: Madison Books).

Olivas, Michael. 2012. *No Undocumented Child Left Behind: Plyler v. Doe and the Education of Undocumented Schoolchildren* (New York University Press).

Perez, William. 2009. *We Are Americans: Undocumented Students Pursuing the American Dream* (Stylus Publishing).

Perez, William. 2011. *Americans by Heart: Undocumented Latino Students and the Promise of Higher Education (Multicultural Education Series)* (Teachers College Press).

Rodriguez, Clara. 2000. *Changing Race: Latinos, the Census, and the History of Ethnicity in the United States* (New York University Press).

Shachar, Ayelet. 2009. *The Birthright Lottery: Citizenship and Global Equity* (Harvard University Press).

Spickard, Paul. 2007. *Almost All Aliens: Immigration, Race, and Colonialism in American History and Identity* (Routledge).

Suarez-Orozco, Carola and Marcelo Suarez-Orozco. 2002. *Children of Immigration* (Harvard University Press).

Suarez-Orozco, Carola, Marcelo Suarez-Orozco, and Irina Todorova. 2010. *Learning in a New Land: Immigrant Students in American Society* (Belknap Press of Harvard University Press).

This site seeks to advance economic and social equity. It is "a national research and action institute advancing economic and social equity by Lifting Up What Works." Its mission is those closest to the nation's challenges are central to finding solutions. The site offers publications and analysis ranging from healthy food to the foreclosure crisis.

www.policylink.org

This website is accessed via the Dream Act portal. It offers political and sociological information on the Dream Act, its likelihood of passing, along with information on who is targeted by the act and what they can do in response to the proposed legislation. It is an interesting site in that the student can learn about the legislative process by using the Internet to communicate to elected representatives in Washington. A similar website, www.dreamact2009.org/, provides the same information. Although the Dream Act failed to get through Congress in 2010, interest remains high.

http://dreamact.info/

The Federation for American Immigration Reform (FAIR) website advocates for immigration policies that "will best serve American environmental, societal, and economic interests today and into the future." It offers data, maps, legislative news coverage, and statements on immigration issues. FAIR has been cited as an anti-immigrant hate group by the Southern Poverty Law Center. The site has a clear position on birthright citizenship and labels the children of illegal immigrants born in the United States as "anchor babies."

www.fairus.org

Internet References . . .

Teaching Tolerance

Teaching Tolerance is a web project of the Southern Poverty Law Center, which offers educators and students with a wide range of resources used for promoting multicultural understanding in schools and communities. Also available are an e-newsletter and an online version of the magazine, *Teaching Tolerance*, which is published twice a year.

www.teachingtolerance.org

U.S. Department of State

The U.S. Department of State website enables students to read official texts and speeches dealing with race and immigration issues such as racial profiling, affirmative action, black colleges, racism, voting rights, and immigrant labor.

www.state.gov/s/ocr/

The Sociological Imagination: Race and Ethnicity

This is the "race and ethnicity" part of the "Exercising the Sociological Imagination Tour" from the Trinity University Department of Sociology and Anthropology website. Helpful to students is the "Sociological Tour Through Cyberspace," which offers links to resources in race and ethnicity along with brief reports on American minority groups.

www.trinity.edu/~mkearl/index.html#in

Race in the 21st Century

This is the website of a political science professor at Michigan State University. Among the many offerings dealing with multiculturalism, education, civil rights, standardized tests, and citizenship is William B. Allen's "Race in the 21st Century" (3/22/99), dealing with race as a consideration in college admissions. Allen represents a conservative perspective.

**www.msu.edu/~allenwi/presentations
/Race_in_21st_Century_America.htm**

The Civil Rights Project: UCLA

The Civil Rights Project helps to renew the civil rights movement by "bridging the worlds of ideas and action, and by becoming a preeminent source of intellectual capital and a forum for building consensus within that movement." It is an excellent source of information and research findings in the field of race relations.

www.civilrightsproject.ucla.edu/

Social Science Data Analysis Network (SSDAN)

The Social Science Data Analysis Network (SSDAN) runs this website to research segregation in local communities across the country. It offers students a chance to do original quantitative research on segregation by selecting neighborhoods in cities and then analyzing the data on race. This site is recommended for a wide range of research possibilities.

www.censusscope.org/segregation.html

The Geography of Race and Ethnicity

*A*ny child who has walked or been driven through an American city knows that there is a geography of race and ethnicity in America. Geography implies that there are boundaries that separate or divide different groups of people. Immigrant neighborhoods, racial neighborhoods, the reservation, small towns, rural areas, and the suburb all conjure up images of race and ethnic residential patterns. References to "the hood," "uptown," "the Hispanic section," "Chinatown," and others remain in everyday language. Some boundary lines are visible, as noted in voting districts, zip codes, school districts, and municipal town lines. Many of these legal geographic boundaries across the country separate people along racial and ethnic lines, which can impact property values, public school attendance, and voter representation. Gerrymandering, the practice of dividing a voting district to give one political party an advantage, often occurs with race in mind. Still, other boundaries are invisible such as the spatial patterns established in social situations by school children and others. White children tend to sit with white children, and black children tend to sit with other black children. Is resegregation moving America to a new de facto segregation era? Beyond redistricting, what are the different ways in which the black vote has been suppressed? How is social space constructed by race and ethnic self-segregation? Do the high rates of black incarceration represent a new form of segregation?

- Are America's Public Schools Resegregating?
- Is There a Need for a Permanent Voting Rights Act?
- Do Minorities and Whites Engage in Self-Segregation?
- Is the Mass Incarceration of Blacks the New Jim Crow?

ISSUE 17

Are America's Public Schools Resegregating?

YES: Tim Lockette, from "Unmaking Brown," *Teaching Tolerance* (Spring 2010)

NO: Ingrid Gould Ellen, from "Welcome Neighbors?" *Brookings Review* (Winter 1997)

Learning Outcomes

After reading this issue, the student should be able to:

- Understand de jure as well as de facto segregation.
- Explain why some neighborhoods are integrated.
- Assess the consequences of the 1954 *Brown vs. Board of Education* Supreme Court desegregation decision.
- Use data effectively to illustrate resegregation.
- Understand the relationship between racial housing patterns and public school segregation in America.
- Appreciate the long history of racially segregated public schools in the United States.
- Understand how vital public school desegregation was to the civil rights movement.

ISSUE SUMMARY

YES: Tim Lockette, a freelance writer in Montgomery, Alabama, and former editor of *Teaching Tolerance,* demonstrates that through certain Supreme Court decisions, the elimination of bus programs, and flawed school choice programs, America's public schools are resegregating. The desegregation effects of the historic 1954 *Brown* decision have been reversed.

NO: Ingrid Gould Ellen, writer for *Brookings Review,* argues that neighborhood racial integration is increasing. She thinks researchers must balance their pessimistic findings of resegregation with increased integration.

After the Civil War and the Reconstruction Era, segregation replaced slavery as the primary basis for defining and developing race relations within the United States. In the wake of the *Plessy v. Ferguson* decision of the U.S. Supreme Court in 1896, segregation became the official policy of the U.S. government.

Before and after 1896, segregation took shape and form almost as if designed by an architect. The *Plessy* case, a public transportation issue, led to the "separate but equal" doctrine that extended to most areas of life including transportation, public accommodations, housing, employment, marriage, and education. Blacks who challenged the architecture of segregation risked losing jobs, places to live, and worst of all—especially for young black men—lynching. Countless "forced acts of humiliation" kept blacks separate from whites. It was with the *Brown v. Board of Education* decision of 1954 that legal segregation was reversed. In actuality, there were two *Brown* decisions rendered by the Court. In *Brown I,* the Court ruled that segregated schools are "inherently unequal," and *Plessy* was reversed. In *Brown II,* the Court challenged the school systems of the states to proceed to desegregate public schools "with all deliberate speed." The latter ruling was sufficiently vague and without a time line, so that it provided those who were opposed to integration the social and legal room to remain segregated.

The issues of American public education and residence are inextricably linked. Segregated schools are created through a variety of circumstances. Schools can be segregated because the community is segregated. Within "mixed" communities, schools may be segregated as the result of district mapping practices or neighborhood "redlining." This is known as de jure segregation and is illegal. However, de facto segregation, or school segregation resulting from housing patterns, is pervasive across the country today. And, the *Brown* decision has had little impact on those communities that practice de facto segregation.

Tim Lockette claims that America's public schools are resegregating and this development is perpetuating educational disadvantages faced by black and Latino students, which *Brown v. Board of Education* was expected to overcome. He cites the termination of bus programs, adverse Supreme Court decisions, and flawed school choice programs as sources of the resegregation phenomenon. Lockette's YES selection uses research conducted by Amy Stuart Wells and Gary Orfield, two noted authorities on school resegregation, in support of his presentation. He also offers an interesting and meaningful discussion of how the trend of resegregation of America's public schools might be reversed.

Ingrid Gould Ellen argues that integrated neighborhoods are growing in number and will most likely remain racially mixed in the future. Using census data that link households to neighborhoods, she found that certain demographic groups are more likely to move into racially mixed neighborhoods.

Whites who are more likely to move into racially mixed neighborhoods are young and single. Thus, she argues that communities with a larger proportion of rental housing are more likely to be integrated. Further, Ellen sees no evidence of white flight. Lastly, she points out that stability is an important factor in maintaining integrated neighborhoods and schools. In other words, the longer a community has been integrated, the more likely that it will remain integrated.

To understand resegregation, students must connect patterns of residential neighborhood formation to public education. Ellen's optimistic argument about the possibility of racial integration could be seen as a new way of looking at housing patterns. At the same time, Lockette points to a number of Court decisions that have contributed to an increasing trend of resegregation. What kinds of neighborhoods remain integrated? Segregated? What factors cause neighborhoods to change from integrated to segregated? How has the Court reversed school integration?

With the increase of suburbanization in the 1970s, America has gradually become more segregated. Segregation is generally imposed by a dominant group on a minority racial or ethnic group. Historically, housing practices in the United States have forced minorities into certain specific neighborhoods. At the same time, members of ethnic groups may seek the safety of a community of racial and ethnic peers. Typically, segregated minority neighborhoods are less desirable. Often poverty, poor government services, and low-achieving, segregated schools characterize them. On the other hand, all-white neighborhoods—indeed, they too are segregated—must be recognized as a significant factor in racial isolation today.

According to the Civil Rights Project at Harvard, as of 1999, "more than 70% of all Blacks attended schools that were predominantly Black," whereas white students were even more segregated with the vast majority attending schools "with few or no students of any other race." The Project points out that changes in segregation patterns are taking place in the general context of "an increasingly diverse public schools enrollment." Latinos, for example, have become increasingly segregated. Today more than 7 million Latinos attend public schools. Thus, two interesting trends are developing in the public schools—rising segregation and increasing diversity.

The example of Detroit illustrates the segregation issue. As one of the country's most segregated cities, almost 90 percent of its residents would have to move from segregated neighborhoods to achieve integration. Further, the vast majority of the residents of Buffalo, Chicago, Cincinnati, St. Louis, New York, Atlanta, Boston, Los Angeles, Houston, Dallas, and Washington, DC, would also have to move for their cities to achieve racial integration. So, despite magnet schools, charter schools, and voucher programs, the school systems of these cities are becoming increasingly segregated.

Public schools have contributed to racial inequities. The embrace of education as a basis for social advancement is a core value of American culture. So long as blacks, Latinos, and other students of color are subjected to low-quality, poor-performing schools, their prospects for economic advancement and achieving equity with whites will continue to lag. Indeed, the Civil Rights Project points out that "patterns of segregation by race are strongly linked to segregation by poverty, and poverty concentrations are strongly linked to unequal opportunities and outcomes."

To address the issue of resegregation is to assess public education in America. School populations reflect the ethnic and racial composition of the community. Clearly, if the neighborhoods are all white, then the schools will be too. No policies exist to remedy de facto segregation in the schools. Ellen's finding that stable mixed neighborhoods are increasing obscures the fact that many white neighborhoods are segregated.

In considering this issue, students should be reminded that there is a persistent problem with segregated schools and school districts throughout the country. Despite the *Brown* decision, segregated schools were not completely eliminated in either the south or the north. Students should know that the ever-increasing number of charter schools contributes to school segregation.

YES

Tim Lockette

Unmaking Brown

So much depends on a yellow bus, winding its way across the North Carolina landscape.

For decades, this was how Wake County integrated its schools. Buses would pick up public school students in largely minority communities along the Raleigh Beltline; in affluent Cary, a Raleigh suburb; in dozens of small towns and unincorporated communities around this fast growing state capital.

Most of the students would travel to schools not far from home. But every year, a few would cross the county to a new school, in a neighborhood very different from their own.

The system won Wake County praise from many integration advocates—but locally, people were less enchanted. In late 2008, a wave of anti-busing sentiment swept in new school board members who promised to support neighborhood schools and keep kids closer to home.

Cathy Truitt worries about what will happen next.

"If we end busing abruptly, we'll be taking a rapid step back to resegregation," said Truitt, a retired teacher who was defeated in her bid for a school board seat.

While Truitt worries about the effects of an end to busing, she says voters were exasperated with a system that seemed to randomly reassign their children to schools far from home.

"A child could be reassigned for three out of four years, while another family would go untouched," Truitt said. "While people embraced diversity, they were absolutely tired of losing their choices."

The New Segregation

Stories like that are bound to get a reaction from Amy Stuart Wells.

A professor at Teachers College at Columbia University, Wells has spent much of her career studying the resegregation of American schools—writing the history of the steady march back to separateness that has left our educational system more racially segregated now than it was in 1968.

"We don't have to accept this juxtaposition that puts school choice on one side and a civil rights approach to integration on the other," Wells said. "Our approaches to school choice over the past 20 years have been pretty unimaginative—and children are paying for our lack of imagination."

From *Teaching Tolerance*, Spring 2010, pp. 28, 30–32. Copyright © 2010 by Southern Poverty Law Center. Reprinted by permission. www.tolerance.org

For Wells and other experts on school integration, the Wake County school board election is just another phase in a long-term, city-by-city struggle over how to integrate our schools. It's a struggle that the entire country has been losing for the better part of two decades.

Today, one-third of black students attend school in places where the black population is more than 90 percent. A little less than half of white students attend schools that are more than 90 percent white. One-third of all black and Latino students attend high-poverty schools (where more than 75 percent of students receive free or reduced lunch); only 4 percent of white children do.

Things have been better, and not so long ago. In 1990, more than 40 percent of black students in the South were attending majority-white schools. Today, fewer than 30 percent of students do—roughly the same percentage as in the late 1960s, when many districts were still refusing to implement 1954's *Brown v. Board of Education.*

That trend isn't limited just to the South, according to Gary Orfield, director of the Civil Rights Project at UCLA. According to Orfield, some of the deepest racial divisions in America today are in the Midwest, where old patterns of "white flight" have shaped the suburban landscape, and a new generation of immigrants is settling into communities that were never under orders to desegregate.

Most of the decades-old obstacles to integration still remain. Wake County's debate over active integration measures is a rarity these days: Most busing programs were killed by white backlash in the 1970s. Our schools are still governed by a hodgepodge of districts, some giant and some tiny, many of which were created as enclaves of white privilege. And Americans still are choosing— or being steered toward—home ownership in communities where everyone looks like them.

And there are new challenges. In 2007, the U.S. Supreme Court effectively gutted *Brown* by declaring that school districts can't consider racial diversity as a factor in school assignments. (Where busing still exists, it's done on the basis of family income.) And as the suburbs have spread, we've seen residential segregation on steroids.

"The old paradigm of black cities and white suburbs is no longer true," said Orfield. "Black and Latino communities are expanding into the suburbs— but they're concentrated in specific areas. We're seeing a suburbia that is divided by ethnicity."

Separate Is Still Unequal

Depending on where you stand, the drift back to segregation may be obvious, or it may be entirely invisible.

"Many white students attend schools that are overwhelmingly white, and those schools are actually seeing an increase in diversity," Orfield said. "We have the irony that white students can feel that their educational experience is more integrated, when in fact the level of segregation nationwide has increased."

In the mid-1960s, 80 percent of American students were white. Today, due to immigration and other factors, children of color make up almost 40 percent of the student body. While the student body as a whole has grown much more diverse, many majority-white schools have seen only a slight bump in their minority enrollment.

Meanwhile, growing numbers of black, Latino and Asian American students are finding themselves in what Orfield calls "intensely segregated" schools—schools where students of color make up more than 90 percent of the student body. Typically, these schools have high concentrations of students in poverty—what Orfield calls "double segregation." And increasingly, there is "triple segregation" as English language learners in poverty find themselves concentrated in certain schools.

"These schools are just fundamentally different from other schools," said Erica Frankenberg, a scholar on the Civil Rights Project. "In terms of AP classes available, number of veteran teachers, graduation rates—on almost every measure you see an indication of a school in severe stress."

Students in these intensely segregated environments are far less likely to graduate, or to go on to college. It's a problem that is well known to many people of color. Frankenberg says its time for the entire country to realize that this is a crisis for each of us.

"If we don't start educating black and Latino students better than we are doing now, we are going to see an intergenerational decline in the percentage of high school graduates in the adult population for the first time ever," she noted.

There's strong evidence that integration could help us eliminate the "achievement gap." Frankenberg and Orfield both note that the gap was lowest during the late 1980s and early 1990s—the period in history when our schools were at their most integrated.

"We have never been able to implement *Plessy v. Ferguson*," Frankenberg said. "Separate schools have never been equal. Yet we keep trying to make a segregated system work."

A Hidden History of Choice

How do we reverse a 40-year trend, one that is embedded in our residential landscape? And how do we integrate schools when the Supreme Court has ruled that race and diversity can't be factors in school assignments?

The solution might be as simple as changing the way we think—particularly the way we think about school choice.

"We need to rethink what choice means, and we need to realize that it isn't inimical to the 'civil rights' approach to integration," Wells said.

Experts such as Wells and Orfield point out that many fundamentals of school segregation haven't changed all that much since 1990. There was residential segregation then, and many racially homogenous districts date back to the 1970s.

What did change was a paradigm shift. Court rulings weakened local integration plans, and Americans increasingly began looking for solutions that appealed to their free-market instincts. Charter schools and vouchers began to look like the best way to liberate students from intensely segregated schools— and the best way to create innovative, effective schools.

"By and large, it hasn't worked," Orfield contends.

"Charter schools are the most segregated segment of the school system," he said. "They often appear in highly segregated areas, and they tend to increase segregation."

Again, so much depends on a yellow bus. By not providing transportation and other services commonly found in traditional public schools, charters were limiting their student body to kids who lived nearby—and to parents who had the right social networks.

"With charters, recruitment is largely word-of-mouth, and, as a result, these schools aren't as accessible as they could be," Wells said.

Orfield notes that charters aren't bound by civil rights mandates, the way magnet schools are. But even magnet schools—with their implied mission of providing alternatives—don't have enough capacity to provide parents with a true choice. With waiting lists at every magnet, it's the schools that are doing the selecting.

"The laissez-faire, market-based approaches of the past 20 years have done a really good job of providing schools with a choice of students," Wells said. "But they haven't done a good job of providing students with a choice of schools."

"It didn't have to be that way," Wells said.

"The problem is that there's a whole history of school choice that has been hidden and forgotten," she said.

Wells recently co-authored a major study on school systems that still have voluntary busing. Eight major cities—including Indianapolis, St. Louis, Palo Alto and others—still have voluntary busing systems that allow students from intensely segregated schools to choose to attend other schools—even across district lines.

"These programs aren't thriving—in fact, they're struggling, politically, to survive—but they're hanging on in large part because of support from parents," Wells said.

That includes parents in white, affluent suburbs who want students from other districts to be brought into their schools.

"A lot of white parents in the suburbs bemoan the fact that they're raising kids in an all-white, privileged context," Wells said. "Even the kids realize they're in this bubble."

For Wells, the voluntary busing programs represent an approach to school choice that once was well known—one most parents have forgotten, or believe to be a failure. And that's a shame, she said, because for students in these programs, the achievement gap has shrunk.

"Not only do these programs provide meaningful choices, they provide the intangibles—high expectations, higher academic aspirations, exposure to more ways of seeing the world," she said. . . .

Rethinking Districts

Wells is quick to point out that these are programs that bus students from one district to another. School district boundaries, she says, are "the new Jim Crow," separating poverty from wealth and white from black and brown.

Frankenberg agrees. She notes that the most segregated states today are the ones with the greatest profusion of districts—a legacy of a post-*Brown* movement to establish white and affluent enclaves in the shadow of major cities.

Frankenberg, who grew up in Mobile, uses her home state as an example. Alabama has 67 counties and 167 school districts. Neighboring Florida also has 67 counties—and 69 districts (one for each county and two special districts for university laboratory schools). According to Frankenberg, Alabama is the most segregated state in the South—the only Southern state that consistently shows up in the top 10 of most segregated states.

Consolidating districts in highly segregated areas might be a difficult political battle, but complete consolidation isn't the only option.

"We need to rethink our attitude toward districts," Wells says. "The boundaries can be more permeable than they are now."

In an age of economic hardship, that approach may be more welcome than ever before. Well points to Long Island, New York, which has 125 individual school districts.

"People are starting to understand that this system is wasteful," she said. "Districts are starting to talk about saving money by consolidating back-office operations. There's even talk about consolidating certain employment functions, though I'm not sure the union will approve of that.

"If districts can share these services, why can't we find ways to allow students to attend school across district lines?" she said. "Why can't we create interdistrict magnet programs?"

A Paradigm Shift

Wells, Orfield and Frankenberg all say they're hopeful things will change now that America has its first black president. So far, though, the signals from the Obama Administration have been mixed.

Wells says she hopes a new generation of research on the benefits of a diverse education will help "put integration and civil rights back on the public radar." She cites the work of Scott E. Page, a mathematician who has used computer models to show that diverse groups of thinkers come up with better solutions than homogenous groups.

But the testimony of teachers and parents is just as important. If debates like the one in Wake County reach an unhappy ending, it may be because we're losing sight of the perspectives that only educators can provide.

"We need to be politically active in seeking a change," she said. "And teachers need to be prepared to share what they know—to explain why diversity is important."

Ingrid Gould Ellen  **NO**

Welcome Neighbors?

The conventional wisdom on racial integration in the United States is that there are three kinds of neighborhoods: the all-white neighborhood, the all-black neighborhood, and the exceedingly rare, highly unstable, racially mixed neighborhood. The only real disagreement is about why so few neighborhoods are successfully integrated. Some attribute it to white discrimination pure and simple: whites, that is, have consciously and determinedly excluded blacks from their communities. Others contend that it is a matter of minority choice. Like Norwegians in Brooklyn's Bay Ridge and Italians in Manhattan's Little Italy, African Americans, they explain, prefer to live among their own kind. Finally, others maintain that segregation is driven mainly by income differences across racial groups. But almost all agree that when African Americans do manage to gain a foothold in a previously all-white community, the whites move away in droves—a phenomenon well known as "white flight." Integration is no more than, in the words of Saul Alinsky, the "time between when the first black moves in and last white moves out."

But while there is no denying that the United States remains a remarkably segregated country, such views are too pessimistic. Racially mixed neighborhoods are not as rare as people think. In 1990, according to nationwide census tract data, nearly 20 percent of all census tracts—which generally include a few thousand residents, roughly the size of the typical neighborhood— were racially integrated, defined as between 10 percent and 50 percent black. (Defining an "integrated" neighborhood is inevitably somewhat arbitrary. The 10–50 percent range takes into account both that African Americans make up just 12 percent of the total U.S. population and that most people consider integration to involve a fairly even racial split.) In 1990, more than 15 percent of the non-Hispanic white population and nearly one-third of the black population lived in these mixed neighborhoods. And the proportion is increasing. The number of households, both white and black, living in integrated communities grew markedly between 1970 and 1980 and even faster between 1980 and 1990. Most strikingly, the share of white residents living in overwhelmingly white census tracts—those in which blacks represent less than 1 percent of the total population—fell from 63 percent in 1970 to 36 percent in 1990.

From *Brookings Review,* Winter 1997, pp. 18–21. Copyright © 1997 by the Brookings Institution Press. Reprinted by permission.

Not only are racially mixed neighborhoods more numerous than people think, they are also more stable. An examination of a sample of 34 large U.S. metropolitan areas with significant black populations reveals that more than three quarters of the neighborhoods that were racially mixed in 1980 were still mixed in 1990. And in more than half, the share of non-Hispanic whites remained constant or grew. Most significantly, perhaps, a comparison with data from the 1970s suggests that neighborhoods are becoming more stable over time. The mean white population loss in integrated neighborhoods was lower in the 1980s than in the 1970s; a greater share of integrated tracts remained steady in the 1980s; and fewer tracts experienced dramatic white loss. In sum, neighborhood racial integration appears to be becoming both more widespread and more stable. Again, this is not to claim that America's neighborhoods are no longer dramatically segregated. But it may no longer be accurate to describe them, as have some, as a system of "American Apartheid."

How is it that certain neighborhoods seem to turn rapidly from white to black as soon as a few black households move in, while others hardly seem to change at all? The conventional account of racial mixing has, I think, discouraged people from seriously investigating this question—either by theorizing about what might be different about the more stable areas or by examining matters empirically. Because all mixed neighborhoods are presumed to be highly unstable, explaining the variance in the rate of racial change has hardly seemed pressing. But examining the conditions under which integration seems to thrive offers considerable insight not only into the causes of our nation's racial segregation, but also into the prospects for mitigating it.

Why Are Some Mixed Neighborhoods Stable?

It is possible to devise a variety of theories to explain why some mixed neighborhoods remain integrated. One theory is simply that neighborhoods with fewer minority residents are more likely to be stable. The argument is that white households basically dislike living with minorities and that once the minority population of a given community reaches a concentration greater than they can tolerate, whites abandon the community, which quickly becomes all black. But while this argument has some intuitive appeal in light of our nation's long history of racism, the degree of integration in a mixed community appears to have no bearing on its future racial mix. Whether a community is 10 percent black or 50 percent black, the likelihood of white loss is the same.

A second theory is that communities are more stable when black and white residents have similar incomes and education levels. This theory has an intuitive appeal to those who think that our country has gotten beyond race. But it is not borne out by the data either. Indeed, neighborhoods where blacks and whites are more equal in status are, if anything, less stable.

A third theory—and the one that best fits the evidence—is that residential decisions, especially those of white households, are indeed heavily shaped by negative racial attitudes. But it is not a simple matter of racial animus, of white households being unwilling to live, at any particular moment in time, in neighborhoods with moderately sized black populations. Rather, it is a matter of white households tending to assume that all mixed neighborhoods quickly and inevitably become predominantly black and being uncomfortable with the prospect of living in such an environment in the future.

As for the sources of this discomfort, I would emphasize two. First, whites may simply fear being "left behind" as a racial minority as the community becomes largely black. Second, and more important, white households (and potentially black households as well) may have negative preconceptions about what an all-black neighborhood will be like. Specifically, black neighbors may be thought to bring with them, or at least to portend, a deterioration in what Richard Taub and others have called the "structural position," or strength, of a neighborhood: the aggregate of school quality, public safety, property values, and the like. In other words, white households may not necessarily dislike living next to blacks per se; but many white households, rightly or wrongly, associate blacks with decreasing structural strength. Whether such stereotyped associations should be distinguished from simple racial prejudice on moral grounds deserves lengthy discussion, but certainly they are analytically distinct and have distinct policy implications.

This proposed hypothesis—call it the "racial neighborhood stereotyping" hypothesis—generates some powerful predictions that can be tested empirically. First, it suggests that households who are less invested in the structural strength of the community—renters and households with no children, for instance—will be more open to racial mixing and thus more likely to live in mixed communities. Significantly, if whites simply dislike living near blacks, the opposite should hold true. For white renters—who can enter and exit neighborhoods more easily than homeowners—will be less likely to live in mixed communities.

Second, this hypothesis suggests that—contrary to the conventional view that racial transition is caused by "white flight"—racial concerns are more influential in decisions whether to move into a community than whether to move out. For residents of a community should be fully aware of its structural strength and therefore have less need to rely on race as a signal of this strength. Consequently, entry decisions should be far more important to racial change than exit decisions.

Third, racial mixing should be more stable in communities that seem sheltered in some way from further black growth (either because they are distant from the central area of black residence or because they have been racially stable in the past) or in which school quality, property values, and other neighborhood attributes seem particularly secure.

Testing the Theory

Using a unique census data set that links households to the neighborhoods in which they live, I have tested each of these predictions. The data generally bear them out. First, as predicted, households who are likely to be less invested in the structural strength of a neighborhood appear to be far more open to racial mixing. White households moving into racially mixed areas tend, for instance, to be younger than those opting for predominantly white areas.

They also tend to be single rather than married and not to have children. Significantly, childless black households are similarly more open to increasingly black communities than their counterparts with children. Finally, white renters are considerably more willing to move into and remain in racially mixed areas than homeowners are. Thus, communities with relatively larger proportions of rental housing are more likely to remain integrated. Again, this finding runs counter to the pure-prejudice view of neighborhood choice, since renters can leave much more quickly than homeowners.

The data support the second prediction as well. Indeed, there is virtually no evidence of white flight or accelerated departure rates in the face of racial mixing. White households are no more likely to leave a community that is 80 percent black than one that is 2 percent black. And the moving decisions of black households appear insensitive to racial composition as well. Thus, to the extent that integrated neighborhoods do tip, or become increasingly black, entry decisions, rather than exit decisions, appear to be the cause. The point is, residents living in a community are far less likely to consider race as a signal of neighborhood quality than outsiders considering moving in.

As for the third prediction, the evidence confirms that mixed neighborhoods that seem sheltered from further black growth are more stable. In fact, the most crucial determinant of a community's future course of racial change is its past racial stability. The longer a community has been integrated, the more likely it is to remain so. And analysis of individual decision-making confirms this. Controlling for present racial composition, white households are both less likely to leave a mixed community and more likely to enter one if its black population has been fairly steady in the past and thus seems likely to remain steady in the future. Moreover, integrated neighborhoods located farther from black inner-city communities are more likely to remain stable. Of course, the added distance may discourage blacks from entering these communities as quickly, but it seems likely that white expectations play a role too. For white households may view communities closer to the core black area as both more apt to gain black population and more vulnerable to the social dislocation that whites associate with such gain.

Furthermore, mixed neighborhoods in which the housing market is thriving and in which neighborhood amenities seem particularly secure are more likely to remain stable. For example, the data appear to show that communities with large stabilizing institutions, such as universities or military bases, that promise to provide a continual source of people, both white and black, who desire to live in the area provide just such strength and security.

Policy Implications, Big and Small

To the extent the racial neighborhood stereotyping hypothesis is sound, the obvious question arises: what light does it shed on the moral and economic justification for government intervention to maintain mixed neighborhoods or to promote integration generally, and what kinds of policies would most effectively promote integration consistent with this justification? This is not the place to address such a grand question. Suffice it here simply to point out a few salient implications of the hypothesis for existing government policies designed to maintain mixed communities.

One policy that is occasionally used is the setting of an explicit quota on the number of blacks or minorities who may move into a particular mixed community or development where black or minority demand is high. For example, several years back, the owners of Starrett City, a large middle-income apartment complex in Brooklyn built with substantial government subsidies, set a quota on the number of blacks and Hispanics who could live there. In 1987, a federal court found that the quota violates the Fair Housing Act of 1968. But such quotas may also not make much sense as a matter of policy, since, as noted, no specified level of minority representation triggers white departure from a community.

Mixed communities have also tried to stem panic-selling by restricting realtors' unsolicited efforts to encourage homeowners to sell and by banning the display of "For Sale" signs. But if exit decisions are less sensitive than entry decisions to racial composition and less critical to long-run stability, such strategies are poorly targeted. Integration, my results show, would be more effectively promoted by encouraging outsiders to move in, not discouraging insiders from leaving.

Some communities have tried to do just this. For example, some have tried to attract outsiders by public relations campaigns that advertise their particular strengths: their housing stock, their parks, their community solidarity. Such efforts also directly counter white households' fears about the structural decline they associate with predominantly black neighborhoods.

Efforts in mixed communities to raise amenity levels also address white households' fears of community decline. For example, programs to improve the appearance of a community—restoring local playgrounds, cleaning up commercial strips, repairing broken windows—can build social capital and bolster people's faith in a neighborhood's strength.

Finally, the racial neighborhood stereotyping hypothesis has important implications for government policies that have nothing to do with promoting racial integration. For example, policies designed to increase homeownership, such as the homeowner mortgage interest deduction, may have the unintended consequence of exacerbating racial segregation.

Unwarranted Pessimism

The real story about America's neighborhoods, though far from revealing anything close to a color-blind society, is less pessimistic and more dynamic than we have tended to believe. Integrated neighborhoods may be a minority, but their numbers are growing, and many appear likely to remain racially mixed for many years. Researchers must not overlook them. For the question of when and where households seem content to live in racially mixed environments is in many ways the flip side of the ultimate question of why our nation's residential neighborhoods are as segregated as they are. And any progress toward answering the first question is progress toward answering the second. More important, white households should not overlook the facts either, for their overly pessimistic assumption that rapid racial transition is inevitable has helped, by its self-fulfilling nature, to undermine racial mixing.

In hindsight, the optimism of many people during the civil rights era that integration was just around the corner seems hopelessly naive. But the pessimism that has replaced it in recent years does not seem appropriate either. It seems based more on weariness in the face of an endlessly daunting challenge than on the facts, and it has, in my view, slowed our progress toward understanding neighborhood racial segregation.

EXPLORING THE ISSUE

Are America's Public Schools Resegregating?

Critical Thinking and Reflection

1. What is de jure segregation? What is de facto segregation?
2. Why are some neighborhoods segregated, and others racially integrated?
3. What are the consequences of the *Brown* decision?
4. Specifically, what is the evidence to support the claim of resegregation?
5. How do housing patterns determine the racial composition of public schools? What does the data suggest about resegregation?
6. What is the history of segregated schools in America?
7. How important was public school desegregation to the modern civil rights movement?

Is There Common Ground?

It is possible that the students will find that both positions articulated here reflect contradictory twenty-first century trends. Large cities may reflect increasing diversity. At the same time, the communities and local neighborhoods within those cities continue to remain racially and ethnically isolated. This is a major paradox. One of the outcomes of the struggle to desegregate public schools and other institutions was the phenomenon of white flight. Whites who were concerned with issues of quality and safety in schools along with housing values left cities in large numbers to expanding suburbs. Thus, a vocabulary emerged—white flight, redlining, steering, and vanilla suburb, chocolate city. Despite these trends, Americans are challenged to live in a multicultural, diverse nation. Resegregation is antithetical to the achievement of this goal. There is a common value at stake in educating all children as best the nation can to insure a better future for all Americans. Students should be prepared to contribute to the discussion of a larger issue that emerges here: Is the integration of schools a national goal? If so, how can this goal be achieved? The answer to these questions has major implications for the future of this increasingly multicultural nation.

Additional Resources

Blackmon, Douglas A. 2008. *Slavery by Another Name: The Re-Enslavement of Black Americans From the Civil War to World War II* (Doubleday).

321

D'Angelo, Raymond. 2000. *The American Civil Rights Movement: Readings and Interpretations* (McGraw/Dushkin).

"50 Years Later: Brown v. Board of Education." *Teaching Tolerance* (Spring 2004).

Frankenberg, Erica and Chungmei Lee. 2002. "Race in American Public Schools: Rapidly Resegregating School District." The Civil Rights Project at Harvard University (August).

Hacker, Andrew. 1992. *Two Nations: Black and White, Separate, Hostile, Unequal* (Charles Scribner's Sons).

Kleinfield, N.R. 2012. "Why Don't We Have Any White Kids?" *The New York Times* (May 13).

Kluger, Richard. 1975. *Simple Justice: A History of Brown v. Board of Education and Black America's Struggle for Equality* (Vintage).

Kozol, Jonathan. 1991. *Savage Inequalities: Children in American Schools* (Crown Publishers Inc.).

Martin, Waldo. 1998. *Brown v. Board of Education: A Brief History with Documents* (Bedford).

Massey, Douglas S. and Nancy Denton. 1993. *American Apartheid: Segregation and the Making of the Underclass* (Harvard University Press).

Orfield, Gary and Susan Eaton. 1996. *Dismantling Segregation: The Quiet Reversal of Brown v. Board of Education* (The New Press).

Piliawsky, Monte. 1998. "Remedies to De Facto School Segregation: The Case of Hartford," *The Black Scholar* (Summer).

Smallwood, Arwin D. 1998. *The Atlas of African-American History and Politics: From the Slave Trade to Modern Time* (McGraw-Hill).

The Magazine of History. 2004. Entire issue is devoted to research on Jim Crow. 18: January(2)).

Thernstrom, Abigail and Stephan. 1997. *America in Black and White: One Nation, Indivisible* (Simon & Schuster).

Wilson, William J. 1987. *The Truly Disadvantaged: The Inner City, the Underclass and Public Policy* (University of Chicago Press).

Woodward, C. Vann. 1974. *The Strange Career of Jim Crow* (Oxford University Press).

This website encourages people to develop and apply their sociological imaginations. Appropriate to this issue is a March 30, 2011 article, "2010 Census Data on Residential Segregation" by Gwen Sharp, a sociologist at Nevada State College, that presents information based on recent census reports detailing, among other things, the 10 most segregated metropolitan areas in the country. The site carefully illustrates data on a wide range of social issues.

http://thesocietypages.org/socimages/

The American Communities Project is run as a public service by the Initiative in Spatial Structures in the Social Sciences (Brown University) and the Lewis Mumford Center (University at Albany). The site offers data and analyses of race, ethnicity, and diversity throughout the country. It allows the user to select cities and states to search for school district data on race and ethnicity.

http://mumford1.dyndns.org/cen2000/

The National Poverty Center website (University of Michigan Gerald R. Ford School of Public Policy), a nonpartisan research center, conducts and promotes research on the effects of poverty. Of relevance to the resegregation issue is the site research dealing with race and ethnicity, especially those projects that connect segregation and inequality.

www.npc.umich.edu/publications/working_papers/?publication_id=175&

ISSUE 18

Is There a Need for a Permanent Voting Rights Act?

YES: Richard M. Valelly, from "Ballots in the Balance: Does the 1965 Voting Rights Act Still Matter?" *The Two Reconstructions: The Struggle for Black Enfranchisement* (University of Chicago Press, 2004)

NO: Abigail Thernstrom, from "Redistricting, Race, and the Voting Rights Act," *National Affairs* (Spring 2010)

Learning Outcomes

After reading this issue, the student should be able to:

- Develop a comprehensive understanding of African American voting prior to the passage of the Voting Rights Act of 1965.
- Understand the significance of voting rights as a focal concern of the civil rights movement.
- Understand the protections of civil rights, which are provided by the Voting Rights Act, and their significance.
- Discuss and analyze the political and social impacts of the Voting Rights Act within America.
- Identify and critically examine the challenges that advocates of voting rights for all Americans, including blacks, face in their continuing effort to maintain the act as an effective instrument of racial reform.
- Discuss and analyze the data that illuminate the advances in African American voting rights as a result of the passage of the Voting Rights Act of 1965.

ISSUE SUMMARY

YES: Richard M. Valelly, the author of *The Two Reconstructions: The Struggle for Black Enfranchisement* (University of Chicago Press, 2004), is a professor of political science at Swarthmore College. Pointing to U.S. history, he fears that without key sections, especially Section 5, of the Voting Rights Act, the black vote will be suppressed. What happened in the 1890s to black disfranchisement can happen again.

NO: Abigail Thernstrom, a political scientist, is a senior fellow at the Manhattan Institute in New York. She has written extensively on race and voting rights. She argues that it is time to end race-driven districting and that certain sections, especially Section 5, of the Voting Rights Act of 1965 are no longer needed.

Voting rights are fundamental to citizens' participation in a democratic polity with a representative system of governance. It is noteworthy therefore that the nation entered the twentieth century with a majority of citizens being denied the right to vote. Given this fact, the failure of the Founding Fathers to establish and protect voting rights for all under the original Constitution of the United States was a failure of leadership, given that they claimed to be engaged in "a new experiment in human freedom." Clearly, the right to vote has been a source of conflict throughout the nation's history.

For African Americans, ongoing struggles for the right to the franchise are a focal concern of civil rights advocacy. The slave had no such rights, nor did the freedmen after they were disfranchised during the post–Reconstruction Period of the nineteenth century despite the Fifteenth Amendment of 1870. Voting rights are perceived as vital to the establishment of citizenship and the empowerment and advancement of African Americans. Thus, the passage of the Voting Rights Act of 1965 is a crowning achievement of the civil rights movement.

The struggle to enact the Voting Rights Act was bitter. The segregationists and white supremacist forces, utilized various means, including the states' rights doctrine, to deny passage or to dilute the contents of this legislation. The National Association for the Advancement of Colored People (NAACP) along with Martin Luther King and other civil rights leaders criticized both the scope of the coverage of the proposed bill and aspects of its enforcement mechanisms, especially the paucity of voter registrars to be sent to various jurisdictions, especially in the South, that were included in the legislation. Civil rights advocates were concerned with the tenure of the bill, especially the provision that requires its renewal. Eventually, the Voting Rights Act of 1965 was passed and signed into law by President Lyndon B. Johnson. By his action, America took a great leap forward in addressing the legacy of Jim Crow by securing the right to vote as a pillar of African American citizenship.

Section 5 is one of the most important and controversial components of the Voting Rights Act of 1965. It is designed to prevent racial gerrymandering. Section 5 requires that any jurisdiction seeking changes in election law or procedure must submit the proposed changes to the Justice Department (or DC district court) for preapproval, or "preclearance," before enacting those changes. Additionally, the burden of proof falls on the county or state proposing changes. This key provision was essential to the demise of Jim Crow voting practices in the South. The Voting Rights Act of 1965 banned redistricting that dilutes the voting strength of black and other minority communities.

Despite the gains achieved through the Voting Rights Act, the maintenance of this reform measure is a continuing concern of civil rights proponents.

Many conservatives argue that America is a post-racial nation (see Issue 4), that the voting rights of African Americans and others are now well established and secured, and thus the law is no longer necessary. Abigail Thernstrom and other conservatives would utilize the renewal requirement to simply allow sections of it to expire because they are no longer necessary. She urges the Supreme Court to declare it unconstitutional as soon as it gets the opportunity.

Thernstrom writes that race-conscious districting was appropriate at a time when southern whites would not vote for any black candidates. However, it is her contention that there is sufficient evidence of black voting, black political representation, and black political power and influence to support the termination of Section 5. She is concerned that race-conscious districting has led to segregated voting districts. Thus, she thinks that Section 5 is no longer needed and argues that we need to get beyond race in America.

Progressives such as Richard M. Valelly, on the other hand, assume a contrarian posture and employ today's concerns with the voter suppression of blacks and other minorities and the conflicts over the restoration of voting rights of former prisoners to make their case. By eliminating Section 5, Valelly fears that there will be an erosion of African American and Latino voting rights. He fears that if Section 5 preclearance is allowed to expire, the country may see a return to discriminatory election rules in the South. For him, a permanent Voting Rights Act would protect future black voter participation in the American democracy.

Going beyond the right to vote, historian Darlene Clark Hine writes, "The vote alone is not enough. And as the presidential election of 2000 shows, the South, and Florida in particular, still employs the means to make black ballots count less or not at all." There are many ways to suppress the black vote including, but not limited to, redistricting, racial gerrymandering, misleading, and confusing voting procedures as seen in the Florida recount of the 2000 presidential election, and the constant legislative threats of not renewing provisions of the Voting Rights Act. On the issue of a permanent Voting Rights Act, a number of questions arise and among them are the following: What would America gain by the failure to renew the Voting Rights Act? Would the sensibility that has been gained throughout much of black America that blacks are now more substantially included as American citizens be weakened or undermined by the termination of the Voting Rights Act?

In the wake of the passage of the Voting Rights Act of 1965, blacks have gained significant institutional placement, power, and influence in the United States, including the South. The numbers of black elected officials and those who function in other governmental agencies at all levels are substantial. Despite this progress there are still challenges to African American voting rights in the United States. One area where there has been little progress is in the U.S. Senate. Currently, no blacks serve in the Senate and historically, only six have served. Among the issues with which advocates of African American voting rights are concerned today are voting rights of ex-prisoners, suppression of black votes, and voter identification laws. All of these measures are viewed as critical to an examination of this issue. Against this background, it is clear that blacks will continue to view the Voting Rights Act as a necessary protection of their right to vote.

YES

Richard M. Valelly

Ballots in the Balance: Does the 1965 Voting Rights Act Still Matter?

Forty years ago—in a dramatic response to decades of African American struggle in the courts and the streets and to growing public concern over black disenfranchisement—a large bipartisan majority in Congress framed and passed the 1965 Voting Rights Act. President Lyndon Johnson proudly signed it in a special Capitol Hill ceremony. These officials, much of the public, and key partners such as the Student Nonviolent Coordinating Committee, the NAACP, the Southern Christian Leadership Conference, and the Congress on Racial Equality all intended a restoration of the Reconstruction Amendments, particularly the 14th and 15th Amendments. In that they succeeded. Since 1965 the federal protection afforded by the Voting Rights Act has immeasurably strengthened minority voting and representation. The Voting Rights Act is today widely recognized as perhaps the premier case of a national law that can institute broad and desirable political change.

But will the Voting Rights Act survive its next congressional review? Should it? These questions now animate a growing number of conferences and discussions at law schools and universities around the country. Opponents and supporters of the Voting Rights Act are now meeting and planning for the congressional review. Voting rights issues now flying below the public radar are certain to surface on the national agenda this year or next.

By August 2007 Congress must renew, amend, or drop the Voting Rights Act's temporary enforcement provisions. These measures include (1) federal review of proposed election changes in Southern and some non-Southern states and counties (a process technically known as "Section 5 preclearance"), (2) the federal election observer program, and (3) the requirement—added ten years after Congress first passed the law—that many non-Southern jurisdictions, including Arizona, California, and Texas, provide bilingual balloting materials and assistance.

Some legal experts argue that the most important temporary measure, Section 5 preclearance, cannot survive the upcoming congressional review. They believe that under the doctrine of separation of powers currently advocated by the Supreme Court's majority, Congress cannot enact a prospective prohibition on unconstitutional behavior. Instead, Congress can remedy discrimination or correct systematic public violations of civil rights only *after* discriminatory violations appear. Congress cannot, in other words, enact remedies for problems that do not yet exist or no longer exist. By implication, Section 5 preclearance would be allowed to die a decent death, with thanks for the forty years of work that made America a much more democratic country.

But is that work really finished? Once the deterrent effects of Section 5 preclearance vanish, will there be an erosion of hard-won African American and Latino voting rights? As my new book, *The Two Reconstructions: The Struggle for Black Enfranchisement,* shows, as a country we have been here before. The First Reconstruction, after the Civil War, was successful far longer than we think, but collapsed altogether in the 1890s, as black disenfranchisement spread throughout the South. A regression of that magnitude is unthinkable today. But we are hearing some echoes of it, ironically outside the Deep South. Given our history, we Americans must deliberate together about what we can and must do to avoid any backsliding on our fundamental freedoms.

During the 2000 and 2004 presidential elections black voters experienced— according to a stream of anecdotal evidence and several statistically sound studies—a wide range of difficulties in voting in the key battleground states of Florida and Ohio. These included unconscionably long voting lines because too few machines were provided, high levels of ballot spoilage, and challenges by private citizens and elections officials. Since 2000 there has been mounting anec- dotal evidence of so-called ballot security programs targeted by the Republican Party on minority neighborhoods and localities—a great irony, given the party's proud history in securing black emancipation and voting rights.

Significantly, such attacks on black voting rights have surfaced in juris- dictions that are *not* subject to Section 5 preclearance. To put it another way, with the possible recent exception of still unproven election-day ballot security programs in the 2003 Mississippi gubernatorial election, election-day shenani- gans have all but disappeared in areas subject to Section 5 preclearance—yet they have sprouted up in uncovered jurisdictions when election contests have been uncertain and close.

Once Section 5's deterrent and compliance-inducing effects are removed in places that have been covered since 1965, will the new ballot security programs migrate from uncovered jurisdictions to previously covered juris- dictions? In 1990 Senator Jesse Helms launched a massive ballot security program, mailing tens of thousands of postcards to black North Carolinians falsely warning them of penalties for fraudulent voting. He did this in a very tight campaign in which he trailed a dynamic black Democrat, former Charlotte mayor Harvey Gantt. After the fact Helms was forced by the Depart- ment of Justice to stipulate that his program was impermissible under the Voting Rights Act. Once the Voting Rights Act's temporary enforcement provi- sions go, will the Justice Department have the resources to effectively police a rash of new ballot security programs in tight elections in the previously covered jurisdictions?

In addition, consider minority representation rights, which are secured in principle by a permanent feature of the Voting Rights Act: Section 2. Con- gress added Section 2 in 1982 after thirteen years of massive resistance by Southern governments to the prospect of black officeholders. Such resistance, in fact, continues in some jurisdictions today. Both before and after the 1982 amendment, Section 5 preclearance played a leading role in forcing Southern governments to drop election rules that blocked black office seekers. The obvious question is: if Section 5 preclearance expires, will we see a return of such discriminatory election rules in the South? Or in Arizona, California, New Mexico, Texas, and parts of New York, where they were once used to deny electoral victory to aspiring Latino politicians?

No one knows the answers to these questions. But not knowing the answers hardly lessens their importance. The evidence of *selective* disenfranchisement of minorities in America is plentiful—and growing. Such selective disenfranchisement is rare in jurisdictions that are now covered by the Voting Rights Act. But after 2007 that may change. Congress must soberly weigh that possibility. Indeed, not only must Congress renew the Voting Rights Act's temporary provisions; it must also find ways to take its cue from the Voting Rights Act and curb the selective disenfranchisement that increasingly plagues too many elections all over this country.

Abigail Thernstrom

 **NO**

Redistricting, Race, and the Voting Rights Act

As we have at the beginning of each decade since 1790, Americans this year are participating in a national census. Next year, as has happened after each of those head counts, state legislators around the country will gather to redraw their congressional and state legislative districts. But in the years that follow this redistricting, we will surely be treated to displays of a more recent phenomenon: a slew of controversies over racially gerrymandered districts carefully drawn to ensure that minorities are elected to public office roughly in proportion to their share of the population.

Ironically, these race-conscious districts—and these controversies—are the products not of racism but of the struggle to combat it. They arise from the effort to enforce the Voting Rights Act of 1965: the crowning achievement of the civil-rights movement, and a watershed in the evolution of American democracy.

There can be little doubt that the cause of integrating American politics has triumphed in the years since the act was originally passed. In terms of voter participation and election to local, state, and federal offices, African Americans have made progress that the act's sponsors and champions could barely have imagined. In 2008, a black man was elected president of the United States, garnering 43% of the white vote—roughly the same share secured by his party's white candidates in recent elections—and even winning two former strongholds of southern white racism: Virginia and North Carolina. It seems fair to say that Barack Obama's race was no barrier to (and may even have been an advantage in) securing his election as president.

More broadly, black citizens have made spectacular gains as participants in our civic life, and much of that progress can be traced to the passage of the Voting Rights Act. But today that once-magnificent statute, much changed over four and a half decades, has become a barrier to the political integration that was its original aim.

The Original Voting Rights Act

The 15th Amendment to the Constitution, ratified in 1870, promised to secure black voting rights. It prohibited the denial or abridgement of the right of any American citizen to vote "on account of race, color, or previous condition of servitude," and empowered Congress to enforce that prohibition by statute. But when the last federal troops pulled out of the South in 1877, blacks were left to fend for themselves in a society dominated by white supremacists. By the 1890s, literacy and "understanding" tests, poll taxes, economic coercion, intimidation, and violence prevented most southern blacks from exercising their right to vote.

By 1965, blacks had made some progress. Whereas an appalling 3% of the 5 million southern blacks of voting age were registered in 1940, by 1964, the figure had climbed to 27% in Georgia and 37% in South Carolina. In fact, in every state except Mississippi, white supremacists were losing ground. But they were far from beaten: Florida and Tennessee were the only southern states in which as many as half of all voting-age blacks were registered.

This constitutional travesty finally became the focus of the civil-rights movement in the early 1960s. And in January 1965, safely elected and eager to pursue an ambitious agenda, President Lyndon Johnson called on Congress to restore to the descendants of slaves their most basic political rights. Both houses passed the Voting Rights Act that summer by comfortable bipartisan margins, and Johnson signed it into law in August.

A number of the act's key provisions were categorical and permanent—restating the basic premise of the 15th Amendment, and establishing a system of court-appointed "examiners" (federal election registrars) and observers to oversee racially charged elections around the country. Yet largely overlooked was the original law's most radical provision—a measure that created a temporary, and constitutionally unprecedented, process for keeping state and local authorities from using clever tactics to prevent blacks from voting.

Section 4 of the statute set out an ingenious statistical "trigger" to identify the states clearly deserving of federal intervention (without actually mentioning them). Those who wrote the act knew that literacy tests in the South were utterly fraudulent—illiterate whites could pass them, while black faculty from Tuskegee University often could not—and the act's authors took the well-established correlation between these tests and low voter turnout as evidence of intentional disfranchisement. So states and counties that had employed literacy tests for voting, and that had total (black and white) voter turnouts of less than 50% in the 1964 presidential election, were "covered" by a series of special provisions. The trigger was thus carefully designed to capture Alabama, Georgia, Louisiana, Mississippi, South Carolina, Virginia, and some counties in North Carolina.

This "coverage" had several consequences. In the targeted states and counties, literacy tests were prohibited. At the discretion of the attorney general—and without any need for judicial involvement—federal registrars and monitors could be dispatched to these jurisdictions during elections to ensure black access to the polls. In addition, a separate provision, Section 5, forced all covered jurisdictions to submit their proposed changes in election laws and procedures to the Justice Department or the (seldom used) D.C. district court for "preclearance," or pre-approval.

Remarkably, the preclearance provision was barely discussed in the congressional hearings prior to the passage of the act. But it was utterly unique in

American law. As Loyola University law professor Richard Hasen has written: "Never before or since has a state or local jurisdiction needed permission from the federal government to put its own laws into effect." Over time, Section 5 became the best-known provision of the Voting Rights Act.

Under this provision, the burden of proving that changes in voting procedures were free of racial animus fell upon the jurisdictions proposing them. So a city that submitted for preclearance a proposed enlargement of its governing council, or a change in its districting map, or the relocation of a polling place, had to prove a negative—demonstrating an absence of discriminatory purpose or, even more difficult, future effect. The mere suspicion of discrimination was thus enough to sink a proposed change.

Section 5 was of course not without its adamant critics, including Supreme Court Justice Hugo Black. In a withering dissent in the 1966 case *South Carolina v. Katzenbach,* Black wrote that by compelling states to "beg federal authorities to approve their policies," the provision "so distort[ed] our constitutional structure of government as to render any distinction drawn in the Constitution between state and federal power almost meaningless." Nevertheless, in an 8-1 ruling, the Court upheld the law's constitutionality. The majority asserted that the evidence of what Chief Justice Earl Warren called the South's "unremitting and ingenious defiance of the Constitution" required the kind of severe measure embodied by the preclearance provision. Moreover, the constitutional distortion Justice Black had complained about would only be temporary; Sections 4 and 5 were emergency provisions, slated to expire after just five years.

The brilliant design of the Voting Rights Act—and the Court's strong defense of it—yielded swift results. Black registration rates in the covered states soared: In 1964, fewer than 7% of eligible blacks were registered to vote in Mississippi; by the end of 1966, the figure had risen to nearly 60%. During the same period in Alabama, registration rates climbed from just below 20% to just above 50%.

But it didn't take southern politicians very long to find a loophole. They realized that while it had become nearly impossible to limit black voters' access to the ballot box, it was still possible to limit the power of the votes they cast. And in the years immediately following the enactment of the Voting Rights Act, a growing number of southern jurisdictions replaced geographic districts with at-large voting, eliminated elected positions in favor of appointed ones, and reconfigured state legislative districts—all in an effort to reduce the effect of the newly surging black vote and to maintain white supremacy.

These deliberate attempts to prevent the transfer of political power from whites to blacks were bound to spark legal challenges. They reached the Supreme Court with the 1969 case *Allen v. State Board of Elections,* which forever transformed the meaning of Section 5. The case involved a series of laws, mostly in Mississippi, that replaced single-member districts with county-wide voting in the election of county commissioners. The reasoning went like this: Within a county, some smaller single-member districts would likely have black majorities, and so would elect blacks to represent them. But in the South at the time, if the entire county became one majority-white district, only whites would get elected—and no white was likely to represent black interests. Because African-American voters could still cast ballots, the introduction of at-large voting did not violate the Voting Rights Act (at least as originally conceived). Still, Mississippi and other states were clearly engaging in unacceptable racist mischief that, as the Court put it, could "nullify" the ability of black voters "to elect the candidate of their choice just as would prohibiting some of them from voting."

In proscribing these moves, the Court expanded the definition of discriminatory voting practices under the act to include devices that "diluted" the impact of the black vote. From then on, Section 5 was understood to empower federal officials to object to at-large voting, districting lines, and other methods of structuring elections—any measure that might have the effect of depriving blacks of expected gains in political power.

The act had been irrevocably altered—for better and for worse. Preclearance took on a far broader meaning, one that required the Justice Department to involve itself far more deeply in state and local political judgments. Of these, the most important turned out to be the redrawing of election districts, required after every decennial census—a process that involves what University of California, Los Angeles, law professor Daniel Lowenstein has called "the woof and warp of [a] state's politics and political culture."

The Court's re-reading of the law meant that blacks in areas covered by Section 5 had acquired a new entitlement: the ability "to elect the candidate of their choice." And in response, the Justice Department began to demand electoral districts drawn to ensure that, at every level of government, blacks held office in numbers proportional to the relevant black population. No longer an effort to secure political equality, the act now ensured that blacks would be treated as politically different—entitled to *in*equality, in the form of a unique political privilege. Race-based districting that amounted to legislative quotas became a federal mandate. In such districts, whites would seldom even bother to compete.

Looking back, it is tempting to argue that this was an obviously dangerous decision by the Court. But the South's swift and effective circumvention of the Voting Rights Act in the wake of its passage demonstrated the truth of what many civil-rights activists had argued: that merely providing access to the ballot was insufficient after centuries of slavery, another century of segregation, ongoing white racism, and persistent resistance to black political power. In the Deep South in 1969 (and beyond), the alternative to de facto reserved legislative seats for black candidates would have been the perpetuation of whites-only politics.

The Court made the right decision in *Allen*. And yet its revised reading of the Voting Rights Act set in motion a process that, through reauthorizations and amendments as well as judicial and administrative interpretations, would destroy the legislation's original logic. By 1995, Judge Bruce M. Selya would call the statute a "Serbonian bog" into which "plaintiffs and defendants, pundits and policymakers, judges and justices" had sunk. Most tragically, this process would cause the legislation to actually hinder racial progress.

The Act Transformed

Sections 4 and 5 of the original Voting Rights Act were set to expire in 1970, but five years had not been enough time for the political culture of the South to be meaningfully transformed. The case for reauthorizing Sections 4 and 5 was thus an easy one: The Voting Rights Act had made enormous progress toward its goal, but significant hurdles remained. The act was therefore extended for another five years—reauthorized with amendments that seemed modest on the surface, but would ultimately have quite significant effects.

The most important of these amendments revised the formula for identifying racially suspect jurisdictions. The new trigger preserved the old criteria—flagging jurisdictions that had once employed literacy tests and had voter-turnout rates below 50% in the '64 election—but expanded its reach to include those with below-50% turnout in the '68 election as well.

This "updating" of the trigger made a hash of its original purpose. In 1965, the authors of the Voting Rights Act knew which states they wanted to target, and designed their precise statistical test accordingly. But applying the same benchmark to the 1968 election meant that the Justice Department would have to scrutinize jurisdictions that had no history of racist vote-suppression—like random counties in California and New York. Three boroughs in New York City—Manhattan, Brooklyn, and the Bronx—became subject to DOJ oversight (Queens and Staten Island did not), even though blacks throughout the city had been voting freely since the enactment of the 15th Amendment and had held municipal offices for 50 years. The city had not changed; the doors of political opportunity had not suddenly been closed to minority voters. It was just that in the 1968 presidential election, reflecting the national trend, more voters had stayed home than in 1964—pushing those three boroughs below the 50% threshold.

In fact, when the Voting Rights Act first passed in 1965, New York was the implicit standard against which the racism of southern politics had been judged. But by 1970, three New York City boroughs and Neshoba County, Mississippi—where three voting-rights advocates were murdered in 1964— had come to be equally restricted in their freedom to structure their own electoral arrangements. And these restrictions were not just theoretical: In 1972, the Justice Department used its preclearance power to object to a Brooklyn districting plan. The problem? The plan provided for a state-senate district in which the population was an allegedly insufficient 61% black. The Justice Department demanded that the district be redrawn so that its voting population would be 65% black, in order to better assure the election of a black state senator.

But what necessitated an absolutely secure black legislative seat in a northern state in which blacks had long been political players? And if Section 5 now demanded districts that were 65% black in Brooklyn, why not in the adjacent borough of Queens? The distinction drawn in 1965 between Mississippi and New York had not been arbitrary; that between Brooklyn and Queens in 1970 clearly was. The 1970 amendments destroyed the clean lines and logical construction of the original voting-rights statute.

That process of corruption continued in 1975, when the act was again reauthorized and amended. Ten years after the passage of the original act, the problem of access to the polls had been solved, and it was Section 5 that had come to be seen as the centerpiece of the statute. Civil-rights advocates wanted to build on the concept of the equally effective vote that Section 5 had been interpreted to promise. They argued that the right to vote included the right to representation; that minority representation could be measured only by the number of minority officeholders; and that justice demanded a national commitment to protecting black candidates from white competition. The renewal of the preclearance provision was thus a foregone conclusion in Congress that year.

To be sure, it was still too early to release the South from the federal receivership into which the region had been placed by the original act. In 1975, the nation was far from the point at which it could be said that southern blacks were equal citizens, free to form political coalitions and choose candidates in the same manner as other Americans. But in further amending the act in 1975, Congress largely ignored the statute's original aim of black enfranchisement and expanded its reach far beyond what its authors had originally intended.

The driving force behind this expansion was the Mexican-American Legal Defense and Education Fund (MALDEF), which wanted for its constituents the same extraordinary protection afforded blacks. They complained that cities in Alabama could not draw new districting maps, move polling places, or even expand their municipal boundaries without federal approval—and yet San Antonio, Texas, was free to adopt at-large voting, redraw the districts from which city council members were elected, and make any other alterations to its electoral arrangements. If blacks were entitled to proportional racial representation, why should Hispanics settle for anything less?

Persuaded by MALDEF, Congress brought four additional "language minority" groups under Section 5 coverage: Asian Americans, American Indians, Alaskan Natives, and "persons of Spanish heritage" (although the record compiled in the hearings before that reauthorization made only a feeble case for the inclusion of these groups, whose experience in the United States was so different from that of southern blacks).

Legislators also once again changed the trigger for coverage. Turnout figures for 1972 were added to those of 1964 and 1968, and the literacy test was redefined to include English-only ballots, as if they were equivalent to fraudulent literacy tests in the Jim Crow South. Coverage under the act was thus extended to the entire states of Texas, Arizona, and Alaska, as well as to counties in California, Florida, and South Dakota. These were all jurisdictions in which voting fell short of the 50% mark in 1972, and in which no bilingual ballots were provided for a language-minority group exceeding 5% of the state's or county's population. And all of these changes were set to expire after seven years, rather than five, to ensure that they would influence the redistricting that followed the 1980 census.

By this point, the carefully crafted 1965 statute had become almost unrecognizable. Indisputably, the racial progress that southern blacks had made in the decade since the act's original passage was due in considerable part to the broader definition of disfranchisement adopted by the Supreme Court and subsequently embraced by Congress and the Justice Department. But this definition was very much in line with the act's original intent: to protect southern blacks and allow them to play an equal role in the nation's civic and political life. The extensions of the law beyond that original aim were indefensible.

Yet such extensions continued. When the 1975 reauthorization expired in 1982, a strong case could have been made for another ten-year extension of Section 5 to protect southern blacks in the post-1990 round of redistricting. But important civil-rights spokesmen instead wanted to make Section 5 permanent—an idea so constitutionally radical as to be a non-starter. They settled for a still-extraordinary 25-year extension instead.

The 1982 reauthorization also included an even more significant amendment. Section 2 of the original Voting Rights Act had been nothing but a preamble reiterating the nation's commitment to the principles of the 15th Amendment. But some activists seized on the provision as a means of repairing the damage (as they saw it) wrought two years earlier by the Supreme Court decision in the case of *City of Mobile v. Bolden,* which had addressed the use of at-large voting to select members of the Mobile, Alabama, city council. In its ruling, the Court had held that the equal protection clause required the same showing of discriminatory *intent* in voting-rights cases as it did in employment, school segregation, and other contexts. Plaintiffs in 14th Amendment cases—including those involving alleged electoral inequality between minorities and whites—therefore could not prevail without evidence of discriminatory purpose. In the view of the civil-rights community, that requirement would prove impossible to fulfill (despite much legal precedent to the contrary). So why not avoid the hassle of constitutional litigation in the first place by altering the Voting Rights Act? Section 2 was thus amended to make discriminatory "result," not purpose, the standard by which voting-rights violations would be judged nationwide. Such a "result" would be apparent wherever minority-group members had relatively less opportunity, in the words of the statute, "to participate in the political process and to elect representatives of their choice."

Unlike Section 5, Section 2 had nationwide reach. And whereas Section 5's preclearance applied only to changes in electoral procedure made after the passage of the 1965 act, the new Section 2 allowed lawsuits attacking long-standing election methods. Moreover, unlike Section 5, it was a permanent provision, meaning it would never come up for renewal. The language of the amended Section 2 was a civil-rights lawyer's dream: a disparate-impact test for discrimination, wrapped in the rhetoric of opportunity. Equal results and equal opportunity had become one and the same.

Section 2 quickly became a powerful tool to attack methods of voting that failed to elect minority representatives in proportion to the minority population in jurisdictions across the nation. As Justice Sandra Day O'Connor pointed out, the new Section 2 could mean only one thing: "a right to usual, roughly proportional representation on the part of sizable, compact, cohesive minority groups." As with Section 5, proportionality was the inevitable standard against which racial fairness would come to be judged—for anything short of proportionality would suggest at least partial dilution of a minority vote.

Section 5 was due to expire again in 2007. But as the date for renewal approached, the prospect of racially charged controversy sent both Democrats and Republicans into a state of panic. Thus, an entire year before the expiration date, a Republican-controlled Congress once again renewed Section 5— for another 25 years. The temporary, constitutionally extraordinary emergency provision had turned into a near-permanent rule. Other amendments further strengthened the act in a variety of legally complicated ways, but the trigger for coverage remained the 1972 turnout figures—even less relevant to the question of enfranchisement than they had been 25 years earlier, and now in place through 2032.

A Legacy of Progress

During the 2006 Voting Rights Act reauthorization process, the House Judiciary Committee argued in its official report that "Discrimination today is more subtle than the visible methods used in 1965. However, the effects and results are the same." Rarely in the rich annals of congressional deceit and self-deception have more false and foolish words been written. No meaningful evidence supported this extraordinary claim, which did a disservice to the nation by refusing to recognize the remarkable revolution in race relations that occurred in the second half of the 20th century.

Without question, the Voting Rights Act of 1965 was essential to the demise of the Jim Crow South. It ended whites' exclusive hold on political power, which had made all other forms of southern racial subjugation possible. It was an indispensable and beautifully designed response to a profound moral wrong.

Even the drawing of race-conscious districts in the South was a reasonable way to address a grave problem. And it ultimately proved both effective and justified. The history of whites-only politics in the segregated South had made the emergence of black officeholders both symbolically and substantively important. Moreover, southern blacks came to politics after 1965 with almost no experience of organizing as a conventional political force. Thus, race-based districts in areas that had historically disenfranchised blacks were arguably analogous to the high tariffs that had helped the infant American steel industry get started: They gave the black political "industry" an opportunity to get on its feet before facing the full force of equal competition.

Many conservatives have argued that race-driven legislative maps violate the basic color-blind principles to which America should be committed. But context matters. While it is relatively easy to take an uncompromising stance against many racial classifications in higher education, for instance, it is more difficult when the issue is race-conscious districting lines drawn to increase black office-holding.

Racially gerrymandered districts, like preferential admissions, protect black candidates from white competition. But the realm of politics is not the same as higher education. There are few objective qualifications for political office—the equivalent of a college or professional degree, a minimum score on the SATs, or a certain grade-point average. And the alternative to racially preferential admissions at the University of Michigan, for example, was never an all-white college or law school. The university had had no history of de jure segregation, and blacks had always been a presence on the campus (although one that was too small in the view of civil-rights advocates). Compare this to southern politics before the Voting Rights Act, in which the aim had been to keep black officeholders out entirely. Moreover, strong evidence suggests that racial double standards in higher education do not work as advertised: Rich empirical work by UCLA law professor Richard Sander has shown that black students preferentially admitted to law schools fail the bar exam at dispro-portionately high rates. It is possible, he finds, that racial preferences have reduced, rather than increased, the supply of black attorneys. Race-based dis-tricts, on the other hand, reliably elect blacks and Hispanics to legislative seats.

Consider that in 1964, only five blacks held seats in Congress—none from any southern state—and just 94 blacks served in any of the 50 state leg-islatures, with only 16 in the southern states that were home to half of the nation's black population. But largely as a consequence of race-conscious dis-tricting, the Congressional Black Caucus today has 42 members, 17 of them from the South. And as of 2008, almost 600 blacks held seats in state legisla-tures; another 8,800 were mayors, sheriffs, school-board members, and other officeholders. Fully 47% of these public officials lived in the seven states origi-nally covered by the Voting Rights Act, even though those states now contain only 30% of the nation's black population. Especially striking is the fact that Mississippi—which once had a well-deserved reputation as the most white-supremacist state in the union—now leads the nation in the number of blacks elected to political office.

Blacks who came north, beginning with the Great Migration in 1915, faced nothing like the barriers to political participation evident in the South (indeed, political parties worked hard to mobilize black voters). And yet today, the former Jim Crow states look very much like the more historically open New York, Illinois, and Michigan. The South is back in the union.

A Legacy Endangered

Race-conscious districting, particularly in the South, was thus defensible and appropriate in the years in which few southern whites would vote for black candidates regardless of their qualifications. But they have come with costs. And these costs have increased in importance as some race-conscious districts have devolved into so-called "bug-splat districts"—so contorted to segregate black and white voters that they raise serious 14th Amendment questions—even as racism among white Americans has waned.

Creating safe black districts and safe white ones is plainly an "effort to 'segregate . . . voters' on the basis of race," Justice O'Connor wrote in 1993. As such, she said, the districts threaten "to stigmatize individuals by reason of their membership in a racial group." As voting-rights scholars T. Alexander Aleinikoff and Samuel Issacharoff have observed, racial sorting of this kind cre-ates advantaged and disadvantaged categories—groups that are privileged and groups that are subordinate. Districts drawn to meet the proportional racial representation standard embedded in the Voting Rights Act are designed to privilege blacks, and in such districts whites are reduced to "filler people"— usually irrelevant to the outcomes of elections.

Harvard law professor Cass Sunstein has observed another pertinent phenomenon. Across the political spectrum, when people talk only to those who are of like mind, they end up with more extreme views than they would hold otherwise. The majority of voters in districts drawn for the sole purpose of maximizing black representation are not likely to talk much to people who don't share their left-leaning, race-conscious values. And aspiring politicians who seek office in such settings are free to confine their appeal to these rigid ideological niches.

Black candidates who run in safe black districts thus tend to be to the left of most white voters. Their isolation from white centrists and conservatives deprives them of the broad experience necessary to win higher office. Perhaps this explains why so few members of the Congressional Black Caucus have run for statewide office. It is doubtful that anyone can imagine, for instance, South Carolina representative James Clyburn mounting a campaign for the Senate, let alone the presidency, despite the fact that he is a well-respected, long-serving political figure. He is a *black* politician with a majority-*black* constituency. He ran on his racial identity, but having done so has limited his further prospects.

There are exceptions to this rule, of course. This year, congressman Artur Davis is running for the Democratic nomination to be governor of Alabama; it is worth noting, though, that he is one of the few members of the Congressional Black Caucus rated as relatively centrist by the non-partisan *National Journal*. And the most successful black politician in American history, President Barack Obama, actually failed in his one attempt to run for office in a majority-minority district—a 2000 race for the U.S. House of Representatives. As voting-rights lawyer Michael Carvin has said:

> [T]he best thing that ever happened to Obama was [that] he ran for a heavily minority black congressional district in Chicago and lost. If he had won, he would have just become another mouthpiece for a group that is ghettoized in Congress and perceived as representing certain interest groups in the legislature.

In still another respect, race-conscious districting may act as a brake on black political advancement. The creation of majority-minority constituencies has not overcome the heritage of political apathy created by the long history of systematic disfranchisement. A number of scholars have shown in recent years that black voters, and therefore black-majority districts, are generally less politically engaged and mobilized. Vanderbilt University law professor Carol Swain has found that turnout in black-majority congressional districts across the country is especially low. She notes, for example, that just 13% of eligible voters showed up at the polls in 1986 in then-congressman Major Owens's 78% black district in New York City. If constituents in Owens's district felt more empowered with a black man representing them in Washington, it certainly did not inspire many of them to bother to vote.

James Campbell, a political scientist at the University of Buffalo, has supported Swain's findings. Campbell found that, in 1994, more than 60% of congressional districts in which racial minorities were the majority ranked in the bottom quintile in terms of voter turnout. The most recently published review of the scholarly literature on this subject is a 2007 article by Harvard political scientist Claudine Gay; summing up what we have learned from previous investigations, Gay observed: "Limited electoral competition and low voter turnout are widely viewed as defining features of districts with black or Latino majorities." The "lack of competition" serves to "discourage participation" and reduces "the incentive for candidates or parties to mobilize voters." In the districts from which members of the California Assembly were elected in 1996, Gay found, voter turnout exceeded 60% of registered voters in only *one-quarter* of the majority-minority districts—compared to 90% of the white-majority districts.

Racial gerrymandering also contributes to the larger problem of political polarization. By concentrating black voters in safe black constituencies, it tends to "bleach" adjoining districts. In the more conservative South, those whiter surrounding districts tend to be safely Republican while black districts are safely Democratic. In this and other ways, the Voting Rights Act has had important partisan as well as racial consequences.

Race-driven majority-minority districts are more or less carved in stone as long as the current interpretation of Section 5 endures. The preclearance provision prohibits so-called "retrogression"—districting after a decennial census that reduces the number of safe minority legislative seats. Thus, when new maps are drawn after 2010, safe black districts will remain safe. The Voting Rights Act has made them sacrosanct. As a consequence, to a substantial degree it is race, not politics, that drives the legislative districting process. And when it comes time for elections in these districts, the non-racial agendas of parties, incumbents, and challengers are recklessly ignored.

Getting Beyond Race

In its current incarnation, the Voting Rights Act rests on the assumption that, even today, black voters would be helpless victims of racism without extraordinary federal protection. Everyone knows, however, that this notion is absurd. Black officeholders and black voters have become politically powerful, but it is not their power alone that protects them. American racial attitudes have changed dramatically, even in the South. And in those places where racial exclusion is alleged, an army of federal attorneys and civil-rights activists stands ready to intervene.

Black voters today are largely ready and able to take full part in American political life. Fifteen years ago, one of the most liberal members of the Supreme Court put the matter plainly: "Minority voters," Justice David Souter wrote, "are not immune from the obligation to pull, haul, and trade to find common political ground, the virtue of which is not to be slighted in applying a statute meant to hasten the waning of racism in American politics."

Pulling, hauling, and trading to find common ground describes the post-racial American polity the Voting Rights Act was intended to create. But it is not the direction in which the contemporary enforcement of the act is taking us. The statute compels us to keep race at the center of our political process, suggests to aspiring black politicians that they should confine themselves to racially safe ground, and encourages black voters to retain a deep pessimism about white racial attitudes that no longer seems justified by the realities of American life.

In February 2008, voters in an Alabama county that is more than 96% white sent a black man, James Fields, as their representative to the state House of Representatives. "Really, I never realize he's black," a white woman told a *New York Times* reporter. America has changed, the South has changed, and the voting-rights problems that are now of greatest concern—hanging chads, provisional ballots, glitches in electronic voting, registration hassles, voter identification, and fraud—bear no relationship to those that plagued the South in 1965. As New York University law professor Richard Pildes wrote in 2006, the statute has become "a model from earlier decades that is increasingly irrelevant and not designed for the voting problems of today." At the congressional hearings preceding that year's reauthorization of the act, he and other liberal voting-rights scholars urged Congress to pass a different statute for a new era.

Of course, no one should doubt the importance of the 1965 statute in making America a nation very different from the one in which I grew up not so many years ago. Race-conscious districting was legitimate as a temporary measure to give blacks what Daniel Lowenstein has called "a jumpstart in electoral politics." But Lowenstein makes a further important point: "A jumpstart is one thing, but the guy who comes and charges up your car when the battery's dead, he doesn't stay there trailing behind you with the cable stuck as you drive down the freeway. He lets it go."

It is time to let race-driven districting go. Congress is undoubtedly too timid to act anytime soon, but the Supreme Court should strike down Section 5 in its current form as unconstitutional. The Court had a chance to do so in 2008 and took a pass, but another, stronger case is bound to end up on the docket before long. The result would likely be a substitute statute—one surely still far from perfect, but perhaps better suited to today's cultural and electoral landscape. And if the Court hears a case regarding Section 2, it should at least require that the statute be interpreted as those who pushed for its passage in 1982 originally insisted it would be: as a means to protect against genuine racism.

America is much better off with the increase in the number of black elected officials made possible in large part by the deliberate drawing of majority-minority districts. But black politics has come of age, and black politicians can protect their turf, fight for their interests, and successfully compete—even for the presidency. America should celebrate, and move on.

EXPLORING THE ISSUE

Is There a Need for a Permanent Voting Rights Act?

Critical Thinking and Reflection

1. What is the historical record of black voting prior to 1965?
2. How significant a goal have voting rights been for civil rights advocates in America?
3. What voting rights were established by the Voting Rights Act of 1965?
4. What has been the impact of the Voting Rights Act from its passage to the present?
5. What are the arguments advanced by those opposed to the extension of the Voting Rights Act?
6. What conclusion is to be drawn concerning the effect of the Voting Rights Act from the available data?

Is There Common Ground?

Richard Valelly and Abgail Thernstrom both agree that the denial of voting rights to African Americans has been a significant challenge to American democracy. Further, they agree that race-conscious districting was an appropriate response to the denial of black voting rights in the United States. Voting rights are fundamental to a citizen's participation in a democratic polity. Prior to the passage of the Voting Rights Act of 1965, the voting rights of African Americans were virtually nonexistent in the United States. This Act, a focal concern of the civil rights movement, was a significant remedy for the problem. President Obama and the black legislators, especially those from the south, owe their positions to the Voting Rights Act and the black political empowerment of blacks that it engendered. Considering the question of the need to continue the Voting Rights Act in the United States, it is important to observe that issues of race and politics continue to beset the American landscape, and there is seemingly little basis for any realistic expectation that this reality will change in the near future. There is too much evidence to the contrary. Given the example of the resegregation of schools (see Issue 17) due to courts vacating desegregation orders and other factors, the hostile response to the Obama election in many segments of red state America, and other evidence, one can assume that many Americans, especially blacks and others, have come to depend upon the Voting Rights Act. We urge students to maximize the opportunity to gain an informed understanding of black voting rights, both past and present, and the challenges that persist.

Additional Resources

Blake, Aaron. 2011. "The GOP's Voter ID Gambit." The Fix (politics blog). *The Washington Post* (March 29). Available online at www.washingtonpost.com/blogs/the-fix/post/the-gops-voter-id-gambit/2011/03/28/AFhk1YuB_blog.html/

Chestnut, J.L. 1990. *Black in Selma* (Farrar, Straus and Giroux).

Davenport, Jim. 2011. "SC Voter ID Law Hits Some Black Precincts Harder." *The Associated Press* (October 19).

Foner, Eric. 1990. *A Short History of Reconstruction* (New York: Harper & Row).

Fund, John. 2008. *Stealing Elections: How Voter Fraud Threatens Our Democracy* (Encounter).

Gamboa, Suzanne. 2011. "Voter ID Laws Target Rarely Occurring Voter Fraud." *The Associated Press* (September 24).

Gillman, Todd J. 2012. "Supreme Court Could Be Receptive to Texas' Challenge of Voting Rights Act." *Dallas Morning News* (March 18).

Hasen, Richard. 2011. *The Voting Wars: From Florida 2000 to the Next Election Meltdown* (Yale University Press).

Hine, Diane Clark. 2003. *Black Victory: The Rise and Fall of the White Primary in Texas* (University of Missouri Press).

Keyssar, Alexander. 2009. *The Right to Vote: The Contested History of Democracy in the United States* (Basic Books).

Minnite, Lorraine. 2010. *The Myth of Voter Fraud* (Cornell University Press).

"Redistricting: Are Minority Groups Fairly Represented in Congress." 2001. *CQ Researcher* (11:February (6), 16). Entire issue dedicated to voting and redistricting.

Rosenkranz, Mark. 2009. *White Male Privilege: A Study of Racism in America 50 Years After the Voting Rights Act,* 3rd ed. (Law Dog Books).

Salisbury, Bill. 2012. "Minnesota Voter ID Measure Going on Fall Ballot." *St. Paul Pioneer Press* (April 3).

Thernstrom, Abigail. 1987. *Whose Votes Count? Affirmative Action and Minority Voting Rights* (Harvard University Press).

Thernstrom, Abigail and Stephan Thernstrom. 1997. *American in Black and White: One Nation, Indivisible* (Simon & Schuster).

"Waging a Battle over Voter ID Laws," "PBS NewsHour" (Web video), March 14, 2012. Available online at www.pbs.org/newshour/bb/politics/jan-june12/voterid_03-14.html

Woodward, C. Vann. 1957. *The Strange Career of Jim Crow* (Oxford University Press).

Yarborough, Timothy E. 2002. *Race and Redistricting: The Shaw-Cromartie Cases* (University Press of Kansas).

The United States Department of Justice website contains information about the agency and its mission to enforce law and defend the interests of the United States. The mission extends to crime control and fair administration of justice. It contains a copy of the "The Voting Rights Act of 1965" as well as voting rights law and other current voting rights information. The student will find access to data on research along with news releases on relevant topics.

www.justice.gov/

This is a website dedicated to the history of the southern civil rights movement also referred to as the Southern Freedom Movement (1951–1968). It contains a history, timeline, and bibliography along with copies of original documents dealing with the civil rights movement. For students doing research, the site offers links, categorized by specific topics, to both scholarly and popular sources on the movement. The site offers important information on the history of voter registration in the south including Freedom Summer in Mississippi and voter registration in Selma, Alabama, in 1965.

www.crmvet.org/

The National Voting Rights Museum and Institute website documents "the historic journey for the right to vote that began when the 'Founding Fathers' first planted the seeds of democracy in 1776." It seeks to enhance public knowledge of voting rights through documentation and education programs carried out by the museum and its institute.

www.nvrmi.com/

ISSUE 19

Do Minorities and Whites Engage in Self-Segregation?

YES: Beverly D. Tatum, from "Identity Development in Adolescence," in *Why Are All the Black Kids Sitting Together in the Cafeteria?* (Basic Books, 1997), pp. 52–74

NO: Debra Humphreys, from *Campus Diversity and Student Self-Segregation: Separating Myths from Facts* (Diversity Web Association of American Colleges and Universities, 1999)

Learning Outcomes

After reading this issue, the student should be able to:

- Present an informed understanding of racial identity development of American youth.
- Develop an appreciation of self-segregation as a mode of intergroup relations.
- Understand how this issue illuminates the continuing legacy of Jim Crow living within American society.
- Explain and apply concepts such as social distance, separatism, desegregation, assimilation, multiculturalism, and diversity to the discussion of this issue.
- Identify and examine factors that contribute to self-segregation within institutional settings.

ISSUE SUMMARY

YES: Beverly D. Tatum, an African American clinical psychologist and president of Spelman College, examines identity development among adolescents, especially black youths, and the behavioral outcomes of this phenomenon. She argues that black adolescents' tendency to view themselves in racial terms is due to the totality of personal and environmental responses that they receive from the larger society.

NO: Debra Humphreys is the director of Programs, Office of Education and Diversity Initiatives, at the Association of American Colleges and Universities in Washington, DC. She notes that today's university students are matriculating on very diverse campuses that are "leading to significant educational and social benefits for all college students. In such an environment, students have many opportunities to interact and associate with students of different backgrounds than themselves." She cites research that tends to show that rather than self-segregating, students are interacting across racial and ethnic lines in significant numbers.

In confronting this issue, students are challenged to develop a more comprehensive understanding of the scope and impact of legal segregation that existed in the United States prior to the civil rights movement. Many Americans, especially youth, have a tendency to associate racial segregation solely with the American South. They fail to recognize that segregation of the races was a national phenomenon. Segregation was not a social aberration, rather it was mandated by the *Plessy v. Ferguson* 1896 decision and the separate but equal doctrine that applied throughout the nation. In the wake of the Plessy decision, Jim Crow laws were passed in many states. The substantially desegregated society, which Americans experience today, is very different than the conditions that prevailed during the segregation era. It is the civil rights movement and the resulting legislation upon which today's race relations exist.

Both of the editors of this *Taking Sides* grew up in the north. Both attended overwhelmingly white public schools with segregated faculty. Both experienced public parks (Parvin State Park, South Jersey) where one day per week was designated for African Americans to swim, with the remaining time designated for whites only. In Philadelphia during the 1950s it was virtually impossible for an African American to be hired to drive a delivery truck. High-achieving African American students experienced rejection for employment in institutions such as banks and schools, whereas some less-achieving white counterparts would be hired.

Blacks who experienced Jim Crow were forced to adjust their expectations and behavior to accommodate segregation. They became conditioned to a Jim Crow lifestyle and responded accordingly. Blacks learned not to seek services or employment within a plethora of institutions, including barbershops, bars, golf courses, restaurants, and many other public accommodations that were racially segregated. Private clubs and associations were clearly off limits to blacks. They wanted to avoid the humiliation that rejection due to skin color generated. Meritocracy did not apply to blacks in pursuit of upward mobility. In examining this issue, students should consider whether the response of blacks to such conditions was due to self-segregation or a pragmatic response to the real world.

American colleges and universities are major institutional domains in which the isolation of African American students and other ethnic groups is a reality that has generated interest, concern, and controversy. African American students tend to be the primary focus of such concerns on our campuses, though they are not the only group involved in what many Americans, both scholars and others, characterize as "self-segregation." The clustering and grouping together of whites can also be seen as self-segregation. The focal concern of this social issue is often stated within the question: "Why are all the black kids sitting together in the cafeteria?" However, the larger and perhaps more relevant question is why do all racial groups tend to congregate together?

Beverly D. Tatum notes that the quest for personal identity is a fundamental aspect of human experience. As black youth proceed in their development from childhood through adolescence, the question of identity evolves and grows, according to Tatum and other psychologists.

This identity development of black youth is influenced by an evolving racial consciousness within their perceptions of self. According to Tatum, these racially focused self-perceptions and identities that black youth develop in response to their experiences within an environment intensify due to messages and treatments they receive in interacting with whites. The challenges facing black youth in their attempts to engage the dominant white world range from having to confront and effectively deal with prejudice and discrimination to resisting stereotypes and affirming other more positive definitions of themselves. In response to these challenges, Tatum examines significant coping strategies that are developed by these youth including self-segregation.

Tatum maintains that black youth develop strategies to affirm and protect themselves from the deleterious effects of their involvement within a society with embedded stereotypes concerning blacks. So, Tatum answers the question, "Why are all the black kids sitting together in the cafeteria?" She does so by exploring the responses of black youth to the stresses of race in American society, and their need to seek meaning, sensitivity, understanding, and support from their black peers.

Debra Humphreys, in the NO selection, offers an interesting challenge to Tatum. Humphreys views self-segregation as an advantage that contributes to the overall adjustment of minorities in a new environment. At the same time, she points out that racial minorities increase their social interaction with whites. She reviews studies of self-segregation (homogeneous groups) and additional levels of friendship. Citing studies by Richard Light of Harvard, a 1991 study of student life at Berkeley, and a 1997 study at the University of Michigan, Humphreys points out that all racial and ethnic groups want to meet and become friends with more students from different ethnic and cultural backgrounds than their own. Hence, she sees an increase of multiculturalism and diversity on the college campuses, overtaking the tendency toward self-segregation.

The issue of self-segregation is linked to Issue 1, "Do We Need a Common Identity?" in that it extends the assimilation–pluralism debate. Understanding voluntary segregation, in contrast to exclusion, challenges one to comprehend the complexities of identity. Given the goal of equality, what are the functions of self-segregation? On one hand, as Tatum points out, it offers a means to cope with rejection. Humphreys agrees and goes further to point out that self-segregation among minority college students does not impede intergroup contact. How might self-segregation impact upon social cohesion? What can be understood from John Matlock's article in *Diversity Digest* (Summer 1997),

"Student Expectations and Experiences," which found that white students had the most segregated friendship patterns on campus of all students.

The United States has a legacy of conflict-ridden race and ethnic relations rooted in such institutions as slavery, segregation, and related policies and practices of discrimination. Despite this legacy, minority students are more likely to interact with students of different backgrounds than are whites. Humphreys writes, "the reality is that students of color have much more intergroup contact than do white students but their pattern of interaction needs to be understood in light of their psychological development."

Many of the nation's campuses have not achieved multicultural sensitivity. We still have hate crimes and other manifestations of race and ethnic conflict. Confederate flags and other incendiary symbols of American racist tradition are still able to penetrate communities of higher learning. Given such realities, the black "table in the cafeteria" is expected to persist within the educational institutions of the United States. Essentially, as stated above, Tatum describes black students congregating around these tables as engaging in positive identity formation. Their peers provide them with the reaffirmation and support that they need to affirm that their blackness is a positive quality. The immersion of these youth within the circle of their peers around the black table can facilitate their development of positive senses of self-esteem and self-worth to serve as effective antidotes to the negativity that they often encounter in dealing with the dominant society. Thus, Tatum argues that self-segregation is a social adaptation by blacks and other youth in order to function effectively on campus.

Both Tatum and Humphreys offer the reader insight into the complex problem of race and American identity. Students may want to consider the following questions for further reflection: Is self-segregation truly voluntary? To what extent is self-segregation on campuses a threat to a common American identity?

YES

Beverly D. Tatum

Identity Development
in Adolescence

Walk into any racially mixed high school cafeteria at lunch time and you will instantly notice that in the sea of adolescent faces, there is an identifiable group of Black students sitting together. Conversely, it could be pointed out that there are many groups of White students sitting together as well, though people rarely comment about that. The question on the tip of everyone's tongue is "Why are the Black kids sitting together?" Principals want to know, teachers want to know, White students want to know, the Black students who aren't sitting at the table want to know.

How does it happen that so many Black teenagers end up at the same cafeteria table? They don't start out there. If you walk into racially mixed elementary schools, you will often see young children of diverse racial backgrounds playing with one another, sitting at the snack table together, crossing racial boundaries with an ease uncommon in adolescence. Moving from elementary school to middle school (often at sixth or seventh grade) means interacting with new children from different neighborhoods than before, and a certain degree of clustering by race might therefore be expected, presuming that children who are familiar with one another would form groups. But even in schools where the same children stay together from kindergarten through eighth grade, racial grouping begins by the sixth or seventh grade. What happens?

One thing that happens is puberty. As children enter adolescence, they begin to explore the question of identity, asking "Who am I? Who can I be?" in ways they have not done before. For Black youth, asking "Who am I?" includes thinking about "Who am I ethnically and/or racially? What does it mean to be Black?"

As I write this, I can hear the voice of a White woman who asked me, "Well, all adolescents struggle with questions of identity. They all become more self-conscious about their appearance and more concerned about what their peers think. So what is so different for Black kids?" Of course, she is right that all adolescents look at themselves in new ways, but not all adolescents think about themselves in racial terms.

The search for personal identity that intensifies in adolescence can involve several dimensions of an adolescent's life: vocational plans, religious beliefs, values and preferences, political affiliations and beliefs, gender roles, and ethnic identities. The process of exploration may vary across these identity domains. James Marcia described four identity "statuses" to characterize the variation in the identity search process: (1) *diffuse,* a state in which there has been little exploration or active consideration of a particular domain, and no psychological commitment; (2) *foreclosed,* a state in which a commitment has been made to particular roles or belief systems, often those selected by parents, without actively considering alternatives; (3) *moratorium,* a state of active exploration of roles and beliefs in which no commitment has yet been made; and (4) *achieved,* a state of strong personal commitment to a particular dimension of identity following a period of high exploration.

An individual is not likely to explore all identity domains at once, therefore it is not unusual for an adolescent to be actively exploring one dimension while another remains relatively unexamined. Given the impact of dominant and subordinate status, it is not surprising that researchers have found that adolescents of color are more likely to be actively engaged in an exploration of their racial or ethnic identity than are White adolescents.

Why do Black youths, in particular, think about themselves in terms of race? Because that is how the rest of the world thinks of them. Our self-perceptions are shaped by the messages that we receive from those around us, and when young Black men and women enter adolescence, the racial content of those messages intensifies. A case in point: If you were to ask my ten-year-old son, David, to describe himself, he would tell you many things: that he is smart, that he likes to play computer games, that he has an older brother. Near the top of his list, he would likely mention that he is tall for his age. He would probably not mention that he is Black, though he certainly knows that he is. Why would he mention his height and not his racial group membership? When David meets new adults, one of the first questions they ask is "How old are you?" When David states his age, the inevitable reply is "Gee, you're tall for your age!" It happens so frequently that I once overheard David say to someone, "Don't say it, I know. I'm tall for my age." Height is salient for David because it is salient for others.

When David meets new adults, they don't say, "Gee, you're Black for your age!" If you are saying to yourself, of course they don't, think again. Imagine David at fifteen, six-foot-two, wearing the adolescent attire of the day, passing adults he doesn't know on the sidewalk. Do the women hold their purses a little tighter, maybe even cross the street to avoid him? Does he hear the sound of the automatic door locks on cars as he passes by? Is he being followed around by the security guards at the local mall? As he stops in town with his new bicycle, does a police officer hassle him, asking where he got it, implying that it might be stolen? Do strangers assume he plays basketball? Each of these experiences conveys a racial message. At ten, race is not yet salient for David, because it is not yet salient for society. But it will be.

Understanding Racial Identity Development

Psychologist William Cross, author of *Shades of Black: Diversity in African American Identity,* has offered a theory of racial identity development that I have found to be a very useful framework for understanding what is happening not only with David, but with those Black students in the cafeteria. According to Cross's model, referred to as the psychology of nigrescence, or the psychology of becoming Black, the five stages of racial identity development are *pre-encounter, encounter, immersion/emersion, internalization,* and *internalization-commitment.* For the moment, we will consider the first two stages as those are the most relevant for adolescents.

In the first stage, the Black child absorbs many of the beliefs and values of the dominant White culture, including the idea that it is better to be White. The stereotypes, omissions, and distortions that reinforce notions of White superiority are breathed in by Black children as well as White. Simply as a function of being socialized in a Eurocentric culture, some Black children may begin to value the role models, lifestyles, and images of beauty represented by the dominant group more highly than those of their own cultural group. On the other hand, if Black parents are what I call race-conscious—that is, actively seeking to encourage positive racial identity by providing their children with positive cultural images and messages about what it means to be Black—the impact of the dominant society's messages is reduced. In either case, in the pre-encounter stage, the personal and social significance of one's racial group membership has not yet been realized, and racial identity is not yet under examination. At age ten, David and other children like him would seem to be in the pre-encounter stage. When the environmental cues change and the world begins to reflect his Blackness back to him more clearly, he will probably enter the encounter stage.

Transition to the encounter stage is typically precipitated by an event or series of events that force the young person to acknowledge the personal impact of racism. As the result of a new and heightened awareness of the significance of race, the individual begins to grapple with what it means to be a member of a group targeted by racism. Though Cross describes this process as one that unfolds in late adolescence and early adulthood, research suggests that an examination of one's racial or ethnic identity may begin as early as junior high school.

In a study of Black and White eighth graders from an integrated urban junior high school, Jean Phinney and Steve Tarver found clear evidence for the beginning of the search process in this dimension of identity. Among the forty-eight participants, more than a third had thought about the effects of ethnicity on their future, had discussed the issues with family and friends, and were attempting to learn more about their group. While White students in this integrated school were also beginning to think about ethnic identity, there was evidence to suggest a more active search among Black students, especially Black females. Phinney and Tarver's research is consistent with my own study of Black youth in predominantly White communities, where the environmental cues that trigger an examination of racial identity often become evident in middle school or junior high school.

Some of the environmental cues are institutionalized. Though many elementary schools have self-contained classrooms where children of varying performance levels learn together, many middle and secondary schools use "ability grouping," or tracking. Though school administrators often defend their tracking practices as fair and objective, there usually is a recognizable racial pattern to how children are assigned, which often represents the system of advantage operating in the schools. In racially mixed schools, Black children are much more likely to be in the lower track than in the honors track. Such apparent sorting along racial lines sends a message about what it means to be Black. One young honors student I interviewed described the irony of this resegregation in what was an otherwise integrated environment, and hinted at the identity issues it raised for him.

> It was really a very paradoxical existence, here I am in a school that's 35 percent Black, you know, and I'm the only Black in my classes. . . . That always struck me as odd. I guess I felt that I was different from the other Blacks because of that.

In addition to the changes taking place within school, there are changes in the social dynamics outside school. For many parents, puberty raises anxiety about interracial dating. In racially mixed communities, you begin to see what I call the birthday party effect. Young children's birthday parties in multiracial communities are often a reflection of the community's diversity. The parties of elementary school children may be segregated by gender but not by race. At puberty, when the parties become sleepovers or boy-girl events, they become less and less racially diverse.

Black girls, especially in predominantly White communities, may gradually become aware that something has changed. When their White friends start to date, they do not. The issues of emerging sexuality and the societal messages about who is sexually desirable leave young Black women in a very devalued position. One young woman from a Philadelphia suburb described herself as "pursuing White guys throughout high school" to no avail. Since there were no Black boys in her class, she had little choice. She would feel "really pissed off" that those same White boys would date her White friends. For her, "that prom thing was like out of the question."

Though Black girls living in the context of a larger Black community may have more social choices, they too have to contend with devaluing messages about who they are and who they will become, especially if they are poor or working-class. As social scientists Bonnie Ross Leadbeater and Niobe Way point out,

> The school drop-out, the teenage welfare mother, the drug addict, and the victim of domestic violence or of AIDS are among the most prevalent public images of poor and working-class urban adolescent girls. . . . Yet, despite the risks inherent in economic disadvantage, the majority of poor urban adolescent girls do not fit the stereotypes that are made about them.

Resisting the stereotypes and affirming other definitions of themselves is part of the task facing young Black women in both White and Black communities.

As was illustrated in the example of David, Black boys also face a devalued status in the wider world. The all too familiar media image of a young

Black man with his hands cuffed behind his back, arrested for a violent crime, has primed many to view young Black men with suspicion and fear. In the context of predominantly White schools, however, Black boys may enjoy a degree of social success, particularly if they are athletically talented. The culture has embraced the Black athlete, and the young man who can fulfill that role is often pursued by Black girls and White girls alike. But even these young men will encounter experiences that may trigger an examination of their racial identity.

Sometimes the experience is quite dramatic. *The Autobiography of Malcolm X* is a classic tale of racial identity development, and I assign it to my psychology of racism students for just that reason. As a junior high school student, Malcolm was a star. Despite the fact that he was separated from his family and living in a foster home, he was an A student and was elected president of his class. One day he had a conversation with his English teacher, whom he liked and respected, about his future career goals. Malcolm said he wanted to be a lawyer. His teacher responded, "That's no realistic goal for a nigger," and advised him to consider carpentry instead. The message was clear: You are a Black male, your racial group membership matters, plan accordingly. Malcolm's emotional response was typical—anger, confusion, and alienation. He withdrew from his White classmates, stopped participating in class, and eventually left his predominately White Michigan home to live with his sister in Roxbury, a Black community in Boston.

No teacher would say such a thing now, you may be thinking, but don't be so sure. It is certainly less likely that a teacher would use the word *nigger,* but consider these contemporary examples shared by high school students. A young ninth-grade student was sitting in his homeroom. A substitute teacher was in charge of the class. Because the majority of students from this school go on to college, she used the free time to ask the students about their college plans. As a substitute she had very limited information about their academic performance, but she offered some suggestions. When she turned to this young man, one of few Black males in the class, she suggested that he consider a community college. She had recommended four-year colleges to the other students. Like Malcolm, this student got the message.

In another example, a young Black woman attending a desegregated school to which she was bussed was encouraged by a teacher to attend the upcoming school dance. Most of the Black students did not live in the neighborhood and seldom attended the extracurricular activities. The young woman indicated that she wasn't planning to come. The well-intentioned teacher was persistent. Finally the teacher said, "Oh come on, I know you people love to dance." This young woman got the message, too.

Coping with Encounters: Developing an Oppositional Identity

What do these encounters have to do with the cafeteria? Do experiences with racism inevitably result in so-called self-segregation? While certainly a desire to protect oneself from further offense is understandable, it is not the only factor at work. Imagine the young eighth-grade girl who experienced the teacher's use of "you people" and the dancing stereotype as a racial affront. Upset and struggling with adolescent embarrassment, she bumps into a White friend who can see that something is wrong. She explains. Her White friend responds, in an effort to make her feel better perhaps, and says, "Oh, Mr. Smith is such a nice guy, I'm sure he didn't mean it like that. Don't be so sensitive." Perhaps the White friend is right, and Mr. Smith didn't mean it, but imagine your own response when you are upset, perhaps with a spouse or partner. He or she asks what's wrong and you explain why you are offended. Your partner brushes off your complaint, attributing it to your being oversensitive. What happens to your emotional thermostat? It escalates. When feelings, rational or irrational, are invalidated, most people disengage. They not only choose to discontinue the conversation but are more likely to turn to someone who will understand their perspective.

In much the same way, the eighth-grade girl's White friend doesn't get it. She doesn't see the significance of this racial message, but the girls at the "Black table" do. When she tells her story there, one of them is likely to say, "You know what, Mr. Smith said the same thing to me yesterday!" Not only are Black adolescents encountering racism and reflecting on their identity, but their White peers, even when they are not the perpetrators (and sometimes they are), are unprepared to respond in supportive ways. The Black students turn to each other for the much needed support they are not likely to find anywhere else.

In adolescence, as race becomes personally salient for Black youth, finding the answer to questions such as, "What does it mean to be a young Black person? How should I act? What should I do?" is particularly important. And although Black fathers, mothers, aunts, and uncles may hold the answers by offering themselves as role models, they hold little appeal for most adolescents. The last thing many fourteen-year-olds want to do is to grow up to be like their parents. It is the peer group, the kids in the cafeteria, who hold the answers to these questions. They know how to be Black. They have absorbed the stereotypical images of Black youth in the popular culture and are reflecting those images in their self-presentation.

Based on their fieldwork in U.S. high schools, Signithia Fordham and John Ogbu identified a common psychological pattern found among African American high school students is this stage of identity development. They observed that the anger and resentment that adolescents feel in response to their growing awareness of the systematic exclusion of Black people from full participation in U.S. society leads to the development of an oppositional social identity. This oppositional stance both protects one's identity from the psychological assault of racism and keeps the dominant group at a distance. Fordham and Ogbu write:

> Subordinate minorities regard certain forms of behavior and certain activities or events, symbols, and meanings as *not appropriate* for them because those behaviors, events, symbols, and meanings are characteristic of white Americans. At the same time they emphasize other forms

of behavior as more appropriate for them because these are *not* a part of white Americans' way of life. To behave in the manner defined as falling within a white cultural frame of reference is to "act white" and is negatively sanctioned.

Certain styles of speech, dress, and music, for example, may be embraced as "authentically Black" and become highly valued, while attitudes and behaviors associated with Whites are viewed with disdain. The peer groups's evaluation of what is Black and what is not can have a powerful impact on adolescent behavior.

Reflecting on her high school years, one Black woman from a White neighborhood described both the pain of being rejected by her Black classmates and her attempts to conform to her peer's definition of Blackness:

> "Oh you sound White, you think you're White," they said. And the idea of sounding White was just so absurd to me. . . . So ninth grade was sort of traumatic in that I started listening to rap music, which I really just don't like. [I said] I'm gonna be Black, and it was just that stupid. But it's more than just how one acts, you know. [The other Black women there] were not into me for the longest time. My first year there was hell.

Sometimes the emergence of an oppositional identity can be quite dramatic, as the young person tries on a new persona almost overnight. At the end of one school year, race may not have appeared to be significant, but often some encounter takes place over the summer and the young person returns to school much more aware of his or her Blackness and ready to make sure that the rest of the world is aware of it, too. There is a certain "in your face" quality that these adolescents can take on, which their teachers often experience as threatening. When a group of Black teens are sitting together in the cafeteria, collectively embodying an oppositional stance, school administrators want to know not only why they are sitting together, but what can be done to prevent it.

We need to understand that in racially mixed settings, racial grouping is a developmental process in response to an environmental stressor, racism. Joining with one's peers for support in the face of stress is a positive coping strategy. What is problematic is that the young people are operating with a very limited definition of what it means to be Black, based largely on cultural stereotypes.

Oppositional Identity Development and Academic Achievement

Unfortunately for Black teenagers, those cultural stereotypes do not usually include academic achievement. Academic success is more often associated with being White. During the encounter phase of racial identity development, when the search for identity leads toward cultural stereotypes and away from anything that might be associated with Whiteness, academic performance often declines. Doing well in school becomes identified as trying to be White. Being smart becomes the opposite of being cool.

While this frame of reference is not universally found among adolescents of African descent, it is commonly observed in Black peer groups. Among the Black college students I have interviewed, many described some conflict or alienation from other African American teens because of their academic success in high school. For example, a twenty-year-old female from a Washington, D.C., suburb explained:

> It was weird, even in high school a lot of the Black students were, like, "Well, you're not really Black." Whether it was because I became president of the sixth-grade class or whatever it was, it started pretty much back then. Junior high, it got worse. I was then labeled certain things, whether it was "the oreo" or I wasn't really Black.

Others described avoiding situations that would set them apart from their Black peers. For example, one young woman declined to participate in a gifted program in her school because she knew it would separate her from the other Black students in the school.

In a study of thirty-three eleventh-graders in a Washington, D.C., school, Fordham and Ogbu found that although some of the students had once been academically successful, few of them remained so. These students also knew that to be identified as a "brainiac" would result in peer rejection. The few students who had maintained strong academic records found ways to play down their academic success enough to maintain some level of acceptance among their Black peers.

Academically successful Black students also need a strategy to find acceptance among their White classmates. Fordham describes one such strategy as *racelessness,* wherein individuals assimilate into the dominant group by de-emphasizing characteristics that might identify them as members of the subordinate group. Jon, a young man I interviewed, offered a classic example of this strategy as he described his approach to dealing with his discomfort at being the only Black person in his advanced classes. He said, "At no point did I ever think I was White or did I ever want to be White. . . . I guess it was one of those things where I tried to de-emphasize the fact that I was Black." This strategy led him to avoid activities that were associated with Blackness. He recalled, "I didn't want to do anything that was traditionally Black, like I never played basketball. I ran cross-country. . . . I went for distance running instead of sprints." He felt he had to show his White classmates that there were "exceptions to all these stereotypes." However, this strategy was of limited usefulness. When he traveled outside his home community with his White teammates, he sometimes encountered overt racism. "I quickly realized that I'm Black, and that's the thing that they're going to see first, no matter how much I try to de-emphasize my Blackness."

A Black student can play down Black identity in order to succeed in school and mainstream institutions without rejecting his Black identity and culture. Instead of becoming raceless, an achieving Black student can become an *emissary,* someone who sees his or her own achievements as advancing the cause of the racial group. For example, social scientists Richard Zweigenhaft and G. William Domhoff describe how a successful Black student, in response to the accusation of acting White, connected his achievement to that of other Black men by saying, "Martin Luther King must not have been Black, then, since he had a doctoral degree, and Malcolm X must not have been Black since he educated himself while in prison." In addition, he demonstrated his loyalty to the Black community by taking an openly political stance against the racial discrimination he observed in his school.

It is clear that an oppositional identity can interfere with academic achievement, and it may be tempting for educators to blame the adolescents themselves for their academic decline. However, the questions that educators and other concerned adults must ask are, How did academic achievement become defined as exclusively White behavior? What is it about the curriculum and the wider culture that reinforce the notion that academic excellence is an exclusively White domain? What curricular interventions might we use to encourage the development of an empowered emissary identity?

An oppositional identity that disdains academic achievement has not always been a characteristic of Black adolescent peer groups. It seems to be a post-desegregation phenomenon. Historically, the oppositional identity found among African Americans in the segregated South included a positive attitude toward education. While Black people may have publicly deferred to Whites, they actively encouraged their children to pursue education as a ticket to greater freedom. While Black parents still see education as the key to upward mobility, in today's desegregated schools the models of success—the teachers, administrators, and curricular heroes—are almost always White.

Black Southern schools, though stigmatized by legally sanctioned segregation, were often staffed by African American educators, themselves visible models of academic achievement. These Black educators may have presented a curriculum that included references to the intellectual legacy of other African Americans. As well, in the context of a segregated school, it was given that the high achieving students would all be Black. Academic achievement did not have to mean separation from one's Black peers.

The Search for Alternative Images

This historical example reminds us that an oppositional identity discouraging academic achievement is not inevitable even in a racist society. If young people are exposed to images of African American academic achievement in their early years, they won't have to define school achievement as something for Whites only. They will know that there is a long history of Black intellectual achievement.

This point was made quite eloquently by Jon, the young man I quoted earlier. Though he made the choice to excel in school, he labored under the false assumption that he was "inventing the wheel." It wasn't until he reached college and had the opportunity to take African American studies courses that he learned about other African Americans besides Martin Luther King, Malcolm X, and Frederick Douglass—the same three men he had heard about year after year, from kindergarten to high school graduation. As he reflected on his identity struggle in high school, he said:

> It's like I went through three phases. . . . My first phase was being cool, doing whatever was particularly cool for Black people at the time, and that was like in junior high. Then in high school, you know, I thought being Black was basically all stereotypes, so I tried to avoid all of those things. Now in college, you know, I realize that being Black means a variety of things.

Learning his history in college was of great psychological importance to Jon, providing him with role models he had been missing in high school. He was particularly inspired by learning of the intellectual legacy of Black men at his own college:

> When you look at those guys who were here in the Twenties, they couldn't live on campus. They couldn't eat on campus. They couldn't get their hair cut in town. And yet they were all Phi Beta Kappa. . . . That's what being Black really is, you know, knowing who you are, your history, your accomplishments. . . . When I was in junior high, I had White role models. And then when I got into high school, you know, I wasn't sure but I just didn't think having White role models was a good thing. So I got rid of those. And I basically just, you know, only had my parents for role models. I kind of grew up thinking that we were on the cutting edge. We were doing something radically different than everybody else. And not realizing that there are all kinds of Black people doing the very things that I thought we were the only ones doing. . . . You've got to do the very best you can so that you can continue the great traditions that have already been established.

This young man was not alone in his frustration over having learned little about his own cultural history in grade school. Time and again in the research interviews I conducted, Black students lamented the absence of courses in African American history or literature at the high school level and indicated how significant this new learning was to them in college, how excited and affirmed they felt by this newfound knowledge. Sadly, many Black students never get to college, alienated from the process of education long before high school graduation. They may never get access to the information that might have helped them expand their definition of what it means to be Black and, in the process, might have helped them stay in school. Young people are developmentally ready for this information in adolescence. We ought to provide it.

Not at the Table

As we have seen, Jon felt he had to distance himself from his Black peers in order to be successful in high school. He was one of the kids *not* sitting at the Black table. Continued encounters with racism and access to new culturally relevant information empowered him to give up his racelessness and become an emissary. In college, not only did he sit at the Black table, but he emerged as a campus leader, confident in the support of his Black peers. His example illustrates that one's presence at the Black table is often an expression of one's identity development, which evolves over time.

Some Black students may not be developmentally ready for the Black table in junior or senior high school. They may not yet have had their own encounters with racism, and race may not be very salient for them. Just as we don't all reach puberty and begin developing sexual interest at the same time, racial identity development unfolds in idiosyncratic ways. Though my research suggests that adolescence is a common time, one's own life experiences are also important determinants of the timing. The young person whose racial identity development is out of synch with his or her peers often feels in an awkward position. Adolescents are notoriously egocentric and assume that their experience is the same as everyone else's. Just as girls who have become interested in boys become disdainful of their friends still interested in dolls, the Black teens who are at the table can be quite judgmental toward those who are not. "If I think it is a sign of authentic Blackness to sit at this table, then you should too."

The young Black men and women who still hang around with the White classmates they may have known since early childhood will often be snubbed by their Black peers. This dynamic is particularly apparent in regional schools where children from a variety of neighborhoods are brought together. When Black children from predominantly White neighborhoods go to school with Black children from predominantly Black neighborhoods, the former group is often viewed as trying to be White by the latter group. We all speak the language of the streets we live on. Black children living in White neighborhoods often sound White to their Black peers from across town, and may be teased because of it. This can be a very painful experience, particularly when the young person is not fully accepted as part of the White peer group either.

One young Black woman from a predominantly White community described exactly this situation in an interview. In a school with a lot of racial tension, Terri felt that "the worst thing that happened" was the rejection she experienced from the other Black children who were being bussed to her school. Though she wanted to be friends with them, they teased her, calling her an "oreo cookie" and sometimes beating her up. The only close Black friend Terri had was a biracial girl from her neighborhood.

Racial tensions also affected her relationships with White students. One White friend's parents commented, "I can't believe you're Black. You don't seem like all the Black children. You're nice." Though other parents made similar comments, Terri reported that her White friends didn't start making them until junior high school, when Terri's Blackness became something to be explained. One friend introduced Terri to another White girl by saying, "She's not really Black, she just went to Florida and got a really dark tan." A White sixth-grade "boyfriend" became embarrassed when his friends discovered he had a crush on a Black girl. He stopped telling Terri how pretty she was, and instead called her "nigger" and said, "Your lips are too big. I don't want to see you. I won't be your friend anymore."

Despite supportive parents who expressed concern about her situation, Terri said she was a "very depressed child." Her father would have conversations with her "about being Black and beautiful" and about "the union of people of color that had always existed that I needed to find. And the pride." However, her parents did not have a network of Black friends to help support her.

It was the intervention of a Black junior high school teacher that Terri feels helped her the most. Mrs. Campbell "really exposed me to the good Black community because I was so down on it" by getting Terri involved in singing gospel music and introducing her to other Black students who would accept her. "That's when I started having other Black friends. And I thank her a lot for that."

The significant role that Mrs. Campbell played in helping Terri open up illustrates the constructive potential that informed adults can have in the identity development process. She recognized Terri's need for a same-race peer group and helped her find one. Talking to groups of Black students about the variety of living situations Black people come from, and the unique situation facing Black adolescents in White communities, helps to expand the definition of what it means to be Black and increases intragroup acceptance at a time when that is quite important.

For children in Terri's situation, it is also helpful for Black parents to provide ongoing opportunities for their children to connect with other Black peers even if that means traveling outside the community they live in. Race-conscious parents often do this by attending a Black church or maintaining ties to Black social organizations such as Jack and Jill. Parents who make this effort often find that their children become bicultural, able to move comfortably between Black and White communities, and able to sit at the Black table when they are ready.

Implied in this discussion is the assumption that connecting with one's Black peers in the process of identity development is important and should be encouraged. For young Black people living in predominantly Black communities, such connections occur spontaneously with neighbors and classmates and usually do not require special encouragement. However, for young people in predominantly White communities they may only occur with active parental intervention. One might wonder if this social connection is really necessary. If a young person has found a niche among a circle of White friends, is it really necessary to establish a Black peer group as a reference point? Eventually it is.

As one's awareness of the daily challenges of living in a racist society increase, it is immensely helpful to be able to share one's experiences with others who have lived it. Even when White friends are willing and able to listen and bear witness to one's struggles, they cannot really share the experience. One young woman came to this realization in her senior year of high school:

> [The isolation] never really bothered me until about senior year when I was the only one in the class. . . . That little burden, that constant burden of you always having to strive to do your best and show that you can do just as much as everybody else. Your White friends can't understand that, and it's really hard to communicate to them. Only

someone else of the same racial, same ethnic background would understand something like that.

When one is faced with what Chester Pierce calls the "mundane extreme environmental stress" of racism, in adolescence or in adulthood, the ability to see oneself as part of a larger group from which one can draw support is an important coping strategy. Individuals who do not have such a strategy available to them because they do not experience a shared identity with at least some subset of their racial group are at risk for considerable social isolation.

Of course, who we perceive as sharing our identity may be influenced by other dimensions of identity such as gender, social class, geographical location, skin color, or ethnicity. For example, research indicates that first-generation Black immigrants from the Caribbean tend to emphasize their national origins and ethnic identities, distancing themselves from U.S. Blacks, due in part to their belief that West Indians are viewed more positively by Whites than those American Blacks whose family roots include the experience of U.S. slavery. To relinquish one's ethnic identity as West Indian and take on an African American identity may be understood as downward social mobility. However, second-generation West Indians without an identifiable accent may lose the relative ethnic privilege their parents experienced and seek racial solidarity with Black American peers in the face of encounters with racism. Whether it is the experience of being followed in stores because they are suspected of shoplifting, seeing people respond to them with fear on the street, or feeling overlooked in school, Black youth can benefit from seeking support from those who have had similar experiences.

An Alternative to the Cafeteria Table

The developmental need to explore the meaning of one's identity with others who are engaged in a similar process manifests itself informally in school corridors and cafeterias across the country. Some educational institutions have sought to meet this need programmatically. Several colleagues and I recently evaluated one such effort, initiated at a Massachusetts middle school participating in a voluntary desegregation program known as the Metropolitan Council for Educational Opportunity (METCO) program. Historically, the small number of African American students who are bussed from Boston to this suburban school have achieved disappointing levels of academic success. In an effort to improve academic achievement, the school introduced a program, known as Student Efficacy Training (SET) that allowed Boston students to meet each day as a group with two staff members. Instead of being in physical education or home economics or study hall, they were meeting, talking about homework difficulties, social issues, and encounters with racism. The meeting was mandatory and at first the students were resentful of missing some of their classes. But the impact was dramatic. Said one young woman,

> In the beginning of the year, I didn't want to do SET at all. It took away my study and it was only METCO students doing it. In the beginning all we did was argue over certain problems or it was more like a

rap session and I didn't think it was helping anyone. But then when we looked at records. . . . I know that last year out of all the students, sixth through eighth grade, there was, like, six who were actually good students. Everyone else, it was just pathetic, I mean, like, they were getting like Ds and Fs. . . . The eighth grade is doing much better this year. I mean, they went from Ds and Fs to Bs and Cs and occasional As. . . . And those seventh-graders are doing really good, they have a lot of honor roll students in seventh grade, both guys and girls. Yeah, it's been good. It's really good.

Her report is borne out by an examination of school records. The opportunity to come together in the company of supportive adults allowed these young Black students to talk about the issues that hindered their performance—racial encounters, feelings of isolation, test anxiety, homework dilemmas—in the psychological safety of their own group. In the process, the peer culture changed to one that supported academic performance rather than undermined it, as revealed in these two students' comments:

Well, a lot of the Boston students, the boys and the girls, used to fight all the time. And now, they stopped yelling at each other so much and calling each other stupid.

It's like we've all become like one big family, we share things more with each other. We tease each other like brother and sister. We look out for each other with homework and stuff. We always stay on top of each other 'cause we know it's hard with African American students to go to a predominantly White school and try to succeed with everybody else.

The faculty, too, were very enthusiastic about the outcomes of the intervention, as seen in the comments of these two classroom teachers:

This program has probably produced the most dramatic result of any single change that I've seen at this school. It has produced immediate results that affected behavior and academics and participation in school life.

My students are more engaged. They aren't battling out a lot of the issues of their anger about being in a White community, coming in from Boston, where do I fit, I don't belong here. I feel that those issues that often came out in class aren't coming out in class anymore. I think they are being discussed in the SET room, the kids feel more confidence. The kids' grades are higher, the homework response is greater, they're not afraid to participate in class, and I don't see them isolating themselves within class. They are willing to sit with other students happily. . . . I think it's made a very positive impact on their place in the school and on their individual self-esteem. I see them enjoying themselves and able to enjoy all of us as individuals. I can't say enough, it's been the best thing that's happened to the METCO program as far as I'm concerned.

Although this intervention is not a miracle cure for every school, it does highlight what can happen when we think about the developmental needs of

Black adolescents coming to terms with their own sense of identity. It might seem counterintuitive that a school involved in a voluntary desegregation program could improve both academic performance and social relationships among students by *separating* the Black students for one period every day. But if we understand the unique challenges facing adolescents of color and the legitimate need they have to feel supported in their identity development, it makes perfect sense.

Though they may not use the language of racial identity development theory to describe it, most Black parents want their children to achieve an internalized sense of personal security, to be able to acknowledge the reality of racism and to respond effectively to it. Our educational institutions should do what they can to encourage this development rather than impede it. When I talk to educators about the need to provide adolescents with identity-affirming experiences and information about their own cultural groups, they sometimes flounder because this information has not been part of their own education. Their understanding of adolescent development has been limited to the White middle-class norms included in most textbooks, their knowledge of Black history limited to Martin Luther King, Jr., and Rosa Parks. They sometimes say with frustration that parents should provide this kind of education for their children. Unfortunately Black parents often attended the same schools the teachers did and have the same informational gaps. We need to acknowledge that an important part of interrupting the cycle of oppression is constant re-education, and sharing what we learn with the next generation.

Debra Humphreys

NO

Campus Diversity and Student Self-Segregation: Separating Myths From Facts

When students went off to college this Fall, they entered more diverse campuses than ever before. For many students, in fact, their college community is the most diverse they have ever encountered. Most students entering college today come from high schools that are predominantly or exclusively one racial or ethnic group. Given this reality, how are students interacting with one another educationally and socially in college? How socially segregated are college campuses? Is campus diversity leading to educational benefits for today's college students or are students too separated into enclaves on campus to benefit from campus diversity?

> A survey of the most recent research suggests that, indeed, campus diversity is leading to significant educational and social benefits for all college students. It also suggests that, contrary to popular reports, student self-segregation is not, in fact, a dominant feature of campus life today. This paper summarizes new research on campus diversity and on the actual extent of student self-segregation and interaction across racial/ethnic lines on college campuses today.

This new research is little known outside of the academic community and critics have ignored it as they describe campus life today to reflect their own political agendas. Critics of both affirmative action and campus diversity programs are skeptical about the educational benefits of campus diversity; they allege that racial and ethnic self-segregation among students is widespread and that it undermines the educational promise of a genuinely multicultural college community. In addition, some critics suggest that campus diversity programs themselves, including African American and Ethnic Studies programs, racial/ethnic student groups, theme houses and dorms, encourage separation rather than community and undermine intergroup contact and the learning that can result from it.

The latest educational research suggests a very different picture of campus life.

While the phenomenon does not appear to be widespread, given the degree of continuing segregation in America's schools and communities, it isn't surprising that college students today do sometimes choose to live, socialize, or study together with other students from similar backgrounds. Contrary to many commentators' claims, however, research suggests that this clustering isn't widespread; it doesn't prevent students from interacting across racial/ethnic lines; and it may be an essential ingredient in many students' persistence and success in college.

Is Student Self-Segregation Prevalent on Today's Diverse College Campuses?

While there are situations in which college students may cluster in racial/ethnic groups, research suggests that there is a high degree of intergroup contact on college campuses and that self-segregation by race/ethnicity is not a dominant feature on diverse college campuses today.

In a recent study, Anthony Lising Antonio, assistant professor of education at Stanford University, examined the extent to which students perceive racial balkanization at the University of California, Los Angeles (UCLA) and whether their perceptions reflect the reality of actual close friendship patterns.[1]

Compared to many American colleges and universities, UCLA is a very diverse campus. When this study was conducted (between 1994 and 1997), the undergraduate student body was approximately 40% white, 35% Asian American, 16% Latino, 6% African American, and just over 1% Native American.

Antonio found that students at UCLA do, indeed, view their campus as racially balkanized.

More than 90% of students in his surveys agreed that students predominantly cluster by race and ethnicity on campus. A small majority (52%) said that students rarely socialize across racial lines.

Antonio, however, didn't stop at just measuring perceptions. He also calculated the actual racial/ethnic diversity or homogeneity of close friendship groups on campus. Antonio categorized the racial diversity of each student's friendship groups as one of the following: 1) Homogenous—the largest racial/ethnic group makes up 100% of the friendship group; 2) Predominantly one race/ethnicity—the largest racial/ethnic group makes up 75–99% of the friendship group; 3) Majority one race/ethnicity—the largest racial/ethnic group makes up 51–74% of the friendship group; and 4) No majority—the largest racial/ethnic group makes up 50% or less of the friendship group.

Just 17% of UCLA students, or about one in six, reported having friendship groups that were racially and ethnically homogenous.

Homogenous groups and those groups with predominantly one race/ethnicity together account for about one-quarter of the sample.

The most common friendship group on campus (46%), however, was racially and ethnically mixed with no racial or ethnic group constituting a majority.

At the level of student friendship groups, then, racial and ethnic balkanization is not a dominant, overall campus characteristic at UCLA. Several other earlier studies also suggest a high degree of student interaction across racial and ethnic lines at campuses across the country, especially among students of color.

A 1991 study that examined patterns of intergroup contact at 390 institutions across the country confirmed that self-segregation is not a general pattern among students of color. The authors of this study examined the frequency with which students dined, roomed, socialized, or dated someone from a racial/ethnic group different from their own.[2]

Chicano, Asian American, and African American students reported widespread and frequent interaction across race/ethnicity in these informal situations. White students were least likely to report engaging in any of these activities across race/ethnicity.

Sixty-nine percent of Asian Americans and 78% of Mexican American students frequently dined with someone of a different ethnic or racial background compared with 55% of African American students and 21% of white students.

Nearly 42% of Asian American students reported interracial or interethnic dating compared with 24% of Mexican Americans, 13% of African Americans, and 4% of white students.

What Characterizes Student Interactions within and across Racial/Ethnic Lines on Campus? Why Do Some Students Cluster by Race/ Ethnicity on College Campuses?

Understanding student interactions across racial/ethnic lines requires an appreciation of the influence of the widespread residential segregation that characterizes American society. It also requires an appreciation of how white American higher education still is, despite its increasing diversity. Most students of color who do not attend historically black colleges or universities attend overwhelmingly white institutions.

A 1991 study of student life at Berkeley, an unusually diverse college campus, describes the experience of campus life as a complex phenomenon that encompasses both some student-initiated racial/ethnic clustering and substantial amounts of interracial interactions.[3]

This study also found, however, that 70% of all undergraduates agreed with the statement, I'd like to meet more students from ethnic and cultural backgrounds that are different from my own.

A forthcoming book by Richard Light of Harvard University also suggests that students from a wide array of racial/ethnic groups desire intergroup contact and see the educational and social benefits of such interactions.

The widespread segregation by race that still characterizes much of the rest of American life is, however, having an impact on how students interact with one another on college campuses.

A 1997 study at the University of Michigan found that students' friendship patterns closely reflected the make-ups of their high schools and home neighborhoods. This study confirmed that a majority of all students, but a very high percentage of white students, came from highly segregated high schools and neighborhoods.

The Michigan study also found that white students had the most segregated friendship patterns on campus of all ethnic groups.[4]

The reality is that students of color have much more intergroup contact than do white students, but their patterns of interaction need to be understood in light of their psychological development. Research by psychologist Beverly Daniel Tatum, Dean of the College at Mt. Holyoke College, suggests that there are complex psychological reasons why college students may choose to cluster in racial/ethnic groups. She argues that racial grouping is a developmental process in response to an environmental stressor, racism. Joining with one's peers for support in the face of stress is a positive coping strategy. There is a developmental need on the part of many college students to explore the meaning of one's identity with others who are engaged in a similar process.[5]

What Difference Does Racial/Ethnic Clustering Make When It Does Occur?

Recent research, including Tatum's and that of others, suggests that racial/ethnic clustering can be an important component contributing to the psychological health and educational success of many students. Research also suggests that this clustering need not prevent students from achieving the educational benefits of intergroup contact within college classrooms and on college campuses.

The 1991 study of 390 institutions cited above found that ethnic-specific activities were not impeding intergroup contact for the students who participated in them. Programs like racial/ethnic theme houses and study groups seem to help students of color persist and succeed in college and seem to increase their involvement overall with other areas of college life in which they interact frequently across racial/ethnic lines.

Other studies confirm these findings:

- A 1994 study of Latino students suggests that students belonging to Latino organizations increased their adjustment and attachment to their colleges and universities.[6]
- Two other studies, one in 1994 and another in 1996, also found positive benefits of participation in racial and ethnic groups and that these groups also fostered rather than impeded intergroup contact.[7]
- Another 1989 study found that a targeted student support program was positively related to African American students' persistence in college and their degree status.[8]

Given the Relatively High Level of Intergroup Contact and the Existence of Some Racial/Ethnic Clustering, What Is the Impact of Campus Diversity on Today's College Students?

Research suggests a variety of positive educational outcomes that result from being educated in a diverse environment. It also suggests a positive impact for those students with high degrees of intergroup contact.

Patricia Gurin, professor of psychology at the University of Michigan, recently compiled a report summarizing three parallel empirical analyses of university students. Her report suggests that,

> A racially and ethnically diverse university student body has far-ranging and significant benefits for all students, non-minorities and minorities alike. Students learn better in such an environment and are better prepared to become active participants in our pluralistic, democratic society once they leave school. In fact, patterns of racial segregation and separation historically rooted in our national life can be broken by diversity experiences in higher education.

Gurin's research demonstrates that the diverse environment provided by many colleges today contributes to students' intellectual and social development. She suggests that racial diversity in a college or university student body provides the very features that research has determined are central to producing the conscious mode of thought educators demand from their students.

Gurin also found that these positive effects of campus diversity extend beyond graduation.

Diversity experiences during college had impressive effects on the extent to which graduates in the national study were living racially and ethnically integrated lives in the post-college world. Students with the most diversity experiences during college had the most cross-racial interactions five years after leaving college.[9]

The study by Antonio mentioned above also confirms that campus diversity is having a positive impact on today's college students.

Antonio examined the impact of the diverse friendship groups he found to be common at UCLA. Controlling for important background information such as gender, socio-economic status, and the racial diversity of pre-college friendship groups, Antonio found that friendship group diversity contributed to greater interracial interaction outside the friendship group and stronger commitments to racial understanding.

Another important arena of college life, of course, is the classroom. On diverse campuses, many students are now being educated in highly diverse classrooms in which they are studying a much wider array of subjects that include content about previously neglected groups. These classes are also having a significant positive educational impact on both majority and minority students as well.[10]

Conclusions: Is There Cause for Alarm, Hope, or Celebration?

There is little cause for alarm, some cause for celebration and much hope for what lies ahead. The reality is that while there is still a long way to go before American higher education will truly reflect the full diversity of American society, college campuses are becoming much more diverse and their diverse campus environments are having a significant positive effect on this generation of students.

College campuses are not dominated by widespread racial/ethnic segregation and the racial/ethnic clustering that does occur isn't impeding intergroup contact. In fact, the existence of racial/ethnic groups and activities, along with other comprehensive campus diversity initiatives, is contributing to the success of today's college students and preparing them to help build a healthier multicultural America for the future.

Notes

1. Antonio, Anthony Lising, "Racial Diversity and Friendship Groups in College: What The Research Tells Us," *Diversity Digest,* Summer, 1999, (Washington, DC: Association of American Colleges and Universities, 1999): 6–7.

2. Hurtado, S., Dey, E., and Treviëo, J., "Exclusion or Self-Segregation? Interaction Across Racial/Ethnic Groups on College Campuses," paper presented at American Educational Research Association Conference, New Orleans, LA, 1994.

3. Duster, Troy, "The Diversity Project: Final Report," Institute for the Study of Social Change. University of California, Berkeley, 1991.

4. Matlock, John, "Student Expectations and Experiences: The Michigan Study," *Diversity Digest,* Summer, 1997, (Washington, DC: Association of American Colleges and Universities, 1997): 11.

5. Tatum, Beverly Daniel. *Why Are All the Black Kids Sitting Together in the Cafeteria?* (New York: Basic Books, 1997): 62;71.

6. Hurtado, S., and D.F. Carter, "Latino Students' Sense of Belonging in the College Community: Rethinking the Concept of Integration on Campus," paper presented at the annual meeting of the American Educational Research Association, New Orleans, LA, 1994.

7. Gilliard, M. D., "Racial Climate and Institutional Support Factors Affecting Success in Predominantly White Institutions: An Examination of African American and White Student Experiences," unpublished Ph.D. dissertation, University of Michigan, 1996; Hurtado, S., Dey, E., and Treviëo, J., "Exclusion or Self-Segregation? Interaction Across Racial/Ethnic Groups on College Campuses," paper presented at American Educational Research Association Conference, New Orleans, LA, 1994.

8. Trippi, J., and H.E. Cheatham, "Effects of Special Counseling Programs for Black Freshman on a Predominantly White Campus," *Journal of College Student Development* 30, (1989): 35–40.

9. Gurin, Patricia, "New Research on the Benefits of Diversity in College and Beyond: An Empirical Analysis," *Diversity Digest,* Spring, 1999, (Washington, DC: Association of American Colleges and Universities, 1999): 5/15.

10. For information on the impact of diversity courses, see "Diversity and The College Curriculum," http://www.inform.umd.edu/EdRes/Topic/Diversity/ Response/ Web/Leadersguide/CT/curriculum_briefing.html.

EXPLORING THE ISSUE

Do Minorities and Whites Engage in Self-Segregation?

Critical Thinking and Reflection

1. How do adolescents develop a sense of racial identity? How is the understanding of racial identity developed among adolescents important for understanding this issue?
2. Why do young people choose self-segregation as their way of dealing with interracial environments?
3. What is the link between Jim Crow society and self-segregation?
4. How do these concepts inform the discussion of this issue?
5. What social and psychological factors lead to self-segregation of adolescents? How may self-segregation extend to areas of life beyond high school and college?

Is There Common Ground?

The separation of blacks from whites within American society is the prevailing context within which race relations develop throughout history. The long-standing tradition of segregated schools, neighborhoods, and even churches in the United States is being challenged by the growing multiculturalism and the diversity ideal. However, some levels of segregation persist, especially in the area of housing (Issue 17). It is important to note that any tendency toward self-segregation is an outcome of the traditional Jim Crow that dominated the country for many years. Neither Tatum nor Humphreys challenges the reality of self-segregation within institutional settings today. Both Tatum and Humphreys recognize that self-segregation is part of the collegiate experience, as it is in other areas of life. For many students, the university is the first truly integrated experience of their lives. At the same time, Humphreys points out that college campuses are not dominated by widespread self-segregation and, when it occurs, the self-segregation does not impede intergroup contact. Additionally, Tatum and Humphreys both view self-segregation as a means for all students—whites and minorities—to adjust to a new experience. Campus diversity is having a positive impact on today's college students.

Additional Resources

Anderson, Elijah. 1978. *A Place on the Corner* (University of Chicago Press).

Anderson, Elijah. 1999. *Code of the Street: Decency, Violence, and the Moral Life of the Inner City* (W.W. Norton & Co.).

Anderson, Elijah. 2012. *The Cosmopolitan Canopy: Race and Civility in Everyday Life* (W.W. Norton & Co.).

Antonio, Anthony Lising. 1999. "Racial Diversity and Friendship Groups in College: What the Research Tells Us," *Diversity Digest* (Summer, 6–7).

Bow, Leslie. 2010. *Partly Colored: Asian Americans and Racial Anomaly in the Segregated South* (New York University Press).

Chan, Priscilla. 2004. "Drawing the Boundaries," in Arar Han and John Hsu, eds. *Asian American X: An Intersection of 21st Century Asian American Voices* (University of Michigan Press).

Conley, Dalton. 2000. *Honky* (Vintage).

Cose, Ellis. 1993. *The Rage of a Privileged Class* (HarperCollins, 1993).

DuBois, W.E.B. 1951. *The Souls of Black Folk* (Fawcett World Library).

Duster, Troy. 1991. "The Diversity Project: Final Report" (Institute for the Study of Social Change, University of California, Berkeley, CA).

Hurtado, Sylvia. 1994. *Exclusion of Self-Segregation?: Interaction Across Racial/ Ethnic Groups Across College Campuses* (S. Hurtado, distributor).

Massey, Douglas and Nancy Denton. 1993. *American Apartheid: Segregation and the Making of the Underclass* (Harvard University Press).

Matlock. 1997. "Student Expectations and Experiences: The Michigan Study," *Diversity Digest* (Summer, 11).

Nathan, Rebekah. 2005. *My Freshman Year: What a Professor Learned by Becoming a Student* (Penguin Books).

Norman, Brian. 2010. *Neo-Segregation Narratives: Jim Crow in Post-Civil Rights Literature* (University of Georgia Press).

Royster, Deidre A. 2003. *Race and the Invisible Hand: How White Networks Exclude Black Men from Blue Collar Jobs* (University of California).

Thurman, Howard. 1986. *The Search for Common Ground* (Friends United Press).

Thurman, Howard. 1989. *The Luminous Darkness: A Personal Interpretation of the Anatomy of Segregation and the Ground of Hope* (Friends United Press).

West, Cornel. 1993. *Race Matters* (New York: Vintage Books).

Wilson, William Julius. 1980. *The Declining Significance of Race* (University of Chicago).

This website seeks to "connect, amplify, and advance campus diversity." Its focus is on higher education as it helps colleges and universities "to establish diversity as a comprehensive institutional commitment and educational priority." It is home to *Diversity & Democracy* and *Diversity Digest*, the Association of American Colleges and Universities publications on diversity, global learning, and civic engagement in higher education. It contains links to numerous articles on self-segregation including some by Beverly Tatum and Debra Humphreys.

www.diversityweb.org/

ISSUE 20

Is the Mass Incarceration of Blacks the New Jim Crow?

YES: **Michelle Alexander,** from *The New Jim Crow* (The New Press, 2011)

NO: **James Forman, Jr.,** from "Racial Critiques of Mass Incarceration: Beyond the New Jim Crow," *Racial Critiques* (vol. 87, February 26, 2012)

Learning Outcomes

After reading this issue, the student should be able to:

- Understand the racial composition of the prison population.
- Compare and contrast the new Jim Crow with early American segregation.
- Understand the relationship between race and criminal justice policies throughout America.
- Apply new concepts to an analysis of the criminal justice system.
- Understand the role and impact of incarceration in society.

ISSUE SUMMARY

YES: Michelle Alexander is an associate professor of law at Ohio State University with a joint appointment at the Kirwan Institute for the Study of Race and Ethnicity. She draws attention to the racial imbalance in America's prison population and presents a compelling analysis of the wide-ranging social costs and divisive racial impact of mass incarceration.

NO: James Forman, Jr., a clinical professor of law at Yale Law School and a noted constitutional law scholar, affirms the utility of the new Jim Crow paradigm but argues that it has significant limitations. It obscures significant facts regarding the history of mass incarceration as well as black support for punitive criminal justice policy among other deficiencies.

Racial justice is a critical issue for those who are concerned with the fairness and efficacy of criminal justice policy in the United States. Historically, there has been a concern that the mass arrests and incarceration of people of color, especially African Americans, are measures employed to maintain their subordination within society.

During early Reconstruction, a body of laws called the Black Codes was passed in southern states. The laws were an attempt on the part of these defeated Confederate states to define a status for the newly emancipated African Americans that limited the rights that would be available to them. A significant feature of such laws was the criminal clauses which they contained that applied to blacks only. These codes were mechanisms of social control that were designed to "keep the Negroes in their place."

More recently, since the 1960s, politicians emphasizing a concern for crime, law, and order supported a legislative agenda that has led to the mass incarceration of blacks and others that we are witnessing today. Among the initiatives associated with this development are the War on Drugs and the Three Strikes Laws that were passed by legislatures across the nation. They are the source of the mass incarceration of people of color, which is referred to as "the new Jim Crow."

In her book, *The New Jim Crow*, Michelle Alexander offers a significant critique of important matters of race and criminal justice. She examines the substantial racial disparity of arrest and incarceration in the United States and concludes that this is a new form of segregation. Clearly, the prison population of approximately 2.5 million includes whites, Asians, and Latinos as well. However, it is the disproportionate black rate of incarceration that is the subject of this issue.

Alexander argues that, "Similar to black people living under the old Jim Crow, a convicted criminal of today becomes a member of a stigmatized past, virtually condemned to a lifetime of second class citizenship." Essentially for her, this is the creation of a new caste in the American class system. Blacks emerge from incarceration labeled as "ex-cons" or "felons" with little opportunity for success and upward mobility. Their future is further compromised.

In "Racial Critiques of Mass Incarceration: Beyond the New Jim Crow," James Forman is concerned that the idea of a new Jim Crow is limiting in that it ignores the mass incarceration of whites and Latinos. Additionally, he is concerned that the focus of the new Jim Crow thesis fails to address the support given to these measures by some African Americans, especially those living in high-crime areas. Forman is concerned that readers understand the nature and scope of mass incarceration and its social impacts on contemporary society.

Forman agrees with Alexander that mass incarceration and an ever-expanding prison population have created a profound social crisis within the nation. Today's economic reality and the pressures to cut budgets at all levels of government raise serious questions regarding the true costs that mass incarceration incurs for the American taxpayer. Alexander gives attention to the growth of the American underclass that arises from the ever-increasing recycling of African Americans within the prison system. She understands that, as a result of their imprisonment, they are stigmatized and the labels that they bear delimit opportunities for meaningful employment. To have a sector of American citizens with little hope for achieving the American Dream is a recipe for discontent and social conflict. For such a situation to persist is a challenge to the interest of the nation.

Alexander and Forman disagree on the scope of the problem and what group or groups are impacted by it. Alexander focuses on blacks, whereas Forman includes blacks, whites, and Latinos in his approach. Students should be aware that in today's society commentators ranging from academics to prison officials to politicians are questioning mass incarceration and the cost that our nation is incurring for this policy. It is important that students critically examine the data on mass incarceration that is relevant to this issue. They should be prepared to answer questions such as: What is the prison rate of the United States? How does it compare with other countries? What is the racial composition of the prison population? What is the prison industrial complex? What is its relationship to the rest of the economy?

Perhaps the most striking example of the new Jim Crow is the prison industry in Louisiana. Currently considered the prison capital of the world, the state of Louisiana prison system currently holds 1,619 prisoners per 100,000 residents in contrast to the U.S. average, which is at 730 per 100,000 residents. Two-thirds of Louisiana prisoners are nonviolent offenders and the state leads the nation in percentage of prisoners serving life without parole. Many of the prisons are for-profit and the local prisons have entered the lucrative business of housing prisoners serving state time. Although blacks constitute 32 percent of the state's population, they comprise 78 percent of its prison inmates. A worthy project for students is to research the Louisiana prison system and evaluate Alexander's thesis as well as Forman's ideas. The situation that Louisiana faces is a microcosm of the challenges of mass incarceration to the nation as a whole.

YES

Michelle Alexander

The New Jim Crow

The law and order perspective, first introduced during the peak of the Civil Rights Movement by rabid segregationists, had become nearly hegemonic two decades later. By the mid-1990s, no serious alternatives to the War on Drugs and "get tough" movement were being entertained in mainstream political discourse. Once again, in response to a major disruption in the prevailing racial order—this time the civil rights gains of the 1960s—a new system of racialized social control was created by exploiting the vulnerabilities and racial resentments of poor and working-class whites. More than 2 million people found themselves behind bars at the turn of the twenty-first century, and millions more were relegated to the margins of mainstream society, banished to a political and social space not unlike Jim Crow, where discrimination in employment, housing, and access to education was perfectly legal, and where they could be denied the right to vote. The system functioned relatively automatically, and the prevailing system of racial meanings, identities and ideologies already seemed natural. Ninety percent of those admitted to prison for drug offenses in many states were black or Latino, yet the mass incarceration of communities of color was explained in race-neutral terms, an adaptation to the needs and demands of the current political climate. The New Jim Crow was born.

QUESTIONS TO CONSIDER

If one were to look at who is incarcerated in the United States for drug crimes, one might conclude that black and Latino men are more likely to carry, use, and distribute illegal drugs. What we learn from, Michelle Alexander, however, is that national studies on drug use find that whites are in fact more likely to carry and use drugs like cocaine, marijuana, and heroin. If it is the case that whites have more contact with illegal drugs, why are African Americans and Latinos overrepresented in our prisons? Why is it that certain racial and ethnic groups are more likely to be stopped, searched, or arrested by the police? How might the very act of policing be linked to rates of incarceration?

Imagine you are Emma Faye Stewart, a thirty-year-old, single African American mother of two who was arrested as part of a drug sweep in Hearne, Texas. All but one of the people arrested were African American. You are innocent. After a week in jail, you have no one to care for your two small children and are eager to get home. Your court-appointed attorney urges you to plead guilty to a drug distribution charge, saying the prosecutor has offered probation. You refuse, steadfastly proclaiming your innocence. Finally, after almost a month in jail, you decide to plead guilty so you can return home to your children. Unwilling to risk a trial and years of imprisonment, you are sentenced to ten years' probation and ordered to pay $1,000 in fines, as well as court and probation costs. You are also now branded a drug felon. You are no longer eligible for food stamps; you may be discriminated against in employment; you cannot vote for at least twelve years; and you are about to be evicted from public housing. Once homeless, your children will be taken from you and put in foster care.

A judge eventually dismisses all cases against the defendants who did not plead guilty. At trial, the judge finds that the entire sweep was based on the testimony of a single informant who lied to the prosecution. You, however, are still a drug felon, homeless, and desperate to regain custody of your children.

Now place yourself in the shoes of Clifford Runoalds, another African American victim of the Hearne drug bust. You returned home to Bryan, Texas, to attend the funeral of your eighteen-month-old daughter. Before the funeral services begin, the police show up and hand-cuff you. You beg the officers to let you take one last look at your daughter before she is buried. The police refuse. You are told by prosecutors that you are needed to testify against one of the defendants in a recent drug bust. You deny witnessing any drug transaction; you don't know what they are talking about. Because of your refusal to cooperate, you are indicted on felony charges. After a month of being held in jail, the charges against you are dropped. You are technically free, but as a result of your arrest and period of incarceration, you lose your job, your apartment, your furniture, and your car. Not to mention the chance to say good-bye to your baby girl.

This is the War on Drugs. The brutal stories described above are not isolated incidents, nor are the racial identities of Emma Faye Stewart and Clifford Runoalds random or accidental. In every state across our nation, African Americans—particularly in the poorest neighborhoods—are subjected to tactics and practices that would result in public outrage and scandal if committed in middle-class white neighborhoods. In the drug war, the enemy is racially defined. The law enforcement methods described [earlier] have been employed almost exclusively in poor communities of color, resulting in jaw-dropping numbers of African Americans and Latinos filling our nation's prisons and jails every year. We are told by drug warriors that the enemy in this war is a thing—drugs—not a group of people, but the facts prove otherwise.

Human Rights Watch reported in 2000 that, in seven states, African Americans constitute 80 percent to 90 percent of all drug offenders sent to prison. In at least fifteen states, blacks are admitted to prison on drug charges at a rate from twenty to fifty-seven times greater than that of white men. In fact, nationwide, the rate of incarceration for African American drug offenders dwarfs the rate of whites. When the War on Drugs gained full steam in the mid-1980s, prison admissions for African Americans skyrocketed, nearly quadrupling in three years, and then increasing steadily until it reached in 2000 a level *more than twenty-six times* the level in 1983. The number of 2000 drug admissions for Latinos was twenty-two times the number of 1983 admissions. Whites have been admitted to prison for drug offenses at increased rates as well—the number of whites admitted for drug offenses in 2000 was eight times the number admitted in 1983—but their relative numbers are small compared to blacks' and Latinos'. Although the majority of illegal drug users and dealers nationwide are white, three-fourths of all people imprisoned for drug offenses have been black or Latino. In recent years, rates of black imprisonment for drug offenses have dipped somewhat—declining approximately 25 percent from their zenith in the mid-1990s—but it remains the case that African Americans are incarcerated at grossly disproportionate rates throughout the United States.

There is, of course, an official explanation for all this: crime rates. This explanation has tremendous appeal—before you know the facts—for it is consistent with, and reinforces, dominant racial narratives about crime and criminality dating back to slavery. The truth, however, is that rates and patterns of drug crime do not explain the glaring racial disparities in our criminal justice system. People of all races use and sell illegal drugs at remarkably similar rates. If there are significant differences in the surveys to be found, they frequently suggest that whites, particularly white youth, are more likely to engage in illegal drug dealing than people of color. One study, for example, published in 2000 by the National Institute on Drug Abuse reported that white students use cocaine at seven times the rate of black students, use crack cocaine at eight times the rate of black students, and use heroin at seven times the rate of black students. That same survey revealed that nearly identical percentages of white and black high school seniors use marijuana. The National Household Survey on Drug Abuse reported in 2000 that white youth aged 12–17 are more than a third more likely to have sold illegal drugs than African American youth. Thus the very same year Human Rights Watch was reporting that African Americans were being arrested and imprisoned at unprecedented rates, government data revealed that blacks were no more likely to be guilty of drug crimes than whites and that white youth were actually the *most likely* of any racial or ethnic group to be guilty of illegal drug possession and sales. Any notion that drug use among blacks is more severe or dangerous is belied by the data; white youth have about three times the number of drug-related emergency room visits as their African American counterparts.

The notion that whites comprise the vast majority of drug users and dealers—and may well be more likely than other racial groups to commit drug crimes—may seem implausible to some, given the media imagery we are fed on a daily basis and the racial composition of our prisons and jails. Upon reflection, however, the prevalence of white drug crime—including drug dealing—should not be surprising. After all, where do whites get their illegal drugs? Do they all drive to the ghetto to purchase them from somebody standing on a street corner?

No. Studies consistently indicate that drug markets, like American society generally, reflect our nation's racial and socioeconomic boundaries. Whites tend to sell to whites; blacks to blacks. University students tend to sell to each other. Rural whites, for their part, don't make a special trip to the 'hood to purchase marijuana. They buy it from somebody down the road. White high school students typically buy drugs from white classmates, friends, or older relatives. Even Barry McCaffrey, former director of the White House Office of National Drug Control Policy, once remarked, if your child bought drugs, "it was from a student of their own race generally." The notion that most illegal drug use and sales happens in the ghetto is pure fiction. Drug trafficking occurs there, but it occurs everywhere else in America as well. Nevertheless, black men have been admitted to state prison on drug charges at a rate that is more than thirteen times higher than white men. The racial bias inherent in the drug war is a major reason that 1 in every 14 black men was behind bars in 2006, compared with 1 in 106 white men. For young black men, the statistics are even worse. One in 9 black men between the ages of twenty and thirty-five was behind bars in 2006, and far more were under some form of penal control—such as probation or parole. These gross racial disparities simply cannot be explained by rates of illegal drug activity among African Americans.

What, then, does explain the extraordinary racial disparities in our criminal justice system? Old-fashioned racism seems out of the question. No politicians and law enforcement officials today endorse racially biased practices, and most of them fiercely condemn racial discrimination of any kind. When accused of racial bias, police and prosecutors—like most Americans—express horror and outrage. Forms of race discrimination that were open and notorious for centuries were transformed in the 1960s and 1970s into something unAmerican—an affront to our newly conceived ethic of color-blindness. By the early 1980s, survey data indicated that 90 percent of whites thought black and white children should attend the same schools, 71 percent disagreed with the idea that whites have a right to keep blacks out of their neighborhoods, 80 percent indicated they would support a black candidate for president, and 66 percent opposed laws prohibiting intermarriage. Although far fewer supported specific policies designed to achieve racial equality or integration (such as busing), the mere fact that large majorities of whites were, by the 1980s, supporting the antidiscrimination principle reflected a profound shift in racial attitudes. The margin of support for color-blind norms has only increased since then.

This dramatically changed racial climate has led defenders of mass incarceration to insist that our criminal justice system, whatever its past sins, is now largely fair and nondiscriminatory. They point to violent crime rates in the African American community as a justification for the staggering number of black men who find themselves behind bars. Black men, they say, have much higher rates of violent crime; that's why so many of them are locked in prisons.

Typically, this is where the discussion ends.

The problem with this abbreviated analysis is that violent crime is *not* responsible for the prison boom. As numerous researchers have shown, violent crime rates have fluctuated over the years and bear little relationship to incarceration rates—which have soared during the past three decades regardless of whether violent crime was going up or down. Today violent crime rates are at historically low levels, yet incarceration rates continue to climb.

Murder convictions tend to receive a tremendous amount of media attention, which feeds the public's sense that violent crime is rampant and forever on the rise. But like violent crime in general, the murder rate cannot explain the prison boom. Homicide convictions account for a tiny fraction of the growth in the prison population. In the federal system, for example, homicide offenders account for 0.4 percent of the past decade's growth in the federal prison population, while drug offenders account for nearly 61 percent of that expansion. In the state system, less than 3 percent of new court commitments to state prison typically involve people convicted of homicide. As much as a third of state prisoners are violent offenders, but that statistic can easily be misinterpreted. Violent offenders tend to get longer prison sentences than nonviolent offenders, and therefore comprise a much larger share of the prison population than they would if they had earlier release dates. The uncomfortable reality is that convictions for drug offenses—not violent crime—are the single most important cause of the prison boom in the United States, and people of color are convicted of drug offenses at rates out of all proportion to their drug crimes.

These facts may still leave some readers unsatisfied. The idea that the criminal justice system discriminates in such a terrific fashion when few people openly express or endorse racial discrimination may seem far-fetched, if not absurd. How could the War on Drugs operate in a discriminatory manner, on such a large scale, when hardly anyone advocates or engages in explicit race discrimination? That question is the subject of this chapter. As we shall see, despite the color-blind rhetoric and fanfare of recent years, the design of the drug war effectively guarantees that those who are swept into the nation's new undercaste are largely black and brown.

This sort of claim invites skepticism. Nonracial explanations and excuses for the systematic mass incarceration of people of color are plentiful. It is the genius of the new system of control that it can always be defended on nonracial grounds, given the rarity of a noose or a racial slur in connection with any particular criminal case. Moreover, because blacks and whites are almost never similarly situated (given extreme racial segregation in housing and disparate life experiences), trying to "control for race" in an effort to evaluate whether the mass incarceration of people of color is really about race or something else—anything else—is difficult. But it is not impossible.

A bit of common sense is overdue in public discussions about racial bias in the criminal justice system. The great debate over whether black men have been targeted by the criminal justice system or unfairly treated in the War on Drugs often overlooks the obvious. What is painfully obvious when one steps back from individual cases and specific policies is that the system of mass incarceration operates with stunning efficiency to sweep people of color off the streets, lock them in cages, and then release them into an inferior second-class status. Nowhere is this more true than in the War on Drugs.

The central question, then, is how exactly does a formally color-blind criminal justice system achieve such racially discriminatory results? Rather easily, it turns out. The process occurs in two stages. The first step is to grant law enforcement officials extraordinary discretion regarding whom to stop, search, arrest, and charge for drug offenses, thus ensuring the conscious and unconscious racial beliefs and stereotypes will be given free reign. Unbridled discretion inevitably creates huge racial disparities. Then, the damning step: Close the courthouse doors to all claims by defendants and private litigants that the criminal justice system operates in a racially discriminatory fashion. Demand that anyone who wants to challenge racial bias in the system offer, in advance, clear proof that the racial disparities are the product of intentional racial discrimination—i.e., the work of a bigot. This evidence will almost never be available in the era of color-blindness, because everyone knows—but does not say—that the enemy in the War on Drugs can be identified by race. This simple design has helped to produce one of the most extraordinary systems of racialized social control the world has ever seen.

Race as a Factor

The dirty little secret of policing is that the Supreme Court has actually granted the police license to discriminate. This fact is not advertised by police departments, because law enforcement officials know that the public would not respond well to this fact in the era of colorblindness. It is the sort of thing that is better left unsaid. Civil rights lawyers—including those litigating racial profiling cases—have been complicit in this silence, fearing that any acknowledgment that race-based policing is authorized by law would legitimate in the public mind the very practice they are hoping to eradicate.

The truth, however, is this: At other stages of the criminal justice process, the Court has indicated that overt racial bias necessarily triggers strict scrutiny—a concession that has not been costly, as very few law enforcement officials today are foolish enough to admit bias openly. But the Supreme Court has indicated that in policing, race can be used as a factor in discretionary decision making. In *United States v. Brjgnoni-Ponce* the Court concluded it was permissible under the equal protection clause of the Fourteenth Amendment for the police to use race as a factor in making decisions about which motorists to stop and search. In that case, the Court concluded that the police could take a person's Mexican appearance into account when developing reasonable suspicion that a vehicle may contain undocumented immigrants. The Court said that "the likelihood that any person of Mexican ancestry is an alien is high enough to make Mexican appearance a relevant factor." Some commentators have argued that *Brignoni-Ponce* may be limited to the immigration context; the Court might not apply the same principle to drug-law enforcement. It is not obvious what the rational basis would be for limiting overt race discrimination by police to immigration. The likelihood that a person of Mexican ancestry is an "alien" could not be significantly higher than the likelihood that any random black person is a drug criminal.

The Court's quiet blessing of race-based traffic stops has led to something of an Orwellian public discourse regarding racial profiling. Police departments and highway patrol agencies frequently declare, "We do not engage in racial profiling," even though their officers routinely use race as a factor when making decisions whom to stop and search. The justification for the implicit doublespeak—"we do not racial-profile; we just stop people based on race"—can be explained in part by the Supreme Court's jurisprudence. Because the Supreme Court has authorized the police to use race as a factor when making decisions regarding whom to stop and search, police departments believe that racial profiling exists only when race is the *sole* factor. Thus, if race is one factor but not the only factor, then it doesn't really count as a factor at all.

The absurdity of this logic is evidenced by the fact that police almost never stop anyone because of race. A young black male wearing baggy pants, standing in front of his high school surrounded by a group or similarly dressed black friends, may be stopped and searched because police believe he "looks like" a drug dealer. Clearly, race is not the only reason for that conclusion. Gender, age, attire, and location play a role. The police would likely ignore an eighty-five-year-old black man standing in the same spot surrounded by a group of elderly black women.

The problem is that although race is rarely the sole reason for a stop or search, it is frequently a *determinative* reason. A young white male wearing baggy pants, standing in front of his high school and surrounded by his friends, might well be ignored by police officers. It might never occur to them that a group of white kids might be dealing dope in front of their high school. Similarly situated people inevitably are treated differently when police are granted permission to rely on racial stereotypes when making discretionary decisions.

Equally important, though, the sole-factor test ignores the ways in which seemingly race-neutral factors—such as location—operate in a highly discriminatory fashion. Some law enforcement officials claim that they would stop and search white kids wearing baggy jeans in the ghetto (that would be suspicious)—it just so happens they're rarely there. Subjecting people to stops and searches because they live in "high crime" ghettos cannot be said to be truly race-neutral, given that the ghetto itself was constructed to contain and control groups of people defined by race. Even seemingly race-neutral factors such as "prior criminal history" are not truly race-neutral. A black kid arrested twice for possession of marijuana may be no more of a repeat offender than a white frat boy who regularly smokes pot in his dorm room. But because of his race and his confinement to a racially segregated ghetto, the black kid has a criminal record, while the white frat boy, because of his race and relative privilege, docs not. Thus, when prosecutors throw the book at black repeat offenders or when police stalk ex-offenders and subject them to regular frisks and searches on the grounds that it makes sense to "watch criminals closely," they arc often exacerbating racial disparities created by the discretionary decision to wage the War on Drugs almost exclusively in poor communities of color.

Defending against claims of racial bias in policing is easy. Because race is never the only reason for a stop or search, any police officer with a fifth-grade education will be able to cite multiple nonracial reasons for initiating an encounter, including any number of the so-called "indicators" of drug trafficking discussed [previously], such as appearing too nervous or too calm. Police officers (like prosecutors) are highly adept at offering race-neutral reasons for actions that consistently disadvantage African Americans. Whereas prosecutors claim they strike black jurors not because of their race but because of their hairstyle, police officers have their own stock excuses—e.g., "Your honor, we didn't stop him because he's black; we stopped him because he failed to use his turn signal at the right time," or "It wasn't just because he was black; it was also because he seemed nervous when he saw the police car." Judges are just as reluctant to second-guess an officer's motives as they are to second-guess prosecutors'. So long as officers refrain from uttering racial epithets and so long as they show the good sense not to say "the only reason I stopped him was because he's black," courts generally turn a blind eye to patterns of discrimination by the police.

Studies of racial profiling have shown that police do, in fact, exercise their discretion regarding whom to stop and search in the drug war in a highly discriminatory manner. Not only do police discriminate in their determinations regarding where to wage the war, but they also discriminate in their judgments regarding whom to target outside of the ghetto's invisible walls.

The most famous of these studies were conducted in New Jersey and Maryland in the 1990s. Allegations of racial profiling in federally funded drug interdiction operations resulted in numerous investigations and comprehensive data demonstrating a dramatic pattern of racial bias in highway patrol stops and searches. These drug interdiction programs were the brainchild of the DEA, part of the federally funded program known as Operation Pipeline.

In New Jersey, the data showed that only 15 percent of all drivers on the New Jersey Turnpike were racial minorities, yet 42 percent of all stops and 73 percent of all arrests were of black motorists—despite the fact that blacks and whites violated traffic laws at almost exactly the same rate. While radar stops were relatively consistent with the percentage of minority violators, discretionary stops made by officers involved in drug interdiction resulted in double the number of stops of minorities. A subsequent study conducted by the attorney general of New Jersey found that searches on the turnpike were even more discriminatory than the initial stops—77 percent of all consent searches were of minorities. The Maryland studies produced similar results: African Americans comprised only 17 percent of drivers along a stretch of 1-95 outside of Baltimore, yet they were 70 percent of those who were stopped and searched. Only 21 percent of all drivers along that stretch of highway were racial minorities (Latinos, Asians, and African Americans), yet those groups comprised nearly 80 percent of those pulled over and searched.

What most surprised many analysts was that, in both studies, whites were actually *more likely* than people of color to be carrying illegal drugs or contraband in their vehicles. In fact, in New Jersey, whites were almost twice as likely to be found with illegal drugs or contraband as African Americans, and five times as likely to be found with contraband as Latinos. Although whites were more likely to be guilty of carrying drugs, they were far less likely to be viewed as suspicious, resulting in relatively few stops, searches, and arrests of whites. The former New Jersey attorney general dubbed this phenomenon the "circular illogic of racial profiling." Law enforcement officials, he explained, often point to the racial composition of our prisons and jails as a justification for targeting racial minorities, but the empirical evidence actually suggested the opposite conclusion was warranted. The disproportionate imprisonment of people of color was, in part a product of racial profiling—not a justification for it.

In the years following the release of the New Jersey and Maryland data, dozens of other studies of racial profiling have been conducted. A brief sampling:

- In Volusia County, Florida, a reporter obtained 148 hours of video footage documenting more than 1,000 highway stops conducted by state troopers. Only 5 percent of the drivers on the road were African American or Latino, but more them 80 percent of the people stopped and searched were minorities.
- In Illinois, the state police initiated a drug interdiction program known as Operation Valkyrie that targeted Latino motorists. While Latinos comprised less than 8 percent of the Illinois population and took fewer than 3 percent of the personal vehicle trips in Illinois, they comprised approximately 30 percent of the motorists stopped by drug interdiction officers for discretionary offenses, such as failure to signal a lane change. Latinos, however, were significantly less likely than whites to have illegal contraband in their vehicles.
- A racial profiling study in Oakland, California, in 2001 showed that African Americans were approximately twice as likely as whites to be stopped, and three times as likely to be searched.

Pedestrian stops, too, have been the subject of study and controversy. The New York Police Department released statistics in February 2007 showing that during the prior year its officers stopped an astounding 508,540 people—an average of 1,393 per day—who were walking down the street, perhaps on their way to the subway, grocery store, or bus stop. Often the stops included searches for illegal drugs or guns—searches that frequently required people to lie face down on the pavement or stand spread-eagled against a wall while police officers aggressively groped all over their bodies while bystanders watched or walked by. The vast majority of those stopped and searched were racial minorities, and more than half were African American.

The NYPD began collecting data on pedestrian stops following the shooting of Amadou Diallo, an African immigrant who died in a hail of police bullets on the front steps of his own home in February 1999. Diallo was followed to his apartment building by four white police officers—members of the elite Street Crime Unit—who viewed him as suspicious and wanted to interrogate him. They ordered him to stop, but, according to the officers, Diallo did not respond immediately. He walked a bit further to his apartment building, opened the door, and retrieved his wallet—probably to produce identification. The officers said they thought the wallet was a gun, and fired forty-one times. Amadou Diallo died at the age of twenty-two. He was unarmed and had no criminal record.

Diallo's murder sparked huge protests, resulting in a series of studies commissioned by the attorney general of New York. The first study found that

African Americans were stopped six times more frequently than whites, and that stops of African Americans were less likely to result in arrests than stops of whites—presumably because blacks were less likely to be found with drugs or other contraband. Although the NYPD attempted to justify the stops on the grounds that they were designed to get guns off the street, stops by the Street Crime Unit—the group of officers who supposedly are specially trained to identify gun-toting thugs—yielded a weapon in only 2.5 percent of all stops.

Rather than reducing reliance on stop-and-frisk tactics following the Diallo shooting and the release of this disturbing data, the NYPD dramatically *increased* its number of pedestrian stops and continued to stop and frisk African Americans at grossly disproportionate rates. The NYPD stopped five times more people in 2005 than in 2002—the overwhelming majority of whom were African American or Latino.

In Los Angeles, mass stops of young African American men and boys resulted in the creation of a database containing the names, addresses, and other biographical information of the overwhelming majority of young black men in the entire city. The LAPD justified its database as a tool for tracking gang or "gang-related" activity. However, the criterion for inclusion in the database is notoriously vague and discriminatory. Having a relative or friend in a gang and wearing baggy jeans is enough to put youth on what the ACLU calls a Black List. In Denver, displaying any two of a list of attributes—including slang, "clothing of a particular color," pagers, hairstyles, or jewelry—earns youth a spot in the Denver Police's gang database. In 1992, citizen activism led to an investigation, which revealed that eight out of every ten people of color in the entire city were on the list of suspected criminals.

The End of an Era

The litigation that swept the nation in the 1990s challenging racial profiling practices has nearly vanished. The news stories about people being stopped and searched on their way to church or work or school have faded from evening news. This is not because the problem has been solved or because the experience of being stopped, interrogated, and searched on the basis of race has become less humiliating, alienating, or demoralizing as time has gone by. The lawsuits have disappeared because, in a little noticed case called *Alexander v. Sandoval,* decided in 2001, the Supreme Court eliminated the last remaining avenue available for challenging racial bias in the criminal justice system.

Sandoval was not, on its face, even about criminal justice. It was a case challenging the Alabama Department of Public Safety's decision to administer state driver's license examinations only in English. The plaintiffs argued that the department's policy violated Title VI of the Civil Rights Act of 1964 and its implementing regulations, because the policy had the effect of subjecting non—English speakers to discrimination based on their national origin. The Supreme Court did not reach the merits of the case, ruling instead that the plaintiffs lacked the legal right even to file the lawsuit. It concluded that Title VI does not provide a "private right of action" to ordinary citizens and civil rights groups, meaning that victims of discrimination can no longer sue under the law.

The *Sandoval* decision virtually wiped out racial profiling litigation nationwide. Nearly all of the cases alleging racial profiling in drug-law enforcement were brought pursuant to Title VI of the Civil Rights Act of 1964 and its implementing regulations. Title VI prohibits federally funded programs or activities from discriminating on the basis of race, and the regulations employ a "disparate impact test" for discrimination—meaning that plaintiffs could prevail in claims of race discrimination without proving discriminatory intent. Under the regulations, a federally funded law enforcement program or activity is unlawful if it has a racially discriminatory impact and if that impact cannot be justified by law enforcement necessity. Because nearly all law enforcement agencies receive federal funding in the drug war, and because drug war tactics—such as pretext stops and consent searches—have a grossly discriminatory impact and are largely ineffective, plaintiffs were able to argue persuasively that the tactics could not be justified by law enforcement necessity.

In 1999, for example, the ACLU of Northern California filed a class action lawsuit against the California Highway Patrol (CHP), alleging that its highway drug interdiction program violated Title VI of the Civil Rights Act because it relied heavily on discretionary pretext stops and consent searches that are employed overwhelmingly against African American and Latino motorists. During the course of the litigation, the CHP produced data that showed African Americans were twice as likely, and Latinos three times as likely, to be stopped and searched by its officers as were whites. The data further showed that consent searches were ineffective; only a tiny percentage of the discriminatory searches resulted in the discovery of drugs or other contraband, yet thousands of black and brown motorists were subjected to baseless interrogations, searches, and seizures as a result of having committed a minor traffic violation. The CHP entered into a consent decree that provided for a three-year moratorium on consent searches and pretext stops statewide and the collection of comprehensive data on the race and ethnicity of motorists stopped and searched by the police, so that it would be possible to determine whether discriminatory practices were continuing. Similar results were obtained in New Jersey, as a result of landmark litigation filed against the New Jersey State Police. After *Sandoval,* these cases can no longer be brought under Title VI by private litigants. Only the federal government can sue to enforce Title VI's antidiscrimination provisions—something it has neither the inclination nor the capacity to do in most racial profiling cases due to its limited resources and institutional reluctance to antagonize local law enforcement. Since the War on Drugs, private litigants represented by organizations such as the ACLU have been at the forefront of racial profiling litigation. Those days, however, have come to an end. The racial profiling cases that swept the nation in the 1990s may well be the last wave of litigation challenging racial bias in the criminal justice system that we see for a very long time.

The Supreme Court has now closed the courthouse doors to claims of racial bias at every stage of the criminal justice process, from stops and searches to plea bargaining and sentencing. The system of mass incarceration is now, for all practical purposes, thoroughly immunized from claims of racial bias. Staggering racial disparities in the drug war continue but rarely make the news. The Obama administration has indicated it supports abolition of the hundred-to-one disparity in sentencing for crack versus powder cocaine–the most obvious and embarrassing example of racial bias in a system that purports to be colorblind. But that disparity is just the tip of the iceberg. This system depends primarily on the prison label, not prison time. What matters most is who gets swept into this system of control and then ushered into an undercaste. The legal rules adopted by the Supreme Court guarantee that those who find themselves locked up and permanently locked out due to the drug war are overwhelmingly black and brown.

James Forman, Jr.

Racial Critiques of Mass Incarceration: Beyond the New Jim Crow

Introduction

In the five decades since African Americans won their civil rights, hundreds of thousands have lost their liberty. Blacks now make up a larger portion of the prison population than they did at the time of *Brown v. Board of Education*, and their lifetime risk of incarceration has doubled As the United States has become the world's largest jailer and its prison population has exploded, black men have been particularly affected. Today, black men are imprisoned at 6.5 times the rate of white men.

While scholars have long analyzed the connection between race and America's criminal justice system, an emerging group of scholars and advocates has highlighted the issue with a provocative claim: They argue that our growing penal system, with its black tinge, constitutes nothing less than a new form of Jim Crow. This Article examines the Jim Crow analogy. Part I tracks the analogy's history, documenting its increasing prominence in the scholarly literature on race and crime. Part II explores the analogy's usefulness, pointing out that it is extraordinarily compelling in some respects. The Jim Crow analogy effectively draws attention to the plight of black men whose opportunities in life have been permanently diminished by the loss of citizenship rights and the stigma they suffer as convicted offenders. It highlights how ostensibly race-neutral criminal justice policies unfairly target black communities. In these ways, the analogy shines a light on injustices that are too often hidden from view.

But, as I argue in Parts III through VIII, the Jim Crow analogy also obscures much that matters. Part III shows how the Jim Crow analogy, by highlighting the role of politicians seeking to exploit racial fears while minimizing other social factors, oversimplifies the origins of mass incarceration. Part IV demonstrates that the analogy has too little to say about black attitudes toward crime and punishment, masking the nature and extent of black support for punitive crime policy. Part V explains how the analogy's myopic focus on the War on Drugs diverts us from discussing violent crime—a troubling oversight given that violence destroys so many lives in low-income black communities and that violent offenders make up a plurality of the prison population. Part VI argues that the Jim Crow analogy obscures the fact that mass incarceration's impact has been almost exclusively concentrated among the most disadvantaged African Americans. Part VII argues that the analogy draws our attention away from the harms that mass incarceration inflicts on other racial groups, including whites and Hispanics. Part VIII argues that the analogy diminishes our understanding of the particular harms associated with the Old Jim Crow.

Before I turn to the argument itself, I would like to address a question that arose when I began presenting versions of this Article to readers familiar with my own opposition to our nation's overly punitive criminal justice system. As an academic, I have written extensively about the toll that mass incarceration has taken on the African-American community, and especially on young people in that community. I am also a former public defender who co-founded a school that educates young people who have been involved with the juvenile justice system. This history prompted one friend familiar with this project to ask the following questions: 1) "Don't you agree with much of what the New Jim Crow writers have to say?" and 2) "Why are you critiquing a point of view that is so closely aligned with your own?" I hope to clarify this Article's broader goals by providing brief answers to those questions here.

Don't you agree with much of what the New Jim Crow writers have to say? In a word, yes. The New Jim Crow writers have drawn attention to a profound social crisis, and I applaud them for that. Low-income and undereducated African Americans are currently incarcerated at unprecedented levels. The damage is felt not just by those who are locked up, but by their children, families, neighbors, and the nation as a whole. In Part II, I recognize some of the signal contributions of the New Jim Crow writers, especially their description of how our criminal justice system makes permanent outcasts of convicted criminals and stigmatizes other low-income blacks as threats to public safety. I also single out Michelle Alexander's contribution to the literature because her elaboration of the argument is the most comprehensive and persuasive to date.

Why are you critiquing a point of view that is so closely aligned with your own? Although the New Jim Crow writers and I agree more often than we disagree, the disagreements matter. 1 believe that the Jim Crow analogy neglects some important truths and must be criticized in the service of truth. I also believe that we who seek to counter mass incarceration will be hobbled in our efforts if we misunderstand its causes and consequences in the ways that the Jim Crow analogy invites us to do. In Part V, for example, I note that the New Jim Crow writers encourage us to view mass incarceration as exclusively (or overwhelmingly) a result of the War on Drugs. But drug offenders constitute only a quarter of our nation's prisoners, while violent offenders make up a much larger share: one-half. Accordingly, an effective response to mass incarceration will require directly confronting the issue of violent crime and developing policy responses that can compete with the punitive approach that currently dominates American criminal policy. The idea that the Jim Crow analogy leads to a distorted view of mass incarceration—and therefore hampers our ability to challenge it effectively—is the central theme of this Article.

I A Brief History of the "New Jim Crow"

. . .The Jim Crow analogy has gained adherents in the past decade—most prominently, Michelle Alexander in her recent book, *The New Jim Crow: Mass Incarceration in the Age of Colorblindness*. Alexander reports that she initially resisted the analogy when she encountered it as a young ACLU lawyer in the Bay Area. Upon noticing a sign on a telephone pole proclaiming that "THE DRUG WAR IS THE NEW JIM CROW," she remembers thinking: "Yeah, the criminal justice system is racist in many ways, but it really doesn't help to make such an absurd comparison. People will just think you're crazy." Over the years, however, she has come to believe that the flyer was right. "Quite belatedly, I came to see that mass incarceration in the United States had, in fact, emerged as a stunningly comprehensive and well-disguised system of racialized social control that functions in a manner strikingly similar to Jim Crow."

II The Value of the Jim Crow Analogy

The Jim Crow analogy has much to recommend it, especially as applied to the predicament of convicted offenders. Building on the work of legal scholars who have examined the collateral consequences of criminal convictions, the New Jim Crow writers document how casually, almost carelessly, our society ostracizes offenders. Our mantra is "Do the Crime, Do the Time." But, increasingly, "the time" is endless, as people with criminal records are permanently locked out of civil society. . . .

While the Jim Crow analogy is most compelling as applied to those convicted of crimes, it applies more broadly as well. Just as Jim Crow defined blacks as inferior, mass imprisonment encourages the larger society to see a subset of the black population—young black men in low-income communities—as potential threats. This stigma increases their social and economic marginalization and encourages the routine violation of their rights. Intense police surveillance of black youths becomes accepted practice. Their misbehavior in school is reported to the police and leads to juvenile court. Employers are reluctant to hire them. Thus, even young, low-income black men who are never arrested or imprisoned endure the consequences of a stigma associated with race.

Taken together, these two forms of exclusion—making permanent outcasts of convicted criminals while stigmatizing other poor blacks as potential threats—have had devastating effects on low-income black communities. While the New Jim Crow writers are not the first to have raised these issues, their analogy usefully connects the dots: It highlights the cumulative impact of a disparate set of race-related disabilities. Alexander is especially persuasive in this regard. Invoking the "birdcage" metaphor associated with structural racism theorists, she documents in depressing detail how mass incarceration intersects with a wide variety of laws and institutions to trap low-income black men in a virtual cage. Her elaboration of the Jim Crow analogy is also useful because, by skillfully deploying a rhetorically provocative claim, she has drawn significant media attention to the often ignored phenomenon of mass imprisonment.

My objection to the Jim Crow analogy is based on what it obscures. Proponents of the analogy focus on those aspects of mass incarceration that most resemble Jim Crow and minimize or ignore many important dissimilarities. As a result, the analogy generates an incomplete account of mass incarceration—one in which most prisoners are drug offenders, violent crime and its victims merit only passing mention, and white prisoners are largely invisible. In sum, as I argue in the Parts that follow, the analogy directs our attention away from features of crime and punishment in America that require our attention if we are to understand mass incarceration in all of its dimensions.

III Obscuring History: The Birth of Mass Incarceration

The New Jim Crow writers typically start their argument with a historical claim, grounded in a theory of backlash. The narrative is as follows: Just as Jim Crow was a response to Reconstruction and the late–nineteenth century Populist movement that threatened Southern elites, mass incarceration was a response to the civil rights movement and the tumult of the 1960s. Beginning in the mid-1960s, Republican politicians—led by presidential candidates Goldwater and Nixon—focused on crime in an effort to tap into white voters' anxiety over increased racial equality and a growing welfare state. Barry Goldwater cleared the way in 1964 when he declared, "Choose the way of [the Johnson] Administration and you have the way of mobs in the street." In 1968, Nixon perfected Goldwater's strategy. In the words of his advisor H.R. Haldeman, Nixon "emphasized that you have to face the fact that the whole problem is really the blacks. The key is to devise a system that recognizes this while not appearing to." John Ehrlichman, another advisor, characterized Nixon's campaign strategy as follows: "We'll go after the racists."

There is much truth to this account, and its telling demonstrates part of what is useful about the Jim Crow analogy. Today, too many Americans refuse to acknowledge the continuing impact of race and prejudice on public policy. By documenting mass imprisonment's roots in race-baiting political appeals, the New Jim Crow writers effectively demolish the notion that our prison system's origins are exclusively colorblind.

But in emphasizing mass incarceration's racial roots, the New Jim Crow writers overlook other critical factors. The most important of these is that crime shot up dramatically just before the beginning of the prison boom. Reported street crime quadrupled in the twelve years from 1959 to 1971. Homicide rates doubled between 1963 and 1974, and robbery rates tripled. Proponents of the Jim Crow analogy tend to ignore or minimize the role that crime and violence played in creating such a receptive audience for Goldwater's and Nixon's appeals. Alexander, for example, characterizes crime and fear of crime as follows:

Unfortunately, at the same time that civil rights were being identified as a threat to law and order, the FBI was reporting fairly significant increases in the national crime rate. Despite significant controversy over the accuracy of the statistics, these reports received a great deal of publicity and were offered as further evidence of the breakdown in lawfulness, morality, and social stability.

In this account, the stress is not on crime itself but on the FBI's reporting, about which we are told there is "significant controversy." But even accounting for problems with the FBI's crime statistics, there is no doubt that crime increased dramatically.

Nor were white conservatives such as Nixon and Goldwater alone in demanding more punitive crime policy. In *The Politics of Imprisonment,* Vanessa Barker describes how, in the late 1960s, black activists in Harlem fought for what would become the notorious Rockefeller drug laws, some of the harshest in the nation. Harlem residents were outraged over rising crime (including drug crime) in their neighborhoods and demanded increased police presence and stiffer penalties. The NAACP Citizens' Mobilization Against Crime demanded "lengthening minimum prison terms for muggers, pushers, [and first] degree murderers." The city's leading black newspaper, *The Amsterdam News,* advocated mandatory life sentences for the "non-addict drug pusher of hard drugs" because such drug dealing "is an act of cold, calculated, premeditated, indiscriminate murder of our community."

Rising levels of violent crime and demands by black activists for harsher sentences have no place in the New Jim Crow account of mass incarceration's rise. As a result, the Jim Crow analogy promotes a reductive account of mass incarceration's complex history in which, as Alexander puts it, "proponents of racial hierarchy found they could install a new racial caste system."

IV Obscuring Black Support for Punitive Crime Policy

. . . The Jim Crow analogy encourages us to understand mass incarceration as another policy enacted by whites and helplessly suffered by blacks. But today, blacks are much more than subjects; they are actors in determining the policies that sustain mass incarceration in ways simply unimaginable to past generations.

. . . While racial animus or indifference might explain the sky-high African American incarceration rates in Baltimore and Detroit, they do not explain those in Washington, D.C. And just as the analogy fails to explain why a majority black jurisdiction would lock up so many of its own, it says little about blacks who embrace a tough-on-crime position as a matter of racial justice. . . .

V Ignoring Violence

To this point, I have focused principally on crimes of violence and the state's response to such crimes. I part company with the New Jim Crow writers in this regard. They focus almost exclusively on the War on Drugs. This approach made sense for early ACLU advocates such as Glasser and Boyd, whose only objective was to curtail the drug war. It makes less sense for more recent proponents of the analogy, who attack the broader phenomenon of mass incarceration but restrict their attention to punishments for drug offenders. Other crimes—especially violent crimes—are rarely mentioned.

The choice to focus on drug crimes is a natural—even necessary—byproduct of framing mass incarceration as a new form of Jim Crow. One of Jim Crow's defining features was that it treated similarly situated blacks and whites differently. For writers seeking analogues in today's criminal justice system, drug arrests and prosecutions provide natural targets, along with racial profiling in traffic stops. Blacks and whites use drugs at roughly the same rates, but African Americans are significantly more likely to be arrested and imprisoned for drug crimes. As with Jim Crow, the difference lies in government practice, not in the underlying behavior. The statistics on selling drugs are less clear-cut, but here too the racial disparities in arrest and incarceration rates exceed any disparities that might exist in the race of drug sellers.

But violent crime is a different matter. While rates of drug offenses are roughly the same throughout the population, blacks are overrepresented among the population for violent offenses. For example, the African American arrest rate for murder is seven to eight times higher than the white arrest rate; the black arrest rate for robbery is ten times higher than the white arrest rate. Murder and robbery are the two offenses for which the arrest data are considered most reliable as an indicator of offending.

In making this point, I do not mean to suggest that discrimination in the criminal justice system is no longer a concern. There is overwhelming evidence that discriminatory practices in drug law enforcement contribute to racial disparities in arrests and prosecutions, and even for violent offenses there remain unexplained disparities between arrest rates and incarceration rates. Instead, I make the point to highlight the problem with framing mass incarceration as a new form of Jim Crow. Because the analogy leads proponents to search for disparities in the criminal justice system that resemble those of the Old Jim Crow, they confine their attention to cases where blacks are like whites in all relevant respects, yet are treated worse by law. Such a search usefully exposes the abuses associated with racial profiling and the drug war. But it does not lead to a comprehensive understanding of mass incarceration.

Does it matter that the Jim Crow analogy diverts our attention from violent crime and the state's response to it, if it gives us tools needed to criticize the War on Drugs? I think it does, because contrary to the impression left by many of mass incarceration's critics, the majority of America's prisoners are not locked up for drug offenses. Some facts worth considering: According to the Bureau of Justice Statistics, in 2006 there were 1.3 million prisoners in state prisons, 760,000 in local jails, and 190,000 in federal prisons. Among the state prisoners, 50% were serving time for violent offenses, 21% for property offenses, 20% for drug offenses, and 8% for public order offenses. In jails, the split among the various categories was more equal, with roughly 25% of inmates being held for each of the four main crime categories (violent, drug, property, and public order). Federal prisons are the only type of facility in which drug offenders constitute a majority (52%) of prisoners, but federal prisons hold many fewer people overall. Considering all forms of penal institutions together, more prisoners are locked up for violent offenses than for any other type, and just under 25% (550,000) of our nation's 2.3 million prisoners are drug offenders. This is still an extraordinary and appalling number. But even if every single one of these drug offenders were released tomorrow, the United States would still have the world's largest prison system.

Moreover, our prison system has grown so large in part because we have changed our sentencing policies for *all* offenders, not just drug offenders. We divert fewer offenders than we once did, send more of them to prison, and keep them in prison for much longer. An exclusive focus on the drug war misses this larger point about sentencing choices. This is why it is not enough to dismiss talk of violent offenders by saying that "violent crime is not responsible for the prison boom." It is true that the prison population in this country continued to grow even after violent crime began to decline dramatically. However, the *state's response* to violent crime—less diversion and longer sentences—has been a major cause of mass incarceration. Thus, changing how governments respond to *all* crime, not just drug crime, is critical to reducing the size of prison populations.

I am sympathetic to the impulse to avoid discussing violent crime. Like other progressives, the New Jim Crow writers are frustrated by decades of losing the crime debate to those who condemn violence while refusing to acknowledge or ameliorate the conditions that give rise to it. "As a society," Alexander writes, "our decision to heap shame and contempt upon those who struggle and fail in a system designed to keep them locked up and locked out says far more about ourselves than it does about them." Since it is especially difficult to suspend moral judgment when the discussion turns to violent crime, progressives tend to avoid or change the subject.

To see how reticent mass incarceration's critics can be regarding the subject of violence, consider how Alexander describes Jarvious Cotton, whose story opens *The New Jim Crow*:

> Cotton's great-great grandfather could not vote as a slave. His great-grandfather was beaten to death by the Ku Klux Klan for attempting to vote. His grandfather was prevented from voting by Klan intimidation. His father was barred from voting by poll taxes and literacy tests. Today, Jarvious Cotton cannot vote because he, like many black men in the United States, has been labeled a felon and is currently on parole.

Cotton is like his ancestors in that he cannot vote. But there is one salient difference between Cotton and his ancestors. They couldn't vote because they were black; Cotton lost his right to vote when he was convicted of murder. But Alexander nowhere mentions Cotton's crime, and her passive construction—Cotton "has been labeled a felon"—suggests that he had no choice in the matter. Now, I agree with Alexander that *even though* Cotton was convicted of murder, his status as a felon should not carry with it a lifetime of disenfranchisement. But Alexander does not strengthen her case, or help us understand the problem of mass incarceration in all of its dimensions, by declining to acknowledge his violent offense.

Avoiding the topic of violence in this manner is a mistake, not least because it disserves the very people on whose behalf the New Jim Crow writers advocate. After all, the same low-income young people of color who disproportionately enter prisons are disproportionately victimized by crime. And the two phenomena are mutually reinforcing. . . .

VI Obscuring Class

In the previous Part, I argued that one of Jim Crow's defining characteristics was that it treated similarly situated blacks and whites differently, and that the New Jim Crow writers are forced by the pressure of the analogy to find modern-day parallels. This leads them to overlook violent crime by limiting their inquiry to the War on Drugs. Jim Crow has another distinctive characteristic that threatens to lead us astray when contemplating mass incarceration. Just as Jim Crow treated similarly situated blacks and whites differently, it treated differently situated blacks similarly. An essential quality of Jim Crow was its uniform and demeaning treatment of all blacks. Jim Crow was designed to ensure the separation, disenfranchisement, and political and economic subordination of *all* black Americans—young or old, rich or poor, educated or illiterate. . . .

. . . Historically, racial justice advocates have been reluctant to acknowledge how class privilege mitigates racial disadvantage. This reluctance is partly a byproduct of the structure of the affirmative action argument. One of the most potent arguments against race-based preferences is the claim that wealthier blacks do not deserve them. Affirmative action's defenders often respond by pointing out the various ways in which even privileged blacks suffer racial discrimination. At the same time, racial profiling reinforces the notion that class differences within the black community matter little. After all, racial profiling is the area in which skin color routinely trumps one's bank account or accumulated graduate degrees. As David Harris argues, "'driving while black' is not only an experience of the young black male, or those blacks at the bottom of the socio-economic ladder. All blacks confront the issue directly, regardless of age, dress, occupation or social station.". . .

. . . Alexander suggests that perhaps "the most important parallel between mass incarceration and Jim Crow is that both have served to define the meaning and significance of race in America." Specifically, she says, "Slavery defined what it meant to be black (a slave), and Jim Crow defined what it meant to be black (a second-class citizen). Today mass incarceration defines the meaning of blackness in America: black people, especially black men, are criminals. That is what it means to be black."

This claim reflects the limitations of the Jim Crow analogy. Today nothing "defines the meaning of blackness in America." In Mississippi in 1950, the totalizing nature of Jim Crow ensured that to be black meant to be second class; there were no blacks free of its strictures. But mass incarceration is much less totalizing. In 2011, *no* institution can define what it "means to be black" in the way that Jim Crow or slavery once did.

VII Overlooking Race

The Jim Crow analogy also obscures the extent to which whites, too, are mass incarceration's targets. Since whites were not direct victims of Jim Crow, it should come as little surprise that whites do not figure prominently in the New Jim Crow writers' accounts of mass incarceration. Most who invoke the analogy simply ignore white prisoners entirely. Alexander mentions them only in passing; she says that mass imprisonment's true targets are blacks, and that incarcerated whites are "collateral damage.". . .

Thus, the data on white and Hispanic prisoners reminds us that while African Americans are incarcerated in numbers grossly disproportionate to their percentage of the overall population, the fact remains that 60% of prisoners are not African American. As I will argue in the conclusion, anyone analyzing mass incarceration must keep that 60% squarely in mind.

VIII Diminishing History: The Old Jim Crow

Having analyzed the Jim Crow analogy's impact on discussions of modern crime and penal policy, I will now evaluate how the analogy influences our understanding of the past. Specifically, I will argue that by invoking the Jim Crow era in an effort to highlight the injustice of mass incarceration, the New Jim Crow writers end up diminishing our collective memory of the Old Jim Crow. My fear is that writers seeking to establish parallels between the Old Jim Crow and mass incarceration overlook (or underemphasize) important aspects of what made the Old Jim Crow so horrible.

The New Jim Crow writers devote little attention to the Old Jim Crow. The choice to say so little is understandable. After all, most people know what Jim Crow was, and the point of these contributions is to tell people a story they do not know—the one about mass incarceration. But I suspect something else is at work as well. In the interest of drawing the parallels between Jim Crow and mass incarceration as tightly as possible, the New Jim Crow writers typically avoid dwelling on the aspects of the Old Jim Crow that have fewer modern parallels. As a result, much that matters is lost. . . .

EXPLORING THE ISSUE

Is the Mass Incarceration of Blacks the New Jim Crow?

Critical Thinking and Reflection

1. What is the racial composition of American prisoners?
2. What factors contribute to the New Jim Crow?
3. What is the difference between the New Jim Crow and early American segregation?
4. What are the new concepts to which you were introduced in the YES and NO selections that are significant to an analysis of the criminal justice system? How does race influence American criminal justice policies?
5. Is the present prison system a means of controlling a segment of the African American male population? How?

Is There Common Ground?

Alexander and Forman are aware that America imprisons more of its citizens than any other nation in the world. Therefore, they agree that mass incarceration is a significant issue confronting American society. Given the fact that African Americans are approximately 13 percent of the American population, they both agree that African Americans are disproportionally represented within the population of U.S. prisoners. Each of these writers is cognizant of the fact that imprisonment and ultimately bearing the label ex-con limit the chance of a person for meaningful employment and social advancement. Alexander and Forman are African American scholars who are well aware of persistent racial segregation despite advancements that have been achieved. For those interested in the racial reality of the demographic distribution of groups that make up the American population, the black ghettos are available for all to see. In developing her thesis that mass incarceration of blacks is creating the New Jim Crow, Alexander is utilizing the traditional black–white paradigm for analyzing race relations. In contrast, Forman challenges those who embrace the New Jim Crow thesis to be more inclusive and to include other groups, especially whites and Latinos, who he claims are also victims of mass incarceration. In developing their conclusions, students should be careful to do proper data analysis. Within that process they will have opportunities to question assertions such as the claim that mass incarceration is a problem for all races not just blacks. Currently, there is growing advocacy in southern-border states to criminalize undocumented immigrants and subject them to arrest, trial, and imprisonment. The current economic recession and the budgetary constraints that it has generated are giving impetus to a reconsideration of mass incarceration. If this development is fully realized, it will intensify the problem of mass incarceration. What new public policy will emerge to deal with this problem fairly and effectively?

Additional Resources

"A Nation Behind Bars?" 2012. *Civil Liberties: The American Civil Liberties Union National Newsletter* (Winter (1), 6).

Alexander, Michelle. 2010. "Go To Trial: Crash the Justice System," *New York Times* (March 11).

Beckett, Katherine and Theodore Sasson. 2004. *The Politics of Injustice: Crime and Punishment in America* (Thousand Oaks, CA: Sage Publications).

Braman, Donald. 2004. *Doing Time on the Outside: Incarceration and Family Life in Urban America* (Ann Arbor, MI: University of Michigan Press).

Chang, Cindy, Scott Threlkeld, and Ryan Smith. 2012."Louisiana Incarcerated: How We Built the World's Prison Capital." Eight part series. *The New Orleans Times-Picayune* (May 13–20).

Clear, Todd R. 2007. *Imprisoning Communities: How Mass Incarceration Makes Disadvantaged Neighborhoods Work* (New York: Oxford University Press).

Jacobs, Andrew. 2008. "Crime-Ridden Newark Tried Getting Jobs for Ex-convicts but Finds Success Elusive," *New York Times* (April 27).

Legal Action Center. 2004. *After Prison: Roadblocks to Reentry, A Report on State Legal Barriers Facing People with Criminal Records* (New York: Legal Action Center).

Loury, Glenn C. 2008. *Race, Incarceration and American Values* (Cambridge, MA: MIT Press).

Pager, Devah. 2007. *Marked: Race, Crime, and Finding Work in an Era of Mass Incarceration* (University of Chicago Press).

Russell-Brown, Katheryn K. 2008. *The Color of Crime: Racial Hoaxes, White Fear, Black Protectionism, Police Harassment, and Other Macroaggressions* (New York University Press).

Street, Paul. 2002. *The Vicious Circle: Race, Prison, Jobs, and Community in Chicago, Illinois and the Nation* (Chicago Urban League).

Wideman, John Edgar. 1995. "Doing Time, Marking Race," *The Nation* (October 30).

X, Malcolm with Alex Haley. 1965. *The Autobiography of Malcolm X* (Grove Press).

Established at Ohio State University in 2003, the Kirwan Institute for the Study of Race and Ethnicity employs an interdisciplinary approach to enhance and deepen understanding of racial and ethnic disparities in American society.

www.kirwaninstitute.org/

With a special focus on racial disparity, the Sentencing Project site is dedicated to research and advocating for reform. The site contains race and justice news along with additional accounts of current events. Other special sections include race, sentencing policy, drug policy, juvenile justice, women, and felony disfranchisement.

www.sentencingproject.org/

The National Poverty Center website (University of Michigan Gerald R. Ford School of Public Policy), a nonpartisan research center, conducts and promotes research on the effects of poverty. Of relevance to the New Jim Crow issue is the site research dealing with race and ethnicity, especially those projects that connect segregation and inequality.

www.npc.umich.edu/publications/working_papers/?publication_id=175&

Project America is a nonpartisan website dedicated to helping Americans understand social issues such as the mass incarceration of blacks. It offers up-to-date information from government and nongovernmental sources. The website strives to maintain nonpartisanship. In terms of current, nonbiased data, it is one of most informative websites on the Internet.

www.project.org/info.php?recordID=174

Contributors to This Volume

EDITORS

RAYMOND D'ANGELO is a professor of sociology at St. Joseph's College in New York where he serves as chair of the Department of Social Sciences. He graduated from Duquesne University, completed an MA from the New School for Social Research, and received his PhD from Bryn Mawr College. D'Angelo has been involved with teaching and research in race and ethnicity throughout his academic career. He is recipient of two fellowships from the National Science Foundation for the study of population, and a research award from the National Institute of Justice to study recidivism in Philadelphia. In 1998, D'Angelo was a National Endowment for the Humanities research fellow in the seminar, "Teaching the History of the Southern Civil Rights Movement." He is author and editor of *The American Civil Rights Movement: Readings and Interpretations* (McGraw Hill/Dushkin, 2000), and has contributed to the *Arena Review: Journal for the Study of Sport and Sociology,* and *Civil Rights in the United States* (MacMillan, 2000). He is active in the preservation of historic sites, especially those of significance to the civil rights movement. Most recently, D'Angelo was a participant in the New York University Faculty Resources Network summer seminar on immigration, "Changing Places, Changing Faces: Recent Immigrant Settlement in the United States and Its Consequences."

HERBERT DOUGLAS is a professor of law and justice studies at Rowan University in Glassboro, New Jersey, where he serves as an African American Studies and International Studies faculty member. He graduated from Duquesne University and received his PhD from the University of Toledo. In 1990, he was recipient of a Fulbright-Hays Fellowship to study conflict resolution in the Soviet Union. Recently, he received the Rosa Parks Award for long-term contributions and leadership for civil rights and social justice, and the Gary Hunter Award for Excellence in Mentoring at Rowan University. Douglas is involved in social causes including membership on the governing board of the Fair Share Housing Center in Camden, New Jersey. He contributed, "Migration and Adaptations of African American Families within Urban America," to *Minority Voices: Linking Personal Ethnic History and the Sociological Imagination* (Allyn & Bacon, 2005) edited by John Myers. He has been involved with teaching and research in race and ethnic studies throughout his academic career.

AUTHORS

MICHELLE ALEXANDER is an associate professor of law at the Ohio State University with a joint appointment at the Kirwan Institute of Race and Ethnicity. She is author of *The New Jim Crow: Mass Incarceration in the Age of Colorblindness* (The New Press, 2011).

GORDON W. ALLPORT (1897–1967) was a social psychologist and author of *The Nature of Prejudice* (1954).

LAWRENCE AUSTER is a conservative essayist and blogger. He has written extensively on immigration and multiculturalism including *The Path to National Suicide* (American Immigration Control Foundation, 1990). He blogs from his website, *View from the Right,* www.amnation.com/vfr.

DERRICK BELL is a visiting professor of law at New York University School of Law. He is author of many books including *Faces at the Bottom of the Well: The Permanence of Racism* (Basic Books, 1992) and the classic *Race, Racism and American Law* (Aspen Publishers Inc., 2000).

HERBERT BLUMER (1900–1987) was a former professional football player who became a sociology professor at the University of Chicago and the University of California, Berkeley. He helped to establish symbolic interactionism as a major paradigm in sociology.

EDUARDO BONILLA-SILVA is a professor of sociology at Texas A&M University and the author of several books on race and ethnicity including *Racism Without Racists* (Rowan & Littlefield, 2003).

PETER BRIMELOW is senior editor of *Forbes* and *National Review*. He is the author of *Alien Nation: Common Sense About America's Immigration Disaster* (Perennial, 1996).

PATRICK J. BUCHANAN is a well-known conservative columnist and the author of *The Death of the West: How Dying Populations and Immigrant Invasions Imperil Our Country and Civilizations* (St. Martin's Griffin, 2002) and *State of Emergency: The Third World Invasion and Conquest of America* (St. Martin's Griffin, 2007).

ROGER CLEGG is general council of the Center for Equal Opportunity and frequent contributor to *The Chronicle of Higher Education.*

WARD CONNERLY is a political activist and conservative commentator. He is best identified with Proposition 209, a California ballot initiative in opposition to affirmative action programs.

SUSAN P. CRAWFORD is a professor of law at the Benjamin N. Cardozo School of Law. She was special assistant to President Obama for Science, Technology and Innovation Policy during 2009. Currently, she is a visiting professor of the First Amendment at Harvard's Kennedy School, a visiting professor at Harvard Law School, and a columnist for *Bloomberg View* and *Wired.*

ELLIS COSE is the author of *The Press, A Nation of Strangers* and *The Rage of a Privileged Class.* He is now a writer and essayist for *Newsweek.*

INGRID GOULD ELLEN is a writer for *Brookings Review*. She is author of *Sharing America's Neighborhoods: The Prospects for Stable Racial Integration* (Harvard University Press, 2000).

ERIC FONER is Dewitt Clinton professor of history at Columbia University and author of numerous books including *A Short History of Reconstruction* (Harper

Perennial, 1990) and, most recently, *The Fiery Trial: Abraham Lincoln and American Slavery* (W.W. Norton & Co., 2011).

JAMES FORMAN, JR., is a clinical professor of law at Yale Law School and a noted constitutional law scholar. He has written many articles including "Beyond The New Jim Crow," (NYU Law Review, April 2012) and "Race and Class in the 21st Century: From Martin Luther King, Jr. to Bill Cosby" (Villanova Law Review, 2005).

CARLOS FUENTES is a social commentator and distinguished Mexican writer.

CHARLES A. GALLAGHER is a professor of sociology at Georgia State University and author of *Rethinking the Color Line: Readings in Race and Ethnicity* (McGraw-Hill, 2006).

HENRY A. GIROUX, an expert on cultural studies, education, multiculturalism, and related topics, is current chair of communication studies at McMaster University, Ontario, Canada. He is the author of several books including *Education Still Under Siege*, coauthored with Stanley Aronowitz (Bergin & Garvey, 1993).

KENDRA HAMILTON is the editor of *Black Issues in Higher Education*. Her background is in English and creative writing. She has published poems in *Callaloo* and written and researched on Gullah, the language and culture of the South Carolina and Georgia's Low Country.

DAVID A. HARRIS is a professor of law and values at the University of Toledo College of Law and Soros senior justice fellow at the Center of Crime, Communities and Justice in New York City. He is author of *Profiles in Injustice: Why Racial Profiling Cannot Work* (New Press, 2003).

DEBRA HUMPHREYS is a former director of Programs, Office of Education and Diversity, Equity and Global Initiatives, at the Association of American Colleges and Universities in Washington, DC. Currently, she is vice president for Communications and Public Affairs at AACU. She has written columns in *The Chronicle of Higher Education* and *USA Today*.

SAMUEL HUNTINGTON is a political scientist and Albert J. Weatherhead III University Professor at Harvard University. He is author of *The Clash of Civilizations and the Remaking of World Order* (Touchstone, 1996).

SCOTT JOHNSON is a fellow of the Claremont Institute, an attorney, and senior vice president of TCF National Bank in Minnesota. Also, he is coauthor of The Power Line blog.

SONIA K. KATYAL is a professor of law at Fordham Law School and the author of *Property Outlaws* (Yale University Press, 2010).

PAUL KIVEL is a teacher, writer, and antiracist social activist. He is author of *Uprooting Racism: How White People Can Work for Racial Justice* (New Society Publishers, 1995).

MELISSA V. HARRIS-LACEWELL is an associate professor of politics and African American studies at Princeton University. She is author of *Barbershops, Bibles, and BET: Everyday Talk and Black Political Thought* (Princeton 2004) and a regular contributor to *The Nation*.

PHILIPPE LEGRAIN is a British journalist, economist, and author of *Immigrants: Your Country Needs Them* (Princeton University Press, 2007) and *Open World: The Truth about Globalisation* (Ivan R. Dee Publishers, 2003).

TIM LOCKETTE is a freelance writer in Montgomery, Alabama. He is the former editor of *Teaching Tolerance.*

RUSSELL NIELE is a lecturer in politics at Princeton University, who has written numerous articles on social policy including affirmative action and the emergence of the urban black underclass.

ALVIN POUSSAINT is a professor of psychiatry at the Harvard Medical School. He has authored many books on child psychiatry with emphasis on African American children including *Come On People: On the Path from Victims to Victors* (Thomas Nelson, 2009) with Bill Cosby.

ROSALIE PEDALINO PORTER is the author of *Forked Tongue: The Politics of Bilingual Education* (Basic Books, 1990) and *Educating Language Minority Children: An Agenda for the Future* (Transaction Publishers, 2000). She is the chairman and director of the READ Institute (Research in English Acquisition and Development).

ARTHUR J. REMILLARD is a professor of religious studies at St. Francis University in Loretto, Pennsylvania. He is author of *Southern Civil Religions* (University of Georgia Press, 2011).

LARRY SCHWEIKART is a professor of history at Dayton University and co-author with Michael Allen of *A Patriot's History of the United States: From Columbus's Great Discovery to the War on Terror* (Sentinel Trade, 2007).

ROBERT STAPLES is a professor of sociology at the University of California, San Francisco, and author of *Black Masculinity: The Black Male's Role in American Society* (Black Scholar Press, 1982) and *Families at the Crossroads: Challenges and Prospects* (Jossey-Bass Inc., 1993), coauthored with Leanor Boulin Johnson.

BEVERLY D. TATUM is a clinical psychologist and current president of Spelman College. She is author of *Why Are All the Black Kids Sitting Together in the Cafeteria? And Other Conversations About Race* (Basic Books, 1997).

ABIGAIL THERNSTROM, a political scientist, is a senior fellow at the Manhattan Institute in New York. She has written extensively on race and voting rights including *Whose Votes Count? Affirmative Action and Minority Voting Rights* (Harvard University Press, 1987); and *American in Black and White: One Nation, Indivisible,* with Stephan Thernstrom, (Simon & Schuster, 1997).

RICHARD M. VALELLY is a professor of political science at Swarthmore College and author of *The Two Reconstructions: The Struggle for Black Enfranchisement* (The University of Chicago Press, 2004). His most recent book is *The Voting Rights Act* (CQ Press, 2005).

MICHAEL WALZER is a political philosopher and professor at the Institute for Advanced Study. He is author of *On Toleration* (Yale University Press, 1997) and *Exodus and Revolution* (Basic Books, 2000).

GEORGE F. WILL is a noted conservative columnist at *Newsweek* and former Pulitzer-Prize winning author. He is author of several books including *The Woven Figure: Conservatism and America's Fabric* (Touchstone, 1998).

TIM WISE is author of *White Like Me: Reflections on Race from a Privileged Son* (Soft Skull Press, 2005) and director of the newly formed Association for White Anti-Racist Education (AWARE) in Nashville, Tennessee.